Cooking Light®

ANNUAL
RECIPES 2013

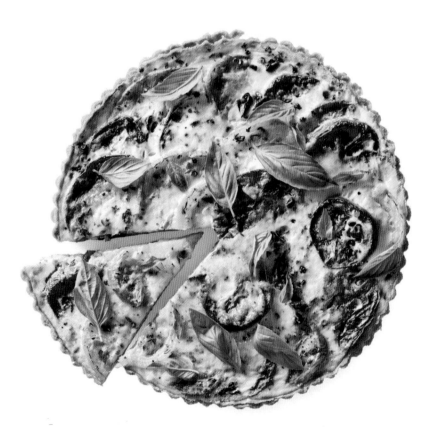

Oxmoor House®

A Year at Cooking Light

2012 was a great year in the *Cooking Light* Test Kitchen. As we celebrated our 25th anniversary year, we retested many of our best recipes and focused on developing our best-ever fast dishes. We also continued to expand our global horizons, using flavorful ingredients in new ways. Our commitment continues to be innovative recipes that put healthy food into the hands of busy cooks who want daily inspiration. But we know those same cooks enjoy soulful weekend cooking for friends and family—comfort food, holiday food, indulgent desserts, great food off the grill, and more.

Bacon and Butternut Pasta
(page 34)
Pasta and sauce canoodle in the oven so that the former absorbs the flavor of the latter and softens deliciously, while the cheese topping merrily bubbles and browns.

Here are some of the year's highlights:

- In January we scoured our archives to find the best, most delicious, most chocolaty recipes ever and held a head-to-head competition: cake against cupcake, pudding vs. mousse, fudge sauce against fondue, and pastry against candy. We narrowed down our Sweet 16 contenders to a final winner—with much debate and argument along the way—that delivers intense, deep chocolate satisfaction in a deliciously lighter package. (page 27)

- We know our readers are busy, but hectic schedules don't have to mean sacrificing a healthy dinner. April featured a collection of 40 meals that are all ready in less than 40 minutes. The goal: healthy recipes that are easy to prepare and can be on the dinner table fast. (page 77)

- We tackled restaurant dishes in May, transforming some classic calorie-bomb favorites into lighter versions of themselves—significantly slashing the calories, sodium, and saturated fat. This section shared the ingredients and tips that made that possible. (page 111)

- Our Summer Cookbook (page 132) is our annual homage to the glories of summer flavors. It includes a wide selection of fresh, healthy recipes using the season's best produce.

- In August, we shared our Food Lover's Guide to Super Simple Cooking (page 188). Twenty-five tips help you get ahead in the kitchen, offer shopping advice, and share strategies on ingredients, prep, equipment, and cooking techniques that save time without sacrificing flavor.

- And we began the holidays with our reader-favorite Holiday Cookbook (page 293) in November. Around the holidays, tradition trumps innovation, but tinkering with flavor can help keep things interesting from year to year. Here, we offer two birds with an array of trimmings to choose from.

Readers are the reason we do what we do, and we enjoy hearing from you. We receive so much positive feedback—mail, e-mail, Instagram comments, and more. To all who cook from *Cooking Light* and share their insights with us: thanks.

Scott Mowbray
Editor

▲ **Beef Filets with Red Wine Sauce and Roasted Veggie Fries** *(page 112)*
Finishing the sauce for the filet mignon, a dab of butter rounds out the flavor and adds a supple, silky texture with rich buttery notes. Roasted cornmeal-dusted baby carrots add color, sweetness, and interesting shapes when paired with potato wedges for a stunning side.

Our Favorite Recipes

Not all recipes are created equal.

At *Cooking Light,* only those that have received a passing grade from our Test Kitchen staff and food editors—a group with very high standards—make it onto the pages of our magazine. We test each recipe rigorously, often two or three times, to ensure that it's healthy, reliable, and tastes as good as it possibly can. So which of our recipes are our favorites? They're the dishes that we can't forget: The ones readers write or call us about, the ones our staff regularly make for their own families and friends.

▶ **Vietnamese Pork Tenderloin** *(page 167)*
Mild-tasting pork tenderloin pairs with big, strong flavors: salty umami-rich soy and fish sauces, peppery ginger, tangy rice vinegar, and fiery Thai chile. It's the perfect setup for a casual, serve-yourself kind of gathering.

▼ **Crab Cakes with Spicy Rémoulade** *(page 80)*
Panko (Japanese breadcrumbs) act as a unique binder for lump crabmeat, keeping the cakes light and the crab front and center. A zesty rémoulade with capers, Dijon mustard, and cayenne pepper enhances every bite.

Lemony Grilled Potato Salad *(page 139)*
Grilling the potatoes, onion, and bell pepper adds smokiness to familiar picnic fare. It's even better a day after it's made.

Vegetable Lasagna *(page 112)*
Lots of colorful, delicious baby vegetables between layers of tender noodles without the typical mounds of cheese.

Tomato Stack Salad with Corn and Avocado *(page 192)*
A whole meal can be built around one superstar ingredient—here, tomatoes. A tangy fresh herb and buttermilk dressing makes this first course worthy of seconds.

Cilantro-Jalapeño Limeade *(page 134)*
Served in a tall glass with a sugared rim,
this sipper begs for a lawn chair and
a hot summer afternoon. A splash of
tequila would make it an adult favorite.

Spicy Squash Pickles
(page 133)
Maple syrup and crushed
red pepper update the iconic
summer condiment, adding
a bright twist and new sizzle.

Spicy Thai Coconut Chicken Soup
(page 31)
Coconut milk tames the heat and combines deliciously with the chicken, smoothing the edges of tart lime, salty fish sauce, and fiery chile paste.

Filipino Arroz Caldo *(page 250)*
Ginger and a touch of saffron make this
comforting porridge richly fragrant. It's
the perfect dish for chilly nights.

Dak Bokkeum with Spinach *(page 53)*
This stew is lick-the-bowl good, something you'll have no trouble doing despite its fiery flavor. Korean food is the soul food of Asia. In this one-pot dish, budget cuts of meat are coaxed to comfort perfection in a spicy-sweet sauce.

▲ All-American Meat Loaf *(page 60)*
We stayed true to the essence of the loaf even with Mom's ketchup topping, but we tried it Italian-style with chunks of melty cheese.

▲ Reuben Sandwiches *(page 111)*
This classic received a makeover: We shrank the portion size, used a lower-sodium sauerkraut, and created a home-made mayo with delicious results.

▲ Cherry-Peach Sangria *(page 175)*
Who could resist the refreshing combination of fruit, fresh herbs, and wine? Use either Bing or Rainier cherries to create fruity, summery flavor.

▲ Chicken Piccata *(page 20)*
Briny capers and bright lemon really make this bird sing. Serve with green beans and creamy polenta for a full meal.

Slow-Braised Lamb Shanks *(page 64)*
The tasty browned bits at the bottom of the pan add deep complex notes to an already hearty dish. Buttery, fork-tender meat falls off the bone from a long, gentle simmer.

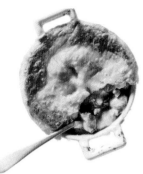

◀ Chicken, Potato, and Leek Pie
(page 193)

Smoky bacon, savory chicken thighs, and the subtle sweetness of carrots and leeks make for a winning combination. America, meet your new favorite potpie.

Chocolate-Hazelnut Banana Bread
(page 276)

Keep some napkins handy—a slice falls apart in the best possible way. Chocolate glaze puts the flavor over the top.

Green Curry Fritters
(page 273)

These are spicy-good! You won't believe how much flavor is packed into these little patties. Thai green curry is a sauce of lemongrass, ginger, chiles, and herbs. It's spicy and fragrant, and turns pedestrian chicken patties into spicy powerhouses.

◀ Lemon Squares *(page 202)*

Refreshingly tangy and buttery-crisp, a creamy citrus filling meets nutty cookie goodness in these lighter, brighter squares.

Pizza Rustica *(page 97)*

A quick vegetarian tour of the Italian boot brings home the flavors of a savory veggie-packed pie. Extra-virgin olive oil is the secret ingredient in the tender, flaky crust. Ciao down!

Ramen Noodle Bowl *(page 273)*

Miso, soy sauce, chile paste, and porcini mushrooms ramp up chicken noodle soup with a Japanese twist. Chewy noodles and deep, umami-rich broth—it's like a steaming bowl of comfort.

◀ Philly Cheesesteak
(page 68)

Our version of the sandwich that put Philly on the comfort-food map keeps its meaty, cheesy soul. Out with the artificial cheese sauce, in with a lean white sauce with real cheese—just enough Parm-Regg and provolone to deliver full satisfaction with less sodium and saturated fat.

Tex-Mex Hash Brown Casserole *(page 57)*

Use a cast-iron skillet to get a delicious browned crust on the bottom of the potatoes, and then bake them with smoky chorizo under a blanket of melty cheese. This approach is all about texture: crisp golden outside, starchy goodness within.

▶ Bread Pudding with Salted Caramel Sauce
(page 41)

A recipe makeover of the classic decadent dessert—bread cubes drenched in heavy cream and eggs—is trimmer and slimmer without sacrificing its velvety interior. Bourbon, vanilla, and cinnamon offer a rich, smoky-spiced flavor punch to the creamy sauce.

Moroccan Chicken and Butternut Squash Soup
(page 31)

Moroccans take great comfort in their wonderful tagines stewed with fragrant spices. This dish is basically a tagine thinned to soup consistency, with couscous to starch it up. Sugary butternut squash and meaty chicken thighs remind us how well sweet and savory flavors play together in Moroccan cuisine.

Pork Chops with Roasted Apples and Onions
(page 270)

Apples, pearl onions, butter, and fresh thyme combine to make a saucy side dish that pairs perfectly with pork chops. Green beans with a mustard vinaigrette complete the easy weeknight dinner.

Tomato Tart
(page 193)

This popular brunch entrée checks in at less than 300 calories a serving. A summery spectacular, it's meat free—olives add satisfying richness.

◀ Grapefruit Pound Cake
(page 40)

There's a surprising, exotic depth of flavor from the grapefruit rind and the juice in the cake. A citrusy glaze adds the finishing touch.

Chocolate Cake with Fluffy Frosting *(page 312)*

Soft, fine-crumbed, moist chocolate cake gets star treatment with a glossy icing. Marshmallow creme is the key to the magnificent texture of this tangy-sweet frosting.

Cranberry-Whiskey Sour Slush *(page 304)*

Intensely delicious cocktail or icy dessert? You decide. This well-balanced combination of high-quality liquor and tangy cranberries is fruity, boozy, and not-too-sweet.

Phyllo Cups with Ricotta, Chèvre, and Thyme
(page 322)

These delightfully crisp little hors d'oeuvres cups are filled with ricotta, goat cheese, and thyme. They're the perfect predinner nibble to offer your guests along with a flute of fizzy Champagne.

CONTENTS

ISBN-13: 978-0-8487-3658-3
ISBN-10: 0-8487-3658-3

Printed in the United States of America
First Printing 2012

Be sure to check with your health-care provider before making any changes in your diet.

Oxmoor House
Editorial Director: Leah McLaughlin
Creative Director: Felicity Keane
Brand Manager: Michelle Turner Aycock
Senior Editor: Heather Averett
Managing Editor: Rebecca Benton
Art Director: Claire Cormany

Cooking Light Annual Recipes 2013
Editor: Rachel Quinlivan West, R.D.
Project Editor: Sarah H. Doss
Senior Production Manager: Greg A. Amason
Assistant Production Manager: Diane Rose

Contributors
Designer: Carol Damsky
Assistant Editors: Emily Robinson, Katie Strasser
Copy Editor: Jacqueline Giovanelli
Proofreader: Julie Bosché
Indexer: Mary Ann Laurens
Interns: Laura Hoxworth, Susan Kemp

Time Home Entertainment Inc.
Publisher: Jim Childs
VP, Strategy & Business Development: Steven Sandonato
Executive Director, Marketing Services: Carol Pittard
Executive Director, Retail & Special Sales: Tom Mifsud
Director, Bookazine Development & Marketing: Laura Adam
Executive Publishing Director: Joy Butts
Finance Director: Glenn Buonocore
Associate General Counsel: Helen Wan

Cooking Light
Editor: Scott Mowbray
Creative Director: Carla Frank
Executive Managing Editor: Phillip Rhodes
Executive Editor, Food: Ann Taylor Pittman
Special Publications Editor: Mary Simpson Creel, MS, RD
Senior Food Editors: Timothy Q. Cebula, Julianna Grimes
Senior Editor: Cindy Hatcher
Assistant Editor, Nutrition: Sidney Fry, MS RD
Assistant Editors: Kimberly Holland, Phoebe Wu
Test Kitchen Director: Vanessa T. Pruett
Assistant Test Kitchen Director: Tiffany Vickers Davis
Recipe Testers and Developers: Robin Bashinsky, Adam Hickman, Deb Wise
Art Directors: Fernande Bondarenko, Shawna Kalish
Associate Art Director: Rachel Cardina Lasserre
Designers: Hagen Stegall, Dréa Zacharenko
Assistant Designer: Nicole Gerrity
Photo Director: Kristen Schaefer
Assistant Photo Editor: Amy Delaune
Senior Photographer: Randy Mayor
Senior Photo Stylist: Cindy Barr
Chief Food Stylist: Kellie Gerber Kelley
Food Styling Assistant: Blakeslee Wright
Production Director: Liz Rhoades
Production Editor: Hazel R. Eddins
Assistant Production Editor: Josh Rutledge
Copy Chief: Maria Parker Hopkins
Assistant Copy Chief: Susan Roberts
Research Editor: Michelle Gibson Daniels
Administrative Coordinator: Carol D. Johnson
CookingLight.com Editor: Allison Long Lowery
CookingLight.com Nutrition Editor: Holley Johnson Grainger, MS, RD
CookingLight.com Production Assistant: Mallory Daughtery Brasseale

To order additional publications, call 1-800-765-6400 or 1-800-491-0551.

For more books to enrich your life, visit **oxmoorhouse.com**

To search, savor, and share thousands of recipes, visit **myrecipes.com**

Cover: *Pork Chops with Roasted Apples and Onions (page 270)*
Back Cover (left to right): *Garlicky Meatball Pasta (page 91),*
Beef Tenderloin Steaks and Balsamic Green Beans (page 44),
Double-Cherry Upside-Down Cake (page 176)
Front Flap: *Chicken and Prosciutto Salad with Arugula and Asiago*
(page 101)
Page 1: *Tomato Tart (page 193)*

ALL HAIL THE KING OF THE DINNER BIRDS

25 chicken recipes! 5 preparation methods! It all adds up to a chick-tacular flock of fresh ideas for simple and healthful dinners.

SAUTÉ

This high-heat, quick-cooking method puts a chicken dinner on the table in a flash. Dust the bird with a supersheer layer of flour for a crisp, golden exterior, or simply season with salt and pepper.

Kid Friendly • Quick & Easy

Sautéed Chicken with Warm Bacon Vinaigrette

Hands-on time: 26 min. Total time: 26 min. If you can't find arugula, substitute mixed salad greens or fresh baby spinach.

1 tablespoon olive oil
4 (6-ounce) skinless, boneless chicken breast halves
5/8 teaspoon kosher salt, divided
1/2 teaspoon black pepper
3 applewood-smoked bacon slices
1/4 cup finely chopped shallots
2 tablespoons white wine vinegar
1/3 cup fat-free, lower-sodium chicken broth
1 tablespoon maple syrup
2 1/2 teaspoons Dijon mustard
6 cups arugula

1. Heat a large skillet over medium-high heat. Add oil to pan; swirl to coat. Sprinkle chicken evenly with 1/2 teaspoon salt and pepper. Add chicken to pan; sauté 6 minutes on each side or until done. Remove chicken; let stand 8 minutes. Slice and keep warm.
2. Reduce heat to medium. Add bacon to pan; cook 6 minutes or until crisp, turning once. Remove bacon from pan, reserving drippings; drain. Crumble bacon. Add shallots to drippings in pan, and cook 30 seconds, stirring constantly. Stir in vinegar, scraping pan to loosen browned bits. Stir in broth, syrup, and mustard; cook 1 minute, stirring frequently. Remove from heat. Arrange 1 1/2 cups arugula on each of 4 plates; sprinkle evenly with remaining 1/8 teaspoon salt. Top each serving with 1 chicken breast half. Drizzle 2 tablespoons dressing over each serving; top evenly with crumbled bacon. Serves 4.

CALORIES 350; **FAT** 15.7g (sat 4.1g, mono 6.9g, poly 1.7g); **PROTEIN** 43g; **CARB** 6.8g; **FIBER** 0.6g; **CHOL** 106mg; **IRON** 1.9mg; **SODIUM** 697mg; **CALC** 71mg

Kid Friendly • Quick & Easy

Open-Faced Chicken Club Sandwiches

Hands-on time: 23 min. Total time: 23 min. This flavorful sandwich will add brightness to even the coldest winter day. Serve it with fresh seasonal citrus or other fruit.

1 tablespoon olive oil
4 (6-ounce) skinless, boneless chicken breast halves
1/4 teaspoon kosher salt, divided
1/4 teaspoon freshly ground black pepper
2 teaspoons fresh lemon juice
3 tablespoons canola mayonnaise
1 ripe peeled avocado, coarsely mashed
4 (1-ounce) slices sourdough bread, toasted
4 pieces green leaf lettuce
2 plum tomatoes, each cut into 6 slices
4 center-cut bacon slices, cooked and drained

1. Heat a large skillet over medium-high heat. Add oil to pan; swirl to coat. Sprinkle chicken evenly with 1/8 teaspoon salt and pepper. Add chicken to pan; sauté 6 minutes on each side or until done. Remove from pan; let stand 5 minutes. Slice.
2. Combine remaining 1/8 teaspoon salt, juice, mayonnaise, and avocado in a small bowl; stir until well blended. Spread about 3 tablespoons avocado mixture over each bread slice. Top each sandwich with 1 lettuce leaf, 1 chicken breast half, 3 tomato slices, and 1 bacon slice. Serves 4.

CALORIES 400; **FAT** 18g (sat 3.3g, mono 9.2g, poly 3.4g); **PROTEIN** 36g; **CARB** 22.5g; **FIBER** 4.8g; **CHOL** 85mg; **IRON** 2.5mg; **SODIUM** 597mg; **CALC** 45mg

Maple-Brined Chicken with Sautéed Brussels Sprouts

Bring ⅓ cup maple syrup; ¼ cup fat-free, lower-sodium chicken broth; 2 tablespoons kosher salt; 2 tablespoons black peppercorns; and 4 crushed garlic cloves to a boil. Remove from heat; stir in 3 cups cold water. Place 4 (6-ounce) skinless, boneless chicken breast halves in a zip-top plastic bag; add brine. Seal; chill 2 hours. Remove chicken; discard brine. Sprinkle chicken with ¼ teaspoon freshly ground black pepper and ⅛ teaspoon kosher salt. Heat a large skillet over medium-high heat. Add 1 tablespoon olive oil; swirl to coat. Add chicken; sauté 5 minutes on each side or until done. Remove chicken from pan. Keep warm. Heat 2 tablespoons butter in a pan. Add 4 cups quartered Brussels sprouts and ½ cup sliced shallots; sauté 6 minutes. Stir in ¼ cup fat-free, lower-sodium chicken broth; cook 6 minutes. Stir in ½ cup chopped pecans. Serves 4 (serving size: 1 breast half and 1 cup Brussels sprouts).

CALORIES 437; **FAT** 22.9g (sat 5.8g); **SODIUM** 496mg

Quick & Easy
If you like olives try:

Sautéed Chicken with Olive Tapenade

Place 1 crushed garlic clove in a mini food processor; process until finely chopped. Add ⅓ cup pitted Castelvetrano (or other fruity) olives, 3 tablespoons pitted kalamata olives, and 1 teaspoon drained capers.

Pulse 10 times or until very finely chopped. With processor on, add 1½ tablespoons extra-virgin olive oil, ¾ teaspoon grated lemon rind, and ⅛ teaspoon crushed red pepper to mixture through food chute; process until combined. Heat a large skillet over medium-high heat. Coat pan lightly with cooking spray. Sprinkle both sides of 4 (6-ounce) skinless, boneless chicken breast halves evenly with ¼ teaspoon freshly ground black pepper and ⅛ teaspoon kosher salt. Add chicken to pan; sauté 6 minutes on each side or until done. Serve with tapenade. Serves 4.

CALORIES 242; **FAT** 11.5g (sat 1.5g); **SODIUM** 581mg

Quick & Easy
If you like onions try:

Sautéed Chicken with Onion Jam

Heat a large nonstick skillet over medium-high heat. Add 2 teaspoons olive oil to pan; swirl to coat. Add 5 cups vertically sliced red onion, 1 tablespoon chopped fresh thyme, and 1 minced garlic clove to pan; sauté 8 minutes, stirring frequently. Add 1½ tablespoons balsamic vinegar and ¼ teaspoon salt. Cover, reduce heat, and cook 15 minutes or until onion is very tender, stirring occasionally. Remove from heat; stir in 1 tablespoon chopped fresh chives, 1 tablespoon butter, and 1 teaspoon fresh lemon juice. Heat a large skillet over medium-high heat. Add 1 tablespoon olive oil; swirl. Sprinkle 4 (6-ounce) skinless, boneless chicken breast halves with ¼ teaspoon salt and ¼ teaspoon freshly ground black pepper. Add chicken to pan; sauté 6 minutes on each side or until done. Serve with jam. Serves 4 (serving size: 1 breast half and about ⅓ cup jam).

CALORIES 281; **FAT** 10.3g (sat 3.1g); **SODIUM** 406mg

Staff Favorite • Quick & Easy

Chicken Piccata
(pictured on page 217)

Hands-on time: 31 min. Total time: 31 min.
Serve this tangy dish with mashed potatoes or roasted seasonal root vegetables.

4 (6-ounce) skinless, boneless chicken breast halves
½ cup all-purpose flour, divided
½ teaspoon kosher salt
¼ teaspoon freshly ground black pepper
2½ tablespoons butter, divided
2 tablespoons olive oil, divided
¼ cup finely chopped shallots
4 medium garlic cloves, thinly sliced
½ cup dry white wine
¾ cup fat-free, lower-sodium chicken broth, divided
2 tablespoons fresh lemon juice
1½ tablespoons drained capers
3 tablespoons coarsely chopped fresh flat-leaf parsley

1. Place each chicken breast half between 2 sheets of heavy-duty plastic wrap; pound to ½-inch thickness using a meat mallet or small heavy skillet. Place 1 teaspoon flour in a small bowl; place remaining flour in a shallow dish. Sprinkle both sides of chicken evenly with salt and pepper. Dredge chicken in flour in shallow dish; shake off excess.
2. Melt 1 tablespoon butter in a large skillet over medium-high heat. Add 1 tablespoon oil to pan; swirl to coat. Add chicken to pan; sauté 4 minutes on each side or until done. Remove chicken from pan; keep warm.
3. Heat remaining 1 tablespoon oil in pan; swirl to coat. Add shallots to pan; cook 3 minutes, stirring frequently. Add garlic; cook 1 minute, stirring constantly. Add wine; bring to a boil, scraping pan to loosen browned bits. Cook until liquid almost evaporates, stirring occasionally. Add ¼ cup broth to reserved 1 teaspoon flour; stir until smooth. Add remaining ½ cup broth

to pan; bring to a boil. Cook until reduced by half (about 5 minutes). Stir in flour mixture; cook 1 minute or until slightly thick, stirring frequently. Remove from heat; stir in remaining 1½ tablespoons butter, juice, and capers. Place 1 chicken breast half on each of 4 plates; top each serving with about 2 tablespoons sauce. Sprinkle each serving with about 2 teaspoons parsley. Serves 4.

CALORIES 365; FAT 16.3g (sat 6.1g, mono 7.3g, poly 1.5g); PROTEIN 41.1g; CARB 9.3g; FIBER 0.7g; CHOL 118mg; IRON 2.1mg; SODIUM 574mg; CALC 41mg

BAKE

Assemble the ingredients in a baking dish or oven-safe pan, and then bake for a short time. Meanwhile, pull together your side dish hands-free while the entrée cooks.

Chicken with Olives and Lemons

Hands-on time: 8 min. Total time: 46 min.
Briny olives and tart lemons combine with fresh herbs for a Mediterranean-influenced chicken dish. Serve with hot cooked orzo.

2 teaspoons grated lemon rind
¼ cup fresh lemon juice
1 tablespoon extra-virgin olive oil
1½ tablespoons minced fresh garlic
4 (6-ounce) skinless, boneless chicken breast halves, halved crosswise
Cooking spray
2 teaspoons chopped fresh oregano
½ teaspoon chopped fresh rosemary
½ teaspoon freshly ground black pepper
15 oil-cured olives, pitted and sliced
1 large shallot, sliced
1 lemon, thinly sliced

1. Preheat oven to 400°.
2. Combine first 4 ingredients in a large zip-top plastic bag. Add chicken to bag; seal. Shake to coat chicken.

Marinate 15 minutes at room temperature. Arrange chicken mixture in a broiler-safe 11 x 7–inch glass or ceramic baking dish coated with cooking spray. Sprinkle chicken evenly with oregano and next 4 ingredients (through shallot); top with lemon slices. Bake at 400° for 20 minutes.
3. Remove chicken from oven. Preheat broiler to HIGH.
4. Place chicken 3 inches from broiler element; broil on HIGH 3 minutes or until chicken is browned and done. Serves 4 (serving size: 1 breast half, ¼ lemon, and about 4 olives).

CALORIES 271; FAT 7.5g (sat 1.3g, mono 4.3g, poly 1g); PROTEIN 40.7g; CARB 9.9g; FIBER 1.3g; CHOL 99mg; IRON 2.2mg; SODIUM 255mg; CALC 54mg

Quick & Easy
Double Plum Baked Chicken
(pictured on page 209)

Hands-on time: 20 min. Total time: 28 min.
If you can't find plum wine, substitute a sweet white wine, such as riesling or plum brandy.

1 tablespoon olive oil, divided
⅓ cup sliced shallots
2 teaspoons minced peeled fresh ginger
½ cup plum wine
¾ cup fat-free, lower-sodium chicken broth
1 teaspoon sambal oelek (such as ground fresh chile paste)
1 teaspoon Chinese mustard
½ cup halved dried plums (about 9)
4 (6-ounce) skinless, boneless chicken breast halves
¼ teaspoon salt
¼ teaspoon freshly ground black pepper
¼ cup (½-inch) slices green onions

1. Preheat oven to 425°.
2. Heat a medium saucepan over medium-high heat. Add 1 teaspoon oil to pan; swirl to coat. Add shallots

and ginger; sauté 1 minute. Add wine; bring to a boil. Cook 1 minute. Add broth, chili paste, and mustard; bring to a boil. Cook until reduced to ¾ cup (about 8 minutes). Stir in dried plums. Remove from heat.
3. Heat a large ovenproof skillet over medium-high heat. Add remaining 2 teaspoons oil to pan; swirl to coat. Sprinkle chicken with salt and pepper. Add chicken to pan, and sauté 3 minutes. Turn chicken over; pour plum mixture over chicken. Bake at 425° for 6 minutes or until done. Let chicken stand 5 minutes. Sprinkle with green onions. Serves 4 (serving size: 1 breast half, 2 tablespoons sauce, and 1 tablespoon green onions).

CALORIES 313; FAT 5.6g (sat 1g, mono 3g, poly 0.8g); PROTEIN 40.4g; CARB 17.6g; FIBER 1.4g; CHOL 99mg; IRON 1.7mg; SODIUM 376mg; CALC 37mg

Kid Friendly • Make Ahead
If you like pepper Jack cheese try:
Chicken and Rice

Preheat oven to 375°. Cut 12 ounces skinless, boneless chicken breast halves into strips. Heat a medium skillet over medium-high heat. Coat pan with cooking spray. Add chicken; sauté 1 minute. Remove chicken. Add 1½ cups chopped onion, 1 cup red bell pepper strips, and 1 cup yellow bell pepper strips to pan; sauté 5 minutes. Stir in 1 tablespoon all-purpose flour and 1 teaspoon ground cumin; cook 1 minute. Add ¾ cup fat-free, lower-sodium chicken broth, stirring until smooth. Cook 2 minutes. Add 8 ounces cubed processed pepper Jack cheese; stir until smooth. Remove from heat; stir in chicken and 2 cups cooked brown rice. Spoon mixture into an 11 x 7–inch glass or ceramic baking dish. Sprinkle mixture with 2 ounces shredded Monterey Jack cheese; bake at 375° for 25 minutes. Serves 6 (serving size: about 1½ cups).

CALORIES 357; FAT 12.9g (sat 6.9g); SODIUM 733mg

If you like sweet potato try:

Chicken with Root Vegetables

Preheat oven to 450°. Combine 2½ cups cubed peeled sweet potato, 2 cups peeled turnip wedges, 1 cup 1-inch carrot slices, 2 tablespoons maple syrup, and 5 halved shallots with 1½ tablespoons olive oil, 1 tablespoon minced fresh garlic, ½ teaspoon freshly ground black pepper, and ¼ teaspoon salt. Arrange mixture in a 13 x 9–inch glass or ceramic baking dish. Bake at 450° for 40 minutes, stirring once. Sprinkle 4 (6-ounce) skinless, boneless chicken breast halves with ½ teaspoon salt and ¼ teaspoon black pepper. Arrange chicken over vegetable mixture. Reduce oven temperature to 350°; bake at 350° for 20 minutes or until chicken is done. Let chicken stand 5 minutes; slice. Toss vegetable mixture with 1 tablespoon white balsamic vinegar. Shave 1 ounce fresh Parmigiano-Reggiano cheese (about ¼ cup) over mixture, and sprinkle with 1 tablespoon chopped fresh thyme. Serves 4 (serving size: 1 breast half, 1 cup vegetables, and about 1 tablespoon cheese).

CALORIES 409; FAT 9.2g (sat 1.8g); SODIUM 660mg

WHAT'S THE BEST BIRD?

If it's best flavor you're after, look for humanely raised, fresh (never frozen) chicken that hasn't been "marinated"— code for a 15% saline injection, which can make chicken taste like broth. To us, "air-chilling" is important. Many mass-produced birds are chilled in cold water, which waters down the flavor. Air-chilled birds taste rich and almost gamey, and our tasters deemed them worth the extra cost.

For our taste test, we gathered a variety of skinless, boneless chicken breast halves: fresh and frozen, low-priced to specialty. We cooked them without seasoning, and then sampled.

CHOP

Chop or cube chicken for fastest possible cooking. More exposed surface area allows the chicken to absorb flavor from sauces or other high-flavor ingredients.

Kid Friendly

Chicken Pizza

Hands-on time: 40 min. Total time: 1 hr.

1 (12-ounce) portion fresh pizza dough
2½ tablespoons olive oil, divided
2 (6-ounce) skinless, boneless chicken breast halves, cubed
1 (4-ounce) link sweet Italian sausage, casing removed
¼ cup vertically sliced onion
4 ounces cremini mushrooms, sliced
1 tablespoon chopped fresh garlic
2 teaspoons cornmeal
4 ounces fontina cheese, shredded
1 red bell pepper, seeded and sliced
¾ teaspoon crushed red pepper
2 tablespoons chopped fresh parsley
2 teaspoons chopped fresh thyme

1. Let dough rest, covered, at room temperature 30 minutes.
2. Preheat oven to 450°.
3. Heat a large skillet over medium-high heat. Add 1½ teaspoons oil, chicken, and sausage to pan; sauté 5 minutes. Remove mixture from pan. Add 1 tablespoon oil to pan; swirl to coat. Add onion, mushrooms, and garlic; sauté 5 minutes, stirring constantly.
4. Punch dough down. Sprinkle a baking sheet with cornmeal. Roll dough out to a 14-inch circle on baking sheet. Brush dough with 1 tablespoon oil; sprinkle with 2 ounces cheese. Arrange chicken mixture, vegetable mixture, and bell pepper over cheese, leaving a ¼-inch border. Top with remaining cheese and crushed red pepper. Bake at 450° for 20 minutes or until golden. Sprinkle with herbs. Serves 6 (serving size: 2 slices).

CALORIES 414; FAT 19.4g (sat 5.8g, mono 7g, poly 2.6g); PROTEIN 25.9g; CARB 33.9g; FIBER 1.9g; CHOL 64mg; IRON 2.9mg; SODIUM 641mg; CALC 154mg

Kid Friendly • Make Ahead

Chicken Spaghetti

Hands-on time: 60 min. Total time: 60 min.

1 cup boiling water
½ ounce dried porcini mushrooms
8 ounces uncooked spaghetti
2¼ teaspoons kosher salt, divided
2 tablespoons extra-virgin olive oil, divided
3 (6-ounce) skinless, boneless chicken breast halves, cut into bite-sized pieces
½ teaspoon black pepper
2 tablespoons butter
8 ounces cremini mushrooms, sliced
2 teaspoons minced fresh garlic
3 tablespoons all-purpose flour
1¼ cups fat-free, lower-sodium chicken broth
1¼ cups 2% reduced-fat milk
4 ounces processed cheese, cubed
3 ounces ⅓-less-fat cream cheese
2 ounces Gruyère cheese, shredded (about ½ cup)
1½ cups frozen English peas, thawed
⅓ cup finely chopped fresh chives
1½ ounces French bread, torn into pieces

1. Combine 1 cup boiling water and porcini mushrooms in a bowl; let stand 20 minutes. Drain in a colander over a bowl, reserving ½ cup soaking liquid. Chop porcini.
2. Cook pasta in boiling water with 2 teaspoons salt until almost al dente; drain. Rinse pasta with cold water; drain.
3. Heat a large saucepan over medium-high heat. Add 1 tablespoon oil, chicken, remaining ¼ teaspoon salt, and pepper; sauté 5 minutes, turning to brown. Remove chicken. Melt butter in pan. Add cremini mushrooms and garlic; sauté 3 minutes, stirring frequently. Add flour; sauté 1 minute, stirring constantly.
4. Arrange rack in middle of oven. Preheat broiler to HIGH.
5. Combine reserved porcini liquid, broth, and milk. Gradually add broth mixture to pan, stirring constantly;

bring to a boil. Reduce heat, and cook 1 minute or until slightly thick, stirring frequently. Stir in processed cheese and cream cheese. Remove from heat; stir until smooth. Stir in Gruyère. Add porcini, pasta, chicken, peas, and chives; toss. Scrape pasta mixture into a broiler-safe 13 x 9–inch glass or ceramic baking dish.

6. Place bread in a food processor; drizzle with remaining 1 tablespoon oil. Process until coarse crumbs form. Sprinkle crumbs over pasta mixture. Place dish on middle rack in oven; broil 6 minutes or until golden. Serves 8 (serving size: about 1½ cups).

CALORIES 413; FAT 16.4g (sat 7.9g, mono 5g, poly 1.2g); PROTEIN 29g; CARB 36g; FIBER 3.1g; CHOL 75mg; IRON 2.8mg; SODIUM 583mg; CALC 228mg

Quick & Easy

Szechuan Chicken Stir-Fry

Hands-on time: 25 min. Total time: 25 min.

1 tablespoon dark sesame oil, divided
½ cup fat-free, lower-sodium chicken broth
2 tablespoons lower-sodium soy sauce
1 tablespoon rice vinegar
2 teaspoons sambal oelek (such as ground fresh chile paste)
2 teaspoons cornstarch
¼ teaspoon salt
2 tablespoons canola oil, divided
1 pound skinless, boneless chicken breast halves, cut into bite-sized pieces
1 yellow bell pepper, cut into strips
1 red bell pepper, cut into strips
1 cup diagonally cut snow peas
½ cup vertically sliced onion
1 tablespoon grated peeled fresh ginger
1 tablespoon minced fresh garlic
2 cups hot cooked long-grain white rice
¼ cup (1-inch) slices green onions
¼ cup chopped unsalted roasted peanuts

1. Combine 2 teaspoons sesame oil and next 6 ingredients in a small bowl. Heat a large skillet over medium-high heat. Add remaining 1 teaspoon sesame oil and 1 tablespoon canola oil to pan; swirl to coat. Add chicken; stir-fry 2 minutes. Remove chicken from pan. **2.** Add remaining 1 tablespoon canola oil to pan; swirl to coat. Add bell peppers and next 4 ingredients; stir-fry 1 minute. Add broth mixture; cook 30 seconds or until thick. Return chicken to pan; cook 4 minutes or until chicken is done. Spoon ½ cup rice onto each of 4 plates; top each with 1 cup chicken mixture, green onions, and peanuts. Serves 4.

CALORIES 420; FAT 16.7g (sat 2g, mono 8.2g, poly 5.1g); PROTEIN 32.3g; CARB 32.3g; FIBER 2.7g; CHOL 66mg; IRON 2.7mg; SODIUM 478mg; CALC 45mg

Quick & Easy
If you like butternut squash try:

Moroccan-Style Chicken Tagine

Combine ½ teaspoon salt, ½ teaspoon ground cumin, ½ teaspoon ground cinnamon, ¼ teaspoon ground ginger, and ½ teaspoon ground red pepper. Sprinkle mixture over 2½ cups chopped skinless, boneless chicken breast. Heat a large skillet over medium-high heat. Add 1 tablespoon olive oil to pan; swirl to coat. Add chicken, and sauté 4 minutes. Stir in 1 cup (½-inch) cubed peeled butternut squash; ½ cup fat-free, lower-sodium chicken broth; 1 (15-ounce) can no-salt-added drained chickpeas; and 1 (14.5-ounce) can diced tomatoes; bring to a boil. Reduce heat, and simmer 5 minutes or until squash is tender. Combine 1½ cups boiling water and 1 cup uncooked couscous. Cover; let stand 5 minutes. Stir in ¼ cup toasted sliced almonds and 1 teaspoon grated orange rind. Serves 4 (serving size: 1¼ cups chicken mixture and ¾ cup couscous).

CALORIES 431; FAT 8.2g (sat 1g); SODIUM 658mg

If you like Brie try:
Chicken Quesadillas

Preheat oven to 400°. Heat a large skillet over medium-high heat. Coat with cooking spray. Add 3 cups chopped skinless, boneless chicken breast; sauté chicken 4 minutes. Add 2 tablespoons minced fresh garlic and 1 seeded, minced jalapeño; sauté 2 minutes. Stir in ½ cup chopped plum tomato and ¼ cup chopped green onions. Brush 1 tablespoon olive oil over a jelly-roll pan; arrange 4 (8-inch) fat-free flour tortillas on pan. Spread 1 ounce Brie cheese over half of each tortilla; top with about ⅓ cup chicken mixture. Bake at 400° for 5 minutes. Fold each tortilla in half. Bake 12 minutes, turning once. Combine ¾ cup chopped pear, 2 tablespoons chopped fresh cilantro, 3 tablespoons minced red onion, 1 tablespoon fresh lemon juice, 2 teaspoons olive oil, ⅛ teaspoon ground cumin, and ⅛ teaspoon ground red pepper. Serve with quesadillas. Serves 4 (serving size: 1 quesadilla and about ¼ cup salsa).

CALORIES 420; FAT 15.3g (sat 6.2g); SODIUM 620mg

If you like coconut milk try:

Green Curry Chicken

Combine 2 tablespoons minced shallots, 2 tablespoons green curry paste, 1 tablespoon lower-sodium soy sauce, 1 tablespoon dark sesame oil, 2 teaspoons grated peeled fresh ginger, 2 teaspoons minced fresh garlic, ½ teaspoon sugar, ½ teaspoon ground cumin, and ½ teaspoon sambal oelek (such as ground fresh chile paste). Heat a large skillet over medium-high heat. Add 1 tablespoon canola oil to pan; swirl to coat. Add 12 ounces cubed skinless, boneless chicken breast to pan; sauté 2 minutes. Add curry mixture and 1 (13.5-ounce) can light coconut milk; bring to a boil. Reduce heat, and simmer 4 minutes. Stir in 2 cups chopped bok choy, ¼ cup sliced green onions, and ¼ cup chopped fresh cilantro; cook 2 minutes. Reduce heat, and simmer 8 minutes or until chicken is done, stirring occasionally. Serve with 2 cups hot cooked long-grain rice. Serves 4 (serving size: ½ cup rice and ¾ cup chicken mixture).

CALORIES 402; **FAT** 12.9g (sat 5.4g); **SODIUM** 352mg

GLAZE

Brush chicken with a savory-sweet glaze for gorgeous results. Browning in a skillet first gives it a delicious crust and pretty appearance. Finishing it in liquid ensures it will be moist.

Maple-Mustard Glazed Chicken

Hands-on time: 15 min. Total time: 25 min. The tangy-sweet flavor combination of this sauce will work equally well with chicken thighs or pork. Serve with hot cooked rice and steamed haricots verts or a tossed green salad.

2 teaspoons olive oil
4 (6-ounce) skinless, boneless chicken breast halves
½ teaspoon freshly ground black pepper
¼ teaspoon salt
¼ cup fat-free, lower-sodium chicken broth
¼ cup maple syrup
2 teaspoons chopped fresh thyme
2 medium garlic cloves, thinly sliced
1 tablespoon cider vinegar
1 tablespoon stone-ground mustard

1. Preheat oven to 400°.
2. Heat a large ovenproof skillet over medium-high heat. Add oil to pan; swirl to coat. Sprinkle chicken with pepper and salt. Add chicken to pan; sauté 2 minutes on each side or until browned. Remove chicken from pan. Add broth, syrup, thyme, and garlic to pan; bring to a boil, scraping pan to loosen browned bits. Cook 2 minutes, stirring frequently. Add vinegar and mustard; cook 1 minute, stirring constantly. Return chicken to pan, and spoon mustard mixture over chicken. Bake at 400° for 10 minutes or until chicken is done. Remove chicken from pan; let stand 5 minutes. Place pan over medium heat; cook mustard mixture 2 minutes or until liquid is syrupy, stirring frequently. Serve with chicken. Serves 4 (serving size: 1 breast half and about 1 tablespoon sauce).

CALORIES 264; **FAT** 4.4g (sat 0.9g, mono 2.2g, poly 0.7g); **PROTEIN** 39.5g; **CARB** 14.2g; **FIBER** 0.2g; **CHOL** 99mg; **IRON** 1.6mg; **SODIUM** 337mg; **CALC** 38mg

If you like pomegranate try:

Pomegranate Chicken

Heat a small saucepan over medium-high heat. Add 1 teaspoon olive oil to pan; swirl to coat. Add 2 tablespoons minced shallots and ½ teaspoon chopped fresh rosemary; sauté 1 minute. Stir in 1 cup pomegranate juice, ¼ cup agave nectar, and 2 tablespoons red wine vinegar; bring to a boil. Cook until reduced to ½ cup (about 15 minutes), stirring occasionally. Remove from heat; stir in 1 tablespoon butter. Heat a large skillet over medium-high heat. Add 1 tablespoon olive oil to pan; swirl to coat. Sprinkle 4 (6-ounce) skinless, boneless chicken breast halves with ¼ teaspoon salt and ¼ teaspoon freshly ground black pepper. Add chicken to pan; sauté 4 minutes on each side or until browned. Brush chicken with ¼ cup glaze; cook 1 minute. Turn chicken over; brush with remaining glaze. Cook 1 minute or until chicken is done. Garnish with pomegranate arils, if desired. Serves 4 (serving size: 1 breast half).

CALORIES 363; **FAT** 9.5g (sat 3g); **SODIUM** 287mg

If you like chipotle try:

Chipotle Chicken

Preheat oven to 350°. Combine ¼ cup minced onion; ¼ cup agave nectar; 3 tablespoons fat-free, lower-sodium chicken broth; 1 minced chipotle chile; and 1 tablespoon adobo sauce from chipotle can. Heat an ovenproof skillet over medium-high heat. Add 2 teaspoons olive oil to pan; swirl to coat. Sprinkle 4 (6-ounce) skinless, boneless chicken breast halves with ½ teaspoon salt and ½ teaspoon freshly ground black pepper. Add chicken to pan; cook 3 minutes on each side or until browned. Add onion mixture to pan; bring to a boil. Bake at 350° for 8 minutes or until done, turning and basting once. Remove chicken from pan. Return pan to medium heat. Bring glaze to a boil; cook 2 minutes or until thick and bubbly. Stir in 1 tablespoon fresh lime juice. Brush over chicken. Serves 4 (serving size: 1 breast half).

CALORIES 276; **FAT** 4.5g (sat 0.9g); **SODIUM** 495mg

If you like balsamic vinegar try:
Balsamic Chicken

Combine ⅓ cup balsamic vinegar, ¼ cup lower-sodium soy sauce, ¼ cup minced shallots, 3 tablespoons brown sugar, 1 tablespoon minced garlic, and 1 tablespoon olive oil. Place 4 (6-ounce) skinless, boneless chicken breast halves in a zip-top plastic bag. Add vinegar mixture; seal. Marinate in refrigerator 1 hour. Preheat oven to 400°. Remove chicken from bag; reserve marinade. Place marinade in a small, heavy saucepan over medium heat; bring to a boil. Boil 2 minutes or until syrupy, stirring frequently. Remove from heat; divide mixture in half. Heat a large ovenproof skillet over medium-high heat. Add 1 tablespoon olive oil to pan; swirl to coat. Add chicken; sauté 4 minutes. Turn chicken over; brush with half of vinegar mixture. Bake at 400° for 6 minutes or until done. Remove chicken from oven; brush with remaining vinegar mixture. Serves 4 (serving size: 1 breast half).

CALORIES 320; **FAT** 8.9g (sat 1.5g); **SODIUM** 510mg

Miso Chicken

Hands-on time: 22 min. Total time: 1 hr. 22 min. *If you can't find miso, substitute 2 teaspoons anchovy paste and 1 teaspoon tahini instead. With miso, the darker the color, the more pronounced the salty flavor.*

- **¼ cup rice vinegar**
- **3 tablespoons lower-sodium soy sauce**
- **2½ tablespoons honey**
- **1½ tablespoons white miso**
- **1½ teaspoons sambal oelek (such as ground fresh chile paste)**
- **2 tablespoons minced fresh garlic**
- **2 tablespoons dark sesame oil, divided**
- **4 (6-ounce) skinless, boneless chicken breast halves**
- **2 tablespoons chopped fresh cilantro (optional)**

1. Combine first 6 ingredients, stirring well with a whisk. Stir in 1 tablespoon oil. Place chicken in a zip-top plastic bag. Add vinegar mixture; seal. Marinate in refrigerator 1 hour, turning once.
2. Preheat oven to 400°.
3. Remove chicken from bag; reserve marinade. Place marinade in a small, heavy saucepan over medium heat; bring to a boil. Boil 2 minutes or until syrupy, stirring frequently. Remove from heat; divide mixture in half. Heat a large ovenproof skillet over medium-high heat. Add remaining 1 tablespoon oil to pan; swirl to coat. Add chicken; sauté 4 minutes. Turn chicken over; brush chicken with half of marinade mixture. Place pan in oven; bake at 400° for 6 minutes or until done. Remove chicken from oven; brush with remaining half of marinade mixture, turning to coat. Sprinkle with cilantro, if desired. Serves 4 (serving size: 1 breast half).

CALORIES 314; **FAT** 9.1g (sat 1.6g, mono 3.5g, poly 3.5g); **PROTEIN** 41.5g; **CARB** 15.7g; **FIBER** 1.3g; **CHOL** 99mg; **IRON** 1.9mg; **SODIUM** 608mg; **CALC** 29mg

---

POACH

Poaching is a gentle cooking method, less popular but absolutely worthwhile. Beautiful flavor and moist meat result, and the cooking liquid can double as a tasty element in the recipe.

Make Ahead
Chicken Enchiladas

Hands-on time: 47 min. Total time: 1 hr. 52 min. *Use the freshest tortillas you can find since older ones tend to dry out and crack even though they're moistened in the sauce.*

- **4 cups cold water**
- **2 cups fat-free, lower-sodium chicken broth**
- **1 tablespoon whole black peppercorns**
- **5 garlic cloves, crushed**
- **2 (6-ounce) skinless, boneless chicken breast halves**
- **1 celery stalk, coarsely chopped**
- **1 large carrot, peeled and cut into ½-inch pieces**
- **1 jalapeño pepper, halved**
- **½ medium onion, cut into wedges**
- **1 (7-ounce) can salsa verde**
- **¼ cup heavy whipping cream**
- **1 cup chopped seeded tomato**
- **¼ cup chopped fresh cilantro**
- **¼ teaspoon kosher salt**
- **½ teaspoon ground cumin**
- **¼ teaspoon ground red pepper**
- **4 ounces ⅓-less-fat cream cheese, softened**
- **12 (6-inch) corn tortillas**
- **Cooking spray**
- **1 ounce sharp cheddar cheese, shredded (about ¼ cup)**

1. Combine first 9 ingredients in a saucepan over medium heat; bring to a simmer. Cook 8 minutes or until chicken is done. Remove chicken from pan using a slotted spoon; let stand 10 minutes. Shred chicken, and set aside. Drain cooking liquid through a sieve over a bowl; reserve cooking liquid. Discard solids.

continued

2. Combine reserved cooking liquid and salsa verde in a saucepan; bring to a boil over medium-high heat. Cook until reduced to 1½ cups (about 30 minutes). Reduce heat to low; stir in whipping cream. Place pan over low heat.
3. Preheat oven to 400°.
4. Place chicken in a medium bowl. Add tomato and next 5 ingredients to chicken; toss. Dip each tortilla in sauce mixture 10 seconds. Fill each tortilla with about ⅓ cup chicken mixture; roll up. Arrange filled tortillas, seam sides down, in an 11 x 7–inch glass or ceramic baking dish coated with cooking spray. Spoon sauce over tortillas; top evenly with cheddar cheese. Bake at 400° for 20 minutes or until lightly browned. Serves 6 (serving size: 2 enchiladas).

CALORIES 262; **FAT** 10.8g (sat 5.7g, mono 0.2g, poly 0.7g); **PROTEIN** 18.3g; **CARB** 22.8g; **FIBER** 2.5g; **CHOL** 65mg; **IRON** 0.6mg; **SODIUM** 715mg; **CALC** 79mg

Make Ahead
Chicken and Chorizo Stew

Hands-on time: 40 min. Total time: 56 min.

2 cups fat-free, lower-sodium chicken broth
2 cups water
1 bunch fresh flat-leaf parsley
3 garlic cloves
1 onion, quartered
1 medium carrot, chopped
2 (6-ounce) skinless, boneless chicken breast halves
6 ounces chopped Spanish chorizo
3 cups cubed red potato
1½ cups chopped onion
1 medium red bell pepper, chopped
1 tablespoon minced fresh garlic
½ teaspoon ground cumin
¼ teaspoon kosher salt
¼ teaspoon saffron threads
1½ tablespoons sherry vinegar
2 tablespoons chopped fresh parsley

1. Combine first 6 ingredients in a saucepan over medium-high heat. Add chicken to pan; bring mixture to a boil. Reduce heat, and simmer 14 minutes or until chicken is done. Remove chicken, reserving cooking liquid; cool. Shred chicken. Strain cooking liquid through a fine sieve over a bowl; discard solids.
2. Wipe pan with paper towels. Sauté sausage over medium-high heat 2 minutes. Add potato, onion, and bell pepper; sauté 8 minutes, stirring occasionally. Add garlic and next 3 ingredients (through saffron); sauté 2 minutes, stirring constantly. Add reserved cooking liquid; bring to a simmer. Simmer 12 minutes, stirring occasionally. Add shredded chicken; simmer 5 minutes. Remove from heat; stir in vinegar. Ladle about 1 cup stew into each of 4 bowls; top each serving with 2 tablespoons chopped parsley. Serves 4.

CALORIES 357; **FAT** 14.8g (sat 5.2g, mono 6.9g, poly 2.2g); **PROTEIN** 27.1g; **CARB** 27.5g; **FIBER** 3.5g; **CHOL** 69mg; **IRON** 2.2mg; **SODIUM** 751mg; **CALC** 63mg

Kid Friendly • Make Ahead
If you like crème fraîche try:
Creamy Chicken and Mushrooms

Combine 4 cups fat-free, lower-sodium chicken broth; 2 cups water; ⅓ cup chopped onion; 3 thyme sprigs; and 1 celery stalk in a saucepan. Add 4 (6-ounce) skinless, boneless chicken breast halves; bring to a simmer. Simmer gently 15 minutes or until chicken is done. Remove chicken from pan; cool. Shred chicken. Strain cooking liquid through a sieve over a bowl, reserving 1 cup cooking liquid; reserve remaining cooking liquid for another use. Discard solids. Heat a skillet over medium-high heat. Add 1 tablespoon olive oil, ½ cup thinly sliced shallots, and 2 teaspoons minced garlic; sauté 1 minute, stirring frequently. Add

8 ounces sliced cremini mushrooms, ½ teaspoon kosher salt, and ¼ teaspoon freshly ground black pepper; sauté 3 minutes. Add ½ cup dry white wine; cook until liquid evaporates. Stir in 2 teaspoons all-purpose flour; cook 1 minute. Stir in reserved cooking liquid; bring to a boil. Cook 1 minute. Remove from heat; stir in chicken and ½ cup crème fraîche. Serve over 6 (2-ounce) toasted whole-grain bread slices. Serves 6.

CALORIES 404; **FAT** 13g (sat 5.5g); **SODIUM** 708mg

Make Ahead
If you like brown rice try:
Chicken and Rice Salad

Place 4 cups cold water; 2 cups fat-free, lower-sodium chicken broth; and 3 (6-ounce) skinless, boneless chicken breast halves in a saucepan over high heat; bring to a simmer. Reduce heat, and simmer 15 minutes or until chicken is done. Remove chicken from pan, reserving cooking liquid; cool. Shred chicken. Increase heat to medium-high; bring cooking liquid to a boil. Add 1 cup brown and wild rice blend to pan. Cover, reduce heat, and simmer 28 minutes. Add 1 cup chopped peeled carrot to rice; cook 7 minutes or until rice is tender. Drain. Combine 2 tablespoons white wine vinegar, 2 tablespoons olive oil, and 2 teaspoons Dijon mustard. Toss dressing with rice mixture. Stir in shredded chicken, ½ cup toasted chopped pecans, ⅓ cup sweetened dried cranberries, ¼ cup chopped red onion, 3 tablespoons chopped fresh parsley, ½ teaspoon kosher salt, and ¼ teaspoon freshly ground black pepper. Spoon 1½ cups rice mixture into each of 6 bowls. Sprinkle evenly with 2 ounces crumbled goat cheese. Serves 6.

CALORIES 372; **FAT** 15.8g (sat 3.6g); **SODIUM** 467mg

OUR BEST CHOCOLATE RECIPE EVER

Sixteen recipes battle head-to-head, tournament-style, in a bake-off to find our most intense, most chocolaty treat of the past 25 years.

So we were talking chocolate. How would we surface the best recipes published in our first quarter-century? Taste them all, obviously! But that meant hundreds of dishes. Using our own ratings and those of web users, we narrowed the list to a Sweet 16: cake against cupcake, pudding against mousse, pastry against candy. Tastings followed, and much passionate argument.

"Best" is subjective, but also technical and nuanced. Was it important for us to distinguish between a great recipe that happens to contain chocolate and a great chocolate recipe—a paragon of chocolatiness? We decided it was. Above all, the winner had to deliver intense, deep chocolate satisfaction to anyone with a serious chocolate jones, while showing off deft use of the star ingredient (or cocoa, or a combo) in a convincingly lighter context—which brought into focus changing tastes and techniques. Some older recipes were eliminated because flavors seemed too tangy or textures too bouncy. Cooks will spot a pattern in a lot of the best contenders: Unsweetened cocoa (low in calories and fat) sets the chocolate foundation for a rich, bittersweet base, then some amount of "real" chocolate and cocoa butter adds depth. Dairy butter pushed the two finalists to the top, delivering an extra bit of richness that enhances a full-on hit of chocolate oomph.

[No. 4]

Kid Friendly • Freezable
Make Ahead

Double Chocolate Ice Cream

Hands-on time: 35 min. Total time: 2 hr. 5 min. A combo of cocoa powder and melted chocolate makes for a rich, ultra-chocolaty dessert. We updated the recipe to use heavy cream in place of the half-and-half in the original. Note: If you're using a 1½-quart tabletop ice-cream maker, it'll be pretty full.
Recipe by Julianna Grimes, July 2006

1⅓ cups sugar
⅓ cup unsweetened cocoa
2½ cups 2% reduced-fat milk, divided
3 large egg yolks
⅓ cup heavy whipping cream
2½ ounces bittersweet chocolate, chopped

1. Combine sugar and cocoa in a medium, heavy saucepan over medium-low heat. Add ½ cup milk and egg yolks, stirring well. Stir in remaining 2 cups milk. Cook 12 minutes or until a thermometer registers 160°, stirring constantly. Remove from heat.
2. Place cream in a microwave-safe bowl; microwave at HIGH 1½ minutes or until cream boils. Add chocolate; stir until smooth. Add cream mixture to pan; stir until smooth. Place pan in a large ice-filled bowl. Cool completely, stirring occasionally.
3. Pour mixture into freezer can of an ice-cream freezer; freeze according to manufacturer's instructions. Spoon ice cream into a freezer-safe container; cover and freeze 1 hour or until firm. Serves 10 (serving size: about ½ cup).

CALORIES 226; **FAT** 8.9g (sat 4.6g, mono 1.5g, poly 0.3g); **PROTEIN** 4g; **CARB** 35.6g; **FIBER** 1g; **CHOL** 79mg; **IRON** 0.7mg; **SODIUM** 37mg; **CALC** 75mg

[No. 3]

Quick & Easy

Chocolate-Frangelico Fondue

Hands-on time: 35 min. Total time: 35 min.
Recipe by Marge Perry, October 2000

⅓ cup half-and-half
¼ cup fat-free milk
8 ounces semisweet chocolate, chopped
1¼ cups sifted powdered sugar
2 tablespoons dark corn syrup
2 tablespoons Frangelico (hazelnut-flavored liqueur)
4 cups (1-inch) cubed angel food cake
2 cups quartered small strawberries

1. Combine first 3 ingredients in a medium saucepan; cook over medium-low heat 5 minutes or until smooth, stirring constantly. Stir in sugar and syrup. Cook 10 minutes or until mixture is smooth, stirring constantly. Stir in liqueur. Pour into a fondue pot. Keep warm over low flame. Serve with cake and strawberries. Serves 8 (serving size: ½ cup cake, ¼ cup strawberries, and about 3½ tablespoons fondue).

CALORIES 319; **FAT** 9.4g (sat 5.8g, mono 2.6g, poly 0.4g); **PROTEIN** 3.9g; **CARB** 57.5g; **FIBER** 2.5g; **CHOL** 4mg; **IRON** 0.3mg; **SODIUM** 148mg; **CALC** 52mg

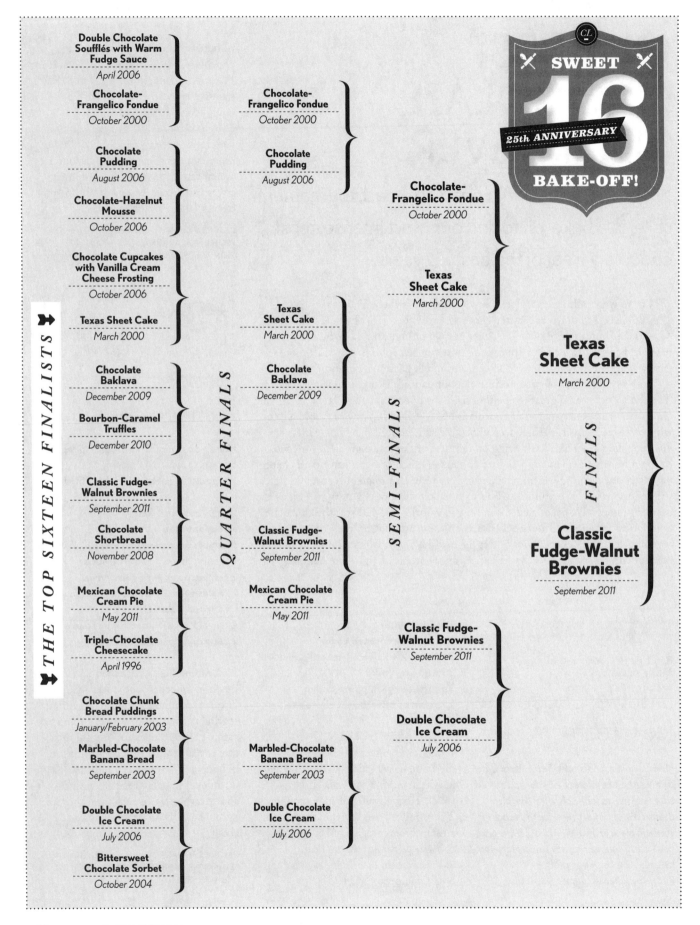

THE TOP SIXTEEN FINALISTS

Double Chocolate Soufflés with Warm Fudge Sauce
April 2006

Chocolate-Frangelico Fondue
October 2000

Chocolate Pudding
August 2006

Chocolate-Hazelnut Mousse
October 2006

Chocolate Cupcakes with Vanilla Cream Cheese Frosting
October 2006

Texas Sheet Cake
March 2000

Chocolate Baklava
December 2009

Bourbon-Caramel Truffles
December 2010

Classic Fudge-Walnut Brownies
September 2011

Chocolate Shortbread
November 2008

Mexican Chocolate Cream Pie
May 2011

Triple-Chocolate Cheesecake
April 1996

Chocolate Chunk Bread Puddings
January/February 2003

Marbled-Chocolate Banana Bread
September 2003

Double Chocolate Ice Cream
July 2006

Bittersweet Chocolate Sorbet
October 2004

QUARTER FINALS

Chocolate-Frangelico Fondue
October 2000

Chocolate Pudding
August 2006

Texas Sheet Cake
March 2000

Chocolate Baklava
December 2009

Classic Fudge-Walnut Brownies
September 2011

Mexican Chocolate Cream Pie
May 2011

Marbled-Chocolate Banana Bread
September 2003

Double Chocolate Ice Cream
July 2006

SEMI-FINALS

Chocolate-Frangelico Fondue
October 2000

Texas Sheet Cake
March 2000

Classic Fudge-Walnut Brownies
September 2011

Double Chocolate Ice Cream
July 2006

FINALS

Texas Sheet Cake
March 2000

Classic Fudge-Walnut Brownies
September 2011

SWEET 16 BAKE-OFF!
25th ANNIVERSARY

[No. 2]

Kid Friendly • Make Ahead

Texas Sheet Cake

***Hands-on time: 17 min. Total time:
1 hr. 5 min.*** *With a presence as large as its
namesake state, this humble, easy-to-prepare
cake made it all the way to the finals. Since it
first appeared in the magazine 12 years ago,
it's been a staff and reader favorite.*
Recipe by Maureen Callahan, March 2000

Cooking spray
2 teaspoons all-purpose flour
**9 ounces all-purpose flour (about
   2 cups)**
2 cups granulated sugar
1 teaspoon baking soda
1 teaspoon ground cinnamon
¼ teaspoon salt
¾ cup water
½ cup butter
½ cup unsweetened cocoa, divided
½ cup low-fat buttermilk
**1 tablespoon vanilla extract,
   divided**
2 large eggs
6 tablespoons butter
⅓ cup fat-free milk
3 cups powdered sugar
¼ cup chopped pecans, toasted

1. Preheat oven to 375°.
2. Coat a 15 x 10–inch jelly-roll pan
with cooking spray; dust with 2 teaspoons flour. Set aside.
3. Weigh or lightly spoon 9 ounces
flour (about 2 cups) into dry measuring cups; level with a knife. Combine 9
ounces flour and next 4 ingredients in
a large bowl. Combine ¾ cup water, ½
cup butter, and ¼ cup cocoa in a saucepan; bring to a boil, stirring frequently.
Pour into flour mixture. Beat with
a mixer at medium speed until well
blended. Add buttermilk, 1 teaspoon
vanilla, and eggs; beat well. Pour batter

into prepared pan. Bake at 375° for 17
minutes or until a wooden pick inserted
in center comes out clean. Place on a
wire rack.
4. Combine 6 tablespoons butter,
fat-free milk, and remaining ¼ cup
cocoa in a saucepan. Bring to a boil,
stirring constantly. Remove from heat.
Gradually stir in powdered sugar; stir
in remaining 2 teaspoons vanilla and
pecans. Spread over hot cake. Cool
completely on wire rack. Serves 20
(serving size: 1 piece).

CALORIES 298; **FAT** 10g (sat 5.5g, mono 3.2g, poly 0.7g);
PROTEIN 3.1g; **CARB** 49.8g; **FIBER** 0.5g; **CHOL** 44mg;
IRON 1.1mg; **SODIUM** 188mg; **CALC** 25mg

[No. 1]

Kid Friendly • Make Ahead

Classic Fudge-Walnut Brownies

Hands-on time: 15 min. Total time: 45 min.
*The most recent recipe in the competition,
it won unanimously because of the intense
richness from cocoa, melted chocolate, and
chocolate chunks.*
*Recipe by Maureen Callahan, September
2011*

**3.38 ounces all-purpose flour (about
   ¾ cup)**
1 cup granulated sugar
¾ cup unsweetened cocoa
½ cup packed brown sugar
½ teaspoon baking powder
¼ teaspoon salt
**1 cup bittersweet chocolate chunks,
   divided**
⅓ cup fat-free milk
6 tablespoons butter, melted
1 teaspoon vanilla extract
2 large eggs, lightly beaten
½ cup chopped walnuts, divided
Cooking spray

1. Preheat oven to 350°.
2. Weigh or lightly spoon flour into
dry measuring cups; level with a knife.
Combine flour and next 5 ingredients
in a large bowl. Combine ½ cup
chocolate and milk in a microwave-
safe bowl; microwave at HIGH 1
minute, stirring after 30 seconds. Stir
in butter, vanilla, and eggs. Add milk
mixture, remaining ½ cup chocolate,
and ¼ cup nuts to flour mixture; stir
to combine.
3. Pour batter into a 9-inch square
metal baking pan coated with cooking
spray; sprinkle with remaining ¼ cup
nuts. Bake at 350° for 22 minutes or
until a wooden pick inserted in center
comes out with moist crumbs clinging.
Cool in pan on a wire rack. Cut into
20 pieces. Serves 20 (serving size: 1
brownie).

CALORIES 186; **FAT** 9.1g (sat 4.2g, mono 2.2g, poly 1.7g);
PROTEIN 2.8g; **CARB** 25.4g; **FIBER** 1.4g; **CHOL** 30mg;
IRON 0.9mg; **SODIUM** 74mg; **CALC** 23mg

WAS IT THE NUTS
THAT PUSHED
THESE TWO RECIPES
TO THE TOP?
POSSIBLY.
BUT BEYOND
THE NUTS IS THE
NIRVANA OF TRUE
FUDGINESS.

ALL SOUPED UP

Anywhere a chicken walks the earth, a cook stalks behind with a big soup pot. Chicken soup is simply the gold standard of global comfort food. Here are our favorites from six countries.

Quick & Easy • Make Ahead

Chicken Soup with Cabbage and Apple

(pictured on page 211)

Hands-on time: 29 min. Total time: 39 min.
Few cooks put cabbage to more inspired use than the Germans. This soup is the definition of hearty in a bowl: Earthy green cabbage mingles with moist shredded chicken and chicken sausage; broth-soaked potatoes; and tart, crunchy apple that adds a fruity counterpoint.

2 teaspoons caraway seeds
1/2 teaspoon fennel seeds
1 tablespoon olive oil
1 1/2 cups chopped onion
1/2 cup chopped carrot
1/2 cup chopped celery
3 garlic cloves, minced
4 ounces chicken apple sausage, sliced
5 cups Chicken Stock (page 32) or fat-free, lower-sodium chicken broth
8 ounces chopped Yukon gold potato
3 cups thinly sliced green cabbage
2 cups shredded cooked chicken breast (about 8 ounces)
2 cups sliced Granny Smith apple
1 tablespoon cider vinegar
1/4 teaspoon kosher salt
1/4 teaspoon freshly ground black pepper

1. Heat a skillet over medium heat. Add caraway and fennel; cook 2 minutes, stirring constantly. Place in a spice or coffee grinder; process until ground.
2. Heat a Dutch oven over medium heat. Add oil; swirl to coat. Add onion, carrot, celery, and garlic; cook 6 minutes. Add sausage; cook 1 minute. Add ground spices, and cook 30 seconds, stirring constantly. Add Chicken Stock and potato; bring to a boil. Cover, reduce heat, and simmer 10 minutes. Increase heat to medium-high. Add cabbage and remaining ingredients; cook 3 minutes. Serves 4 (serving size: about 1 1/2 cups).

CALORIES 328; FAT 9.8g (sat 2.2g, mono 3.7g, poly 1.2g); PROTEIN 28.5g; CARB 33.2g; FIBER 6.4g; CHOL 85mg; IRON 2.5mg; SODIUM 369mg; CALC 94mg

---

SHORTCUT: CANNED BROTH

Nothing quite beats the taste of homemade chicken stock, but few are the cooks who have time or freezer space for all the fresh stock they could use.

Store-bought is the practical alternative, but beware the salt. Look for reduced-sodium options. Our staff favorite is a mouthful to say: Swanson Natural Goodness Chicken Broth 33% Less Sodium. It has rich, roasted-chicken flavor. It also has about 547mg more sodium per cup than our Chicken Stock recipe (page 32), so you'll want to reduce or skip the added salt in the soup.

Kid Friendly • Freezable
Make Ahead

Old-Fashioned Chicken Noodle Soup

Hands-on time: 51 min. Total time: 1 hr. 1 min. *This soup is classic American comfort food. But it can cross to the wrong side of the road if there are too many odds and ends, if noodles bloat and meat gets dry. Here's a cure, if common chicken soup leaves you cold: a purist's ideal, using flavorful stock, fresh-cooked chicken, traditional veggies, and egg noodles that lend starchy body to the broth.*

8 cups Chicken Stock (page 32) or fat-free, lower-sodium chicken broth
2 (4-ounce) skinless, bone-in chicken thighs
1 (12-ounce) skinless, bone-in chicken breast half
2 cups diagonally sliced carrot
2 cups diagonally sliced celery
1 cup chopped onion
6 ounces uncooked medium egg noodles
1/2 teaspoon kosher salt
1/2 teaspoon freshly ground black pepper
Celery leaves (optional)

1. Combine first 3 ingredients in a Dutch oven over medium-high heat; bring to a boil. Reduce heat; simmer 20 minutes. Remove chicken from pan; let stand 10 minutes. Remove chicken from bones; shred meat into bite-sized pieces. Discard bones.
2. Add carrot, celery, and onion to pan; cover and simmer 10 minutes. Add noodles, and simmer 6 minutes. Add chicken, salt, and black pepper; cook 2 minutes or until noodles are done. Garnish with celery leaves, if desired. Serves 4 (serving size: about 1 1/2 cups).

CALORIES 423; FAT 7.7g (sat 2.2g, mono 1.6g, poly 1.4g); PROTEIN 44.4g; CARB 42.2g; FIBER 4.8g; CHOL 171mg; IRON 3.3mg; SODIUM 474mg; CALC 98mg

Moroccan Chicken and Butternut Squash Soup

Hands-on time: 40 min. Total time: 48 min.
This soup is basically a tagine—lamb or poultry slowly stewed with fragrant spices— thinned to soup consistency, with couscous to starch it up.

1 tablespoon olive oil
1 cup chopped onion
3 (4-ounce) skinless, boneless chicken thighs, cut into bite-sized pieces
1 teaspoon ground cumin
¼ teaspoon ground cinnamon
⅛ to ¼ teaspoon ground red pepper
3 cups (½-inch) cubed peeled butternut squash
2 tablespoons no-salt-added tomato paste
4 cups Chicken Stock (page 32) or fat-free, lower-sodium chicken broth
⅓ cup uncooked couscous
¾ teaspoon kosher salt
1 zucchini, quartered lengthwise and sliced into ¾-inch pieces
½ cup coarsely chopped fresh basil
2 teaspoons grated orange rind

1. Heat a Dutch oven over medium heat. Add oil to pan; swirl to coat. Add onion; cook 4 minutes, stirring occasionally. Add chicken; cook 4 minutes, browning on all sides. Add cumin, cinnamon, and pepper to pan; cook 1 minute, stirring constantly. Add butternut squash and tomato paste; cook 1 minute. Stir in Chicken Stock, scraping pan to loosen browned bits. Bring to a boil. Reduce heat, and simmer 8 minutes. Stir in couscous, salt, and zucchini; cook 5 minutes or until squash is tender. Remove pan from heat. Stir in basil and orange rind. Serves 4 (serving size: 1½ cups).

CALORIES 292; **FAT** 8g (sat 1.6g, mono 3.8g, poly 1.6g); **PROTEIN** 24.4g; **CARB** 31.7g; **FIBER** 5g; **CHOL** 83mg; **IRON** 2.8mg; **SODIUM** 474mg; **CALC** 109mg

Avgolemono

Hands-on time: 21 min. Total time: 37 min.
Avgolemono is an amazingly creamy soup without a drop of cream. Egg-thickened broth is spiked with tart lemon juice, all enrobing a beautiful chicken core. Greeks serve it chilled in the summer. In winter, it's cooked with rice and dished up piping hot. Folks who hit the ouzo too hard have been said to find relief the next day in a steaming bowlful. Sounds likely. Whisk constantly as you add the egg mixture to the hot soup so that the egg thickens but doesn't scramble.

2 teaspoons olive oil
½ cup chopped onion
3 garlic cloves, minced
6½ cups Chicken Stock (page 32) or fat-free, lower-sodium chicken broth
½ cup uncooked long-grain rice
⅓ cup fresh lemon juice
2 teaspoons cornstarch
½ teaspoon salt
½ teaspoon freshly ground black pepper
1 large egg, lightly beaten
2 cups shredded cooked chicken breast (about 8 ounces)
2 tablespoons chopped fresh parsley
2 tablespoons torn fresh basil

1. Heat a Dutch oven over medium-high heat. Add oil to pan; swirl to coat. Add onion and garlic; sauté 2 minutes. Add Chicken Stock; bring to a boil. Stir in rice; reduce heat, and simmer 16 minutes. Combine juice, cornstarch, salt, pepper, and egg in a small bowl, stirring with a whisk. Slowly pour egg mixture into broth mixture, stirring constantly with a whisk. Add chicken to broth mixture; cook until mixture thickens and rice is done (about 3 minutes). Top with parsley and basil. Serves 4 (serving size: about 1½ cups).

CALORIES 269; **FAT** 7g (sat 1.5g, mono 3.5g, poly 1.1g); **PROTEIN** 25.4g; **CARB** 25.7g; **FIBER** 1.1g; **CHOL** 116mg; **IRON** 2.1mg; **SODIUM** 541mg; **CALC** 54mg

Spicy Thai Coconut Chicken Soup

Hands-on time: 25 min. Total time: 32 min.
The Thais are among the world's great soup-makers. It's hot over there, but they like their soup piping hot and often incredibly spicy. Coconut milk tames the heat and combines deliciously with chicken in this soup. This version of tom kha ga smooths the edges of tart lime, salty fish sauce, and fiery chile paste. It all comes into perfect chicken-y balance.

2 teaspoons canola oil
1 cup sliced mushrooms
½ cup chopped red bell pepper
4 teaspoons minced peeled fresh ginger
4 garlic cloves, minced
1 (3-inch) stalk lemongrass, halved lengthwise
2 teaspoons sambal oelek (such as ground fresh chile paste)
3 cups Chicken Stock (page 32) or fat-free, lower-sodium chicken broth
1¼ cups light coconut milk
4 teaspoons fish sauce
1 tablespoon sugar
2 cups shredded cooked chicken breast (about 8 ounces)
½ cup green onion strips
3 tablespoons chopped fresh cilantro
2 tablespoons fresh lime juice

1. Heat a Dutch oven over medium heat. Add oil to pan; swirl to coat. Add mushrooms and next 4 ingredients; cook 3 minutes, stirring occasionally. Add chile paste; cook 1 minute. Add Chicken Stock, coconut milk, fish sauce, and sugar; bring to a simmer. Reduce heat to low; simmer 10 minutes. Add chicken to pan; cook 1 minute or until thoroughly heated. Discard lemongrass. Top with onions, cilantro, and juice. Serves 4 (serving size: about 1⅓ cups).

CALORIES 224; **FAT** 9g (sat 4.5g, mono 2.4g, poly 1.3g); **PROTEIN** 22.7g; **CARB** 15g; **FIBER** 1.1g; **CHOL** 58mg; **IRON** 1.1mg; **SODIUM** 463mg; **CALC** 35mg

Freezable • Make Ahead

Chicken-Udon Soup

Hands-on time: 32 min. Total time:
***1 hr. 2 min.** Yummy, thick Japanese udon noodles are the soul of this soup: slippery enough to slurp, fat enough to lend a satisfying chew. Shiitake mushrooms, fragrant star anise, and a touch of dry rice wine deepen the broth's flavor.*

1 (3½-ounce) package fresh shiitake
   mushrooms
4 cups Chicken Stock (at right) or
   fat-free, lower-sodium chicken broth
6 (¼-inch) slices peeled fresh ginger
3 garlic cloves, crushed
1 green onion, cut into 2-inch pieces
1 star anise
6 ounces dried udon noodles (thick
   Japanese wheat noodles)
1 tablespoon canola oil
2 teaspoons minced peeled fresh ginger
1 garlic clove, minced
¼ cup sake (rice wine) or sherry or dry
   white wine
2 cups shredded cooked chicken breast
1 tablespoon lower-sodium soy sauce
1 tablespoon honey
¼ teaspoon kosher salt
¼ cup diagonally cut green onions

1. Remove stems from mushrooms; reserve stems. Thinly slice mushroom caps; set aside. Combine mushroom stems, Chicken Stock, and next 4 ingredients (through anise) in a large saucepan. Bring to a boil. Cover, reduce heat, and simmer 20 minutes. Remove from heat. Let stand 10 minutes. Strain stock through a sieve over a bowl; discard solids.
2. Cook udon noodles according to package directions, omitting salt and fat. Drain and rinse with cold water; drain well.
3. Heat a large saucepan over medium-high heat. Add canola oil to pan; swirl to coat. Add reserved sliced mushroom caps to pan, and sauté 2 minutes. Add minced ginger and minced garlic; sauté 1 minute. Add sake, and cook 4 minutes, scraping pan to loosen browned bits. Add stock to pan. Bring to a boil, and reduce heat to medium-low. Add chicken, soy sauce, 1 tablespoon honey, and salt; simmer 2 minutes or until chicken is thoroughly heated. Divide noodles evenly among 4 bowls. Add 1½ cups soup to each bowl. Sprinkle each serving with 1 tablespoon green onions. Serves 4.

CALORIES 354; FAT 7.8g (sat 1.1g, mono 3.2g, poly 1.7g); PROTEIN 28.4g; CARB 37.8g; FIBER 3.1g; CHOL 61mg; IRON 2.7mg; SODIUM 345mg; CALC 45mg

Freezable • Make Ahead

Chicken Stock

Hands-on time: 30 min. Total time: 12 hr.

15 black peppercorns
12 parsley sprigs
10 thyme sprigs
8 pounds chicken backs, necks,
   or wings
5 carrots, chopped
5 celery stalks, chopped
4 bay leaves
3 large onions, chopped
5 quarts cold water

1. Combine all ingredients in a 12-quart stockpot. Bring to a boil over medium-high heat. Reduce heat to low; simmer 4 hours, skimming and discarding foam as needed. Strain through a cheesecloth-lined colander into a large bowl; discard solids. Cool stock to room temperature. Cover and refrigerate 6 hours or overnight. Skim fat from surface; discard fat. Serves 20 (serving size: 1 cup).

CALORIES 28; FAT 1.1g (sat 0.3g, mono 0.3g, poly 0.3g); PROTEIN 3.6g; CARB 0.7g; FIBER 0.1g; CHOL 15mg; IRON 0.2mg; SODIUM 23mg; CALC 12mg

TODAY'S LESSON: BAKED PASTA

The casserole idea is this: Disparate elements are combined, sauced, topped, and baked until yummy. In the noodle casserole, pasta and sauce canoodle in the oven so that the former absorbs the flavor of the latter and softens deliciously, while the cheese topping merrily bubbles and browns. In this class, we apply these principles to lighter expressions of casserole perfection. Let's get gooey.

Kid Friendly • Make Ahead Vegetarian

Mushroom Lasagna

Hands-on time: 40 min. Total time: 1 hr. 25 min. *Rich porcini broth and nutty Parmigiano-Reggiano add deep umami taste to this vegetarian lasagna. Plain white button mushrooms will work in place of cremini.*

1 cup boiling water
1 ounce dried porcini mushrooms
1 tablespoon butter
2 tablespoons olive oil, divided
1¼ cups chopped shallots (about 4)
1 (8-ounce) package presliced cremini mushrooms
1 (4-ounce) package presliced exotic mushroom blend
1 teaspoon salt, divided
½ teaspoon black pepper, divided
1½ tablespoons chopped fresh thyme
6 garlic cloves, minced and divided
½ cup white wine
3 ounces ⅓-less-fat cream cheese (about ⅓ cup)
2 tablespoons chopped fresh chives, divided
3 cups 2% reduced-fat milk, divided
1.1 ounces all-purpose flour (about ¼ cup)
Cooking spray
9 no-boil lasagna noodles
2 ounces grated Parmigiano-Reggiano cheese (about ½ cup)

1. Preheat oven to 350°.
2. Combine 1 cup boiling water and porcini. Cover and let stand 30 minutes, and strain mixture through a cheesecloth-lined sieve over a bowl, reserving liquid and mushrooms.
3. Melt butter in a large skillet over medium-high heat. Add 1 tablespoon oil to pan; swirl to coat. Add shallots to pan; sauté 3 minutes. Add cremini and exotic mushrooms, ½ teaspoon salt, and ¼ teaspoon pepper; sauté 6 minutes or until mushrooms are browned. Add thyme and 3 garlic cloves; sauté 1 minute. Stir in wine; bring to a boil. Cook 1 minute or until liquid almost evaporates, scraping pan to loosen browned bits. Remove from heat; stir in cream cheese and 1 tablespoon chives. Add reserved porcini mushrooms.
4. Heat a saucepan over medium-high heat. Add remaining 1 tablespoon oil to pan; swirl to coat. Add remaining 3 garlic cloves to pan; sauté 30 seconds. Add reserved porcini liquid, 2¾ cups milk, remaining ½ teaspoon salt, and remaining ¼ teaspoon pepper; bring to a boil. Weigh or lightly spoon flour into a dry measuring cup; level with a knife. Combine flour and remaining ¼ cup milk in a small bowl; stir with a whisk. Add flour mixture to milk mixture, and simmer 2 minutes or until slightly thick, stirring constantly with a whisk.
5. Spoon ½ cup sauce into an 11 x 7–inch glass or ceramic baking dish coated with cooking spray, and top with 3 noodles. Spread half of mushroom mixture over noodles. Repeat layers, ending with remaining sauce. Sprinkle cheese over top. Bake at 350° for 45 minutes or until golden. Top with remaining 1 tablespoon chopped chives. Serves 6.

CALORIES 396; FAT 15.4g (sat 7.1g, mono 5.5g, poly 0.8g); PROTEIN 17.1g; CARB 43.5g; FIBER 3.2g; CHOL 33mg; IRON 3.1mg; SODIUM 668mg; CALC 288mg

BROWNING

What separates baked pasta from regular sauced pasta is the gorgeously golden top layer of cheese. If the bake time doesn't get the top as browned as you'd like, give it a minute or two under the broiler (as long as your dish is broiler-safe).

OVEN-BOUND PASTA

1. BOIL WATER
Start with a big pot of water to give the pasta plenty of room to move. As a general rule, use about 5 quarts of water for every pound of pasta. (This much water returns to a boil faster after the pasta is added.) Stir the pasta occasionally for the first few minutes to help prevent sticking.

2. DON'T OVERCOOK
With baked pasta dishes—except for lasagnas that use no-boil noodles—the pasta cooks twice: once when boiled, and a second time in the oven. To prevent mushiness, boil noodles only until they're almost al dente.

3. GET SAUCY
The sauce in baked pasta is one of its main flavorings. Season it boldly with fresh herbs, garlic, and spices. But the sauce is also the medium for cooking the pasta again, so it should have enough liquid for the noodles to absorb as they bake.

Kid Friendly • Make Ahead

Bacon and Butternut Pasta

Hands-on time: 38 min. Total time: 1 hr. 15 min. *Broth, thickened with flour and enriched with crème fraîche, forms the savory sauce in this dish. We like the earthy heartiness of kale, which helps balance the sweetness from the squash. You could also use Swiss chard, or for a more peppery bite, try substituting mustard greens.*

5 cups (¹/₂-inch) cubed peeled butternut squash
1 tablespoon olive oil
Cooking spray
12 ounces uncooked ziti (short tube-shaped pasta), campanile, or other short pasta
4 cups chopped kale
2 bacon slices
2 cups vertically sliced onion
1 teaspoon salt, divided
5 garlic cloves, minced
2 cups fat-free, lower-sodium chicken broth, divided
2 tablespoons all-purpose flour
¹/₂ teaspoon crushed red pepper
1 cup crème fraîche
1¹/₂ ounces shredded Gruyère cheese (about ¹/₃ cup)

1. Preheat oven to 400°.
2. Combine squash and oil in a large bowl; toss well. Arrange squash mixture in a single layer on a baking sheet coated with cooking spray. Bake at 400° for 30 minutes or until squash is tender.
3. Cook pasta 7 minutes or until almost al dente, omitting salt and fat. Add kale to pan during last 2 minutes of cooking. Drain pasta mixture.
4. Cook bacon in a large nonstick skillet over medium heat until crisp. Remove bacon from pan; crumble. Add onion to drippings in pan; cook 6 minutes, stirring occasionally. Add ¹/₂ teaspoon salt and garlic; cook 1 minute, stirring occasionally.

5. Bring 1¾ cups broth to a boil in a small saucepan. Combine remaining ¹/₄ cup broth and flour in a small bowl, stirring with a whisk. Add flour mixture, remaining ¹/₂ teaspoon salt, and pepper to broth. Cook 2 minutes or until slightly thickened. Remove from heat; stir in crème fraîche.
6. Combine squash, pasta mixture, bacon, onion mixture, and sauce in a large bowl; toss gently. Place pasta mixture in a 13 x 9–inch glass or ceramic baking dish coated with cooking spray, and sprinkle evenly with cheese. Bake at 400° for 25 minutes or until bubbly and slightly browned. Serves 8 (serving size: about 1¹/₂ cups).

CALORIES 388; FAT 15.4g (sat 8.2g, mono 1.8g, poly 0.4g); PROTEIN 12.1g; CARB 51.4g; FIBER 4.8g; CHOL 36mg; IRON 2.9mg; SODIUM 475mg; CALC 166mg

---

Kid Friendly • Make Ahead

Shrimp-Stuffed Shells

Hands-on time: 22 min. Total time: 1 hr. 10 min. *Look for potato starch near the cornstarch in your supermarket.*

20 uncooked jumbo pasta shells (about 8 ounces)
1¹/₂ tablespoons olive oil
¹/₂ cup chopped shallots
2 tablespoons minced garlic (about 6 cloves)
4 ounces ¹/₃-less-fat cream cheese (about ¹/₂ cup)
¹/₄ cup 2% reduced-fat milk
¹/₄ teaspoon ground red pepper
¹/₃ cup chopped fresh basil
1 pound medium shrimp, peeled, deveined, and coarsely chopped
1 tablespoon potato starch
Cooking spray
3 cups lower-sodium marinara sauce (such as McCutcheon's), divided
1¹/₂ ounces grated fresh Parmigiano-Reggiano cheese (about ¹/₃ cup)

1. Preheat oven to 400°.

2. Cook pasta 7 minutes or until almost al dente, omitting salt and fat. Drain well.

3. Heat a medium skillet over medium heat. Add oil to pan; swirl to coat. Add shallots; cook 4 minutes, stirring occasionally. Add garlic; cook 1 minute, stirring constantly. Add cream cheese, milk, and pepper; cook until cheese melts, stirring until smooth. Remove from heat. Stir in basil. Place shrimp in a bowl. Sprinkle with potato starch; toss well to coat. Add cream cheese mixture to shrimp; toss well.

4. Divide shrimp mixture evenly among pasta shells. Coat a 13 x 9–inch glass or ceramic baking dish with cooking spray; spread 1 cup marinara over bottom of dish. Arrange shells in prepared dish; top with remaining 2 cups marinara. Sprinkle shells evenly with Parmigiano-Reggiano cheese. Bake at 400° for 30 minutes or until shrimp is done. Serves 5 (serving size: 4 stuffed shells).

CALORIES 496; **FAT** 16g (sat 6.2g, mono 5.3g, poly 1.4g); **PROTEIN** 31.1g; **CARB** 85.6g; **FIBER** 1.6g; **CHOL** 163mg; **IRON** 4.1mg; **SODIUM** 575mg; **CALC** 208mg

THE SHRIMP GOES INTO THE PASTA SHELLS RAW TO PREVENT IT FROM OVERCOOKING WHILE THE PASTA BAKES.

LESS MEAT, MORE FLAVOR

WHOLE-GRAIN RISOTTOS

By Mark Bittman

These vegetable-packed recipes feature the nutty flavor and chewy texture of farro and brown rice.

Risotto is among my favorite winter rituals. You stand over a pot, adding liquid and stirring rice, adding more liquid and stirring. The smell keeps you happy, the steam keeps you warm, and at a certain point the rice reaches that perfect balance of creaminess and bite. Put down your spoon, pick up the cheese grater, and then it's time to eat. There are worse ways to cook dinner.

Risotto is usually made with Arborio rice, a white Italian variety that oozes unctuous starch as you cook and stir. It's toasted with fat and aromatics, plied with flavor-packed liquids, and often finished with butter and/or cheese. But you're not obligated to stick to Arborio, and for that matter you're not obligated to make your vegetables play second fiddle to the rice. Whole grains make excellent risotto. Here, I make one with short-grain brown rice (par-cooked to give it a head start) and one with farro (an ancient wheat variety); I ratchet up the vegetable-to-starch ratio in the process.

The key to great risotto (no matter what kind of grain you choose) is building up flavor in the liquid that you use to cook the rice. You can go about that in a number of different ways. I use the soaking water for dried porcini as my cooking liquid for the brown rice; it infuses an inimitably intense mushroom flavor throughout the dish. For the farro, I start by sautéing a good bit of sliced leeks in olive oil. Both dishes get a splash of white wine (why not?) and chopped wintry herbs to further boost the flavor of the liquid. Of course, a rich chicken or vegetable stock in place of water improves things somewhat.

Risotto typically relies on the al dente bite of Arborio for its texture. Here, the whole grains give you that same satisfying chew and are laced with (and outnumbered by) vegetables that add even more texture, flavor, and body. In addition to the smattering of dried porcini, the brown rice gets a whole pound of fresh mushrooms and a shower of chopped green beans (you could use any fresh, crunchy vegetable with a short cooking time). They're sautéed together to intensify their flavor but preserve their respective chew and crunch. The dish is finished off with parsley and Parmesan, at once turning it brighter and richer.

After the farro and the first installments of liquid are added to the sautéed leeks, I stir in a generous amount of diced squash. If you time it right (which you will if you follow this recipe), the squash becomes just tender as the farro reaches al dente. The cubes of squash hold their shape and bite, and stand out wonderfully against the farro background. Any fall or winter root vegetable (like sweet potatoes, parsnips, or celery root) could be used in the same way. Grated Gruyère and chopped hazelnuts add the perfect touch of fat and salt at the end.

With whole grains instead of Arborio, lots of veggies instead of few, these risottos are every bit as pleasurable as the classic; worthy, I might even say, of becoming a new winter ritual.

continued

"Farrotto" with Butternut, Gruyère, and Hazelnuts

Hands-on time: 50 min. Total time: 1 hr. 20 min.

1 tablespoon olive oil
1½ cups thinly sliced leek (about 1 large)
1 cup uncooked farro
1 garlic clove, minced
½ cup white wine
4 cups water, divided
4 cups (½-inch) cubed peeled butternut squash
1 tablespoon chopped fresh sage
¾ teaspoon kosher salt
½ teaspoon freshly ground black pepper
2 ounces Gruyère cheese, grated (about ½ cup)
½ cup chopped hazelnuts, toasted

1. Heat a Dutch oven over medium-high heat. Add oil to pan; swirl to coat. Add leek; sauté 5 minutes or until tender, stirring frequently. Add farro and garlic; cook 1 minute, stirring constantly. Stir in wine; cook 1 minute or until wine evaporates. Add 1 cup water; cook 8 minutes or until liquid is nearly absorbed, stirring frequently. Add 2 more cups water, 1 cup at a time, stirring until each portion is absorbed before adding the next (about 30 minutes total). Stir in remaining 1 cup water, squash, sage, salt, and pepper. Cover, reduce heat, and simmer 30 minutes or until squash is just tender, stirring occasionally. Stir in cheese; sprinkle with nuts. Serve immediately. Serves 4 (serving size: about 1⅓ cups).

CALORIES 449; FAT 17.7g (sat 3.7g, mono 10.4g, poly 1.8g); PROTEIN 15g; CARB 58.1g; FIBER 9.6g; CHOL 15mg; IRON 4.4mg; SODIUM 417mg; CALC 261mg

Mushroom–Brown Rice Risotto

Hands-on time: 51 min. Total time: 1 hr. 6 min. *If the rice isn't tender enough after you've stirred in all the porcini liquid, add water and continue cooking and stirring until it's done.*

1½ teaspoons kosher salt, divided
1 cup short-grain brown rice
½ cup dried porcini mushrooms (about ½ ounce)
3 cups hot water
2 tablespoons olive oil, divided
1 pound button or cremini mushrooms, sliced
3 cups (1-inch) cut green beans
½ teaspoon black pepper, divided
½ cup chopped shallots
½ cup white wine
2 ounces Parmigiano-Reggiano cheese, grated (about ½ cup)
¼ cup chopped fresh flat-leaf parsley
2 teaspoons chopped fresh thyme

1. Bring a medium saucepan of water to a boil, and add 1 teaspoon salt. Stir in rice; reduce heat, and simmer 15 minutes (rice will not be done). Drain. Set aside.
2. Place porcini in a medium bowl; add 3 cups hot water. Let stand 15 minutes. Drain through a sieve over a bowl; reserve liquid. Chop porcini.
3. Heat a large skillet over medium-high heat. Add 1 tablespoon oil; swirl to coat. Add sliced fresh mushrooms; sauté 8 minutes or until moisture evaporates and mushrooms begin to brown, stirring occasionally. Stir in reserved porcini, green beans, ¼ teaspoon salt, and ¼ teaspoon black pepper; cook 2 minutes or until beans are crisp-tender. Place mushroom mixture in a large bowl; keep warm.
4. Return pan to medium-high heat; add remaining 1 tablespoon oil, and swirl to coat. Add shallots; sauté 4 minutes or until tender. Add rice; cook 2 minutes, stirring

occasionally. Stir in remaining ¼ teaspoon salt and remaining ¼ teaspoon black pepper. Stir in wine; cook 2 minutes or until wine evaporates, stirring constantly. Add ½ cup reserved mushroom liquid to rice mixture; cook 3 minutes or until liquid is nearly absorbed, stirring constantly. Stir in remaining mushroom liquid, ½ cup at a time, stirring constantly until each portion is absorbed before adding the next (about 30 minutes total). Stir in mushroom mixture, Parmigiano-Reggiano, and parsley; sprinkle with thyme. Serve immediately. Serves 4 (serving size: about 1¾ cups).

CALORIES 434; FAT 11.8g (sat 2.8g, mono 6.1g, poly 1.3g); PROTEIN 19.1g; CARB 60.6g; FIBER 9.1g; CHOL 9mg; IRON 6.6mg; SODIUM 534mg; CALC 180mg

5-INGREDIENT COOKING

Pan-Grilled Ginger-Honey Pork Tenderloin

Hands-on time: 10 min. Total time: 25 min.

Directions: Combine ginger, honey, juice, and soy sauce in a bowl, stirring with a whisk until smooth. Heat a grill pan over medium-high heat, and coat with cooking spray. Sprinkle pork with ½ teaspoon salt and ¼ teaspoon freshly ground black pepper. Add pork to grill pan; cook 15 minutes or until a thermometer registers 145° or until desired degree of doneness, basting frequently with sauce. Let stand 5 minutes before serving. Serves 4 (serving size: 3 ounces).

CALORIES 178; FAT 2.7g (sat 0.8g, mono 0.9g, poly 0.4g); PROTEIN 24.1g; CARB 14g; FIBER 0.1g; CHOL 74mg; IRON 1.3mg; SODIUM 489mg; CALC 8mg

THE FIVE INGREDIENTS

1 tablespoon grated peeled fresh ginger

+

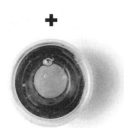

3 tablespoons honey

+

1 tablespoon fresh lemon juice

+

1 tablespoon lower-sodium soy sauce

+

1 (1-pound) pork tenderloin, trimmed

SECRET INGREDIENT

THE TRUFFLE OIL TRICK

Ignore the naysayers. Just a tiny drizzle turns a pan of mac and cheese into an earthy delight.

Much of the oil on the market is synthetic truffle-*flavored* oil. But you can find truffle oil that contains bits of real truffle—expensive (roughly $15 for a small, less-than-2-ounce bottle), but with a staggering, unique character. Our recipe transforms mac and cheese with less than 2 teaspoons of the stuff. Look for white truffle oil, garlicky and pungent, and buy the smallest bottle: A little goes a mile. After you've had your way with mac and cheese, try it in risotto, soup, or pasta tosses.

Kid Friendly • Vegetarian

Truffled Mac and Cheese

Hands-on time: 36 min. Total time: 44 min. White truffle oil has an intense earthy flavor that wakes up ordinary mac and cheese. We also get extra flavor by steeping the milk with onion and bay leaf.

2¼ cups 1% low-fat milk, divided
2 cups sliced onion (about 1 medium)
1 bay leaf
12 ounces uncooked elbow macaroni
2 tablespoons all-purpose flour
¾ teaspoon kosher salt
3 ounces shredded fontina cheese (about ¾ cup)
2 ounces shredded Comté or Gruyère cheese (about ½ cup)
1½ teaspoons white truffle oil
2 ounces French bread baguette, torn
2 tablespoons grated fresh Parmesan cheese
2 garlic cloves, crushed
1 tablespoon olive oil

1. Heat 1¾ cups milk, onion, and bay leaf in a large saucepan to 180° or until tiny bubbles form around edges (do not boil). Cover and remove from heat; let stand 15 minutes.
2. Cook pasta according to package directions; drain.
3. Strain milk mixture through a colander over a bowl; discard solids. Return milk to saucepan over medium heat. Combine remaining ½ cup milk and flour in a small bowl, stirring with a whisk until well blended. Gradually stir flour mixture and salt into warm milk, stirring constantly with a whisk. Bring mixture to a boil, stirring frequently; cook 1 minute, stirring constantly. Remove from heat; let stand 6 minutes or until mixture cools to 155°. Gradually add fontina and Comté cheeses, stirring until cheeses melt. Stir in pasta and truffle oil. Spoon mixture into a 2-quart broiler-safe glass or ceramic baking dish.
4. Preheat broiler.
5. Place bread, Parmesan cheese, and garlic in a food processor; process until coarse crumbs form. Drizzle with olive oil; pulse until fine crumbs form. Sprinkle breadcrumb mixture over pasta. Place dish on middle rack in oven; broil 2 minutes or until golden brown. Serves 6 (serving size: about 1 cup).

CALORIES 418; **FAT** 13.2g (sat 6.1g, mono 5.2g, poly 1.1g); **PROTEIN** 18.9g; **CARB** 55.2g; **FIBER** 2.1g; **CHOL** 33mg; **IRON** 2.4mg; **SODIUM** 528mg; **CALC** 325mg

HEARTY BEANS AND HEALTHY GREENS

Flavor-packed, deliciously textured: There's nothing as satisfying and comforting as these combinations.

Make Ahead • Vegetarian

Tuscan White Bean Soup with Escarole

Hands-on time: 15 min. Total time: 50 min.
Don't toss those rinds from Parmesan or other hard cheeses; store in the freezer, and simmer in soup for added richness and flavor.

1 tablespoon olive oil
2 cups finely chopped onion
5 garlic cloves, minced
2 cups organic vegetable broth
1 cup water
1 teaspoon chopped fresh rosemary
2 (15-ounce) cans no-salt-added Great Northern beans, rinsed and drained
2 thyme sprigs
1 (1½-ounce) piece Parmigiano-Reggiano cheese rind
8 cups chopped escarole (about 1 pound)
1 cup chopped carrot
½ teaspoon crushed red pepper
¼ teaspoon salt
¼ teaspoon freshly ground black pepper
1 teaspoon white wine vinegar
6 tablespoons shaved fresh Parmesan cheese

1. Heat a large Dutch oven over medium-high heat. Add oil to pan; swirl to coat. Add onion, and sauté 4 minutes, stirring frequently. Add garlic, and sauté 30 seconds. Add vegetable broth and next 5 ingredients (through cheese rind); bring to a boil. Reduce heat, and simmer 10 minutes. Stir in escarole and carrot; cover and simmer 15 minutes or until carrot is tender. Stir in red pepper, salt, black pepper, and vinegar. Remove and discard rind; sprinkle soup with shaved cheese. Serves 4 (serving size: about 2 cups soup and 1½ tablespoons cheese).

CALORIES 225; **FAT** 7.1g (sat 2.1g, mono 3.2g, poly 0.6g); **PROTEIN** 10.9g; **CARB** 31.2g; **FIBER** 9.7g; **CHOL** 8mg; **IRON** 2.7mg; **SODIUM** 644mg; **CALC** 220mg

Vegetarian

Butternut Squash and Smoky Black Bean Salad

Hands-on time: 47 min. Total time: 47 min. *You'll find chipotle chiles canned in adobo sauce on the Latin food aisle. Use just the sauce here; reserve chiles for another use.*

4 cups (½-inch) cubed peeled butternut squash
7 teaspoons extra-virgin olive oil, divided
½ cup walnuts, chopped
Cooking spray
½ teaspoon kosher salt, divided
2 tablespoons red wine vinegar
1 tablespoon Dijon mustard
1 tablespoon honey
1 tablespoon adobo sauce
2 garlic cloves, thinly sliced
¼ teaspoon black pepper
1 (15-ounce) can no-salt-added black beans, rinsed and drained
1 (9-ounce) package baby arugula
2 ounces crumbled goat cheese (about ½ cup)

1. Preheat oven to 425°.
2. Combine squash and 1 tablespoon oil; toss to coat. Arrange squash on a jelly-roll pan. Bake at 425° for 25 minutes or until tender.
3. Arrange walnuts on jelly-roll pan; coat with cooking spray. Sprinkle ⅛ teaspoon salt over nuts; toss. Bake at 425° for 10 minutes or until toasted, stirring once.
4. Combine 1 tablespoon olive oil, vinegar, mustard, honey, and adobo sauce in a bowl; stir with a whisk.
5. Heat a medium nonstick skillet over medium heat. Add remaining 1 teaspoon oil to pan; swirl to coat. Add garlic; sauté 1 minute. Add squash, remaining ⅜ teaspoon salt, pepper, and beans; cook 3 minutes or until heated through. Remove from heat; stir in 3 tablespoons adobo dressing; toss to coat.
6. Combine remaining dressing and arugula; toss to coat. Divide arugula mixture evenly among 4 plates; top with bean mixture. Sprinkle evenly with nuts and cheese. Serves 4 (serving size: 2 cups arugula, ¾ cup bean mixture, 2 tablespoons nuts, and 2 tablespoons cheese).

CALORIES 369; **FAT** 20.1g (sat 4g, mono 7.1g, poly 7.8g); **PROTEIN** 10.7g; **CARB** 39.8g; **FIBER** 10.2g; **CHOL** 10mg; **IRON** 4.5mg; **SODIUM** 544mg; **CALC** 170mg

Black-Eyed Pea Cakes and Beer-Braised Turnip Greens

Hands-on time: 35 min. Total time: 1 hr. 25 min. *You could serve this hearty dish on New Year's Day for prosperity and good fortune.*

Cakes:
1/4 cup uncooked quinoa
1/2 cup organic vegetable broth
2 cups canned black-eyed peas, rinsed, drained, and divided
2 garlic cloves, chopped
1/2 cup panko (Japanese breadcrumbs)
1/2 cup finely chopped red onion
1 1/2 teaspoons ground cumin
1/2 teaspoon black pepper
1/4 teaspoon kosher salt
1/8 teaspoon ground red pepper
2 large eggs, lightly beaten
1 tablespoon olive oil, divided

Greens:
2 teaspoons olive oil
1 1/2 pounds turnip greens, coarsely chopped
6 ounces light beer
1/2 teaspoon sugar
1/4 teaspoon black pepper
1/4 teaspoon kosher salt
4 garlic cloves, chopped
1 tablespoon red wine vinegar
2 tablespoons pine nuts, toasted

1. To prepare cakes, place quinoa in a fine sieve; place sieve in a large bowl. Cover quinoa with water. Using your hands, rub grains together 30 seconds; rinse and drain well. Combine broth and quinoa in a small saucepan, and bring to a boil. Cover, reduce heat, and simmer 20 minutes or until liquid is absorbed. Remove from heat, and fluff with a fork.

2. Place 1 cup peas and 2 garlic cloves in a food processor; process until peas make a thick paste. Combine pea mixture, remaining 1 cup peas, panko, and next 6 ingredients (through eggs) in a large bowl. Stir in quinoa. Divide mixture into 8 portions, shaping each into a 1/2-inch-thick patty.

3. Heat a large nonstick skillet over medium-high heat. Add 1 1/2 teaspoons oil, and swirl to coat. Add 4 patties, and cook 4 minutes on each side or until golden. Repeat procedure with remaining 1 1/2 teaspoons oil and patties. Keep warm.

4. To prepare greens, heat a large Dutch oven over medium heat. Add 2 teaspoons oil; swirl to coat. Add greens, beer, and next 4 ingredients (through garlic); bring to a boil. Cover, reduce heat, and simmer 30 minutes or until tender, stirring occasionally. Stir in vinegar. Serve with pea cakes; sprinkle with nuts. Serves 4 (serving size: 1 cup greens, 2 cakes, and 1 1/2 teaspoons nuts).

CALORIES 344; FAT 13.1g (sat 2.1g, mono 6.1g, poly 3.2g); PROTEIN 14g; CARB 42.9g; FIBER 10.5g; CHOL 106mg; IRON 4.4mg; SODIUM 716mg; CALC 383mg

FROM A READER'S KITCHEN

MUFFINS, PERKED UP

When a friend of Sarah Engeler-Young's husband showed her the recipe for a chocolate and coffee muffin, this mocha-lover knew it'd be an instant favorite—if only there were a way to trim the fat and calories. "People asked for the recipe, and I felt like the angel of death giving it to them," she said. So Engeler-Young experimented, making test batches to find the perfect balance of butter, egg, and sugar. Now these muffins are a guilt-free treat, perfect for breakfast or a snack.

Kid Friendly • Quick & Easy
Freezable • Make Ahead

Chocolate Chip–Coffee Muffins

Hands-on time: 17 min. Total time: 35 min. *"Watch the muffins carefully—they will toughen if baked too long."*
—Sarah Engeler-Young, Conway, Ark.

2/3 cup whole milk
5 tablespoons butter, melted
3 tablespoons instant coffee granules
1 1/2 teaspoons vanilla extract
1 large egg, lightly beaten
9 ounces all-purpose flour (about 2 cups)
2/3 cup sugar
1/2 cup semisweet chocolate chips
2 teaspoons baking powder
1/4 teaspoon salt
Cooking spray

1. Preheat oven to 400°.

2. Combine first 5 ingredients in a medium bowl.

3. Weigh or lightly spoon flour into dry measuring cups; level with a knife. Combine flour and next 4 ingredients (through salt) in a large bowl; stir well with a whisk. Make a well in center of flour mixture. Add milk mixture to flour mixture; stir just until moist.

4. Spoon batter into 12 muffin cups coated with cooking spray. Bake at 400° for 18 minutes or until done. Remove muffins from pan immediately; place on a wire rack. Serves 12 (serving size: 1 muffin).

CALORIES 214; FAT 7.9g (sat 4.8g, mono 2.2g, poly 0.4g); PROTEIN 3.6g; CARB 32.9g; FIBER 1g; CHOL 29mg; IRON 1.3mg; SODIUM 163mg; CALC 66mg

GRAPEFRUIT

Grapefruits pack a bracing jolt of refreshing flavor in the deep freeze of winter. Bright acids and a beautifully bitter edge are tempered by a kiss of sweetness. White, pink, or ruby fruits add zest to salads, whether you use tangy segments or fresh juice. Desserts, like our pound cake, blossom from the floral essence of grated rind.

Staff Favorite • Freezable Make Ahead

Grapefruit Pound Cake

Hands-on time: 20 min. Total time: 2 hr.

Baking spray with flour
9 ounces all-purpose flour (about 2 cups)
1 teaspoon baking powder
⁵/₈ teaspoon salt, divided
1²/₃ cups granulated sugar
6 tablespoons butter, softened
6 ounces ¹/₃-less-fat cream cheese
2 large eggs
¹/₄ cup canola oil
2 tablespoons grated grapefruit rind
¹/₂ teaspoon vanilla extract
¹/₂ cup 2% reduced-fat milk
¹/₂ cup fresh grapefruit juice
1¹/₄ cups powdered sugar

1. Preheat oven to 325°.
2. Coat a 10-inch tube pan with baking spray. Weigh or lightly spoon flour into dry measuring cups; level with a knife. Combine flour, baking powder, and ¹/₂ teaspoon salt, stirring well. Place granulated sugar, butter, and cream cheese in a large bowl; beat with a mixer at high speed until light and fluffy. Add eggs, 1 at a time, beating well after each addition. Beat in oil, rind, and vanilla.
3. Add flour mixture and milk alternately to batter, beginning and ending with flour. Spoon batter into pan; bake at 325° for 1 hour and 10 minutes or until a wooden pick inserted in center comes out with moist crumbs clinging. Cool 10 minutes in pan on a wire rack. Invert cake. Cool on wire rack.
4. Place juice in a saucepan over medium-high heat; bring to a boil. Cook until reduced to 3 tablespoons (about 4 minutes). Cool slightly. Stir in powdered sugar and remaining ¹/₈ teaspoon salt. Drizzle over cake. Serves 16 servings (serving size: 1 slice).

CALORIES 289; **FAT** 10.9g (sat 4.8g, mono 3.6g, poly 1.3g); **PROTEIN** 3.5g; **CARB** 44.8g; **FIBER** 0.5g; **CHOL** 42mg; **IRON** 0.9mg; **SODIUM** 202mg; **CALC** 41mg

PUCKER UP

Grapefruits are hybrids, usually a cross between the orange and the pummelo. These are the most common varieties.

WHITE GRAPEFRUIT
Also called golden grapefruit, they are tangier than the pink- or red-fleshed fruits.

PINK AND RUBY GRAPEFRUIT
Pinkish-red flesh tastes sweeter and contains lycopene and more vitamins.

PUMMELO
The largest of all citrus. Very sweet fruit under a thick blanket of pith.

DID YOU KNOW? GRAPEFRUITS ARE NAMED FOR THE GRAPE-LIKE CLUSTERS THEY GROW IN.

PERMISSION GRANTED: BREAD PUDDING

No, we're not sabotaging your resolution! This has just 300 calories.

Can a decadent, rich pudding really be made from plain old white bread? Yes, especially when that bread is drenched in heavy cream and eggs, and then drowned in a butter-based caramel sauce. This hearty dessert can weigh in at 800 calories and 30 grams of saturated fat per warm, gooey bowl. Thanks, but no thanks for a New Year's treat.

To ensure a rich, velvety interior without all the calories and fat, we first dry out French bread by toasting it; this maximizes its ability to soak up the custard. Instead of cream, low-fat milk combines with the concentrated, slightly caramelized flavor of fat-free evaporated milk, while bourbon, cinnamon, and vanilla offer a smoky-spiced flavor punch. The sauce blends brown sugar, bourbon, and a dash of salt (to balance the sweetness)—it's so good that we layer some in the middle of the pudding, and then drizzle the rest on top. It gets baked in a loaf pan for the perfect crust-to-creamy interior ratio. Our bread pudding is a slimmer, trimmer, and top-rated (by our picky Test Kitchen judges) redesign for the New Year.

Bread Pudding with Salted Caramel Sauce

Hands-on time: 25 min. Total time: 1 hr. 50 min. The sauce in the middle of the pudding is the secret to this velvety-rich interior.

Bread Pudding:
5 cups (½-inch) cubed French bread (about 8 ounces)
1 cup evaporated fat-free milk
¾ cup 1% low-fat milk
⅓ cup granulated sugar
2 tablespoons bourbon
1 tablespoon vanilla extract
1 teaspoon ground cinnamon
¼ teaspoon kosher salt
2 large eggs
Sauce:
¾ cup packed light brown sugar
3 tablespoons bourbon
1 tablespoon unsalted butter
6 tablespoons half-and-half, divided
1 teaspoon vanilla extract
⅛ teaspoon kosher salt
Cooking spray

1. Preheat oven to 350°.
2. To prepare bread pudding, arrange bread in a single layer on a baking sheet. Bake at 350° for 8 minutes or until lightly toasted.
3. Combine evaporated milk and next 7 ingredients (through eggs) in a large bowl, and stir with a whisk. Add bread cubes. Let stand 20 minutes, occasionally pressing on bread to soak up milk.
4. To prepare sauce, combine brown sugar, 3 tablespoons bourbon, and butter in a small saucepan over medium-high heat; bring to a boil. Simmer 2 minutes or until sugar dissolves, stirring frequently. Stir in 5 tablespoons half-and-half; simmer 10 minutes or until reduced to about 1 cup. Remove pan from heat. Stir in remaining 1 tablespoon half-and-half, 1 teaspoon vanilla, and ⅛ teaspoon salt. Keep warm.
5. Spoon half of bread mixture into a 9 x 5–inch loaf pan coated with cooking spray. Drizzle 3 tablespoons sauce over bread mixture. Spoon remaining half of bread mixture over sauce. Bake at 350° for 45 minutes or until a knife inserted in center comes out clean. Serve warm sauce with bread pudding. Serves 8 (serving size: 1 slice bread pudding and about 1½ tablespoons sauce).

CALORIES 300; **FAT** 4.8g (sat 2.4g, mono 1.4g, poly 0.5g); **PROTEIN** 8.5g; **CARB** 50.6g; **FIBER** 0.9g; **CHOL** 63mg; **IRON** 1.6mg; **SODIUM** 349mg; **CALC** 172mg

CLASSIC	MAKEOVER
843 calories per serving	300 calories per serving
50.3 grams total fat	4.8 grams total fat
30.2 grams saturated fat	2.4 grams saturated fat

BREAD PUDDING POINTERS

The success of this succulent pudding starts with how you treat the bread. Here's how to obtain that perfectly moist, creamy interior with a crisp outer crust.

1. Toast the bread cubes in the oven until lightly browned. This dries them out and allows them to soak up more of the creamy custard.

2. Soak the bread cubes in the egg-milk mixture for at least 20 minutes to ensure maximum custard absorption. Gently press on the bread once or twice while the cubes soak.

3. Drizzle a thin layer of sauce in the middle of the pudding to keep the bread supermoist while baking. Bake in a loaf pan to create a crispy crust around the creamy interior.

DINNER TONIGHT

Here is a batch of fast weeknight menus from the *Cooking Light* Test Kitchen.

READY IN 40 MINUTES

The
SHOPPING LIST

Seafood Cioppino
Onion (1 large)
Garlic
Fresh basil
Fresh oregano
Fresh flat-leaf parsley
Lemon (1)
Extra-virgin olive oil
Organic vegetable broth (1 cup)
35-ounce can whole tomatoes with basil (1)
Dry white wine (1 cup)
Crushed red pepper
10-ounce yellowtail snapper fillet (1)
Sea scallops (4)
Medium peeled and deveined shrimp (8)
Littleneck clams (12)

Garlic Sourdough
1.5-ounce slices sourdough bread (4)

The
GAME PLAN

Cook broth base.
While broiler preheats:
■ Brown snapper and scallops.
While seafood cooks in broth:
■ Toast bread.

Quick & Easy
Seafood Cioppino
With Garlic Sourdough

2 tablespoons extra-virgin olive oil, divided
2 cups vertically sliced onion
4 garlic cloves, sliced
1 cup dry white wine
1 cup organic vegetable broth
2 tablespoons chopped fresh basil
2 tablespoons chopped fresh oregano
½ teaspoon crushed red pepper
1 (35-ounce) can whole tomatoes with basil, rinsed, drained, and coarsely chopped
1 (10-ounce) yellowtail snapper fillet, cut into 8 (1-inch) cubes
4 sea scallops (about 6 ounces)
½ teaspoon black pepper
8 medium peeled and deveined shrimp (about 5 ounces)
12 littleneck clams, scrubbed
2 tablespoons chopped flat-leaf parsley
1 tablespoon fresh lemon juice

1. Heat a Dutch oven over medium-high heat. Add 1 tablespoon oil; swirl to coat. Add onion; sauté 1 minute. Add garlic; reduce heat to medium. Cover and cook 8 minutes, stirring occasionally. Add wine and next 5 ingredients (through tomatoes); cover. Bring to a boil; reduce heat and simmer, uncovered, 15 minutes.
2. Sprinkle snapper and scallops with black pepper. Heat a large skillet over high heat. Add remaining 1 tablespoon oil; swirl to coat. Add snapper and scallops; cook 90 seconds on each side or until golden brown. Add snapper, scallops, shrimp, and clams to broth mixture. Cover and cook 4 minutes or until clams open; discard any unopened shells. Stir in parsley and lemon juice. Serves 4 (serving size: about 1¾ cups).

Sustainable Choice — *Look for wild-caught yellowtail snapper.*

CALORIES 319; **FAT** 8.8g (sat 1.3g, mono 5.2g, poly 1.4g); **PROTEIN** 33.4g; **CARB** 13.9g; **FIBER** 1.8g; **CHOL** 103mg; **IRON** 6.5mg; **SODIUM** 596mg; **CALC** 109mg

---

Kid Friendly ● Quick & Easy
Vegetarian
For the Garlic Sourdough:
Preheat broiler. Broil 4 (1.5-ounce) slices sourdough bread 90 seconds, turning once. Rub toasted bread with cut sides of 2 halved garlic cloves. Brush with 2 tablespoons extra-virgin olive oil. Serves 4 (serving size: 1 toast slice).

CALORIES 167; **FAT** 7.7g (sat 0.9g); **SODIUM** 242mg

READY IN 40 MINUTES

The
SHOPPING LIST

Cheesy Potato Soup
Onion (1)
Red potatoes (1 pound)
Green onions
All-purpose flour
Ground red pepper
Fat-free, lower-sodium chicken broth (¾ cup)
Butter
1% low-fat milk (1¼ cups)
Reduced-fat sharp cheddar cheese (2 ounces)

Mini Ham Sandwiches
Fresh chives
Dijon mustard
Canola mayonnaise
Hawaiian rolls (8)
1-ounce reduced-sodium ham slices (4)

The
GAME PLAN

While oven preheats:
■ Simmer soup.
■ Prepare rolls.
Bake rolls; assemble sandwiches.

Cheesy Potato Soup

With Mini Ham Sandwiches

(pictured on page 211)

Technique Tip: Stir in cheese and remove from heat as soon as it melts to prevent curdling.

1 tablespoon butter
1 cup chopped onion
2¹⁄₂ tablespoons all-purpose flour
3 cups chopped red potato (about 1 pound)
1¹⁄₄ cups 1% low-fat milk
³⁄₄ cup fat-free, lower-sodium chicken broth
¹⁄₂ cup water
2 ounces shredded reduced-fat sharp cheddar cheese (about ¹⁄₂ cup)
¹⁄₈ teaspoon ground red pepper
2 tablespoons chopped green onions

1. Melt butter in a medium saucepan over medium-high heat. Add onion to pan; sauté 5 minutes or until onion is tender. Sprinkle with flour; cook 1 minute, stirring onion mixture constantly. Add potato, milk, broth, and ¹⁄₂ cup water to pan; bring to a boil. Cover, reduce heat, and simmer 10 minutes. Add cheese and red pepper; cook 2 minutes or until cheese melts, stirring frequently. Top each serving evenly with 1¹⁄₂ teaspoons green onions. Serves 4 (serving size: 1 cup).

CALORIES 225; **FAT** 6.9g (sat 4.1g, mono 1g, poly 0.2g); **PROTEIN** 9.9g; **CARB** 32.7g; **FIBER** 2.6g; **CHOL** 21mg; **IRON** 1.5mg; **SODIUM** 250mg; **CALC** 322mg

Kid Friendly • Quick & Easy
For the Mini Ham Sandwiches:
Preheat oven to 400°. Combine 1 tablespoon minced fresh chives, 2 tablespoons canola mayonnaise, and 1 teaspoon Dijon mustard. Cut 8 (1-ounce) Hawaiian rolls in half horizontally, cutting to, but not through, other side. Place rolls, cut sides up, on a baking sheet; bake at 400° for 5 minutes or until golden. Spread cut sides evenly with mayonnaise mixture. Divide 4 ounces reduced-sodium thinly sliced ham (such as Boar's Head) evenly among bottoms of rolls. Cover with roll tops; cut into individual rolls. Serves 4 (serving size: 2 sandwiches).

CALORIES 282; **FAT** 9g (sat 3.5g); **SODIUM** 539mg

READY IN 40 MINUTES

The SHOPPING LIST

Enchilada Casserole
Garlic
Onion (1)
Fat-free, lower-sodium beef broth (1 cup)
40%-less-sodium taco seasoning mix
8-ounce can no-salt-added tomato sauce (1)
All-purpose flour
8-inch whole-wheat flour tortillas (4)
Monterey Jack cheese with jalapeños
Ground sirloin (1 pound)
Butter

Spicy Black Beans
Lime (1)
Red bell pepper (1)
Jalapeño pepper (1)
Canola oil
15-ounce can organic no-salt-added black beans (1)
Fresh cilantro

The GAME PLAN

Cook beef mixture.
While oven preheats:
▪ Cook tomato mixture.
▪ Assemble casserole.
While casserole bakes:
▪ Cook beans.

Enchilada Casserole

With Spicy Black Beans

Simple Sub: Use ground turkey and chicken broth instead of beef, if desired.

1 pound ground sirloin
1 cup chopped onion
1 tablespoon butter
1 tablespoon minced garlic
1¹⁄₂ tablespoons all-purpose flour
1 cup fat-free, lower-sodium beef broth
1 tablespoon 40%-less-sodium taco seasoning mix (such as Old El Paso)
1 (8-ounce) can no-salt-added tomato sauce
4 (8-inch) whole-wheat flour tortillas
1¹⁄₂ ounces shredded Monterey Jack cheese with jalapeño peppers (about ¹⁄₃ cup)

1. Heat a large nonstick skillet over medium-high heat. Add beef and onion to pan; cook 6 minutes, stirring to crumble.
2. Preheat oven to 400°.
3. Melt butter in a medium saucepan over medium-high heat. Add garlic; sauté 1 minute. Sprinkle with flour; cook 30 seconds, stirring constantly. Add broth, taco seasoning, and tomato sauce to pan. Bring to a boil; cook 2 minutes, stirring occasionally. Add 1¹⁄₂ cups tomato mixture to beef mixture; reserve ¹⁄₂ cup tomato mixture.
4. Place 1 tortilla in a 9-inch pie plate. Top with 1 cup beef mixture. Repeat layers, ending with tortilla. Spread reserved tomato mixture over tortilla. Top with cheese. Bake at 400° for 10 minutes or until cheese melts. Cool slightly. Cut into 4 wedges. Serves 4 (serving size: 1 wedge).

CALORIES 377; **FAT** 14.6g (sat 7g, mono 5.3g, poly 1.6g); **PROTEIN** 30.2g; **CARB** 32.4g; **FIBER** 4.7g; **CHOL** 76mg; **IRON** 2.5mg; **SODIUM** 650mg; **CALC** 91mg

continued

Quick & Easy • Vegetarian
For the Spicy Black Beans:

Heat a large nonstick skillet over medium-high heat. Add 2 teaspoons canola oil to pan; swirl to coat. Add 1 cup chopped red bell pepper and 1 minced jalapeño pepper; sauté 4 minutes. Add 2 tablespoons fresh lime juice, ¼ teaspoon salt, and 1 (15-ounce) can rinsed and drained organic no-salt-added black beans. Cook 3 minutes or until thoroughly heated. Sprinkle with 1 tablespoon chopped fresh cilantro. Serves 4 (serving size: about ½ cup).

CALORIES 83; **FAT** 2.5g (sat 0.2g); **SODIUM** 156mg

READY IN 40 MINUTES

The
SHOPPING LIST

Beef Tenderloin Steaks and Balsamic Green Beans
Yellow onion (1)
Red onion (1)
Shallots (2)
Garlic
Green beans (2 cups)
Balsamic vinegar
Fat-free, lower-sodium beef broth (½ cup)
4-ounce beef tenderloin steaks (4)
Butter

Parmesan Potatoes
Green onions
Refrigerated mashed potatoes (2 cups)
Parmesan cheese (2 ounces)

The
GAME PLAN

While bean mixture cooks:
- Cook steaks.

While steaks rest:
- Prepare potatoes.

Kid Friendly • Quick & Easy
Beef Tenderloin Steaks and Balsamic Green Beans

With Parmesan Potatoes
(pictured on page 211)

Budget Buy: Substitute 1 (1-pound) flank steak for tenderloin.

2 teaspoons butter, divided
1 cup vertically sliced yellow onion
1 cup vertically sliced red onion
¼ cup sliced shallots
3 garlic cloves, minced
½ cup fat-free, lower-sodium beef broth
2 cups green beans, trimmed
2 tablespoons balsamic vinegar
¼ teaspoon salt, divided
4 (4-ounce) beef tenderloin steaks
¼ teaspoon freshly ground black pepper
Cooking spray

1. Melt 1 teaspoon butter in a medium saucepan over medium-high heat. Add onions and shallots; sauté 6 minutes. Add garlic; sauté 1 minute. Add broth; cook 4 minutes or until onions are tender and liquid almost evaporates. Add beans and vinegar; cover and cook 4 minutes or until beans are crisp-tender. Remove from heat. Stir in remaining 1 teaspoon butter and ⅛ teaspoon salt; keep warm.
2. Sprinkle steaks with remaining ⅛ teaspoon salt and pepper. Heat a cast-iron skillet over medium-high heat. Coat pan with cooking spray. Add steaks to pan; cook 3 minutes on each side or until desired degree of doneness. Let stand 5 minutes. Serve with bean mixture. Serves 4 (serving size: 1 steak and ½ cup bean mixture).

CALORIES 244; **FAT** 9.4g (sat 4g, mono 3.5g, poly 0.4g); **PROTEIN** 27.1g; **CARB** 12.4g; **FIBER** 3.1g; **CHOL** 81mg; **IRON** 2.4mg; **SODIUM** 285mg; **CALC** 78mg

---

Kid Friendly • Vegetarian
For the Parmesan Potatoes:

Heat a small saucepan over medium heat. Add 2 cups refrigerated mashed potatoes (such as Simply Potatoes); cover and cook 5 minutes or until thoroughly heated, stirring occasionally. Stir in 2 ounces grated fresh Parmesan cheese (about ½ cup), ¼ cup thinly sliced green onions, and ⅛ teaspoon freshly ground black pepper. Serves 4 (serving size: about ½ cup).

CALORIES 131; **FAT** 5.4g (sat 3.7g); **SODIUM** 294mg

SUPERFAST

Welcome the year with bright flavors from warm places: saffron-infused shrimp, a quesadilla with a kick, toasty chai-inspired rice pudding, and more.

Kid Friendly • Quick & Easy
Make Ahead
White Chocolate-Cherry Bark

Pack a cherry-spiked piece in your child's bag (or your own) for a creamy-crunchy treat.

2 tablespoons sliced almonds
⅓ cup dried cherries, chopped
1 ounce small salted pretzel sticks, broken into ¼-inch pieces (about ⅔ cup)
1 (12-ounce) package premium white chocolate chips

1. Place almonds in a skillet over high heat. Cook 2 minutes or until lightly browned, stirring frequently. Remove from heat. Combine almonds, cherries, and pretzels in a bowl. Set aside half of mixture.
2. Place chocolate in a 1-quart glass measure. Microwave at HIGH 1½ minutes or until chocolate melts, stirring every 30 seconds. Add chocolate to bowl with pretzel mixture;

stir well. Spread chocolate mixture evenly into a 12 x 7–inch rectangle on a jelly-roll pan lined with parchment paper. Sprinkle remaining pretzel mixture evenly over chocolate, pressing lightly to adhere. Freeze 10 minutes. Break into 16 pieces. Serves 16.

CALORIES 137; **FAT** 7.2g (sat 4.2g, mono 2.2g, poly 0.3g); **PROTEIN** 1.6g; **CARB** 16.8g; **FIBER** 0.5g; **CHOL** 4mg; **IRON** 0.2mg; **SODIUM** 49mg; **CALC** 48mg

Quick & Easy
Spicy Chicken Quesadillas

To make these quesadillas kid friendly, omit the pickled jalapeño peppers.

1 cup chopped skinless, boneless rotisserie chicken breast
1/3 cup refrigerated fresh salsa
1/4 cup canned no-salt-added black beans, rinsed and drained
1/4 cup frozen whole-kernel corn, thawed
1 1/2 tablespoons chopped pickled jalapeño pepper
8 (6-inch) flour tortillas
1 cup shredded reduced-fat Monterey Jack cheese
Cooking spray
1/4 cup reduced-fat sour cream

1. Combine first 5 ingredients in a medium bowl. Divide chicken mixture evenly over 4 tortillas. Sprinkle quesadillas evenly with cheese. Top with remaining 4 tortillas.
2. Heat a large skillet over medium-high heat. Coat pan with cooking spray. Add 1 quesadilla to pan; cook 1 minute on each side or until golden. Remove from pan, and repeat with remaining quesadillas. Serve with sour cream. Serves 4 (serving size: 1 quesadilla and 1 tablespoon sour cream).

CALORIES 372; **FAT** 14.1g (sat 6.2g, mono 5g, poly 1.3g); **PROTEIN** 24.2g; **CARB** 36.7g; **FIBER** 2.7g; **CHOL** 56mg; **IRON** 2.6mg; **SODIUM** 743mg; **CALC** 307mg

Quick & Easy
Pan-Seared Halibut with Bell Pepper Relish

(pictured on page 211)

This relish also works well with grilled chicken. Serve with a simple spinach salad.

1 1/2 tablespoons olive oil, divided
4 (6-ounce) halibut fillets
1/4 teaspoon salt
1/4 teaspoon freshly ground black pepper
2 tablespoons chopped shallots
1 teaspoon minced fresh garlic
1 cup chopped yellow bell pepper
1/2 cup chopped plum tomato
1 tablespoon sherry vinegar
1/2 teaspoon smoked paprika
1 tablespoon chopped fresh flat-leaf parsley

1. Heat a large nonstick skillet over medium-high heat. Add 2¼ teaspoons oil to pan; swirl to coat. Sprinkle halibut evenly with salt and black pepper. Add fish to pan; cook 3 minutes on each side or until fish flakes easily when tested with a fork. Carefully remove fish from pan, and keep warm.
2. Add remaining 2¼ teaspoons oil to pan; swirl to coat. Add shallots and garlic to pan; sauté 1 minute. Add bell pepper and next 3 ingredients (through paprika); sauté 3 minutes or until bell pepper is tender. Stir in parsley. Serve relish with fish. Serves 4 (serving size: 1 fillet and about ¼ cup relish).

 Be sure to purchase wild Alaskan halibut for a sustainable choice; avoid Atlantic halibut.
Sustainable Choice

CALORIES 252; **FAT** 10.2g (sat 2g, mono 5.7g, poly 2.2g); **PROTEIN** 35.7g; **CARB** 4.5g; **FIBER** 1.2g; **CHOL** 122mg; **IRON** 0.9mg; **SODIUM** 286mg; **CALC** 44mg

Quick & Easy
Shrimp with Lemon-Saffron Rice

(pictured on page 210)

This recipe combines all the flavors of a traditional paella in a weeknight-friendly dish.

1 tablespoon extra-virgin olive oil
1/2 cup chopped onion
1/2 cup chopped green bell pepper
1 teaspoon minced fresh garlic
1 pound peeled and deveined large shrimp
2 cups uncooked instant rice
1/2 cup water
1 1/2 teaspoons chopped fresh oregano
1/4 teaspoon salt
1/4 teaspoon saffron threads, crushed
1/4 teaspoon paprika
1/4 teaspoon freshly ground black pepper
1 (14-ounce) can fat-free, lower-sodium chicken broth
1 cup frozen green peas
2 1/2 tablespoons fresh lemon juice

1. Heat a large Dutch oven over medium-high heat. Add oil to pan; swirl to coat. Add onion and bell pepper; sauté 3 minutes or until vegetables are tender, stirring frequently. Add garlic; cook 30 seconds, stirring constantly. Add shrimp to pan; cook 30 seconds, stirring frequently. Add rice and next 7 ingredients (through broth). Bring rice mixture to a boil; cover pan. Reduce heat, and simmer 5 minutes or until rice is done. Remove from heat; stir in peas and lemon juice. Serves 4 (serving size: 1 cup).

 Look for U.S. Pacific or West Coast white shrimp farmed in recirculating systems or inland ponds.
Sustainable Choice

CALORIES 394; **FAT** 6.5g (sat 0.9g, mono 2.9g, poly 1.3g); **PROTEIN** 29.9g; **CARB** 51.8g; **FIBER** 3.7g; **CHOL** 172mg; **IRON** 6.6mg; **SODIUM** 517mg; **CALC** 97mg

Chicken with Pepperoni-Marinara Sauce

Cooking spray
½ teaspoon minced fresh garlic
16 slices pepperoni, coarsely chopped
¼ teaspoon dried oregano
1½ cups lower-sodium marinara sauce (such as McCutcheon's)
2 tablespoons chopped fresh basil
2 teaspoons olive oil
1½ pounds chicken cutlets
¼ teaspoon freshly ground black pepper
1 cup shredded part-skim mozzarella cheese

1. Preheat broiler to high.
2. Heat a saucepan over medium-high heat. Coat pan with cooking spray. Add garlic and pepperoni; cook 2 minutes or until garlic begins to brown, stirring frequently. Add oregano; cook 30 seconds. Add marinara sauce; bring to a boil. Reduce heat, and simmer 5 minutes. Remove from heat; stir in basil.
3. Heat a large ovenproof skillet over medium-high heat. Add oil; swirl to coat. Sprinkle chicken with pepper. Add chicken to skillet; cook 5 minutes or until lightly browned, turning after 3 minutes. Spoon sauce over chicken; sprinkle evenly with cheese. Broil 2 minutes or until cheese melts. Serves 4 (serving size: 5 ounces chicken and about ⅓ cup sauce).

CALORIES 380; **FAT** 14.7g (sat 6g, mono 5.2g, poly 1.2g); **PROTEIN** 48.5g; **CARB** 28.7g; **FIBER** 0.1g; **CHOL** 122mg; **IRON** 1.5mg; **SODIUM** 533mg; **CALC** 231mg

Warm Coconut Rice Pudding

1 cup water
1 cup uncooked instant rice
½ cup sugar
3 tablespoons cornstarch
¼ teaspoon salt
1½ cups 2% reduced-fat milk, divided
2 large egg yolks
1 cup light coconut milk
¼ cup flaked sweetened coconut
1 teaspoon vanilla extract
¼ teaspoon ground cinnamon
¼ teaspoon ground cardamom
1 tablespoon chopped pistachios

1. Bring 1 cup water to a boil in a saucepan. Stir in rice; cover and reduce heat to medium-low. Simmer 5 minutes. Remove from heat; uncover. Set aside.
2. Combine sugar, cornstarch, and salt in a small bowl.
3. Combine ¼ cup milk and yolks in a bowl, stirring with a whisk. Add sugar mixture to milk mixture, stirring with a whisk until blended.
4. Bring remaining 1¼ cups milk and coconut milk to a boil in a small saucepan. Gradually add hot milk mixture to yolk mixture, stirring with a whisk. Return milk mixture to pan. Bring to a boil, and cook 1 minute, stirring constantly. Remove from heat; stir in cooked rice, coconut, and next 3 ingredients (through cardamom). Top with pistachios. Serves 6 (serving size: ½ cup pudding and ½ teaspoon pistachios).

CALORIES 228; **FAT** 5.4g (sat 3g, mono 1.4g, poly 0.5g); **PROTEIN** 4.6g; **CARB** 40g; **FIBER** 0.8g; **CHOL** 75mg; **IRON** 1.3mg; **SODIUM** 141mg; **CALC** 87mg

CONVENIENCE COOKING
START WITH A BAG OF SPINACH

Keep fresh, prewashed greens in the refrigerator as a starting point for healthy, easy salads, soups, sandwiches, and more.

Spinach and Lentil Soup with Cheese and Basil

Hands-on time: 30 min. Total time: 1 hr. 30 min. *This recipe can be made ahead—just wait to stir in spinach until after you reheat the soup.*

1 tablespoon extra-virgin olive oil
¼ cup chopped pancetta (about 1 ounce)
1¼ cups chopped onion
¾ cup chopped celery
¾ cup chopped carrot
1 teaspoon chopped fresh thyme
1 bay leaf
1 cup dried brown lentils
3 cups fat-free, lower-sodium chicken broth
2 cups water
1 (6-ounce) package fresh baby spinach
½ cup chopped fresh basil
1 ounce grated fresh Parmesan cheese (about ¼ cup)
1 tablespoon fresh lemon juice
⅛ teaspoon freshly ground black pepper

1. Heat a Dutch oven over medium heat. Add oil to pan; swirl to coat. Add pancetta; cook 1 minute or until pancetta begins to brown, stirring occasionally. Add onion and next 4 ingredients (through bay leaf); cook

8 minutes or until vegetables are tender, stirring occasionally. Add lentils, broth, and 2 cups water; bring to a boil. Cover, reduce heat, and simmer 40 minutes or until lentils are tender and mixture is slightly thickened. Remove from heat. Discard bay leaf.

2. Place 2 cups lentil mixture in a blender. Remove the center piece of blender lid (to allow steam to escape), and secure blender lid on blender. Place a clean towel over opening in blender lid (to avoid splatters), and blend until smooth. Return pureed lentil mixture to pan. Add baby spinach, chopped basil, Parmesan cheese, lemon juice, and black pepper; stir until spinach wilts. Serve immediately. Serves 4 (serving size: about 1¾ cups).

CALORIES 295; **FAT** 7.9g (sat 2.5g, mono 3g, poly 0.8g); **PROTEIN** 18.4g; **CARB** 38.7g; **FIBER** 17.5g; **CHOL** 10mg; **IRON** 5.3mg; **SODIUM** 601mg; **CALC** 162mg

Kid Friendly

Sausage and Spinach Risotto

Hands-on time: 44 min. Total time: 44 min.

3 cups fat-free, lower-sodium chicken broth
1 cup water
1 tablespoon extra-virgin olive oil
⅛ teaspoon salt
1 (8-ounce) package presliced mushrooms
5 ounces sweet Italian sausage, casings removed (about 2 links)
½ cup chopped shallots
3 garlic cloves, minced
1 cup uncooked Arborio rice
⅓ cup dry white wine
1 (6-ounce) package fresh baby spinach
1 ounce shaved fresh Romano cheese (about ¼ cup)

1. Bring broth and 1 cup water to a simmer in a small saucepan (do not boil); keep warm over low heat.

2. Heat a Dutch oven over medium-high heat. Add oil; swirl to coat. Add salt and mushrooms; cook 8 minutes or until browned, stirring occasionally. Remove mushrooms from pan; set aside.

3. Add sausage to pan; cook 3 minutes or until browned, stirring to crumble. Add shallots and garlic; cook 1 minute, stirring constantly. Reduce heat to medium. Add rice; cook 1 minute, stirring constantly. Stir in wine; cook until liquid is nearly absorbed, scraping pan to loosen browned bits.

4. Stir in 1 cup broth mixture; cook 2 minutes or until liquid is nearly absorbed, stirring constantly. Add remaining broth mixture, ½ cup at a time, stirring constantly until each portion of broth mixture is absorbed before adding the next (about 30 minutes total). Remove pan from heat. Add mushrooms and spinach; stir until spinach wilts. Top evenly with cheese. Serve immediately. Serves 4 (serving size: 1½ cups).

CALORIES 331; **FAT** 9g (sat 3g, mono 3.8g, poly 0.7g); **PROTEIN** 15.9g; **CARB** 46.5g; **FIBER** 3.6g; **CHOL** 15mg; **IRON** 2.3mg; **SODIUM** 768mg; **CALC** 153mg

Rosemary-Chicken Panini with Spinach and Sun-Dried Tomatoes

Hands-on time: 40 min. Total time: 1 hr. 10 min.

2 tablespoons extra-virgin olive oil, divided
1 teaspoon chopped fresh rosemary
4 (4-ounce) chicken cutlets
¼ cup chopped drained oil-packed sun-dried tomato
⅛ teaspoon crushed red pepper
8 garlic cloves, thinly sliced
1 (6-ounce) package fresh baby spinach

⅜ teaspoon salt, divided
Cooking spray
⅛ teaspoon freshly ground black pepper
8 (1-ounce) slices country-style Italian bread
2 ounces shredded fresh mozzarella cheese (about ½ cup)

1. Combine 2 teaspoons olive oil, rosemary, and chicken in a large zip-top plastic bag. Seal and marinate in refrigerator 30 minutes.

2. Heat a large nonstick skillet over medium-high heat. Add remaining 4 teaspoons oil to pan; swirl to coat. Add sun-dried tomato, red pepper, and garlic; sauté 1 minute or until garlic begins to brown. Add spinach; cook 1 minute or until spinach barely wilts. Stir in ⅛ teaspoon salt; set aside.

3. Heat a grill pan over medium-high heat; coat with cooking spray. Remove chicken from marinade; discard marinade. Sprinkle chicken with remaining ¼ teaspoon salt and black pepper. Cook chicken 3 minutes on each side or until done. Remove chicken from pan; keep pan on medium-high heat.

4. Top each of 4 bread slices with 1 tablespoon cheese, 1 chicken cutlet, one-fourth of spinach mixture, 1 additional tablespoon cheese, and remaining 4 bread slices.

5. Recoat grill pan with cooking spray. Arrange 2 sandwiches in pan. Place a cast-iron or heavy skillet on top of sandwiches; press gently to flatten. Cook 4 minutes on each side (leave skillet on sandwiches while they cook). Repeat procedure with remaining 2 sandwiches. Cut each sandwich in half; serve immediately. Serves 4 (serving size: 1 sandwich).

CALORIES 414; **FAT** 14.8g (sat 3.9g, mono 6.3g, poly 2.1g); **PROTEIN** 35.5g; **CARB** 33.6g; **FIBER** 3.1g; **CHOL** 77mg; **IRON** 4mg; **SODIUM** 687mg; **CALC** 114mg

Quick & Easy

Fennel and Spinach Salad with Shrimp and Balsamic Vinaigrette

Hands-on time: 18 min. Total time: 18 min.

3 center-cut bacon slices
1 pound jumbo shrimp, peeled and deveined
2 cups thinly sliced fennel bulb (about 1 medium bulb)
1 cup grape tomatoes, halved
1/2 cup thinly sliced red onion
1 (9-ounce) package fresh baby spinach
2 tablespoons finely chopped shallots
3 tablespoons extra-virgin olive oil
1 tablespoon balsamic vinegar
1 teaspoon Dijon mustard
1/4 teaspoon salt
1/4 teaspoon freshly ground black pepper

1. Cook bacon in a skillet over medium heat until crisp. Remove bacon from pan, reserving drippings, and crumble. Add shrimp to drippings in pan, and cook 2 minutes, turning once.
2. Combine bacon, fennel, and next 3 ingredients (through spinach) in a bowl. Combine shallots and remaining ingredients in a small bowl, stirring with a whisk. Add shrimp and balsamic mixture to spinach mixture; toss well. Serves 4 (serving size: about 3½ cups).

CALORIES 274; FAT 13.5g (sat 2.2g, mono 7.7g, poly 1.9g); PROTEIN 27.5g; CARB 11.2g; FIBER 3.5g; CHOL 176mg; IRON 5mg; SODIUM 487mg; CALC 156mg

BUDGET COOKING

FEED 4 FOR LESS THAN $10

Meat sauce with polenta will satisfy the whole family. Kids will dig our breakfast-for-dinner "muffins."

Kid Friendly
Quick & Easy

$1.58/serving, $6.33 total

Mini Bacon and Egg Tarts

Hands-on time: 24 min. Total time: 39 min. *Green onions add color and flavor, but they're optional. Omit them, if you prefer.*

8 (1-ounce) slices whole-wheat white sandwich bread, crusts removed
Cooking spray
1/2 cup 2% reduced-fat milk
4 large eggs, lightly beaten
2 tablespoons chopped green onions (optional)
2 smoked bacon slices, cooked and crumbled
2 ounces shredded sharp cheddar cheese (about 1/2 cup)

1. Preheat oven to 425°.
2. Lightly coat both sides of bread with cooking spray. Press each bread slice into the cup of a muffin tin. Bake at 425° for 10 minutes or until bread is lightly toasted. Cool slightly.
3. Reduce oven temperature to 350°.
4. Combine milk and eggs, stirring well with a whisk. Divide egg mixture evenly among bread cups. Sprinkle onions, if desired, and bacon evenly over tarts; top each tart with 1 tablespoon cheese. Bake at 350° for 15 minutes or until set. Serves 4 (serving size: 2 tarts).

CALORIES 316; FAT 12.8g (sat 5.6g, mono 2.8g, poly 1.5g); PROTEIN 18.3g; CARB 31.2g; FIBER 3g; CHOL 202mg; IRON 1mg; SODIUM 515mg; CALC 163mg

Kid Friendly

Sausage Ragù over Creamy Polenta

$2.45/serving, $9.80 total

Hands-on time: 40 min. Total time: 50 min. *Turkey sausage and bottled marinara combine for a quick, affordable twist on this Italian classic. Serve with a romaine salad tossed with red wine vinegar and olive oil.*

3 (4-ounce) links sweet turkey Italian sausage, casings removed
1 tablespoon olive oil
1 cup finely chopped onion
4 garlic cloves, minced
1½ cups lower-sodium marinara sauce
2⅓ cups water, divided
1 cup whole milk
3/4 cup instant polenta
1 ounce fresh pecorino Romano cheese, grated
1/8 teaspoon black pepper
1/4 cup coarsely chopped fresh flat-leaf parsley

1. Heat a large skillet over medium-high heat. Add sausage; sauté 6 minutes, stirring to crumble. Remove sausage from pan; drain. Wipe pan clean with paper towels; return to medium-high heat. Add oil to pan; swirl to coat. Add onion; sauté 4 minutes. Add garlic; sauté 1 minute. Stir in sausage, marinara, and 1/3 cup water; bring to a boil. Reduce heat; simmer 20 minutes.
2. Bring remaining 2 cups water and milk to a boil in a medium saucepan over medium heat; reduce heat to low. Gradually add polenta; cook 3 minutes or until thick, stirring constantly. Remove from heat; stir in cheese and pepper. Serve with sausage mixture; top with parsley. Serves 4 (serving size: 3/4 cup polenta, 1/2 cup sausage mixture, and 1 tablespoon parsley).

CALORIES 357; FAT 14g (sat 4.8g, mono 5.2g, poly 2.3g); PROTEIN 17.2g; CARB 50.8g; FIBER 3.7g; CHOL 65mg; IRON 1.1mg; SODIUM 712mg; CALC 137mg

Chicken and Rice with Mushrooms

$2.31/serving, $9.25 total

Hands-on time: 25 min. Total time: 1 hr. 45 min. *A small amount of dried porcini mushrooms goes a long way. Using the reconstituted mushrooms and their soaking liquid gives this one-dish meal a rich, earthy flavor.*

2 cups boiling water
¼ cup dried porcini mushrooms (about ¼ ounce)
2 tablespoons olive oil, divided
1 pound skinless, boneless chicken thighs, cut into 1-inch pieces
1 teaspoon sweet paprika
¾ teaspoon salt, divided
½ teaspoon freshly ground black pepper, divided
¾ cup chopped onion
8 ounces cremini mushrooms, sliced
¾ cup uncooked brown basmati rice
2 cups frozen green peas, thawed
1 tablespoon chopped fresh thyme

1. Combine 2 cups boiling water and porcini mushrooms; let stand 20 minutes. Drain through a sieve over a bowl, reserving soaking liquid. Finely chop mushrooms.
2. Heat a large nonstick skillet over medium-high heat. Add 1 tablespoon oil to pan; swirl to coat. Sprinkle chicken evenly with paprika, ½ teaspoon salt, and ¼ teaspoon pepper. Add chicken mixture to pan; sauté 5 minutes or until chicken is browned, stirring occasionally. Remove chicken from pan.
3. Return pan to medium-high heat. Add remaining 1 tablespoon oil to pan; swirl to coat. Add onion and cremini mushrooms; sprinkle with remaining ¼ teaspoon salt and remaining ¼ teaspoon pepper; sauté 4 minutes or until lightly browned, stirring occasionally. Stir in reserved porcini liquid, chopped porcini, and rice; bring to a boil. Cover, reduce heat to medium-low, and simmer gently 35 minutes. Stir in reserved chicken, peas, and thyme. Cover and cook 10 minutes or until rice is tender and chicken is done. Serves 4 (serving size: 1½ cups).

CALORIES 398; FAT 12.8g (sat 2.4g, mono 6.7g, poly 2.4g); PROTEIN 30.8g; CARB 40.7g; FIBER 6.1g; CHOL 94mg; IRON 3.6mg; SODIUM 620mg; CALC 49mg

Pork Tenderloin with Mushroom Sauce

$2.45/serving, $9.80 total

Hands-on time: 25 min. Total time: 53 min. *Serve with stone-ground yellow grits to soak up the tangy, creamy sauce.*

1 (1-pound) pork tenderloin, trimmed
¾ teaspoon kosher salt, divided
½ teaspoon freshly ground black pepper
2 tablespoons olive oil, divided
1 (8-ounce) package button mushrooms, thinly sliced
3 garlic cloves, minced
2 tablespoons white wine vinegar
1 cup fat-free, lower-sodium chicken broth
¼ cup crème fraîche or sour cream
2 teaspoons Dijon mustard
3 tablespoons chopped fresh flat-leaf parsley

1. Place a small roasting pan in oven. Preheat oven to 425°.
2. Sprinkle pork evenly with ½ teaspoon salt and pepper. Add 1 tablespoon oil to preheated pan; swirl to coat. Add pork to pan. Roast at 425° for 20 minutes or until a thermometer inserted in the thickest portion of pork registers 145°, turning after 10 minutes. Remove pork from pan, and let stand 10 minutes.
3. Place roasting pan over medium-high heat. Add remaining 1 tablespoon oil to pan; swirl to coat. Add mushrooms; sauté 4 minutes, stirring occasionally. Add garlic, and sauté 1 minute, stirring constantly. Stir in vinegar, and bring to a boil, scraping pan to loosen browned bits. Cook 1 minute or until liquid almost evaporates, stirring occasionally. Stir in remaining ¼ teaspoon salt and broth; bring to a boil. Cook until liquid is reduced to ⅓ cup (about 7 minutes). Remove from heat, and stir in crème fraîche and mustard. Cut pork crosswise into slices. Place 3 ounces pork on each of 4 plates, and top each serving with about 2½ tablespoons sauce. Garnish with parsley. Serves 4.

CALORIES 257; FAT 15.2g (sat 5.2g, mono 6.1g, poly 1.2g); PROTEIN 25.3g; CARB 3.7g; FIBER 1g; CHOL 76mg; IRON 1.7mg; SODIUM 575mg; CALC 20mg

KITCHEN SECRET: QUICKER "WHOLE" GRAINS

Whole grains often require anywhere from 45 minutes to more than an hour to prepare, in part because of the tough bran exterior. That puts them out of reach of many weeknight cooks, unless they prep grains on the weekend and store in the fridge or freezer (a good habit to get into). To speed things up while retaining a lot of the same chewy texture and goodness, we like to use pearled farro or barley. Now, pearled (or "pearl") grains aren't quite whole. The pearling (polishing) process removes part of the outer bran layer, which tenderizes the grain. That said, these nutty morsels still retain nearly as many nutrients and plenty of the original fiber (about 75%, according to the Whole Grains Council). Plus, you'll shave an average of 15 to 20 minutes off the cook time—a wholly beneficial thing if you're in a squeeze.

WHAT IS BUDGET COOKING?

Prices derived from mid-sized city supermarkets. Side dishes mentioned in recipe notes are included in the cost of the meal. For specialty or highly perishable ingredients, like some Asian sauces or fresh herbs, we account for the entire cost of the ingredient. For staples and other ingredients, we include the cost for only the amount used. Salt, pepper, and cooking spray are freebies.

OOPS!

YOUR FLAPJACKS FLAME OUT

For pancake perfection, prep the pan.

Too often, pancake cooks put up with a few poor specimens at the beginning—splotchy and greasy—and a few more duds at the end; the latter can be scorched from a too-dry pan yet perversely underdone within. This is not a heat problem or a batter problem: It's a pan-prepping problem.

The solution: Don't pour oil directly into the pan. Hot oil will spread, pooling in some areas, leaving other parts dry. Just a scant amount of cooking oil creates a smooth, even cooking surface throughout, so pancakes cook evenly from start to finish.

If you're using a pristine nonstick pan, you may not need oil at all. Otherwise, here's how to apply it: Heat a skillet (any variety) over medium heat, and then grasp a wadded paper towel with tongs and douse it with 1 tablespoon canola oil. Brush the pan with the soaked towel. You could also use cooking spray, except with nonstick pans: It leaves sticky residue on Teflon surfaces.

Add the batter, flipping only when bubbles form on the surface of each pancake, about two to three minutes. Resist the urge to peek, which breaks the seal between the pan and the batter; that seal is what ensures even cooking. Swab the pan with the oiled paper towel between batches to keep it properly greased.

(Good as gold!)

(The dog's breakfast)

COMFORT FOOD OF THE CHEFS

We asked food experts from various lands to tell their comfort food tales, then created lighter—but still comforting—recipes inspired by their stories.

JACQUES PÉPIN
Godfather of French food in America

French food, like all great cuisines, can go high and fancy or low and rustic. Jacques Pépin's early memories lean toward the latter. He grew up during World War II, his dad away in the service and his mother left with meager means to feed her children. Pépin remembers her simple but magical dishes prepared almost out of thin air.

Pépin's comfort foods are quintessentially simple: bread and butter, mashed potatoes, soup. Soup has a special place in Pépin's psyche: He opened a French soup restaurant, La Potagerie, in New York in the 1970s.

Bean soup, split pea soup, and fish soup are all on his list of comfort favorites, but onion soup seems a perfect Pépin match: Humble ingredients are transformed into a deliciously hearty and comforting dish in a recipe that was synonymous with French cooking in the '60s (when Pépin began his American journey) and that, today, deserves remembering and reviving. In his wonderful new summing-up cookbook, *Essential Pépin*, he recalls: "When I was a young man, I often made it with my friends at 2 or 3 a.m. after returning home from a night of dancing."

Pépin sometimes adds a splash of port or egg to his broth to add flavor and richness. Our version hews to classic, comforting principles: Silky soft caramelized onions are stirred into a rich, meaty broth and topped with crusty bread and melty cheese. But it is far lighter.

Make Ahead
French Onion Soup

Hands-on time: 1 hr. 20 min. Total time: 5 hr. 39 min. *It's worth the effort to make your own stock for this simple soup, but if you want to save time, you can use store-bought lower-sodium broth. You'll need to halve the amount of salt you add to the soup.*

Stock:
- 1½ pounds meaty beef bones
- 1 pound beef shanks
- 2 large carrots, peeled and coarsely chopped
- 2 celery stalks, coarsely chopped
- 1 medium onion, cut into wedges
- 3 quarts cold water
- 1 tablespoon whole black peppercorns
- 3 thyme sprigs
- 1 bunch fresh flat-leaf parsley
- 1 bay leaf

Soup:
- 2 tablespoons olive oil
- 1 tablespoon butter
- 3 large onions, vertically sliced (about 13 cups)
- 1⅛ teaspoons kosher salt
- ½ teaspoon freshly ground black pepper
- 1 teaspoon chopped fresh thyme
- ¼ cup chopped fresh chives
- 12 (½-ounce) slices French bread baguette
- 4 ounces Gruyère cheese, shredded (about 1 cup)

1. Preheat oven to 450°.

2. To prepare stock, arrange first 5 ingredients in a single layer on a large baking sheet. Bake at 450° for 35 minutes or until browned. Scrape beef mixture and pan drippings into a large Dutch oven. Stir in 3 quarts cold water and next 4 ingredients; bring to a boil over medium heat. Reduce heat to low, and simmer 2½ hours, skimming surface as necessary. Strain mixture through a fine-mesh sieve lined with a double layer of cheesecloth over a bowl; discard solids. Wipe pan clean with paper towels.

3. To prepare soup, return Dutch oven to medium heat. Add oil to pan; swirl to coat. Melt butter in oil. Add sliced onion to pan; cook 5 minutes, stirring occasionally. Partially cover, reduce heat to medium-low, and cook 15 minutes, stirring occasionally. Add salt and ground pepper; cook, uncovered, until deep golden brown (about 35 minutes), stirring frequently. Add reserved stock and chopped thyme; bring to a boil. Reduce heat, and simmer until reduced to 8 cups (about 50 minutes). Stir in chives.

4. Preheat broiler to high.

5. Arrange bread slices in a single layer on a jelly-roll pan, and broil 2 minutes or until toasted, turning after 1 minute. Ladle 1⅓ cups soup into each of 6 broiler-safe soup bowls. Top each serving with 2 bread slices, and sprinkle evenly with cheese. Place soup bowls on jelly-roll pan, and broil 4 minutes or until tops are golden brown and cheese bubbles. Serves 6.

CALORIES 346; FAT 14.1g (sat 5.9g, mono 6.2g, poly 1.2g); PROTEIN 16.1g; CARB 40.5g; FIBER 5.3g; CHOL 33mg; IRON 2.3mg; SODIUM 649mg; CALC 274mg

Andrew Zimmern plays the role of the food guy who'll eat anything. But anyone who watches *Bizzare Foods* soon realizes he eats these foods not so much as a stunt but as an affirmation that one man's "ick" can be another's true passion and joy: Zimmern will play the goof, but he's an ambassador of comfort and connection through food. For him, the ultimate comfort food, the world over, is soup. "A warm mug or whole bowl slurped or scooped puts you in very close proximity with your food."

He tells this story with typical, infectious Zimmern detail: "We're in Morocco, and we're in the souk in Marrakech, and there are 10 different lamb stalls, starting with whole roast lamb. And as you went down the lines, the pickings got slimmer, all the way to a thin lamb broth, made just with the bones. The merchant would walk up to the top stand and give [the vendor] the roasted lamb bones, and he would make broth in the little tin cups. He always had a bigger line than anywhere else. Everyone remembered the broth from their childhood. There were more smiles at that stall than anywhere else in the city!"

Childhood soup memories can mean *posole* in Mexico or *udon* in Japan, but, "I'm a Jewish kid from New York, so for me it's chicken in the pan."

He poaches a whole chicken in rich chicken stock, reinforcing the flavor. In this version of matzo ball soup, we roast chicken wings to make a rich broth and use flavorful dark meat for the soup. We cut the *schmaltz*—chicken fat, unctuous but calorie-packed—and added a bit of chopped fresh dill with the matzo balls for a surprising but comforting zing. It's a beautiful thing.

COMFORT FOODS, SAYS GLOBE-TROTTING ZIMMERN, "PANG IN THE BACK OF YOUR MIND."

Kid Friendly • Make Ahead

Chicken–Matzo Ball Soup

Hands-on time: 35 min. Total time: 5 hr. 10 min. *For a shortcut version of this recipe, use store-bought, unsalted chicken stock instead of making your own. (Adapted from a recipe from AndrewZimmern.com.)*

Stock:
3 pounds chicken wings
2 large carrots, peeled and coarsely chopped
2 celery stalks, coarsely chopped
1 medium onion, cut into wedges
3 quarts cold water
1 tablespoon whole black peppercorns
1 bunch fresh flat-leaf parsley
1 bay leaf
Soup:
¼ cup club soda
1 tablespoon canola oil
2 large eggs
⅔ cup matzo meal
1 tablespoon chopped fresh dill
1 teaspoon kosher salt, divided
½ teaspoon freshly ground black pepper, divided
3 chicken leg quarters, skinned
1 cup diagonally sliced carrot
1 cup sliced celery
1 cup vertically sliced onion
2 tablespoons chopped fresh flat-leaf parsley
1 tablespoon chopped fresh chives

1. To prepare stock, preheat oven to 425°. Spread chicken wings and next 3 ingredients in a single layer on a large baking sheet; bake at 425° for 40 minutes or until golden. Scrape chicken wing mixture and pan drippings into a large Dutch oven. Add 3 quarts cold water and next 3 ingredients; bring to a boil over medium heat. Reduce heat to low, and simmer very gently 2½ hours, skimming surface as necessary. Strain mixture through a fine-mesh sieve lined with a double layer of cheesecloth over a bowl; discard solids. Wipe pan with paper towels. Return stock to pan; bring to a boil. Cook until reduced to 6 cups.

2. To prepare soup, combine club soda, oil, and eggs in a medium bowl, stirring well. Stir in matzo meal, dill, ¼ teaspoon salt, and ¼ teaspoon ground pepper; chill 30 minutes. Shape dough into 24 (½-inch) balls.

3. Combine reduced stock and chicken leg quarters in a large Dutch oven over medium-high heat; bring to a simmer. Reduce heat, and cook 30 minutes or until chicken is done, skimming surface as necessary. Remove chicken from pan; cool slightly. Shred chicken with 2 forks; discard bones. Add matzo balls, 1 cup sliced carrot, and 1 cup sliced celery to stock in pan; bring to a simmer. Cook 20 minutes. Stir in vertically sliced onion; cook 5 minutes or until matzo balls are thoroughly cooked. Remove from heat; stir in shredded chicken, remaining ¾ teaspoon salt, remaining ¼ teaspoon pepper, 2 tablespoons parsley, and chives. Serves 6 (serving size: about 1¼ cups).

CALORIES 240; **FAT** 8.7g (sat 1.9g, mono 3.7g, poly 2g); **PROTEIN** 20g; **CARB** 21g; **FIBER** 2.6g; **CHOL** 132mg; **IRON** 1.7mg; **SODIUM** 447mg; **CALC** 52mg

MARJA VONGERICHTEN

Cookbook author, TV series host

Dak bokkeum, spicy Korean chicken stew, is Korean-born Marja Vongerichten's favorite comfort food—a nice culinary coda to the story of an adopted girl who came to America from South Korea at age 3 and rediscovered her food roots when reunited with her mother at the age of 19. Vongerichten—now married to superstar chef Jean-Georges Vongerichten—wove her tale into the PBS series *Kimchi Chronicles* and companion book of the same name.

Born outside Seoul to a Korean single mother, Vongerichten never knew her father, an America soldier stationed in Korea who left her mother two months before she was born. She was put up for adoption and came to northern Virginia, where she grew up with her adoptive African-American family, out of touch with her Korean roots and Korean food. But she had dreamlike memories of her early childhood. One food memory persisted like a wisp of steam: the smell of *jajangmyeon*—noodles with black bean sauce.

When, at 19, she found and met her birth mother—who had moved to Brooklyn—the mother-daughter duo ate a meal her mother had spent the day preparing: *bulgogi* (grilled marinated beef), kimchi (the ubiquitous spicy fermented cabbage), and more.

Having deeply explored the food of her birth country, Vongerichten calls Korean food the "soul food of Asia." Much like American soul food, she says, the cuisine was born of struggle: cooks making do with waves of privation as Korea was invaded time and again. Cheap cuts of meat are coaxed to comfort perfection with rich ingredients. "And," she adds, "food had to be medicine, as well."

Dak bokkeum, adapted here, is often a one-pot dish of chicken, carrot, onion, and potato, all stewed in a spicy-sweet sauce. But you can adapt it to a mix of your favorite veggies. Our version features spinach and flavorful chicken thighs.

Staff Favorite

Dak Bokkeum with Spinach (Korean Stewed Chicken with Spinach)

Hands-on time: 35 min. Total time: 1 hr. 25 min. *Gochujang is an indispensable Korean sauce based on fermented soybeans and chiles. You'll find it in Asian markets, or seek out Annie Chun's brand, which is more widely available.*

$1/3$ cup gochujang (Korean chile sauce)

$1/4$ cup ($1/2$-inch) slices green onion bottoms

$2^{1/2}$ tablespoons lower-sodium soy sauce

2 tablespoons minced fresh garlic

2 tablespoons minced peeled ginger

2 tablespoons dark sesame oil

1 tablespoon brown sugar

$3/4$ teaspoon crushed red pepper

2 pounds skinless, boneless chicken thighs, cut into $1/2$-inch strips

$1^{1/2}$ cups uncooked short-grain white rice

$1^{1/2}$ cups water

$1/3$ cup water

$3/4$ cup ($1^{1/2}$-inch) slices green onion tops

1 (5-ounce) bag fresh baby spinach

1 tablespoon toasted sesame seeds

1. Combine first 8 ingredients in a large bowl. Stir in chicken. Cover and marinate 30 minutes.

2. Place rice in a medium saucepan; cover with water to 2 inches above rice. Stir rice; drain. Repeat procedure twice. Add $1^{1/2}$ cups water to drained rice in pan. Bring to a boil over medium-high heat. Cover, reduce heat, and simmer 20 minutes. Remove from heat; let stand 10 minutes.

3. While rice cooks, bring $1/3$ cup water to a boil in a Dutch oven. Add chicken mixture; bring to a simmer. Cover, reduce heat, and simmer 20 minutes. Uncover and simmer 10 minutes or until mixture thickens, stirring occasionally. Remove from heat; stir in green onion tops and spinach. Sprinkle with sesame seeds. Serve with rice. Serves 6 (serving size: 1 cup chicken mixture and $3/4$ cup rice).

CALORIES 433; FAT 12g (sat 2.2g, mono 3.9g, poly 3.6g); PROTEIN 33.5g; CARB 45.2g; FIBER 2.9g; CHOL 125mg; IRON 6.3mg; SODIUM 649mg; CALC 54mg

HAVING DEEPLY EXPLORED THE FOOD OF HER BIRTH COUNTRY, MARJA VONGERICHTEN CALLS KOREAN FOOD THE "SOUL FOOD OF ASIA."

ANISSA HELOU
Cookbook author, art historian, teacher

When London-based chef, cookbook author, and cooking instructor Anissa Helou talks expansively about comfort food, it comes as no surprise that she's been a Sotheby's rep, antiques shop owner, and art consultant to the Kuwaiti ruling family. Food has to be appealing, of course, and have a generous look, but that doesn't mean it should lack refinement. Lebanese-born Helou likes Middle Eastern cuisine for this balance. "It can be very refined in the way that it's prepared, but it's not very aesthetic, like Japanese food or French," she explains. Helou's recollections of childhood are tinged with images, sounds, and smells of Lebanese street vendors and the galettes, *shawarma*, and falafel they sold. Family is another important element. She remembers the women of her family gathered in the kitchen stuffing vegetables like zucchini or peppers for their meals.

There are meat-stuffed veggies and meatless versions, but Helou prefers the soft texture of vegetables stuffed with meat and rice. Because they simmer in flavorful broth until the grains and meats are fully tender, the entire dish takes on a soft, soothing, and supple texture. The Lebanese often use ground lamb, but our version calls for ground beef, and the grains are precooked to ensure there are no crunchy bits in the flavorful meat mixture.

FOODS THAT BRING GREAT COMFORT TASTE OF THE PAST, SIMPLY.

Make Ahead
Lebanese Peppers

Hands-on time: 50 min. Total time: 1 hr. 10 min.

4 medium red bell peppers
1 teaspoon black pepper, divided
½ cup fat-free, lower-sodium beef broth, divided
1 cup cooked long-grain white rice, cooled
½ teaspoon ground allspice
½ teaspoon salt
¼ teaspoon ground cinnamon
¾ pound ground sirloin
2 cups water
½ cup chopped fresh parsley, divided
2 teaspoons olive oil
¾ cup chopped onion
1 teaspoon minced garlic
1 cup canned crushed tomatoes
¼ cup water
¼ teaspoon sugar
¼ teaspoon dried oregano
⅛ teaspoon crushed red pepper
2 tablespoons plain 2% reduced-fat Greek yogurt
4 lemon wedges

1. Preheat oven to 400°.
2. Cut tops off bell peppers; reserve. Discard seeds. Place peppers in a microwave-safe baking dish; cover with damp paper towels. Microwave at HIGH 6 minutes. Let stand 5 minutes.
3. Combine ½ teaspoon black pepper, ¼ cup broth, and next 5 ingredients. Divide beef mixture among peppers; top with tops. Pour 2 cups water into dish; cover. Bake at 400° for 45 minutes. Sprinkle peppers with ¼ cup parsley.
4. Heat a medium skillet over medium-high heat. Add oil to pan; swirl to coat. Add onion; sauté 8 minutes, stirring occasionally. Add garlic; sauté 30 seconds. Add remaining ½ teaspoon black pepper, remaining ¼ cup broth, tomatoes, and next 4 ingredients; bring to a boil. Reduce heat; simmer 30 minutes. Stir in remaining ¼ cup parsley and yogurt. Serve with lemons. Serves 4 (serving size: 1 stuffed pepper, about 3 tablespoons sauce, and 1 lemon wedge).

CALORIES 454; FAT 12.1g (sat 4.1g, mono 5.5g, poly 0.9g); PROTEIN 25.2g; CARB 60g; FIBER 6.2g; CHOL 56mg; IRON 5.8mg; SODIUM 507mg; CALC 90mg

---

LIDIA BASTIANICH
Restaurateur, cookbook author, grandmother

Family, love, food: for Lidia Bastianich, this was the texture of childhood in Istria—now part of Croatia. Bastianich's grandmother made homemade pasta or gnocchi at least once a week, pairing it with produce from the garden. "It was all the best of fresh, seasonal ingredients," Bastianich says. "It was never masquerading. You could really tell what the ingredients were." When she ate her grandmother's gnocchi, she remembers, it was as if her mouth was "filled with velvetiness, like a hug from the inside out." If that doesn't define comfort food, what does?

As with so many big families of the time, thrift was built into their lives. Leftovers became new meals, down to the last crumb or noodle; gnocchi from dinnertime would be stuffed with prunes, rolled in cinnamon and sugar, and served as a sweet snack at room temperature.

Bastianich and her family moved to America when she was 12. Her mother worked in a bakery, and dinner preparation often fell to young Lidia—early training for the revered New York restaurant leader she became while earning her matriarchal stripes as mother and grandmother. Bastianich still follows the wisdom of her grandmother's kitchen: fresh ingredients, proper technique, foods made with love. And her table is always filled with family—four generations. Now she makes gnocchi for the grandchildren.

Here we present a healthy adaptation of gnocchi that's served in the generous spirit of Bastianich: The potato pillows are enrobed in a rich browned butter sauce and topped with grated Parmigiano-Reggiano and toasted walnuts.

Gnocchi with Browned Butter

Hands-on time: 35 min. Total time: 1 hr. 52 min. *Bastianich loves fresh sage with buttery gnocchi.*

2 (12-ounce) baking potatoes,
  unpeeled
1 teaspoon kosher salt
4.5 ounces all-purpose flour (about
  1 cup)
1/4 cup chopped fresh chives, divided
1/4 teaspoon freshly ground black
  pepper
2 large eggs, lightly beaten
6 quarts boiling water
3 tablespoons butter
1 large garlic clove, crushed
1/4 cup coarsely chopped walnut halves
1/2 ounce fresh Parmigiano-Reggiano or
  Grana Padano cheese, grated

1. Place potatoes in a saucepan; cover with water. Bring to a boil over medium-high heat. Cook 40 minutes; drain. Cool; peel. Press potato flesh through a ricer. Spread potatoes on a baking sheet; sprinkle with salt. Cool.
2. Scoop potatoes into a large bowl. Weigh or lightly spoon flour into a dry measuring cup; level with a knife. Add flour, and toss. Form a well in center. Add 2 tablespoons chives, pepper, and eggs; stir. Turn dough out onto a lightly floured surface. Gently knead just until dough comes together (about 1 minute).
3. Cut dough into 4 equal portions, and roll each into a 22-inch-long rope. Cut each rope into 22 pieces. Score gnocchi with a fork. Cook half of gnocchi 3 minutes in boiling water. Repeat with remaining gnocchi; drain.
4. Melt butter in a large skillet over medium heat. Add garlic; cook 2 minutes. Add nuts; cook 2 minutes or until butter browns. Discard garlic. Set aside half of butter mixture. Add half of gnocchi to pan; toss. Cook 1 minute or until browned. Repeat with remaining butter and gnocchi. Divide gnocchi evenly among 6 shallow bowls. Sprinkle with 2 tablespoons chives and cheese. Serves 4 (serving size: 22 gnocchi).

CALORIES 398; FAT 15.2g (sat 6.8g, mono 3.5g, poly 3.7g); PROTEIN 10.6g; CARB 56.4g; FIBER 3.6g; CHOL 78mg; IRON 3.4mg; SODIUM 606mg; CALC 73mg

LESS MEAT, MORE FLAVOR

MAC AND CHEESE, WITH VEGGIES

By Mark Bittman

When you add meaty mushrooms, earthy spinach, or rich sweet potatoes, the ultimate comfort food gets even more delicious.

Macaroni and cheese is perhaps the greatest comfort food. It meets all the criteria: butter, cheese, and pasta in nearly equal measure, composed of ingredients that are uniformly pale yellow, fatty, creamy, oozy, and crispy. It's as easy to cook as it is to devour. However, the ultimate comfort food does not contain vegetables.

Well, it does now.

The point of adding vegetables is not to punish mac and cheese for being sinful, but to add body, texture, and flavor to a dish that most of us probably don't tinker with too often. Not unlike a pot of grains or beans, pasta with melted cheese is a fairly blank canvas. There's no reason vegetables can't play a part. They provide a hit of brightness (both flavor and color), a touch of meatiness, a creamy richness, and even that crisp crust—the requisite crown on a great mac and cheese. Here, we have the best of all possibilities.

Sweet potatoes in mac and cheese may be a surprise (though it's not unprecedented). But when you cook them until very tender, and then layer in moisture and cheese, they form a rich, creamy base for pasta that makes dairy overload unnecessary. For a really smooth sauce, peel and cube the sweet potatoes; simmer in milk, stock, water, or a combination; then puree them in a blender.

I opt for roasting the potatoes whole, and then mashing them together with the rest of the ingredients in a bowl. The flavor from roasting is a bit deeper than when you simmer them, and the texture of the sauce (something like not-completely-smooth mashed potatoes) is heartier.

One of the all-time great flavor combinations is sweet potatoes and chipotle chiles (which are smoked jalapeños). The mix of sweet, rich, smoky, and spicy is addictive. Here, I spike the sweet potato and cheese mixture with a few tablespoons of chopped canned chipotles in adobo sauce before stirring in the pasta (you can add as much or as little as you like, depending on your tolerance for heat). An extra touch of spice (plus the must-have crunch) comes from fresh Mexican-style chorizo, sautéed until crisp and then scattered over the top before a quick pass under the broiler. A generous sprinkling of scallions and cilantro finishes it off.

My other version of veggie mac is a tribute to a place that probably doesn't make you think of vegetables at all: the steak house. It combines elements of three classic steak house side dishes: creamed spinach, roasted mushrooms, and salad with blue cheese and bacon. I sauté mushroom quarters until nicely browned, and then stir in minced garlic and a lot of baby spinach. Once the spinach wilts, I add the veggies to not-quite-tender pasta, along with a mixture of crumbled blue cheese and thick Greek yogurt. The mushrooms and spinach add a meaty

continued

chew and earthy flavor, and garlic adds a sharp bite, while the blue cheese and yogurt—melted in the residual heat—form a thin, tangy sauce. As for the topping, I use crumbles of crisp bacon tossed with breadcrumbs. Enough said.

Vegetables may not have the comfort-food cachet of knobs of butter or heaps of cheese, but they are no less comforting if you know how to use them. Take advantage of the ones that turn seductively rich and creamy like potatoes, cauliflower, parsnips, or winter squash, or the ones that are hearty and meaty like mushrooms, Brussels sprouts, or kale. Try them on their own or in combination, and you will soon find that the ultimate comfort food can get even better.

Sweet Potato Chile Mac

Hands-on time: 22 min. Total time: 1 hr. 32 min. *Crispy bits of Mexican chorizo (fresh, crumbly sausage—not to be confused with Spanish chorizo) create a delicious topping for this sweet-spicy take on mac and cheese. There's a fair amount of heat here, so if you prefer mild food, use even less chipotle.*

3 medium sweet potatoes (about 2 pounds)
1 cup fat-free milk
1½ to 2 tablespoons chopped chipotle chile, canned in adobo sauce
³⁄₈ teaspoon kosher salt
¼ teaspoon freshly ground black pepper
3 ounces Monterey Jack cheese, shredded (about ³⁄₄ cup)
8 ounces uncooked whole-wheat macaroni or penne pasta
1 tablespoon olive oil
6 ounces fresh Mexican chorizo, casings removed
¼ cup chopped green onions
2 tablespoons chopped fresh cilantro

1. Preheat oven to 425°.
2. Pierce potatoes several times with a fork; place on a foil-lined baking sheet. Bake at 425° for 1 hour or until tender. Cool slightly; peel and mash in a large bowl. Stir in milk and next 4 ingredients.
3. Cook pasta according to package directions, omitting salt and fat; drain. Add pasta to sweet potato mixture; set aside.
4. Preheat broiler to high.
5. Heat a large ovenproof skillet over medium heat. Add oil to pan; swirl to coat. Add chorizo to pan; cook 4 minutes or until browned, stirring to crumble. Place chorizo in a small bowl. Wipe pan clean. Spoon sweet potato mixture into pan; sprinkle evenly with chorizo. Broil 2 minutes or until lightly browned and crisp. Sprinkle with onions and cilantro. Serves 6 (serving size: about 1 cup).

CALORIES 456; FAT 15.5g (sat 6.2g, mono 6.9g, poly 1.4g); PROTEIN 18.6g; CARB 63.2g; FIBER 8.8g; CHOL 32mg; IRON 3.1mg; SODIUM 589mg; CALC 235mg

Steak House Side Mac and Cheese

Hands-on time: 20 min. Total time: 50 min. *This recipe combines flavors of classic steak house side dishes: creamed spinach, sautéed mushrooms, and blue cheese dressing.*

4 teaspoons olive oil, divided
2 teaspoons salt
8 ounces uncooked whole-wheat penne pasta or macaroni
3 bacon slices
10 ounces mushrooms, quartered
¼ teaspoon black pepper
2 garlic cloves, minced
2 (5-ounce) packages fresh baby spinach
¼ cup plain 2% Greek yogurt
4 ounces blue cheese, crumbled
½ cup whole-wheat panko (Japanese breadcrumbs)
2 tablespoons chopped fresh parsley

1. Preheat oven to 400°.
2. Coat a 2-quart glass or ceramic baking dish with 1 teaspoon oil. Set aside.
3. Bring a large saucepan of water to a boil; add salt and pasta. Cook 6 minutes or until just barely tender. Drain pasta in a colander over a bowl; reserve 1 cup cooking liquid.
4. Cook bacon in a large skillet over medium heat until crisp. Remove bacon from pan, reserving 2 tablespoons drippings in pan; crumble bacon. Add mushrooms to drippings in pan; cook 8 minutes or until browned, stirring occasionally. Add pepper, garlic, and spinach (in batches); cook 3 minutes or until spinach wilts, tossing occasionally.
5. Combine yogurt and cheese in a large bowl, stirring until almost smooth. Add pasta and mushroom mixture; toss to combine. Stir in ½ cup reserved cooking liquid (or more if mixture looks dry). Spoon pasta mixture into prepared dish. Combine crumbled bacon, panko, and parsley. Drizzle with remaining 3 teaspoons oil; toss to combine. Sprinkle evenly over top of pasta. Bake at 400° for 20 minutes or until golden and bubbly. Serves 6 (serving size: about 1½ cups).

CALORIES 347; FAT 15.4g (sat 6.4g, mono 6.4g, poly 1.4g); PROTEIN 15.5g; CARB 40.9g; FIBER 6.6g; CHOL 23mg; IRON 3.6mg; SODIUM 553mg; CALC 160m

KITCHEN SECRET: GARLIC TIPS

Although we often call for minced garlic, smaller or larger cuts might be better suited to certain dishes. Remember: The more intact the clove, the less pungent.

WHOLE
roasts, braises

THINLY SLICED
stir-fries, sautés

CRUSHED
marinades, stocks, oil infusions

PASTE
meat rubs, dressings, marinades

HASHED, MASHED & STUFFED

The potato is the humble star of the comfort-food pantry. Here, three essential techniques.

HASHED

Whether the spuds are diced or shredded, this approach is all about texture: crisp and golden outside, starchy goodness within.

Kid Friendly • Vegetarian

Home Fries

Hands-on time: 42 min. Total time: 1 hr. 12 min. Briefly microwaving the potatoes gives them a head start on cooking. Adding butter not only helps them brown better, but also lends rich flavor. Waxy potatoes won't break down in the pan when cubed and sautéed.

2 pounds Yukon gold or red potato, cubed
2¹⁄₂ tablespoons canola oil, divided
3 cups chopped yellow onion
6 garlic cloves, minced
2 tablespoons butter
¹⁄₂ teaspoon kosher salt
¹⁄₂ teaspoon freshly ground black pepper
¹⁄₄ cup coarsely chopped fresh flat-leaf parsley

1. Place potatoes in a microwave-safe dish, and cover with plastic wrap. Microwave at HIGH 5 minutes. Uncover and cool slightly.
2. Heat a large skillet over medium heat. Add 1¹⁄₂ tablespoons oil to pan; swirl to coat. Add onion; cook 20 minutes or until golden and tender, stirring occasionally. Add garlic; cook 1 minute, stirring constantly. Remove onion mixture from pan. Wipe pan clean with paper towels.
3. Increase heat to medium-high. Add remaining 1 tablespoon oil and butter to pan, and swirl to coat. Add potato, and cook 4 minutes, without stirring. Turn potatoes over. Cook 6 minutes or until browned, without stirring. Reduce heat to medium-low, and cook 10 minutes or until tender and golden brown, stirring occasionally. Remove from heat. Stir in onion mixture, salt, and black pepper; toss. Sprinkle with parsley. Serves 6 (serving size: about ¾ cup).

CALORIES 248; **FAT** 9.8g (sat 2.9g, mono 4.7g, poly 1.8g); **PROTEIN** 4.8g; **CARB** 35.4g; **FIBER** 3.3g; **CHOL** 10mg; **IRON** 1.7mg; **SODIUM** 201mg; **CALC** 29mg

THE KEY TO MAKING AMAZING HOME FRIES: RESIST THE URGE TO STIR. LEAVE THE POTATOES TO COOK AT THE RIGHT TEMPERATURE, AND THEY'LL BROWN GORGEOUSLY.

Kid Friendly • Make Ahead

Tex-Mex Hash Brown Casserole

(pictured on page 213)

Hands-on time: 45 min. Total time: 1 hr. 15 min.

4 teaspoons canola oil, divided
4 ounces Mexican chorizo
3 garlic cloves, minced
1 cup enchilada sauce
¹⁄₃ cup grated white onion
¹⁄₄ teaspoon kosher salt
¹⁄₂ teaspoon black pepper
3 pounds Yukon gold or baking potatoes, peeled and shredded
1 large egg, lightly beaten
4 ounces shredded sharp cheddar cheese (about 1 cup)
¹⁄₂ cup chopped avocado
1¹⁄₂ teaspoons fresh lemon juice
¹⁄₄ cup fresh cilantro leaves
¹⁄₄ cup chopped white onion
6 radishes, thinly sliced

1. Preheat oven to 450°.
2. Heat a 10-inch cast-iron skillet over medium-high heat. Add 1 teaspoon oil to pan; swirl to coat. Remove casings from chorizo. Add chorizo to pan; sauté 3 minutes, stirring to crumble. Add garlic; sauté 30 seconds. Remove sausage mixture from pan. Combine sausage mixture and enchilada sauce.
3. Add remaining 3 teaspoons oil to pan; swirl to coat. Combine grated onion, salt, pepper, potato, and egg; toss. Add potato mixture to pan, pressing gently; cook 10 minutes (do not stir). Spread enchilada sauce mixture over potato mixture; sprinkle with cheese. Bake at 450° for 20 minutes. Remove from oven; let stand 10 minutes.
4. Combine avocado and juice; toss gently. Stir in cilantro and remaining ingredients. Serve with casserole. Serves 6 (serving size: 1 wedge).

CALORIES 432; **FAT** 20.2g (sat 7.5g, mono 9.2g, poly 2.1g); **PROTEIN** 17g; **CARB** 47.1g; **FIBER** 4.9g; **CHOL** 72mg; **IRON** 2.9mg; **SODIUM** 686mg; **CALC** 152mg

MASHED

Fluffy, soft, warmly satisfying, simple, and—with endless stir-in and topping possibilities—never dull. But there isn't one definitive smoothness. It varies with the dish.

Kid Friendly • Quick & Easy
Vegetarian

Potato and Root Vegetable Mashers

Hands-on time: 30 min. Total time: 55 min. Sweet potato and turnip turn an otherwise straightforward mash into an intriguing dish with subtle earthy, sweet notes.

4 cups (1-inch) cubed Yukon gold or baking potato (about 1½ pounds)
2 cups cubed peeled turnip
2 cups cubed peeled sweet potato
2 tablespoons butter
⅓ cup light sour cream
¼ cup 1% low-fat milk
½ teaspoon salt
½ teaspoon freshly ground black pepper

1. Combine first 3 ingredients in a large saucepan; cover with water. Bring to a boil. Reduce heat and simmer, covered, 20 minutes or until tender. Drain well; return to pan over medium-low heat. Add butter; mash potato mixture with a potato masher. Stir in sour cream and remaining ingredients. Serves 6 (serving size: about ⅔ cup).

CALORIES 215; **FAT** 5g (sat 3.2g, mono 1g, poly 0.2g); **PROTEIN** 4.9g; **CARB** 38.4g; **FIBER** 4.8g; **CHOL** 15mg; **IRON** 1.6mg; **SODIUM** 311mg; **CALC** 61mg

A COARSE MASH GIVES THE DISH RUSTIC APPEAL; LEAVE SMALL CHUNKS OF THE VEGGIES IN POTATO AND ROOT VEGETABLE MASHERS TO ADD TEXTURE TO THE DISH.

Kid Friendly • Quick & Easy

Bacon and Cheddar Mashed Potatoes

Hands-on time: 10 min. Total time: 40 min. A loaded baked potato in a creamy format—with sour cream, cheddar, scallions, and bacon.

2½ pounds Yukon gold or baking potato, peeled and coarsely chopped
½ cup fat-free milk
2 ounces shredded extra-sharp cheddar cheese (about ½ cup)
½ cup fat-free sour cream
½ teaspoon freshly ground black pepper
¼ teaspoon kosher salt
⅓ cup sliced green onions
2 applewood-smoked bacon slices, cooked and finely chopped

1. Place potato in a large saucepan; cover with cold water. Bring to a boil. Reduce heat; simmer 15 minutes or until tender. Drain well; return potato to pan over medium-low heat. Add milk; mash potato mixture with a potato masher to desired consistency. Cook 2 minutes or until thoroughly heated, stirring constantly. Remove from heat. Add cheese, and stir until cheese melts. Stir in sour cream, pepper, and salt. Top with green onions and bacon. Serves 6 (serving size: about 1 cup).

CALORIES 237; **FAT** 4.5g (sat 2.5g, mono 1.4g, poly 0.2g); **PROTEIN** 9.5g; **CARB** 38.3g; **FIBER** 2.5g; **CHOL** 15mg; **IRON** 1.8mg; **SODIUM** 238mg; **CALC** 129mg

PICK THE RIGHT POTATO

BAKING POTATOES, also known as russets, fall into the "starchy" category. They break down and become fluffy when cooked, making them great for mashing and baking, but bad for cubing and sautéing.

FINGERLINGS and **RED POTATOES,** on the other hand, are "waxy." Their denser, firm texture (gluey when mashed) helps keep their shape for home fries and potato salads.

YUKON GOLDS, finally, are the great all-purpose potatoes.

SELECTING AND STORING

Choose firm potatoes without soft spots, bruises, sprouts, or a green tint to the skin. Green skin means the potato has been exposed to light too long and can be bitter or even toxic. Trim off small sprouts before cooking. Keep potatoes in a dark, dry place, ideally under 55°, but don't refrigerate. Store away from other produce, which may give off gases that shorten shelf life. Wash just before using.

DON'T WRAP POTATOES IN FOIL BEFORE BAKING: THAT PRODUCES SOGGY SKIN. TRY A LIGHT COATING OF COOKING SPRAY OR OIL TO MAKE THE JACKETS IRRESISTIBLY CRISP.

STUFFED

Baked potatoes are hot, starchy bowls ready to hold tasty fillings—self-contained suppers ideal for cold nights.

Kid Friendly

Cajun-Stuffed Potatoes

Hands-on time: 38 min. Total time: 1 hr. 28 min. Substitute chopped cooked shrimp if crawfish are unavailable.

6 medium Yukon gold or small baking
 potatoes (about 3 pounds)
2 tablespoons olive oil, divided
1 1/2 cups chopped yellow onion
3/4 cup chopped green bell pepper
1/2 cup thinly sliced celery
1 tablespoon minced fresh garlic
3/4 teaspoon salt
3/4 teaspoon Hungarian sweet paprika
1/2 teaspoon onion powder
1/2 teaspoon ground red pepper
3/4 cup 1/3-less-fat cream cheese,
 softened (about 6 ounces)
2 tablespoons butter, softened
1 tablespoon chopped fresh oregano
2 teaspoons chopped fresh thyme
1 1/2 pounds frozen cooked crawfish
 meat, thawed

1. Preheat oven to 450°.
2. Pierce potatoes with a fork, and brush with 1 teaspoon olive oil. Bake at 450° for 50 minutes or until tender. Remove potatoes from oven; cool slightly. Cut potatoes in half lengthwise, and scoop pulp out of skins, leaving a 1/4-inch-thick shell. Place pulp in a large bowl, and coarsely mash pulp.
3. Preheat broiler to high.
4. Heat a large skillet over medium-high heat. Add remaining 5 teaspoons oil to pan, and swirl to coat. Add onion, bell pepper, and celery to pan; sauté 4 minutes. Add garlic and next 4 ingredients, and sauté 1 minute. Remove from heat. Add cheese, butter, and herbs, stirring until smooth.
5. Stir cheese mixture and crawfish into potato pulp. Place 1/2 cup crawfish mixture in each potato shell. Arrange stuffed potatoes on a baking sheet. Broil 5 minutes or until browned. Serves 6 (serving size: 2 potato halves).

CALORIES 451; **FAT** 16.5g (sat 7g, mono 6.3g, poly 1.6g); **PROTEIN** 27.8g; **CARB** 46.8g; **FIBER** 3.9g; **CHOL** 182mg; **IRON** 3.2mg; **SODIUM** 546mg; **CALC** 124mg

Kid Friendly • Make Ahead

Chicken and White BBQ Potatoes

Hands-on time: 20 min. Total time: 1 hr. Baking potatoes (russets) can get huge, tipping the scales at a pound or more each, but smaller ones should also be readily available. If not, go with Yukon golds, which tend to be smaller.

4 (6-ounce) Yukon gold or baking
 potatoes
Cooking spray
2/3 cup canola mayonnaise
3 tablespoons white vinegar
1 tablespoon Dijon mustard
2 teaspoons freshly ground black pepper
1/2 teaspoon sugar
1/4 teaspoon salt
2 garlic cloves, minced
1 1/2 cups shredded skinless, boneless
 rotisserie chicken breast
3 tablespoons sweet pickle relish
1/4 cup sliced green onions

1. Preheat oven to 450°.
2. Pierce potatoes with a fork, and coat lightly with cooking spray. Bake at 450° for 50 minutes or until tender. Remove potatoes from oven, and cool slightly. Cut a lengthwise slit in each potato that goes to, but not through, other side, and squeeze ends to loosen potato flesh.
3. Combine mayonnaise and next 6 ingredients in a medium bowl. Stir in chicken and relish. Divide chicken mixture evenly among potatoes. Top each potato with 1 tablespoon onions. Serves 4 (serving size: 1 stuffed potato).

CALORIES 489; **FAT** 30.8g (sat 3g, mono 16.6g, poly 8.2g); **PROTEIN** 14.6g; **CARB** 36.9g; **FIBER** 2.7g; **CHOL** 45mg; **IRON** 1.9mg; **SODIUM** 730mg; **CALC** 17mg

TODAY'S LESSON: MEAT LOAF

Meat loaf, once the pride and triumph of the thrifty American housewife, now pops up in urban hot spots. It's souped up with exotic chiles, tahini, or truffle oil. Anyone for Foie Gras–Stuffed Kobe Beef Meat Loaf? But at heart, it's humble food. Our goal here was to cut fat while staying true to the Essence of the Loaf. Then we tried it Italian-style. Then we decided to try a vegetarian version...

Kid Friendly • Make Ahead

All-American Meat Loaf
(pictured on page 212)

Hands-on time: 15 min. Total time: 1 hr. 10 min.

1½ ounces French bread, torn into
    pieces
½ cup ketchup, divided
1 cup coarsely chopped onion
5 tablespoons chopped fresh flat-leaf
    parsley, divided
¼ cup nonfat buttermilk
1 tablespoon minced fresh garlic
1 tablespoon Dijon mustard
½ teaspoon freshly ground black
    pepper
¼ teaspoon kosher salt
2 ounces sharp cheddar cheese, diced
2 large eggs, lightly beaten
1 pound ground sirloin
Cooking spray

1. Preheat oven to 350°.
2. Place bread in a food processor; pulse 10 times or until coarse crumbs measure 1 cup. Arrange breadcrumbs in an even layer on a baking sheet. Bake at 350° for 6 minutes or until lightly toasted; cool. Combine toasted breadcrumbs, ¼ cup ketchup, onion, 3 tablespoons parsley, and next 8 ingredients in a bowl; gently mix until just combined.
3. Transfer mixture to a 9 x 5–inch loaf pan coated with cooking spray; do not pack. Bake at 350° for 30 minutes. Brush top of loaf with remaining ¼ cup ketchup. Bake an additional 25 minutes or until thermometer registers 160°. Let stand 10 minutes, and cut into 6 slices. Sprinkle with remaining parsley. Serves 6 (serving size: 1 slice).

CALORIES 258; FAT 12.6g (sat 5.8g, mono 4g, poly 0.6g); PROTEIN 21.2g; CARB 14g; FIBER 0.8g; CHOL 119mg; IRON 2.6mg; SODIUM 557mg; CALC 104mg

STEP-BY-STEPS

KEEP IT MOIST
To avoid loaves that are tough and dense, it's important to add filler ingredients like breadcrumbs, rice, or other grains. If using breadcrumbs, fresh is best. Process a torn baguette or other crusty bread to form coarse crumbs, and be sure to toast them before stirring them into the meat mixture.

ADD MORE FLAVOR
Aromatic ingredients, such as onion or other veggies, and cheese add flavor and moisture. Shred the cheese and chop the aromatics finely, and they'll blend into the loaf seamlessly. For a rustic appearance and texture, chop the veggies coarsely and leave the cheese chunky, as we did.

MIX, SHAPE, AND BAKE
Especially when using ground meats, mix as little as possible, just until the ingredients are blended. Overmixing will compact the mixture and yield a tough, dense loaf. Also take care to avoid packing the meat when transferring it to the pan or shaping it.

Make Ahead • Vegetarian

Vegetable "Meat" Loaf

Hands-on time: 1 hr. Total time: 1 hr. 47 min. *Vegetarians and carnivores alike will love this ingenious twist on meat loaf. The meaty-flavored, umami-rich recipe received our Test Kitchen's highest rating. Ordinarily you wouldn't pack a meat loaf into the pan, but since we're using a vegetable mixture, you will to make sure it holds together.*

Meat loaf:
1 large red bell pepper
1 large green bell pepper
2 pounds cremini mushrooms, coarsely chopped
1 tablespoon olive oil
1 cup ($1/2$-inch) asparagus pieces
$1/2$ cup chopped red onion
1 cup panko (Japanese breadcrumbs)
1 cup chopped walnuts, toasted
2 tablespoons chopped fresh basil
1 tablespoon ketchup
1 teaspoon Dijon mustard
$1/2$ teaspoon kosher salt
$1/2$ teaspoon freshly ground black pepper
4 ounces fresh Parmigiano-Reggiano cheese, grated
2 large eggs, lightly beaten
Cooking spray
Topping:
2 tablespoons ketchup
1 tablespoon vodka or vegetable broth
$1/4$ teaspoon Dijon mustard

1. Preheat broiler to high.
2. To prepare meat loaf, cut bell peppers in half lengthwise; discard seeds and membranes. Place pepper halves, skin sides up, on a foil-lined baking sheet; flatten with hand. Broil 12 minutes or until blackened. Place in a paper bag; fold to close tightly. Let stand 10 minutes. Peel and finely chop. Place bell peppers in a large bowl.
3. Reduce oven temperature to 350°.
4. Place about one-fourth of mushrooms in a food processor; pulse 10 times or until finely chopped. Transfer chopped mushrooms to a bowl. Repeat procedure 3 times with remaining mushrooms.
5. Heat a large nonstick skillet over medium-high heat. Add oil to pan; swirl to coat. Add mushrooms to pan; sauté 15 minutes or until liquid evaporates, stirring occasionally. Add mushrooms to bell peppers. Wipe pan with paper towels. Add asparagus and onion to pan; sauté 6 minutes or until just tender, stirring occasionally. Add onion mixture to mushroom mixture.
6. Arrange breadcrumbs in an even layer on a baking sheet; bake at 350° for 10 minutes or until golden. Add breadcrumbs and next 8 ingredients to mushroom mixture, stirring well. Spoon mixture into a 9 x 5–inch loaf pan coated with cooking spray; press gently to pack. Bake at 350° for 45 minutes or until a thermometer registers 155°.
7. To prepare topping, combine 2 tablespoons ketchup and remaining ingredients in a small bowl; brush ketchup mixture over meat loaf. Bake an additional 10 minutes. Let stand 10 minutes; cut into 6 slices. Serves 6 (serving size: 1 slice).

CALORIES 338; **FAT** 21.2g (sat 4.3g, mono 5.1g, poly 10.1g); **PROTEIN** 17.5g; **CARB** 22.6g; **FIBER** 4.9g; **CHOL** 72mg; **IRON** 2.6mg; **SODIUM** 535mg; **CALC** 197mg

Kid Friendly • Make Ahead

Meat Loaf Bolognese

Hands-on time: 55 min. Total time: 1 hr. *This dish contains many of the flavors of sauce Bolognese, the classic Italian ragù of pancetta, a mixture of ground meats, and aromatic ingredients stewed together. Round out the meal with polenta. Garnish with chopped fresh rosemary, if desired.*

Meat loaf:
1 ounce French bread, torn
Cooking spray
2 ounces pancetta, chopped
$1/2$ cup finely chopped shallots
$1/2$ cup finely chopped carrot
1 tablespoon tomato paste
$1/4$ cup fruity red wine
$1/4$ cup 2% reduced-fat milk
$1/2$ teaspoon kosher salt
$1/2$ teaspoon freshly ground black pepper
1 large egg, lightly beaten
$1/3$ pound ground sirloin
$1/3$ pound lean ground pork
$1/3$ pound ground veal
Mushroom sauce:
1 tablespoon butter
4 ounces finely chopped cremini mushrooms
2 tablespoons minced shallots
4 teaspoons all-purpose flour
1 cup fat-free, lower-sodium beef broth
2 tablespoons half-and-half
$1/4$ teaspoon freshly ground black pepper
Dash of salt

1. Preheat oven to 350°.
2. To make meat loaf, place bread in a food processor; pulse 10 times or until coarse crumbs measure $3/4$ cup. Arrange breadcrumbs on a baking sheet; bake at 350° for 8 minutes.
3. Heat a small skillet over medium-high heat. Coat pan with cooking spray. Add pancetta; sauté 2 minutes. Add $1/2$ cup shallots and carrot; sauté

continued

8 minutes, stirring occasionally. Add tomato paste; cook 1 minute. Add wine; cook 2 minutes or until liquid almost evaporates, scraping pan to loosen browned bits. Remove pan from heat; cool 5 minutes. Combine breadcrumbs, pancetta mixture, milk, and next 6 ingredients in a large bowl; gently mix until just combined.

4. Transfer mixture to a 9 x 5–inch loaf pan coated with cooking spray; do not pack. Bake at 350° for 40 minutes or until a thermometer registers 160°. Let stand 10 minutes; cut into 6 slices.

5. To prepare sauce, melt butter in a medium saucepan over medium-high heat. Add cremini mushrooms and 2 tablespoons shallots; sauté 6 minutes, stirring occasionally. Add flour, and cook 1 minute. Add 1 cup beef broth; cook 2 minutes, stirring frequently. Stir in half-and-half, ¼ teaspoon black pepper, and dash of salt. Cook 30 seconds. Serve with meat loaf. Serves 6 (serving size: 1 slice meat loaf and about 2 tablespoons sauce).

CALORIES 251; **FAT** 13.2g (sat 5.9g, mono 4g, poly 0.8g); **PROTEIN** 20g; **CARB** 10.5g; **FIBER** 0.8g; **CHOL** 100mg; **IRON** 1.6mg; **SODIUM** 597mg; **CALC** 47mg

START WITH A JAR OF PASTA SAUCE

Use its rich, slow-simmered herb-and-tomato goodness as a starting point for dinner, be it chili, braised lamb, poached eggs, or baked pasta. Of all the shortcut ingredients for the healthy cook, a good marinara is one of the finest because it delivers the pleasures of slow-cooking—in a jar.

Kid Friendly • Make Ahead

Chicken Cacciatore

Hands-on time: 37 min. Total time: 1 hr. 7 min. Serve on a bed of spaghetti or with a short pasta like penne or cavatappi for a complete meal.

8 bone-in chicken thighs, skinned (about 2½ pounds)
³⁄₈ teaspoon salt, divided
¼ teaspoon freshly ground black pepper
2 tablespoons olive oil, divided
1½ cups chopped red bell pepper
¾ cup chopped green bell pepper
1 cup chopped onion
½ cup chopped celery
2 teaspoons chopped fresh rosemary
4 garlic cloves, minced
8 ounces sliced mushrooms
1⅓ cups lower-sodium marinara sauce (such as McCutcheon's)
1 ounce Parmigiano-Reggiano cheese, shaved

1. Preheat oven to 350°.

2. Heat a large nonstick skillet over medium-high heat. Sprinkle chicken with ¼ teaspoon salt and black pepper. Add 2 teaspoons oil to pan; swirl to coat. Add 4 chicken thighs to pan; cook 4 minutes on each side or until browned. Remove chicken from pan; keep warm. Repeat procedure with 2 teaspoons oil and remaining chicken.

3. Add remaining 2 teaspoons oil to pan; swirl to coat. Add bell peppers, 1 cup onion, celery, rosemary, minced garlic, and remaining ⅛ teaspoon salt; cook 3 minutes, stirring frequently. Add mushrooms; cook 6 minutes, stirring occasionally. Stir in marinara sauce; cook 1 minute.

4. Spread vegetable mixture in bottom of a 13 x 9–inch glass or ceramic baking dish. Arrange chicken on top of vegetable mixture. Bake at 350° for 30 minutes or until a thermometer inserted into chicken registers 160°. Sprinkle with cheese. Serves 4 (serving size: 2 chicken thighs, 1 cup vegetable mixture, and about 1 tablespoon cheese).

CALORIES 352; **FAT** 15.5g (sat 3.9g, mono 7.2g, poly 2.3g); **PROTEIN** 32.9g; **CARB** 36.3g; **FIBER** 3.2g; **CHOL** 119mg; **IRON** 2.4mg; **SODIUM** 596mg; **CALC** 128mg

VEGETARIAN DELIGHT: A CHUNK OF HEARTY TOAST SOAKS UP SAVORY DELICIOUSNESS FROM TANGY SAUCE AND CREAMY EGG YOLK.

Quick & Easy • Vegetarian

Eggs Poached in Tomato Sauce with Onions and Peppers

Hands-on time: 18 min. Total time: 25 min. *This saucy dish makes a great savory breakfast, or pair with a side salad for a lighter dinner option.*

1 tablespoon extra-virgin olive oil
2 cups sliced red bell pepper
1 cup sliced green bell pepper
1 cup sliced onion
2 garlic cloves, minced
2 cups lower-sodium marinara sauce (such as McCutcheon's)
1 teaspoon dried oregano
4 large eggs
¼ teaspoon salt
¼ teaspoon freshly ground black pepper
4 (1½-ounce) slices 100% whole-wheat bread, toasted
2 tablespoons chopped fresh parsley
4 teaspoons shaved fresh Parmesan cheese

1. Heat a medium nonstick skillet over medium heat. Add olive oil to pan; swirl to coat. Add bell peppers and onion; cook 6 minutes, stirring occasionally. Add garlic, and cook 2 minutes, stirring frequently. Reduce heat to medium-low. Stir in marinara sauce and oregano; cook 3 minutes, stirring occasionally.
2. Form 4 (3-inch) indentations in vegetable mixture using back of a spoon. Break 1 egg into each indentation; sprinkle salt and black pepper evenly over eggs. Cover and cook 6 minutes or until eggs are desired degree of doneness.
3. Arrange 1 toast slice on each of 4 plates. Top each slice with ½ cup sauce and 1 egg. Sprinkle each serving with 1½ teaspoons parsley and 1 teaspoon cheese. Serves 4.

CALORIES 303; **FAT** 12g (sat 2.5g, mono 5.4g, poly 1.3g); **PROTEIN** 14.4g; **CARB** 59.4g; **FIBER** 6.8g; **CHOL** 181mg; **IRON** 2.7mg; **SODIUM** 640mg; **CALC** 129mg

THE RIGHT SAUCE FOR THE JOB

We sorted through the billion pasta sauce choices now on supermarket shelves, focused on marinara (the most basic and most versatile), and evaluated using two criteria: sodium and flavor. Sodium can be particularly high, as much as 540mg per half-cup serving. Generally, we recommend seeking out sauces with less than 350mg sodium per half-cup serving. Some sauces also contain a lot of added sugar, which means you'll want to add salt to rebalance. Others have a too-pronounced dried-herb flavor. Our favorites from the marinara tasting:

MCCUTCHEON'S MARINARA PASTA SAUCE
Not labeled as lower-sodium, but it is—only 185mg in a half cup. No added sugar, so it's decidedly savory, with just the right amount of herby-garlicky kick. The unanimous favorite, it has become our default pasta sauce. (We buy ours at Whole Foods.)

AMY'S LIGHT IN SODIUM FAMILY MARINARA PASTA SAUCE
Sweeter than McCutcheon's (it contains "organic evaporated cane juice," which is basically sugar), but it's nicely balanced by savory onions and garlic. A half-cup serving has 290mg sodium.

Freezable • Make Ahead

Chicken and Sausage Stew

Hands-on time: 25 min. Total time: 1 hr. 10 min. *Gumbo-ish at heart, a full-bodied stew that's intensely satisfying. The cooked flour and oil mixture, known as roux, thickens this gumbo-inspired stew. Marinara sauce adds body, enriches the color and taste, and provides slightly tangy notes for a more rounded flavor.*

3 tablespoons all-purpose flour
2 tablespoons olive oil
2 cups chopped onion
1 cup chopped green bell pepper
1 cup chopped celery
¼ teaspoon dried thyme
4 ounces diced chicken andouille sausage
4 garlic cloves, minced
¼ teaspoon ground red pepper
12 ounces skinless, boneless chicken thighs, cut into 1-inch pieces
1½ cups lower-sodium marinara sauce (such as McCutcheon's)
1½ cups fat-free, lower-sodium chicken broth
½ cup chopped green onions
3 cups hot cooked white rice

1. Heat flour and oil in a Dutch oven over medium-low heat; cook 5 minutes or until lightly browned, stirring frequently with a whisk. Add onion, bell pepper, celery, thyme, sausage, and garlic; increase heat to medium-high, and cook 5 minutes, stirring mixture frequently. Add ground red pepper and chicken; cook 1 minute. Stir in marinara sauce and chicken broth; bring to a boil, stirring frequently. Cover, reduce heat, and simmer 20 minutes or until chicken is tender. Remove from heat; stir in green onions. Serve over rice. Serves 6 (servings size: 1 cup stew and ½ cup rice).

CALORIES 323; **FAT** 9.2g (sat 2.1g, mono 4.1g, poly 1.2g); **PROTEIN** 18.7g; **CARB** 51.8g; **FIBER** 2.4g; **CHOL** 67mg; **IRON** 2.6mg; **SODIUM** 677mg; **CALC** 67mg

Slow-Braised Lamb Shanks

Hands-on time: 30 min. Total time: 2 hr. 45 min. *Buttery, fork-tender meat from a long, gentle simmer. Serve over mashed potatoes, polenta, or couscous.*

4 (12-ounce) lamb shanks, trimmed
¼ teaspoon black pepper
1 teaspoon olive oil
1 cup chopped onion
1 teaspoon chopped fresh thyme
3 garlic cloves, minced
½ cup red wine
3 cups lower-sodium marinara sauce (such as McCutcheon's)
½ cup fat-free, lower-sodium chicken broth
¼ cup thinly sliced fresh basil
2 teaspoons grated lemon rind

1. Heat a large Dutch oven over medium-high heat. Sprinkle lamb evenly with pepper. Add oil to pan; swirl to coat. Add lamb to pan; cook 8 minutes, browning on all sides. Remove lamb from pan. Add onion, thyme, and garlic to pan; cook 2 minutes, stirring occasionally. Add wine to pan, scraping pan to loosen browned bits; cook until liquid evaporates (about 2 minutes). Stir in marinara sauce and broth; cook 4 minutes, stirring occasionally. Return lamb to pan. Cover; reduce heat to low, and simmer 2 hours or until very tender and meat pulls easily from the bone. Remove lamb from pan; skim any fat from surface of sauce, and discard. Increase heat to medium-high; bring sauce to a boil, and cook until sauce thickens (about 6 minutes). Add lamb; cook 2 minutes or until thoroughly heated. Remove pan from heat; stir in basil and rind. Serves 4 (serving size: 1 shank and ¾ cup sauce).

CALORIES 426; **FAT** 18.7g (sat 7.3g, mono 7.3g, poly 1.2g); **PROTEIN** 3.3g; **CARB** 60.3g; **FIBER** 0.9g; **CHOL** 120mg; **IRON** 2.8mg; **SODIUM** 422mg; **CALC** 46mg

Poblano-Jalapeño Chili

(*pictured on page 215*)

Hands-on time: 34 min. Total time: 1 hr. 4 min. *Meaty, juicy, and moderately spicy. For a bit of crunch, top with thinly sliced radishes.*

Cooking spray
1½ pounds ground sirloin
2 jalapeño peppers
1 tablespoon canola oil
3 cups chopped onion (about 1 large)
1 cup chopped seeded poblano chile (about 2 large)
8 garlic cloves, minced
1 (12-ounce) Mexican beer
1 tablespoon chili powder
1½ teaspoons ground cumin
¾ teaspoon kosher salt
2½ cups lower-sodium marinara sauce (such as McCutcheon's)
1 cup fat-free, lower-sodium chicken broth
2 (15-ounce) cans no-salt-added kidney beans, rinsed and drained
1 (14.5-ounce) can diced fire-roasted tomatoes, undrained
3 ounces sharp cheddar cheese, shredded (about ¾ cup)
½ cup light sour cream
¼ cup fresh cilantro leaves

1. Heat a Dutch oven over medium-high heat. Coat pan with cooking spray. Add beef; cook 10 minutes or until browned, stirring to crumble. Remove beef from pan; drain. Wipe pan clean.
2. Remove and discard seeds and membranes from 1 jalapeño; finely chop both jalapeños. Heat pan over medium-high heat. Add oil; swirl to coat. Add jalapeños, onion, poblano, and garlic; sauté 10 minutes or until onion is tender. Add beer; scrape pan to loosen browned bits. Cook 12 minutes or until half of liquid evaporates. Add chili powder, cumin, and salt; cook 1 minute, stirring frequently. Stir in beef, marinara, broth, beans, and tomatoes; bring to a boil. Reduce heat; simmer, uncovered, 30 minutes or until slightly thickened. Ladle about 1½ cups chili into each of 8 bowls; top each serving with 1½ tablespoons cheese, 1 tablespoon sour cream, and 1½ teaspoons cilantro. Serves 8.

CALORIES 349; **FAT** 14.4g (sat 5.9g, mono 5.1g, poly 1g); **PROTEIN** 25.6g; **CARB** 44.9g; **FIBER** 6.5g; **CHOL** 71mg; **IRON** 3.2mg; **SODIUM** 625mg; **CALC** 142mg

Cheesy Pasta Bake

Hands-on time: 39 min. Total time: 59 min. *Classic formula of pasta plus sauce plus sausage plus cheese. Tasty!*

14 ounces uncooked ziti or mostaccioli
12 ounces ground turkey breast
8 ounces sweet turkey Italian sausage, casings removed
Cooking spray
1½ tablespoons olive oil
2 cups chopped onion
¼ teaspoon crushed red pepper
6 garlic cloves, minced
½ cup red wine
5 cups lower-sodium marinara sauce
½ cup chopped fresh basil
6 ounces whole-milk mozzarella cheese, thinly sliced
2 ounces grated Parmigiano-Reggiano cheese, divided (about ½ cup)
2 tablespoons small basil leaves or torn basil

1. Preheat oven to 350°.
2. Cook pasta according to package directions, omitting salt and fat; drain and set aside.
3. Place ground turkey and sausage in a medium bowl, and mix well with hands to combine. Heat a Dutch oven over medium-high heat. Coat pan with cooking spray. Add turkey mixture to pan; cook 8 minutes or until browned, stirring to crumble. Remove from pan.
4. Add oil to pan; swirl to coat. Add onion and pepper; sauté 4 minutes.

Add garlic; sauté 5 minutes or until onion is tender. Add wine, scraping pan to loosen browned bits, and cook 4 minutes or until liquid almost evaporates. Stir in pasta, turkey mixture, marinara sauce, and ½ cup basil. Spoon mixture into a 13 x 9–inch glass or ceramic baking dish coated with cooking spray. Top with mozzarella and ¼ cup Parmigiano-Reggiano. Bake at 350° for 25 minutes or until bubbly and cheese melts and begins to brown. Remove from oven, and sprinkle with basil leaves and remaining ¼ cup Parmigiano-Reggiano cheese. Serves 8 (serving size: about 1½ cups).

CALORIES 492; **FAT** 14.2g (sat 6.1g, mono 4.8g, poly 1.4g); **PROTEIN** 30.2g; **CARB** 88g; **FIBER** 2.4g; **CHOL** 72mg; **IRON** 2.8mg; **SODIUM** 708mg; **CALC** 224mg

KID-FRIENDLY COOKING

A KID IN THE KITCHEN

This month, 11-year-old Matisse Reid introduces her BFFs to fresh fish tacos with creamy guac.

"To field-test one of our kid-friendly recipes, I contacted the food-savviest kid I know, Matisse Reid, who loves lobster and squid and likes to add a splash of olive brine to her mussels. Her assignment: Prepare our fresh tuna tacos for some of her friends. She got her two besties to come over, and here's what she told me."

—Ann Taylor Pittman

"Today I made some Tuna-Guacamole Tacos. The recipe was really easy to make. I had my friends take turns at scooping out and mashing the avocado—saved me the work! Because the guacamole recipe was very basic, you could really appreciate the lime, which gave it a tart taste without overwhelming the delicate flavor of the tuna. The guacamole was REALLY creamy and yummy to eat on its own. The fish was very succulent—I gave it an extra squeeze of lime because I like the tart taste. I cooked the tuna so it was still pink in the middle—very rare (still swimming). My two BFFs don't normally like fish, but they loved the tuna and did not mind that it was rare (maybe because I did not tell them it was rare)."

Kid Friendly • Quick & Easy

Tuna-Guacamole Tacos

Hands-on time: 15 min. Total time: 15 min.

½ cup thinly sliced red onion
1 tablespoon fresh lime juice
¾ teaspoon kosher salt, divided
2 ripe peeled avocados, mashed
Cooking spray
2 (10-ounce) Yellowfin tuna steaks (about 1 inch thick)
8 (6-inch) corn tortillas

1. Combine onion, lime juice, ¼ teaspoon salt, and avocados.
2. Heat a grill pan over medium-high heat; coat pan with cooking spray. Sprinkle tuna with remaining ½ teaspoon salt. Add tuna to pan; cook 4 minutes on each side or to desired degree of doneness. Cut tuna into ¼-inch-thick slices. Warm tortillas according to package directions. Divide avocado mixture evenly among tortillas. Divide tuna evenly among tortillas. Serves 4 (serving size: 2 tacos).

CALORIES 402; **FAT** 17.3g (sat 2.5g, mono 10.1g, poly 2.7g); **PROTEIN** 37.3g; **CARB** 28.2g; **FIBER** 9g; **CHOL** 64mg; **IRON** 1.6mg; **SODIUM** 430mg; **CALC** 59mg

THE VERDICT

MEGS (AGE 11)
Normally hates fish, but she gave the recipe **10/10.**

JOC (AGE 10)
Eats lots of guac but loved this one best! She gave it **10/10.**

MATISSE
I gave it **9/10.** I felt it needed more color. I would definitely make this recipe again because it is really quick to make, lots of fun, and it is yummy in your tummy!!!

MATISSE SAYS: "BEFORE SQUEEZING THE LIME, ROLL IT ON YOUR BOARD. THIS RELEASES THE JUICE TO MAKE IT EASIER TO SQUEEZE."

WHEN RICE MET VEGGIES ...

... a wonderful marriage happened. Savor the world's most popular grain in a quick-and-easy stir-fry, a cheesy casserole, and a Korean favorite.

Freezable • Make Ahead • Vegetarian

Cheesy Brown Rice Gratin with Zucchini and Eggplant

***Hands-on time: 45 min. Total time: 1 hr. 15 min.** The walnuts in this gratin offer a crunchy contrast to the roasted vegetables and cheesy rice mixture, while the splash of half-and-half adds creamy richness. The rice mixture can be made ahead and refrigerated. When ready to prepare, bring to room temperature, spoon into the baking dish, and proceed as directed at the end of step 5.*

¾ cup uncooked long-grain brown rice
1 pound eggplant, cut into 1-inch cubes
1 pound zucchini, halved lengthwise
    and cut into 1-inch pieces
¾ teaspoon salt, divided
2 tablespoons extra-virgin olive oil,
    divided
Cooking spray
1 cup chopped onion
3 garlic cloves, minced
4 ounces Parmigiano-Reggiano cheese,
    grated and divided (about 1 cup)
¼ cup half-and-half
¼ teaspoon freshly ground black
    pepper
2 large eggs, lightly beaten
2 ounces French bread, cut into 1-inch
    cubes
½ cup chopped walnuts
2 tablespoons chopped fresh parsley

1. Cook rice according to package directions, omitting salt and fat.
2. Preheat oven to 400°.
3. Combine eggplant, zucchini, ¼ teaspoon salt, and 1 tablespoon olive oil in a bowl; toss to combine. Place eggplant mixture evenly on a large baking sheet coated with cooking spray. Bake at 400° for 15 minutes. Place vegetables in a large bowl.
4. Reduce oven temperature to 375°.
5. Heat a large nonstick skillet over medium heat. Add 2 teaspoons olive oil to pan, and swirl to coat. Add onion and garlic; cook 12 minutes or until tender. Add onion mixture to eggplant mixture. Add cooked rice, remaining ½ teaspoon salt, ¾ cup cheese, and next 3 ingredients, and stir well to combine. Spoon rice mixture into an 11 x 7–inch glass or ceramic baking dish coated with cooking spray. Cover with foil, and bake at 375° for 15 minutes.
6. Place bread in a food processor; pulse 10 times or until coarse crumbs measure 1 cup. Heat a large skillet over medium-high heat. Add remaining 1 teaspoon oil to pan, and swirl to coat. Add breadcrumbs, and cook 3 minutes or until toasted, stirring frequently. Remove pan from heat; stir in remaining ¼ cup cheese, walnuts, and parsley.
7. Remove foil from rice mixture. Top evenly with breadcrumb mixture. Bake, uncovered, at 375° for 15 minutes or until vegetables are tender and topping is browned. Serves 6 (serving size: about 1½ cups).

CALORIES 354; FAT 18.7g (sat 5g, mono 6.6g, poly 5.9g); PROTEIN 14.1g; CARB 35.5g; FIBER 5.6g; CHOL 86mg; IRON 2mg; SODIUM 596mg; CALC 215mg

Quick & Easy • Vegetarian

Tempeh and Broccolini Stir-Fry

***Hands-on time: 30 min. Total time: 30 min.** For a whole-grain base, use brown rice.*

½ pound Broccolini
6 tablespoons chopped green onions,
    divided
4½ tablespoons rice vinegar
3 tablespoons lower-sodium soy sauce
2 tablespoons hoisin sauce
2 teaspoons honey
¼ teaspoon crushed red pepper
5 teaspoons canola oil, divided
1 (8-ounce) package organic tempeh,
    cut into ½-inch cubes
1 cup diagonally cut snow peas
2⅔ cups hot cooked long-grain
    white rice
3 tablespoons chopped unsalted,
    dry-roasted peanuts

1. Cook Broccolini in boiling water 2 minutes or until crisp-tender. Drain and plunge into ice water; drain. Squeeze dry. Cut into 1-inch pieces.
2. Combine 3 tablespoons green onions and next 5 ingredients in a bowl.
3. Heat a large, heavy skillet or wok over medium-high heat. Add 1 tablespoon oil to pan; swirl to coat. Add tempeh; stir-fry 5 minutes or until golden brown on all sides. Remove tempeh from pan; keep warm. Add remaining 2 teaspoons oil to pan; swirl to coat. Add Broccolini and snow peas; stir-fry 2 minutes, stirring occasionally. Add tempeh and vinegar mixture to pan; bring to a boil. Divide rice evenly among 4 bowls; top with tempeh mixture. Sprinkle with remaining 3 tablespoons green onions and peanuts. Serves 4 (serving size: ⅔ cup rice, 1¼ cups tempeh mixture, about 2 teaspoons green onions, and about 2 teaspoons peanuts).

CALORIES 410; FAT 16g (sat 2.3g, mono 7.3g, poly 5.1g); PROTEIN 18.6g; CARB 50.6g; FIBER 7.5g; CHOL 0mg; IRON 4.4mg; SODIUM 558mg; CALC 140mg

Vegetarian

Bibimbop

Hands-on time: 50 min. Total time: 1 hr. 6 min. A combination of rice and vegetables, this signature Korean dish is worth the effort. As you prepare each component, place hot food on a jelly-roll pan and keep in a warm oven.

8 ounces extra-firm tofu, drained
⅓ cup water
¼ cup apple cider vinegar
2 teaspoons sugar, divided
2 teaspoons minced garlic, divided
1 teaspoon minced peeled fresh ginger, divided
¼ teaspoon crushed red pepper
1 cup julienne-cut carrot
2 tablespoons lower-sodium soy sauce
3 tablespoons plus 2 teaspoons dark sesame oil, divided
3 cups hot cooked short-grain rice
1 cup fresh bean sprouts
1 (5-ounce) package sliced shiitake mushroom caps
1 (9-ounce) package fresh baby spinach
1 teaspoon unsalted butter
4 large eggs
4 teaspoons gochujang (Korean chili paste, such as Annie Chun's)
¼ teaspoon kosher salt

1. Cut tofu into ¾-inch-thick slices. Place tofu in a single layer on several layers of paper towels; cover with additional paper towels. Let stand 30 minutes, pressing down occasionally.
2. Combine ⅓ cup water, vinegar, 1 teaspoon sugar, ½ teaspoon garlic, ½ teaspoon ginger, and crushed red pepper in a small saucepan. Bring to a boil. Add carrot, and remove from heat; let stand 30 minutes. Drain.
3. Remove tofu from paper towels; cut into ¾-inch cubes. Place tofu in a medium bowl. Combine remaining 1 teaspoon sugar, ½ teaspoon garlic, remaining ½ teaspoon ginger, soy sauce, and 1 tablespoon oil, stirring with a whisk. Add 1 tablespoon soy sauce mixture to tofu; toss gently. Let stand 15 minutes.

4. Heat a 10-inch cast-iron skillet over high heat 4 minutes. Add 1 tablespoon sesame oil to pan; swirl to coat. Add rice to pan in a single layer; cook 1 minute (do not stir). Remove from heat; let stand 20 minutes.
5. Heat a large nonstick skillet over medium-high heat. Add 1 teaspoon oil to pan; swirl to coat. Add 1½ teaspoons soy sauce mixture and bean sprouts to pan; sauté 1 minute. Remove sprouts from pan; keep warm. Add 1 teaspoon oil to pan; swirl to coat. Add mushrooms to pan; sauté 2 minutes. Stir in 1½ teaspoons soy sauce mixture; sauté 1 minute. Remove mushrooms from pan; keep warm. Add 2 teaspoons oil to pan; swirl to coat. Add tofu to pan; sauté 7 minutes or until golden brown. Remove tofu from pan; keep warm. Add remaining 1 teaspoon oil to pan; swirl to coat. Add remaining 1 teaspoon garlic and remaining 1 tablespoon soy sauce mixture; sauté 30 seconds. Add spinach to pan; sauté 1 minute or until spinach wilts. Remove spinach from pan; keep warm. Reduce heat to medium. Melt butter in pan. Crack eggs into pan; cook 4 minutes or until whites are set. Remove from heat.
6. Place ¾ cup rice in each of 4 shallow bowls. Top each serving evenly with carrots, sprouts, mushrooms, tofu, and spinach. Top each serving with 1 egg and 1 teaspoon chili paste. Sprinkle evenly with salt. Serves 4 (serving size: 1 bowl).

CALORIES 502; FAT 23.4g (sat 4.5g, mono 9.9g, poly 7.1g); PROTEIN 20.9g; CARB 56.4g; FIBER 6.1g; CHOL 214mg; IRON 6.8mg; SODIUM 698mg; CALC 199mg

WHAT TO EAT RIGHT NOW

MAPLE SYRUP

March in New England brings syrup season. Nights remain cold, but warming days signal time to tap the maple trees. Many maple syrup producers have been at it for generations and still do much of the work manually, collecting sap daily by hand, bucket by bucket. Then water is boiled off, leaving behind the amber gold. Of course, old-fashioned is as trendy with syrup as it is with cheese or bread.

Quick & Easy

Maple-Bourbon Sour

Combine 6 tablespoons bourbon, 2 tablespoons maple syrup, and 2 tablespoons fresh lemon juice, stirring well. Pour mixture into a cocktail shaker filled with ½ cup ice. Cover and shake. Strain mixture; divide evenly between 2 glasses. Serve over ice, if desired. Serves 2 (serving size: about ⅓ cup).

CALORIES 139; FAT 0g; SODIUM 2mg

DID YOU KNOW? THE SEASON'S EARLIEST SAP CONTAINS LESS WATER.

LIGHTER, BETTER CHEESESTEAK

The sandwich that put Philly on the comfort-food map keeps its meaty, cheesy soul but loses 750 calories.

What hot dogs are to Coney Island and wings are to Buffalo, the cheesesteak is to Philadelphia: iconic, tasty, and loaded with salt and fat. The Philly cheesesteak is a heap of chopped meat drowning in melted cheese "product" on a long bun, with more than a day's worth of saturated fat.

To hit all the comforting notes, we start with flank steak, thinly sliced and modestly seasoned—this is a much leaner cut than the traditional rib-eye. The meat gets further beefing up with portobellos and savory grilled peppers and onions. And just forget the artificial cheese sauce: We create a lean white sauce with real cheese—just enough Parm-Regg and provolone to deliver full satisfaction with less sodium and saturated fat. Meaty, gooey, and delightfully messy, this is the type of sandwich you'll crave all year.

MEAT AND CHEESES

FLANK STEAK VS. RIB-EYE STEAK
A hearty 12-ounce portion of flank steak and meaty mushrooms sub in for the pound and a half of fatty, marbled rib-eye to save 346 calories and 13.6g of saturated fat per sandwich.

PROVOLONE AND PARMIGIANO-REGGIANO CHEESES VS. PROCESSED CHEESE PRODUCT
Processed cheese doesn't deliver the real flavor, and the swap saves 20 calories, 5.8g of saturated fat, and 820mg of sodium.

Kid Friendly
Philly Cheesesteak

Hands-on time: 35 min. Total time: 45 min.

1 (12-ounce) flank steak, trimmed
¼ teaspoon kosher salt
¼ teaspoon freshly ground black pepper
2 (5-inch) portobello mushroom caps
2 teaspoons extra-virgin olive oil, divided
1 cup thinly sliced onion
1½ cups thinly sliced green bell pepper
2 teaspoons minced garlic
½ teaspoon Worcestershire sauce
½ teaspoon lower-sodium soy sauce
2 teaspoons all-purpose flour
½ cup 1% low-fat milk
1 ounce provolone cheese, torn into small pieces
2 tablespoons grated Parmigiano-Reggiano cheese
¼ teaspoon dry mustard
4 (3-ounce) hoagie rolls, toasted

1. Place beef in freezer 15 minutes. Cut beef across grain into thin slices. Sprinkle beef with salt and pepper. Remove brown gills from undersides of mushroom caps using a spoon; discard gills. Remove stems; discard. Thinly slice mushroom caps; cut slices in half crosswise.
2. Heat a large nonstick skillet over medium-high heat. Add 1 teaspoon oil to pan; swirl to coat. Add beef to pan; sauté 2 minutes or until beef loses its pink color, stirring constantly. Remove beef from pan. Add remaining 1 teaspoon oil to pan. Add onion; sauté 3 minutes. Add mushrooms, bell pepper, and garlic; sauté 6 minutes. Return beef to pan; sauté 1 minute or until thoroughly heated and vegetables are tender. Remove from heat. Stir in Worcestershire and soy sauce, and keep warm.
3. Place flour in a small saucepan; gradually add milk, stirring with a whisk until blended. Bring to a simmer over medium heat; cook 1 minute or until slightly thickened. Remove from heat. Add cheeses and mustard, stirring until smooth. Keep warm (mixture will thicken as it cools).
4. Hollow out top and bottom halves of bread, leaving a ½-inch-thick shell; reserve torn bread for another use. Divide beef mixture evenly among bottom halves of hoagies. Drizzle sauce evenly over beef mixture; replace top halves. Serves 4 (serving size: 1 sandwich).

CALORIES 397; **FAT** 12.4g (sat 4.9g, mono 4.7g, poly 1.6g); **PROTEIN** 30.8g; **CARB** 44.1g; **FIBER** 3.7g; **CHOL** 37mg; **IRON** 4.6mg; **SODIUM** 637mg; **CALC** 213mg

CLASSIC	MAKEOVER
1,151 calories per sandwich	397 calories per serving
27.3 grams saturated fat	4.9 grams saturated fat
1,480 milligrams sodium	637 milligrams sodium

FLANK MANEUVERS

A memorable cheesesteak depends on the juicy quality of the meat. Here's how to get tender, tasty bites from a leaner cut.

1. Partially freeze the meat to allow for thinner slicing. Slice across the grain, not with it. Use a sharp knife, and hold it at a slight diagonal.

2. Salt boosts flavor and tenderizes. Use kosher salt and freshly ground black pepper. Season the steak after slicing to ensure maximum coverage.

3. Bring the steak to room temperature before searing. Heat the oil to a shimmer in a hot pan, and quickly sear the steak just until no longer pink. Stir constantly for an even sear.

5-INGREDIENT COOKING

Vegetarian
Potato-Beet Gnocchi

Hands-on time: 23 min. Total time: 1 hr. 45 min. *Wilted beet greens top tender, ruby-hued dumplings.*

Directions: Preheat oven to 400°. Remove greens and stems from beet. Chop greens to measure 2 cups. Pierce beet and potatoes with a fork. Bake potatoes 1 hour; bake beet 1 hour 15 minutes. Peel beet and potatoes; press through a potato ricer into a bowl. Weigh or lightly spoon 4.5 ounces flour (about 1 cup) into a dry measuring cup. Combine potato mixture, 4.5 ounces flour, and ½ teaspoon kosher salt. Stir to form dough. Knead on a floured surface until smooth. Divide into 4 equal portions. Shape each into a 16-inch-long rope, dusting with remaining flour to prevent sticking. Cut each rope into 20 pieces. Roll each piece down tines of a lightly floured fork; place on a baking sheet coated with cooking spray. Bring 6 quarts water to a boil in a stockpot. Add half of gnocchi; cook 2½ minutes or until done. Remove gnocchi with a slotted spoon; place in a colander to drain. Repeat with remaining gnocchi. Heat a nonstick skillet over medium-high heat. Add onion; sauté 4 minutes. Add gnocchi, greens, ½ teaspoon pepper, and ¼ teaspoon kosher salt; cook 2 minutes. Sprinkle with cheese. Serves 4 (serving size: 1½ cups gnocchi mixture and 1 tablespoon cheese).

CALORIES 362; **FAT** 3g (sat 1.4g, mono 0.7g, poly 0.4g); **PROTEIN** 11.8g; **CARB** 73.3g; **FIBER** 8.1g; **CHOL** 6mg; **IRON** 3.5mg; **SODIUM** 568mg; **CALC** 162mg

THE FIVE INGREDIENTS

1 (8-ounce) red beet with greens

+

1 pound medium baking potatoes

+

5.6 ounces all-purpose flour (about 1¼ cups), divided

+

4 cups vertically sliced onion

+

1 ounce shaved fresh Parmesan cheese (about ¼ cup)

FEED 4 FOR LESS THAN $10

Give kids what they'd really love for dinner: cheesy pigs in blankets! Grown-ups will enjoy zingy shrimp tacos and chunky chickpea soup.

$2.50/serving, $9.99 for four

Kid Friendly

Shrimp Tacos with Green Apple Salsa

Hands-on time: 37 min. Total time: 49 min. *Serve with mashed black beans.*

1½ tablespoons olive oil, divided
4 teaspoons fresh lime juice, divided
¼ teaspoon ground cumin
¼ teaspoon hot smoked paprika
¼ teaspoon ground red pepper
1 pound medium shrimp, peeled and deveined
⅓ cup sliced green onions
¼ teaspoon salt, divided
½ teaspoon grated lime rind
1 Granny Smith apple, thinly sliced
1 minced seeded jalapeño pepper
8 (6-inch) corn tortillas
1 ounce crumbled queso fresco

1. Combine 1 tablespoon olive oil, 2 teaspoons lime juice, cumin, paprika, and red pepper in a small bowl. Combine shrimp and spice mixture in a zip-top plastic bag, and seal. Let stand 15 minutes.
2. Combine 1½ teaspoons oil, remaining 2 teaspoons juice, onions, ⅛ teaspoon salt, rind, apple, and jalapeño in a small bowl; toss.
3. Remove shrimp from bag; discard marinade. Heat a grill pan over medium-high heat. Sprinkle shrimp with remaining ⅛ teaspoon salt. Arrange half of shrimp in pan; grill

2 minutes on each side or until done. Remove from pan; keep warm. Repeat procedure with remaining shrimp. Toast tortillas in grill pan, if desired. Place 2 tortillas on each of 4 plates, and divide shrimp evenly among tortillas. Divide salsa evenly among tacos, and top with queso fresco. Serves 4 (serving size: 2 tacos).

CALORIES 259; FAT 9.4g (sat 1.6g, mono 5.3g, poly 1.7g); PROTEIN 21.2g; CARB 24.3g; FIBER 3g; CHOL 170mg; IRON 3mg; SODIUM 364mg; CALC 87mg

Kid Friendly • Quick & Easy

Cheesy Pigs in Blankets

$1.54/serving, $6.15 for four

Hands-on time: 15 min. Total time: 27 min. *Serve with steamed broccoli and apple wedges.*

1 (6-ounce) portion fresh pizza dough
1½ ounces part-skim mozzarella cheese, shredded
4 turkey hot dogs, halved crosswise
Cooking spray
2 tablespoons ketchup
1 tablespoon barbecue sauce
1 teaspoon prepared mustard

1. Preheat oven to 425°.
2. Let dough stand, covered, 20 minutes. On a lightly floured surface, roll dough into a 12 x 4–inch rectangle. Cut rectangle into 4 (4 x 3–inch) rectangles; cut each rectangle in half diagonally to form 8 triangles. Divide cheese evenly among triangles; place in center of wide ends. Place ½ hot dog at wide end of each triangle; roll up, pinching ends to seal. Arrange rolls on a baking sheet coated with cooking spray. Bake at 425° for 12 minutes. Combine ketchup and remaining ingredients. Serve with rolls. Serves 4 (serving size: 2 rolls and 2½ teaspoons sauce).

CALORIES 215; FAT 6.4g (sat 2.1g, mono 0.5g, poly 0.8g); PROTEIN 13.5g; CARB 27.5g; FIBER 0.8g; CHOL 32mg; IRON 1.4mg; SODIUM 825mg; CALC 85mg

Make Ahead

$2.45/serving, $9.80 for four

Roasted Fennel, Tomato, and Chickpea Soup

Hands-on time: 15 min. Total time: 1 hr.

2 cups chopped fennel bulb (about 1 small bulb)
2 cups chopped onion
Cooking spray
1 (15½-ounce) can organic chickpeas (garbanzo beans), rinsed and drained
2 teaspoons butter
3 garlic cloves, minced
2 (14-ounce) cans fat-free, lower-sodium chicken broth
2 (14.5-ounce) cans organic diced tomatoes, undrained
½ teaspoon freshly ground black pepper
¼ teaspoon salt
Fresh flat-leaf parsley
2 (6-inch) pitas, each cut into 8 wedges

1. Preheat oven to 425°.
2. Arrange fennel and onion in a single layer on a jelly-roll pan coated with cooking spray. Bake at 425° for 25 minutes, stirring after 15 minutes. Add chickpeas to vegetable mixture. Bake an additional 20 minutes or until fennel is tender and chickpeas start to brown, stirring after 10 minutes.
3. Melt butter in a large saucepan over medium heat. Add garlic to pan, and cook 1 minute, stirring occasionally. Add vegetable mixture, broth, and next 3 ingredients to pan, and bring to a boil. Cook 3 minutes or until thoroughly heated. Remove from heat, and garnish with parsley. Serve with pita wedges. Serves 4 (serving size: 2 cups soup and 4 pita wedges).

CALORIES 301; FAT 3.3g (sat 1.4g, mono 0.6g, poly 0.3g); PROTEIN 12.5g; CARB 55.9g; FIBER 10.7g; CHOL 5mg; IRON 3mg; SODIUM 739mg; CALC 157mg

DINNER TONIGHT

Here is a batch of fast weeknight menus from the *Cooking Light* Test Kitchen.

READY IN 40 MINUTES

············ *The* ············

SHOPPING LIST

Crispy Herbed Shrimp with Chive Aioli
Fresh parsley
Fresh thyme
Fresh chives
Lemon (1)
Panko (Japanese breadcrumbs)
Crushed red pepper
Ground red pepper
Cornstarch
Olive oil
2% Greek yogurt
Canola mayonnaise
Large eggs (2)
Large shrimp, peeled and deveined

Roasted Asparagus and Tomatoes
Asparagus (1 pound)
Cherry tomatoes (½ cup)
Shallots (2)
Fresh thyme

············ *The* ············

GAME PLAN

While oven preheats:
  ■ Trim asparagus.
  ■ Dredge shrimp.
While asparagus roasts:
  ■ Cook shrimp.

Kid Friendly • Quick & Easy

Crispy Herbed Shrimp with Chive Aioli

With Roasted Asparagus and Tomatoes

Prep Pointer: Trim and discard tough, fibrous ends from the asparagus.
Kid Pleaser: Omit red pepper for a milder mayo sauce.
Flavor Hit: Fresh herbs brighten up the shrimp coating.

¾ cup panko (Japanese breadcrumbs), divided
1 tablespoon chopped fresh parsley
2 teaspoons chopped fresh thyme
⅛ teaspoon crushed red pepper
2 tablespoons cornstarch
2 large egg whites, lightly beaten
1½ pounds large shrimp, peeled and deveined
¼ teaspoon salt
¼ teaspoon freshly ground black pepper
2 tablespoons olive oil, divided
½ cup plain 2% reduced-fat Greek yogurt
¼ cup canola mayonnaise
3 tablespoons chopped fresh chives
1 tablespoon fresh lemon juice
¼ teaspoon ground red pepper

1. Place ¼ cup panko, parsley, thyme, and crushed red pepper in a mini food processor; pulse to combine. Combine herb mixture and remaining ½ cup panko in a shallow dish. Place cornstarch and egg whites in separate shallow dishes. Sprinkle shrimp with salt and black pepper. Dredge half of shrimp in cornstarch, shaking off excess; dip into egg whites. Dredge shrimp in panko mixture, and press to adhere. Repeat procedure with remaining shrimp.
2. Heat a large nonstick skillet over medium-high heat. Add 1 tablespoon oil to pan; swirl to coat. Add half of shrimp to pan; cook 3 minutes on each side or until done. Repeat with remaining oil and shrimp.
3. Combine yogurt and remaining ingredients in a small bowl. Serve with shrimp. Serves 4 (serving size: about 5 shrimp and 2 tablespoons sauce).

CALORIES 430; FAT 21.7g (sat 2.9g, mono 11.4g, poly 4.9g); PROTEIN 41.3g; CARB 14.8g; FIBER 0.7g; CHOL 265mg; IRON 4.4mg; SODIUM 583mg; CALC 115mg

Quick & Easy • Vegetarian
For the Roasted Asparagus and Tomatoes:
Preheat oven to 400°. Combine 1 pound trimmed asparagus, ½ cup cherry or grape tomatoes, ⅓ cup sliced shallots, 1½ teaspoons chopped fresh thyme, ¼ teaspoon salt, and ¼ teaspoon freshly ground black pepper on a jelly-roll pan. Coat lightly with cooking spray. Bake at 400° for 6 minutes or until crisp-tender. Serves 4.

CALORIES 38; FAT 0.3g (sat 0.1g); SODIUM 152mg

READY IN 40 MINUTES

Italian Meatball Sliders
Garlic
Shallots (3)
Fresh parsley
Fresh basil
Olive oil
Panko (Japanese breadcrumbs)
Crushed red pepper
Lower-sodium marinara sauce
Slider buns (12)
Part-skim ricotta cheese
Large egg (1)
Lean ground pork (8 ounces)
4-ounce links turkey Italian sausage (2)

Spinach and Mozzarella Salad
Large red bell pepper (1)
Red onion (1)
Baby spinach (6 cups)
Olive oil
Balsamic vinegar
Fresh mozzarella

The
GAME PLAN

While pepper and onion marinate:
- Make and shape meatballs.

While meatballs cook:
- Finish salad.

Kid Friendly • Quick & Easy
Italian Meatball Sliders

With Spinach and Mozzarella Salad

Prep Pointer: Adding ricotta to the meatballs keeps them moist.

1 tablespoon olive oil, divided
3 garlic cloves, minced
3 shallots, finely diced
⅓ cup part-skim ricotta cheese
¼ cup chopped fresh parsley
¼ cup panko (Japanese breadcrumbs),
  toasted
½ teaspoon freshly ground black
  pepper
¼ teaspoon crushed red pepper
⅛ teaspoon salt
8 ounces lean ground pork
2 (4-ounce) links turkey Italian
  sausage, casings removed
1 large egg
1½ cups lower-sodium marinara sauce
12 slider buns, toasted
12 fresh basil leaves

1. Heat a large skillet over medium heat. Add 1 teaspoon oil to pan; swirl to coat. Add garlic and shallots to pan; sauté 3 minutes or until shallots are softened, stirring frequently. Combine shallot mixture, ricotta, and next 8 ingredients in a medium bowl. Shape mixture into 12 (1-inch) meatballs; flatten each meatball slightly.
2. Return pan to medium-high heat. Add remaining 2 teaspoons oil to pan. Add meatballs to pan; cook 6 minutes, turning once. Add marinara sauce; bring to a boil, scraping pan to loosen browned bits. Cover, reduce heat, and simmer 8 minutes or until meatballs are done. Top bottom half of each bun with 1½ tablespoons sauce, 1 meatball, 1 basil leaf, and top half of bun. Serves 6 (serving size: 2 sliders).

CALORIES 429; **FAT** 16.3g (sat 4g, mono 5.1g, poly 4.2g); **PROTEIN** 25.4g; **CARB** 60.5g; **FIBER** 2.3g; **CHOL** 85mg; **IRON** 2.7mg; **SODIUM** 764mg; **CALC** 131mg

---

Quick & Easy • Vegetarian
For the Spinach and Mozzarella Salad:
Combine 1 cup julienne-cut red bell pepper, 1 cup sliced red onion, 2 table-spoons olive oil, and 1 tablespoon bal-samic vinegar in a large bowl; let stand 15 minutes. Add 6 cups baby spinach, ¼ teaspoon salt, and ¼ teaspoon black pepper. Toss. Top with 6 tablespoons finely chopped fresh mozzarella. Serves 6 (serving size: 1 cup).

CALORIES 98; **FAT** 7.3g (sat 2.3g); **SODIUM** 167mg

READY IN 40 MINUTES

Poached Eggs with Spinach and Walnuts
10-ounce bag baby spinach
Shallots (3)
Garlic
Fresh sage
Fresh thyme
8-ounce package cremini mushrooms
Olive oil
Walnuts (¾ cup)
Red wine vinegar
White vinegar
Gruyère cheese (2 ounces)
Large eggs (4)

Roasted Acorn Squash
Small acorn squash (1)
Butter

The
GAME PLAN

While oven preheats:
- Cut and season squash.

While squash roasts:
- Sauté mushroom mixture.

While mushroom mixture cooks:
- Poach eggs.

Poached Eggs with Spinach and Walnuts

With Roasted Acorn Squash

1 tablespoon olive oil, divided
1 (10-ounce) bag baby spinach, chopped
3 garlic cloves, minced
3 vertically sliced shallots
1 tablespoon chopped fresh sage
³⁄₄ teaspoon chopped fresh thyme, divided
½ teaspoon black pepper, divided
¼ teaspoon salt
1 (8-ounce) package cremini mushrooms, quartered
³⁄₄ cup toasted walnuts, chopped and divided
2 tablespoons red wine vinegar
2 ounces shredded Gruyère cheese
8 cups water
2 tablespoons white vinegar
4 large eggs

1. Heat a large Dutch oven over medium-high heat. Add 1 teaspoon oil; swirl to coat. Add spinach; sauté 2 minutes. Remove spinach from pan; drain, cool slightly, and squeeze out excess moisture. Add remaining 2 teaspoons oil to pan. Add garlic and shallots; sauté 3 minutes. Add sage, ½ teaspoon thyme, ¼ teaspoon pepper, salt, and mushrooms; sauté 7 minutes. Stir in spinach, ½ cup walnuts, red wine vinegar, and cheese; cook 30 seconds.
2. Combine 8 cups water and white vinegar in a large saucepan, and bring to a simmer. Break each egg gently into pan. Cook 3 minutes. Remove eggs using a slotted spoon. Spoon ⅔ cup mushroom mixture onto each of 4 plates. Top each serving with 1 egg. Sprinkle evenly with remaining thyme, pepper, and walnuts. Serves 4.

CALORIES 350; FAT 24.3g (sat 5.5g, mono 7.5g, poly 10.2g); PROTEIN 17.4g; CARB 18.4g; FIBER 5.1g; CHOL 196mg; IRON 4.4mg; SODIUM 383mg; CALC 257mg

---

For the Roasted Acorn Squash:
Preheat oven to 400°. Cut 1 acorn squash in half lengthwise; discard seeds. Cut each half into 6 wedges. Melt 2 tablespoons butter in a large ovenproof skillet over medium heat. Add squash; cook 3 minutes or until browned on one side. Turn wedges; sprinkle with ¼ teaspoon salt. Place pan in oven; bake at 400° for 12 minutes or until tender. Serves 4 (serving size: 3 wedges).

CALORIES 94; FAT 5.9g (sat 3.7g); SODIUM 192mg

READY IN
40
MINUTES

The
SHOPPING LIST

Potato, Mushroom, and Leek Croquettes
Yukon gold potatoes (8 ounces)
Sliced cremini mushrooms (4 ounces)
Sliced button mushrooms (4 ounces)
Leek (1)
Fresh thyme
All-purpose flour
Panko (Japanese breadcrumbs)
Olive oil
Gruyère cheese (2 ounces)
Parmigiano-Reggiano cheese (1 ounce)
Large egg (1)

Greens and Shallot Vinaigrette
Shallot (1)
Gourmet salad greens (6 cups)
Olive oil
Sherry vinegar

The
GAME PLAN

While potatoes cook:
■ Cook mushroom mixture.
While croquettes cook:
■ Make salad.

Potato, Mushroom, and Leek Croquettes

With Greens and Shallot Vinaigrette

Prep Pointer: Halve leeks lengthwise, and rinse thoroughly.
Time-Saver: Use packages of presliced mushrooms.
Technique Tip: A food mill gives the potatoes a smooth texture.

8 ounces coarsely chopped peeled Yukon gold potato
4 ounces sliced cremini mushrooms
4 ounces sliced button mushrooms
½ cup chopped leek
1 teaspoon chopped fresh thyme
Cooking spray
2 ounces shredded Gruyère cheese (about ½ cup)
1 ounce grated Parmigiano-Reggiano cheese (about ¼ cup), divided
½ teaspoon kosher salt
½ teaspoon freshly ground black pepper
1 large egg yolk
⅓ cup all-purpose flour
1 large egg white
2 teaspoons water
½ cup panko (Japanese breadcrumbs)
1 tablespoon olive oil

1. Place potato in a saucepan; cover with water. Bring to a boil. Reduce heat; simmer 8 minutes or until tender. Drain. Press potato through a ricer or food mill into a bowl.
2. Place mushrooms, leek, and thyme in a food processor; pulse until finely chopped. Heat a large skillet over medium heat. Coat pan with cooking spray. Add mushroom mixture; cook 6 minutes, stirring occasionally. Add mixture to potato. Add Gruyère, 2 tablespoons Parmigiano-Reggiano,
continued

salt, pepper, and egg yolk; stir until blended. Shape mixture into 8 (2-inch) round patties.

3. Place flour in a shallow dish. Combine egg white and 2 teaspoons water in a shallow dish, stirring with a whisk. Combine remaining 2 tablespoons Parmigiano-Reggiano and panko in a shallow dish. Dredge patties in flour. Dip in egg mixture; dredge in panko mixture. Heat a large nonstick skillet over medium-high heat. Add oil to pan; swirl to coat. Add patties; cook 4 minutes on each side or until golden. Serves 4 (serving size: 2 patties).

CALORIES 266; FAT 10.9g (sat 4.2g, mono 4.7g, poly 1g); PROTEIN 12.4g; CARB 29.3g; FIBER 2g; CHOL 64mg; IRON 2mg; SODIUM 412mg; CALC 229mg

Quick & Easy • Vegetarian
For the Greens and Shallot Vinaigrette:
Combine 2 tablespoons olive oil, 2 tablespoons sherry vinegar, ¼ teaspoon black pepper, and ⅛ teaspoon salt in a medium bowl. Add 6 cups gourmet salad greens and 1 sliced shallot to bowl; toss gently. Serves 4 (serving size: 1½ cups salad).

CALORIES 82; FAT 6.8g (sat 0.9g); SODIUM 120mg

KITCHEN SECRET: WHY TO WEIGH CHEESE

Cheese is precious in our Test Kitchen, and with our sodium and saturated fat guidelines, we make the most of every shred. As with flour, we call for both a weighed measurement and a cup measurement— because depending on the cook and how densely a cup is packed, too much (or too little!) cheese can be used. If you don't have a scale, use freshly grated or shredded cheese. The pre-cut, packaged variety often comes coated in a food starch to keep the cheese from clumping, which also adds bulk, making it tough to pack the right amount into a measuring cup.

SUPERFAST

Inspired, flavor-packed dishes for busy nights: buttery steak, nutty mushroom panini, creamy tomato-basil soup, plus other speedy options.

Freezable • Make Ahead
Tomato-Basil Soup

1 tablespoon extra-virgin olive oil
1½ cups prechopped onion
3 garlic cloves, chopped
¾ cup chopped fresh basil
1 (28-ounce) can fire-roasted diced tomatoes, undrained
4 ounces ⅓-less-fat cream cheese, cut into cubes (about ½ cup)
2 cups 1% low-fat milk
¼ teaspoon salt
¼ teaspoon freshly ground black pepper
12 (½-inch-thick) slices French bread
Cooking spray
1 garlic clove, halved
1 ounce shredded Asiago cheese

1. Preheat broiler to high.
2. Heat a saucepan over medium-high heat. Add olive oil to pan; swirl to coat. Add onion; sauté 3 minutes. Stir in garlic; cook 1 minute. Add basil and tomatoes; bring to a boil. Stir in cheese until melted. Place mixture in a blender, and blend until smooth. Return to pan; stir in milk, salt, and pepper. Return to medium-high heat; cook 2 minutes.
3. Place bread on a baking sheet; lightly coat with cooking spray. Broil 1 minute. Rub garlic over toasted side; turn bread over. Top with Asiago; broil 1 minute. Serves 4 (serving size: 1¼ cups soup and 3 toasts).

CALORIES 312; FAT 13.9g (sat 6.3g, mono 4.5g, poly 0.9g); PROTEIN 13.2g; CARB 33.8g; FIBER 3.4g; CHOL 33mg; IRON 1.4mg; SODIUM 506mg; CALC 281mg

Quick & Easy
Grilled Sirloin with Anchovy-Lemon Butter and Broccoli Rabe
(pictured on page 215)

Cooking spray
1 (1-pound) boneless sirloin steak
½ teaspoon kosher salt, divided
⅜ teaspoon black pepper
2 tablespoons unsalted butter
1½ teaspoons grated lemon rind, divided
1 teaspoon fresh lemon juice
½ teaspoon anchovy paste
1 teaspoon extra-virgin olive oil
¼ cup presliced onion
2 garlic cloves, sliced
¼ teaspoon crushed red pepper
½ cup fat-free, lower-sodium chicken broth
8 ounces broccoli rabe (rapini), cut into 1-inch pieces

1. Heat a grill pan over medium-high heat. Coat pan with cooking spray. Sprinkle steak with ¼ teaspoon salt and ¼ teaspoon pepper. Add steak to pan; cook 3 minutes on each side. Let stand 5 minutes. Cut across grain into slices.
2. Place butter in a bowl. Microwave at HIGH 10 seconds. Add ⅛ teaspoon salt, remaining ⅛ teaspoon pepper, ½ teaspoon rind, juice, and anchovy paste; stir until combined. Set aside.
3. Heat a skillet over medium-high heat. Add oil; swirl to coat. Add onion; sauté 2 minutes. Add garlic and red pepper; sauté 30 seconds. Stir in broth and rabe; bring to a boil. Cover and simmer 3 minutes. Remove from heat; stir in remaining rind and salt.
4. Place 3 ounces steak and ½ cup rabe on each of 4 plates. Top each steak with 1½ teaspoons butter. Serves 4.

CALORIES 223; FAT 11.6g (sat 5.5g, mono 4.1g, poly 0.5g); PROTEIN 24.8g; CARB 4.3g; FIBER 0.3g; CHOL 59mg; IRON 2mg; SODIUM 400mg; CALC 49mg

Mushroom and Manchego Panini

1 teaspoon unsalted butter
¼ cup minced shallots
1 tablespoon chopped fresh thyme
2 teaspoons minced fresh garlic
½ teaspoon freshly ground black pepper
¼ teaspoon kosher salt
2 (4-ounce) packages presliced exotic mushroom blend (such as shiitake, cremini, and oyster)
1 (8-ounce) package presliced cremini mushrooms
1½ tablespoons sherry vinegar
8 (1½-ounce) slices sourdough bread
3 ounces shaved Manchego cheese
Cooking spray
1 garlic clove, halved

1. Melt butter in a large skillet over medium-high heat; add shallots and next 6 ingredients (through cremini mushrooms). Cook 10 minutes or until mushrooms are tender and liquid almost evaporates, stirring frequently. Add vinegar; cook 30 seconds or until liquid almost evaporates.
2. Divide mushroom mixture evenly among bread slices. Top evenly with Manchego cheese and remaining bread slices.
3. Heat a large grill pan over medium-high heat. Coat pan with cooking spray. Add sandwiches to pan. Place a cast-iron or heavy skillet on top of sandwiches; press gently to flatten. Cook sandwiches 2 minutes on each side or until cheese melts and bread is toasted (leave skillet on sandwiches while they cook). Rub top and bottom of each sandwich with cut side of garlic clove. Serves 4 (serving size: 1 sandwich).

CALORIES 352; **FAT** 10.9g (sat 6g, mono 2.4g, poly 1g); **PROTEIN** 16.8g; **CARB** 48.8g; **FIBER** 3.7g; **CHOL** 25mg; **IRON** 4.3mg; **SODIUM** 741mg; **CALC** 375mg

Creamy Potato Salad

1 large egg
¾ pound fingerling potatoes
2 tablespoons light mayonnaise
1 tablespoon plain fat-free Greek yogurt
1½ teaspoons prepared mustard
⅓ cup prechopped celery
3 tablespoons prechopped red onion
¼ teaspoon kosher salt
¼ teaspoon freshly ground black pepper

1. Place a saucepan filled two-thirds with water over high heat; add egg, and cover. Cut potatoes into 1-inch pieces. Add potatoes to pan; cover and bring to a boil. Reduce heat to medium-high; cook 5 minutes or until tender. Drain.
2. Combine remaining ingredients in a medium bowl; add potatoes. Peel and coarsely chop egg; add to potatoes. Serves 6 (serving size: ½ cup).

CALORIES 74; **FAT** 2.5g (sat 0.5g, mono 0.8g, poly 1.1g); **PROTEIN** 2.5g; **CARB** 10.5g; **FIBER** 1.2g; **CHOL** 32mg; **IRON** 0.6mg; **SODIUM** 148mg; **CALC** 16mg

Quick & Easy • Make Ahead Vegetarian
Variation 1: Sour Cream–Dill

Prepare base recipe through step 1; omit egg. Combine ½ cup diced English cucumber, 2 tablespoons reduced-fat sour cream, 1½ tablespoons plain fat-free Greek yogurt, 1½ teaspoons chopped fresh dill, ¼ teaspoon kosher salt, and ¼ teaspoon freshly ground black pepper in a large bowl. Add drained potatoes to cucumber mixture, and toss gently to coat. Serves 6 (serving size: ½ cup).

CALORIES 50; **FAT** 0.7g (sat 0.4g); **SODIUM** 87mg

Variation 2: German-Style

Prepare recipe through step 1; omit egg. Cook 2 center-cut bacon slices over medium-high until crisp; crumble. Add 1 tablespoon olive oil to drippings in pan. Return pan to medium-high. Add 2 teaspoons brown sugar, 1 teaspoon minced garlic, and 2 teaspoons Dijon mustard; cook 1 minute. Add 3 tablespoons cider vinegar; bring to a boil. Remove from heat; stir in ¼ teaspoon freshly ground black pepper and ⅛ teaspoon kosher salt. Combine sugar mixture, potatoes, and ⅓ cup sliced green onions. Top with bacon. Serves 6 (serving size: ⅓ cup).

CALORIES 82; **FAT** 3.1g (sat 0.7g); **SODIUM** 132mg

Quick & Easy • Vegetarian
Variation 3: Lemon-Herb

Prepare base recipe through step 1; omit egg. Whisk together 1 tablespoon olive oil, ¼ teaspoon grated lemon rind, 1 tablespoon lemon juice, 1 teaspoon Dijon mustard, and ¼ teaspoon freshly ground black pepper in a bowl. Stir in ⅓ cup chopped arugula, 2 tablespoons sliced kalamata olives, 1 tablespoon chopped fresh parsley, 1 tablespoon chopped fresh basil, and 1 tablespoon chopped fresh chives. Add drained potatoes; toss gently to coat. Serves 6 (serving size: ⅓ cup).

CALORIES 75; **FAT** 3.6g (sat 0.5g); **SODIUM** 101mg

Fettuccine with Turkey Meatballs

1 (9-ounce) package refrigerated fettuccine
3 (4-ounce) links sweet Italian turkey sausage
1 tablespoon extra-virgin olive oil
2 cups sliced onion
1/4 teaspoon crushed red pepper
2 large garlic cloves, crushed
2 cups lower-sodium marinara sauce (such as McCutcheon's)
1/2 ounce pecorino cheese, grated (about 2 tablespoons)
8 fresh basil leaves, torn

1. Cook pasta according to package directions, omitting salt and fat; drain.
2. Remove casing from sausages. Shape sausages into 12 (1-inch) balls. Heat a large skillet over medium-high heat. Add oil to pan; swirl to coat. Add meatballs to pan; cook 7 minutes, browning on all sides. Remove meatballs from pan. Add onion, red pepper, and garlic to pan; sauté 2 minutes. Return meatballs and add marinara sauce to pan, and bring to a simmer over medium heat, scraping pan to loosen browned bits. Reduce heat to medium-low, and simmer 5 minutes or until meatballs are done. Add pasta to sauce mixture; toss well. Sprinkle with cheese and basil. Serves 4 (serving size: about 1¼ cups).

CALORIES 412; FAT 14g (sat 4.2g, mono 5.4g, poly 3.1g); PROTEIN 19.2g; CARB 77.7g; FIBER 2.6g; CHOL 77mg; IRON 2.6mg; SODIUM 632mg; CALC 43mg

OOPS!

YOUR OVEN FRIES FIZZLE

For perfect comfort fries, give spuds a bath.

(Sob.)

(Yum!)

Great oven fries can mimic, if not entirely duplicate, the best qualities of their deep-fried cousins—golden, with a crisp exterior and fluffy middle—yet remain much lower in fat. Bad oven fries, however, can turn out pale and soggy, or dry up and burn, sometimes achieving both states in the same batch.

The solution: It seems counterintuitive, but you need to presoak. Nearly half a potato's weight is accounted for by water. Soaking pulls out starch, which reduces the water content of the potatoes: less water, less steaming in the oven.

Start with baking potatoes (russets): They're drier than waxy varieties. Cut each peeled potato in half lengthwise, halve again, and slice each quarter into ¼-inch-thick strips (a mandoline is nice but not essential). Even thickness and wide surface area prevent burning and give you more crispy real estate. Soak in cold water for 30 minutes, and then dry thoroughly with paper towels.

Toss with olive oil, and then spread on a parchment-lined baking sheet. Don't overcrowd the fries, or it will be a steam bath in there. Bake on the bottom rack at 400° for 35 minutes. Flip once, halfway through.

40 MEALS UNDER 40 MINUTES

We offer quick, simple, delicious menus to satisfy every weeknight hunger. Or you can build your own meals from mains, salads, and sides.

USE THIS MEAL GUIDE

to pick menus that suit your weeknight fancy, and then flag the recipes. Or simply pick an entrée and juggle sides and sauces for your own custom menu. Nutrition information follows every recipe.

$ indicates a **budget meal** that costs less than $15 • V indicates a **vegetarian** meal

CHICKEN DINNERS

MEAL NO. 1
Blackened Chicken with Dirty Rice, p.81
Avocado–Butter Lettuce Salad, p.83

MEAL NO. 2
Chicken and Broccoli Rice Bowl, p.93
Sautéed Butter-Thyme Mushrooms, p.83

MEAL NO. 3 ($)
Grill Pan Chicken, p.86
White BBQ Sauce, p.87
Garlicky Asparagus, p.84
Wheat Rolls with Orange Butter, p.82

MEAL NO. 4
Grill Pan Chicken, p.86
Mushroom Sauce, p.85
Creamed Spinach and Mushrooms, p.84
Garlic Mashed Potatoes, p.82

FOR SEAFOOD LOVERS

MEAL NO. 5
Pecan-Crusted Trout, p.81
Creamed Spinach and Mushrooms, p.84
Steamed Sugar Snap Peas, p. 84

MEAL NO. 6
Hazelnut-Crusted Halibut with Roasted Asparagus, p. 80
Roasted Red Potatoes, p.84

MEAL NO. 7 ($)
Shrimp and Pea Rice Bowl, p. 93
Wheat Rolls with Orange Butter, p.82

MEAL NO. 8
Basic Striped Bass, p.86
Warm Bacon Vinaigrette, p. 87
Garlic Mashed Potatoes, p.82
Sautéed Butter-Thyme Mushrooms, p.83

SANDWICH NIGHT

MEAL NO. 9 ($, V)
Hummus-Stuffed Pitas, p.92
Steamed Sugar Snap Peas, p.84

MEAL NO. 10
Pan-Seared Flank Steak, p.86
Cheddar Cheese Sauce, p.86
Sourdough toast
Mixed Greens Salad, p.82

MEAL NO. 11 (V)
Grilled Veggie and Hummus Wraps, p.92
Avocado–Butter Lettuce Salad, p. 83

MEAL NO. 12 (V)
Open-Faced Hummus Sandwiches, p.92
Garlicky Asparagus, p.84

MEAL NO. 13 (V)
Hummus "Cheesesteak" Hoagies, p.92
Napa Cabbage Slaw, p.83

MEAL NO. 14
Roasted Pork Tenderloin, p.86
Tzatziki, p.85
Pita bread
Avocado–Butter Lettuce Salad, p. 83

SALAD MEALS

MEAL NO. 15
Romaine, Asparagus, and Watercress Salad with Shrimp, p.81
Wheat Rolls with Orange Butter, p.82

MEAL NO. 16
Avocado Chicken Salad on tortilla chips, p.94
Garlicky Asparagus, p.84

MEAL NO. 17
Tzatziki Chicken Salad on pita chips, p.94
Mixed Greens Salad, p.82

MEAL NO. 18
Creamy Tarragon Chicken Salad on whole-grain crackers, p.95
Steamed Sugar Snap Peas, p.84

MEAL NO. 19 ($)
Chicken and Green Bean Salad on crostini, p.94
Roasted Red Potatoes, p.84

continued

MEATY MEALS

MEAL NO. 20
Pan-Grilled Flank Steak with Soy-Mustard Sauce, p.79
Garlicky Asparagus, p.84
Garlic Mashed Potatoes, p.82

MEAL NO. 21 ($)
Sausage-Spinach Rice Bowl, p. 93
Garlicky Asparagus, p.84

MEAL NO. 22
Pan-Seared Flank Steak, p.86
Mushroom Sauce, p.85
Garlic Mashed Potatoes, p.82
Butter-Roasted Carrots, p.82

MEAL NO. 23
Roasted Pork Tenderloin, p.86
Quick Gravy, p.87
Roasted Red Potatoes, p.84
Steamed Sugar Snap Peas, p.84

GLOBAL FUSIONS

MEAL NO. 24
Sesame Tuna with Edamame and Soba, p.80
Napa Cabbage Slaw, p.83

MEAL NO. 25 ($)
Grill Pan Chicken, p.86
Ponzu, p.87
Brown Rice with Sesame, p.84
Sautéed Snow Peas and Peppers, p.83

MEAL NO. 26
Basic Striped Bass, p.86
Chimichurri, p.85
Roasted Red Potatoes, p.84
Garlicky Asparagus, p.84

MEAL NO. 27
Sautéed Shrimp, p. 86
Saffron Aioli, p. 86
Garlic Mashed Potatoes, p.82
Mixed Greens Salad, p.82

FIERY FLAVORS

MEAL NO. 28 ($)
Spicy Basil Chicken, p.79
Brown Rice with Sesame, p.84
Sautéed Snow Peas and Peppers, p.83

MEAL NO. 29
Sautéed Shrimp, p. 86
Wasabi Cream, p.86
Brown Rice with Sesame, p.84
Napa Cabbage Slaw, p.83

MEAL NO. 30
Tex-Mex Rice Bowl, p.94
Avocado–Butter Lettuce Salad, p. 83

MEAL NO. 31
Crab Cakes with Spicy Rémoulade, p. 80
Mixed Greens Salad, p.82

HEALTHY PIZZAS

MEAL NO. 32 (V)
Beet Salad Pizza, p.89

MEAL NO. 33 ($, V)
Sunny-Side-Up Pizza, p.90

MEAL NO. 34
Tuna Salad Pizza, p.90

MEAL NO. 35
Steak House Pizza, p.90

PASTA DINNERS

MEAL NO. 36 ($)
Creamy Spring Pasta, p.78
Butter-Roasted Carrots, p.82

MEAL NO. 37
Shrimp Vodka Pasta, p. 90
Creamed Spinach and Mushrooms, p.84

MEAL NO. 38 (V)
Ricotta-Spinach Pasta, p.91
Orange and Olive Salad, p.85

MEAL NO. 39
Pasta Pork Bolognese, p.91
Steamed Sugar Snap Peas, p.84

MEAL NO. 40
Garlicky Meatball Pasta, p.91
Avocado–Butter Lettuce Salad, p.83

NINE FAST AND EASY ENTRÉES

Dishes for every taste, matched with simple sides to get a healthy meal on the table in 30 to 40 minutes.

Kid Friendly • Quick & Easy Vegetarian

Creamy Spring Pasta
(pictured on page 215)

Hands-on time: 30 min. Total time: 30 min. *This dish is luxuriously creamy, but the pasta soaks up the sauce quickly. Be sure to serve it right away. Use refrigerated pasta to cut several minutes off the cook time. Serve with Butter-Roasted Carrots, page 82.*

3 quarts water
2 ounces French bread baguette, torn into pieces
1 tablespoon butter
3 garlic cloves, minced and divided
1½ cups (2-inch) diagonally cut asparagus
1 cup frozen green peas
6 ounces uncooked fettuccine
2 teaspoons olive oil
⅓ cup finely chopped sweet onion
1 tablespoon all-purpose flour
¼ cup fat-free, lower-sodium chicken broth
1 cup 1% low-fat milk
3 ounces ⅓-less-fat cream cheese
1 ounce grated fresh Parmigiano-Reggiano cheese, grated (about ¼ cup packed)
½ teaspoon kosher salt
¼ teaspoon freshly ground black pepper
2 tablespoons chopped fresh tarragon

1. Bring 3 quarts water to a boil in a Dutch oven.
2. Place torn bread in a food processor; process until coarse crumbs form. Melt butter in a large skillet over medium-

high heat. Add 1 garlic clove to pan; sauté 1 minute. Add breadcrumbs, and sauté 3 minutes or until golden brown and toasted. Remove breadcrumb mixture from pan; wipe pan clean with paper towels.

3. Add asparagus and peas to boiling water; cook 3 minutes or until crisp-tender. Remove from pan with a slotted spoon. Rinse under cold water; drain.

4. Add pasta to boiling water; cook 10 minutes or until al dente. Drain and keep warm.

5. Heat a large skillet over medium heat. Add oil to pan; swirl to coat. Add onion and remaining 2 garlic cloves; cook 3 minutes or until tender, stirring frequently. Place flour in a small bowl; gradually whisk in chicken broth. Add broth mixture and milk to pan, stirring constantly with a whisk; bring to a boil. Reduce heat; cook 1 minute or until thickened. Remove from heat; add cheeses, salt, and pepper, stirring until cheeses melt. Add pasta, asparagus, and peas; toss well. Sprinkle with breadcrumbs and tarragon. Serves 4 (serving size: about 1¼ cups).

CALORIES 408; **FAT** 13.8g (sat 6.7g, mono 4.5g, poly 1.1g); **PROTEIN** 17.6g; **CARB** 54g; **FIBER** 4.6g; **CHOL** 33mg; **IRON** 3.9mg; **SODIUM** 625mg; **CALC** 225mg

REACH FOR CONVENIENT, HIGH-FLAVOR INGREDIENTS— ASIAN SAUCES, BOLD SPICES, PUNGENT HERBS, AND FRAGRANT NUTS—TO JAZZ UP QUICK ENTRÉES.

Quick & Easy

Spicy Basil Chicken

Hands-on time: 19 min. Total time: 19 min. Substitute lower-sodium soy sauce if fish sauce is difficult to find. The flavor won't be as complex, but soy sauce will still add a salty note. You can also substitute thinly sliced Thai bird chiles or jalapeño for the sambal oelek—or leave it out completely if you'd rather enjoy a mild dish. Serve with Brown Rice with Sesame, page 84, and Sautéed Snow Peas and Peppers, page 83.

2 teaspoons canola oil
¼ cup minced shallots
3 garlic cloves, thinly sliced
6 (4-ounce) skinless, boneless chicken thighs, cut into 1-inch pieces
1 tablespoon fish sauce
2 teaspoons sugar
2 teaspoons lower-sodium soy sauce
1¼ teaspoons sambal oelek (such as ground fresh chile paste)
1 teaspoon water
½ teaspoon cornstarch
⅛ teaspoon salt
⅓ cup sliced fresh basil leaves

1. Heat a large nonstick skillet over medium-high heat. Add oil to pan; swirl to coat. Add shallots and garlic to pan; cook 30 seconds or until fragrant. Add chicken to pan; cook 13 minutes or until chicken is done. Combine fish sauce and next 6 ingredients in a small bowl, stirring with a whisk. Add fish sauce mixture to pan, and cook 1 minute or until mixture thickens, stirring to coat chicken. Remove from heat. Stir in basil. Serves 4 (serving size: ¾ cup).

CALORIES 291; **FAT** 15.2g (sat 3.7g, mono 6.4g, poly 3.6g); **PROTEIN** 31.3g; **CARB** 5.6g; **FIBER** 0.1g; **CHOL** 112mg; **IRON** 1.9mg; **SODIUM** 615mg; **CALC** 31mg

Quick & Easy

Pan-Grilled Flank Steak with Soy-Mustard Sauce

Hands-on time: 16 min. Total time: 16 min. Serve with Garlicky Asparagus, page 84, and Garlic Mashed Potatoes, page 82.

1 pound flank steak, trimmed
⅜ teaspoon kosher salt
¼ teaspoon freshly ground black pepper
Cooking spray
1 teaspoon canola oil
1½ teaspoons minced fresh garlic
2 tablespoons lower-sodium soy sauce
1 teaspoon Dijon mustard
¾ teaspoon sugar
1½ tablespoons heavy whipping cream
2 tablespoons chopped fresh cilantro, divided

1. Heat a grill pan over high heat. Sprinkle steak evenly with salt and pepper. Lightly coat steak with cooking spray. Add steak to pan, and grill 5 minutes on each side or until desired degree of doneness. Let stand 3 minutes.

2. Heat a small skillet over medium-high heat. Add oil to pan; swirl to coat. Add garlic; cook 30 seconds or until fragrant. Add soy sauce, mustard, and sugar; cook 1 minute or until bubbly. Remove pan from heat. Stir in cream and 1 tablespoon cilantro. Cut steak diagonally across grain into thin slices. Sprinkle with remaining 1 tablespoon cilantro. Serve sauce with steak. Serves 4 (serving size: about 3 ounces steak and about 1 tablespoon sauce).

CALORIES 202; **FAT** 9.7g (sat 3.7g, mono 3.6g, poly 0.6g); **PROTEIN** 25g; **CARB** 2.3g; **FIBER** 0.1g; **CHOL** 45mg; **IRON** 2mg; **SODIUM** 541mg; **CALC** 35mg

Crab Cakes with Spicy Rémoulade

Hands-on time: 20 min. Total time: 20 min. *Serve with Mixed Greens Salad, page 82.*

Crab cakes:
1 pound jumbo lump crabmeat, shell pieces removed
2 tablespoons finely chopped green bell pepper
1½ tablespoons canola mayonnaise
¼ teaspoon black pepper
2 green onions, finely chopped
1 large egg, lightly beaten
1 cup panko, divided
2 tablespoons canola oil, divided
Rémoulade:
¼ cup canola mayonnaise
2 teaspoons minced shallots
1 teaspoon chopped fresh tarragon
1 teaspoon chopped fresh parsley
1½ teaspoons Dijon mustard
¾ teaspoon capers, chopped
¾ teaspoon white wine vinegar
¼ teaspoon ground red pepper

1. To prepare crab cakes, drain crabmeat on several layers of paper towels. Combine crabmeat, bell pepper, and next 4 ingredients, tossing gently. Stir in ¼ cup panko. Place remaining ¾ cup panko in a shallow dish.
2. Divide crab mixture into 8 equal portions. Shape portions into ¾-inch-thick patties; dredge in panko. Heat a large nonstick skillet over medium-high heat. Add 1 tablespoon oil; swirl to coat. Add 4 dredged patties; cook 3 minutes on each side or until golden. Remove from pan. Repeat procedure with remaining patties and oil.
3. To prepare rémoulade, combine ¼ cup mayonnaise and remaining ingredients; serve with crab cakes. Serves 4 (serving size: 2 crab cakes and about 2 tablespoons sauce).

CALORIES 320; **FAT** 17g (sat 1.2g, mono 8.7g, poly 5g); **PROTEIN** 26.8g; **CARB** 11.7g; **FIBER** 0.9g; **CHOL** 166mg; **IRON** 1.5mg; **SODIUM** 555mg; **CALC** 133mg

Hazelnut-Crusted Halibut with Roasted Asparagus

Hands-on time: 28 min. Total time: 28 min. *Fish is a great choice for quick dinners—most fillets cook to perfection in less than 10 minutes. You can use pecans, walnuts, or pine nuts in place of hazelnuts. To streamline prep, roast the asparagus together with the suggested potato side dish. Serve with Roasted Red Potatoes, page 84.*

1 tablespoon butter
2 teaspoons extra-virgin olive oil, divided
4 (6-ounce) halibut fillets, skinned
1 egg white, lightly beaten
½ teaspoon salt, divided
½ teaspoon freshly ground black pepper, divided
½ cup finely chopped hazelnuts
2 garlic cloves, thinly sliced
1 pound asparagus, trimmed
Cooking spray
1 teaspoon chopped fresh thyme
4 lemon wedges

1. Preheat oven to 400°.
2. Heat butter and 1 teaspoon oil in a large nonstick skillet over medium-high heat. Brush tops of fish fillets with egg white; sprinkle fish evenly with ¼ teaspoon salt and ¼ teaspoon pepper. Coat tops of fish with nuts, pressing gently to adhere. Place half of fish, nuts side down, in pan; cook 3 minutes or until browned. Turn fish over; cook 4 minutes or until desired degree of doneness.
3. Combine remaining 1 teaspoon olive oil, garlic, and asparagus on a jelly-roll pan coated with cooking spray; toss to combine. Sprinkle with remaining ¼ teaspoon salt, remaining ¼ teaspoon pepper, and thyme. Bake at 400° for 8 minutes or until crisp-tender. Serve with fish and lemon wedges. Serves 4 (serving size: 1 fish fillet, about 5 asparagus spears, and 1 lemon wedge).

CALORIES 356; **FAT** 18.1g (sat 3.4g, mono 10.2g, poly 2.8g); **PROTEIN** 41.2g; **CARB** 8.2g; **FIBER** 4g; **CHOL** 62mg; **IRON** 4.7mg; **SODIUM** 424mg; **CALC** 131mg

Sesame Tuna with Edamame and Soba

Hands-on time: 27 min. Total time: 27 min. *Use all white sesame seeds if black seeds are unavailable. Serve with Napa Cabbage Slaw, page 83.*

4 ounces soba (Japanese buckwheat noodles)
1 cup frozen shelled edamame (green soybeans)
2 tablespoons lower-sodium soy sauce
1½ tablespoons fresh lime juice
1½ tablespoons sweet chili sauce
1 tablespoon dark sesame oil
¼ cup chopped fresh cilantro
1 tablespoon white sesame seeds
1 tablespoon black sesame seeds
4 (6-ounce) U.S. yellowfin or albacore tuna steaks
Cooking spray
½ teaspoon kosher salt
2 teaspoons canola oil

1. Cook soba noodles according to package directions, omitting salt and fat; add edamame for last 3 minutes. Rinse with warm water; drain well.
2. Combine 2 tablespoons soy sauce, lime juice, chili sauce, and sesame oil in a medium bowl. Add soba mixture and cilantro; keep warm.
3. Combine white and black sesame seeds in a shallow dish. Coat tuna with cooking spray, and sprinkle evenly with salt. Coat both sides of each steak with sesame seeds, pressing gently to adhere. Heat a large nonstick skillet over medium-high heat. Add oil to pan; swirl to coat. Add steaks to pan;

cook 3 minutes on each side or until desired degree of doneness. Slice tuna thinly against grain. Serve with noodle mixture. Serves 4 (serving size: 1 tuna steak and ¾ cup noodle mixture).

CALORIES 413; FAT 11.8g (sat 1.4g, mono 4.1g, poly 3.7g); PROTEIN 50.2g; CARB 26.7g; FIBER 2.6g; CHOL 77mg; IRON 4.1mg; SODIUM 606mg; CALC 103mg

Romaine, Asparagus, and Watercress Salad with Shrimp

Hands-on time: 17 min. Total time: 17 min. Serve with Wheat Rolls with Orange Butter, page 82.

1 teaspoon grated lemon rind
⅓ cup fresh lemon juice
¼ cup chopped fresh basil
1½ teaspoons paprika
½ teaspoon salt
¼ teaspoon crushed red pepper
¼ teaspoon black pepper
3 garlic cloves, minced
4 tablespoons olive oil, divided
1 pound peeled and deveined large shrimp
2 cups (1-inch) cut asparagus
7 cups torn romaine lettuce
1 cup trimmed watercress

1. Combine first 8 ingredients; gradually whisk in 3 tablespoons oil.
2. Heat a large skillet over medium-high heat. Add remaining 1 tablespoon oil to pan; swirl to coat. Add shrimp; cook 2 minutes. Add juice mixture; cook 1 minute. Stir in asparagus. Place romaine in a large bowl; add shrimp mixture, and toss. Divide salad among 4 plates; top each with ¼ cup watercress. Serves 4 (serving size: 2 cups).

CALORIES 281; FAT 16g (sat 2.3g, mono 10.2g, poly 2.5g); PROTEIN 26.2g; CARB 9.8g; FIBER 3.8g; CHOL 172mg; IRON 5.4mg; SODIUM 476mg; CALC 126mg

Pecan-Crusted Trout

Hands-on time: 18 min. Total time: 18 min. Breading the flesh side of the fish allows the skin to crisp up on the other side. Serve with Creamed Spinach and Mushrooms, page 84, and Steamed Sugar Snap Peas, page 84.

2 tablespoons all-purpose flour
¼ cup nonfat buttermilk
⅓ cup pecan halves, ground
⅓ cup panko (Japanese breadcrumbs)
4 (6-ounce) trout fillets, divided
½ teaspoon salt
¼ teaspoon freshly ground black pepper
1 tablespoon butter, divided
1 tablespoon olive oil, divided
1 tablespoon chopped fresh parsley
4 lemon wedges

1. Place flour in a shallow dish. Place buttermilk in a dish. Combine pecans and panko in a dish. Sprinkle fish with salt and pepper. Dredge flesh side of 2 fillets in flour; dip in buttermilk. Dredge in panko mixture.
2. Melt 1½ teaspoons butter in a large nonstick skillet over medium-high heat. Add 1½ teaspoons oil. Add dredged fillets, crust-side down; cook 3 minutes on each side or until done. Remove from pan. Repeat procedure with remaining flour, buttermilk, panko mixture, fillets, butter, and oil. Top evenly with parsley. Serve with lemon wedges. Serves 4 (serving size: 1 fillet and 1 lemon wedge).

CALORIES 355; FAT 20.1g (sat 6.3g, mono 7.5g, poly 4.6g); PROTEIN 32.7g; CARB 10.8g; FIBER 1.3g; CHOL 106mg; IRON 1mg; SODIUM 439mg; CALC 144mg

Blackened Chicken with Dirty Rice

Hands-on time: 29 min. Total time: 29 min. Serve with Avocado–Butter Lettuce Salad, page 83.

Rice:
1 tablespoon olive oil
⅓ cup chopped onion
⅓ cup chopped celery
⅓ cup chopped green bell pepper
1 tablespoon chopped fresh thyme
1 cup long-grain white rice
2 teaspoons paprika
¼ teaspoon ground red pepper
3 garlic cloves, minced
2 cups water
¼ teaspoon kosher salt
Cooking spray
4 ounces chicken livers, finely chopped
2 green onions, thinly sliced
⅛ teaspoon hot pepper sauce
Chicken:
1½ teaspoons ground cumin
1 teaspoon smoked paprika
1 teaspoon ground coriander
½ teaspoon kosher salt
½ teaspoon black pepper
¼ teaspoon ground red pepper
4 (6-ounce) skinless, boneless chicken breast halves
2 teaspoons olive oil
½ cup fat-free, lower-sodium chicken broth

1. To prepare rice, heat a medium saucepan over medium-high heat. Add oil to pan; swirl to coat. Add onion and next 3 ingredients; sauté 4 minutes. Add rice, paprika, ¼ teaspoon red pepper, and garlic; sauté 1 minute. Add 2 cups water and ¼ teaspoon salt; bring to a boil. Reduce heat, cover, and simmer 12 minutes. Let stand 5 minutes.
2. Heat a medium skillet over medium-high heat. Coat pan with cooking spray. Add livers; sauté 4 minutes or until lightly browned and
continued

cooked through. Stir in green onions. Add liver mixture and hot pepper sauce to rice; fluff with a fork.

3. Preheat oven to 400°.

4. To prepare chicken, combine cumin and next 5 ingredients; rub evenly over chicken. Heat a large ovenproof skillet over medium-high heat. Add oil to pan; swirl to coat. Add chicken to pan; cook 3 minutes. Turn chicken; place pan in oven. Bake at 400° for 6 minutes or until chicken is done. Remove chicken from pan. Add broth to pan; bring to a boil. Cook until liquid is reduced to ¼ cup (about 2 minutes). Spoon sauce over chicken; serve with rice. Serves 4 (serving size: 1 chicken breast half, about ⅔ cup rice, and 1 tablespoon sauce).

CALORIES 467; **FAT** 10g (sat 1.9g, mono 5.1g, poly 1.7g); **PROTEIN** 48.7g; **CARB** 42.2g; **FIBER** 2.6g; **CHOL** 196mg; **IRON** 6.9mg; **SODIUM** 557mg; **CALC** 65mg

SPEEDY SIDES & SALADS

Match these with almost any main dish, or see the menus on pages 77-78.

Kid Friendly • Make Ahead
Wheat Rolls with Orange Butter

Hands-on time: 3 min. Total time: 8 min.

2 teaspoons unsalted butter, softened
1 teaspoon honey
½ teaspoon grated orange rind
4 (1-ounce) whole-wheat dinner rolls

1. Combine butter, honey, and rind; stir well. Serve each roll with butter mixture. Serves 4 (serving size: 1 roll and about ¾ teaspoon butter).

CALORIES 98; **FAT** 3.3g (sat 1.5g, mono 0.8g, poly 0.7g); **PROTEIN** 2.5g; **CARB** 16g; **FIBER** 2.2g; **CHOL** 5mg; **IRON** 0.7mg; **SODIUM** 136mg; **CALC** 32mg

Kid Friendly • Quick & Easy
Vegetarian
Garlic Mashed Potatoes

Hands-on time: 10 min. Total time: 30 min.

2 pounds cubed peeled red potatoes
2 garlic cloves, halved
½ cup 2% reduced-fat milk
1 tablespoon butter
¼ teaspoon salt
¼ teaspoon freshly ground black pepper

1. Place potatoes and garlic in a medium saucepan; cover with cold water. Bring to a boil. Reduce heat, and simmer 12 minutes or until potatoes are very tender. Drain. Return potato mixture to pan. Add milk, 1 tablespoon butter, salt, and black pepper; mash with a potato masher to desired consistency. Serves 4 (serving size: about 1 cup).

CALORIES 202; **FAT** 3.8g (sat 2.3g, mono 0.9g, poly 0.3g); **PROTEIN** 5.4g; **CARB** 38.1g; **FIBER** 3.9g; **CHOL** 10mg; **IRON** 1.7mg; **SODIUM** 194mg; **CALC** 63mg

BUSY COOKS CAN WORK IN REAL MASHED POTATOES OR ROASTED FRESH CARROTS! GET THE VEGGIES COOKING, AND THEN SET ABOUT PULLING THE REST OF THE MEAL TOGETHER.

Kid Friendly • Quick & Easy
Vegetarian
Butter-Roasted Carrots

Hands-on time: 5 min. Total time: 20 min.

2 cups (2-inch) diagonally cut carrot
1 tablespoon butter, melted
1 teaspoon olive oil
¼ teaspoon kosher salt
¼ teaspoon black pepper
Cooking spray

1. Preheat oven to 425°.

2. Combine first 5 ingredients on a baking sheet coated with cooking spray. Bake at 425° for 15 minutes. Serves 4 (serving size: about ½ cup).

CALORIES 61; **FAT** 4.2g (sat 2g, mono 1.6g, poly 0.3g); **PROTEIN** 0.6g; **CARB** 5.9g; **FIBER** 1.7g; **CHOL** 8mg; **IRON** 0.2mg; **SODIUM** 183mg; **CALC** 22mg

Quick & Easy • Vegetarian
Mixed Greens Salad

Hands-on time: 5 min. Total time: 5 min.

For delicate zucchini and yellow squash ribbons, draw a vegetable peeler down the length of the squash. For paper-thin shavings, use a mandoline.

6 cups mixed baby salad greens
1 cup shaved summer squash (such as zucchini and yellow squash)
⅓ cup thinly sliced radishes
3 tablespoons bottled Italian vinaigrette dressing

1. Combine greens, squash, radishes, and vinaigrette in a large bowl; toss gently to coat. Serves 4 (serving size: about 1½ cups).

CALORIES 36; **FAT** 1.6g (sat 0.1g, mono 1.1g, poly 0.1g); **PROTEIN** 1.9g; **CARB** 6g; **FIBER** 2g; **CHOL** 0mg; **IRON** 2.8mg; **SODIUM** 214mg; **CALC** 67mg

SPEEDY SALADS NEED NOT BE BORING. FRESH AVOCADO AND ONIONS ADD CREAM AND CRUNCH TO GREENS. CHILI SAUCE PERKS UP A FAST NAPA CABBAGE SLAW.

Quick & Easy • Vegetarian

Sautéed Butter-Thyme Mushrooms

Hands-on time: 17 min. Total time: 17 min.

1 tablespoon butter
1 tablespoon canola oil
1/4 cup finely chopped shallots
3/8 teaspoon salt
2 (8-ounce) packages presliced cremini
  mushrooms
1/3 cup dry white wine
4 teaspoons chopped fresh thyme

1. Melt butter in a large skillet over medium-high heat. Add oil and shallots; cook 1 minute or until tender. Add salt and mushrooms to pan; cook 13 minutes or until mushrooms are brown and liquid evaporates. Add wine to pan; cook 2 minutes or until liquid almost evaporates. Stir in thyme, and cook 30 seconds. Serves 4 (serving size: 1/2 cup).

CALORIES 103; FAT 6.5g (sat 2.1g, mono 3g, poly 1.2g); PROTEIN 3.2g; CARB 6.8g; FIBER 0.8g; CHOL 8mg; IRON 0.7mg; SODIUM 250mg; CALC 29mg

Quick & Easy • Make Ahead
Vegetarian

Napa Cabbage Slaw

Hands-on time: 15 min. Total time: 25 min.

1 tablespoon lower-sodium soy sauce
1 tablespoon dark sesame oil
1 tablespoon rice vinegar
1 1/2 teaspoons sweet chili sauce
1 teaspoon grated peeled fresh ginger
1/4 teaspoon crushed red pepper
2 cups thinly sliced Napa cabbage
1/2 cup julienne-cut yellow squash
1/2 cup matchstick-cut carrot
1/4 cup diagonally cut green onions

1. Combine first 6 ingredients in a large bowl. Add remaining ingredients; toss well. Let stand 10 minutes. Serves 4 (serving size: 3/4 cup).

CALORIES 52; FAT 3.5g (sat 0.5g, mono 1.4g, poly 1.5g); PROTEIN 1.1g; CARB 4.4g; FIBER 1.4g; CHOL 0mg; IRON 0.2mg; SODIUM 117mg; CALC 43mg

Quick & Easy • Vegetarian

Avocado-Butter Lettuce Salad

Hands-on time: 10 min. Total time: 20 min.

1 cup thinly sliced red onion
2 tablespoons olive oil
1 tablespoon fresh lime juice
1/4 teaspoon salt
1/4 teaspoon black pepper
3 cups torn butter lettuce
1 cup sliced avocado

1. Combine first 5 ingredients in a large bowl. Let stand 10 minutes. Add lettuce and avocado; toss gently. Serves 4 (serving size: 1 cup).

CALORIES 119; FAT 9.7g (sat 1.4g, mono 6.6g, poly 1.2g); PROTEIN 1.9g; CARB 8.3g; FIBER 4.4g; CHOL 0mg; IRON 0.9mg; SODIUM 154mg; CALC 28mg

Quick & Easy • Vegetarian

Sautéed Snow Peas and Peppers

Hands-on time: 4 min. Total time: 12 min.

2 teaspoons dark sesame oil, divided
2 1/2 cups fresh snow peas, trimmed
1 cup thinly sliced red bell pepper
1/4 teaspoon salt
1/8 teaspoon freshly ground black
  pepper

1. Heat a large skillet over medium-high heat. Add 1 teaspoon sesame oil to pan; swirl to coat. Add snow peas and bell pepper to pan; sauté 4 minutes or until vegetables are crisp-tender, stirring occasionally. Remove pan from heat. Drizzle vegetable mixture with remaining 1 teaspoon sesame oil. Sprinkle with salt and black pepper, and toss well to combine. Serves 4 (serving size: about 3/4 cup).

CALORIES 46; FAT 2.4g (sat 0.4g, mono 0.9g, poly 1g); PROTEIN 1.4g; CARB 4.8g; FIBER 1.6g; CHOL 0mg; IRON 1mg; SODIUM 150mg; CALC 19mg

TAKE A TIP FROM THE BEST CHEFS: BUY THE BEST POSSIBLE FRESH INGREDIENTS. THEY OFTEN NEED THE LEAST HELP AND FUSS IN THE KITCHEN.

Kid Friendly • Quick & Easy Vegetarian

Steamed Sugar Snap Peas

Hands-on time: 4 min. Total time: 12 min. Fresh, crunchy, and (as the name implies) remarkably sweet, these snap peas are a versatile spring side dish. With mint, the flavors are bright; with tarragon, they go slightly earthy.

3 cups fresh sugar snap peas
1 tablespoon chopped fresh mint or tarragon
1 tablespoon butter
1/8 teaspoon salt
1/8 teaspoon freshly ground black pepper

1. Steam peas 5 minutes or until crisp-tender; drain. Combine peas, mint or tarragon, butter, salt, and pepper; toss well. Serves 4 (serving size: 3/4 cup).

CALORIES 46; **FAT** 3g (sat 1.8g, mono 0.8g, poly 0.2g); **PROTEIN** 1.4g; **CARB** 3.7g; **FIBER** 1.3g; **CHOL** 8mg; **IRON** 1mg; **SODIUM** 96mg; **CALC** 22mg

Kid Friendly • Quick & Easy Vegetarian

Brown Rice with Sesame

Hands-on time: 4 min. Total time: 18 min.

1 cup uncooked instant brown rice
2 tablespoons fresh lime juice
1/4 teaspoon salt
1 tablespoon toasted sesame seeds

1. Cook rice according to package directions, omitting fat. Stir in juice and salt. Sprinkle with seeds. Serves 4 (serving size: about 3/4 cup).

CALORIES 187; **FAT** 2.5g (sat 0.4g, mono 0.9g, poly 1g); **PROTEIN** 4.4g; **CARB** 36.7g; **FIBER** 3.1g; **CHOL** 0mg; **IRON** 1mg; **SODIUM** 153mg; **CALC** 39mg

Quick & Easy • Vegetarian

Garlicky Asparagus

Hands-on time: 7 min. Total time: 15 min.

1 pound asparagus spears, trimmed
1 tablespoon olive oil
2 garlic cloves, thinly sliced
1/8 teaspoon salt
1/8 teaspoon black pepper

1. Steam asparagus 4 minutes or until crisp-tender.
2. While asparagus steams, heat a large skillet over medium heat. Add oil to pan; swirl to coat. Add garlic; cook 2 minutes or until fragrant, stirring frequently. Add asparagus, salt, and pepper, and toss to combine. Serves 4 (serving size: about 3 ounces asparagus).

CALORIES 57; **FAT** 3.4g (sat 0.5g, mono 2.5g, poly 0.4g); **PROTEIN** 2.5g; **CARB** 5.4g; **FIBER** 2.5g; **CHOL** 0mg; **IRON** 0.5mg; **SODIUM** 74mg; **CALC** 27mg

Kid Friendly • Quick & Easy Vegetarian

Roasted Red Potatoes

Hands-on time: 4 min. Total time: 30 min.

1 tablespoon olive oil
1/4 teaspoon kosher salt
1/4 teaspoon black pepper
2 shallots, thinly sliced
1 (20-ounce) bag refrigerated potato wedges

1. Preheat oven to 400°.
2. Combine all ingredients on a large jelly-roll pan; toss well. Roast at 400° for 20 minutes or until done, stirring after 15 minutes. Serves 4 (serving size: about 3/4 cup).

CALORIES 123; **FAT** 3.4g (sat 0.5g, mono 2.5g, poly 0.4g); **PROTEIN** 3.8g; **CARB** 18.8g; **FIBER** 3.5g; **CHOL** 0mg; **IRON** 0.7mg; **SODIUM** 269mg; **CALC** 1mg

Quick & Easy • Vegetarian

Creamed Spinach and Mushrooms

Hands-on & total time: 19 min.

4 teaspoons canola oil, divided
8 ounces sliced cremini mushrooms
1 (10-ounce) package baby spinach
1/3 cup finely chopped shallots
2 teaspoons minced fresh garlic
3/4 cup fat-free milk
1 tablespoon all-purpose flour
3/8 teaspoon salt
1/4 teaspoon freshly ground black pepper
Dash of nutmeg
2 1/2 ounces 1/3-less-fat cream cheese

1. Heat a large skillet over medium-high heat. Add 1 1/2 teaspoons oil; swirl to coat. Add mushrooms; cook 6 minutes or until liquid evaporates. Remove mushrooms from pan. Add 1 1/2 teaspoons oil to pan; swirl to coat. Add spinach; cook 1 minute or until spinach wilts. Remove from heat.
2. Heat a Dutch oven over medium heat. Add remaining 1 teaspoon oil; swirl to coat. Add shallots and garlic; cook 1 minute, stirring constantly. Combine milk and flour, stirring with a whisk. Add milk mixture, salt, pepper, and nutmeg to pan; bring to a boil, stirring constantly. Cook 3 minutes or until thickened, stirring constantly. Add cheese; stir until cheese melts and mixture is smooth. Add mushrooms and spinach to milk mixture, and toss gently to coat. Serves 6 (serving size: 1/2 cup).

CALORIES 102; **FAT** 6.1g (sat 1.8g, mono 2.7g, poly 1.1g); **PROTEIN** 4.8g; **CARB** 8.1g; **FIBER** 1.4g; **CHOL** 9mg; **IRON** 1.7mg; **SODIUM** 241mg; **CALC** 111mg

Orange and Olive Salad

Hands-on & total time: 13 min.

2 tablespoons extra-virgin olive oil
1 tablespoon fresh lemon juice
1½ teaspoons honey
¼ teaspoon black pepper
⅛ teaspoon salt
4 cups torn Bibb lettuce
1 cup fresh orange sections
½ cup sliced fennel bulb
1 ounce oil-cured olives, halved

1. Combine first 5 ingredients in a large bowl. Add remaining ingredients; toss gently. Serves 4 (serving size: about 1 cup).

CALORIES 118; FAT 9.5g (sat 1.5g, mono 4.9g, poly 0.8g); PROTEIN 1.3g; CARB 10.3g; FIBER 3.1g; CHOL 0mg; IRON 0.9mg; SODIUM 249mg; CALC 43mg

SIMPLE 10-MINUTE SAUCES

Supersimple ways to jazz up chicken, beef, fish, and veggies. Many need no cooking!

Quick & Easy • Make Ahead
Vegetarian

Tzatziki

Taste and Texture: Yogurt sauce with a Greek accent: chunky from grated cukes, fragrant from dill, and pungent from fresh garlic.
Tips: Avoid garlic cloves with green sprouts inside—they'll be bitter. Be sure to reach for Greek yogurt to achieve the creamiest texture.
Try with: Beef, lamb, or chicken kebabs; pita sandwiches or burgers; crudités or baked pita chips.

¾ cup plain low-fat Greek yogurt
¼ cup grated peeled English cucumber
1 tablespoon chopped fresh dill
2 teaspoons red wine vinegar
¼ teaspoon salt
⅛ teaspoon black pepper
2 garlic cloves, minced

1. Combine all ingredients in a medium bowl. Serves 4 (serving size: 3 tablespoons).

CALORIES 36; FAT 1g (sat 0.8g, mono 0g, poly 0g); PROTEIN 4.4g; CARB 2.7g; FIBER 0.1g; CHOL 3mg; IRON 0.1mg; SODIUM 162mg; CALC 50mg

Quick & Easy • Make Ahead
Vegetarian

Chimichurri

Taste and Texture: This classic Argentinian meat condiment is bright with a touch of heat.
Tips: Use the freshest herbs for the best flavor. Stick to the leaves and try not to incorporate the thick stems, which can taste bitter.
Try with: Grilled steak, chicken, or fish; roasted leg of lamb; roasted potatoes or baby carrots; sandwiches as a dipping sauce; grilled bread; raw oysters on the half shell.
To Your Health: A smidgen of heart-smart olive oil is the only significant source of fat.

1 cup fresh flat-leaf parsley leaves
1 cup fresh cilantro leaves
¼ cup fresh oregano leaves
2 garlic cloves
½ teaspoon grated lime rind
2 tablespoons fresh lime juice
2 tablespoons extra-virgin olive oil
¼ teaspoon salt
¼ teaspoon crushed red pepper

1. Place first 4 ingredients in a food processor; process until finely chopped. Add lime rind and remaining ingredients to herb mixture; process until herbs are very finely chopped and mixture is well combined. Serves 4 (serving size: 2 tablespoons).

CALORIES 79; FAT 7.2g (sat 1g, mono 5g, poly 0.9g); PROTEIN 0.9g; CARB 4.2g; FIBER 1.9g; CHOL 0mg; IRON 2.4mg; SODIUM 155mg; CALC 73mg

Quick & Easy

Mushroom Sauce

Taste and Texture: Plenty of sautéed mushrooms give this sauce deep, meaty, umami flavor, balanced by a touch of acid from white wine. Medium-bodied texture.
Tips: Make sure the sauce is bubbling as it cooks so the cornstarch can effectively thicken it. A couple of tablespoons of butter round out the flavors and add richness to this sauce.
Try with: Steak; roasted or grilled chicken or pork; mashed potatoes; shepherd's pie filling; hot cooked rice or egg noodles.

Cooking spray
1 (8-ounce) package presliced mushrooms
1 teaspoon chopped fresh thyme
½ cup fat-free, lower-sodium chicken broth
¼ cup white wine
2 teaspoons cornstarch
⅛ teaspoon salt
⅛ teaspoon black pepper
2 tablespoons butter

1. Heat a large skillet over medium-high heat. Coat pan with cooking spray. Add mushrooms and thyme to pan; sauté 4 minutes or until mushrooms are lightly browned. Stir in broth, wine, cornstarch, salt, and pepper; cook 2 minutes or until sauce is slightly thickened. Remove from heat; add butter, stirring until butter melts. Serves 8 (serving size: about 3 tablespoons).

CALORIES 37; FAT 2.9g (sat 1.8g, mono 0.8g, poly 0.1g); PROTEIN 0.8g; CARB 1.9g; FIBER 0.2g; CHOL 8mg; IRON 0.2mg; SODIUM 87mg; CALC 7mg

Wasabi Cream

Taste and Texture: *Forward, horseradish-y heat from wasabi (a classic Japanese flavoring), with pleasant tang from sour cream and lime. Thick consistency, great for dolloping.*
Tips: *Be sure to use wasabi paste rather than powder.*
Try with: *Grilled or roasted beef, chicken, or pork; sautéed or grilled shrimp; baked potato; raw veggies.*

1 cup reduced-fat sour cream
2 tablespoons chopped fresh cilantro
2 tablespoons fresh lime juice
2 teaspoons wasabi paste

1. Combine all ingredients in a bowl. Serves 8 (serving size: 2 tablespoons).

CALORIES 57; FAT 3.9g (sat 2.4g, mono 1g, poly 0.2g); PROTEIN 1.4g; CARB 3.1g; FIBER 0.1g; CHOL 16mg; IRON 0mg; SODIUM 43mg; CALC 50mg

Saffron Aioli

Taste and Texture: *Garlicky, with saffron's faint honey-vanilla sweetness balanced by a light bitterness. Thick and creamy.*
Tips: *Saffron doesn't fully release its color, flavor, or fragrance until it blends with warm liquid, which is why you make the saffron-water blend in the microwave.*
Try with: *Poached, grilled, sautéed, or roasted fin fish; scallops, shrimp, or lobster; toasted bread; oven fries; steamed or sautéed asparagus, broccoli, or carrots.*

1½ tablespoons water
⅛ teaspoon crushed saffron threads
1 garlic clove, minced
½ cup canola mayonnaise
1 teaspoon fresh lemon juice

1. Combine first 3 ingredients in a small microwave-safe bowl; microwave at HIGH 30 seconds. Cool slightly. Stir in mayonnaise and juice, stirring until well blended. Serves 8 (serving size: 1 tablespoon).

CALORIES 46; FAT 4.5g (sat 0g, mono 2.5g, poly 1.5g); PROTEIN 0g; CARB 0.2g; FIBER 0g; CHOL 0mg; IRON 0mg; SODIUM 90mg; CALC 1mg

---

SIMPLE PARTNERS, SIMPLE SAUCES

Fish, chicken, and more, pan-cooked. Match them with a sauce that strikes your fancy.

BASIC STRIPED BASS

Heat a grill pan over medium-high heat. Coat pan with cooking spray. Sprinkle 4 (6-ounce) striped bass fillets with ½ teaspoon salt and ¼ teaspoon freshly ground black pepper. Add fish to pan; cook 4 minutes on each side or until desired degree of doneness. Serves 4 (serving size: 1 fillet).

CALORIES 159; FAT 3.8g (sat 0.8g); SODIUM 403mg

GRILL PAN CHICKEN

Heat a grill pan over medium-high heat. Coat pan with cooking spray. Sprinkle 4 (6-ounce) skinless, boneless chicken breast halves with ½ teaspoon salt and ¼ teaspoon freshly ground black pepper. Add chicken to pan; cook 6 minutes on each side or until done. Serves 4 (serving size: 1 breast half).

CALORIES 183; FAT 4g (sat 1.1g); SODIUM 373mg

SAUTÉED SHRIMP

Heat a large nonstick skillet over medium-high heat. Add 1 tablespoon olive oil to pan; swirl to coat. Sprinkle ½ teaspoon freshly ground black pepper and ¼ teaspoon salt over 1½ pounds large peeled and deveined shrimp. Add shrimp to pan; cook 2 minutes on each side or until shrimp are done. Serves 4 (serving size: about 6 ounces).

CALORIES 211; FAT 6.3g (sat 1g); SODIUM 399mg

ROASTED PORK TENDERLOIN

Sprinkle ½ teaspoon salt and ¼ teaspoon freshly ground black pepper over 1 (1-pound) pork tenderloin. Heat a large skillet over medium-high heat. Add 1 tablespoon olive oil to pan; swirl to coat. Add pork to pan; cook 3 minutes, browning on all sides. Bake pork at 400° for 17 minutes or until a thermometer registers 145°. Let stand 10 minutes; cut across the grain into thin slices. Serves 4 (serving size: about 3 ounces).

CALORIES 170; FAT 7.5g (sat 1.9g); SODIUM 338mg

PAN-SEARED FLANK STEAK

Heat a grill pan over medium-high heat. Coat pan with cooking spray. Sprinkle 1 (1-pound) flank steak with ½ teaspoon salt and ½ teaspoon freshly ground black pepper. Add steak to pan; cook 8 minutes on each side or until desired degree of doneness. Let steak stand 10 minutes; cut steak diagonally across the grain into thin slices. Serves 4 (serving size: 3 ounces).

CALORIES 152; FAT 5.5g (sat 2.3g); SODIUM 341mg

Cheddar Cheese Sauce

Taste and Texture: *A mild, kid-friendly sauce with a subtle tang from sharp cheddar.*
Tips: *Remove from heat, and then stir in the cheese to ensure that the sauce doesn't curdle. The flour helps stabilize the dairy mixture, but if it's boiled after the cheese is added, the sauce will separate or curdle.*
Try with: *Steamed or sautéed veggies; baked potatoes; roast beef sandwiches; pasta.*
To Your Health: *This slimmed-down sauce boasts a fraction of the fat you'd find in regular or processed cheese sauces.*

1 cup 1% low-fat milk, divided
4 teaspoons all-purpose flour
¼ teaspoon salt
1.5 ounces sharp cheddar cheese, shredded (about ⅓ cup)
¼ teaspoon freshly ground black pepper

1. Combine ¼ cup milk and flour in a saucepan; stir with a whisk. Stir in remaining ¾ cup milk and salt; bring to a boil over medium heat, stirring frequently. Reduce heat to low; simmer 2 minutes or until slightly thickened, stirring constantly. Remove from heat. Stir in cheese and pepper, stirring until cheese melts. Serves 8 (serving size: 1½ tablespoons).

CALORIES 37; FAT 1.9g (sat 1.2g, mono 0.5g, poly 0.1g); PROTEIN 2.3g; CARB 2.6g; FIBER 0.1g; CHOL 6mg; IRON 0.1mg; SODIUM 115mg; CALC 71mg

Quick & Easy • Make Ahead
Ponzu

Taste and Texture: Salty, tangy, lightly sweet, with a little heat; a traditional Japanese sauce.
Tips: If mirin is unavailable, you can substitute 1 tablespoon rice wine vinegar and 1 tablespoon water or 2 tablespoons dry sherry—just bump up the sugar to 2 teaspoons.
Try with: Rice; Asian noodles like soba and udon; beef and chicken; shrimp; scallops; sushi.
To Your Health: Huge flavor, no fat. But sodium is a little high, so use sparingly if that's your dietary concern.

1 tablespoon chopped green onions
3 tablespoons fresh lemon juice
2 tablespoons mirin (sweet rice wine)
2 tablespoons lower-sodium soy sauce
1 teaspoon brown sugar
¼ teaspoon crushed red pepper
¼ teaspoon fish sauce

1. Combine all ingredients in a bowl; stir with a whisk until sugar dissolves. Serves 4 (serving size: 2 tablespoons).

CALORIES 30; FAT 0g; PROTEIN 0.6g; CARB 5.2g; FIBER 0.1g; CHOL 0mg; IRON 0.1mg; SODIUM 225mg; CALC 5mg

Kid Friendly • Quick & Easy
Quick Gravy

Taste and Texture: The lightly meaty, flour-thickened chicken broth base is enriched with cream cheese for a smooth, medium-bodied, herb-flecked sauce.
Tips: Bring your cream cheese to room temperature before stirring it into the sauce—it blends more smoothly this way, without clumping or curdling.
Try with: Grilled or roasted chicken, pork, or turkey; meatballs; potpie fillings; mashed potatoes, savory bread pudding, or oven fries.

1 cup fat-free, lower-sodium chicken broth, divided
1 tablespoon all-purpose flour
2 tablespoons minced shallots
1 bay leaf
1 tablespoon chopped fresh flat-leaf parsley
2 tablespoons ⅓-less-fat cream cheese
⅛ teaspoon black pepper

1. Combine ¼ cup broth and flour in a small saucepan, stirring well with a whisk. Stir in remaining ¾ cup chicken broth, shallots, and bay leaf; bring to a boil. Reduce heat; simmer 3 minutes or until slightly thickened, stirring constantly. Let stand 1 minute; discard bay leaf. Stir in parsley, cheese, and pepper, stirring until cheese melts. Serves 4 (serving size: about 3 tablespoons).

CALORIES 30; FAT 1.6g (sat 1g, mono 0.4g, poly 0.1g); PROTEIN 1.1g; CARB 2.9g; FIBER 0.1g; CHOL 5mg; IRON 0.2mg; SODIUM 142mg; CALC 9mg

Quick & Easy • Make Ahead
Vegetarian
White BBQ Sauce

Taste and Texture: An Alabama staple condiment—peppery, creamy, and tangy.
Tips: Fresh ground pepper is key in this sauce—it's meant to be a little spicy.
Try with: Grilled, roasted, or smoked chicken; shredded cabbage (for coleslaw); chicken or turkey sandwiches.

1 cup canola mayonnaise
¼ cup white vinegar
1 teaspoon freshly ground black pepper
¼ teaspoon salt

1. Combine all ingredients in a medium bowl. Serves 16 (serving size: 1 tablespoon).

CALORIES 100; FAT 11g (sat 1g, mono 6g, poly 3g); PROTEIN 0g; CARB 0.1g; FIBER 0g; CHOL 5mg; IRON 0mg; SODIUM 136mg; CALC 1mg

Kid Friendly • Quick & Easy
Warm Bacon Vinaigrette

Taste and Texture: Salty, smoky, and tart. Thin-bodied.
Tips: Add the oil slowly, drop by drop at first, stirring constantly with a whisk to get an emulsion. Mustard is an emulsifier and helps stabilize the blend.
Try with: Main-dish green salad with shredded rotisserie chicken; grilled or roasted chicken or trout; seared scallops; steamed or sautéed green beans or asparagus; roasted Brussels sprouts.

4 center-cut bacon slices
2 tablespoons chopped shallots
3 tablespoons red wine vinegar
1 teaspoon Dijon mustard
¼ teaspoon black pepper
⅛ teaspoon sugar
3 tablespoons olive oil

1. Heat a medium nonstick skillet over medium heat. Add bacon to pan; cook until crisp. Remove bacon, reserving 1½ tablespoons drippings in pan. Crumble bacon. Add crumbled bacon and shallots to pan; cook 1 minute, stirring frequently. Remove from heat, and stir in vinegar and next 3 ingredients. Gradually add oil to vinegar mixture, stirring constantly with a whisk. Serves 8 (serving size: 1 tablespoon).

CALORIES 59; FAT 5.7g (sat 1g, mono 3.7g, poly 0.5g); PROTEIN 1.1g; CARB 0.7g; FIBER 0g; CHOL 3mg; IRON 0.1mg; SODIUM 59mg; CALC 2mg

ALMOST INSTANT DESSERTS

Extra! Extra! We put together a few sweets along parfait, pudding, and sundae lines—the perfect punctuation to any quick meal.

Kid Friendly • Quick & Easy
Make Ahead

Last-Minute Tropical Sherbet

Hands-on time: 12 min. Total time: 12 min.

Frozen fruit and yogurt get whirred together to make a tangy sherbet that's the texture of soft-serve. You can make it ahead, but don't freeze overnight; the mixture will become icy.

1 (12-ounce) package frozen mango chunks (about 2½ cups)
1 cup frozen pineapple chunks
1 (6-ounce) carton lemon low-fat yogurt
1 teaspoon grated lime rind

1. Remove mango and pineapple from freezer, and let stand at room temperature 10 minutes. Place mango, pineapple, yogurt, and rind in a food processor; process until smooth. Serve immediately (for soft-serve texture), or freeze in an airtight container 1 hour and 30 minutes (for firmer texture). Serves 4 (serving size: ¾ cup).

CALORIES 144; FAT 0.6g (sat 0.4g, mono 0.2g, poly 0g); PROTEIN 3g; CARB 34.1g; FIBER 2.5g; CHOL 2mg; IRON 0.3mg; SODIUM 78mg; CALC 29mg

Kid Friendly • Quick & Easy

Mango-Ginger Parfaits

Hands-on time: 12 min. Total time: 12 min.

2 cups plain 2% reduced-fat Greek yogurt
2 tablespoons mascarpone cheese
2 tablespoons brown sugar
2 tablespoons fresh lime juice
2 peeled mangoes, chopped
¼ cup gingersnap crumbs
2 tablespoons flaked sweetened coconut, toasted

1. Combine 2 cups yogurt and mascarpone.
2. Combine sugar, lime juice, and mango.
3. Combine gingersnaps and coconut.
4. Place ¼ cup yogurt mixture into each of 4 parfait glasses. Top with ¼ cup mango mixture and 1½ teaspoons gingersnap mixture. Repeat layers. Serves 4 (serving size: 1 parfait).

CALORIES 270; FAT 10.5g (sat 5.9g, mono 2.6g, poly 0.3g); PROTEIN 11.5g; CARB 35.9g; FIBER 2.2g; CHOL 25mg; IRON 0.7mg; SODIUM 95mg; CALC 118mg

A SMALL AMOUNT OF MASCARPONE CHEESE GIVES THE MANGO-GINGER PARFAITS RICHNESS.

Kid Friendly • Quick & Easy

Greek Yogurt with Warm Berry Sauce

Hands-on time: 10 min. Total time: 20 min.

Although this is dessert, there's enough protein to consider it for breakfast.

⅔ cup frozen blueberries
⅔ cup frozen blackberries
½ cup water
¼ cup sugar
2 tablespoons fresh lemon juice
1 tablespoon butter
2 cups plain 2% reduced-fat Greek yogurt

1. Combine first 5 ingredients in a small saucepan. Bring mixture to a boil. Reduce heat to medium-low; gently boil 10 minutes or until sauce thickens. Stir in butter.
2. Spoon ½ cup yogurt into each of 4 bowls; top each serving with about ¼ cup sauce. Serves 4.

CALORIES 192; FAT 5.8g (sat 3.8g, mono 0.8g, poly 0.2g); PROTEIN 11.8g; CARB 25.7g; FIBER 2g; CHOL 14.3mg; IRON 0.3mg; SODIUM 64mg; CALC 131mg

Quick & Easy

Coffee-Drenched Ice Cream with Banana and Nuts

Hands-on time: 7 min. Total time: 7 min.

Use a vegetable peeler to make chocolate curls.

1 cup vanilla low-fat ice cream
1 medium banana, sliced
¼ cup hot brewed espresso
1 tablespoon chopped dry-roasted peanuts
1 tablespoon chocolate curls (about ¼ ounce)

1. Spoon ½ cup ice cream into each of 2 bowls. Top each with half of banana, 2 tablespoons espresso, 1½ teaspoons peanuts, and 1½ teaspoons chocolate. Serves 2.

CALORIES 226; FAT 6.8g (sat 2.2g, mono 1.8g, poly 1.1g); PROTEIN 5.5g; CARB 37.5g; FIBER 3.4g; CHOL 5.3mg; IRON 0.5mg; SODIUM 107mg; CALC 104mg

Quick & Easy
Warm Mocha Pudding

Hands-on time: 22 min. Total time: 32 min.

If you've never tried a warm pudding, this is the one to try. The flavors are more up front when the pudding is warm.

½ cup sugar
1 large egg
2 cups 1% low-fat milk
⅓ cup unsweetened cocoa
1 tablespoon cornstarch
1 tablespoon instant espresso granules
⅛ teaspoon salt
1 ounce bittersweet chocolate
1 teaspoon unsalted butter
1 teaspoon vanilla extract

1. Combine sugar and egg in a medium bowl; stir with a whisk. Add milk and next 4 ingredients; stir to combine. Transfer milk mixture to a medium saucepan; cook over medium heat 14 minutes or until thick and bubbly, stirring constantly. Remove from heat; stir in chocolate, butter, and vanilla. Cool 10 minutes before serving. Serves 4 (serving size: about ½ cup).

CALORIES 250; FAT 6.9g (sat 3.2g, mono 2.1g, poly 0.4g); PROTEIN 7.6g; CARB 41.4g; FIBER 1.9g; CHOL 53.6mg; IRON 1.5mg; SODIUM 146mg; CALC 153mg

Quick & Easy
Limoncello Freeze

Hands-on time: 10 min. Total time: 10 min.

Mush together purchased ice cream, lemon curd (found near the jellies and jams), and limoncello, and you get a delicious lemony version of a Creamsicle—fruity-tangy and creamy-milky at the same time. Meringue cookies add welcome crunch.

¼ cup lemon curd
2½ tablespoons limoncello (lemon liqueur)
2 cups vanilla low-fat ice cream, softened
12 mini vanilla meringue cookies

1. Combine curd and liqueur in a small bowl, stirring with a whisk to blend. Add ice cream to curd mixture; stir gently to swirl. Spoon ½ cup ice-cream mixture into each of 4 bowls; top each with 3 meringue cookies. Serves 4.

CALORIES 231; FAT 4.7g (sat 2.7g, mono 1g, poly 0.2g); PROTEIN 3.7g; CARB 40.1g; FIBER 2.2g; CHOL 36mg; IRON 0.1mg; SODIUM 73mg; CALC 122mg

SUPERMARKET SHORTCUT SOLUTIONS

Five off-the-shelf and out-of-the-fridge convenience foods make possible fast meals that are full of fresh flavors and healthy goodness.

KITCHEN TIP

If the dough starts retracting and fighting you as you shape it, walk away for a couple of minutes; let it relax, and it will cooperate.

PIZZA DOUGH

In the roster of shortcut ingredients, fresh pizza dough is an all-star. In as little as 30 minutes, you can make a fantastic pie with a crispy-chewy, deliciously browned crust, hot from the oven. And when you load it with fresh veggies: voilà, a wonderfully healthy salad pizza. Fresh dough, from the supermarket bakery section or from a local pizzeria, is our favorite to work with, though canned dough and prebaked crusts work fine in a pinch.

Quick & Easy
Beet Salad Pizza

Hands-on & total time: 28 min.

1 pound fresh pizza dough
2 tablespoons olive oil
1 (5-ounce) golden beet, peeled
4 cups loosely packed arugula
1 shallot, thinly sliced
3 tablespoons balsamic vinaigrette
¼ teaspoon freshly ground black pepper
3 ounces crumbled goat cheese
1 ounce Parmesan cheese, shaved
2 ounces shaved prosciutto

1. Preheat oven to 450°.
2. Place dough in a microwave-safe bowl; microwave at MEDIUM (50% power) 45 seconds. Let stand 5 minutes. Roll into a 14-inch circle. Place on pizza pan; pierce with fork. Brush with oil. Bake at 450° for 14 minutes.
3. Wrap beet in parchment paper. Microwave at HIGH until tender (about 2½ minutes). Thinly slice.
4. Combine arugula, shallot, beet, vinaigrette, and pepper; arrange on crust with cheeses and prosciutto. Serves 6.

CALORIES 349; FAT 13.7g (sat 4g, mono 4.8g, poly 2.1g); PROTEIN 14g; CARB 44.4g; FIBER 2.2g; CHOL 15mg; IRON 3.3mg; SODIUM 813mg; CALC 102mg

Sunny-Side-Up Pizza

Hands-on & total time: 30 min.

1 pound fresh pizza dough
2 tablespoons olive oil, divided
2 garlic cloves, minced
6 large eggs
1/8 teaspoon kosher salt
4 cups mâche or baby spinach
1/4 cup thinly sliced red onion
3 tablespoons balsamic vinaigrette
2 ounces Parmesan cheese, shaved
3/8 teaspoon freshly ground black pepper

1. Preheat oven to 450°.
2. Place dough in a microwave-safe bowl; microwave at MEDIUM (50% power) 45 seconds. Let stand 5 minutes. Roll dough into a 14-inch circle. Place on a pizza pan; pierce with a fork. Combine 1 1/2 tablespoons oil and garlic; brush over dough. Bake at 450° for 14 minutes.
3. Heat a large nonstick skillet over medium heat. Add remaining 1 1/2 teaspoons oil; swirl to coat. Crack eggs into pan; cook 4 minutes or until whites are set. Sprinkle with salt.
4. Combine mâche, onion, and vinaigrette. Arrange on crust; top with eggs, cheese, and pepper. Serves 6.

CALORIES 385; FAT 15.2g (sat 3.6g, mono 5.9g, poly 2.6g); PROTEIN 17.3g; CARB 44.9g; FIBER 2.4g; CHOL 186mg; IRON 4.3mg; SODIUM 814mg; CALC 184mg

Quick & Easy

Tuna Salad Pizza

Hands-on & total time: 28 min.

1 pound fresh pizza dough
3 tablespoons olive oil, divided
1 1/2 tablespoons fresh lemon juice
1/8 teaspoon kosher salt
4 cups mixed salad greens
1/2 cup halved grape tomatoes
1 ounce chopped kalamata olives
1 (6-ounce) can albacore tuna packed in oil, drained
1 1/2 ounces Parmesan cheese, shaved
1/4 teaspoon freshly ground black pepper

1. Preheat oven to 450°.
2. Place dough in a microwave-safe bowl; microwave at MEDIUM (50% power) 45 seconds. Let stand 5 minutes. Roll dough into a 14-inch circle. Place dough on a pizza pan; pierce with a fork. Brush 1 tablespoon oil over dough. Bake at 450° for 14 minutes or until crisp.
3. Combine remaining 2 tablespoons oil, juice, and salt in a large bowl. Add greens and tomatoes; toss. Arrange salad over crust. Top with olives and tuna; sprinkle with cheese and pepper. Cut into 12 wedges. Serves 6 (serving size: 2 wedges).

CALORIES 361; FAT 14g (sat 2.6g, mono 7.2g, poly 3g); PROTEIN 17.4g; CARB 43.1g; FIBER 2.5g; CHOL 10mg; IRON 3.2mg; SODIUM 801mg; CALC 92mg

Quick & Easy

Steak House Pizza

Hands-on & total time: 30 min.

1 pound fresh pizza dough
8 teaspoons olive oil, divided
2 garlic cloves, minced
2 (4-ounce) beef tenderloin steaks
1/8 teaspoon kosher salt
4 cups loosely packed arugula
1/4 cup thinly sliced red onion
3 tablespoons balsamic vinaigrette
2 ounces crumbled blue cheese
1/4 teaspoon freshly ground black pepper

1. Preheat oven to 450°.
2. Place dough in a bowl; microwave at MEDIUM (50% power) 45 seconds. Let stand 5 minutes. Roll dough into a 14-inch circle. Place on a pizza pan; pierce with fork. Combine 2 tablespoons oil and garlic; brush over dough. Bake at 450° for 14 minutes.
3. Heat a large skillet over medium-high heat. Add remaining 2 teaspoons oil to pan; swirl to coat. Sprinkle steaks with salt. Add steaks to pan; cook 3 minutes on each side. Remove from pan; let stand 5 minutes. Cut across grain into slices.
4. Combine arugula, onion, and vinaigrette. Arrange over crust; top with steak, cheese, and pepper. Serves 6.

CALORIES 370; FAT 15.3g (sat 3.7g, mono 6g, poly 2.2g); PROTEIN 17.2g; CARB 42.1g; FIBER 1.7g; CHOL 29mg; IRON 3.2mg; SODIUM 744mg; CALC 80mg

FRESH PASTA

For those nights when you just don't have the 12 minutes to cook dried fettuccine, reach for refrigerated fresh pasta: It's done in about two minutes. The texture is deliciously different: more delicate, with a slightly springy bounce. Yet, it's not too refined for a bold Bolognese, a meatball treatment, or a creamy vodka-tomato sauce.

Quick & Easy

Shrimp Vodka Pasta

Hands-on & total time: 18 min. Serve with Creamed Spinach and Mushrooms, page 84.

9 ounces refrigerated fettuccine
1 tablespoon olive oil, divided
12 ounces large shrimp, peeled and deveined
3 garlic cloves, thinly sliced
1/3 cup vodka
1 1/3 cups lower-sodium marinara sauce
1/3 cup chopped fresh basil, divided
1/4 cup heavy whipping cream
1/2 teaspoon kosher salt
1/4 teaspoon black pepper

1. Cook pasta according to package directions. Drain.

2. Heat a large skillet over medium-high heat. Add 1½ teaspoons oil to pan; swirl to coat. Add shrimp; sauté 4 minutes or until done. Remove shrimp from pan.

3. Add remaining 1½ teaspoons oil and garlic to pan; sauté 1 minute. Carefully add vodka; cook 1 minute. Add marinara, ¼ cup basil, cream, salt, and pepper; bring to a simmer. Stir in pasta and shrimp. Sprinkle with remaining basil. Serves 4 (serving size: 1¼ cups).

CALORIES 427; **FAT** 12.6g (sat 4.9g, mono 4.8g, poly 1.4g); **PROTEIN** 24.6g; **CARB** 60.1g; **FIBER** 2.4g; **CHOL** 184mg; **IRON** 2.2mg; **SODIUM** 632mg; **CALC** 65mg

Kid Friendly • Quick & Easy

Pasta Pork Bolognese

Hands-on & total time: 14 min. *Serve with Steamed Sugar Snap Peas, page 84.*

9 ounces refrigerated fettuccine
2 teaspoons olive oil
12 ounces lean ground pork
½ cup grated carrot
3 garlic cloves, minced
⅓ cup red wine
1⅔ cups lower-sodium marinara sauce
½ cup chopped fresh basil, divided
½ teaspoon kosher salt
¼ teaspoon freshly ground black pepper

1. Cook pasta according to package directions. Drain.
2. Heat a large skillet over medium-high heat. Add olive oil to pan; swirl to coat. Add pork, carrot, and garlic; sauté 4 minutes or until pork is done. Add wine; cook 1 minute. Add marinara, ¼ cup basil, salt, and pepper; bring to a simmer. Pour sauce over pasta. Sprinkle with remaining ¼ cup basil. Serves 4 (serving size: 1¼ cups).

CALORIES 412; **FAT** 13.1g (sat 4.6g, mono 5.1g, poly 1g); **PROTEIN** 24.9g; **CARB** 67.6g; **FIBER** 2.1g; **CHOL** 102mg; **IRON** 1.7mg; **SODIUM** 468mg; **CALC** 35mg

Kid Friendly • Quick & Easy

Garlicky Meatball Pasta

(pictured on page 215)

Hands-on & total time: 31 min. *Serve with Avocado–Butter Lettuce Salad, page 83.*

9 ounces refrigerated fettuccine
12 ounces ground sirloin
½ cup panko (Japanese breadcrumbs)
⅓ cup chopped fresh basil
2 garlic cloves, minced
⅜ teaspoon kosher salt
¼ teaspoon freshly ground black pepper
1 large egg, lightly beaten
2 teaspoons olive oil
1¾ cups lower-sodium marinara sauce
1 ounce Parmesan cheese, grated

1. Cook pasta according to package directions. Drain over a bowl, and reserve ⅓ cup pasta water.
2. While pasta cooks, combine beef and next 6 ingredients; shape mixture into 16 meatballs. Heat a large skillet over medium-high heat. Add olive oil to pan; swirl to coat. Add meatballs; cook 5 minutes, browning on all sides. Reduce heat to medium-low. Add marinara and ⅓ cup pasta water. Cover and cook 11 minutes or until meatballs are done. Divide the pasta evenly among 4 plates; top evenly with sauce, meatballs, and cheese. Serves 4.

CALORIES 489; **FAT** 16.6g (sat 6.1g, mono 6.9g, poly 1g); **PROTEIN** 29.1g; **CARB** 71.6g; **FIBER** 2.6g; **CHOL** 147mg; **IRON** 2.4mg; **SODIUM** 688mg; **CALC** 110mg

Quick & Easy • Vegetarian

Ricotta-Spinach Pasta

Hands-on & total time: 18 min. *Serve with Orange and Olive Salad, page 85.*

9 ounces refrigerated fettuccine
⅔ cup whole-milk ricotta cheese
1 teaspoon grated lemon rind
¾ teaspoon kosher salt, divided
½ teaspoon freshly ground black pepper
2 tablespoons olive oil, divided
1½ cups diced red bell pepper
⅓ cup chopped walnuts
4 garlic cloves, thinly sliced
1 tablespoon fresh lemon juice
3 cups fresh baby spinach
Lemon rind strips (optional)

1. Cook pasta according to package directions. Drain in a colander over a bowl; reserve ½ cup pasta water.
2. Combine ricotta, 1 teaspoon rind, ¼ teaspoon salt, and black pepper.
3. Heat a large skillet over medium-high heat. Add 1 tablespoon oil to pan; swirl to coat. Add bell pepper; sauté 2 minutes. Add walnuts, ½ teaspoon salt, and garlic; sauté 2 minutes. Stir in 1 tablespoon oil and juice. Add pasta, pasta water, and spinach; cook 1 minute or until spinach wilts. Top with ricotta mixture and, if desired, rind strips. Serves 4 (serving size: 1 cup).

CALORIES 407; **FAT** 20.5g (sat 5.7g, mono 7.3g, poly 5.5g); **PROTEIN** 14.9g; **CARB** 43.2g; **FIBER** 4.3g; **CHOL** 59mg; **IRON** 2.7mg; **SODIUM** 442mg; **CALC** 134mg

HUMMUS

This dip, the ringer in our shortcut lineup, is far more versatile than you might think. Here, it's a tasty base for a wide range of easy, veggie-packed vegetarian sandwiches made special with the robust flavors of garlic and nutty tahini. And hummus is loaded with protein and fiber. We love Tribe Classic Hummus (and gave it a Taste Test Award in 2010), but use any brand you like.

Quick & Easy • Vegetarian

Open-Faced Hummus Sandwiches

***Hands-on & total time: 18 min.** Serve with Garlicky Asparagus, page 84.*

4 (1¹⁄₂-ounce) slices sourdough bread
1¹⁄₂ cups quartered grape tomatoes
¹⁄₃ cup chopped green onions
¹⁄₄ cup chopped pitted kalamata olives
1 tablespoon olive oil
¹⁄₄ teaspoon freshly ground black
    pepper
¹⁄₈ teaspoon kosher salt
1 garlic clove, minced
1 (8-ounce) container plain hummus
¹⁄₂ cup crumbled goat cheese

1. Preheat broiler.
2. Arrange bread on a baking sheet. Broil 1 minute or until toasted.
3. Combine tomatoes and next 6 ingredients. Spread about ¼ cup hummus over each bread slice. Divide tomato mixture evenly among bread slices. Top each serving with 2 tablespoons cheese. Serves 4 (serving size: 1 sandwich).

CALORIES 358; **FAT** 20.1g (sat 3.1g, mono 11.9g, poly 3.9g); **PROTEIN** 12.3g; **CARB** 36.5g; **FIBER** 4.3g; **CHOL** 7mg; **IRON** 3.5mg; **SODIUM** 811mg; **CALC** 100mg

Quick & Easy • Make Ahead
Vegetarian

Hummus-Stuffed Pitas

***Hands-on & total time: 15 min.** Serve with Steamed Sugar Snap Peas, page 84.*

1 teaspoon grated lemon rind
1 (8-ounce) container plain hummus
4 (6-inch) whole-wheat pitas, halved
4 green leaf lettuce leaves, halved
1¹⁄₄ cups thinly sliced English cucumber
³⁄₄ cup thinly sliced radishes
¹⁄₃ cup thinly sliced red onion
¹⁄₂ cup crumbled feta cheese
Freshly ground black pepper

1. Combine rind and hummus. Divide hummus mixture evenly among 8 pita halves (about 1½ tablespoons each). Divide lettuce, cucumber, radishes, onion, and cheese evenly among pita halves. Sprinkle with pepper. Serves 4 (serving size: 2 pita halves).

CALORIES 344; **FAT** 14.9g (sat 2.4g, mono 7.4g, poly 3.6g); **PROTEIN** 13.1g; **CARB** 47.1g; **FIBER** 7.7g; **CHOL** 13mg; **IRON** 3.9mg; **SODIUM** 758mg; **CALC** 141mg

Quick & Easy • Vegetarian

Grilled Veggie and Hummus Wraps

***Hands-on & total time: 20 min.** Serve with Avocado–Butter Lettuce Salad, page 83.*

4 (¹⁄₂-inch-thick) slices red onion
1 red bell pepper, seeded and
    quartered
1 (12-ounce) eggplant, cut into ¹⁄₂-inch-
    thick slices
2 tablespoons olive oil, divided
¹⁄₄ cup chopped fresh flat-leaf parsley
¹⁄₈ teaspoon kosher salt
1 (8-ounce) container plain hummus
4 (1.9-ounce) whole-grain flatbreads
    (such as Flatout Light)
¹⁄₂ cup crumbled feta cheese

1. Heat a large grill pan over medium-high heat. Brush onion, bell pepper, and eggplant with 1 tablespoon oil. Add onion and bell pepper to pan; cook 3 minutes on each side or until grill marks appear. Remove from pan. Add eggplant to pan; cook 3 minutes on each side or until grill marks appear. Remove from pan; coarsely chop vegetables. Combine vegetables, remaining 1 tablespoon oil, parsley, and salt; toss to combine.
2. Spread ¼ cup hummus over each flatbread, leaving a ½-inch border around edges. Divide vegetables over each flatbread; top each serving with 2 tablespoons cheese. Roll up wraps, and cut diagonally in half. Serves 4 (serving size: 1 wrap).

CALORIES 356; **FAT** 22.7g (sat 3.1g, mono 13.6g, poly 4.4g); **PROTEIN** 16.8g; **CARB** 35.4g; **FIBER** 15.3g; **CHOL** 13mg; **IRON** 3.6mg; **SODIUM** 788mg; **CALC** 156mg

Quick & Easy • Vegetarian

Hummus "Cheesesteak" Hoagies

***Hands-on & total time: 18 min.** Serve with Napa Cabbage Slaw, page 83.*

4 (3-ounce) hoagie rolls, split
1 tablespoon olive oil
1 cup vertically sliced yellow onion
1 cup thinly sliced red bell pepper
1 cup thinly sliced poblano chile
3 garlic cloves, thinly sliced
¹⁄₄ teaspoon crushed red pepper
¹⁄₄ teaspoon black pepper
1 (8-ounce) container plain hummus
4 (¹⁄₂-ounce) slices provolone
    cheese

1. Preheat broiler to high.
2. Hollow out top and bottom halves of bread, leaving a ½-inch-thick shell; reserve torn bread for another use. Place rolls, cut sides up, on a baking sheet. Broil 1 minute or until toasted.

3. Heat a large skillet over medium-high heat. Add oil to pan; swirl to coat. Add onion and next 5 ingredients; sauté 5 minutes or until vegetables are tender.

4. Spread about ¼ cup hummus over bottom half of each roll; top with ½ cup onion mixture and 1 cheese slice. Broil 2 minutes or until cheese melts. Top hoagies with top halves of rolls. Serves 4 (serving size: 1 sandwich).

CALORIES 410; FAT 20.3g (sat 3.3g, mono 12.1g, poly 3.6g); PROTEIN 14.3g; CARB 49.8g; FIBER 4.5g; CHOL 10mg; IRON 3.7mg; SODIUM 807mg; CALC 161mg

PRECOOKED BROWN RICE

We all need to eat more whole grains, but they're not exactly an easy choice for the fast cook; brown rice can take an hour. Until now: Say hello to precooked brown rice, which is cooked and then put into a shelf-stable pouch, with little added (i.e. it's not a sodium bomb).

Kid Friendly • Quick & Easy

Chicken and Broccoli Rice Bowl

Hands-on & total time: 22 min. Serve with Sautéed Butter-Thyme Mushrooms, page 83.

3 cups small broccoli florets
1 (8.8-ounce) pouch precooked brown rice (such as Uncle Ben's)
1 tablespoon olive oil
8 ounces skinless, boneless chicken breast, cut into bite-size pieces
¼ teaspoon kosher salt
¼ teaspoon black pepper
½ cup chopped green onions
3 ounces light processed cheese (such as Velveeta Light), cut into 1-inch pieces
2 tablespoons sliced almonds, toasted

1. Steam broccoli 5 minutes or until crisp-tender.
2. Heat rice according to directions.
3. Heat a large nonstick skillet over medium-high heat. Add oil to pan; swirl to coat. Add chicken; sprinkle with salt and pepper. Cook 4 minutes or until done, stirring occasionally. Add onions and cheese, stirring until cheese begins to melt. Stir in rice; fold in broccoli. Cook 1 minute or until thoroughly heated. Sprinkle with almonds. Serves 3 (serving size: 1 cup).

CALORIES 366; FAT 13g (sat 3.4g, mono 5.6g, poly 2.2g); PROTEIN 28.9g; CARB 33.7g; FIBER 4.5g; CHOL 56mg; IRON 2.1mg; SODIUM 688mg; CALC 229mg

Quick & Easy

Sausage-Spinach Rice Bowl

Hands-on & total time: 10 min. Serve with Garlicky Asparagus, page 84.

1 (8.8-ounce) pouch precooked brown rice (such as Uncle Ben's)
1 tablespoon olive oil
6 ounces hot turkey Italian sausage, casings removed
⅛ teaspoon crushed red pepper
5 garlic cloves, thinly sliced
1 (6-ounce) package fresh baby spinach
1 ounce Parmigiano-Reggiano cheese, shaved (about ¼ cup)

1. Heat rice according to directions.
2. Heat a large skillet over medium-high heat. Add oil to pan; swirl to coat. Add sausage and pepper; cook 4 minutes or until sausage is browned, stirring to crumble. Add garlic; cook 30 seconds, stirring constantly. Add spinach; cook 30 seconds or until spinach begins to wilt, tossing constantly. Stir in rice; cook 1 minute or until heated. Sprinkle with cheese. Serves 3 (serving size: 1 cup).

CALORIES 333; FAT 15.4g (sat 4.3g, mono 7g, poly 3.6g); PROTEIN 17.5g; CARB 33g; FIBER 4g; CHOL 40mg; IRON 3.4mg; SODIUM 610mg; CALC 161mg

Quick & Easy

Shrimp and Pea Rice Bowl

Hands-on & total time: 20 min. Serve with Wheat Rolls with Orange Butter, page 82.

1 (8.8-ounce) pouch precooked brown rice (such as Uncle Ben's)
1 tablespoon olive oil
8 ounces medium shrimp, peeled and deveined
3 garlic cloves, minced
¼ cup water
⅔ cup frozen green peas
1 tablespoon white wine vinegar
¾ teaspoon kosher salt
¼ teaspoon crushed red pepper
¼ teaspoon ground turmeric
2 tablespoons chopped fresh flat-leaf parsley

1. Heat rice according to directions.
2. Heat a large skillet over medium-high heat. Add oil to pan; swirl to coat. Add shrimp; sauté 2 minutes. Add garlic; sauté 1 minute or until shrimp are done. Remove mixture from pan. Add ¼ cup water to pan. Bring water to a simmer. Add peas; cover and cook 2 minutes or until done. Stir in rice, shrimp, vinegar, salt, pepper, and turmeric; cook 1 minute or until heated. Sprinkle with parsley. Serves 3 (serving size: 1 cup).

CALORIES 280; FAT 8.4g (sat 1.2g, mono 4.4g, poly 2g); PROTEIN 20.2g; CARB 30.5g; FIBER 2.8g; CHOL 115mg; IRON 3mg; SODIUM 629mg; CALC 55mg

WE LIKE:

Uncle Ben's Ready Rice, which heats in 90 seconds and contains only 15mg sodium per serving. Other brands, like Minute Rice, have similar products that are also great choices—use 2 cups of the rice for our recipes.

Tex-Mex Rice Bowl

Hands-on & total time: 11 min. *Serve with Avocado–Butter Lettuce Salad, page 83.*

1 (8.8-ounce) pouch precooked brown rice (such as Uncle Ben's)
8 ounces ground sirloin
¼ cup water
1½ tablespoons 40%-less-sodium taco seasoning (such as Ortega)
½ cup frozen whole-kernel corn
1 (15-ounce) can organic black beans, rinsed and drained
1 cup fresh pico de gallo
1 jalapeño pepper, minced
4 teaspoons chopped fresh cilantro

1. Heat rice according to directions.
2. Heat a large skillet over medium-high heat. Add beef; cook 3 minutes or until done, stirring to crumble. Stir in ¼ cup water and taco seasoning; bring to a simmer. Stir in corn and beans; cook 1 minute or until heated. Stir in rice. Top with pico de gallo and jalapeño. Sprinkle with cilantro. Serves 4 (serving size: 1 cup).

CALORIES 306; FAT 7.6g (sat 2.5g, mono 2.5g, poly 0.3g); PROTEIN 18.1g; CARB 44.4g; FIBER 4.3g; CHOL 37mg; IRON 2.7mg; SODIUM 503mg; CALC 28mg

ROTISSERIE CHICKEN

Supermarket rotisserie chicken is a help to the quick cook—a moist, plump, savory bird just waiting for you to pick up and carry home to put in soups, stews, tacos, casseroles. But they're equally handy kept in the fridge for tomorrow's quick salad meals. We spotlight rotisserie chicken in four riffs on chicken salad. Choose your favorite style: creamy, herby, with the tang of vinaigrette, or with the heat of salsa.

Chicken and Green Bean Salad

Hands-on & total time: 20 min. *Crunchy green beans and juicy tomatoes create a beautiful salad. Serve with Roasted Red Potatoes, page 84.*

4 ounces French bread baguette, cut into 12 thin slices
1½ cups trimmed green beans, cut in half
3 tablespoons extra-virgin olive oil
1½ tablespoons fresh lemon juice
1½ tablespoons whole-grain Dijon mustard
1 teaspoon chopped fresh thyme
¼ teaspoon kosher salt
¼ teaspoon freshly ground black pepper
2 cups shredded skinless, boneless rotisserie chicken (white and dark meat)
1 cup halved cherry tomatoes

1. Preheat broiler.
2. Arrange bread in a single layer on a baking sheet. Broil 1 minute or until toasted.
3. Steam green beans 3 minutes or until crisp-tender. Drain and rinse with cold water; drain.
4. Combine oil and next 5 ingredients in a medium bowl, stirring with a whisk. Add chicken, beans, and tomatoes; toss to combine. Serve with toast. Serves 4 (serving size: 1 cup salad and 3 toasts).

CALORIES 286; FAT 14.3g (sat 2.5g, mono 9.2g, poly 1.7g); PROTEIN 18.4g; CARB 22.6g; FIBER 2.5g; CHOL 62mg; IRON 1.7mg; SODIUM 633mg; CALC 33mg

WHAT TO BUY

Plain or classic flavor, because stronger seasonings will unbalance these recipes.

Avocado Chicken Salad

Hands-on & total time: 16 min. *Tortilla chips are fun scoopers. Serve with Garlicky Asparagus, page 84.*

2 tablespoons olive oil
2 tablespoons fresh lime juice
⅜ teaspoon kosher salt
⅛ teaspoon freshly ground black pepper
2 cups shredded skinless, boneless rotisserie chicken breast
¼ cup chopped fresh cilantro
¾ cup refrigerated fresh salsa
1 ripe avocado, peeled and chopped
3 ounces tortilla chips

1. Combine first 4 ingredients in a medium bowl, stirring with a whisk. Add chicken and cilantro; toss to combine. Gently fold in salsa and avocado. Serve with chips. Serves 4 (serving size: 1 cup salad and about ½ cup chips).

CALORIES 345; FAT 21.1g (sat 3.1g, mono 12.1g, poly 4.5g); PROTEIN 19.2g; CARB 20.4g; FIBER 4.5g; CHOL 50mg; IRON 1.1mg; SODIUM 579mg; CALC 52mg

Tzatziki Chicken Salad

Hands-on & total time: 16 min. *We made a classic Greek sauce of creamy yogurt and cucumber for the base of this tangy salad. Serve with Mixed Greens Salad, page 82.*

⅔ cup plain 2% reduced-fat Greek yogurt
¼ cup finely chopped red onion
1 tablespoon fresh lemon juice
2 teaspoons chopped fresh dill
⅜ teaspoon kosher salt
¼ teaspoon freshly ground black pepper

1 cucumber, seeded and shredded
1 garlic clove, minced
2 cups shredded skinless, boneless
   rotisserie chicken breast
3 ounces multigrain pita chips

1. Combine first 8 ingredients in a medium bowl, stirring with a whisk. Add chicken; toss to coat. Serve with pita chips. Serves 4 (serving size: about ⅔ cup salad and ½ cup chips).

CALORIES 230; FAT 7.5g (sat 1.5g, mono 1.4g, poly 2.1g); PROTEIN 23g; CARB 18.7g; FIBER 2.1g; CHOL 53mg; IRON 1mg; SODIUM 569mg; CALC 60mg

---

Quick & Easy • Make Ahead

Creamy Tarragon Chicken Salad

Hands-on & total time: 11 min. *A combo of yogurt and mayo gives a traditional chicken salad more zip. We like the richness of white and dark meat, but you can use all one type. Serve with Steamed Sugar Snap Peas, page 84.*

⅓ cup plain 2% reduced-fat Greek
   yogurt
¼ cup canola mayonnaise
1 tablespoon chopped fresh tarragon
¼ teaspoon kosher salt
¼ teaspoon freshly ground black
   pepper
2 cups shredded skinless, boneless
   rotisserie chicken (white and dark
   meat)
¼ cup thinly sliced red onion
3 ounces whole-grain crackers

1. Combine first 5 ingredients in a medium bowl, stirring with a whisk. Add chicken and onion; toss to combine. Serve with crackers. Serves 4 (serving size: ½ cup salad and ½ cup crackers).

CALORIES 319; FAT 19.7g (sat 3.1g, mono 9.2g, poly 5.2g); PROTEIN 19.2g; CARB 16.1g; FIBER 0.8g; CHOL 68mg; IRON 1.2mg; SODIUM 612mg; CALC 46mg

---

LESS MEAT, MORE FLAVOR

SWEET GRAPES, SAVORY DISHES

By Mark Bittman

How to deploy this rarely cooked fruit in healthy main courses

When you reach into your savory-recipe arsenal, I'm guessing that you don't often come up with a plan to deploy grapes. Grapes are for wine and juice, jelly and jam, fruit salad and pie, but not for pasta, stir-fry, or roast chicken. This should change—and we'll all be happier cooks when it does. Grapes can be a great addition to savory dishes, familiar and exotic alike.

So, red or green? This is in part a decision about which color will look best in your dish. It's also a choice between slightly sweeter red grapes and more tart green. No need to agonize over this one. A much more important decision is whether to cook the grapes for a while or leave them a little closer to raw. Mostly raw grapes will give you exactly what you think they will: a plump, firm texture, sweetness with a hint of sour, and that unmistakable burst of juice. Cooking grapes (dry cooking, that is, like roasting) softens them up, begins to dry them out—or turn them into raisins if you wait long enough—and concentrates their sweetness.

Grapes fit seamlessly into Moroccan food, which, with its warm, cinnamon-laced spiced blends, already tends toward the sweet. Wherever you see a raisin—which you do often in Moroccan cuisine—you can probably use a grape. In the recipe on page 96, I send red grapes down the path to raisin-dom but stop them wonderfully short. I put a few cups on a baking sheet, toss them with salt, pepper, and oil, and roast them at high heat until beautifully charred and slightly shriveled but still holding on to some juice. A spice rub of cumin, coriander, cinnamon, and red pepper goes on bone-in chicken thighs, which roast atop carrots and onion until the chicken skin is irresistibly crisp. I combine the chicken, vegetables, and grapes, and sprinkle with chopped parsley to add a burst of freshness. Served over bulgur, this is hard to beat.

The other dish features a classic Italian combination that you may not have heard of before: grapes and sausage. I brown chunks of hot or sweet Italian sausage, and then stir in halved green grapes just long enough to coat them in the rendered fat and soften them slightly. I remove the grapes and sausage and cook thinly sliced red onion and garlic before piling in chopped broccoli rabe and steaming it with a little white wine. I mix everything back together with a touch of vinegar and finish it off with a dusting of Parmesan cheese. The green grapes retain much of their refreshing juice but develop enough sweetness—along with the red onions—to balance the trademark bitterness of the broccoli rabe. The wine and vinegar add a hint of acid to go along with the grapes, while the sausage and Parmesan provide a fatty richness that pulls everything together.

Where else can grapes work? Scattered into Asian stir-fries; tossed with pasta, Parmesan, and pine nuts; added to almost any vegetable, grain, or chicken salad (a classic); or simply roasted alongside whole chicken or pork loin. Try doing that with jelly.

continued

Sautéed Sausage and Grapes with Broccoli Rabe

Hands-on time: 38 min. Total time: 38 min. *This is a classic Italian combo—grapes and sausage—paired with pleasantly bitter broccoli rabe to balance the sweetness.*

- **1 pound broccoli rabe, trimmed and coarsely chopped**
- **2 tablespoons olive oil, divided**
- **2 (4-ounce) links hot or sweet pork Italian sausage, casings removed**
- **3 cups green grapes, sliced in half lengthwise**
- **¼ teaspoon kosher salt, divided**
- **¼ teaspoon freshly ground black pepper, divided**
- **1 cup thinly sliced red onion**
- **1 tablespoon minced garlic**
- **¼ cup white wine or water**
- **1 teaspoon red wine vinegar**
- **1 ounce Parmesan cheese, shaved (about ¼ cup)**

1. Cook broccoli rabe in boiling water 1½ minutes; drain and rinse with cold water. Drain well. Place in a large bowl. Set aside.
2. Heat a large skillet over medium-high heat. Add 1 tablespoon olive oil to pan; swirl to coat. Add sausage; cook 6 minutes or until browned, stirring to crumble. Add grapes, ⅛ teaspoon salt, and ⅛ teaspoon pepper; cook 2 minutes or until grapes begin to soften. Add sausage mixture to broccoli rabe.
3. Return pan to medium-high heat. Add remaining 1 tablespoon oil to pan; swirl to coat. Add onion; cook 2 minutes or until soft. Add garlic; cook 30 seconds or until fragrant. Add wine; cook 2 minutes or until liquid almost evaporates. Add remaining ⅛ teaspoon salt, remaining ⅛ teaspoon pepper, sausage mixture, and vinegar. Toss to combine; cook 1 minute or until thoroughly heated. Sprinkle with cheese; serve immediately. Serves 4 (serving size: 1¾ cups).

CALORIES 310; **FAT** 16.7g (sat 4.9g, mono 8.9g, poly 1.8g); **PROTEIN** 13.3g; **CARB** 29.9g; **FIBER** 1.4g; **CHOL** 21mg; **IRON** 2.1mg; **SODIUM** 621mg; **CALC** 164mg

Roasted Moroccan-Spiced Grapes and Chicken

Hands-on time: 32 min. Total time: 52 min. *Though we usually call for removing skin from dark-meat chicken, here it stays on for delicious flavor, crispy texture, and extra richness. The serving size is small, so saturated fat isn't a problem. The grapes will collapse soon after they come out of the oven, so serve right away.*

- **1½ cups sliced yellow onion**
- **4 large carrots, quartered lengthwise and cut into ½-inch pieces (about 3 cups)**
- **5 teaspoons olive oil, divided**
- **¾ teaspoon kosher salt, divided**
- **½ teaspoon freshly ground black pepper, divided**
- **½ teaspoon ground cumin**
- **½ teaspoon ground coriander**
- **¼ teaspoon ground cinnamon**
- **⅛ teaspoon ground red pepper**
- **4 bone-in, skin-on chicken thighs, trimmed (about 1½ pounds)**
- **3 cups seedless red grapes**
- **¼ cup picholine olives, pitted**
- **2 tablespoons chopped fresh flat-leaf parsley**

1. Place 2 jelly-roll pans in oven. Preheat oven to 450°.
2. Combine onion, carrot, and 1 tablespoon oil in a bowl; toss well. Arrange carrot mixture on 1 preheated pan; sprinkle with ¼ teaspoon salt. Bake at 450° for 10 minutes.
3. Combine ⅜ teaspoon salt, ¼ teaspoon black pepper, and next 4 ingredients in a small bowl. Sprinkle chicken evenly with spice mixture. Heat a small skillet over medium-high heat. Add 1 teaspoon oil to pan; swirl to coat. Add chicken to pan, skin side down; cook 5 minutes or until browned and skin is crisp. Remove chicken from pan. Add chicken to vegetable mixture, skin side up. Bake at 450° for 20 minutes or until chicken is done and vegetables are tender.
4. Combine remaining 1 teaspoon oil, grapes, remaining ⅛ teaspoon salt, remaining ¼ teaspoon black pepper, and olives in a medium bowl; toss well. Place grape mixture on remaining preheated jelly-roll pan. Bake at 450° for 15 minutes or until grapes are charred and beginning to soften, stirring occasionally. Place ½ cup vegetable mixture and ½ cup grape mixture on each of 4 plates. Top each serving with 1 chicken thigh. Sprinkle with parsley. Serve immediately. Serves 4.

CALORIES 406; **FAT** 23.3g (sat 5.4g, mono 12.4g, poly 4.3g); **PROTEIN** 18.6g; **CARB** 33g; **FIBER** 4.2g; **CHOL** 79mg; **IRON** 2.1mg; **SODIUM** 661mg; **CALC** 68mg

CIAO DOWN!

A quick vegetarian tour of the Italian boot brings home the flavors of baked eggplant; a rustic savory pie; and a thin, crispy chickpea cake.

Vegetarian • Make Ahead

Pizza Rustica

Hands-on time: 40 min. Total time: 2 hr. 30 min. A time-worthy Italian treasure, this savory pie is tasty both warm and at room temperature.

Crust:
7.75 ounces all-purpose flour (about 1³⁄₄ cups), divided
¹⁄₂ teaspoon salt
¹⁄₂ teaspoon baking powder
¹⁄₃ cup extra-virgin olive oil
¹⁄₄ cup water
Torta:
2 medium-sized red bell peppers
2 tablespoons extra-virgin olive oil, divided
1 pound Swiss chard, trimmed and thinly sliced
2 tablespoons chopped shallots
2 teaspoons minced garlic
2 (8-ounce) packages cremini mushrooms, sliced
8 ounces part-skim ricotta cheese
2 ounces fontina cheese, shredded (about ¹⁄₂ cup)
1 ounce Parmigiano-Reggiano cheese, grated (about ¹⁄₄ cup)
1 tablespoon chopped fresh thyme
¹⁄₂ teaspoon kosher salt
¹⁄₄ teaspoon freshly ground black pepper
2 large eggs, lightly beaten
1 large egg white
Cooking spray
1 tablespoon fat-free milk

1. To prepare crust, weigh or lightly spoon 7.25 ounces flour (about 1²⁄₃ cups) into dry measuring cups; level with a knife. Place 7.25 ounces flour, ¹⁄₂ teaspoon salt, and baking powder in a food processor; pulse 2 times to combine. Combine ¹⁄₃ cup olive oil and ¹⁄₄ cup water in a small bowl. With processor on, slowly add oil mixture through food chute, and process just until dough begins to form a ball (dough will be crumbly). Turn dough out onto a lightly floured surface. Knead 3 minutes; add enough of the remaining 2 tablespoons flour to prevent dough from sticking to hands. Divide dough into 2 equal portions. Press each portion into a 5-inch circle on plastic wrap. Cover with additional plastic wrap. Chill at least 30 minutes.
2. To prepare torta, preheat broiler to high.
3. Cut bell peppers in half lengthwise; discard seeds and membranes. Place pepper halves, skin sides up, on a foil-lined baking sheet; flatten with hand. Broil 10 minutes or until blackened. Place in a paper bag; fold to close tightly. Let stand 10 minutes. Peel and coarsely chop.
4. Heat a large nonstick skillet over medium heat. Add 1 tablespoon oil; swirl to coat. Add chard to pan; cook 1 minute or until greens begin to wilt. Place chard and bell peppers in a large bowl. Return pan to medium heat. Add remaining 1 tablespoon oil to pan; swirl to coat. Add shallots and garlic to pan; cook 1 minute. Add mushrooms; cook 5 minutes, stirring occasionally. Place mushroom mixture and chard mixture in a fine sieve; let drain 5 minutes. Place vegetable mixture in a large bowl. Add ricotta and next 7 ingredients to vegetable mixture, stirring to combine.
5. Preheat oven to 375°.
6. Slightly overlap 2 sheets of plastic wrap on a slightly damp surface. Unwrap one dough portion, and place on plastic wrap. Cover dough with 2 additional sheets of overlapping plastic wrap. Roll dough, still covered, into an 11-inch circle. Place dough in freezer 5 minutes or until plastic wrap can be easily removed. Remove top sheets of plastic wrap; fit dough, plastic wrap side up, into a 9-inch pie plate coated with cooking spray. Remove remaining plastic wrap. Spoon vegetable mixture into prepared pie plate.
7. Slightly overlap 2 sheets of plastic wrap on a slightly damp surface. Unwrap remaining dough portion, and place on plastic wrap. Cover dough with 2 additional sheets of overlapping plastic wrap. Roll dough, still covered, into an 11-inch circle. Place dough in freezer 5 minutes or until plastic wrap can be easily removed. Remove top sheets of plastic wrap; fit dough, plastic wrap side up, over vegetable mixture. Remove remaining plastic wrap. Press edges of dough together. Fold edges under, and flute. Brush top of dough with milk. Cut several slits in top of dough to allow steam to escape.
8. Bake at 375° for 45 minutes or until crust is golden brown. Cool 30 minutes. Cut into 8 wedges. Serves 8 (serving size: 1 wedge).

CALORIES 348; **FAT** 19.8g (sat 5.6g, mono 11.1g, poly 2g); **PROTEIN** 14.5g; **CARB** 29.4g; **FIBER** 2.9g; **CHOL** 73mg; **IRON** 3.3mg; **SODIUM** 589mg; **CALC** 220mg

DOUGH TRICK

For fast pizzas, we like to use refrigerated dough from our grocer's bakery section, and let it stand at room temperature for 15 minutes to make it easier to roll. But when there isn't time to spare, try this trick: Put the dough in a bowl, and microwave at HIGH for 30 seconds or at 50% power for 45 seconds. If the dough shrinks or snaps back as you roll it out, let it rest for several minutes—the gluten will relax, letting it stretch to the desired size.

Eggplant Involtini

Hands-on time: 1 hr. 8 min. Total time: 1 hr. 33 min.

1 tablespoon extra-virgin olive oil
2 pounds tomatoes, seeded and coarsely chopped (about 3 large)
$\frac{1}{2}$ teaspoon kosher salt, divided
4 garlic cloves, crushed and divided
12 ($\frac{1}{4}$-inch-thick) lengthwise slices eggplant (about 2 medium)
$\frac{1}{4}$ teaspoon black pepper
Cooking spray
2 tablespoons pine nuts, lightly toasted
1 ounce whole-wheat French bread, toasted and torn into pieces
8 ounces part-skim ricotta cheese
1 teaspoon grated lemon rind
1 large egg
$\frac{3}{4}$ cup chopped fresh basil leaves, divided
2 ounces Parmigiano-Reggiano cheese, grated (about $\frac{1}{2}$ cup) and divided

1. Combine oil and tomatoes in a medium saucepan; stir in $\frac{1}{4}$ teaspoon salt and 2 garlic cloves. Bring to a boil over medium-high heat; reduce heat, and simmer 15 minutes or until reduced to 2 cups. Cool 10 minutes. Place mixture in a food processor; process until smooth. Set aside.
2. Preheat broiler to high.
3. Sprinkle eggplant slices evenly with remaining $\frac{1}{4}$ teaspoon salt and pepper; arrange slices in a single layer on a foil-lined baking sheet. Lightly coat eggplant with cooking spray. Broil 4 minutes on each side or until lightly browned. Cool 10 minutes.
4. Preheat oven to 375°.
5. Place remaining 2 garlic cloves in a mini food processor; pulse until chopped. Add nuts and bread; pulse 10 times or until coarse crumbs form. Add ricotta, rind, and egg; process until smooth. Stir in $\frac{1}{2}$ cup basil and $\frac{1}{4}$ cup Parmigiano-Reggiano.
6. Spread $1\frac{1}{2}$ cups tomato sauce over bottom of an 8-inch square glass or ceramic baking dish coated with cooking spray. Spread 2 tablespoons ricotta mixture onto each eggplant slice; roll up jelly-roll fashion. Place rolls, seam sides down, over sauce in dish. Spoon remaining sauce over rolls. Sprinkle with remaining $\frac{1}{4}$ cup Parmigiano-Reggiano. Bake at 375° for 25 minutes or until bubbly. Sprinkle with remaining basil. Serves 4 (serving size: 3 eggplant rolls).

CALORIES 323; **FAT** 16.2g (sat 6g, mono 5.2g, poly 2.6g); **PROTEIN** 18.3g; **CARB** 32.3g; **FIBER** 12.4g; **CHOL** 79mg; **IRON** 2.3mg; **SODIUM** 442mg; **CALC** 374mg

Asparagus, Tomato, and Onion Farinata

Hands-on time: 42 min. Total time: 1 hr. 22 min.

1 pint cherry tomatoes, halved
4 tablespoons olive oil, divided
$2\frac{1}{4}$ teaspoons chopped fresh rosemary, divided
$\frac{3}{8}$ teaspoon freshly ground black pepper, divided
3.18 ounces chickpea (garbanzo bean) flour (about $\frac{3}{4}$ cup)
1 cup water
$\frac{1}{2}$ teaspoon salt
$2\frac{1}{2}$ cups thinly vertically sliced yellow onion
$\frac{1}{8}$ teaspoon crushed red pepper
3 garlic cloves, chopped
1 cup (1-inch) slices asparagus
2 tablespoons shaved pecorino Romano cheese
1 teaspoon fresh lemon juice
2 teaspoons balsamic vinegar
4 cups baby arugula
3 tablespoons pine nuts, toasted

1. Preheat oven to 450°.
2. Combine tomatoes, $1\frac{1}{2}$ teaspoons oil, $\frac{1}{4}$ teaspoon rosemary, and $\frac{1}{8}$ teaspoon black pepper in a small bowl, tossing to coat. Arrange tomatoes in a single layer on a jelly-roll pan; bake at 450° for 20 minutes, stirring once. Cool slightly.
3. Weigh or lightly spoon flour into dry measuring cups; level with a knife. Combine flour, 1 cup water, 1 tablespoon olive oil, remaining 2 teaspoons rosemary, salt, and remaining $\frac{1}{4}$ teaspoon black pepper in a large bowl, stirring with a whisk until smooth. Let stand 30 minutes.
4. Place a 10-inch cast-iron skillet in oven.
5. Heat a large skillet over medium-high heat. Add $1\frac{1}{2}$ teaspoons olive oil; swirl to coat. Add onion; cover and cook 8 minutes or until tender, stirring occasionally. Stir in $\frac{1}{8}$ teaspoon red pepper and garlic. Cook, uncovered, 18 minutes or until onions are golden, stirring frequently. Remove from heat; stir in asparagus.
6. Carefully remove cast-iron skillet from oven. Add 1 tablespoon oil; swirl to coat. Stir batter once; pour batter into skillet. Bake at 450° for 20 minutes. Top evenly with onion mixture and tomatoes; sprinkle evenly with cheese. Bake 12 minutes or until center of dough is set. Remove from oven; let stand 10 minutes. Cut into 4 wedges.
7. Combine remaining 1 tablespoon oil, juice, and vinegar in a medium bowl, stirring with a whisk. Add arugula; toss to coat. Arrange 1 cup arugula on each of 4 plates; sprinkle each serving with about 2 teaspoons nuts. Serve with 1 wedge farinata. Serves 4.

CALORIES 321; **FAT** 20.5g (sat 2.9g, mono 11.7g, poly 4.5g); **PROTEIN** 9.8g; **CARB** 27.2g; **FIBER** 6g; **CHOL** 2mg; **IRON** 3.1mg; **SODIUM** 358mg; **CALC** 110mg

FEED 4 FOR LESS THAN $10

Mighty pleasing weeknight dinners: cheesy pasta with bacon, flatbread topped with prosciutto, and chile-spiked pork

Kid Friendly • Quick & Easy

$0.94/serving, $3.75 for four

Bacon and Broccoli Mac and Cheese

Hands-on time: 12 min. Total time: 36 min. *This one-dish meal will win over adults and children alike. Substitute English peas or fresh spinach for the broccoli, if you prefer.*

3 cups broccoli florets
8 ounces uncooked rigatoni
1 tablespoon butter
1¹/₂ tablespoons all-purpose flour
1¹/₄ cups 2% reduced-fat milk
2 ounces reduced-fat processed American cheese, cut into pieces
¹/₄ cup thinly sliced green onions
¹/₂ teaspoon salt
¹/₄ teaspoon freshly ground black pepper
2 center-cut bacon slices, cooked and crumbled
2 ounces extra-sharp cheddar cheese, shredded (about ¹/₂ cup packed)

1. Steam broccoli 5 minutes or until crisp-tender; drain. Pat dry, and keep warm. Cook pasta in boiling water in a large saucepan 8 minutes or until al dente; drain and keep warm. Wipe pan with paper towels, and return to medium heat. Melt butter in pan. Sprinkle flour over melted butter; cook 1 minute, stirring constantly with a whisk. Gradually add milk to flour mixture in pan, and bring to a boil, stirring constantly with a whisk. Cook 1 minute or until slightly thick, and remove from heat. Add American cheese; stir until smooth. Stir in sliced green onions and remaining ingredients. Stir in broccoli and pasta; serve immediately. Serves 4 (serving size: 1¹/₂ cups).

CALORIES 413; **FAT** 13.3g (sat 7.5g, mono 3.4g, poly 0.9g); **PROTEIN** 19.6g; **CARB** 53.4g; **FIBER** 3.8g; **CHOL** 39mg; **IRON** 2.8mg; **SODIUM** 772mg; **CALC** 317mg

$1.95/serving, $7.81 for four

Prosciutto and Cheese Tartine

Hands-on time: 36 min. Total time: 2 hr. 11 min. *Although the name tartine often refers to a French open-faced sandwich, this version is closer to Italian focaccia topped with piquant salad. Because it's inexpensive to make your own flatbread, you can splurge on real Italian Parmigiano-Reggiano, which makes a huge difference in a simple recipe like this one. You'll also have room in the budget for 2 ounces thinly sliced prosciutto for a salty, savory note.*

¹/₂ cup warm water (100° to 110°)
1 teaspoon sugar
1 package dry yeast
5.6 ounces all-purpose flour (about 1¹/₄ cups)
3 tablespoons olive oil, divided
⁵/₈ teaspoon kosher salt, divided
¹/₄ teaspoon freshly ground black pepper
Cooking spray
¹/₂ cup coarsely chopped walnuts
¹/₃ cup very thinly sliced red onion
1 teaspoon chopped fresh thyme
2 cups arugula
1 teaspoon fresh lemon juice
2 ounces thinly sliced imported prosciutto
1 ounce fresh Parmigiano-Reggiano cheese, shaved

1. Preheat oven to 450°.
2. Combine first 3 ingredients in a medium bowl, and let stand 5 minutes or until bubbly. Weigh or lightly spoon 5.6 ounces flour (about 1¹/₄ cups) into dry measuring cups, and level with a knife. Stir 4 teaspoons olive oil into yeast mixture. Add flour, ¹/₄ teaspoon salt, and ¹/₄ teaspoon black pepper to yeast mixture, stirring until a soft dough forms. Knead dough on a lightly floured surface until smooth and elastic (dough will be soft and tacky).
3. Place dough in a large bowl coated with cooking spray, turning to coat top. Cover and let rise in a warm place (85°), free from drafts, 45 minutes or until doubled in size. Punch dough down; cover and let rest 5 minutes.
4. Drizzle 2 teaspoons oil into an 11 x 7–inch glass or ceramic baking dish. Press dough into dish. Cover loosely with plastic wrap, and let rise in a warm place (85°), free from drafts, 30 minutes or until puffy; sprinkle dough with ¹/₄ teaspoon salt, nuts, onion, and thyme. Bake at 450° for 18 minutes or until golden.
5. Place arugula in a bowl; drizzle with remaining 1 tablespoon oil and juice. Toss. Turn bread out onto a work surface; top evenly with prosciutto. Slice bread into 4 (2³/₄ x 7–inch) rectangles. Top each serving with about ¹/₂ cup arugula mixture; sprinkle evenly with remaining ¹/₈ teaspoon salt. Top with cheese. Serves 4.

CALORIES 408; **FAT** 23.9g (sat 4.1g, mono 9.4g, poly 8.3g); **PROTEIN** 14.2g; **CARB** 36.3g; **FIBER** 2.8g; **CHOL** 17mg; **IRON** 3.1mg; **SODIUM** 793mg; **CALC** 120mg

Make Ahead

Chipotle Pork

$2.37/serving, $9.49 for four

Hands-on time: 31 min. Total time: 4 hr. 1 min. *Serve with rice and a salad of torn romaine, orange segments, and avocado dressed with olive oil and the juices you capture from the oranges as you cut the sections.*

1/2 cup chopped onion
1 1/2 tablespoons honey
1 teaspoon ground cumin
1/8 teaspoon ground cinnamon
9 large garlic cloves, peeled
3 chipotle chiles, canned in adobo sauce
1 lime
2 tablespoons olive oil, divided
1 (1 1/4-pound) boneless pork shoulder (Boston butt), trimmed
3/4 teaspoon kosher salt
1/2 cup fat-free, lower-sodium chicken broth

1. Place first 6 ingredients in a food processor; pulse until finely chopped. Peel and section lime over a bowl, catching juices; discard peel. Add lime juice, lime sections, and 1 tablespoon olive oil to food processor; process until smooth. Scrape chipotle mixture into a zip-top plastic bag. Add pork; seal. Marinate in refrigerator 1 hour.
2. Preheat oven to 325°.
3. Heat a small Dutch oven over medium-high heat. Add remaining 1 tablespoon oil to pan; swirl. Remove pork from bag; reserve marinade. Sprinkle pork with salt. Add pork to pan; sauté 8 minutes, browning on all sides. Remove pork from pan. Add broth and reserved marinade to pan; bring to a boil, scraping pan to loosen browned bits. Return pork to pan; cover and bake at 325° for 2 1/2 hours or until pork is fork-tender. Shred pork; toss with sauce. Serves 4 (serving size: 3 ounces pork and about 2 tablespoons sauce).

CALORIES 344; **FAT** 22.1g (sat 6.6g, mono 11.7g, poly 2.5g); **PROTEIN** 22.3g; **CARB** 14.1g; **FIBER** 2.3g; **CHOL** 83mg; **IRON** 2.1mg; **SODIUM** 591mg; **CALC** 45mg

KID-FRIENDLY COOKING

A KID IN THE KITCHEN

This month, 11-year-old Matisse Reid serves up spaghetti squash to her two toughest critics.

To field-test one of our kid-friendly recipes, I once again turned to the food-savviest kid I know, Matisse Reid, who loves simply cooked squid and the briny taste of olives. Her assignment: make spaghetti squash and see how other kids like it. Here's her report.
–Ann Taylor Pittman

"I made Spaghetti Squash with Tomato-Basil Sauce. The recipe was supereasy, and I was able to cook the squash while I did my homework (which was not fun)! I expected the squash to be more spaghetti-like, but at first mine turned into mash. That wasn't a bad thing, but now I know how to make the spaghetti strands properly. I did like scraping the squash pulp with a fork, and it was so easy even my little brother could do it. For the sauce, I cheated and used one can of pureed tomatoes with one can of diced—hey, a girl as busy as I am needs to cut corners, and I like a smooth sauce. The sauce was pretty tart; I would probably add a little sugar next time. I plated the spaghetti squash, poured over the sauce, and presented it to two of my biggest critics—MY BROTHERS!!!"

Kid Friendly • Vegetarian

Spaghetti Squash with Tomato-Basil Sauce

Hands-on time: 25 min. Total time: 1 hr. 30 min. *Parents may need to help out a bit by cutting the hard squash in half, but kids can have fun scraping up strands of spaghetti-like pulp. You can serve this as a side dish, or add sausage or ground beef to the sauce to turn it into an entrée.*

1 (3-pound) spaghetti squash
Cooking spray
1 tablespoon olive oil
2 garlic cloves, minced
1 (14.5-ounce) can no-salt-added diced tomatoes
1 (14.5-ounce) can diced tomatoes
1/2 cup chopped fresh basil, divided
6 tablespoons shredded fresh pecorino Romano cheese

1. Preheat oven to 350°.
2. Cut squash in half lengthwise. Scoop out seeds; discard. Place squash halves, cut sides down, on a baking sheet coated with cooking spray. Bake at 350° for 1 hour or until tender.
3. Heat a medium saucepan over medium heat. Add oil to pan; swirl to coat. Add garlic; cook 3 minutes, stirring occasionally. Add tomatoes;

bring to a simmer. Cook 15 minutes or until thickened. Remove from heat; stir in ⅓ cup basil.

4. Cool squash at room temperature 10 minutes or until cool enough to handle. Scrape inside of squash with a fork to remove spaghetti-like strands to measure about 5 cups. Divide squash evenly among 6 plates, and top each serving with about ⅓ cup sauce and 1 tablespoon cheese. Top with remaining basil. Serves 6.

CALORIES 133; FAT 4.6g (sat 1.8g, mono 1.7g, poly 0.6g); PROTEIN 4.3g; CARB 19.2g; FIBER 3.8g; CHOL 4mg; IRON 1.5mg; SODIUM 311mg; CALC 158mg

MATISSE SAYS, "TO GET STRANDS (NOT MASH), USE A FORK TO SCRAPE AROUND THE OUTSIDE OF THE SQUASH AND PULL FROM THE SIDES INTO THE CENTER."

"BE CAREFUL WHEN ADDING TOMATOES TO THE PAN AFTER COOKING GARLIC, AS THE OIL FROM THE GARLIC MIGHT SPIT."

SUPERFAST

A weekday dinner gets very easy and very tasty with this standout salad. Kids will like our beefy mac and cheese. See other fast-cooking recipes starting on page 77.

Quick & Easy

Chicken and Prosciutto Salad with Arugula and Asiago

(pictured on page 214)

2 (1-ounce) slices sourdough bread, cut into ½-inch cubes
Cooking spray
½ teaspoon dried basil
⅛ teaspoon garlic powder
3 tablespoons extra-virgin olive oil, divided
2 ounces very thin slices prosciutto, chopped
2 tablespoons fresh lemon juice
¼ teaspoon salt
2 (5-ounce) packages baby arugula
1½ ounces Asiago cheese, shaved and divided (about ⅓ cup)
6 ounces shredded skinless, boneless rotisserie chicken breast
1 cup grape tomatoes, halved

1. Preheat oven to 425°.
2. Place bread cubes on a baking sheet, and lightly coat with cooking spray. Add basil and garlic powder; toss well. Place bread mixture in preheating oven; bake for 8 minutes or until crisp.
3. Heat a large nonstick skillet over medium-high heat. Add 1 teaspoon oil to pan; swirl to coat. Add prosciutto; sauté 4 minutes or until prosciutto is crisp. Drain on paper towels.
4. Combine remaining 2 tablespoons plus 2 teaspoons oil, juice, and salt in a small bowl; stir well with a whisk. Place arugula, half of cheese, and juice mixture in a large bowl; toss well to coat. Divide arugula mixture evenly among 6 plates; divide chicken, prosciutto, tomatoes, remaining cheese, and croutons evenly over salads. Serves 6 (serving size: about 2 cups).

CALORIES 193; FAT 11.5g (sat 2.9g, mono 5.8g, poly 1.3g); PROTEIN 14.4g; CARB 8.9g; FIBER 1.5g; CHOL 37mg; IRON 1.4mg; SODIUM 481mg; CALC 142mg

Kid Friendly • Quick & Easy

Chili-Cheese Mac

1 teaspoon canola oil
¾ pound ground round
1 teaspoon garlic powder
1 teaspoon ground coriander
1 teaspoon ground cumin
2 teaspoons chili powder
2 cups fat-free, lower-sodium beef broth
1 cup water
1 (10-ounce) can mild diced tomatoes and green chiles, undrained
8 ounces uncooked elbow macaroni
½ cup fat-free milk
4 ounces ⅓-less-fat cream cheese
4½ ounces finely shredded reduced-fat sharp cheddar cheese

1. Heat a Dutch oven over medium-high heat. Add oil to pan; swirl to coat. Add beef and next 4 ingredients; cook 3 minutes. Add broth, water, and tomatoes; bring to a boil. Stir in macaroni; cover and cook 10 minutes or until macaroni is done.
2. Heat milk and cream cheese in a saucepan over medium heat. Cook 4 minutes or until cheese melts, stirring frequently. Remove from heat. Stir in cheddar. Add cheese sauce to macaroni mixture; toss well to coat. Serves 6 (serving size: 1 cup).

CALORIES 342; FAT 12.3g (sat 6g, mono 3.7g, poly 1.1g); PROTEIN 25.7g; CARB 32.7g; FIBER 1.8g; CHOL 60mg; IRON 2.3mg; SODIUM 652mg; CALC 363mg

Creamy Ranch-Style Dip

Serve this dip with baby carrots, broccoli florets, or other fresh vegetables.

4 ounces 1/3-less-fat cream cheese, softened
3 tablespoons nonfat buttermilk
2 tablespoons chopped fresh flat-leaf parsley
1 teaspoon chopped fresh dill
1/2 teaspoon minced garlic
1/4 teaspoon onion powder
1/4 teaspoon salt
1/4 teaspoon freshly ground black pepper

1. Combine cream cheese and buttermilk in a small bowl, stirring with a whisk until blended. Stir in remaining ingredients. Serves 6 (serving size: about 2 tablespoons).

CALORIES 52; FAT 4.3g (sat 2.4g, mono 1.1g, poly 0.2g); PROTEIN 2.1g; CARB 1.4g; FIBER 0.1g; CHOL 14mg; IRON 0.1mg; SODIUM 170mg; CALC 34mg

WHAT TO EAT RIGHT NOW

RHUBARB

Rhubarb appears like celery's wilder cousin, stalking the land briefly and throwing a jolt of electric acidity to any dish it graces. These days, hothouse rhubarb is available year-round, but now's the time for the fresh, field-grown stuff, which tends to have maximum color and zing. With just a little water and plenty of sugar, the stringy stalks quickly collapse into a luscious compote in a saucepan, beautiful with Greek yogurt or even oatmeal. We love homemade Rhubarb Liqueur, a sweet-tart song to the season. Sip it straight or top it with a splash of cava or your favorite dry sparkling wine.

Rhubarb Liqueur

Bring 6 tablespoons sugar and 1/4 cup water to a boil in a small saucepan, stirring just until sugar dissolves; remove from heat. Cool. Place 1½ pounds coarsely chopped rhubarb in a wide-mouth jar. Add 3 cups vodka, ½ cup Grand Marnier or other orange-flavored liqueur, and cooled sugar syrup; stir. Screw lid on tightly; let stand at room temperature for 2 to 3 weeks or until all the color leaches out of rhubarb. Strain mixture through a sieve over a bowl; discard solids. Serves 20 (serving size: about 1½ ounces).

CALORIES 107; FAT 0g; SODIUM 1mg

Rhubarb-Apple Pie

Hands-on time: 28 min. Total time: 1 hr. 13 min.

1/2 (14.1-ounce) package refrigerated pie dough (such as Pillsbury)
Cooking spray
3½ cups sliced fresh rhubarb (about 1¼ pounds)
1 cup granulated sugar
1 tablespoon fresh lemon juice
2 Granny Smith apples, peeled, cored, and sliced
1/2 teaspoon ground cinnamon
3/8 teaspoon salt, divided
4.22 ounces all-purpose flour (about 1 cup), divided
1/2 cup packed brown sugar
6 tablespoons cold butter, cut into small pieces
1/3 cup chopped walnut halves

1. Preheat oven to 425°.
2. Place pie dough on a lightly floured work surface; roll into a 12-inch circle. Fit dough into a 9-inch pie plate coated with cooking spray. Turn edges under; flute. Combine rhubarb, granulated sugar, juice, and apples; toss. Sprinkle rhubarb mixture with cinnamon, 1/4 teaspoon salt, and 3 tablespoons flour; toss. Spoon rhubarb mixture into prepared crust.
3. Weigh or lightly spoon remaining 3.38 ounces flour (about 3/4 cup) into a dry measuring cup; level with a knife. Combine 3.38 ounces flour, remaining 1/8 teaspoon salt, and brown sugar in a medium bowl; cut butter into flour mixture with a pastry blender or two knives until mixture resembles coarse meal. Stir in walnuts. Sprinkle butter mixture evenly over rhubarb mixture. Bake at 425° for 15 minutes.
4. Reduce oven temperature to 375° (do not remove pie). Bake at 375° for 30 minutes or until golden and bubbly (shield edges of crust with foil if it gets too brown). Let pie stand on a cooling rack 15 minutes before slicing. Serves 12 (serving size: 1 wedge).

CALORIES 296; FAT 12.4g (sat 5.4g, mono 1.8g, poly 1.8g); PROTEIN 2.6g; CARB 46.2g; FIBER 1.5g; CHOL 15mg; IRON 0.8mg; SODIUM 192mg; CALC 47mg

RECIPE MAKEOVER

EASTER ROLLS MADE BETTER

Hot Cross Buns! Hot Cross Buns! Less butter, more whole grains—baked and iced for everyone!

These rich, sweet yeast bread delights show up every spring, fresh-baked according to English tradition on Good Friday. Topped with a cross of creamy white icing, the popable treats are more like mini cakes, filled with lots of buttery goodness, candied fruits, and warm spices. But each sweet little bun can set you back about 270 calories, and that's if you stop at just one. We wondered if we could lighten this buttery Easter favorite, while keeping all the irresistibility of the classic.

We blend whole-grain pastry flour into all-purpose flour for a more nutrient-dense base that still maintains a light, fluffy crumb. Golden raisins and currants are plumped in orange juice, and fresh citrus peel takes the place of sugary crystallized fruit. A touch of sweet butter maintains that moist, cakelike texture—with more than a stick less than the original. A hint of warm spices balances a sweet glaze to finish. Less heft, more flavor and fluff, these delicate Easter buns deserve attention all year.

Kid Friendly • Freezable
Make Ahead

Hot Cross Buns

Hands-on time: 40 min. Total time: 3 hr. 15 min.

Rolls:
1/2 cup golden raisins
1/2 cup dried currants
1/4 cup warm orange juice (120° to 130°)
19 ounces all-purpose flour (about 4 1/4 cups), divided
4.5 ounces whole-grain pastry flour (about 1 cup)
1 teaspoon salt
1 teaspoon grated lemon rind
1 teaspoon grated orange rind
1/2 teaspoon ground cinnamon
1/4 teaspoon grated whole nutmeg
1 package quick-rise yeast (about 2 1/4 teaspoons)
1 cup warm fat-free milk (120° to 130°)
1/4 cup honey
1/4 cup unsalted butter, melted
2 large eggs, lightly beaten
Cooking spray
1 tablespoon water
1 large egg white

Glaze:
1 cup powdered sugar
1 tablespoon 2% reduced-fat milk
1 teaspoon fresh lemon juice

1. To prepare rolls, combine first 3 ingredients in a small bowl; let stand 10 minutes. Drain fruit in a colander over a bowl, reserving fruit and juice.
2. Weigh or lightly spoon 18.5 ounces (about 4 cups plus 2 tablespoons) all-purpose flour and pastry flour into dry measuring cups; level with a knife. Combine flours, salt, and next 5 ingredients in bowl of a stand mixer with dough hook attached; mix until combined. Combine reserved orange juice, fat-free milk, honey, butter, and 2 eggs in a bowl, stirring with a whisk. With mixer on, slowly add milk mixture to flour mixture; mix at medium-low speed 7 minutes. Turn dough out onto a lightly floured surface. Add reserved fruit. Knead 2 minutes or until smooth and elastic; add enough of remaining 2 tablespoons all-purpose flour, 1 tablespoon at a time, to prevent dough from sticking. Place dough in a large bowl coated with cooking spray, turning to coat top. Cover and let rise in a warm, dry place, free from drafts, 1 hour or until doubled in size. (Gently press two fingers into dough. If indentation remains, dough has risen enough.) Punch dough down; cover and let rest 5 minutes. Divide into 24 equal portions; roll each portion into a ball. Place rolls in muffin cups coated with cooking spray. Cover and let rise 1 hour or until almost doubled in size.

3. Preheat oven to 350°.
4. Combine 1 tablespoon water and egg white; stir with a whisk. Gently brush rolls with egg white mixture. Bake at 350° for 20 minutes or until golden, rotating pans once during baking. Remove from pans; cool 10 minutes on a wire rack.
5. To prepare glaze, combine powdered sugar and remaining ingredients in a bowl, stirring with a whisk. Microwave at HIGH 20 seconds or until warm. Spoon glaze into a zip-top plastic bag. Seal bag; snip a tiny hole in 1 corner of bag. Pipe a cross on top of each warm roll. Serves 24 (serving size: 1 roll).

CALORIES 179; FAT 2.8g (sat 1.4g, mono 0.7g, poly 0.2g); PROTEIN 4.5g; CARB 34.8g; FIBER 1.6g; CHOL 23mg; IRON 1.4mg; SODIUM 111mg; CALC 29mg

FOR BETTER BUNS

Add whole grains, use less butter, and brighten with citrus.

WHOLE-GRAIN FLOUR VS. REFINED FLOUR
Nutty whole-grain pastry flour replaces some of the refined flour to boost the fiber to 1.6 grams per roll.

A TOUCH OF BUTTER
You only need a little for a light, fluffy crumb. We decreased by two-thirds to save 42 calories and 3 grams of sat fat per roll.

FRESH CITRUS PEEL VS. CANDIED
Fresh citrus rind offers a more natural, refreshing flavor, with less sugar and fewer calories than candied peel.

CLASSIC	MAKEOVER
268 calories per roll	179 calories per roll
227 milligrams sodium	111 milligrams sodium
4.8 grams saturated fat	1.4 grams saturated fat

(Stayed perky)

OOPS!

YOUR LETTUCE IS LIFELESS

How to baby the most important part of a green salad

Nice lettuce is a mighty pretty thing, until it shrivels and withers 'twixt store and salad bowl—or, worse, rots and blackens around the edges. Once opened, even relatively shelf-stable bagged lettuces suffer this fate. And lettuce leaves are prone to nasty bruising when roughly handled. This is among the most delicate of foods.

The main storage problem is usually too much moisture. Wet lettuce spoils faster as water condenses on the leaves and suffocates them. More moisture also means more gases, like ethylene, which speed up ripening and spoilage in fruits and vegetables. But here's the rub: Lettuce needs some water to stay crisp—otherwise leaves dry out and droop.

The solution: Keep lettuce moist, but just barely. Loosely wrap a head (or the contents of bagged lettuce) in slightly damp paper towels, and seal in a zip-top bag. This will absorb excess water without dehydrating the leaves. Store in your crisper drawer—the best spot for consistent, controlled humidity. Don't wash lettuce until you're ready to use it.

(Gone limp)

TACOS, BURRITOS, Y ENCHILADAS!

Five delicious, light, tortilla-wrapped goodies—just in time for those Cinco de Mayo margaritas.

The wrap rivals the noodle for versatility: There are wraps in India, China, Southeast Asia, and all over Latin America. Lovers of Mexican food find supermarkets bursting with new tortilla options in the bread and Latin food aisles, and in the produce and refrigerated sections. You'll find small, fragrant corn tortillas (5 to 6 inches in diameter); white and whole-wheat flour tortillas that range from 6 to a mighty 12 inches; and now a wide variety of flavored tortillas with ingredients such as sun-dried tomatoes and flax.

Burritos are flour tortillas stuffed with a savory filling. Enchiladas are stuffed corn tortillas that are topped with sauce and cheese, and then baked—the gooier, saucier, corn-tortilla riff on the burrito.

Corn tortillas make authentic tacos and enchiladas. They're small and often low in sodium. For burritos, reach for flour tortillas, but know that sodium levels rise. Know, too, that as the diameter goes up, the stuffing capacity goes up a lot.

Heat tortillas before filling so they're more pliable. For tacos, toast in a dry cast-iron skillet for 10 seconds on each side for a charred look and flavor. For burritos and enchiladas, warm per package directions.

Vegetarian

Vegetable and Rice Burritos with Quesadilla Cheese

Hands-on time: 40 min. Total time: 40 min. *Most grocery stores have a refrigerated section of Mexican cheeses; look for quesadilla cheese there. Use the more commonly found crumbly queso fresco if quesadilla cheese is not available, or opt for melty Monterey Jack. Warming tortillas prior to adding your filling will help keep the tortillas from tearing or cracking during the rolling process—a must-do step for perfect burritos.*

4 teaspoons canola oil, divided
1/3 cup uncooked long-grain white rice
1 teaspoon chopped garlic, divided
2/3 cup water
1/4 teaspoon salt, divided
1 tablespoon chopped jalapeño pepper
1/4 cup reduced-fat sour cream
1 tablespoon chopped fresh cilantro
1 teaspoon fresh lemon juice
1/8 teaspoon ground red pepper
1 cup chopped onion
1 cup sliced cremini mushrooms
1/2 cup fresh corn kernels
1 small zucchini, halved lengthwise and sliced (about 3/4 cup)
3/4 cup halved grape tomatoes
4 (7- to 8-inch) whole-wheat tortillas
4 ounces quesadilla cheese, shredded (about 1 cup packed)
Cilantro leaves (optional)

1. Heat a small saucepan over medium-high heat. Add 1 teaspoon canola oil to pan; swirl to coat. Add rice and 1/2 teaspoon garlic; sauté 1 minute, stirring constantly. Add 2/3 cup water and 1/8 teaspoon salt; bring to a boil. Cover, reduce heat, and simmer 15 minutes. Remove from heat; let stand 10 minutes. Fluff with a fork; stir in jalapeño.
2. Combine sour cream, chopped cilantro, juice, and red pepper in a small bowl.
3. Heat a large nonstick skillet over medium-high heat. Add remaining 1 tablespoon oil to pan; swirl to coat. Add onion; sauté 2 minutes, stirring frequently. Add remaining 1/2 teaspoon garlic and mushrooms; sauté 1 minute, stirring frequently. Add corn and zucchini; sauté 2 minutes, stirring frequently. Add remaining 1/8 teaspoon salt and tomatoes; sauté 30 seconds or until tomatoes are thoroughly heated. Remove vegetable mixture from pan. Wipe pan clean with a paper towel.
4. Heat tortillas according to package directions. Divide sour cream mixture evenly among tortillas; spread to a thin layer, leaving a 1/2-inch border. Top each tortilla with 1/4 cup cheese, about 1/4 cup rice mixture, and about 1/2 cup vegetable mixture. Roll up each, jelly-roll fashion. Return skillet to medium heat. Add 2 burritos to pan, seam side down; cook 1 minute on each side or until browned. Repeat procedure with remaining burritos. Garnish with cilantro leaves, if desired. Serves 4 (serving size: 1 burrito).

CALORIES 363; **FAT** 12.4g (sat 4.1g, mono 4.9g, poly 1.7g); **PROTEIN** 11.1g; **CARB** 51.6g; **FIBER** 5g; **CHOL** 18mg; **IRON** 1.6mg; **SODIUM** 543mg; **CALC** 101mg

Cumin-Spiced Fish Tacos with Avocado-Mango Salsa

Hands-on time: 23 min. Total time: 23 min. The superb flavor you get from toasting and grinding cumin seeds is well worth the little bit of effort. Clean the grinder to remove flavors that could permeate the next item ground. Wipe the grinder clean with a soft cloth, add a few tablespoons of uncooked white rice, and grind until rice turns into powder; repeat until the ground rice comes out white.

1 tablespoon cumin seeds
3/4 teaspoon salt, divided
1/2 teaspoon paprika
1/4 teaspoon black pepper
2 garlic cloves, minced
1 pound tilapia fillets
1 tablespoon canola oil
1 cup sliced peeled avocado
2/3 cup finely chopped peeled ripe
   mango
1/4 cup chopped green onions
1/4 cup finely chopped red onion
2 tablespoons finely chopped fresh
   cilantro
1 tablespoon fresh lime juice
1/4 teaspoon ground red pepper
1 jalapeño pepper, thinly sliced
   (optional)
8 (6-inch) corn tortillas

1. Heat a large skillet over medium heat. Add cumin seeds, and cook 2 minutes or until toasted, shaking pan frequently. Place cumin, 1/2 teaspoon salt, paprika, and black pepper in a spice grinder; process until finely ground. Combine cumin mixture and garlic, and rub over fish. Return skillet to medium-high heat. Add oil to pan; swirl to coat. Add fish; cook 2 minutes on each side or until done. Remove from heat; keep warm.

2. Combine remaining 1/4 teaspoon salt, avocado, and next 6 ingredients. Stir in jalapeño, if desired.
3. Heat tortillas according to package directions. Break fish into pieces; divide evenly among tortillas. Top each tortilla with 2 tablespoons salsa. Fold tortillas in half; serve immediately. Serves 4 (serving size: 2 tacos).

CALORIES 315; **FAT** 12.4g (sat 1.9g, mono 6.8g, poly 2.8g); **PROTEIN** 26.2g; **CARB** 29.1g; **FIBER** 5.8g; **CHOL** 57mg; **IRON** 2.1mg; **SODIUM** 521mg; **CALC** 65mg

Potato, Chorizo, and Green Chile Burritos

Hands-on time: 36 min. Total time: 36 min. Chorizo and potato make a classic Mexican combination; be sure to use highly spiced, raw, and crumbly Mexican chorizo—not the firm, cured Spanish kind. For the best browning and a bit of crunch, resist the urge to stir the potatoes often.

10 ounces red potatoes, cut into
   1/2-inch cubes
1 cup chopped tomato
2 tablespoons diced white onion
1 tablespoon chopped fresh cilantro
2 teaspoons fresh lime juice
6 ounces Mexican raw chorizo
1 cup chopped white onion
1/3 cup thinly sliced poblano chile
2 teaspoons olive oil
1/8 teaspoon salt
4 (7- to 8-inch) whole-wheat flour
   tortillas
2 ounces queso fresco, crumbled
   (about 1/2 cup)

1. Place red potatoes in a saucepan, and cover with cold water. Bring to a boil. Remove pan from heat, and let stand 5 minutes. Drain; pat potatoes dry with paper towels.
2. Combine 1 cup tomato, 2 tablespoons onion, cilantro, and lime juice.

3. Heat a large skillet over medium-high heat. Add chorizo; cook 3 minutes, stirring to crumble. Add 1 cup onion and poblano to pan; cook 2 minutes or until onion is tender and chorizo is done, stirring frequently. Remove chorizo mixture from pan. Add oil to pan; swirl to coat. Add potatoes; cook 8 minutes or until lightly browned, stirring occasionally. Remove pan from heat. Stir in chorizo mixture and salt.
4. Heat tortillas according to package directions. Divide potato mixture evenly among tortillas; top evenly with salsa and cheese. Roll up, jelly-roll fashion.
5. Heat a large nonstick skillet over medium heat. Add 2 burritos to pan, seam side down; cook 1 minute on each side or until browned. Repeat with remaining burritos. Serves 4 (serving size: 1 burrito).

CALORIES 349; **FAT** 15.4g (sat 4.6g, mono 7g, poly 1.8g); **PROTEIN** 14.5g; **CARB** 39.6g; **FIBER** 5.8g; **CHOL** 77mg; **IRON** 1.4mg; **SODIUM** 669mg; **CALC** 135mg

OUR FAVORITE TORTILLAS

CORN "HYBRID" TORTILLAS
La Tortilla Factory's Handmade-Style Yellow Corn Tortillas are a combo of corn and wheat. They're thick, pliable, and have a nutty-corn flavor. Sodium creeps higher in these: 200mg for each 90-calorie tortilla.

CORN TORTILLAS
La Tortilla Factory's Smart & Delicious Whole-Grain Fiber & Flax Yellow Corn Tortillas stand out. Made from stone-ground corn with just a hint of flaxseed, these have rich, roasted corn flavor. They're not too thick, so they don't split as easily as other corn tortillas when you try to fold them. The numbers are great, too: A serving of two tortillas contains only 90 calories and 15mg sodium.

FLOUR TORTILLAS
We love the nutty, grain-y flavor and visible bits of seeds and hulls in Mission Multigrain Artisan-Style Tortillas. They're thicker than many flour tortillas we tried, with a pleasant chew. Each 100-calorie, 7-inch tortilla contains a reasonable 230mg sodium. (We saw others that had more than 500mg!)

Steak and Charred Vegetable Tacos

Hands-on time: 16 min. Total time: 1 hr. 9 min.

2 tablespoons canola oil, divided
1 tablespoon fresh lime juice
1 teaspoon brown sugar
1 1/2 teaspoons chipotle chile powder
2 large garlic cloves, minced and divided
1 (1-pound) skirt steak, trimmed and chopped
1/2 medium onion, cut into 1/2-inch-thick slices
1/2 pound plum tomatoes, halved lengthwise
1 red bell pepper, halved and seeded
5/8 teaspoon salt, divided
1/4 teaspoon dried oregano
1/4 teaspoon black pepper
Cooking spray
8 (6-inch) corn tortillas
1/4 cup reduced-fat sour cream

1. Combine 1 tablespoon oil, juice, sugar, chile powder, and 1 minced garlic clove in a large zip-top plastic bag. Add steak; seal and toss to coat. Marinate at room temperature 30 minutes.
2. Heat a large grill pan over medium-high heat. Brush remaining 1 tablespoon oil over onion slices, tomatoes, and bell pepper. Arrange vegetables in pan; cook 4 minutes on each side or until charred and softened.
3. Place tomato, 1/4 teaspoon salt, and remaining garlic clove in a food processor; pulse until almost pureed. Place tomato mixture in a bowl. Coarsely chop onion and bell pepper; add to bowl. Stir in oregano and black pepper.
4. Heat a large cast-iron skillet over high heat. Coat pan with cooking spray. Add steak mixture to pan; cook 6 minutes or until done, stirring frequently. Stir in remaining 3/8 teaspoon salt.
5. Heat tortillas according to package directions. Arrange about 1 1/2 ounces steak on each tortilla; top each tortilla with about 2 tablespoons salsa and 1 1/2 teaspoons sour cream. Serves 4 (serving size: 2 tacos).

CALORIES 336; FAT 17.3g (sat 4.3g, mono 8.6g, poly 2.9g); PROTEIN 21.4g; CARB 26g; FIBER 3.6g; CHOL 54mg; IRON 2.3mg; SODIUM 477mg; CALC 58mg

Pork and Plantain Enchiladas with Black Bean Puree

Hands-on time: 44 min. Total time: 1 hr. 44 min.

1/2 teaspoon ground cumin
1/2 teaspoon dried oregano
5/8 teaspoon ground red pepper, divided
1/2 teaspoon salt, divided
1 (1-pound) pork tenderloin, trimmed
2 tablespoons canola oil, divided
1 2/3 cups chopped onion, divided
1 1/3 cups fat-free, lower-sodium chicken broth, divided
3/4 pound tomatillos, husked, rinsed, and coarsely chopped (about 6 large)
2 garlic cloves, chopped and divided
1 serrano chile, seeded and thinly sliced
1 cup fresh cilantro leaves
1 tablespoon fresh lime juice
1 (15-ounce) can organic black beans, rinsed and drained
1 teaspoon brown sugar
1 soft black plantain, peeled and coarsely chopped
Cooking spray
12 (6-inch) corn tortillas
6 ounces Monterey Jack cheese, shredded (about 1 1/2 cups)

1. Preheat oven to 350°.
2. Combine cumin, oregano, 1/2 teaspoon ground red pepper, and 1/4 teaspoon salt; rub evenly over pork. Heat a large ovenproof skillet over medium-high heat. Add 2 teaspoons oil to pan; swirl to coat. Add pork; cook 5 minutes, browning on all sides. Place pan in oven, and bake at 350° for 20 minutes or until pork is done. Remove pork from pan; let rest 15 minutes. Cut pork into 1/2-inch pieces.
3. Combine 1 cup onion, 1 cup broth, tomatillos, 1 garlic clove, and serrano in a saucepan. Bring to a boil; reduce heat, and simmer 15 minutes or until tomatillos are tender. Cool 10 minutes. Place tomatillo mixture, cilantro, lime juice, and remaining 1/4 teaspoon salt in a blender; process until smooth. Pour into a large measuring cup.
4. Place skillet over medium heat. Add 1 teaspoon oil to pan; swirl to coat. Add remaining 2/3 cup onion; cook 3 minutes or until tender, stirring frequently. Add remaining garlic clove; cook 30 seconds, stirring constantly. Add remaining 1/3 cup broth, and cook 1 minute, scraping pan to loosen browned bits. Add black beans; cook 2 minutes, stirring frequently. Cool slightly. Place black bean mixture in blender. Pulse 15 times, scraping occasionally until mixture is a thick puree.
5. Heat a nonstick skillet over medium-high heat. Add remaining 1 tablespoon oil to pan; swirl to coat. Combine remaining 1/8 teaspoon red pepper, brown sugar, and plantain in a medium bowl, tossing to coat plantain. Add plantain mixture to pan; sauté 3 minutes or until golden brown, stirring frequently. Cool slightly; finely chop. Combine pork and plantain mixture in a medium bowl.
6. Spread 1/3 cup tomatillo mixture in a 13 x 9–inch glass or ceramic baking dish coated with cooking spray. Heat tortillas according to package directions. Spread about 1 1/2 tablespoons black bean puree down center of each tortilla; top with about 2 tablespoons pork mixture. Sprinkle each tortilla with 1 tablespoon cheese; roll up. Place seam sides down in baking dish. Pour remaining tomatillo mixture over filled tortillas; sprinkle with remaining cheese. Bake at 350° for 25 minutes or until cheese melts and filling is thoroughly heated. Serves 6 (serving size: 2 enchiladas).

CALORIES 428; FAT 16.6g (sat 6.4g, mono 6.1g, poly 2.5g); PROTEIN 29.5g; CARB 43.5g; FIBER 6.3g; CHOL 74mg; IRON 2.2mg; SODIUM 573mg; CALC 268mg

THE FLEETING PERFECTION OF THE STRAWBERRY

May brings to stores and markets that lovely, candy-sweet fragrance that can signal only one thing: the arrival of the sweetest, prettiest, most strawberry-like strawberries of the year. You'll find strawberries year-round, of course, but they won't be as good as they are now. Out of season, the fruit lacks sweetness and juiciness, and the texture is often cottony. Load up now and get to making classic strawberry shortcake and fluffy mousse, or start new berry traditions like berry-ricotta napoleons or a fizzy strawberry limeade spiked with sparkling wine. This sweet moment doesn't last long. Seize it!

WILL WE EVER SEE A BETTER SUPERMARKET STRAWBERRY?

Those big berries can break your heart. For durability, they're often picked on the firmer, green side, meaning they will redden, but not ripen, after picking. This is the strawberry version of the tomato problem: pretty fruit, underflavored.

The tomato problem was solved in part by the grape tomato, which delivers concentrated flavor in a durable little package. The goal is similar for strawberries: Breeders are working on a berry that's both fit for supermarket shipping and succulently sweet. Vance Whitaker, PhD, a strawberry breeder at the University of Florida, has consumers taste-testing varieties to identify the genetic recipe for a better berry. "We have made a lot of progress in firmness and shipability," he says. "We have leeway to put more effort on flavor."

That's only one example of the attempt to breed a better strawberry. The North Carolina Strawberry Project, meanwhile, is a partnership between N.C. State University researchers and chefs at Johnson and Wales University to pinpoint the best qualities in 20 strawberry breeds, then find the perfect breed.

For now, just reconcile yourself to the fleeting nature of the strawberry season, and dive right in while they're here. Whether they're from a small farm or large, it's a good idea to choose organic: Strawberries rank high on "The Dirty Dozen," the Environmental Working Group's list of fruits and vegetables with the most pesticide residues.

Quick & Easy
Strawberry-Mint Sparkling Limeade

Hands-on time: 10 min. Total time: 10 min. *For a kid-friendly version, substitute 3 cups chilled club soda for the wine. When adding the wine or soda, pour slowly down the edge of the glass to tame the foam.*

3 cups sliced strawberries
1/2 cup loosely packed fresh mint leaves
1/2 cup fresh lime juice
1/4 cup water
1/4 cup agave nectar
1 (750-milliliter) bottle sparkling wine, chilled
Whole strawberries (optional)

1. Place first 5 ingredients in a blender; process until smooth (about 1 minute). Pour about 1/2 cup strawberry mixture into each of 6 glasses. Slowly pour about 1/2 cup wine into each glass; gently stir to combine. Garnish with whole berries, if desired. Serves 6 (serving size: 1 cup).

CALORIES 163; FAT 0.3g (sat 0g, mono 0.1g, poly 0.1g); PROTEIN 0.7g; CARB 21.2g; FIBER 1.9g; CHOL 0mg; IRON 0.5mg; SODIUM 2mg; CALC 21mg

Ricotta-Strawberry Napoleons

Hands-on time: 30 min. Total time: 1 hr.

- 2 tablespoons slivered almonds, toasted
- 2 tablespoons granulated sugar
- 3 (14 x 9-inch) sheets frozen phyllo dough, thawed
- 2 tablespoons butter, melted
- 1½ teaspoons canola oil
- 2 tablespoons turbinado sugar
- 1 cup part-skim ricotta cheese (such as Calabro)
- 1½ tablespoons honey
- 2 cups chopped strawberries
- 1 tablespoon granulated sugar
- 1½ teaspoons Grand Marnier (orange-flavored liqueur)

1. Preheat oven to 350°.
2. Place almonds in a mini chopper; process until finely ground. Add granulated sugar; pulse to combine.
3. Line a baking sheet with parchment paper. Place 1 phyllo sheet on pan (cover remaining phyllo to prevent drying). Combine butter and oil; brush lightly over phyllo. Sprinkle phyllo sheet with about 1½ tablespoons almond mixture. Top with another phyllo sheet; brush lightly with butter mixture, and sprinkle with remaining almond mixture. Top with 1 phyllo sheet; brush lightly with butter mixture, and sprinkle with turbinado sugar. Using a sharp knife or pizza cutter, cut phyllo into 15 (3 x 2¾-inch) pieces. Separate phyllo pieces on baking sheet. Cover phyllo with another sheet of parchment paper. Top with another baking sheet. Bake at 350° for 10 minutes or until golden brown. Carefully remove top baking sheet and parchment paper. Cool phyllo on a wire rack.
4. Combine ricotta and honey. Combine berries, 1 tablespoon granulated sugar, and liqueur; let stand 10 minutes.

Place 1 phyllo piece on each of 5 dessert plates; top each with 1½ tablespoons ricotta mixture and about 2 tablespoons strawberry mixture. Repeat layers once; top each with 1 phyllo piece. Serves 5 (serving size: 1 napoleon).

CALORIES 240; FAT 11.8g (sat 5.7g, mono 4.3g, poly 1.2g); PROTEIN 7.1g; CARB 27.9g; FIBER 1.8g; CHOL 28mg; IRON 0.8mg; SODIUM 123mg; CALC 155mg

Kid Friendly • Make Ahead

No-Bake Fresh Strawberry Pie

Hands-on time: 35 min. Total time: 1 hr. 15 min. Glorious spring berries are the focus here—tons of them, piled atop a layer of creamy filling. You can leave small berries whole.

- 25 chocolate wafers
- 3 ounces bittersweet chocolate, finely chopped
- 2 teaspoons canola oil
- Cooking spray
- 6 ounces ⅓-less-fat cream cheese, softened
- ⅓ cup powdered sugar
- ¾ teaspoon vanilla extract
- 2 cups frozen fat-free whipped topping, thawed
- 2 tablespoons seedless strawberry fruit spread
- 1 tablespoon Chambord (raspberry-flavored liqueur)
- ½ teaspoon fresh lemon juice
- 1 pound small strawberries, hulled and cut in half

1. Place chocolate wafers in a food processor, and process until finely ground. Place chopped chocolate in a small microwave-safe bowl. Microwave at HIGH 45 seconds or until chocolate melts, stirring every 15 seconds. Add melted chocolate and oil to processor; process until well combined. Gently press mixture into bottom and up sides of a 9-inch pie plate or removable-bottom tart pan coated with cooking spray. Place in freezer 15 minutes or until set.
2. Place cream cheese, sugar, and vanilla in a medium bowl; beat with a mixer at medium speed until smooth. Fold in whipped topping. Carefully spread over bottom of crust. Place fruit spread in a large microwave-safe bowl; microwave at HIGH 10 seconds or until softened. Add Chambord and juice; stir with a whisk until smooth. Add berry halves; toss to combine. Arrange berry halves over pie. Chill 30 minutes before serving. Serves 8 (serving size: 1 wedge).

CALORIES 294; FAT 11.5g (sat 5.5g, mono 2.9g, poly 0.9g); PROTEIN 4.3g; CARB 41.5g; FIBER 1.8g; CHOL 19mg; IRON 0.9mg; SODIUM 225mg; CALC 34mg

THE TASTE OF A FRESH SPRING STRAWBERRY IS A BEAUTIFUL BALANCE OF INTENSE SWEETNESS AND JUST ENOUGH TANG TO LIFT THE FLAVOR.

Simple Strawberry Mousse

Hands-on time: 25 min. Total time: 2 hr. 25 min.

1 cup finely chopped strawberries
1/2 cup sugar, divided
5 tablespoons water, divided
3/4 teaspoon unflavored gelatin
Dash of salt
2 large egg whites
1/4 teaspoon vanilla extract
1/2 cup heavy whipping cream

1. Place strawberries and 1 tablespoon sugar in a mini chopper or food processor; toss gently. Let stand 10 minutes. Process until smooth.
2. Pour 2 tablespoons water in a large bowl, and sprinkle with gelatin. Let stand 5 minutes.
3. Place 6 tablespoons sugar, remaining 3 tablespoons water, and dash of salt in a small heavy saucepan over medium-high heat; bring to a boil, stirring just until sugar dissolves. Cook, without stirring, until a candy thermometer registers 240° (about 4 minutes). Add egg whites to gelatin mixture; beat with a mixer at high speed until foamy. Gradually add remaining 1 tablespoon sugar, beating at high speed until soft peaks form. Gradually pour hot sugar syrup into egg white mixture, beating first at medium speed and then at high speed until stiff peaks form. Beat in vanilla.
4. Place cream in a large bowl; beat with a mixer at high speed until stiff peaks form. Gently fold one-fourth of egg white mixture into whipped cream. Fold in remaining egg white mixture. Fold in strawberry mixture. Spoon about 1/2 cup mousse into each of 6 dessert glasses; chill 2 hours or until set. Serves 6.

CALORIES 150; **FAT** 7.5g (sat 4.6g, mono 2.2g, poly 0.3g); **PROTEIN** 2.1g; **CARB** 19.6g; **FIBER** 0.6g; **CHOL** 27mg; **IRON** 0.1mg; **SODIUM** 52mg; **CALC** 19mg

Strawberry-Lemon Shortcakes

Hands-on time: 35 min. Total time: 1 hr. 30 min. *Tender biscuits get a little lift from sweet, floral lemon rind. For slightly taller shortcakes with soft sides, pack biscuits into a round cake pan; for separate shortcakes with crisp edges, arrange onto a baking sheet with space between.*

9 ounces all-purpose flour (about 2 cups)
1/4 cup granulated sugar
1 tablespoon baking powder
1/2 teaspoon baking soda
1/4 teaspoon salt
6 tablespoons chilled butter, cut into small pieces
1 1/4 cups low-fat buttermilk
1 tablespoon grated lemon rind
Cooking spray
1/2 cup all-purpose flour
1 tablespoon butter, melted
1 tablespoon turbinado sugar
4 cups sliced strawberries
1/4 cup granulated sugar
1 tablespoon fresh lemon juice
1 1/4 cups frozen fat-free whipped topping, thawed

1. Preheat oven to 425°.
2. Weigh or lightly spoon 9 ounces flour (about 2 cups) into dry measuring cups; level with a knife. Combine 9 ounces flour, 1/4 cup granulated sugar, baking powder, baking soda, and 1/4 teaspoon salt in a large bowl. Cut in chilled butter with a pastry blender until mixture resembles coarse meal. Combine 1 1/4 cups buttermilk and grated lemon rind. Add buttermilk mixture to flour mixture, and toss gently with a fork to combine. (Dough should be wet and about the texture of cottage cheese.)
3. Coat a 9-inch round metal cake pan or baking sheet with cooking spray. Place 1/2 cup flour in a shallow dish. Scoop 10 equal dough portions into

dish. Gently shape each portion into a round by tossing in flour to help shape dough. Arrange in prepared pan. Discard excess flour. Brush dough with melted butter, and sprinkle evenly with 1 tablespoon turbinado sugar. Bake at 425° for 22 minutes or until shortcakes are lightly browned. Cool in pan on a wire rack 10 minutes. Remove shortcakes from pan. Cool on wire rack.
4. Combine berries, 1/4 cup granulated sugar, and lemon juice; toss to coat. Let stand 15 minutes. Split each shortcake in half; spoon about 1/3 cup berry mixture and 2 tablespoons whipped topping into each. Serves 10 (serving size: 1 filled shortcake).

CALORIES 267; **FAT** 8.8g (sat 5.3g, mono 2.2g, poly 0.5g); **PROTEIN** 4.5g; **CARB** 46.2g; **FIBER** 2.2g; **CHOL** 23mg; **IRON** 1.6mg; **SODIUM** 338mg; **CALC** 126mg

Strawberry-Buttermilk Sherbet

Hands-on time: 10 min. Total time: 1 hr. 40 min. *This recipe is one of those refreshingly light desserts that can be so satisfying.*

2 cups chopped strawberries
1/3 cup agave nectar
1 1/2 cups whole buttermilk
3 tablespoons Chambord (raspberry-flavored liqueur)
1 tablespoon fresh lemon juice (optional)

1. Place berries and nectar in a blender; process until smooth (about 1 minute). Add buttermilk; process until well blended. Add liqueur; pulse to mix. Add juice, if desired. Chill mixture 1 hour. Pour into freezer can of an ice-cream freezer; freeze according to manufacturer's instructions. Serves 6 (serving size: about 3/4 cup).

CALORIES 135; **FAT** 2.2g (sat 1.3g, mono 0.6g, poly 0.2g); **PROTEIN** 2.4g; **CARB** 24.4g; **FIBER** 1.1g; **CHOL** 9mg; **IRON** 0.2mg; **SODIUM** 73mg; **CALC** 9mg

HALF THE CALORIES!

We took classic restaurant dishes, kept the meal appeal, and cut the calories by a huge amount. Here are the ingredients and techniques that make that possible.

HOW WE DID IT

• Deli sandwiches can get ridiculously big—some piled so high they're impossible to eat. You don't need sodium-heavy corned beef layered 3 inches high to get plenty of savory flavor. So we shrank the portion size to reap significant nutritional savings.

• Started with a whole loaf of unsliced bread, and then cut it into sensible-sized DIY slices to trim calories.

• Made a full-flavored sauce from canola mayo to save on saturated fat, calories, and sodium.

• Shaved the cheese with a vegetable peeler or box grater to stretch a small amount further.

• Bonus: Using organic sauerkraut reduced the amount of sodium.

Quick & Easy

Reuben Sandwiches
(pictured on page 216)

Hands-on time: 18 min. Total time: 18 min. *With sauerkraut, corned beef, and rye bread, sodium is a serious issue in a traditional Reuben. Add dressing and cheese, and the saturated fat and calories start to climb, too. Not to fear: Our lighter, lower-sodium version is just as delicious. If you can't find chili sauce, substitute ketchup.*

Dressing:
¼ cup canola mayonnaise
1 tablespoon chili sauce
2 teaspoons finely minced dill pickle
1 teaspoon Worcestershire sauce
½ teaspoon grated onion
Sandwiches:
8 (¾-ounce) slices rye bread
3 ounces Swiss cheese, shaved (about ¾ cup)
4 ounces lower-sodium corned beef, thinly sliced (such as Boar's Head corned beef, top round, cap-off)
1 cup organic sauerkraut, drained well

1. Preheat broiler to high.
2. To prepare dressing, combine first 5 ingredients in a small bowl, stirring well.
3. To prepare sandwiches, place bread slices in a single layer on a heavy baking sheet. Broil bread 1½ minutes or until toasted. Turn bread over; broil 1 minute or until lightly toasted. Remove 4 slices. Divide cheese evenly among remaining 4 slices, sprinkling it over lightly toasted sides. Broil 1 minute or until cheese melts. Spread about 1½ tablespoons dressing over cheese-coated side of each bread slice; top each serving with 1 ounce corned beef, ¼ cup sauerkraut, and remaining bread slices. Serve immediately. Serves 4 (serving size: 1 sandwich).

CALORIES 336; **FAT** 19.9g (sat 5.6g, mono 8.1g, poly 3.6g); **PROTEIN** 14.7g; **CARB** 24.2g; **FIBER** 3.4g; **CHOL** 40mg; **IRON** 1.9mg; **SODIUM** 790mg; **CALC** 212mg

CANOLA MAYONNAISE HELPS DELIVER A FULL-FLAVORED SAUCE WITH FEWER CALORIES AND LESS SAT FAT AND SODIUM THAN A TRADITONAL SAUCE.

CLASSIC	MAKEOVER
860 calories per serving	336 calories per serving
15 grams saturated fat	5.6 grams saturated fat
4,186 milligrams sodium	790 milligrams sodium

Kid Friendly

Vegetable Lasagna

Hands-on time: 29 min. Total time: 2 hr.

Vegetables:
**3 large shallots, peeled and cut into
  1/2-inch-thick slices**
2 pounds baby pattypan squash
3 tablespoons olive oil, divided
3/4 teaspoon kosher salt, divided
3/4 teaspoon black pepper, divided
2 pints cherry tomatoes
1/4 cup chopped fresh basil
2 tablespoons chopped fresh chives
2 teaspoons minced garlic
Sauce:
**3 1/2 cups fat-free, lower-sodium
  chicken broth**
5 tablespoons all-purpose flour
1/4 cup heavy whipping cream
1 1/2 tablespoons Dijon mustard
1 large egg, lightly beaten
Cooking spray
9 cooked lasagna noodles
**1 1/2 ounces grated fresh Parmigiano-
  Reggiano cheese (about 1/3 cup)**
**3 ounces fontina cheese, shredded
  (about 3/4 cup)**
2 tablespoons torn fresh basil

1. To prepare vegetables, place a small metal roasting pan in oven. Preheat oven to 450°.
2. Combine shallots and squash; drizzle with 2 tablespoons oil. Sprinkle with 1/2 teaspoon salt and 1/2 teaspoon pepper; toss. Arrange vegetables in preheated pan; roast at 450° for 30 minutes, stirring once.

3. Preheat broiler to high.
4. Place tomatoes in a roasting pan; broil 10 minutes or until blistered. Combine squash mixture, tomatoes, 1/4 cup basil, chives, and garlic; toss gently.
5. Reduce oven temperature to 350°.
6. To prepare sauce, heat a small saucepan over medium heat. Add remaining 1 tablespoon oil; swirl to coat. Combine broth and flour, stirring with a whisk; add broth mixture to oil. Bring to a simmer, stirring constantly with a whisk. Stir in cream, mustard, remaining 1/4 teaspoon salt, and remaining 1/4 teaspoon pepper; simmer gently 4 minutes or until mixture begins to thicken, stirring constantly. Remove from heat; let stand 5 minutes. Place egg in a small bowl; slowly add 1 1/2 cups sauce to egg, stirring constantly. Return sauce to pan.
7. Spread 1/2 cup sauce over bottom of a broiler-safe 13 x 9–inch glass or ceramic baking dish coated with cooking spray. Arrange 3 lasagna noodles over sauce; spread half of squash mixture over noodles. Sprinkle with half of Parmigiano-Reggiano cheese. Repeat layers with remaining noodles, vegetable mixture, and Parmigiano-Reggiano, ending with noodles. Pour remaining sauce over noodles. Sprinkle with fontina. Bake at 350° for 30 minutes or until bubbly.
8. Preheat broiler to high.
9. Broil lasagna 4 minutes or until top is lightly browned. Sprinkle with 2 tablespoons fresh basil. Let stand 12 minutes. Serves 6.

CALORIES 401; FAT 18.7g (sat 7.5g, mono 8.2g, poly 1.4g); PROTEIN 16.7g; CARB 42g; FIBER 4.9g; CHOL 72mg; IRON 1.6mg; SODIUM 802mg; CALC 205mg

CLASSIC	MAKEOVER
850 calories per serving	401 calories per serving
25 grams saturated fat	7.5 grams saturated fat
2,830 milligrams sodium	802 milligrams sodium

HOW WE DID IT

• Lots of colorful, delicious baby veggies between pasta layers to reduce the typical mounds of cheese.

• Red sauce often contains fatty meats like sausage, and standard white sauces rely on cream. Our white sauce is based on fat-free broth, and we add just a bit of cream and an egg to give it a silky texture.

• Boosted the amount of Parmigiano-Reggiano. Aged cheeses have rich, concentrated flavor, so you can get away with using less. We sprinkled the Parm within the layers to supplement the fontina that's used to give a crunchy-cheesy crust on top.

Kid Friendly

Beef Filets with Red Wine Sauce and Roasted Veggie Fries

Hands-on time: 58 min. Total time: 1 hr. 28 min. Coat the potato wedges and baby carrots with a mixture of cornmeal and grated fresh Parmigiano-Reggiano cheese to add crunchy texture and golden-brown color to the plate.

Veggies:
2 tablespoons yellow cornmeal
**1/2 ounce finely grated fresh
  Parmigiano-Reggiano cheese (about
  2 tablespoons)**
**1 pound Yukon gold potato, cut into
  wedges**
**1 1/2 pounds baby carrots with tops,
  peeled and trimmed**
2 tablespoons olive oil
1/4 teaspoon kosher salt
**1/4 teaspoon freshly ground black
  pepper**
Steaks:
**1/2 cup earthy red wine (such as pinot
  noir)**
3 thyme sprigs
2 garlic cloves, crushed

1 medium shallot, sliced
1 rosemary sprig
1½ cups fat-free, lower-sodium beef
  broth
1 tablespoon olive oil
4 (4-ounce) beef tenderloin steaks
⅜ teaspoon kosher salt, divided
¼ teaspoon freshly ground black
  pepper
2 teaspoons Dijon mustard
2 tablespoons cold butter, cut into
  pieces
2 teaspoons fresh thyme leaves
  (optional)

1. Place a large baking sheet in oven. Preheat oven to 450°.
2. To prepare veggies, combine cornmeal and cheese in a small bowl, stirring well. Place potato and carrots in a large bowl. Drizzle vegetables with 2 tablespoons oil. Sprinkle vegetables with ¼ teaspoon salt and ¼ teaspoon pepper; toss. Sprinkle cornmeal mixture over vegetables; toss. Arrange vegetables in a single layer on preheated baking sheet; bake at 450° for 15 minutes. Turn vegetables over; bake an additional 8 minutes or until golden and tender.
3. To prepare steaks, heat a medium saucepan over medium-high heat. Add wine and next 4 ingredients to pan, and bring to a boil. Cook until liquid almost evaporates (about 8 minutes). Add broth; bring to a boil. Cook until reduced to about ½ cup (about 13 minutes). Remove from heat; strain mixture through a sieve over a bowl. Discard solids.
4. Heat a cast-iron skillet over medium-high heat. Add 1 tablespoon

oil to pan, and swirl to coat. Sprinkle both sides of steaks evenly with ¼ teaspoon salt and ¼ teaspoon black pepper. Add steaks to pan, and sauté 3 minutes on each side or until desired degree of doneness. Let steaks stand 5 minutes.
5. Heat pan to high heat. Add reduced broth mixture to pan, and stir in mustard and remaining ⅛ teaspoon salt. Remove from heat. Add butter to pan, 1 piece at a time, stirring with a whisk until each addition is incorporated. Place 1 steak on each of 4 plates; drizzle each serving with about 1 tablespoon sauce. Sprinkle each steak with ½ teaspoon thyme leaves, if desired. Divide vegetable fries evenly among servings. Serves 4.

CALORIES 521; FAT 24g (sat 8.3g, mono 11.9g, poly 1.8g); PROTEIN 31.1g; CARB 41.6g; FIBER 6.3g; CHOL 86mg; IRON 3.4mg; SODIUM 795mg; CALC 116mg

HOW WE DID IT

• 4 ounces uncooked lean filet mignon is a satisfying portion size.

• Cooked steaks in a little olive oil, which is tasty and a great source of healthy fat.

• Finished the sauce with a nice dab of butter. Just a little goes a long way; stirring it into the cooked sauce rounds out the flavor and adds a supple, silky texture and rich, buttery notes.

• Roasted cornmeal-dusted baby carrots and potato wedges for a delicious and stunning side. We replaced some of the potatoes in the usual pile of fries with lower-calorie carrots, which add color, sweetness, and interesting shapes to the mix.

CLASSIC	MAKEOVER
1,560 calories per serving	521 calories per serving
36 grams saturated fat	8.3 grams saturated fat
2,080 milligrams sodium	795 milligrams sodium

Make Ahead

Beef and Black Bean Enchiladas

Hands-on time: 1 hr. Total time: 1 hr. 30 min. You can make all the components ahead and simply assemble the enchiladas just before baking.

Sauce:
2 dried ancho chiles, stemmed
3 cups fat-free, lower-sodium chicken
  broth
1 (6-inch) corn tortilla, torn into small
  pieces
⅓ cup fresh cilantro leaves
2 teaspoons minced fresh garlic
2 green onions, coarsely chopped
Enchiladas:
8 ounces ground sirloin
2 teaspoons olive oil
2 cups chopped onion
4 teaspoons minced garlic
1 teaspoon dried Mexican oregano
½ teaspoon ground cumin
¼ teaspoon kosher salt
1 tablespoon no-salt-added tomato
  paste
⅔ cup rinsed and drained organic
  black beans
½ cup fat-free, lower-sodium chicken
  broth
1 tablespoon fresh lime juice
4 cups water
12 (6-inch) corn tortillas, at room
  temperature
Cooking spray
2½ ounces sharp cheddar cheese,
  shredded (about ⅔ cup)
2 ounces Monterey Jack cheese,
  shredded (about ½ cup)
3 green onions, thinly sliced and
  divided
6 tablespoons Mexican crema

1. Preheat oven to 400°.
2. To prepare sauce, place ancho chiles in a medium saucepan. Add 3 cups broth; bring to a boil. Reduce heat, and simmer 5 minutes. Stir in 1 torn

continued

CLASSIC	MAKEOVER
730 calories per serving (two enchiladas; no garnish)	343 calories per serving (two enchiladas; garnish included)
22 grams saturated fat	5.8 grams saturated fat
2,155 milligrams sodium	540 milligrams sodium

tortilla; simmer 5 minutes, stirring occasionally. Pour chile mixture into a blender; let stand 10 minutes. Add cilantro, 2 teaspoons garlic, and 2 coarsely chopped green onions to blender; process until smooth. Return mixture to pan; bring to a boil over medium heat. Cook until reduced to 2 cups (about 7 minutes), stirring occasionally. Remove sauce from heat.

3. To prepare enchiladas, heat a large skillet over medium-high heat. Add beef; sauté 5 minutes or until browned. Remove beef from pan using a slotted spoon; drain on paper towels. Wipe pan with paper towels. Return pan to medium heat. Add oil to pan; swirl to coat. Add onion; cook 8 minutes or until tender, stirring occasionally. Add garlic and next 3 ingredients; cook 2 minutes, stirring constantly. Stir in tomato paste; cook 1 minute, stirring frequently. Stir in drained beef, beans, and ½ cup broth; bring to a boil, scraping pan to loosen browned bits. Cook 1 minute, stirring occasionally. Remove from heat; stir in lime juice.

4. Place 4 cups water in a saucepan over medium-high heat; bring to a simmer. Working with 1 tortilla at a time, dip tortillas in simmering water 2 to 3 seconds each or until softened. Place 1 tortilla on a flat work surface; spoon 3 tablespoons beef mixture onto 1 end of each tortilla. Roll enchiladas up jelly-roll style. Repeat procedure with remaining tortillas and beef mixture. Spread ½ cup sauce in bottom of a 13 x 9–inch glass or ceramic baking dish coated with cooking spray. Arrange enchiladas, seam sides down, in prepared dish. Pour remaining sauce

over enchiladas. Top with cheeses. Bake at 400° for 20 minutes or until lightly browned and bubbly. Let stand 10 minutes. Sprinkle with 3 sliced green onions; serve with crema. Serves 6 (serving size: 2 enchiladas and 1 tablespoon crema).

CALORIES 343; FAT 15.4g (sat 5.8g, mono 5.1g, poly 1.4g); PROTEIN 18.2g; CARB 35.7g; FIBER 6.9g; CHOL 48mg; IRON 2.6mg; SODIUM 540mg; CALC 236mg

HOW WE DID IT

• Used lean ground beef for the enchilada filling. We drained the cooked beef and wiped the pan of any remaining grease and were able to cut a few more calories.

• Used less beef and bulked up the filling by adding black beans, a good source of lean protein. An ounce of beans also has one-third of the calories of an ounce of beef.

• Pumped up the flavor of the sauce by using ancho chile peppers, which add smoky depth but almost no calories.

• Moistened tortillas in water. With traditional enchiladas, tortillas are often fried in oil to soften them before filling them.

• Relied on broth in the sauce instead of cream to cut down on both calories and saturated fat.

Kid Friendly • Quick & Easy
Shrimp Fried Rice
(pictured on page 216)

Hands-on time: 31 min. Total time: 31 min. *This dish is best if you use day-old rice. Cook it and spread in a single layer on a baking sheet to cool completely. Then refrigerate overnight to allow it to lose any excess moisture.*

1 cup broccoli florets
7 teaspoons canola oil, divided
1 medium-sized red bell pepper, cut into thin strips
1 medium-sized yellow bell pepper, cut into thin strips
1 cup sugar snap peas, trimmed and halved crosswise
1 tablespoon grated peeled fresh ginger
1 cup cooked long-grain white rice, chilled
1 tablespoon dark sesame oil
12 ounces peeled and deveined medium shrimp
1½ cups frozen edamame, thawed
¼ cup lower-sodium soy sauce
1½ tablespoons rice vinegar
1 teaspoon Sriracha (hot chile sauce, such as Huy Fong)
¼ cup thinly diagonally sliced green onions

1. Steam broccoli 4 minutes or until crisp-tender; set aside. Heat a large skillet or wok over medium-high heat. Add 1 teaspoon canola oil to pan. Add bell peppers and sugar snap peas to pan, and stir-fry 2 minutes. Place vegetable mixture in a large bowl. Add remaining 2 tablespoons canola oil to pan; swirl to coat. Add ginger,

CLASSIC	MAKEOVER
1,154 calories per serving	368 calories per serving
4 grams saturated fat	1.5 grams saturated fat
3,352 milligrams sodium	560 milligrams sodium

and stir-fry 10 seconds. Add rice, and stir-fry 5 minutes or until rice is lightly browned. Remove rice mixture from pan, and add rice to bowl with vegetable mixture.

2. Wipe pan with paper towels. Return pan to medium-high heat. Add sesame oil to pan; swirl to coat. Add shrimp; stir-fry 1 minute. Add edamame; stir-fry 1 minute. Stir in soy sauce, vinegar, and Sriracha; bring to a boil. Cook 3 minutes or until liquid thickens slightly. Add vegetable mixture, broccoli, and green onions; stir to combine. Cook 1 minute or until thoroughly heated, stirring frequently. Serve immediately. Serves 4 (serving size: about 2 cups).

CALORIES 368; **FAT** 15.7g (sat 1.5g, mono 6.9g, poly 4.5g); **PROTEIN** 26.6g; **CARB** 27.1g; **FIBER** 5.8g; **CHOL** 129mg; **IRON** 4.7mg; **SODIUM** 560mg; **CALC** 122mg

HOW WE DID IT

• Used less rice. Our recipe calls for just 1 cup of cooked rice for the entire dish.

• Added edamame, bell pepper, snap peas, and broccoli to bulk up the portion size without inflating calories.

• Reduced the amount of total oil used—a little canola to stir-fry aromatic ingredients and rice, and a small amount of heart-healthy sesame oil to cook the shrimp.

• Cut salt by drizzling in just enough lower-sodium soy sauce to nicely flavor the dish.

TODAY'S LESSON: CUSTARDS

Think custard, and you likely picture silken, creamy desserts. Pudding, ice cream, and crème brûlée are all products of the happy entanglement of milk and eggs. But here's today's lesson: Don't ignore the savory side. Savory custards make dazzling first courses and sides, as we were reminded while adding smoky bacon and nutty Swiss cheese to the mix. Of course, we've got your sweets fix covered, too, with velvety lemon curd and rich, supercreamy butterscotch pudding.

Make Ahead

Lemon Curd with Berries

Hands-on time: 14 min. Total time: 2 hr.
In this custard, citrus juice stands in for milk as the base liquid, thickened by egg yolks. Butter gives the curd a glorious sheen.

²/₃ cup sugar
½ cup fresh lemon juice
¼ cup fresh orange juice
⅛ teaspoon salt
6 large egg yolks
3 tablespoons butter, cut into small pieces
2 teaspoons grated lemon rind
1½ cups blueberries
1½ cups raspberries
8 teaspoons graham cracker crumbs

1. Combine first 5 ingredients in a small, heavy saucepan over medium heat. Heat to 180° or until thick (about 6 minutes), stirring constantly with a whisk; remove from heat. Add butter and rind, stirring until butter melts. Place curd in a medium bowl. Cover surface of curd with plastic wrap, and chill completely. Spoon 2 tablespoons curd into each of 8 small cups. Top each serving with 1½ tablespoons blueberries and 1½ tablespoons raspberries. Repeat layers of curd and berries. Top each serving with 1 teaspoon crumbs. Serves 8.

CALORIES 174; **FAT** 8.1g (sat 4g, mono 2.7g, poly 0.9g); **PROTEIN** 2.7g; **CARB** 24.4g; **FIBER** 2.1g; **CHOL** 169mg; **IRON** 0.7mg; **SODIUM** 85mg; **CALC** 30mg

Bacon and Cheese Custards

***Hands-on time: 15 min. Total time: 1 hr. 5 min.** Serve these savory, smoky treats as a first course, or set them out for brunch as crustless mini quiches.*

4 center-cut bacon slices
¹⁄₃ cup finely chopped red bell pepper
2 garlic cloves, minced
¹⁄₂ cup thinly sliced green onions
1¹⁄₂ ounces shredded reduced-fat Swiss cheese (about ¹⁄₃ cup)
Cooking spray
2 cups 2% reduced-fat milk
1 ounce grated fresh Parmigiano-Reggiano cheese (about ¹⁄₄ cup)
¹⁄₄ teaspoon kosher salt
¹⁄₈ teaspoon ground red pepper
3 large eggs
2 large egg whites

1. Preheat oven to 350°.
2. Cook bacon in a medium nonstick skillet over medium heat until crisp. Remove bacon from pan; crumble. Reserve 1 tablespoon drippings in pan; increase heat to medium-high. Add bell pepper and garlic; sauté 3 minutes. Add green onions; sauté 1 minute. Remove from heat; stir in crumbled bacon and Swiss cheese. Divide bacon mixture evenly among 6 (6-ounce) ramekins or custard cups coated with cooking spray.
3. Heat 2 cups milk in a saucepan over medium heat to 180° or until tiny bubbles form around the edge (do not boil). Place Parmigiano-Reggiano and remaining ingredients in a large bowl; stir with a whisk. Gradually add hot milk to egg mixture, stirring constantly with a whisk. Divide egg mixture evenly among ramekins. Place ramekins in a roasting pan, and add hot water to pan to a depth of 1 inch. Bake at 350° for 32 minutes or until center barely moves when ramekin is touched. Remove ramekins from pan, and let stand 10 minutes. Serve warm. Serves 6 (serving size: 1 custard).

CALORIES 142; **FAT** 7.1g (sat 3.5g, mono 1.7g, poly 0.5g); **PROTEIN** 12g; **CARB** 6.2g; **FIBER** 0.4g; **CHOL** 104mg; **IRON** 0.7mg; **SODIUM** 342mg; **CALC** 218mg

Butterscotch Pudding

Hands-on time: 20 min. Total time: 3 hr. 20 min.

1 cup whole milk, divided
2¹⁄₂ tablespoons cornstarch
1¹⁄₂ cups 2% reduced-fat milk
1 cup packed dark brown sugar
1¹⁄₂ teaspoons vanilla extract
¹⁄₈ teaspoon salt
2 large egg yolks
1 tablespoon cold butter

1. Combine ¼ cup whole milk and cornstarch in a bowl, stirring well with a whisk. Combine remaining ¾ cup whole milk and 2% milk in a medium saucepan over medium heat, and bring to a simmer.
2. Add 1 cup brown sugar, vanilla extract, salt, and 2 egg yolks to cornstarch mixture, and stir well with a whisk. Gradually add warm milk to sugar mixture, stirring constantly with a whisk. Pour mixture into saucepan, and cook over medium heat until mixture begins to boil, stirring constantly with a whisk. Cook 1 minute or until mixture is thick, stirring constantly. Remove from heat. Add 1 tablespoon butter, and stir until butter melts.
3. Place pan in a large ice-filled bowl 6 minutes or until mixture cools, and stir occasionally. Cover surface of pudding with plastic wrap. Chill at least 3 hours before serving. Serves 6 (serving size: ½ cup).

CALORIES 245; **FAT** 6g (sat 3.3g, mono 1.8g, poly 0.4g); **PROTEIN** 4.3g; **CARB** 44.2g; **FIBER** 0g; **CHOL** 84mg; **IRON** 0.5mg; **SODIUM** 117mg; **CALC** 156mg

BAKED CUSTARD BASICS

HEAT MILK, DON'T BOIL
Custard success is all about temperature control. Look for small bubbles around the rim of the pan as you heat the milk, and don't heat it to more than 180° or it may curdle. Have an instant-read digital thermometer on hand to check the temperature.

TEMPER THE EGGS FIRST
Whisking hot milk gradually into the eggs raises their temperature slowly and safely, ensuring they won't curdle. Pour slowly; whisk constantly. And again, as long as your milk mixture isn't hotter than 180°, you should have no trouble.

BAKE IN A WATER BATH
A water bath is just one more way to make sure your custards cook evenly and don't overheat. Set the ramekins in a roasting pan or a metal baking pan, and then pour hot water into the pan to a depth of about 1 inch. Set the pan carefully in the oven.

WARM YOUR GREENS

By Mark Bittman

Open up new flavors by heating the leaves you love to toss.

The side salad is ubiquitous, and it should be: It's fast and healthy, and you can make it up as you go along. But amazing things happen when you start to think of salad greens not merely as pristine products ready to toss and serve, but as ingredients ready to be transformed.

I like to tinker with greens by applying a gentle amount of heat, not so much that they completely wilt or lose their vibrant color, but enough to soften their flavor and texture just a bit. This is an especially nice way to treat them in the spring, when you're done with the long, slow cooking of winter but not yet ready to succumb to the ovenless cooking of summer.

Spinach was probably the first green to blur the line between raw and cooked—spinach salads with warm dressings turned up in a lot of restaurants, and of course spinach can be completely cooked in lasagna or creamed side dishes. Lettuces and arugula, though, have not crossed over and are perfect candidates for a little creativity and a kiss of heat.

The first recipe is a hearty side salad, but it bears only slight resemblance to a standard bowl of greens. It's based on a BLT, about as worthy a combination of ingredients as I can think of. The lettuce here is romaine. I slice it in half the long way—with the core still intact so that it holds together—then put it faceup in the broiler or facedown on the grill until it's nicely charred. The charred face is warm, crackly crisp, and slightly sweet, but as you dig down, the romaine becomes cooler, fresher, and more familiar.

The accompaniments are a progression of ingredients cooked one after the other in a skillet. First: little strips of prosciutto (instead of bacon) that are crisped. Then I cook small cubes of whole-grain bread in the remaining fat until golden brown and crunchy. After the bread comes out (the pan will be nearly dry), whole grape or cherry tomatoes go in. They cook in the skillet until charred and just starting to burst open. Everything gets scattered over the romaine along with some chopped scallions and crumbled blue cheese, which begins to melt when it hits the warm lettuce.

The next step is to get a bit more aggressive in the way that you use cooked salad greens. They can be pureed into cream-based soups, sautéed and tossed with pasta, or quickly stir-fried with meat or vegetables. The French classically poach spring peas and onions with lettuce. The point is that greens can move much closer to the main event than a side salad allows.

The final transformation of greens happens when you swap them in for another ingredient. In the case of the second recipe, I use arugula instead of basil and pistachios instead of pine nuts for a pesto-infused potato salad. The arugula gives it a great peppery bite, and the pistachios add a richness to balance out the bite (they also make it wonderfully crunchy and very green). If you coat the potatoes with pesto while they're still quite hot from roasting, they'll drink in the flavor, and the residual heat will take the edge off the raw garlic without taming the arugula too much. You could toss the pesto with pasta, chicken, shrimp, ripe tomatoes, cubes of toasted bread, or any other roasted vegetables. In any case, you've moved a traditional cool-temperature green right to the middle of the table.

Quick & Easy

Charred BLT Salad

Hands-on time: 27 min. Total time: 27 min.

- 3 tablespoons extra-virgin olive oil, divided
- 2 ounces thinly sliced prosciutto, cut crosswise into ribbons
- 1½ cups (½-inch) cubed whole-grain bread (about 2 ounces)
- 1 pint grape tomatoes
- ⅛ teaspoon kosher salt
- ¼ teaspoon freshly ground black pepper
- 2 romaine hearts, halved lengthwise
- Cooking spray
- ¼ cup chopped green onions
- 2 ounces blue cheese, crumbled

1. Heat a large skillet over medium heat. Add 2 tablespoons oil; swirl to coat. Add prosciutto; cook 4 minutes or until crisp, stirring occasionally. Remove prosciutto with a slotted spoon. Drain on paper towels. Add bread to pan; cook 3 minutes or until browned, stirring frequently. Combine prosciutto and bread. Add remaining 1 tablespoon oil to pan. Add tomatoes; cook 5 minutes or until skins begin to split, stirring frequently. Pour tomatoes and olive oil into a small bowl. Sprinkle with salt and pepper.
2. Preheat grill to medium-high heat.
3. Coat cut sides of lettuce with cooking spray. Place lettuce, cut sides down, on a grill rack coated with cooking spray. Cook 2 minutes or until well marked. Place 1 lettuce half on each of 4 plates. Divide prosciutto mixture and tomato mixture among servings. Top each serving with 1 tablespoon onions and ½ ounce cheese. Serves 4.

CALORIES 226; FAT 16g (sat 4.5g, mono 9.1g, poly 1.4g); PROTEIN 9g; CARB 12.9g; FIBER 2.9g; CHOL 19mg; IRON 1.5mg; SODIUM 559mg; CALC 120mg

Roasted Potatoes with Arugula-Pistachio Pesto

Hands-on time: 18 min. Total time: 58 min.

2 pounds fingerling potatoes, halved lengthwise
1/4 cup extra-virgin olive oil, divided
3/4 teaspoon kosher salt, divided
3/8 teaspoon freshly ground black pepper, divided
1 1/2 cups packed arugula leaves (about 1 1/2 ounces)
3 tablespoons grated fresh Parmesan cheese
1 1/2 tablespoons pistachios
2 teaspoons water
1 1/2 teaspoons fresh lemon juice
1 garlic clove

1. Place a jelly-roll pan in oven. Preheat oven to 400°.
2. Combine potatoes and 1 tablespoon oil in a medium bowl; toss well. Arrange potatoes in a single layer on preheated pan. Sprinkle potatoes with 1/2 teaspoon salt and 1/4 teaspoon pepper. Bake at 400° for 20 minutes; toss potatoes. Bake an additional 25 minutes or until tender, stirring every 10 minutes.
3. Place remaining 3 tablespoons oil, remaining 1/4 teaspoon salt, remaining 1/8 teaspoon pepper, arugula leaves, Parmesan cheese, pistachios, 2 teaspoons water, lemon juice, and garlic in a food processor; process until smooth. Combine arugula mixture and hot potatoes in a medium bowl; toss well. Serves 6 (serving size: 1 cup).

CALORIES 245; FAT 10.8g (sat 1.8g, mono 7.3g, poly 1.4g); PROTEIN 5.3g; CARB 33.1g; FIBER 3.7g; CHOL 2mg; IRON 1.9mg; SODIUM 303mg; CALC 62mg

---

A PEACHIER TURNOVER

A rich, juicy filling and flaky crust keep this portable treat deliciously grease-free and picnic-ready.

Buttery, flaky pockets of deep-fried fruit are a guaranteed success at any picnic. No utensils needed for these peach-packed, lard-laden mini pies (charmingly known as "hand pies" in the South)—just a hearty napkin to wipe the grease and gooey filling off your cheeks. With nearly 730 calories and 19 grams of saturated fat each, we just had to rescue these treats.

Tender, flaky layers of crust require fat and liquid. We drop the lard and decrease the butter to reduce the fat by nearly half. And because too much water yields too much gluten (and thus a tougher crust), our solution was … vodka! The alcohol provides moisture in the reduced-butter dough, and then vaporizes mid-bake (a technique disabled by a deep fryer), leaving no trace of alcohol flavor and a light, flaky crust. Plumped dried peaches offer a concentrated flavor boost for our succulent filling. These fruit-filled party pies are lighter, flakier, and finger-licking good.

Peach "Fried" Pie

Hands-on time: 40 min. Total time: 3 hr.
Dried peaches make this dessert a year-round option. Keeping dough ingredients chilled every step of the way ensures a crisp, tender crust that can stand up to the warm, gooey filling.

Crust:
12.4 ounces all-purpose flour (about 2 3/4 cups), divided
1 teaspoon salt
2 tablespoons sugar
9 tablespoons frozen unsalted butter, cut into small pieces
1/4 cup vodka, chilled
1/4 cup cold water
Filling:
8 ounces dried peaches
1 cup water
1/2 cup orange juice
3/4 cup sugar
1 teaspoon ground cinnamon
1 tablespoon fat-free milk
1 large egg, lightly beaten
Cooking spray

1. To prepare crust, weigh or lightly spoon flour into dry measuring cups; level with a knife. Place 2 1/2 cups flour, salt, and 2 tablespoons sugar in a food processor; pulse 10 times. Add frozen butter, and process until mixture resembles coarse meal. Place food processor bowl and flour mixture in freezer 15 minutes.
2. Place bowl back on processor. Combine vodka and cold water. Add vodka mixture slowly through food chute, pulsing just until combined.
3. Divide dough into 12 equal portions. Shape each dough portion into a ball; flatten each ball into a 3-inch circle on a lightly floured surface. Roll each dough portion into a 5-inch circle, adding remaining 1/4 cup flour as needed to prevent dough from sticking. Stack dough circles between single layers of wax paper or plastic wrap to prevent sticking. Cover stack with

plastic wrap; refrigerate at least 2 hours or overnight.

4. To prepare filling, combine peaches, 1 cup water, orange juice, ¾ cup sugar, and cinnamon in a medium saucepan. Bring to a simmer; cover and cook 1 hour, stirring occasionally. Remove from heat, and mash with a potato masher; cool.

5. Preheat oven to 425°. Place a large foil-lined baking sheet in oven.

6. Remove dough from refrigerator. Working with 1 circle at a time, spoon 2 level tablespoons peach mixture into center of each circle. Fold dough over filling; press edges together with a fork to seal.

7. Combine milk and egg in a small bowl, stirring with a whisk. Brush pies evenly with egg mixture. Cut three diagonal slits across top of each pie. Remove hot baking sheet from oven, and coat with cooking spray. Place pies, cut sides up, on baking sheet, and place on middle oven rack. Bake at 425° for 18 minutes or until lightly browned. Cool slightly on a wire rack. Serves 12 (serving size: 1 pie).

CALORIES 312; **FAT** 9.4g (sat 5.7g, mono 2.4g, poly 0.5g); **PROTEIN** 4.6g; **CARB** 49.7g; **FIBER** 2.3g; **CHOL** 41mg; **IRON** 2mg; **SODIUM** 203mg; **CALC** 15mg

LIGHT-CRUST SECRETS

LESS BUTTER
We decrease the fat in the dough by nearly half, saving 202 calories and 12 grams of sat fat per pie.

OVEN-BAKED GOODNESS
No need to deep-fry. Oven-bake on a preheated baking sheet to save 107 calories and 2 grams of sat fat per pie.

DISAPPEARING VODKA
This little trick adds moisture to the dough without the need for added fat. The alcohol bakes off in the oven.

PIE DOUGH, PERFECTED

Lighter homemade dough requires care in each step. The results are well worth it.

1. Make the most of a smaller amount of fat. Butter goes a *longer* way when frozen and pulsed into the flour, creating pockets of butter throughout.

2. Pulse in vodka, which moistens the dough and limits gluten formation to keep the crust tender. Be careful not to overmix.

3. Roll the dough into thin, 5-inch circles for perfectly portioned treats. Refrigerate 2 hours to make pie assembly easier.

4. Vent the filled pies to allow steam to escape during baking, preventing that fiber-rich filling from overflowing.

CLASSIC	MAKEOVER
730 calories per pie	312 calories per pie
45 grams total fat	9.4 grams total fat
19 grams saturated fat	5.7 grams saturated fat

FEED 4 FOR LESS THAN $10

Budget heads East for a bit of spice action: Indian grilled chicken, nut-crusted tofu tacos, and fiery mango salsa with pork.

Tandoori Chicken Thighs

$2.46/serving, $9.85 total

Hands-on time: 28 min. Total time: 2 hr. 35 min. *Slice half an onion into wedges, and halve and seed six mini sweet peppers. Brush the veggies with a bit of oil, grill them, and serve along with naan bread to round out the meal.*

1 cup plain 2% reduced-fat Greek yogurt
¼ cup grated onion
1½ tablespoons grated peeled fresh ginger
1 tablespoon ground cumin
1 teaspoon ground red pepper
½ teaspoon ground turmeric
5 garlic cloves, minced
8 skinless, boneless chicken thighs
½ teaspoon kosher salt
1 tablespoon canola oil

1. Combine first 7 ingredients in a bowl, stirring well. Scrape yogurt mixture into a large zip-top plastic bag. Add chicken to yogurt mixture in bag; seal. Marinate in refrigerator 2 hours. Remove chicken from bag; discard marinade. Sprinkle both sides of chicken evenly with salt.
2. Preheat grill to medium-high heat.
3. Brush grill rack with oil. Arrange chicken on grill rack. Grill 6 minutes on each side or until done. Serves 4 (serving size: 2 chicken thighs).

CALORIES 298; **FAT** 16.1g (sat 4g, mono 6.6g, poly 3.6g); **PROTEIN** 31g; **CARB** 6g; **FIBER** 1.2g; **CHOL** 101mg; **IRON** 2.1mg; **SODIUM** 349mg; **CALC** 63mg

Pork Tenderloin with Mango Salsa

$2.40/serving, $9.58 total

Hands-on time: 23 min. Total time: 38 min. *Serve this pork and vibrant salsa over hot cooked couscous.*

Cooking spray
1 (1-pound) pork tenderloin, trimmed
½ teaspoon salt, divided
¼ teaspoon freshly ground black pepper
¼ cup chopped red onion
2 tablespoons olive oil
1 tablespoon cider vinegar
2 teaspoons sugar
½ teaspoon grated lemon rind
1 ripe mango, peeled and chopped
1 serrano pepper, seeded and finely chopped
¼ cup small fresh mint leaves

1. Heat a skillet over medium-high heat. Coat pan with cooking spray. Sprinkle pork with ¼ teaspoon salt and black pepper. Add pork to pan; cook 16 minutes or until a thermometer registers 145°, turning to brown on all sides. Remove pork; let stand 10 minutes.
2. Combine red onion and next 6 ingredients; toss. Sprinkle mixture with remaining ¼ teaspoon salt and mint; toss. Slice pork crosswise; serve with mango salsa. Serves 4 (serving size: 3 ounces pork and ½ cup salsa).

CALORIES 232; **FAT** 9.9g (sat 2g, mono 6.1g, poly 1.2g); **PROTEIN** 22.8g; **CARB** 12.7g; **FIBER** 1.4g; **CHOL** 62mg; **IRON** 1.2mg; **SODIUM** 346mg; **CALC** 16mg

Peanut-Crusted Tofu Tacos with Tangy Slaw

$1.86/serving, $7.45 total

Hands-on time: 20 min. Total time: 25 min.

1 (14-ounce) package water-packed extra-firm tofu
½ cup salted, dry-roasted peanuts
½ cup panko (Japanese breadcrumbs)
½ cup light coconut milk
1 large egg, lightly beaten
¾ cup all-purpose flour
3 tablespoons canola oil, divided
2 cups thinly sliced cabbage
⅓ cup sliced green onions
2 tablespoons fresh lime juice
½ teaspoon kosher salt
1 jalapeño pepper, seeded and thinly sliced
8 (6-inch) corn tortillas
Lime wedges (optional)

1. Cut tofu lengthwise into 4 (½-inch-thick) slices. Place tofu slices on several layers of heavy-duty paper towels. Cover tofu with additional paper towels; let stand 5 minutes. Cut each tofu slice lengthwise into ½-inch-thick strips; cut strips in half crosswise.
2. Place peanuts in a food processor; process until ground. Combine peanuts and panko in a shallow dish, stirring well. Combine milk and egg in a shallow dish, stirring well. Place flour in a shallow dish.
3. Heat a large skillet over medium-high heat. Add 1 tablespoon oil to pan; swirl to coat. Dredge half of tofu in flour; dip in egg mixture. Dredge in peanut mixture. Add coated tofu to pan, and sauté 4 minutes or until golden and crisp, turning to brown on all sides. Remove tofu from pan, and drain on paper towels. Repeat procedure with 1 tablespoon canola oil, tofu, flour, egg mixture, and peanut mixture.

4. Combine cabbage and next 4 ingredients. Drizzle cabbage mixture with remaining 1 tablespoon oil; toss to coat. Heat tortillas according to package directions. Place 2 tortillas on each of 4 plates; top each tortilla with ¼ cup slaw. Divide tofu evenly among tacos. Serve with lime wedges, if desired. Serves 4 (serving size: 2 tacos).

CALORIES 506; **FAT** 28.4g (sat 3.9g, mono 12.8g, poly 10.1g); **PROTEIN** 20.5g; **CARB** 46.1g; **FIBER** 5.5g; **CHOL** 53mg; **IRON** 2.9mg; **SODIUM** 301mg; **CALC** 131mg

KITCHEN SECRET: SIZING UP SHRIMP

MEDIUM 26/30*   **LARGE** 16/20*   **JUMBO** Under 10*
number of shrimp per pound

Although the commercial seafood industry has strict sizing standards for shrimp, grocers, fishmongers, and other retailers aren't required to follow these regulations—one store's large might be another's medium. So it's most reliable to purchase these crustaceans by count, which indicates the average number of shrimp per pound. The handy guide above is a good rule of thumb when shopping for shrimp.

EVERYDAY VEGETARIAN

ALL JAZZED UP FOR BRUNCH

Linger over a late-morning meal of mushroom-kale Benedicts or lofty cheese soufflés in honor of Mother's Day...or any lazy Sunday.

Vegetarian

Vegetarian Benedicts with Thyme Sabayon

Hands-on time: 55 min. Total time: 55 min. *Fresh thyme is a welcome addition to this frothy, egg-and-wine–based sauce called sabayon. Substitute curly kale for lacinato kale, if desired.*

Sauce:
1 large egg
2 tablespoons 1% low-fat milk
1 tablespoon dry white wine
1 tablespoon fresh lemon juice
1 teaspoon chopped fresh thyme
2 teaspoons butter, chilled and cut into small pieces
Benedicts:
2 (4-inch) portobello mushroom caps
1 teaspoon extra-virgin olive oil
4 small leaves lacinato kale, trimmed and tough center ribs removed
2 multigrain English muffins, split
1 ounce (about ¼ cup) aged Gouda cheese, shredded
2 tablespoons white wine vinegar
4 large eggs
¼ teaspoon freshly ground black pepper

1. To prepare sauce, combine 1 egg and next 4 ingredients in the top of a double boiler. Cook over simmering water until thick (about 9 minutes), stirring constantly with a whisk. Remove from heat. Add butter, 1 piece at a time, stirring with a whisk until thoroughly incorporated. Keep warm.
2. To prepare Benedicts, remove brown gills from the undersides of portobello mushrooms using a spoon; discard gills. Remove and discard stems. Cut mushroom caps into ½-inch-thick slices.
3. Heat a large skillet over medium-high heat. Add olive oil to pan; swirl to coat. Add mushrooms, and cook 3 minutes on each side or until browned. Keep warm.
4. Bring a large saucepan of water to a boil. Add kale; cook 2 minutes or until just tender. Plunge kale into ice water; drain well.
5. Preheat broiler to high.
6. Place muffin halves, cut sides up, on a baking sheet. Broil 1 minute or until browned. Top each muffin half with 1 tablespoon cheese. Broil 1 minute or until cheese melts. Top cheese with 1 kale leaf; broil 1 minute. Top muffins evenly with mushroom slices. Keep warm.
7. Add water to a large skillet, filling two-thirds full. Bring to a simmer. Add vinegar. Break each egg into a custard cup, and pour gently into pan. Cook 3 minutes or until desired degree of doneness. Remove eggs from pan using a slotted spoon. Top each muffin half with 1 egg. Whisk sabayon over simmering water to reheat; spoon about 1½ tablespoons sauce evenly over each egg. Sprinkle with pepper. Serve immediately. Serves 4 (serving size: 1 Benedict).

CALORIES 242; **FAT** 12g (sat 4.7g, mono 4.6g, poly 1.3g); **PROTEIN** 14.3g; **CARB** 19.9g; **FIBER** 1.8g; **CHOL** 278mg; **IRON** 2.7mg; **SODIUM** 307mg; **CALC** 174mg

Cheese Soufflés with Herb Salad

***Hands-on time: 51 min. Total time: 1 hr. 5 min.** Gruyère cheese grows stronger, earthier, and more complex with age, adding an intensely rich profile to these light, fluffy soufflés.*

Soufflés:

2 teaspoons unsalted butter, softened

8 teaspoons finely grated fresh Parmigiano-Reggiano cheese

2 1/2 tablespoons all-purpose flour

1/8 teaspoon ground red pepper

1/8 teaspoon freshly grated nutmeg

1/8 teaspoon freshly ground black pepper

1/2 cup plus 2 tablespoons 1% low-fat milk

2 tablespoons dry white wine

1/4 teaspoon kosher salt

2 ounces cave-aged Gruyère cheese, shredded (about 1/2 cup)

2 large egg yolks

4 large egg whites

Salad:

4 teaspoons extra-virgin olive oil

4 teaspoons white balsamic vinegar

1/4 teaspoon kosher salt

1/4 teaspoon freshly ground black pepper

4 cups baby arugula

4 cups mixed herbs (such as Italian parsley, mint, dill, cilantro, tarragon, chives, and basil)

1. Preheat oven to 400°.

2. To prepare soufflés, coat each of 4 (1-cup) soufflé dishes evenly with 1/2 teaspoon butter. Sprinkle each soufflé dish with 2 teaspoons Parmigiano-Reggiano cheese, tilting to coat sides and bottom.

3. Combine flour and next 3 ingredients in a small saucepan over medium heat. Gradually add milk and white wine, stirring with a whisk until smooth. Cook 4 minutes or until mixture is thick and bubbly, stirring constantly.

Remove from heat. Add salt and Gruyère cheese; stir until cheese melts. Spoon mixture into a large bowl, and let stand 5 minutes. Stir in egg yolks.

4. Place egg whites in a large bowl; beat with a mixer at high speed until medium peaks form (do not overbeat). Gently stir one-quarter of egg whites into yolk mixture; gently fold in remaining egg whites. Gently spoon mixture into prepared dishes. Place dishes on a baking sheet, and place in 400° oven. Immediately reduce oven temperature to 375°. Bake soufflés at 375° for 17 minutes or until puffy and golden.

5. To prepare salad, combine olive oil, vinegar, salt, and black pepper in a large bowl, stirring well with a whisk. Add arugula and herbs; toss to coat. Serve with soufflés. Serves 4 (serving size: 1 soufflé and 1 1/2 cups salad).

CALORIES 229; FAT 14.8g (sat 6g, mono 6.5g, poly 1.3g); PROTEIN 13.6g; CARB 10.2g; FIBER 1.5g; CHOL 131mg; IRON 3mg; SODIUM 458mg; CALC 310mg

KID-FRIENDLY COOKING

MATISSE'S BREAD ADVENTURE

This month, 11-year-old Matisse Reid shares chai tea–spiced banana bread with family and friends.

To field-test one of our kid-friendly recipes, I contacted the food-savviest kid I know, Matisse Reid, who loves the flavors of squid and olives. This month, we sent her adventurous taste buds home with a tea-spiced twist on classic banana bread to share with family and friends. Here's her report. —Phoebe Wu

"Over the weekend I made Chai Banana Bread. I think this recipe would be really good for a brunch or even a dessert. It has a lot of ingredients, but I think the recipe is well worth it. I did need Mom's help, though, just to make sure that every ingredient got included and all the measurements were correct. The spices in this recipe work really well together and are a good contrast with the sweetness of the banana. The texture of the bread is really nice; it melts in your mouth. Mashing the banana was fun—I used a potato masher, but for little kids who like to get their hands dirty, they can squish the banana through their (clean) hands."

Kid Friendly • Freezable Make Ahead

Chai Banana Bread

Hands-on time: 20 min. Total time: 1 hr. 33 min.

1 1/2 cups mashed ripe banana (about 3)

1/3 cup plain fat-free yogurt

5 tablespoons butter, melted

2 large eggs

1/2 cup granulated sugar

1/2 cup packed brown sugar

10 ounces all-purpose flour (about 2 1/4 cups)

3/4 teaspoon baking soda

1/2 teaspoon salt

3/4 teaspoon ground cardamom

1/2 teaspoon ground cinnamon

1/4 teaspoon ground ginger

1/4 teaspoon ground allspice

1 1/4 teaspoons vanilla extract, divided

Cooking spray

1/3 cup powdered sugar

1 1/2 teaspoons 1% low-fat milk

1. Preheat oven to 350°.
2. Combine first 4 ingredients in a bowl; beat with a mixer at medium speed just until blended. Add sugars; beat at medium just until blended.
3. Weigh or spoon flour into dry measuring cups. Combine flour, soda, and salt. Add flour mixture to banana mixture; beat just until blended.
4. Combine cardamom and next 3 ingredients. Stir 1½ teaspoons spice mixture and 1 teaspoon vanilla into batter. Pour into a 9 x 5–inch loaf pan coated with cooking spray. Bake at 350° for 65 minutes or until a wooden pick inserted in center comes out clean. Cool 10 minutes in pan on a wire rack. Remove from pan; cool.
5. Combine remaining spice mixture, remaining vanilla, powdered sugar, and milk. Drizzle over bread. Serves 16 (serving size: 1 slice).

CALORIES 180; **FAT** 4.4g (sat 2.5g, mono 1.2g, poly 0.3g); **PROTEIN** 3.1g; **CARB** 32.4g; **FIBER** 1.1g; **CHOL** 32mg; **IRON** 1.1mg; **SODIUM** 172mg; **CALC** 20mg

MATISSE SAYS, "DON'T OVERMIX THE BREAD OR IT'LL BE TOUGH AND DRY. JUST MIX IT ENOUGH TO 'WET' ALL THE INGREDIENTS."

"I DIDN'T HAVE GROUND GINGER SO I USED FRESH. I FREEZE MY GINGER BECAUSE IT'S EASIER TO GRATE."

RADICALLY SIMPLE COOKING

VINAIGRETTES GET SAUCY

By Rozanne Gold

Our new columnist plays with the classic high-flavor dressing formula and takes it to salads and beyond.

Clever chefs are shaking up the salad topping idea by using vinaigrettes as quick sauces that lend vibrancy to items other than greens. Tom Colicchio of Craft restaurant and *Top Chef* fame started braising fish in vinaigrette; chef and restaurateur David Burke began reducing vinaigrettes to glaze chicken and lobster; and Dan Barber at Blue Hill Farm created a warm orange vinaigrette to drizzle over fresh figs. One of the most alluring ideas comes from Chef Michel Nischan of Connecticut's Dressing Room—a three-ingredient elixir of apple cider, cider vinegar, and extra-virgin olive oil. It is lovely spooned over roast pork loin, drizzled atop turkey paillards—and not at all bad on a salad.

Inspired by these ideas, I began creating vinaigrettes to spoon atop my main courses. Carrot-ginger vinaigrette, made zippy with orange juice and rice vinegar, is a mouthwatering addition to seared salmon over a tangle of bitter-edged arugula. Another vinaigrette, made from pistachios and lemon and thickened with grated fresh Parmesan, makes simple pork chops taste brand-new.

Dessert vinaigrettes? It's an idea whose time has come. You'll love my riff on Chef Barber's slightly sweet dressing, which I toss with fresh fruit and a chiffonade of basil. It's a whole new world out there.

Kid Friendly • Quick & Easy

Strawberries, Peaches, and Basil with Orange Vinaigrette

Hands-on time: 18 min. Total time: 18 min. *Dan Barber, the chef of the acclaimed locavore restaurant Blue Hill at Stone Barns in Pocantico Hills, New York, created the first dessert vinaigrette I had encountered. This is an adaptation of his recipe, which incorporated much more olive oil and melted butter. The warm vinaigrette releases an intoxicating perfume when poured over the fresh fruit. Serve within 20 minutes of preparing for maximum flavor and optimal temperature.*

1 cup fresh orange juice
1½ tablespoons sugar
1½ tablespoons champagne vinegar
   or white wine vinegar
1 tablespoon extra-virgin olive oil
Dash of salt
1½ cups fresh blueberries
1 pound fresh strawberries, halved
1 large ripe peach or nectarine, cut
   into 16 wedges
¼ cup small fresh basil leaves

1. Combine first 3 ingredients in a small saucepan; bring to a boil. Cook until reduced to ½ cup (about 15 minutes). Add oil and salt to pan, stirring with a whisk. Let stand 2 minutes.
2. Combine berries and peach in a large bowl. Add juice mixture, stirring gently. Sprinkle with basil. Serves 4 (serving size: 1¼ cups).

CALORIES 163; **FAT** 4.2g (sat 0.5g, mono 2.6g, poly 0.7g); **PROTEIN** 2.1g; **CARB** 32.5g; **FIBER** 4.4g; **CHOL** 0mg; **IRON** 1mg; **SODIUM** 39mg; **CALC** 36mg

Crispy Salmon and Arugula Salad with Carrot-Ginger Vinaigrette

Hands-on time: 32 min. Total time: 32 min. *This dressing is so fresh, so addictive, you might want to spoon it over everything. Simply made from a base of carrots and orange juice, it has Asian overtones, as does the salad, with its droplets of roasted sesame oil and rice vinegar. This sophisticated dish comes together quickly and feels healthy as can be.*

¼ **cup grated carrot**
3 **tablespoons fresh orange juice**
2 **tablespoons finely chopped onion or shallots, divided**
2 **tablespoons extra-virgin olive oil, divided**
4 **teaspoons rice vinegar, divided**
1 **teaspoon honey**
1 **teaspoon minced peeled fresh ginger**
¾ **teaspoon salt, divided**
4 **ounces baby arugula (about 6 cups loosely packed)**
1 **cup quartered cherry tomatoes**
1 **large red bell pepper, thinly sliced**
½ **teaspoon dark sesame oil**
4 **(6-ounce) fresh or frozen sustainable salmon fillets (such as wild Alaskan)**
¼ **teaspoon freshly ground black pepper**

1. Place carrot, orange juice, 1 tablespoon onion, 1 tablespoon olive oil, 2 teaspoons rice vinegar, honey, ginger, and ¼ teaspoon salt in a mini food processor; process 1 minute or until well combined.
2. Place arugula, tomatoes, and bell pepper in a large bowl. Add remaining 1 tablespoon onion, 1½ teaspoons olive oil, remaining 2 teaspoons vinegar, and sesame oil; toss well. Sprinkle with ¼ teaspoon salt; toss well.
3. Heat a large nonstick skillet over medium-high heat. Sprinkle fish with

remaining ¼ teaspoon salt and black pepper. Add remaining 1½ teaspoons olive oil to pan; swirl to coat. Add fish to pan, skin sides down; cook 6 minutes or until skin is browned and crisp. Turn fish over; cook 2 minutes or until desired degree of doneness. Arrange 1½ cups salad on each of 4 plates; top each serving with 1 fillet and 2 tablespoons vinaigrette. Serves 4.

Sustainable Choice | *This is the beginning of wild salmon season—a delicious, gorgeous, and sustainable option.*

CALORIES 303; **FAT** 17.1g (sat 2.4g, mono 8.3g, poly 4.8g); **PROTEIN** 29.7g; **CARB** 8.9g; **FIBER** 2.1g; **CHOL** 82mg; **IRON** 1.5mg; **SODIUM** 536mg; **CALC** 68mg

Pork over Couscous with Pistachio-Lemon Vinaigrette

Hands-on time: 28 min. Total time: 28 min. *Here is a stunning "restaurant dish" (that's actually a full meal) you can whip up in your own kitchen. While it contains a cornucopia of ingredients, stealth techniques make it radically simple and radically delicious. Use genuine Dijon mustard from France for the best flavor. The pistachios can be ground in a spice grinder, coffee grinder, or mini food processor.*

¼ **cup extra-virgin olive oil, divided**
2 **tablespoons pistachios, finely ground**
2 **tablespoons grated fresh Parmigiano-Reggiano cheese**
1½ **tablespoons fresh lemon juice**
1 **tablespoon white balsamic vinegar**
2 **teaspoons maple syrup**
2 **teaspoons Dijon mustard**
2 **teaspoons minced garlic, divided**
¾ **teaspoon salt, divided**
1½ **cups water**
1 **cup uncooked couscous**
4 **(4-ounce) boneless center-cut loin pork chops (about ½ inch thick)**

¼ **teaspoon freshly ground black pepper**
1 **pint grape tomatoes**
3 **tablespoons chopped fresh flat-leaf parsley**

1. Combine 3 tablespoons olive oil, pistachios, and next 5 ingredients in a small bowl. Add 1 teaspoon garlic and ⅛ teaspoon salt, stirring with a whisk.
2. Bring 1½ cups water to a boil in a small saucepan. Add ¼ teaspoon salt and couscous. Cover, remove from heat, and let stand 5 minutes. Fluff with a fork.
3. Heat a large skillet over medium-high heat. Rub pork with remaining 1 teaspoon garlic. Sprinkle with ¼ teaspoon salt and pepper. Add 2 teaspoons oil to pan; swirl to coat. Add pork to pan; cook 3 minutes on each side or until done. Remove pork from pan; keep warm. Reduce heat to medium-low. Add remaining 1 teaspoon oil and tomatoes to pan; cook 5 minutes or until skins blister, shaking pan occasionally. Sprinkle with remaining ⅛ teaspoon salt. Stir tomatoes and parsley into couscous; divide couscous mixture evenly among 4 plates. Top each serving with 1 pork chop and about 2 tablespoons vinaigrette. Serves 4.

CALORIES 489; **FAT** 22.1g (sat 4.3g, mono 13.1g, poly 2.8g); **PROTEIN** 29.2g; **CARB** 42.2g; **FIBER** 3.7g; **CHOL** 69mg; **IRON** 1.7mg; **SODIUM** 597mg; **CALC** 84mg

DINNER TONIGHT

Here is a batch of fast weeknight menus from the *Cooking Light* Test Kitchen.

READY IN
40
MINUTES

The
SHOPPING LIST

Crispy Flounder and Roasted Tomatoes
Cherry tomatoes (1 pint)
Fresh basil
Fresh parsley
Fresh thyme
Capers
Olive oil
Panko (Japanese breadcrumbs)
(6-ounce) flounder fillets (4)

Fennel-Potato Hash
Fennel bulb with fronds (1)
Refrigerated shredded hash brown potatoes
Yellow onion (1)

The
GAME PLAN

While oven preheats:
■ Cook hash.
While tomatoes roast:
■ Coat and cook fish.

Quick & Easy
Crispy Flounder and Roasted Tomatoes

With Fennel-Potato Hash

Flavor Hit: Capers give the tomatoes a briny kick.
Technique Tip: A fish spatula is the best tool for flipping thin, delicate fillets like flounder.
Simple Sub: Chopped olives such as kalamata will work in place of capers.

2 tablespoons capers
1 tablespoon olive oil
1 pint cherry tomatoes
¼ teaspoon kosher salt
¼ teaspoon freshly ground black pepper
¼ cup thinly sliced fresh basil
1 cup panko (Japanese breadcrumbs)
1 tablespoon chopped fresh parsley
2 teaspoons chopped fresh thyme
4 (6-ounce) skinless flounder fillets
Cooking spray
¼ teaspoon kosher salt
¼ teaspoon freshly ground black pepper
2 tablespoons olive oil, divided

1. Preheat oven to 400°.
2. Combine first 3 ingredients in a large ovenproof skillet; toss to coat. Sprinkle with ¼ teaspoon salt and ¼ teaspoon pepper. Bake at 400° for 20 minutes. Remove from oven; top with basil.
3. Combine panko, parsley, and thyme in a shallow dish. Coat fillets with cooking spray; sprinkle with ¼

---

teaspoon salt and ¼ teaspoon pepper. Dredge fillets in panko mixture. Heat a nonstick skillet over medium-high heat. Add 1 tablespoon oil to pan; swirl to coat. Add 2 fillets to pan; cook 3 minutes on each side or until fish flakes easily when tested with a fork. Repeat procedure with remaining oil and fillets. Serves 4 (serving size: 1 flounder fillet and ⅓ cup tomatoes).

Sustainable Choice | *Look for wild Pacific flounder or sole.*

CALORIES 317; FAT 13g (sat 1.9g, mono 7.8g, poly 1.7g); PROTEIN 35g; CARB 13.5g; FIBER 1.7g; CHOL 82mg; IRON 1.2mg; SODIUM 552mg; CALC 48mg

Kid Friendly • Quick & Easy Vegetarian

For the Fennel-Potato Hash:
Heat a large nonstick skillet over medium heat. Add 2 tablespoons olive oil to pan; swirl to coat. Add 2 cups cored, thinly sliced fennel bulb, 1½ cups refrigerated shredded hash brown potatoes, and ½ cup vertically sliced yellow onion to pan; cook 12 minutes or until golden brown, stirring frequently. Remove from heat; stir in 1½ tablespoons finely chopped fennel fronds, ¼ teaspoon salt, and ¼ teaspoon black pepper. Serves 4 (serving size: ¾ cup).

CALORIES 132; FAT 6.9g (sat 0.9g); SODIUM 209mg

FLOUNDER GETS GOLDEN CRUNCH FROM PANKO BREADCRUMBS.

READY IN 40 MINUTES

The
SHOPPING LIST

Thai Chicken Soup
Shallot (1)
Garlic
Fresh ginger
5-inch pieces fresh lemongrass (3)
Bok choy (2)
Fresh cilantro
Fresh basil
Lime (1)
Olive oil
14.5-ounce can fat-free, lower-sodium chicken broth
Whole-grain rice noodles (4 ounces)
Crushed red pepper
Rotisserie chicken breast (12 ounces)

Spicy Wontons
Wonton wrappers (8)
Sesame seeds
Ground red pepper
Large egg (1)

The
GAME PLAN

While oven preheats:
- Season wontons.
- Cook soup.
While soup simmers:
- Bake wontons.

CRUSH LEMONGRASS BY BEATING IT A FEW TIMES WITH THE BACK OF A KNIFE.

Quick & Easy
Thai Chicken Soup

With Spicy Wontons

1 teaspoon olive oil
3 tablespoons minced shallots
2 tablespoons minced garlic
1 tablespoon grated peeled fresh ginger
1 (14.5-ounce) can fat-free, lower-sodium chicken broth
3 (5-inch) pieces peeled fresh lemongrass, crushed
2 cups water
2 cups shredded skinless, boneless rotisserie chicken breast
2 cups chopped bok choy
¼ cup fresh cilantro leaves
¼ cup small fresh basil leaves
2 tablespoons fresh lime juice
¼ teaspoon salt
2 cups hot cooked whole-grain rice noodles (such as Annie Chun's)
⅛ teaspoon crushed red pepper

1. Heat a large saucepan over medium-high heat. Add oil to pan; swirl to coat. Add shallots; cook 1 minute, stirring frequently. Add garlic and ginger; cook 30 seconds, stirring constantly. Add broth; bring to a boil, scraping pan to loosen browned bits. Add lemongrass and 2 cups water to broth mixture; bring to a boil. Reduce heat; simmer 10 minutes. Stir in chicken and bok choy; simmer 5 minutes. Discard lemongrass. Remove from heat; stir in cilantro, basil, lime juice, and salt. Place ½ cup noodles in each of 4 bowls; top each serving with 1¼ cups soup. Sprinkle with red pepper. Serves 4.

CALORIES 207; FAT 3.6g (sat 0.8g, mono 1.6g, poly 0.5g); PROTEIN 22.5g; CARB 22.2g; FIBER 1g; CHOL 50mg; IRON 1mg; SODIUM 663mg; CALC 59mg

Kid Friendly • Quick & Easy
Vegetarian
For the Spicy Wontons:
Preheat oven to 425°. Cut 8 wonton wrappers in half; place on a baking sheet coated with cooking spray.

Combine 1 egg white and 2 teaspoons water. Brush tops of wontons with egg white mixture. Combine 2 teaspoons sesame seeds, ⅛ teaspoon salt, and ⅛ teaspoon ground red pepper; sprinkle evenly over wontons. Press mixture into wontons. Bake at 425° for 5 minutes or until golden. Serves 4 (serving size: 4 wontons halves).

CALORIES 61; FAT 1.2g (sat 0.2g); SODIUM 179mg

READY IN 40 MINUTES

The
SHOPPING LIST

Jerk Chicken and Stuffed Mini Bell Peppers
Green onions
Shallots
Limes (2)
Serrano chile (1)
Fresh cilantro
Mini bell peppers (8)
Garlic
Olive oil
Brown sugar
Ground allspice
Bone-in chicken thighs (8)
⅓-less-fat cream cheese
Light sour cream

Grilled Garlic Bread
French bread

The
GAME PLAN

While grill preheats:
- Prepare jerk mixture.
While chicken grills:
- Stuff peppers.
While peppers grill:
- Prepare bread slices.
- Grill bread.

COOL IT: THE DAIRY AND BREAD HELP TAME THE SPICY HEAT.

READY IN
40
MINUTES

Quick & Easy

Jerk Chicken and Stuffed Mini Bell Peppers

With Grilled Garlic Bread

Time-Saver: Boneless chicken thighs will cook even faster.
Flavor It: Seed the serrano for a less spicy dish.

⅓ cup sliced green onions, divided
⅓ cup chopped shallots, divided
1 tablespoon brown sugar
3 tablespoons fresh lime juice, divided
2 tablespoons olive oil
½ teaspoon ground allspice
4 garlic cloves
1 large serrano chile, stemmed
8 bone-in chicken thighs, skinned
¼ teaspoon salt
Cooking spray
⅓ cup (3 ounces) ⅓-less-fat cream cheese
2 tablespoons chopped fresh cilantro
2 tablespoons light sour cream
8 mini bell peppers

1. Preheat grill to medium-high heat. After preheating, reduce one side to low.
2. Place ¼ cup green onions, ¼ cup shallots, sugar, 2 tablespoons juice, oil, allspice, garlic, and serrano in a mini food processor; process until smooth. Combine half of onion mixture and chicken in a medium bowl; toss well. Sprinkle with salt.
3. Place chicken on grill rack coated with cooking spray over medium-high heat. Cover and grill 5 minutes on each side. Move chicken over low heat. Cover and grill 5 minutes on each side or until done. Brush chicken with remaining onion mixture.
4. Combine remaining green onions, remaining shallots, remaining 1 tablespoon juice, cheese, cilantro, and sour cream. Halve bell peppers lengthwise; discard seeds. Divide cheese mixture evenly among pepper halves. Place peppers on grill rack coated with cooking spray over medium-high heat. Grill 7 minutes or until peppers are lightly charred. Serve with chicken. Serves 4 (serving size: 2 thighs and 4 pepper halves).

CALORIES 340; FAT 17.9g (sat 5.9g, mono 8.8g, poly 2.2g); PROTEIN 30.2g; CARB 14g; FIBER 1.6g; CHOL 132mg; IRON 2.1mg; SODIUM 363mg; CALC 67mg

Kid Friendly • Quick & Easy Vegetarian
For the Grilled Garlic Bread:
Preheat grill to medium-high heat. Combine 1½ tablespoons olive oil and 2 minced garlic cloves in a microwave-safe bowl; microwave at HIGH 8 seconds. Brush both sides of 4 (1½-ounce) slices French bread with oil mixture. Place bread on grill rack; grill 1 minute on each side. Serves 4 (serving size: 1 slice).

CALORIES 159; FAT 6.2g (sat 0.7g); SODIUM 269mg

The
SHOPPING LIST

Grilled Salmon and Brown Butter Couscous
Lemon (1)
Pine nuts
14.5-ounce can fat-free, lower-sodium chicken broth
White wine
White pepper
Ground fennel seeds
Ground coriander
Couscous
(6-ounce) skinless salmon fillets (4)
Butter

Grilled Summer Squash
Baby yellow squash
Baby zucchini
Olive oil

The
GAME PLAN

While grill preheats:
■ Cook couscous.
While squashes cook:
■ Prepare spice blend.
■ Grill salmon.

continued

Grilled Salmon and Brown Butter Couscous

With Grilled Summer Squash

Simple Sub: Use thick slices of yellow squash and zucchini in place of baby squash.
Flavor Hit: Browning the pine nuts in butter deepens their taste.
Kid Tweak: Chicken can take the place of strong-flavored fish.

2 tablespoons butter
2 tablespoons pine nuts
1 cup uncooked couscous
2 tablespoons dry white wine
1 (14.5-ounce) can fat-free, lower-sodium chicken broth
1 tablespoon grated lemon rind
1 tablespoon fresh lemon juice
1/4 teaspoon kosher salt
1/4 teaspoon freshly ground black pepper
1/2 teaspoon white pepper
1/2 teaspoon ground fennel seeds
1/2 teaspoon ground coriander
1/4 teaspoon sugar
1/4 teaspoon kosher salt
4 (6-ounce) skinless salmon fillets
Cooking spray

1. Preheat grill to medium-high heat.
2. Heat butter in a small saucepan over medium heat; cook 3 minutes or until browned. Add nuts; cook 1 minute, stirring occasionally. Add couscous; cook 1 minute, stirring occasionally. Add wine and broth; bring to a boil. Cover, remove from heat, and let stand 5 minutes. Fluff with a fork; stir in rind, juice, 1/4 teaspoon salt, and black pepper.
3. Combine white pepper and next 4 ingredients in a small bowl. Coat salmon fillets with cooking spray. Sprinkle fillets with spice mixture. Place salmon on a grill rack coated with cooking spray. Grill over medium-high heat 4 minutes on each side or until desired degree of doneness. Serve with couscous. Serves 4 (serving size: 1 salmon fillet and 1/2 cup couscous).

Sustainable Choice

Look for wild-caught Alaskan salmon.

CALORIES 457; FAT 15g (sat 4.9g, mono 4g, poly 4.1g); PROTEIN 41.2g; CARB 35.8g; FIBER 3.1g; CHOL 104mg; IRON 2.3mg; SODIUM 556mg; CALC 47mg

---

Kid Friendly • Quick & Easy
Vegetarian
For the Grilled Summer Squash:
Preheat grill to medium-high heat. Combine 2 cups baby zucchini, halved lengthwise, and 2 cups baby yellow squash, quartered lengthwise, in a large bowl. Add 2 tablespoons olive oil, 1/2 teaspoon kosher salt, and 1/2 teaspoon freshly ground black pepper; toss well. Place vegetables on a grill rack coated with cooking spray. Grill 5 minutes on each side or until lightly charred and tender. Serves 4 (serving size: 3/4 cup).

CALORIES 86; FAT 7.1g (sat 1g); SODIUM 250mg

SUPERFAST

Spring into warm-weather eating with seared scallops on watercress, gingery salad with meaty salmon, fresh snap pea sides, and more.

Kid Friendly • Quick & Easy

Barbecue Chicken Sandwiches

1/2 cup no-salt-added ketchup
2 tablespoons honey mustard
2 tablespoons water
3/4 teaspoon ancho chile powder
3/4 teaspoon smoked paprika
1/2 teaspoon garlic powder
1/2 teaspoon onion powder
1/2 teaspoon ground cumin
1/2 teaspoon Worcestershire sauce
1/8 teaspoon kosher salt
3 cups shredded skinless, boneless rotisserie chicken
3 tablespoons canola mayonnaise
2 tablespoons cider vinegar
1 teaspoon sugar
3 cups packaged coleslaw
1/3 cup chopped green onions
6 (1 1/2-ounce) hamburger buns, toasted

1. Combine first 10 ingredients in a saucepan. Bring to a simmer; cook 10 minutes. Combine sauce and chicken.
2. Combine mayonnaise, vinegar, and sugar. Add coleslaw and onions; toss.
3. Place about 1/2 cup chicken mixture on bottom half of each bun. Top each serving with about 1/2 cup coleslaw mixture; top with top half of bun. Serves 6 (serving size: 1 sandwich).

CALORIES 316; FAT 9.9g (sat 1.5g, mono 4.3g, poly 2.7g); PROTEIN 21.4g; CARB 35.3g; FIBER 2.1g; CHOL 53mg; IRON 2.1mg; SODIUM 548mg; CALC 91mg

Quick & Easy

Salmon with Spinach Salad and Miso Vinaigrette

(pictured on page 216)

The gingery vinaigrette is also delicious with a steak salad.

8 teaspoons canola oil, divided
4 (6-ounce) salmon fillets (about 1 inch thick)
¼ teaspoon kosher salt
1 tablespoon white miso (soybean paste)
1 tablespoon rice wine vinegar
2 teaspoons minced peeled fresh ginger
1 teaspoon sugar
1 teaspoon dark sesame oil
1½ cups shaved English cucumber
1 (9-ounce) package fresh baby spinach
1 teaspoon sesame seeds, toasted

1. Heat a large nonstick skillet over medium-high heat. Add 2 teaspoons canola oil to pan; swirl to coat. Sprinkle fish with salt. Add fish to pan; cook 4 minutes on each side or until desired degree of doneness. Remove fish from pan; keep warm.
2. Combine remaining 2 tablespoons canola oil, miso, and next 4 ingredients in a large bowl; stir with a whisk. Add cucumber and spinach to bowl; toss well. Arrange 1 fillet and 2 cups salad on each of 4 plates. Sprinkle each serving with ¼ teaspoon sesame seeds. Serves 4.

Sustainable Choice

Wild Alaskan salmon is a sure sustainable choice. Avoid farmed salmon.

CALORIES 339; FAT 16.8g (sat 1.9g, mono 8.1g, poly 5.6g); PROTEIN 36.6g; CARB 11.1g; FIBER 4.1g; CHOL 88mg; IRON 3.8mg; SODIUM 471mg; CALC 81mg

Quick & Easy

Seared Scallops with Wilted Watercress and Bacon

2 teaspoons canola oil
1½ pounds large sea scallops (about 16)
⅜ teaspoon kosher salt, divided
¼ teaspoon sugar
⅛ teaspoon freshly ground black pepper
2 center-cut bacon slices
½ cup sliced shallots
2 large garlic cloves, thinly sliced
3 tablespoons fat-free, lower-sodium chicken broth
2 (4-ounce) packages trimmed watercress

1. Heat a large cast-iron skillet over medium-high heat. Add oil to pan; swirl to coat. Sprinkle both sides of scallops evenly with ¼ teaspoon salt, sugar, and pepper. Add scallops to pan; cook 3 minutes or until done, turning after 2 minutes. Remove from pan; keep warm.
2. Cook bacon in a large nonstick skillet over medium heat until crisp. Remove bacon from pan; crumble. Discard all but 2 teaspoons drippings. Add shallots and garlic to drippings in pan; sauté 2 minutes. Add broth to pan; bring to a boil. Add remaining ⅛ teaspoon salt and watercress to pan; cook 30 seconds or until greens begin to wilt. Place 4 scallops and about 1 cup watercress on each of 4 plates. Sprinkle servings evenly with bacon. Serves 4.

Sustainable Choice

Scallops are a sustainable buy, but for the best choice, pick diver-caught scallops from Mexico.

CALORIES 261; FAT 7.5g (sat 1.7g, mono 3.3g, poly 1.6g); PROTEIN 33.5g; CARB 15.6g; FIBER 0.3g; CHOL 63mg; IRON 1.4mg; SODIUM 594mg; CALC 112mg

Kid Friendly • Quick & Easy

Lemony Snap Peas

(pictured on page 216)

8 cups water
12 ounces sugar snap peas, trimmed
½ teaspoon grated lemon rind
2 tablespoons fresh lemon juice
1 tablespoon extra-virgin olive oil
1 teaspoon Dijon mustard
½ teaspoon sugar
¼ teaspoon kosher salt
¼ teaspoon black pepper
1 shallot, minced

1. Bring 8 cups water to a boil in a large Dutch oven. Add peas; cook 30 seconds or until crisp-tender. Drain and plunge into ice water; drain. Slice half of peas diagonally.
2. Combine rind and remaining ingredients; stir with a whisk. Add peas; toss. Serves 4 (serving size: about 1 cup).

CALORIES 73; FAT 3.6g (sat 0.5g, mono 2.5g, poly 0.4g); PROTEIN 2.5g; CARB 8.4g; FIBER 2.3g; CHOL 0mg; IRON 1.8mg; SODIUM 154mg; CALC 39mg

Variation 1: Radish and Feta
Prepare base recipe, reducing salt to ⅛ teaspoon. Add ½ cup thinly sliced radishes, ⅓ cup (about 1½ ounces) crumbled feta, and 3 tablespoons chopped fresh mint to pea mixture. Toss to combine. Serves 4 (serving size: 1 cup).

CALORIES 104; FAT 5.8g (sat 2.1g); SODIUM 219mg

Variation 2: Israeli Couscous and Dill
Heat a saucepan over medium heat. Add 2 teaspoons olive oil to pan; swirl to coat. Add ⅔ cup Israeli couscous; sauté 3 minutes. Add 1 cup water; bring to a boil. Cover, reduce heat, and simmer 10 minutes. Drain and rinse; drain. Prepare base recipe with 6 ounces peas, increasing salt to ½ teaspoon and substituting ½ teaspoon minced garlic for shallot. Combine pea mixture, couscous, and 1 tablespoon minced dill. Top with 2 tablespoons shaved Parmesan cheese. Serves 4 (serving size: about 1 cup).

CALORIES 211; FAT 6.7g (sat 1.2g); SODIUM 314mg

Variation 3: Toasted Almond and Pecorino

Prepare base recipe. Toast 3 tablespoons sliced almonds in a small skillet; cook over medium heat 3 minutes or until lightly browned. Add almonds to pea mixture; toss gently. Top with 3 tablespoons shaved pecorino Romano cheese. Serves 4 (serving size: about 1 cup).

CALORIES 113; FAT 6.8g (sat 1.4g); SODIUM 221mg

Kid Friendly • Quick & Easy
Vegetarian

Banana-Chocolate French Toast

¼ cup 1% low-fat milk
2 large eggs, lightly beaten
¾ teaspoon vanilla extract
½ teaspoon sugar
⅛ teaspoon salt
6 (1½-ounce) slices whole-grain bread
4½ tablespoons hazelnut-chocolate spread (such as Nutella)
1 cup thinly sliced banana (about 8 ounces)
2 teaspoons canola oil
1½ teaspoons powdered sugar

1. Combine first 5 ingredients in a shallow dish.
2. Spread each of 3 bread slices with 1½ tablespoons hazelnut-chocolate spread; arrange ⅓ cup banana slices over each bread slice. Top sandwiches with remaining 3 bread slices.
3. Heat oil in a large nonstick skillet over medium-high heat. Working with 1 sandwich at a time, place into milk mixture, turning gently to coat both sides. Carefully place coated sandwiches into pan. Cook 2 minutes on each side or until lightly browned. Cut each sandwich into 4 triangles. Sprinkle evenly with powdered sugar. Serves 4 (serving size: 3 triangles).

CALORIES 390; FAT 13.8g (sat 3.6g, mono 6.8g, poly 3.2g); PROTEIN 11.7g; CARB 53.6g; FIBER 6g; CHOL 91mg; IRON 2.6mg; SODIUM 391mg; CALC 115mg

---

WHAT TO EAT RIGHT NOW

BABY ARTICHOKES

If you like the earthy goodness of big globe artichokes but find them fussy, buy a bunch of baby ones instead. Here's the deal: They're choke-free (the choke is that furry part) and almost entirely edible. Less prep work overall. For a light supper and an unforgettable taste of the season, try this stunning tart that pairs baby artichokes with peppery radishes.

Vegetarian

Artichoke Galette

Hands-on time: 49 min. Total time: 1 hr. 19 min.

3 cups water, divided
2 tablespoons fresh lemon juice
8 baby artichokes
½ cup crisp white wine
1½ teaspoons black peppercorns
Cooking spray
5 shallots, peeled and quartered
5 French breakfast radishes, halved lengthwise
½ (14.1-ounce) package refrigerated pie dough (such as Pillsbury)
1 garlic clove, halved
⅓ cup pine nuts, toasted and chopped
3 ounces Asiago cheese, shredded (about ¾ cup)
2 teaspoons fresh thyme leaves
½ teaspoon black pepper
¼ teaspoon kosher salt

1. Preheat oven to 400°.
2. Combine 1 cup water and juice in a bowl. Cut off artichoke tops; trim stems. Quarter artichokes; place in bowl. Combine 2 cups water and wine in a saucepan. Place peppercorns in center of cheesecloth; tie ends. Add sachet to pan; bring to a simmer. Drain artichokes; add to pot. Simmer 5 minutes; drain. Discard sachet. Heat a small skillet over medium-high heat. Coat pan with cooking spray. Add shallots, and sauté 5 minutes. Combine shallots, artichokes, and radishes.
3. Roll dough out to a 15-inch circle; rub with garlic. Place dough on a baking sheet. Sprinkle with nuts and cheese, leaving a 2-inch border. Top with artichoke mixture; sprinkle with thyme, pepper, and salt. Fold edges of dough over to partially cover. Bake at 400° for 30 minutes or until browned. Serves 6 (serving size: 1 wedge).

CALORIES 304; FAT 18.4g (sat 6g, mono 5.5g, poly 5.4g); PROTEIN 9.3g; CARB 30.8g; FIBER 5g; CHOL 13mg; IRON 1.9mg; SODIUM 503mg; CALC 177mg

---

WHAT TO DRINK RIGHT NOW

Cucumber-Mint Tequila Tonic

2 cups chopped English cucumber
½ cup fresh mint leaves
⅓ cup agave nectar
¼ cup fresh cilantro leaves
1 lime, sectioned and juiced
Dash of salt
½ cup tequila blanco
¾ cup chilled tonic water

1. Place first 6 ingredients in a food processor; pulse until smooth. Scrape mixture into a bowl; stir in tequila. Chill. Strain. Stir in tonic water. Serve over ice. Serves 6 (serving size: about ⅓ cup).

CALORIES 114; FAT 0g; SODIUM 45mg

(Nah)

(Dig in)

OOPS!
YOUR GUAC GETS ICKY

The goal is to avoid that khaki color.

Guacamole is a surefire and healthy party pleaser, at least for those who arrive at the party early. Stragglers know they're late by the muddy brown shade the dip has assumed in the bowl.

Obviously, oxygen is the enemy of guac, as it is for sliced potatoes and apples. The question is, can you delay the oxidation process? (Leaving the pit in the dip, an old myth, doesn't help.)

The solution: A two-part strategy involves using acid to delay oxidation and then doling out the dip as needed from an airtight container. The antioxidant property of ascorbic acid, plentiful in lemon or lime juice, is your first line of defense. Toss cubed avocado in citrus juice, about 3 tablespoons per avocado,

and then drain before mashing, reserving the juice. After you've mashed all your ingredients, add some juice back to taste. Still, your dip will brown eventually if you serve it all at once, so serve in small batches, with the rest stored in the fridge like so: Rub a little olive oil onto a sheet of plastic wrap, and then press the wrap, oil side down, onto the surface of the dip—the thin film of oil creates an impermeable barrier, with plastic as a reliable backup. And the dip stays green.

SUMMER COOKBOOK

In our eighth annual homage to the glories of summer, we celebrate with fresh, healthy recipes that run from fruity drinks and zesty pickles to plummy barbecue sauce and a peachy take on shortcake.

STARTERS & DRINKS

Oh, the pleasures of summer, when the preamble of spring turns into a piece of performance art by Mother Nature concerning the bounty of the earth. This is truly the time for market-based food: whatever's fresh. This year we've updated iconic dishes with bright twists and new sizzle. We also invited a few of our favorite chefs to share their hot-weather inspirations. Get ready: It's going to be a long, tasty summer.

Champagne Mango Margaritas
(pictured on page 219)

Ashley James
Executive Chef
Four Seasons Hotel,
Los Angeles at Beverly Hills
Hands-on time: 15 min. Total time:
1 hr. 35 min. *"During my time in Mexico working at the Four Seasons Resort Punta Mita, I lived in Bucerias, halfway between Puerta Vallarta and the hotel. My house was a small casita with beautiful mango groves in the backyard," recalls Chef James. "In the summer, I'd make margaritas with mangoes picked from the trees, fresh lime juice, tamarind, and some chile pequín. I had many of those margaritas, believe you me!"*

Champagne mangoes are also called Ataulfo mangoes. Other varieties may be used but won't be as smooth. Use more mango nectar to compensate.

2 tablespoons water
2 tablespoons sugar
1/2 cup fresh orange juice
1/2 cup tequila
1/4 cup mango nectar
1/4 cup fresh lime juice
1/4 cup Triple Sec
3 Champagne mangoes, peeled, seeded, chopped, and frozen (about 3 cups)
3 dried pequín chiles or chiles de árbol
1 cup ice
1/2 teaspoon kosher salt, divided
3/8 teaspoon sugar
1 lime wedge

1. Combine 2 tablespoons water and 2 tablespoons sugar in a microwave-safe glass measuring cup; microwave at HIGH 2 minutes. Stir until sugar dissolves. Place sugar mixture, orange juice, and next 6 ingredients in a blender, and process until smooth. Add ice to blender; pulse to combine. Stir in 1/8 teaspoon salt. Chill in refrigerator 30 minutes, stirring after 15 minutes.
2. Combine remaining salt and 3/8 teaspoon sugar in a saucer. Rub rims of 6 glasses with 1 lime wedge; spin rim of each glass in salt mixture to coat. Fill each glass with about 2/3 cup margarita. Serves 6.

CALORIES 178; **FAT** 0.4g (sat 0.1g, mono 0.1g, poly 0.1g); **PROTEIN** 0.8g; **CARB** 30.6g; **FIBER** 2.1g; **CHOL** 0mg; **IRON** 0.3mg; **SODIUM** 164mg; **CALC** 16mg

Make Ahead • Vegetarian
Quick Pickled Dilly Green Beans

Hands-on time: 10 min. Total time:
2 hr. 10 min. *A fresh alternative to pickled cukes, these crisp, crunchy treats make a zesty summer snack, garnish for a Bloody Mary, or condiment in a sandwich or salad. They're easy to prepare and will keep up to a week in the refrigerator.*

1/4 cup chopped fresh dill
1/2 pound green beans, trimmed
1 cup white wine vinegar
1 cup water
2 teaspoons sugar
2 teaspoons salt
2 teaspoons pickling spice
1 garlic clove, peeled

1. Combine dill and green beans in a medium bowl.
2. Combine vinegar and remaining ingredients in a small saucepan. Bring to a boil, and cook 1 minute or until sugar and salt dissolve. Pour over bean mixture. Let stand 2 hours. Drain or serve with a slotted spoon. Serves 12 (serving size: about 1/3 cup).

CALORIES 6; **FAT** 0g; **PROTEIN** 0.4g; **CARB** 1.4g; **FIBER** 0.7g; **CHOL** 0mg; **IRON** 0.2mg; **SODIUM** 41mg; **CALC** 7mg

Creole Deviled Eggs

Quick & Easy • Make Ahead
Vegetarian

Chef John Stage
Dinosaur Bar-B-Que, New York City
Hands-on time: 22 min. Total time: 37
min. *Chef Stage remembers his mother's*
deviled eggs, which he updates with vibrant
Creole seasonings.

8 large eggs
1 tablespoon cider vinegar
2 tablespoons (1 ounce) $^{1}/_{3}$-less-fat
   cream cheese
$^{1}/_{4}$ cup plain 2% reduced-fat Greek
   yogurt
1 tablespoon finely chopped green
   bell pepper
1 tablespoon finely chopped celery
1 tablespoon Creole mustard
2 teaspoons minced fresh chives
$^{1}/_{4}$ teaspoon freshly ground black
   pepper
$^{1}/_{4}$ teaspoon hot pepper sauce (such
   as Tabasco)
$^{1}/_{8}$ teaspoon salt
Dash of ground red pepper
2 pieces hot pickled okra, each cut
   into 8 slices

1. Place eggs in a large saucepan. Cover
with water to 1 inch above eggs; stir
in vinegar. Bring just to a rolling boil.
Remove from heat; cover and let stand
15 minutes. Drain and rinse with cold
running water until cool.
2. Peel eggs; cut in half lengthwise.
Place yolks in a medium bowl; add
cream cheese, and mash with a fork
until smooth. Add yogurt and next
8 ingredients. Spoon mixture into egg
white halves (about 1 tablespoon in
each half). Garnish each egg half with
1 okra slice. Serves 8 (serving size: 2
egg halves).

CALORIES 90; **FAT** 4.9g (sat 1.8g, mono 1.9g, poly 0.8g);
PROTEIN 7.2g; **CARB** 2.5g; **FIBER** 0.1g; **CHOL** 183mg;
IRON 1mg; **SODIUM** 163mg; **CALC** 36mg

Make Ahead

Chilled Fresh Corn Soup with King Crab

Hands-on time: 25 min. Total time:
2 hr. 45 min.

1 pound frozen cooked king crab legs,
   thawed
6 cups fresh corn kernels (about 11
   ears)
$4^{1}/_{2}$ cups water
$^{1}/_{8}$ teaspoon ground red pepper
1 cup 2% milk
$^{1}/_{4}$ cup chopped fresh chives
$^{1}/_{2}$ teaspoon freshly ground black
   pepper

1. Cut shells off crab with kitchen
shears; reserve shells. Coarsely chop
crabmeat; chill. Combine shells, corn,
$4^{1}/_{2}$ cups water, and red pepper in a
saucepan; bring to a boil. Reduce heat;
simmer 20 minutes or until corn is
very tender. Discard shells.
2. Place half of corn mixture in a
blender. Remove center piece of blender
lid (to allow steam to escape); secure
blender lid on blender. Place a clean
towel over opening in blender lid (to
avoid splatters). Process until smooth.
Press pureed corn mixture through a
fine sieve over a bowl, reserving liquid;
discard solids. Repeat procedure with
remaining corn mixture. Stir in milk,
chives, and black pepper. Chill 2 hours.
Top with reserved crabmeat. Serves 8
(serving size: about $^{2}/_{3}$ cup soup and
about $^{1}/_{4}$ cup crabmeat).

CALORIES 115; **FAT** 2g (sat 0.6g, mono 0.5g, poly 0.6g);
PROTEIN 10g; **CARB** 16.2g; **FIBER** 2.2g; **CHOL** 20mg;
IRON 0.7mg; **SODIUM** 383mg; **CALC** 59mg

Make Ahead • Vegetarian

Spicy Squash Pickles

Hands-on time: 11 min. Total time:
2 hr. 41 min. *These summer squashes offer*
meatier texture than traditional pickles.

$^{3}/_{4}$ pound zucchini, cut into $^{1}/_{4}$-inch-
   thick slices
$^{3}/_{4}$ pound yellow squash, cut into
   $^{1}/_{4}$-inch-thick slices
2 teaspoons kosher salt, divided
$^{1}/_{2}$ cup thinly sliced sweet onion
   (such as Vidalia)
1 cup water
1 cup cider vinegar
$^{1}/_{4}$ cup maple syrup
$^{1}/_{4}$ to $^{1}/_{2}$ teaspoon crushed red pepper

1. Place a wire rack on a baking sheet.
Arrange zucchini and squash slices on
rack; sprinkle with 1 teaspoon salt. Let
stand 30 minutes. Rinse well under
cold water; pat dry with paper towels.
Place zucchini, squash, and onion in a
medium glass bowl.
2. Combine remaining 1 teaspoon salt,
1 cup water, and remaining ingredients
in a small saucepan; bring to a boil,
and pour over vegetables. Weigh down
vegetables with a plate. Cover and
refrigerate at least 2 hours or overnight. Drain or serve with a slotted
spoon. Serves 12 (serving size: about
$^{1}/_{4}$ cup).

CALORIES 13; **FAT** 0.1g (sat 0g, mono 0g, poly 0.1g);
PROTEIN 0.7g; **CARB** 2.8g; **FIBER** 0.7g; **CHOL** 0mg;
IRON 0.2mg; **SODIUM** 38mg; **CALC** 11mg

Peach Lemonade

Hands-on time: 12 min. Total time: 3 hr. 42 min. *Peaches add sweet, mellow roundness to traditional lemonade. Stir in white rum or bourbon for grown-ups.*

4 cups water
2 cups coarsely chopped peaches
3/4 cup sugar
1 cup fresh lemon juice (about 6 lemons)
4 cups ice
1 peach, cut into 8 wedges

1. Combine first 3 ingredients in a medium saucepan over medium-high heat. Bring to a boil; reduce heat, and simmer 3 minutes. Place peach mixture in a blender; let stand 20 minutes. Remove center piece of blender lid (to allow steam to escape); secure blender lid on blender. Place a clean towel over opening in blender lid. Blend until smooth. Pour into a large bowl. Refrigerate at least 3 hours.
2. Press peach mixture through a sieve over a bowl, reserving liquid; discard solids. Stir in lemon juice. Place ½ cup ice in each of 8 glasses. Pour about ⅔ cup lemonade into each glass; garnish each glass with 1 peach wedge. Serves 8.

CALORIES 98; FAT 0.1g (sat 0g, mono 0g, poly 0g); PROTEIN 0.5g; CARB 25.9g; FIBER 0.8g; CHOL 0mg; IRON 0.1mg; SODIUM 0mg; CALC 4mg

Cilantro-Jalapeño Limeade

Hands-on time: 12 min. Total time: 3 hr. 42 min. *Jalapeño adds a subtle kick, and cilantro brings grassy, herbal notes to classic limeade. Adults might like to stir in a little tequila.*

4½ cups water
3/4 cup sugar
1/2 cup agave nectar
1 cup coarsely chopped fresh cilantro
2 large jalapeño peppers, seeded and chopped (about ½ cup)
2 tablespoons sugar
1/4 teaspoon salt
9 lime wedges, divided
1½ cups fresh lime juice (about 10 limes)
4 cups ice

1. Combine first 3 ingredients in a medium saucepan over medium-high heat; bring to a boil. Remove from heat; stir in cilantro and jalapeño. Let stand 30 minutes. Pour jalapeño mixture into a large bowl; cover and chill at least 3 hours.
2. Combine 2 tablespoons sugar and salt in a shallow dish. Rub rims of 8 glasses with 1 lime wedge. Dip rims of glasses in sugar mixture.
3. Strain cilantro mixture through a fine sieve over a bowl, discarding solids. Stir in lime juice. Fill each prepared glass with ½ cup ice. Add ¾ cup limeade to each glass. Garnish with remaining 8 lime wedges. Serves 8.

CALORIES 155; FAT 0g; PROTEIN 0.2g; CARB 41.3g; FIBER 0.2g; CHOL 0mg; IRON 0.1mg; SODIUM 56mg; CALC 7mg

MAIN DISHES
Balsamic and Shallot Chicken Breasts

James Boyce
Cotton Row and Commerce Kitchen, Huntsville, Ala.
Hands-on time: 23 min. Total time: 43 min. *Chef Boyce remembers his father's chicken from weekly family barbecues when he was a kid. Our take amps up flavor with a balsamic reduction. It starts on the stovetop and finishes in the oven to control doneness.*

6 (8-ounce) bone-in chicken breast halves, skinned
1 teaspoon freshly ground black pepper
1/2 teaspoon salt
1 tablespoon olive oil, divided
1/4 cup chopped shallots
3 garlic cloves, chopped
1 chopped seeded plum tomato
1½ teaspoons tomato paste
1/2 cup fat-free, lower-sodium chicken broth
2/3 cup balsamic vinegar
1/4 cup chopped green onions

1. Preheat oven to 350°.
2. Sprinkle chicken evenly with pepper and salt. Heat a large skillet over medium-high heat. Add 2 teaspoons olive oil to pan; swirl to coat. Add chicken, meat sides down; cook 7 minutes or until browned. Turn chicken over; cook 3 minutes. Place chicken on a jelly-roll pan. Bake at 350° for 23 minutes or until done.
3. Return pan to medium-high heat. Add remaining 1 teaspoon oil, shallots, and garlic to pan, and sauté 1 minute, stirring constantly. Add tomato and tomato paste, and sauté 1 minute, stirring constantly. Add broth; bring to a boil, scraping pan to loosen browned bits. Add vinegar;

reduce heat to medium-low, and cook 20 minutes or until reduced to ⅔ cup, stirring occasionally. Serve sauce with chicken. Sprinkle with green onions. Serves 6 (serving size: 1 chicken breast half, about 2 tablespoons sauce, and 2 teaspoons green onions).

CALORIES 250; FAT 4.6g (sat 0.9g, mono 2.2g, poly 0.8g); PROTEIN 42.6g; CARB 6.9g; FIBER 0.4g; CHOL 105mg; IRON 1.8mg; SODIUM 372mg; CALC 39mg

Cabernet-Balsamic Burgers with Sautéed Mushrooms and Onions

Hands-on time: 57 min. Total time: 57 min. Burgers get irresistible upgrades with creamy blue cheese and caramelized onions spiked with jammy red wine and tart-sweet vinegar. A portion of the onions are mixed into the patties to help keep the lean beef moist.

5 teaspoons olive oil, divided
4 cups thinly sliced red onion
1½ teaspoons chopped fresh thyme
½ cup cabernet sauvignon or other dry red wine
2 tablespoons balsamic vinegar
¾ teaspoon salt, divided
1 (8-ounce) package sliced mushrooms
1½ pounds ground sirloin
Cooking spray
⅓ cup light mayonnaise
1 ounce blue cheese, crumbled (about ¼ cup)
1 garlic clove, minced
6 (1½-ounce) whole-wheat hamburger buns
1½ cups baby arugula

1. Heat a large nonstick skillet over medium-low heat. Add 2 teaspoons oil to pan; swirl to coat. Add onion and thyme; cook 17 minutes or until golden and very tender, stirring occasionally. Increase heat to medium-high; add wine, vinegar, and ¼ teaspoon salt. Cook 6 minutes or until liquid almost evaporates, stirring occasionally. Remove onion mixture from pan.
2. Wipe pan clean with paper towels. Heat pan over medium-high heat. Add remaining 3 teaspoons oil to pan; swirl to coat. Add mushrooms and ¼ teaspoon salt; sauté 8 minutes or until mushrooms brown and liquid mostly evaporates.
3. Preheat grill to medium-high heat.
4. Coarsely chop 1 cup onion mixture, and stir chopped onion mixture into beef. Divide beef mixture into 6 equal portions, gently shaping each into a 1-inch-thick patty. Press a nickel-sized indentation in center of each patty. Sprinkle patties with remaining ¼ teaspoon salt. Place patties on a grill rack coated with cooking spray, and grill 4 minutes on each side or until done.
5. Combine mayonnaise, blue cheese, and garlic in a bowl, and mash well with a fork. Spread top halves of buns evenly with mayonnaise mixture. Arrange ¼ cup arugula on bottom half of each bun; top each bottom half of bun with 1 patty, about 2 tablespoons remaining onion mixture, about ¼ cup mushrooms, and top half of bun. Serves 6 (serving size: 1 burger).

CALORIES 395; FAT 17.1g (sat 4.6g, mono 6.8g, poly 4.3g); PROTEIN 29.2g; CARB 33g; FIBER 5g; CHOL 69mg; IRON 3.4mg; SODIUM 756mg; CALC 106mg

Make Ahead

Tandoori Grilled Chicken with Mint Raita

Hands-on time: 1 hr. 50 min. Total time: 9 hr. 50 min. Barbecued chicken, a backyard summer favorite, marinates here in a heady Indian spice blend and tangy yogurt. A cool, herby raita complements it perfectly.

Marinade:
¾ cup fat-free Greek yogurt
2 tablespoons chopped peeled fresh ginger
1 tablespoon paprika
1 tablespoon fresh lime juice
1 teaspoon chili powder
¾ teaspoon salt
½ teaspoon ground turmeric
½ teaspoon ground cumin
⅛ teaspoon ground red pepper
3 garlic cloves, chopped
4 (12-ounce) bone-in chicken leg-thigh quarters, skinned
Raita:
¾ cup fat-free Greek yogurt
¾ cup chopped seeded cucumber
2 tablespoons chopped fresh mint
½ teaspoon ground cumin
¼ teaspoon salt
Cooking spray

1. To prepare marinade, place first 10 ingredients in a blender; process until smooth. Pour into a large zip-top plastic bag. Add chicken; turn to coat. Marinate chicken in refrigerator at least 4 hours or overnight.
2. To prepare raita, combine ¾ cup yogurt and next 4 ingredients in a small bowl; cover and refrigerate.
3. Remove chicken from refrigerator, and let stand at room temperature 45 minutes.
4. Prepare grill for indirect grilling. If using a gas grill, heat one side to medium-high and leave one side with no heat. If using a charcoal grill, arrange hot coals on either side of charcoal grate, leaving an empty space in middle.
5. Remove chicken from marinade, and discard marinade. Place chicken on unheated part of grill rack coated with cooking spray. Close lid, and grill 90 minutes or until a thermometer inserted into meaty part of thigh registers 165°, turning chicken every 20 minutes. Serves 4 (serving size: 1 chicken quarter and about ⅓ cup raita).

CALORIES 284; FAT 7.9g (sat 2g, mono 2.4g, poly 2g); PROTEIN 45.7g; CARB 4.9g; FIBER 0.7g; CHOL 161mg; IRON 2.5mg; SODIUM 502mg; CALC 76mg

Shrimp and Corn Cakes with Heirloom Tomato Salsa

Hands-on time: 1 hr. Total time: 1 hr.

1/2 cup diced red onion
1/4 cup chopped fresh cilantro
2 tablespoons fresh lime juice
1/4 teaspoon kosher salt
1/4 teaspoon ground cumin
1/8 teaspoon ground red pepper
1 1/2 pounds mixed heirloom tomatoes, seeded and chopped
1 serrano chile, seeded and minced
1.5 ounces masa harina (about 1/3 cup)
1.5 ounces all-purpose flour (about 1/3 cup)
1 teaspoon baking powder
1/2 teaspoon kosher salt
1/2 teaspoon freshly ground black pepper
3 cups fresh corn kernels (about 4 large ears), divided
1 tablespoon low-fat buttermilk
1 tablespoon grated lemon rind
2 teaspoons hot sauce
1 large egg
1/3 cup chopped red bell pepper
12 ounces peeled and deveined shrimp, chopped (about 1 1/2 cups)
2 green onions, thinly sliced
2 garlic cloves, minced
3 tablespoons canola oil, divided

1. Combine first 8 ingredients; set aside.
2. Weigh or lightly spoon flours into dry measuring cups; level with a knife. Combine flours, baking powder, 1/2 teaspoon salt, and black pepper in a bowl.
3. Place 1 1/2 cups corn and next 4 ingredients in bowl of a food processor; process until smooth. Combine pureed corn mixture, remaining 1 1/2 cups corn, bell pepper, shrimp, green onions, and garlic in a large bowl. Add flour mixture, stirring gently until moist.
4. Heat a large nonstick skillet over medium heat. Add 1 tablespoon oil to pan; swirl to coat. Add 4 (1/4-cup) batter mounds to pan, pressing each with the back of a spatula to slightly flatten; cook 3 minutes on each side or until golden and thoroughly cooked. Remove from pan; keep warm. Repeat procedure twice with remaining 2 tablespoons oil and batter. Serve with salsa. Serves 6 (serving size: 2 cakes and about 1/2 cup salsa).

CALORIES 285; FAT 10.2g (sat 1.1g, mono 5.3g, poly 3.2g); PROTEIN 17.9g; CARB 33.4g; FIBER 5g; CHOL 116mg; IRON 3.2mg; SODIUM 466mg; CALC 112mg

Quick & Easy

Pan Bagnat (Niçoise Salad Sandwiches)

Hands-on time: 40 min. Total time: 40 min. *Albacore tuna season runs from June through October.*

2 large eggs
3 (5-ounce) fresh albacore tuna steaks
1/4 teaspoon salt
1/2 teaspoon freshly ground black pepper, divided
Cooking spray
4 (6-inch) pieces French bread baguette, halved lengthwise
24 Quick Pickled Dilly Green Beans (page 132)
8 (1/4-inch-thick) slices tomato
1 cup thinly sliced fennel bulb (about 1/2 small bulb)
5 kalamata olives, pitted and coarsely chopped
2 tablespoons extra-virgin olive oil
1/2 cup arugula leaves

1. Place eggs in a small saucepan. Cover with water to 1 inch above eggs; bring just to a rolling boil. Remove from heat; cover and let stand 15 minutes. Drain and rinse with cold running water until cool. Peel and slice eggs, and set aside.
2. Heat a large cast-iron grill pan over medium-high heat. Sprinkle fish with salt and 1/4 teaspoon pepper. Coat pan with cooking spray. Add fish to pan; cook 3 minutes on each side or until desired degree of doneness. Cut tuna steaks across grain into thin slices.
3. Hollow out top and bottom halves of bread, leaving a 1/3-inch-thick shell; reserve torn bread for another use. Arrange 6 Quick Pickled Dilly Green Beans on each of 4 bottom bread halves. Arrange tuna evenly over green beans. Top each with 2 tomato slices. Arrange fennel evenly over tomato. Divide olives among each of 4 top halves of bread; drizzle each top half of bread with 1 1/2 teaspoons oil. Divide arugula and sliced eggs evenly among top halves of bread, and sprinkle remaining black pepper evenly over eggs. Place top halves of bread on bottom halves; cut each sandwich in half. Serves 4 (serving size: 1 sandwich).

CALORIES 390; FAT 11.4g (sat 2g, mono 7g, poly 1.6g); PROTEIN 32.5g; CARB 39.3g; FIBER 2.7g; CHOL 140mg; IRON 4.1mg; SODIUM 701mg; CALC 69mg

Vegetarian

Baked Tomatoes with Quinoa, Corn, and Green Chiles

Hands-on time: 55 min. Total time: 1 hr. 20 min.

2 poblano chiles
2 cups fresh corn kernels (about 4 ears)
1 cup chopped onion
1 tablespoon chopped fresh oregano
1 tablespoon olive oil
1 tablespoon fresh lime juice
1 teaspoon salt, divided
3/4 teaspoon ground cumin
1/4 teaspoon freshly ground black pepper
6 large ripe tomatoes (about 4 pounds)
1 cup uncooked quinoa
1/4 cup water
4 ounces colby-Jack cheese, shredded (about 1 cup)

1. Preheat broiler to high.
2. Cut chiles in half lengthwise; discard seeds and membranes. Place chile halves, skin sides up, on a foil-lined baking sheet; flatten with hand. Broil 8 minutes or until blackened. Place in a paper bag; close tightly. Let stand 10 minutes. Peel chiles. Coarsely chop chiles; place in a bowl. Add corn and onion to pan; broil 10 minutes, stirring twice. Add corn mixture to chopped chiles; stir in oregano, oil, lime juice, 1/4 teaspoon salt, cumin, and black pepper.
3. Cut tops off tomatoes; set aside. Carefully scoop out tomato pulp, leaving shells intact. Drain pulp through a sieve over a bowl, pressing with the back of a spoon to extract liquid. Reserve 1 1/4 cups liquid, and discard remaining liquid and pulp. Sprinkle tomatoes with 1/2 teaspoon salt. Invert tomatoes on a wire rack; let stand 30 minutes. Dry insides of tomatoes with a paper towel.
4. Place quinoa in a fine sieve, and place sieve in a large bowl. Cover quinoa with water. Using your hands, rub grains together 30 seconds; rinse and drain. Repeat procedure twice. Drain well. Combine reserved tomato liquid, quinoa, 1/4 cup water, and remaining 1/4 teaspoon salt in a medium saucepan; bring to a boil. Cover, reduce heat, and simmer 15 minutes or until liquid is absorbed. Remove from heat; fluff with a fork. Add quinoa mixture to corn mixture; toss well.
5. Preheat oven to 350°.
6. Spoon about 3/4 cup corn mixture into each tomato. Divide cheese evenly among tomatoes. Place tomatoes and tops, if desired, on a jelly-roll pan. Bake at 350° for 15 minutes. Remove from oven. Preheat broiler. Broil tomatoes 1 1/2 minutes or until cheese melts. Place tomato tops on tomatoes, if desired. Serves 6 (serving size: 1 stuffed tomato).

CALORIES 320; FAT 11.2g (sat 4.1g, mono 2.4g, poly 2g); PROTEIN 13.4g; CARB 46.3g; FIBER 8.8g; CHOL 17mg; IRON 3.2mg; SODIUM 550mg; CALC 195mg

Pork Patties with Plum Sauce and Napa Cabbage Slaw

Hands-on time: 48 min. Total time: 48 min. Asian seasonings jazz up these mini pork burgers. We add bulgur to the patties to stretch the ground pork and keep saturated fat in check.

1 1/2 cups coarsely chopped plums (about 1/2 pound)
1 1/2 tablespoons brown sugar
2 tablespoons seasoned rice vinegar
1/2 teaspoon Sriracha (hot chile sauce, such as Huy Fong)
1 cup boiling water
1/2 cup uncooked bulgur
1 1/2 pounds ground pork, 80% lean
1 cup diagonally cut green onions, divided
1/2 cup chopped fresh cilantro, divided
2 tablespoons dry sherry
1 tablespoon minced garlic
1 tablespoon minced peeled fresh ginger
1 teaspoon salt, divided
1/4 teaspoon freshly ground black pepper
Cooking spray
6 cups shredded napa (Chinese) cabbage (about 1/2 large head)
3 tablespoons seasoned rice vinegar
1/4 teaspoon dark sesame oil

1. Combine first 4 ingredients in a small saucepan; bring to a boil. Cover; reduce heat, and simmer 15 minutes, stirring frequently. Remove from heat; let stand 10 minutes. Place plum mixture in a blender or food processor; process until smooth.
2. Combine 1 cup boiling water and bulgur in a medium bowl; cover and let stand 20 minutes. Drain well. Combine bulgur, pork, 1/2 cup onions, 1/4 cup cilantro, sherry, garlic, ginger, 3/4 teaspoon salt, and pepper in a medium bowl. Divide pork mixture into 12 equal portions, gently shaping each into a 3/4-inch-thick patty. Press a nickel-sized indentation in center of each patty. Heat a large skillet or grill pan over medium-high heat. Coat pan with cooking spray. Add 6 patties to pan; cook 5 minutes on each side or until done. Repeat with remaining 6 patties.
3. Combine remaining 1/2 cup onions, remaining 1/4 cup cilantro, remaining 1/4 teaspoon salt, cabbage, vinegar, and oil; toss gently to coat. Serve patties with slaw; drizzle with plum sauce. Serves 6 (serving size: 2 patties, 1 cup slaw, and 2 tablespoons sauce).

CALORIES 296; FAT 10.8g (sat 4.1g, mono 4.3g, poly 1.5g); PROTEIN 25.4g; CARB 24.1g; FIBER 4.2g; CHOL 85mg; IRON 0.7mg; SODIUM 724mg; CALC 85mg

Grilled Maine Lobster Tails with Miso Butter

Bruce and Eric Bromberg
Blue Ribbon Sushi Bar and Grill, The Cosmopolitan of Las Vegas
Hands-on time: 15 min. Total time: 25 min. *The Brombergs fondly recall eating steamed lobsters at the beach on Long Island. Their modern twist is grilled lobster with miso butter. Miso brings salty umami notes to the sweet, succulent lobster.*

3 tablespoons butter
2 teaspoons red miso (soybean paste)
4 (8-ounce) lobster tails, halved lengthwise
Cooking spray

1. Preheat grill to high heat.
2. Place butter and miso in a microwave-safe dish. Microwave at HIGH 30 seconds or until butter melts. Stir to combine.
3. Coat lobster tails with cooking spray. Place tails, flesh sides down, on grill rack coated with cooking spray, and grill 4 minutes. Turn tails over; brush with butter mixture. Grill 3 minutes or until done, brushing occasionally with butter mixture. Serve with remaining butter mixture. Serves 4 (serving size: 1 lobster tail and about 1 tablespoon miso butter).

CALORIES 336; FAT 12.3g (sat 6g, mono 2.9g, poly 1.8g); PROTEIN 47.1g; CARB 6g; FIBER 0g; CHOL 182mg; IRON 2.8mg; SODIUM 586mg; CALC 114mg

SIDES & SALADS

Quick & Easy • Make Ahead
Vegetarian

Cabbage Slaw with Tangy Mustard Seed Dressing

Hands-on time: 20 min. Total time: 35 min. *Mustard seed, cilantro, and cumin give this coleslaw an Indian spin.*

8 cups presliced green cabbage (about 1¹/₂ pounds)
1 cup thinly vertically sliced red onion
¹/₂ cup grated carrot
¹/₂ cup chopped fresh cilantro
2 tablespoons canola oil
2 tablespoons brown mustard seeds
1 tablespoon cumin seeds
1 large garlic clove, minced
¹/₂ jalapeño pepper, finely chopped
¹/₄ cup white wine vinegar
1¹/₂ teaspoons sugar
³/₄ teaspoon salt
³/₄ teaspoon freshly ground black pepper

1. Combine first 4 ingredients in a large bowl.
2. Heat a small saucepan over medium heat. Add oil to pan; swirl to coat. Add mustard and cumin seeds; cook 90 seconds or until mustard seeds begin to pop. Remove from heat. Stir in garlic and jalapeño; let stand 2 minutes. Add vinegar, sugar, salt, and pepper, stirring with a whisk. Pour vinegar mixture over cabbage mixture; toss to coat. Let stand 15 minutes. Serves 10 (serving size: about 1 cup).

CALORIES 67; FAT 3.5g (sat 0.3g, mono 2.3g, poly 0.9g); PROTEIN 1.6g; CARB 7.5g; FIBER 2.4g; CHOL 0mg; IRON 1mg; SODIUM 199mg; CALC 54mg

Melon and Fig Salad with Prosciutto and Balsamic Drizzle

(pictured on page 218)

Hands-on time: 15 min. Total time: 30 min.

¹/₂ cup balsamic vinegar
2 teaspoons extra-virgin olive oil
1 teaspoon fresh lemon juice
¹/₄ teaspoon freshly ground black pepper
¹/₈ teaspoon kosher salt
4 cups gourmet salad greens
¹/₂ pound honeydew melon, peeled, seeded, and thinly sliced
¹/₂ pound cantaloupe, peeled, seeded, and thinly sliced
4 very thin slices prosciutto, torn (about 1 ounce)
4 fresh figs, quartered

1. Bring vinegar to a simmer in a small saucepan over medium-low heat; cook until syrupy and reduced to 3 tablespoons (about 10 minutes), stirring occasionally. Remove from heat.
2. Combine oil, juice, pepper, and salt in a bowl, stirring with a whisk. Add salad greens; toss gently. Divide melon among 4 plates; top with salad greens. Arrange prosciutto and figs over salad greens; drizzle with balsamic syrup. Serves 4 (serving size: ¼ pound melon, about 1 cup salad greens, 1 slice prosciutto, 1 quartered fig, and about 2 teaspoons balsamic syrup).

CALORIES 153; FAT 3.2g (sat 0.6g, mono 1.7g, poly 0.3g); PROTEIN 4.1g; CARB 28.3g; FIBER 3.7g; CHOL 6mg; IRON 1.3mg; SODIUM 299mg; CALC 44mg

Lemony Grilled Potato Salad

Hands-on time: 46 min. Total time: 56 min. *Grilling the vegetables brings unexpected smokiness to a familiar picnic staple.*

2 pounds small Yukon gold potatoes
3 tablespoons extra-virgin olive oil, divided
1 small red onion, cut into 1/2-inch-thick slices
1 red bell pepper, cut in half and seeded
Cooking spray
3 tablespoons chopped fresh basil
2 tablespoons chopped fresh chives
3 tablespoons fresh lemon juice
1 teaspoon capers
3/4 teaspoon salt
1/4 teaspoon freshly ground black pepper

1. Preheat grill to medium-high heat.
2. Place potatoes in a large saucepan; cover with water. Bring to a boil. Reduce heat, and simmer 15 minutes or until tender; drain. Cool slightly. Cut potatoes in half. Combine potatoes and 2 teaspoons oil in a large bowl, and toss well to coat.
3. Brush onion and bell pepper evenly with 1 teaspoon oil. Place potatoes, onion, and bell pepper on a grill rack coated with cooking spray; grill 5 minutes on each side or until tender. Remove vegetables from grill; cool slightly. Cut bell pepper into thin strips. Cut onion slices into quarters.
4. Combine remaining 2 tablespoons oil, basil, and remaining ingredients in a large bowl, stirring with a whisk. Add vegetables to bowl; toss to coat. Serves 6 (serving size: 1 cup).

CALORIES 202; **FAT** 6.9g (sat 1g, mono 4.9g, poly 0.7g); **PROTEIN** 4.1g; **CARB** 30.4g; **FIBER** 2.6g; **CHOL** 0mg; **IRON** 1.5mg; **SODIUM** 320mg; **CALC** 10mg

Black Pepper Pasta Salad with Prosciutto, Asparagus, and Romano

Hands-on time: 35 min. Total time: 35 min. *This mayonnaise-based pasta salad veers from the traditional with salty Italian ham, nutty asparagus, and a generous grinding of pepper.*

8 ounces uncooked cavatappi pasta or elbow macaroni
3 cups (11/2-inch) slices asparagus (about 1 pound)
1 teaspoon olive oil
2 ounces prosciutto, chopped
1/2 cup thinly sliced shallots
6 tablespoons light mayonnaise
1 teaspoon grated lemon rind
1 tablespoon chopped fresh tarragon
2 tablespoons fresh lemon juice
1 teaspoon freshly ground black pepper
Dash of salt
1 cup diced tomato
11/2 ounces pecorino Romano cheese, grated (about 1/3 cup)

1. Cook pasta according to package directions, omitting salt and fat. Add asparagus during last 2 minutes of cooking. Drain and rinse under cold water; drain.
2. Heat a large nonstick skillet over medium-high heat. Add olive oil to pan, and swirl to coat. Add prosciutto, and cook 6 minutes or until crisp, stirring occasionally. Remove prosciutto from pan using a slotted spoon, leaving drippings in pan. Drain prosciutto on paper towels. Add shallots to drippings in pan; cook over medium heat 1 minute or until shallots are tender, stirring frequently.
3. Combine mayonnaise and next 5 ingredients in a large bowl; stir well. Add pasta, asparagus, three-fourths prosciutto, shallots, tomato, and cheese; toss well to coat. Top servings evenly with remaining prosciutto. Serves 8 (serving size: about 1 cup).

CALORIES 208; **FAT** 7g (sat 1.9g, mono 1.8g, poly 2.3g); **PROTEIN** 9.3g; **CARB** 27.9g; **FIBER** 2.5g; **CHOL** 15mg; **IRON** 2.5mg; **SODIUM** 367mg; **CALC** 86mg

Herby Cucumber Salad

Hands-on time: 12 min. Total time: 12 min. *Creamy and tangy, this simple side comes together in a flash. Don't make the salad ahead—the cucumbers will release too much water.*

1/4 cup plain low-fat yogurt
2 tablespoons coarsely chopped fresh dill
1 tablespoon coarsely chopped fresh parsley
2 tablespoons fresh lemon juice
1 tablespoon extra-virgin olive oil
11/2 teaspoons coarsely chopped fresh mint
2 teaspoons Dijon mustard
1/4 teaspoon sugar
1/4 teaspoon salt
1/4 teaspoon freshly ground black pepper
1 garlic clove
51/2 cups thinly sliced cucumber (about 2 large)
21/2 cups thinly sliced red onion

1. Place first 11 ingredients in a food processor or a blender, and process until well blended. Combine cucumber and onion in a large bowl. Drizzle with yogurt mixture, and toss to coat. Serves 6 (serving size: 1 cup).

CALORIES 65; **FAT** 2.6g (sat 0.5g, mono 1.7g, poly 0.3g); **PROTEIN** 1.8g; **CARB** 9.9g; **FIBER** 1.4g; **CHOL** 1mg; **IRON** 0.5mg; **SODIUM** 150mg; **CALC** 48mg

> ## "NOW, FOR EVERY BARBECUE, I ALWAYS HAVE TO MAKE A THREE-BEAN SALAD THAT REMINDS ME OF SUMMER AND MY FAMILY."
>
> —Chef Julian Medina

Quick & Easy • Vegetarian

Pinto, Black, and Red Bean Salad with Grilled Corn and Avocado

Julian Medina
Toloache, Yerba Buena, Coppelia,
New York City
Hands-on time: 42 min. Total time: 42 min. *"When I was growing up in Mexico City, my parents would throw wonderful summer barbecues," says Chef Medina. "We would grill corn on the cob and mix in leftover beans from the weekend and make a delicious, simple corn and bean salad." This Latin-accented three-bean and corn salad is studded with guacamole components: jalapeño, cilantro, white onion, lime, and avocado.*

**1 cup halved heirloom grape or cherry
    tomatoes**
1 teaspoon salt, divided
3 ears shucked corn
**1 medium white onion, cut into ¼-inch-
    thick slices**
1 jalapeño pepper
1 tablespoon olive oil
Cooking spray
⅓ cup chopped fresh cilantro
⅓ cup fresh lime juice
**1 (15-ounce) can no-salt-added pinto
    beans, rinsed and drained**
**1 (15-ounce) can no-salt-added black
    beans, rinsed and drained**
**1 (15-ounce) can no-salt-added kidney
    beans, rinsed and drained**
2 diced peeled avocados

1. Preheat grill to medium-high heat.
2. Place tomatoes in a large bowl, and sprinkle with ½ teaspoon salt. Let stand 10 minutes.
3. Brush corn, onion, and jalapeño evenly with oil. Place vegetables on grill rack coated with cooking spray. Grill corn 12 minutes or until lightly charred, turning after 6 minutes. Grill onion slices and jalapeño 8 minutes or until lightly charred, turning after 4 minutes. Let vegetables stand 5 minutes. Cut kernels from cobs. Coarsely chop onion. Finely chop jalapeño; discard stem. Add corn, onion, and jalapeño to tomato mixture; toss well. Add remaining ½ teaspoon salt, cilantro, and next 4 ingredients to corn mixture; toss well. Top with avocado. Serves 12 (serving size: ⅔ cup).

CALORIES 141; FAT 6.4g (sat 0.9g, mono 4.2g, poly 0.9g); PROTEIN 5g; CARB 18.2g; FIBER 6.8g; CHOL 0mg; IRON 1.2mg; SODIUM 211mg; CALC 38mg

Quick & Easy

Grilled Caesar Salad

Hands-on time: 25 min. Total time: 25 min. *Grilling lettuce gives it a hint of smokiness and lends the leaves crisp-tender contrast. Toasted garlic bread stands in for croutons.*

**10 (½-ounce) slices diagonally cut
    French bread (about ¼ inch thick)**
Cooking spray
3 garlic cloves, divided
**7 canned anchovy fillets, rinsed,
    drained, and divided**
¼ cup fresh lemon juice
1 teaspoon Dijon mustard
**½ teaspoon freshly ground black
    pepper**
¼ teaspoon salt
1 large pasteurized egg yolk
¼ cup extra-virgin olive oil
**3 romaine lettuce hearts, cut in half
    lengthwise (about 24 ounces)**
**½ ounce Parmigiano-Reggiano cheese,
    shaved (about ⅓ cup)**

1. Preheat grill to high.
2. Coat bread slices with cooking spray. Place bread on grill rack coated with cooking spray, and grill 1 minute or until golden, turning once. Remove bread from grill. Cut 1 garlic clove in half; rub both sides of bread with cut sides of garlic clove. Discard clove.
3. Pat anchovy fillets dry with a paper towel. Place remaining 2 garlic cloves, 2 anchovy fillets, juice, and next 4 ingredients in a blender; process until smooth. With blender on, add oil, 1 tablespoon at a time; process until smooth.
4. Place lettuce, cut sides down, on a grill rack coated with cooking spray; grill 2 minutes. Turn; grill 1 minute. Remove from heat; coarsely chop lettuce. Place lettuce in a large bowl; drizzle with dressing, tossing gently to coat.

5. Cut remaining 5 anchovy fillets in half lengthwise. Arrange about ¾ cup salad on each of 10 plates; top each serving with 1 bread slice and 1 anchovy half. Sprinkle each serving with about 1½ teaspoons Parmigiano-Reggiano cheese. Serves 10.

CALORIES 118; **FAT** 7g (sat 1.2g, mono 4.4g, poly 0.7g); **PROTEIN** 3.6g; **CARB** 10.5g; **FIBER** 1.2g; **CHOL** 25mg; **IRON** 1.5mg; **SODIUM** 290mg; **CALC** 66mg

---

Quick & Easy • Vegetarian

Snap Pea and Pea Shoot Stir-Fry with Gingery Orange Sauce

Hands-on time: 22 min. Total time: 22 min. *Asian flavorings elevate a summer veggie side dish.*

¼ cup fresh orange juice
2 tablespoons lower-sodium soy sauce
1¼ teaspoons cornstarch
1 teaspoon ground ginger
1 teaspoon cider vinegar
1 teaspoon dark sesame oil
½ teaspoon Sriracha (hot chile sauce, such as Huy Fong)
2 teaspoons canola oil
⅓ cup sliced red bell pepper
1 pound sugar snap peas, trimmed
2 cups pea shoots

1. Combine first 7 ingredients in a small bowl, and stir well with a whisk.
2. Heat a wok or large, heavy skillet over medium-high heat. Add canola oil to pan; swirl to coat. Add bell pepper and peas; stir-fry 2 minutes. Stir in juice mixture; cook 1 minute or until thick and bubbly, stirring constantly. Top with pea shoots. Serve immediately. Serves 6 (serving size: about ⅔ cup).

CALORIES 79; **FAT** 2.4g (sat 0.2g, mono 1.3g, poly 0.8g); **PROTEIN** 2.5g; **CARB** 8g; **FIBER** 2g; **CHOL** 0mg; **IRON** 0.8mg; **SODIUM** 153mg; **CALC** 52mg

---

DESSERTS

Kid Friendly • Make Ahead

Lemon–Earl Grey Squares

(pictured on page 220)

Hands-on time: 25 min. Total time: 2 hr.

Crust:
Cooking spray
5.6 ounces all-purpose flour (about 1¼ cups)
⅓ cup powdered sugar
2 Earl Grey tea bags, divided
⅛ teaspoon salt
8 tablespoons chilled butter, cut into pieces
Filling:
¼ cup fresh lemon juice
1 cup granulated sugar
2 tablespoons all-purpose flour
½ teaspoon baking powder
2 teaspoons grated lemon rind
3 large eggs
1 tablespoon powdered sugar

1. Preheat oven to 350°.
2. To prepare crust, line an 8-inch square metal baking pan with foil that extends 2 inches beyond sides; coat foil with cooking spray. Weigh or lightly spoon 5.6 ounces flour into dry measuring cups; level with a knife. Combine 5.6 ounces flour, ⅓ cup powdered sugar, 1 teaspoon tea leaves from 1 tea bag (discard remaining tea in bag), and salt in a bowl; cut in butter with a pastry blender or 2 knives until mixture resembles coarse meal. Press into bottom of prepared pan. Bake at 350° for 19 minutes or until lightly browned.
3. To prepare filling, place juice in a medium microwave-safe bowl. Microwave at HIGH 30 seconds. Add remaining 1 tea bag to juice; cover and steep 10 minutes. Squeeze juice from tea bag into bowl; discard tea bag. Combine granulated sugar, 2 tablespoons flour, and baking powder in a bowl. Add rind and eggs to juice; stir with a whisk until combined. Add sugar mixture to juice mixture; stir with a whisk until well combined.
4. Remove crust from oven; pour filling onto hot crust. Bake at 350° for 23 minutes or until set. Cool in pan on a wire rack 30 minutes. Remove from pan by lifting foil. Remove foil, and cut into 16 squares. Sprinkle squares with 1 tablespoon powdered sugar. Serves 16 (serving size: 1 square).

CALORIES 167; **FAT** 6.7g (sat 3.9g, mono 1.9g, poly 0.4g); **PROTEIN** 2.5g; **CARB** 24.5g; **FIBER** 0.4g; **CHOL** 49mg; **IRON** 0.7mg; **SODIUM** 45mg; **CALC** 18mg

STEEPING THE EARL GREY TEA IN THE JUICE ALLOWS ITS SUBTLE FLAVOR TO SHINE IN THIS CLASSIC DESSERT.

Blackberry Merlot Granita

David Myers
Comme Ça, Los Angeles
Hands-on time: 8 min. Total time: 4 hr.
20 min. *"This reminds me of summer after catching lightning bugs," says Chef Myers. "My family would eat fresh-picked black-berries like candy after dinner as the sun was going down."*

4 cups fresh blackberries
¾ cup water
½ cup sugar
½ cup merlot
1 tablespoon lemon juice
1 (3-inch) cinnamon stick

1. Combine all ingredients in a medium saucepan over medium heat; bring to a boil, stirring occasionally. Remove from heat; let stand 15 minutes.
2. Strain mixture through a fine sieve over a bowl, reserving soaking liquid (do not press berries or the mixture will be cloudy). Reserve berries for another use. Pour mixture into an 8-inch square glass or ceramic baking dish. Cover and freeze until partially frozen (about 2 hours). Scrape mixture with a fork, crushing any lumps. Freeze 3 hours or until completely frozen, scraping with a fork every hour. Remove from freezer; scrape mixture with a fork until fluffy. Serves 4 (serving size: ½ cup).

CALORIES 130; **FAT** 0.1g (sat 0g, mono 0g, poly 0.1g);
PROTEIN 0.2g; **CARB** 27.8g; **FIBER** 0.8g; **CHOL** 0mg;
IRON 0.6mg; **SODIUM** 1mg; **CALC** 7mg

Peach and Basil Shortcake

Hands-on time: 29 min. Total time:
3 hr.

Topping:
4 cups sliced peeled peaches (about
 3 pounds)
⅓ cup sugar
⅓ cup small fresh basil leaves
1½ tablespoons fresh lemon juice
Shortcake:
9 ounces cake flour (about 2¼ cups)
½ cup sugar, divided
1 tablespoon baking powder
½ teaspoon baking soda
¼ teaspoon salt
6 tablespoons chilled butter, cut into
 small pieces
1 cup low-fat buttermilk
Cooking spray
1½ teaspoons fat-free milk
¼ cup slivered almonds
¾ cup plain nonfat Greek yogurt

1. To prepare topping, combine first 4 ingredients in a bowl; let stand 1 hour.
2. Preheat oven to 400°.
3. To prepare shortcake, weigh or lightly spoon flour into dry measuring cups, and level with a knife. Combine flour, 7 tablespoons sugar, baking powder, baking soda, and salt in a bowl; stir with a whisk. Cut in butter with a pastry blender or 2 knives until mixture resembles coarse meal. Stir in buttermilk with a fork just until combined (do not overmix). Spoon dough into a 9-inch round metal baking pan coated with cooking spray. Gently brush dough with milk. Sprinkle with remaining 1 tablespoon sugar and almonds.
4. Bake at 400° for 23 minutes or until a wooden pick inserted in center comes out clean. Cool 5 minutes in pan on a wire rack. Remove shortcake from pan; cool completely on wire rack.

5. Cut shortcake into 12 wedges. Top each with ⅓ cup peach mixture and 1 tablespoon yogurt. Serves 12.

CALORIES 261; **FAT** 7.8g (sat 4g, mono 2.4g, poly 0.7g);
PROTEIN 5.5g; **CARB** 44g; **FIBER** 2.3g; **CHOL** 17mg;
IRON 2mg; **SODIUM** 266mg; **CALC** 119mg

Lemon Verbena Ice Cream

Karen Hatfield
Hatfield's, Los Angeles
Hands-on time: 13 min. Total time: 1
hr. 13 min. *"I remember discovering lemon verbena one summer at the greenmarket in New York," says Chef Hatfield. "The smell is intoxicating, and it stays with you forever."*

2½ cups whole milk
1½ cups half-and-half
¾ cup lemon verbena leaves
½ cup sugar
3 large egg yolks

1. Combine first 4 ingredients in a medium, heavy saucepan over medium-high heat. Heat milk mixture to 180° or until tiny bubbles form around edge of pan (do not boil). Remove from heat; let stand 2 minutes. Strain through fine sieve over bowl; discard solids.
2. Place egg yolks in a large bowl; stir with a whisk. Gradually add half of hot milk mixture to yolks, stirring constantly with a whisk. Pour yolk mixture and remaining milk mixture into pan. Cook custard over medium heat 5 minutes or until thermometer registers 160°, stirring constantly. Remove from heat; cool to room temperature.
3. Pour custard into freezer can of an electric ice-cream freezer; freeze according to manufacturer's instructions. Serves 8 (serving size: ½ cup).

CALORIES 174; **FAT** 9.4g (sat 5.3g, mono 1.4g, poly 0.4g);
PROTEIN 4.8g; **CARB** 18.3g; **FIBER** 0g; **CHOL** 103mg;
IRON 0.3mg; **SODIUM** 52mg; **CALC** 144mg

FRESH TAKES ON FIVE SALADS

These are the salad days, when the markets burst with local produce and appetites tilt toward food that's lighter and of-the-moment.

But even now, salad routine can set in—too much of the same good things. Avoid that by playing with your favorite salad themes, as we've done here with five main-course versions that look to Italy, Indonesia, and more for inspiration.

A few tips: Dress lightly for summer—too much vinaigrette drowns the dish. For essential acidic notes, look to interesting vinegars, fresh lemon juice, or a combination. Balance acid with a pinch of sugar, a grating of fragrant orange rind, or a smidgen of peppery Dijon. Play with herbs. And invest in some of those good, healthy oils: hazelnut, pistachio, even avocado.

Vegetarian

Indonesian Vegetable Salad with Peanut Dressing

Hands-on time: 1 hr. 8 min. Total time: 1 hr. 8 min. This is a simplified version of the splendid Indonesian salad called gado gado, *which along with satay is practically a national dish, often served with crunchy shrimp crackers. It uses shortcut ingredients in the sauce—peanut butter, curry paste—to speed things along. For a spicier dressing, stir in sambal oelek or Sriracha.*

Salad:
4 large eggs
1½ cups julienne-cut carrot
1½ cups green beans, trimmed
1½ cups fresh bean sprouts
1 red bell pepper, seeded and cut into thin strips

½ English cucumber, halved lengthwise and cut crosswise into ¼-inch-thick slices (about 2 cups)
Tofu:
1 (14-ounce) package water-packed extra-firm tofu, drained
1 tablespoon cornstarch
2 teaspoons red curry powder or Madras curry powder
¼ teaspoon salt
2 tablespoons canola oil
Dressing:
⅓ cup creamy peanut butter
3 tablespoons hot water
3 tablespoons fresh lime juice
1 tablespoon lower-sodium soy sauce
2 teaspoons brown sugar
2 teaspoons Thai red curry paste
¼ teaspoon salt

1. To prepare salad, place eggs in a large saucepan; cover with water. Bring to a rolling boil; cover, remove from heat, and let stand 12 minutes. Remove eggs from pan with a slotted spoon; rinse with cold water. Peel eggs; cut in half.

2. Return water to a boil. Add carrot, and cook 1 minute. Remove carrot with a slotted spoon; drain and rinse with cold water. Drain and place in a bowl. Add green beans to boiling water, and cook 4 minutes or until crisp-tender. Remove green beans with a slotted spoon; drain and rinse with cold water. Drain and place in a separate bowl. Arrange 2 egg halves, about ⅓ cup carrot, ⅓ cup green beans, ⅓ cup bean sprouts, ¼ cup red bell pepper, and ½ cup cucumber on each of 4 plates.

3. To prepare tofu, cut lengthwise into 4 (½-inch-thick) slices. Place tofu slices on several layers of paper towels. Cover tofu with additional paper towels; let stand 5 minutes. Cut each tofu slice crosswise into ½-inch-thick strips. Combine cornstarch, curry powder, and ¼ teaspoon salt; gently toss with tofu to coat.

4. Heat a large nonstick skillet over medium-high heat. Add oil to pan; swirl to coat. Add tofu to pan; cook 10 minutes or until crisp and browned, turning to brown on all sides. Divide tofu evenly among plates.

5. To prepare dressing, combine peanut butter and next 6 ingredients in a bowl; stir with a whisk until smooth. Serve each salad with about 3 tablespoons dressing. Serves 4.

CALORIES 449; FAT 29.1g (sat 5.6g, mono 12.7g, poly 9.3g); PROTEIN 24.3g; CARB 27.1g; FIBER 5.9g; CHOL 212mg; IRON 4.1mg; SODIUM 645mg; CALC 158mg

THE ASIAN CLASSIC, REIMAGINED

Each plate of this vegetarian salad meal, based on *gado gado*, contains about 4 servings of vegetables and plenty of protein from eggs and tofu. The vibrant colors and crisp texture of the veggies are lovely on their own, but the real star here is the dressing that's draped over all: a creamy, rich, slightly sweet, slightly spicy peanut sauce that is this salad's raison d'être.

Farro, Green Bean, and Fennel Salad with Tuna

Hands-on time: 30 min. Total time: 1 hr. 10 min. We recently tasted—and loved—Wild Planet's wild albacore tuna, jarred in olive oil, which is firm, meaty, rich, and moist. We also love that it's sustainable, 100% pole and troll caught. Visit wildplanetfoods.com to purchase online or locate retailers.

½ cup uncooked whole-grain farro
¾ teaspoon salt, divided
4 cups water
2 cups (2-inch) cut green beans (about ½ pound)
3 tablespoons extra-virgin olive oil
2 tablespoons white wine vinegar
1 tablespoon fresh lemon juice
1 teaspoon Dijon mustard
1 small garlic clove, minced
¼ teaspoon freshly ground black pepper
1 cup grape tomatoes, halved lengthwise
1 cup very thinly sliced fennel bulb (about 1 small bulb)
¼ cup fresh flat-leaf parsley leaves
¼ cup oil-cured olives, pitted and coarsely chopped
5 green onions, thinly sliced
2 (4.5-ounce) jars sustainable oil-packed albacore tuna, drained

1. Combine farro, ½ teaspoon salt, and 4 cups water in a medium saucepan; bring to a boil. Cover and simmer 1 hour or until farro is tender but still slightly chewy. Drain. Cool slightly.
2. While farro cooks, fill another medium saucepan two-thirds full with water; bring to a boil. Add green beans; cook 4 minutes or until crisp-tender. Drain and rinse with cold water; drain.
3. Combine oil, vinegar, juice, mustard, and garlic in a large bowl; stir in remaining ¼ teaspoon salt and pepper. Add farro, beans, tomatoes, and next 4 ingredients; toss well to combine. Flake tuna into large chunks. Add tuna to salad; toss gently to combine. Serves 4 (serving size: about 1½ cups).

CALORIES 393; FAT 27g (sat 4.2g, mono 16.8g, poly 2.6g); PROTEIN 13.9g; CARB 29.4g; FIBER 7.2g; CHOL 15mg; IRON 2.3mg; SODIUM 613mg; CALC 67mg

TO MAKE THIS A FULL WHOLE-GRAIN SALAD, AVOID PEARLED FARRO, WHICH HAS BEEN PARTIALLY PROCESSED. YES, IT TAKES A LITTLE LONGER, BUT TO SAVE TIME, HUNT DOWN SOME PRE-COOKED WHOLE-GRAIN FARRO. IT'S FOUND ON THE RICE AISLE.

Spinach-Pea Salad with Grilled Shrimp

Hands-on time: 45 min. Total time: 45 min. Sweet, briny shrimp are lovely here—seared scallops would be, too. For a beautiful garnish, purchase edible flowers, separate the petals, and scatter them on top. Grilled whole-wheat pita makes wonderfully thin croutons; we like whole-wheat, but you can use white pita, too.

1 cup shelled green peas (about 1 pound unshelled green peas) or frozen green peas
1 (6-inch) whole-wheat pita
Cooking spray
3 tablespoons extra-virgin olive oil, divided
1½ teaspoons grated lemon rind, divided
¼ teaspoon salt
½ teaspoon freshly ground black pepper, divided
1 pound large shrimp, peeled and deveined
1 tablespoon red wine vinegar
1 tablespoon fresh lemon juice
1 small garlic clove, minced
½ cup thinly sliced red onion
3 tablespoons chopped fresh mint
1 (6-ounce) bag fresh baby spinach
1 ounce feta cheese, crumbled (about ¼ cup)

1. Preheat grill to medium-high heat.
2. Bring a small pot of water to a boil. Add peas; cook 5 minutes or until

crisp-tender. Drain and rinse with cold water; drain.

3. Split pita into 2 rounds. Arrange pita rounds on a grill rack coated with cooking spray; grill 1 minute on each side or until toasted. Remove from grill; cool. Break pita into 1-inch pieces.

4. Combine 1 tablespoon oil, 1 teaspoon lemon rind, salt, and ¼ teaspoon black pepper in a large bowl. Add shrimp; toss to coat. Thread shrimp onto 4 (12-inch) skewers. Arrange skewers on grill rack coated with cooking spray; grill 2 minutes on each side or until done.

5. Combine remaining 2 tablespoons oil, remaining ½ teaspoon lemon rind, remaining ¼ teaspoon pepper, vinegar, juice, and garlic in a large bowl. Add peas, onion, mint, and spinach; toss to coat. Arrange about 2 cups salad on each of 4 plates; divide pita and shrimp evenly among salads. Sprinkle each serving with about 1 tablespoon cheese. Serves 4.

CALORIES 328; **FAT** 14.2g (sat 2.9g, mono 8.1g, poly 2.1g); **PROTEIN** 28.9g; **CARB** 22.3g; **FIBER** 5.6g; **CHOL** 179mg; **IRON** 5.4mg; **SODIUM** 551mg; **CALC** 146mg

---

A SICILIAN DIP, TRANSFORMED

Another riff, this one off the flavors of a garlicky Sicilian salad often served as a dip. Our version is more of a full salad. Colorful veggies are cut into a variety of shapes, some grilled to a turn. Eggplant and zucchini should be buttery soft. Use the best juicy-firm tomatoes you can find to play off the creamy-milky cheese and the oily crunch of pine nuts. Like the cherry on top of a sundae sits the caper berry, briny and green.

Vegetarian

Grilled Caponata Salad with Grilled Flatbreads

Hands-on time: 42 min. Total time: 42 min. *Look for caper berries near the olives in the supermarket; they should be next to the capers, but they're much bigger and have a stem. In a pinch, substitute about a tablespoon of chopped capers. Japanese eggplants have thinner skins than typical globe eggplants, so you can leave the peel on. The light purple color is pretty, too.*

Dressing:
2 tablespoons extra-virgin olive oil
1½ tablespoons red wine vinegar
1 teaspoon grated orange rind
½ teaspoon minced fresh oregano
¼ teaspoon salt
¼ teaspoon freshly ground black pepper
⅛ teaspoon crushed red pepper
1 large garlic clove, minced
Flatbreads:
1 (4-ounce) piece fresh pizza dough, halved
1 tablespoon olive oil
Cooking spray
1 garlic clove, halved
Salad:
1 large Japanese eggplant, cut diagonally into ½-inch-thick slices (about 10 ounces)
12 ounces baby zucchini, halved lengthwise (about 8)
1 red bell pepper, quartered and seeded
1 small sweet onion, cut into ½-inch-thick slices
10 large sliced pitted green olives
2 globe tomatoes, each cut into 8 wedges
3 tablespoons pine nuts, toasted
1 cup fresh basil leaves, torn
4 ounces fresh mozzarella cheese, thinly sliced and torn into pieces
4 caper berries with stems, rinsed and drained

1. To prepare dressing, combine first 8 ingredients in a large bowl, stirring with a whisk. Set aside.

2. Preheat grill to medium-high heat.

3. To prepare flatbreads, turn dough out onto a lightly floured surface; let stand 15 minutes. Pat each dough portion into a 5-inch circle. Brush with 1 tablespoon oil. Place dough on grill rack coated with cooking spray; grill 2 minutes on each side or until crisp and well marked. Remove from grill; rub top of each flatbread with cut sides of 1 garlic clove. Tear each flatbread in half.

4. To prepare salad, lightly coat eggplant and next 3 ingredients with cooking spray. Arrange eggplant and zucchini on grill rack coated with cooking spray; grill 1½ minutes on each side or until tender and well marked. Arrange bell pepper and onion on grill rack; grill 3 minutes on each side or until well marked.

5. Separate onion slices into rings. Cut bell pepper into thick strips. Add onion, eggplant, zucchini, bell pepper, green olives, and tomato to dressing; toss gently to combine. Arrange vegetables on a platter. Top with nuts, basil, cheese, and caper berries. Serve with flatbreads. Serves 4 (serving size: about 1½ cups salad, 1 caper berry, and 1 flatbread piece).

CALORIES 373; **FAT** 23.7g (sat 5.9g, mono 9.4g, poly 4.1g); **PROTEIN** 11.8g; **CARB** 32.3g; **FIBER** 6.8g; **CHOL** 23mg; **IRON** 2.8mg; **SODIUM** 621mg; **CALC** 215mg

Grilled Steak Panzanella with Pickled Vegetables

***Hands-on time: 45 min. Total time: 45 min.** Use the bottom part of ciabatta for this salad. The crusty, flat surface is easier to grill and provides more crunch. Don't skip the delicious pickled vegetable topping—it's earthy, crunchy, sweet-sour, and welcome in every bite.*

¼ cup red wine vinegar
1½ tablespoons sugar
3 tablespoons water
½ cup thinly sliced red onion
½ cup julienne-cut carrot
½ cup julienne-cut radishes
3 tablespoons extra-virgin olive oil
1 tablespoon minced garlic
2 teaspoons chopped fresh thyme
½ teaspoon salt, divided
½ teaspoon freshly ground black pepper, divided
2 cups grape tomatoes, halved
1 (4-ounce) piece ciabatta (about 1 inch thick)
Cooking spray
1 (1-pound) flatiron steak, trimmed
1 teaspoon paprika
3 cups baby spinach and arugula mixture
¼ cup chopped fresh basil leaves

1. Preheat grill to medium-high heat.
2. Combine first 3 ingredients in a medium bowl, stirring with a whisk until sugar dissolves. Add onion, carrot, and radishes; toss well. Let stand 30 minutes; drain.
3. Combine olive oil, garlic, thyme, ¼ teaspoon salt, and ¼ teaspoon pepper in a large bowl, stirring with a whisk. Stir in tomatoes; set aside.
4. Lightly coat bread with cooking spray. Place bread on grill rack; grill 3 minutes on each side or until crisp. Sprinkle steak evenly with paprika, remaining ¼ teaspoon salt, and remaining ¼ teaspoon black pepper. Place on grill rack coated with cooking spray; grill 3 minutes on each side or until desired degree of doneness. Let stand 10 minutes. Cut steak across grain into thin slices. Cut each slice in half.
5. Cut bread into (1-inch) cubes. Add bread, greens, steak, and basil to tomato mixture; toss well. Top with carrot mixture. Serves 4 (serving size: about 1⅔ cups salad and ⅓ cup carrot mixture).

CALORIES 417; FAT 22.5g (sat 5.9g, mono 12.9g, poly 1.8g); PROTEIN 25.4g; CARB 29g; FIBER 3.4g; CHOL 71mg; IRON 4.4mg; SODIUM 593mg; CALC 60mg

LESS MEAT, MORE FLAVOR

COLD NOODLE BOWLS

By Mark Bittman

Fresh, perfect-for-summer meals full of vibrant vegetables

It's safe to say that the most popular way to eat a cold noodle in this country is via the basic pasta salad, all too often drenched in mayonnaise or oil and refrigerated until it's chilly enough that you can't really taste the ingredients. There are ways to make excellent pasta salad (namely, cooking a hot pasta dish and letting it come to room temperature), but to my mind, the very best versions of cold noodles have their roots in Asia.

Asian-style noodles are particularly well suited to being eaten at room temperature or just slightly chilled. Here, I use soba and rice noodles, most often from Southeast Asia. You can also use any kind of Chinese wheat noodles, which are often served cold with peanut or sesame sauce, or Japanese ramen or udon noodles. Whichever you use, just give them a rinse under cold water when they're finished cooking to get the starch off and prevent them from overcooking and getting mushy.

The first recipe is Thai-inspired—and an example of how cold Asian noodles are a great way to clean out your vegetable bin. The classic flavors of Southeast Asia—basil, mint, cilantro, green onions, nuts, fish sauce, and lime—make the noodles vibrant and fresh. I also add raw thinly sliced radishes and snow peas stir-fried with garlic, ginger, and chile. The vegetable add-ins could easily be peppers, bean sprouts, carrots, or eggplant instead. The hot snow peas activate the flavor in the fresh herbs, which really brings the noodles to life. Rice noodles may naturally clump up a bit, by the way, so as you rinse them, separate them as best you can.

The second dish is satisfyingly simple: soba noodles, spinach, bok choy, vinaigrette, beef, and sesame seeds. Throwing the bok choy and spinach into the pot with the noodles for the last minute or so of cooking is a great technique for any fairly tender vegetables that you just want to blanch quickly and then cool off, such as snap peas, green beans, broccoli, or asparagus (it also saves you from using an extra dish). Make sure to squeeze the excess water out of the spinach leaves so it doesn't dilute the dressing.

I make the dressing with coconut milk, soy sauce, rice vinegar, lime juice, curry powder, chopped ginger, and a touch of honey to cut the acid. Sliced garlic and hot sauce would be nice additions. I toss the noodles, greens, and vinaigrette together with simple stir-fried beef—chilled in the freezer and sliced very thin—and sesame seeds for a little crunch. It's tangy from the vinegar and earthy from the greens, with just enough richness from the beef.

The key to salads like these is that something warm coaxes the flavor out of ingredients that are not. To improvise, you can toss hot stir-fries into noodles that have been cooled down, or you can also toss warm noodles and/or dressings with any number of raw vegetables, greens, or herbs. Whichever way you choose, you're bound to end up with something infinitely better than traditional American pasta salad. Just remember to leave the mayonnaise in the fridge.

Quick & Easy

Thai-Style Vegetable Rice Noodles

Hands-on time: 35 min. Total time: 35 min.

4 ounces uncooked flat rice noodles (pad Thai noodles)
1 cup thinly sliced radishes
1/2 cup chopped green onions
1/2 cup chopped fresh basil
1/2 cup fresh cilantro leaves
1/4 cup fresh mint leaves
2 tablespoons fresh lime juice
1 tablespoon Thai fish sauce
2 tablespoons peanut oil
1 1/2 tablespoons grated peeled fresh ginger
6 garlic cloves, sliced
2 Thai chiles, finely chopped
1 pound snow peas, trimmed
3/4 teaspoon kosher salt
1/2 cup chopped unsalted, dry-roasted peanuts

1. Cook noodles according to package directions, omitting salt and fat. Drain and rinse under cold water; drain. Place in a medium bowl. Add radishes and next 6 ingredients; toss well.
2. Heat a large skillet over low heat; add oil, ginger, garlic, and chiles, and cook 2 minutes. Increase heat to medium-high; cook 1 minute or until garlic begins to brown. Add snow peas and salt to pan; cook 3 minutes or until crisp-tender, stirring occasionally. Add snow pea mixture to noodle mixture; toss well. Sprinkle with nuts. Serves 4 (serving size: 1 1/4 cups).

CALORIES 326; FAT 15.3g (sat 2.4g, mono 7.2g, poly 4.9g); PROTEIN 10.9g; CARB 41.2g; FIBER 5.8g; CHOL 0mg; IRON 3.9mg; SODIUM 682mg; CALC 103mg

Quick & Easy

Beef Soba Noodles with Spinach and Coconut-Curry Vinaigrette

Hands-on time: 35 min. Total time: 35 min.

1 (8-ounce) boneless sirloin steak
4 quarts water
1 1/2 teaspoons kosher salt, divided
8 ounces uncooked soba noodles
8 cups coarsely chopped bok choy
1 pound bagged prewashed spinach
1/2 cup light coconut milk
2 tablespoons fresh lime juice
2 tablespoons lower-sodium soy sauce
1 tablespoon rice vinegar
1 teaspoon honey
1/2 teaspoon freshly ground black pepper, divided
2 tablespoons peanut oil, divided
1 tablespoon chopped peeled fresh ginger
1 tablespoon sliced garlic
1 1/2 teaspoons Madras curry powder
1 tablespoon sesame seeds, toasted

1. Place beef in freezer.
2. Bring 4 quarts water and 1 teaspoon salt to a boil in a large saucepan. Add noodles to boiling salted water; cook according to package directions. During last 1 minute of cooking, add bok choy and spinach. Cook 1 minute or until greens wilt. Drain and rinse under cold water; drain well.
3. Combine 1/4 teaspoon salt, coconut milk, juice, soy sauce, vinegar, honey, and 1/4 teaspoon pepper in a small bowl, stirring with a whisk.
4. Combine 5 teaspoons oil, ginger, garlic, and curry in a Dutch oven over low heat; cook 5 minutes, stirring frequently. Remove from heat. Add reserved coconut milk mixture and noodle mixture; toss well.
5. Heat a large, heavy skillet over high heat. Cut beef across grain into thin slices; sprinkle with remaining 1/4 teaspoon salt and remaining 1/4 teaspoon pepper. Add remaining 1 teaspoon oil to pan; swirl to coat. Add beef to pan; sauté 2 minutes or until done. Add beef to pasta mixture; toss well. Sprinkle with sesame seeds. Serves 6 (serving size: 1 1/3 cups).

CALORIES 319; FAT 13.2g (sat 4.1g, mono 4.7g, poly 2.2g); PROTEIN 17.4g; CARB 34.4g; FIBER 4.3g; CHOL 20mg; IRON 5.4mg; SODIUM 450mg; CALC 190mg

"BLOOM" THE GINGER, GARLIC, AND CURRY POWDER BY WARMING THEM IN OIL TO ROUND OUT FLAVORS.

FRESH SUMMER PIZZAS

Invite friends over, scoop up some superfresh ingredients, and throw an easy pie party.

That's summer entertaining at its best. Two different pies make for more fun, so we've made these recipes easy. They start with the dough. Fast and simple mean store-bought, not homemade. We love the fresh dough now offered in many supermarkets. You can also wheedle some out of many independent pizza shops. Give the dough time to rest at room temperature to make it easy to stretch—30 minutes, plenty of time to get the oven good and hot.

Decide whether you want your pizza saucy, flatbreadlike, or creamy; you'll find each type here. If you're taking our make-two-kinds advice, pick a contrasting pair.

Finally, and this is the most important part, blast that pizza at superhigh heat so it will cook up crisp and wonderfully blistered in spots. Run a cutter across your pizzas with great verve. Guests will cheer. Party on.

Kid Friendly • Vegetarian

Summer Grilled Vegetable Pizza

Hands-on time: 50 min. Total time: 1 hr.
If you're not in the mood to light up the outdoor grill, cook the vegetables in a grill pan.

1 pound refrigerated fresh pizza dough
1 red bell pepper, seeded and
   quartered
1 (4-ounce) zucchini, cut into 1/4-inch-
   thick diagonal slices
1 (4-ounce) yellow squash, cut into
   1/4-inch-thick diagonal slices
1 small red onion (about 7 ounces),
   cut into 12 wedges
2 tablespoons olive oil, divided
Cooking spray
1 tablespoon yellow cornmeal
1/2 cup lower-sodium marinara sauce
1/2 teaspoon kosher salt
1/4 teaspoon crushed red pepper
6 ounces fresh mozzarella cheese,
   thinly sliced and torn into pieces

1. Preheat grill to medium-high heat.
2. Remove dough from refrigerator. Let stand at room temperature, covered, 30 minutes.
3. Place a pizza stone or heavy baking sheet in oven. Preheat oven to 500° (keep pizza stone or baking sheet in oven as it preheats).
4. Flatten bell pepper pieces with hand. Arrange all vegetables in a single layer on a large cutting board or baking sheet; brush both sides with 1 1/2 tablespoons oil. Arrange onion wedges on skewers, if desired. Arrange vegetables on grill rack coated with cooking spray, and grill 3 minutes on each side or until crisp-tender and grill marks appear. Remove from grill. Coarsely chop bell pepper.
5. Roll dough into a 14-inch circle on a lightly floured surface, and pierce entire surface liberally with a fork. Carefully remove pizza stone from oven. Sprinkle cornmeal over pizza stone; place dough on pizza stone. Bake at 500° for 5 minutes. Remove partially baked crust from oven. Spread

sauce over crust, leaving a 1/2-inch border. Arrange vegetables over dough, and sprinkle evenly with salt and crushed red pepper. Top evenly with cheese. Carefully return pizza to pizza stone. Bake at 500° for an additional 12 minutes or until crust and cheese are browned. Brush edge of dough with remaining 1 1/2 teaspoons olive oil. Cut into 6 large slices. Serves 6 (serving size: 1 slice).

CALORIES 346; FAT 13.5g (sat 4.7g, mono 5.2g, poly 2.3g); PROTEIN 12g; CARB 49.6g; FIBER 2.5g; CHOL 23mg; IRON 2.7mg; SODIUM 675mg; CALC 158mg

KEEP IT FRESH

To prevent the spinach from getting singed in Three-Cheese White Pizza with Spinach, it's added to the pizza toward the end of cooking.

Kid Friendly • Vegetarian

Three-Cheese White Pizza with Spinach

Hands-on time: 15 min. Total time: 55 min. *The higher-quality the ricotta cheese, the creamier and more delicious the pizza; we prefer Calabro brand.*

1 pound refrigerated fresh pizza
   dough
2 tablespoons olive oil, divided
4 garlic cloves, thinly sliced
6 cups fresh baby spinach
1 cup part-skim ricotta cheese
2 ounces shredded part-skim
   mozzarella cheese (about 1/2 cup)
2 ounces pecorino Romano cheese,
   grated (about 1/2 cup)
3 tablespoons 2% reduced-fat milk
1 garlic clove, minced
1 tablespoon cornmeal

1. Remove dough from refrigerator. Let stand at room temperature, covered, 30 minutes.

2. Place a pizza stone or heavy baking sheet in oven. Preheat oven to 500° (keep pizza stone or baking sheet in oven as it preheats).

3. Combine 1½ tablespoons olive oil and sliced garlic in a large skillet. Heat over medium-high heat 1½ minutes or until garlic begins to sizzle. Add 6 cups spinach; sauté 2 minutes or until spinach wilts. Set aside.

4. Combine cheeses, milk, and minced garlic in a bowl.

5. Roll dough into a 14-inch circle on a lightly floured surface, and pierce entire surface liberally with a fork. Carefully remove pizza stone from oven. Sprinkle cornmeal over pizza stone; place dough on pizza stone. Spread cheese mixture over dough, leaving a ½-inch border. Bake at 500° for 10 minutes or until crust is golden and cheese is lightly browned. Top with spinach; bake an additional 2 minutes or until thoroughly heated. Remove from oven; brush outer crust with remaining 1½ teaspoons oil. Cut into 6 large slices. Serves 6 (serving size: 1 slice).

CALORIES 359; **FAT** 12.5g (sat 3.9g, mono 5g, poly 2.4g); **PROTEIN** 15.4g; **CARB** 47g; **FIBER** 2.6g; **CHOL** 17mg; **IRON** 3.5mg; **SODIUM** 655mg; **CALC** 173mg

JUICY TOMATOES ARE GREAT, BUT NOT ON A PIZZA THAT YOU WANT TO STAY CRISP. DRAIN THEM ON PAPER TOWELS FIRST.

Vegetarian
Fresh Tomato-Feta Pizza

Hands-on time: 35 min. Total time: 55 min. *If olives are a deal breaker, leave them off; the pizza is still yummy.*

1 pound refrigerated fresh pizza dough
4 plum tomatoes, sliced
2½ tablespoons olive oil, divided
2 garlic cloves, minced
1 tablespoon cornmeal
4 ounces feta cheese
1 ounce pitted kalamata olives, halved (⅓ cup)
¼ cup fresh basil leaves

1. Remove dough from refrigerator. Let stand at room temperature, covered, 30 minutes.

2. Arrange tomato slices on a jelly-roll pan lined with paper towels; top with more paper towels. Let stand 30 minutes.

3. Place a pizza stone or heavy baking sheet in oven. Preheat oven to 500° (keep pizza stone or baking sheet in oven as it preheats).

4. Combine tomatoes, 2 tablespoons oil, and garlic. Roll dough into a 14-inch circle on a lightly floured surface, and pierce dough liberally with a fork. Carefully remove pizza stone from oven. Sprinkle cornmeal over stone; place dough on stone. Arrange tomato mixture on dough. Crumble cheese; sprinkle over pizza. Bake at 500° for 19 minutes or until crust is golden and cheese is lightly browned. Remove from oven; top with olives and basil. Brush outer crust with remaining 1½ teaspoons oil. Cut pizza into 6 large slices. Serves 6 (serving size: 1 slice).

CALORIES 319; **FAT** 13g (sat 3.6g, mono 5.9g, poly 2.2g); **PROTEIN** 10.6g; **CARB** 42.2g; **FIBER** 1.9g; **CHOL** 10mg; **IRON** 2.6mg; **SODIUM** 665mg; **CALC** 65mg

Kid Friendly
Prosciutto-Mozza Pizza

Hands-on time: 15 min. Total time: 55 min. *For 30 more calories and 1 more gram of sat fat, you can use pepperoni in place of prosciutto.*

1 pound refrigerated fresh pizza dough
1 tablespoon cornmeal
⅔ cup lower-sodium marinara sauce (such as McCutcheon's)
6 ounces fresh mozzarella cheese, thinly sliced
2 teaspoons olive oil
2 ounces thinly sliced prosciutto, torn into ½-inch-wide strips
¼ cup small fresh oregano leaves

1. Remove dough from refrigerator. Let stand at room temperature, covered, 30 minutes.

2. Place a pizza stone or heavy baking sheet in oven. Preheat oven to 500° (keep pizza stone or baking sheet in oven as it preheats).

3. Roll dough into a 14-inch circle on a lightly floured surface, and pierce entire surface liberally with a fork. Carefully remove pizza stone from oven. Sprinkle cornmeal over pizza stone; place dough on pizza stone. Spread sauce over dough, leaving a ½-inch border; top with cheese. Bake at 500° for 14 minutes or until crust is golden and cheese is lightly browned. Remove from oven; brush outer crust with olive oil. Arrange prosciutto over pizza; top with oregano. Cut into 6 large slices. Serves 6 (serving size: 1 slice).

CALORIES 331; **FAT** 11.4g (sat 4.6g, mono 1.5g, poly 1.6g); **PROTEIN** 13.6g; **CARB** 49.6g; **FIBER** 1.4g; **CHOL** 29mg; **IRON** 2.6mg; **SODIUM** 664mg; **CALC** 160mg

TODAY'S LESSON: BURGERS

The constitution ought to be amended to stipulate that the happiness produced by the pursuit of a great, juicy hamburger should not be denied to the American who also wants to eat healthy. But in fact the healthy burger has often been a sad burger: dry, stunted, a pale imitation of this great food—no burger at all. It shall not be so henceforth: Lean meats, handled properly, make for delicious burgers that lend themselves to loads of variations. Calorie and fat savings are huge. Exhibit A is our superb classic cheeseburger with silky caramelized shallots. And then we riff: a hoisin-glazed salmon burger, and a lamb burger with tangy yogurt sauce. Healthy, and happy.

Kid Friendly • Quick & Easy

Cheddar Cheeseburgers with Caramelized Shallots

Hands-on time: 38 min. Total time: 38 min. *Tender, golden shallots lend a lovely sweetness to this classic cheeseburger.*

1 tablespoon olive oil, divided
2 cups thinly sliced shallots
¹/₂ teaspoon kosher salt, divided
1 tablespoon white wine vinegar
2 garlic cloves, minced
1 pound ground beef, 90% lean
2 ounces shredded sharp cheddar cheese (about ¹/₂ cup)
1 cup baby arugula
4 (1¹/₂-ounce) hamburger buns, toasted
3 tablespoons light mayonnaise

1. Heat a nonstick skillet over medium-low heat. Add 2 teaspoons oil; swirl to coat. Add shallots and ¼ teaspoon salt; cook 15 minutes or until golden brown, stirring occasionally. Stir in vinegar; cook 1 minute. Remove from heat; keep warm.

2. Gently combine garlic and beef. Divide meat mixture into 4 equal portions, gently shaping each into a ¹/₂-inch-thick patty. Press a nickel-sized indentation in center of each patty. Sprinkle evenly with remaining ¼ teaspoon salt.

3. Heat a large cast-iron skillet over medium-high heat. Add remaining 1 teaspoon oil to pan; swirl to coat. Add patties, and cook 3 minutes on each side or until desired degree of doneness. Top each patty with 2 tablespoons cheese; cover and cook 1 minute or until cheese melts.

4. Place ¼ cup arugula on bottom half of each bun; top with 1 patty and one-fourth of shallots. Spread about 2 teaspoons mayonnaise on top half of each bun; place on top of burgers. Serves 4 (serving size: 1 burger).

CALORIES 370; FAT 17.7g (sat 6.1g, mono 5.4g, poly 2.9g); PROTEIN 31.1g; CARB 31.7g; FIBER 8.1g; CHOL 77mg; IRON 2.2mg; SODIUM 654mg; CALC 113mg

KITCHEN TIP

Lean ground beef in a 4-ounce patty cuts sat fat by as much as 4 grams. Buy freshly ground beef and cook it to medium at most to help keep it from drying out. Also, a touch of mayo on the bun helps add moisture.

BUILDING BETTER BURGERS

1. USE A LIGHT TOUCH
Form the patties gently and quickly. This is a crucial step and one that many cooks get wrong. Don't overhandle or pack the meat together tightly, or you'll end up with dense, dry, tough burgers. Loosely formed patties make for the juiciest, most tender burgers.

2. DENT THE CENTER
To prevent patties from bloating, make a thumbprint-sized indentation in the middle of each. This compensates for juices that run into the center as the burger cooks and the meat contracts. The result: flat-topped patties that perfectly accommodate the bun.

3. DEVELOP THE CRUST
A good sear in a hot pan or over an open flame will create a dark brown, flavorful crust on the outside of the burger—a wonderful textural contrast to the juicy tenderness inside. A cast-iron pan is your best bet here because it can get much hotter than a nonstick skillet.

Quick & Easy

Hoisin-Glazed Salmon Burgers with Pickled Cucumber

Hands-on time: 30 min. Total time: 38 min. Quick-pickled cukes give these burgers tart crunch. Panko and egg white hold the patties together. Use cilantro leaves on the burgers as you would lettuce for herby freshness.

1/3 cup water
1/4 cup cider vinegar
1 teaspoon sugar
1/2 teaspoon minced garlic
1/2 teaspoon minced peeled fresh
   ginger
1/4 teaspoon crushed red pepper
24 thin English cucumber slices
1/2 cup panko (Japanese breadcrumbs)
1/3 cup thinly sliced green onions
2 tablespoons chopped fresh cilantro
1 tablespoon lower-sodium soy sauce
1 1/2 teaspoons grated peeled fresh
   ginger
1 teaspoon grated lime rind
1 (1-pound) skinless wild fresh or frozen
   Alaskan salmon fillet, finely chopped
1 large egg white
1 1/2 teaspoons dark sesame oil
1 tablespoon hoisin sauce
4 (1 1/2-ounce) hamburger buns with
   sesame seeds, toasted

1. Combine first 6 ingredients in a small saucepan; bring to a boil. Remove from heat; add cucumber. Let stand 30 minutes. Drain.
2. Combine panko and next 7 ingredients in a bowl, and stir well. Divide mixture into 4 equal portions, gently shaping each into a ½-inch-thick patty. Press a nickel-sized indentation in center of each patty.

3. Heat a large cast-iron skillet over medium-high heat. Add sesame oil to pan; swirl to coat. Add patties; cook patties 3 minutes on each side or until desired degree of doneness. Brush tops of patties evenly with hoisin; cook 30 seconds.
4. Place 1 patty on bottom half of each bun; top each patty with 6 cucumber slices and top half of bun. Serves 4 (serving size: 1 burger).

CALORIES 324; **FAT** 8.6g (sat 1.5g, mono, 2.3g, poly 3.1g); **PROTEIN** 29.4g; **CARB** 30.1g; **FIBER** 1.7g; **CHOL** 59mg; **IRON** 2.6mg; **SODIUM** 473mg; **CALC** 89mg

Quick & Easy

Lamb Burgers with Cilantro Raita

Hands-on time: 26 min. Total time: 26 min. The tangy, herby yogurt sauce (raita) stands in for mayonnaise on this blended burger. For more spicy kick, leave the seeds in the serrano chile.

1/3 cup plain fat-free Greek yogurt
1 tablespoon chopped fresh
   cilantro
1 tablespoon chopped fresh mint
1 1/2 teaspoons minced seeded
   serrano chile
1/8 teaspoon kosher salt
1 garlic clove, minced
1/2 English cucumber, grated,
   squeezed dry
1/2 pound ground beef, 90% lean
6 ounces ground lamb
1/4 teaspoon kosher salt
1/8 teaspoon freshly ground black
   pepper
1 teaspoon olive oil
1 cup fresh baby spinach
4 thin slices red onion
4 (1 1/2-ounce) hamburger buns,
   toasted

1. Combine first 7 ingredients in a small bowl; stir well.
2. Gently combine beef and lamb, being careful not to overwork. Divide mixture into 4 equal portions, gently shaping each into a ½-inch-thick patty. Press a nickel-sized indentation in center of each patty. Sprinkle evenly with ¼ teaspoon salt and pepper.
3. Heat a large cast-iron skillet over medium-high heat. Add oil to pan; swirl to coat. Add patties; cook 3 minutes on each side or until desired degree of doneness.
4. Place ¼ cup spinach, 1 onion slice, and 1 patty on bottom half of each hamburger bun. Top each patty with 2 tablespoons raita and top half of bun. Serves 4 (serving size: 1 burger).

CALORIES 341; **FAT** 15g (sat 5.5g, mono 6.4g, poly 1.6g); **PROTEIN** 25.4g; **CARB** 24.3g; **FIBER** 1.6g; **CHOL** 68mg; **IRON** 3.6mg; **SODIUM** 467mg; **CALC** 98mg

GROUND LAMB IS ONLY 80% LEAN AT MOST SUPERMARKETS, SO WE MIX IT WITH LEAN BEEF TO KEEP SATURATED FAT IN CHECK.

THE STUFF-IT STRATEGY

If you think of veggies—whether lettuce or zucchini or eggplant—as containers for tasty ingredients, dinner gets more interesting.

Vegetarian

Persian Rice-Stuffed Zucchini with Pistachios and Dill

Hands-on time: 34 min. Total time: 56 min. *A run under the broiler creates a crunchy crust, an essential for Persian rice dishes.*

6 medium zucchini (6 ounces each)
1 teaspoon kosher salt, divided
3/8 teaspoon freshly ground black
   pepper, divided
3 tablespoons olive oil, divided
3/4 cup jasmine rice
6 cardamom pods
1 (3-inch) cinnamon stick
1/2 teaspoon ground cumin
1/8 teaspoon ground red pepper
1 1/4 cups water
8 dried apricots, coarsely chopped
   (about 1/3 cup)
1/2 teaspoon grated orange rind
2 tablespoons fresh lemon juice
2 tablespoons fresh orange juice
1/3 cup chopped shelled dry-roasted,
   unsalted pistachios
1/4 cup chopped fresh dill
1/4 cup chopped fresh flat-leaf parsley
2 ounces goat cheese, crumbled
   (about 1/4 cup)
1 (15-ounce) can no-salt-added
   chickpeas (garbanzo beans), rinsed
   and drained

1. Preheat oven to 375°.
2. Cut zucchini in half lengthwise; scoop out pulp, leaving a 1/4-inch-thick shell. Chop pulp. Place zucchini halves, cut sides up, on a baking sheet lined with parchment paper; sprinkle with 1/4 teaspoon salt and 1/8 teaspoon black pepper. Bake at 375° for 15 minutes or until tender.
3. Heat a medium saucepan over medium heat. Add 1 tablespoon oil; swirl to coat. Add rice, cardamom, and cinnamon; cook 5 minutes or until rice is opaque, stirring frequently. Add 1/4 teaspoon salt, cumin, red pepper, and 1 1/4 cups water. Bring to a boil; cover, reduce heat, and simmer 12 minutes. Remove from heat; stir in apricots. Cover and let stand 10 minutes; discard cardamom and cinnamon. Spoon rice mixture into a large bowl; cool slightly.
4. Combine remaining 2 tablespoons olive oil, remaining 1/2 teaspoon salt, remaining 1/4 teaspoon black pepper, orange rind, and juices in a small bowl; stir with a whisk. Add dressing, reserved zucchini pulp, pistachios, and remaining ingredients to rice mixture; toss well to combine.
5. Preheat broiler to high.
6. Spoon about 1/4 cup rice mixture into each zucchini shell. Broil 6 minutes or until lightly browned. Serves 6 (serving size: 2 stuffed zucchini halves).

CALORIES 265; FAT 12.7g (sat 2.8g, mono 7.1g, poly 1.9g); PROTEIN 9.2g; CARB 31.6g; FIBER 5.6g; CHOL 4mg; IRON 2.2mg; SODIUM 389mg; CALC 81mg

Vegetarian

Falafel-Stuffed Eggplant with Tahini Sauce and Tomato Relish

Hands-on time: 40 min. Total time: 1 hr. 25 min. *Traditional falafel is made from seasoned, mashed chickpeas that are shaped into patties and deep-fried. Here we use the same components to make a tasty filling for eggplants, baked and topped with a nutty sauce.*

Tahini sauce:
3 tablespoons warm water
2 tablespoons tahini (roasted sesame
   seed paste)
4 teaspoons fresh lemon juice
1 teaspoon honey
1/2 teaspoon ground cumin
1 garlic clove, minced
Eggplant:
2 eggplants (about 12 ounces each)
Cooking spray
3/4 teaspoon kosher salt, divided
1/4 cup chopped onion
1/4 cup fresh breadcrumbs
1/4 cup chopped fresh flat-leaf parsley
1 tablespoon tahini (roasted sesame
   seed paste)
2 teaspoons olive oil
1 1/2 teaspoons ground cumin
1/2 teaspoon ground coriander
1/4 teaspoon black pepper
1/4 teaspoon ground red pepper
2 large eggs
2 garlic cloves, minced
1 (15-ounce) can no-salt-added
   chickpeas (garbanzo beans), rinsed
   and drained
Relish:
1 cup chopped seeded tomato
1/2 cup chopped seeded peeled
   cucumber
1/2 cup vertically sliced red onion
1/2 cup coarsely chopped fresh flat-leaf
   parsley
1 tablespoon fresh lemon juice
1 tablespoon extra-virgin olive oil

1. To prepare sauce, combine first 6 ingredients in a small bowl, and stir with a whisk. Set aside.

2. Preheat oven to 475°.

3. To prepare eggplant, slice eggplants in half lengthwise; score cut sides with a crosshatch pattern. Place eggplant halves, cut sides down, on a baking sheet coated with cooking spray. Bake at 475° for 7 minutes or until slightly tender and browned. Remove from oven; carefully scoop out pulp, leaving a ¾-inch shell. Reserve pulp for another use. Season cut sides with ¼ teaspoon salt.

4. Place remaining ½ teaspoon salt, onion, and next 11 ingredients in a food processor; process until smooth. Spoon ½ cup chickpea mixture into each eggplant shell. Bake at 475° for 25 minutes or until eggplant halves are tender and chickpea mixture is lightly browned.

5. To prepare relish, combine tomato and remaining ingredients in a bowl; stir to combine.

6. Place 1 eggplant half on each of 4 plates. Top each half with ¼ cup relish and 1½ tablespoons sauce. Serves 4 (serving size: 1 stuffed eggplant half).

CALORIES 308; FAT 15.6g (sat 2.5g, mono 7.4g, poly 3.8g); PROTEIN 12.1g; CARB 34.3g; FIBER 10.8g; CHOL 106mg; IRON 3.5mg; SODIUM 450mg; CALC 116mg

FAST, FRESH BREADCRUMBS

If you are throwing a party or perhaps just cooking for a gathering, you might be left with an extra loaf of bread, a quartet of dinner rolls, or half a baguette. Instead of throwing out the leftovers, seal them in an airtight bag in the freezer. That way, whenever a recipe calls for breadcrumbs, you can make them quickly by running the frozen bread down a medium-coarse grater (the one designated for hard cheeses). And as an added bonus, there's no need to lug out (or clean!) your food processor. You can also use the fresh crumbs to bind meatballs, thicken soups, or add crunch to gratins.

Quick & Easy • Vegetarian

Lettuce Wraps with Hoisin-Peanut Sauce

Hands-on time: 25 min. Total time: 39 min.

Sauce:
1 teaspoon canola oil
1 tablespoon minced shallot
⅓ cup water
2 tablespoons creamy peanut butter
4 teaspoons hoisin sauce
⅛ teaspoon crushed red pepper
1 tablespoon fresh lime juice

Filling:
1 (14-ounce) package extra-firm tofu, drained and crumbled
1 tablespoon dark sesame oil
6 thinly sliced green onions (about ⅔ cup), divided
½ cup plus 2 tablespoons chopped fresh cilantro, divided
3 tablespoons lower-sodium soy sauce
1 teaspoon grated fresh ginger
2 teaspoons sugar
½ teaspoon Sriracha (hot chile sauce, such as Huy Fong)
1 cup matchstick-cut cucumbers
1 cup matchstick-cut carrots
2 cups hot cooked sticky rice
8 Bibb lettuce leaves

1. To prepare sauce, heat a small saucepan over medium heat. Add canola oil to pan; swirl to coat. Add shallot, and sauté 2 minutes. Add ⅓ cup water and next 3 ingredients, and stir with a whisk. Bring to a boil; cook 1 minute. Remove from heat; stir in lime juice.

2. To prepare filling, spread crumbled tofu in a single layer on several layers of paper towels; cover with additional paper towels. Let stand 20 minutes, pressing down occasionally.

3. Heat a large nonstick skillet over medium-high heat. Add sesame oil to pan; swirl to coat. Add ⅓ cup green onions; sauté 1 minute. Add tofu; sauté 4 minutes, stirring occasionally. Add 2 tablespoons cilantro, soy sauce, ginger, sugar, and Sriracha; sauté 1 minute. Remove from heat; stir in cucumbers, carrots, and remaining green onions.

4. Spoon ¼ cup rice into each lettuce leaf. Top with about ½ cup tofu mixture; sprinkle with 1 tablespoon cilantro. Serve with sauce. Serves 4 (serving size: 2 lettuce wraps and 2 tablespoons sauce).

CALORIES 355; FAT 15g (sat 2.1g, mono 8.5g, poly 3.7g); PROTEIN 16.2g; CARB 42.6g; FIBER 3.9g; CHOL 0mg; IRON 4.5mg; SODIUM 568mg; CALC 224mg

---

MINCING SHALLOTS

These prized alliums look like copper-skinned garlic cloves and have a mild onion flavor. Release tons of shallot essence by mincing finely.

1. Slice off both the root end and tip of the shallot, and discard. Peel off papery skins. It's OK (and easier) to lose a thin layer of edible flesh.

2. Halve shallot lengthwise, and lay it flat on cutting board; cut into thin slices. Cut across slices at tiny intervals to mince.

OTHER USES FOR FISH SAUCE

By Naomi Duguid

Don't be daunted! This Southeast Asian staple adds depth to many dishes.

A long time ago, when I was making food for my second child, who was about eight months old, I made a soft puree of ripe avocado with cooked potato and a little olive oil. He loved it. I did, too—after I'd seasoned it with a dash of fish sauce for my adult palate. That led me to add fish sauce to guacamole the next time I made it. It turned out to be a great addition: Fish sauce enhances the avocado's richness and gives it extra depth without overpowering. Ever since, I've always added a dash to my guacamole—about a teaspoon. The effect is subtle (there's no taste of fish), but it's not a "hidden" ingredient: Taste the fish sauce version next to an unsauced one; the former is notably deeper, richer, and somehow smokier.

In many parts of mainland Southeast Asia, fish sauce (made from the liquid of, yes, salted fermented fish) is a staple, used for seasoning instead of salt. It gives wonderful depth of flavor—what the Japanese call umami. But unless you're cooking Southeast Asian food every week, a big bottle (it's cheapest in big bottles) can sit in your cupboard unloved and unused for months. It probably hasn't gotten into your regular rotation of cooking ingredients because, undiluted, it gives off an intense fishy smell.

Don't let the first whiff of fish sauce put you off; it's actually a lighter and more subtle seasoning than soy sauce. I prefer Thai fish sauces, though others like more pungent ones from Vietnam. In any case, it has become my most-used seasoning. I add it to soup broths, to vinaigrettes and marinades, and to many Asian dipping sauces (most often with lime juice and a little garlic), which are great for grilled meat, dumplings, or noodle bowls.

Kid Friendly • Quick & Easy

Guacamole with Fish Sauce

Hands-on time: 5 min. Total time: 5 min.
This supersimple recipe is for when you have perfectly ripe avocados—there's no need for tomato or other complications. Avocados' richness shines against the zip of lime and cilantro, their flavor deepened with fish sauce.

2 ripe avocados, peeled and seeded
1 tablespoon fresh lime juice
1 teaspoon Thai fish sauce
¼ teaspoon kosher salt
2 tablespoons chopped fresh cilantro

1. Place avocados in a medium bowl; mash roughly with a fork. Add lime juice, fish sauce, and salt; mash to desired consistency. Stir in cilantro. Serves 4 (serving size: about ¼ cup).

CALORIES 163; FAT 14.7g (sat 2.1g, mono 9.9g, poly 1.8g); PROTEIN 2.1g; CARB 9.3g; FIBER 6.8g; CHOL 0mg; IRON 0.6mg; SODIUM 243mg; CALC 14mg

3 MORE EVERYDAY USES FOR FISH SAUCE

Remember, this stuff is concentrated. You only need a tiny amount to make a flavor impact.

1 Splash into brothy soups to deepen the savory notes.

2 Add a dash to vinaigrettes—it's not so different from anchovies in Caesar dressing.

3 Mix with olive oil and toss with vegetables before grilling; try zucchini or onions.

IF YOU LIKE PIÑA COLADAS

You'll like our way of losing almost all the sat fat while keeping the delicious coconutty goodness.

Nothing says "escape" like a creamy, ice-cold piña colada: cocktail in hand, feet in the sand, music in the background (hopefully not that dreadful piña colada song, the last #1 hit of the 1970s, unless it's a guilty pleasure). Unfortunately, nothing says "better head to the gym" like a piña colada, too: 425 calories, 8 grams of saturated fat, most of which comes from the mysterious goo known as cream of coconut.

But the good thing about a problem ingredient is that if you can reinvent it, you've solved most of the problem in one fell swoop. We discovered an unlikely hero in evaporated fat-free milk, full-bodied in texture with surprisingly rich, nutty notes. When steeped with flaked sweetened coconut, the result is creamy and tasty. The coconut is then strained out (along with most of its calories and sat fat), leaving behind real coconutty essence.

Tart, fresh pineapple gets sweetened with agave nectar, while aged rum adds depth with hints of caramel and molasses. A splash of pineapple juice adds a little more acidity, balancing the drink. At just 158 calories, it's all pleasure, no guilt.

Piña Coladas

Hands-on time: 12 min. Total time: 4 hr. 25 min. *Freezing the pineapple adds a velvety texture and keeps the cocktail frozen longer. The riper the pineapple, the more concentrated the flavor will be.*

2 cups flaked sweetened coconut
1 (12-ounce) can evaporated fat-free milk
2 cups cubed fresh pineapple
2¹⁄₂ cups ice cubes
³⁄₄ cup gold rum (such as Bacardi Gold)
¹⁄₄ cup pineapple juice
2 tablespoons light agave nectar
8 fresh pineapple slices

1. Combine 2 cups coconut and evaporated milk in a medium saucepan over medium heat, and cook until tiny bubbles form around edge (do not boil), about 7 minutes. Remove from heat. Cover and chill at least 4 hours or up to overnight.
2. Arrange pineapple in a single layer on a baking sheet; freeze at least 1 hour or until firm.
3. Strain coconut mixture through a sieve over a medium bowl, pressing coconut with the back of a spoon to remove as much milk as possible. Discard solids.
4. Place pineapple, ice cubes, rum, juice, and agave nectar in a blender; process mixture until smooth. Add milk mixture, and process until smooth. Serve with pineapple slices. Serves 8 (serving size: about ²⁄₃ cup).

CALORIES 158; **FAT** 1.2g (sat 1g, mono 0.1g, poly 0g); **PROTEIN** 3.5g; **CARB** 18.6g; **FIBER** 1.1g; **CHOL** 2mg; **IRON** 0.4mg; **SODIUM** 57mg; **CALC** 124mg

FOR A LIGHTER LIBATION

HOMEMADE COCONUT MILK
We make our own infused coconut milk to replace heavy, sugary cream of coconut. This cuts 176 calories and 8 grams of sat fat per drink. Save day-of prep time by doing this step (step 1) the night before.

FRESH PINEAPPLE
Pineapple peaks in summer; it's sweet, slightly tart, and juicy. Sub fresh fruit for some of the canned juice and save 44 calories per drink. A splash of juice adds more acidity.

GOLD RUM
We opted for the darker variety, with its hints of caramel and molasses, which better complement the creamy coconut and tart pineapple.

CLASSIC	MAKEOVER
425 calories per serving	158 calories per serving
9.4 grams total fat	1.2 grams total fat
8.8 grams saturated fat	1 gram saturated fat

BUDGET COOKING

FEED 4 FOR LESS THAN $10

Dinner inspiration from around the world: savory Korean-style tacos, Moroccan chicken skewers, and an all-American BLT

Kid Friendly • Quick & Easy

Fried Egg BLT Sandwiches

$1.53/serving, $6.11 total

Hands-on time: 15 min. Total time: 15 min. *Opt for focaccia without cheese or herbs, and choose one that doesn't look oily. Serve with a fruit salad.*

1 teaspoon olive oil
4 large eggs
4 (1-ounce) slices focaccia bread, toasted
1 cup packed baby arugula
4 applewood-smoked bacon slices, cooked, drained, and halved crosswise
4 (¹⁄₄-inch-thick) slices tomato
¹⁄₄ teaspoon kosher salt
¹⁄₄ teaspoon freshly ground black pepper

1. Heat a large nonstick skillet over medium heat. Add olive oil to pan; swirl to coat. Crack eggs into pan; cook 2 minutes. Cover and cook 2 minutes or until whites are set or until desired degree of doneness. Remove from heat.
2. Place 1 focaccia slice on each of 4 plates; top each serving with ¹⁄₄ cup arugula, 2 bacon slice halves, and 1 tomato slice. Sprinkle tomatoes evenly with salt and pepper. Top each serving with 1 egg; garnish with additional freshly ground black pepper, if desired. Serves 4 (serving size: 1 sandwich).

CALORIES 241; **FAT** 12.7g (sat 3.5g, mono 4.9g, poly 1.2g); **PROTEIN** 12.7g; **CARB** 18.3g; **FIBER** 1g; **CHOL** 190mg; **IRON** 2mg; **SODIUM** 517mg; **CALC** 38mg

Spicy Moroccan Chicken Skewers

$2.34/serving, $9.35 total

Hands-on time: 9 min. Total time: 2 hr. 9 min. *Serve with hot cooked couscous. Give the couscous nutty flavor by toasting it in a hot pan before you rehydrate it.*

1½ tablespoons minced fresh garlic
1½ tablespoons sambal oelek (such as ground fresh chile paste)
2 tablespoons olive oil
1 teaspoon ground cumin
½ teaspoon ground coriander
⅝ teaspoon kosher salt, divided
4 skinless, boneless chicken thighs, cut into 36 pieces
½ yellow bell pepper, cut into 12 pieces
12 cherry tomatoes
Cooking spray
¼ cup plain 2% reduced-fat Greek yogurt

1. Combine first 5 ingredients in a small bowl; stir in ⅛ teaspoon salt. Scrape mixture into a zip-top plastic bag. Add chicken; seal. Marinate in refrigerator 2 hours, turning after 1 hour.
2. Immerse 12 (8-inch) wooden skewers in water; soak 30 minutes. Drain and pat dry.
3. Preheat grill to medium-high heat.
4. Remove chicken from marinade; discard marinade. Thread 3 chicken pieces, 1 pepper piece, and 1 tomato alternately onto each skewer, beginning and ending with chicken; sprinkle evenly with remaining ½ teaspoon salt. Arrange skewers on grill rack coated with cooking spray; grill 4 minutes on each side or until done. Serve with yogurt. Serves 4 (serving size: 3 skewers and 1 tablespoon yogurt).

CALORIES 204; **FAT** 10.8g (sat 2g, mono 6.1g, poly 1.6g); **PROTEIN** 19.3g; **CARB** 7.8g; **FIBER** 1.5g; **CHOL** 72mg; **IRON** 1.7mg; **SODIUM** 508mg; **CALC** 43mg

Korean-Style Beef Tacos

$2.43/serving, $9.73 total

Hands-on time: 28 min. Total time: 1 hr. 28 min. *Serve with cooked rice tossed with a tablespoon of toasted sesame oil. Shop for your meat at supercenter box stores or discount warehouses like Costco for the best prices.*

⅓ cup sugar
5 tablespoons lower-sodium soy sauce
1½ tablespoons sambal oelek (ground fresh chile paste)
1 tablespoon fresh lime juice
1 tablespoon dark sesame oil
4 garlic cloves, minced
12 ounces flank steak, sliced against the grain into thin strips
⅛ teaspoon salt
Cooking spray
8 (6-inch) corn tortillas
Quick Pickled Cabbage
3 tablespoons sliced green onions

1. Combine first 6 ingredients in a shallow dish. Add steak to dish; cover. Marinate in refrigerator 1 hour, turning after 30 minutes.
2. Preheat grill to medium-high heat.
3. Remove steak from marinade, and discard marinade. Thread steak onto 8 (8-inch) skewers; sprinkle with salt. Place skewers on grill rack coated with cooking spray. Grill 2 minutes on each side or until desired degree of doneness. Grill tortillas 30 seconds on each side or until lightly charred; keep warm. Place 2 tortillas on each of 4 plates, and divide steak evenly among tortillas. Divide Quick Pickled Cabbage evenly among tacos; sprinkle with onions. Serves 4 (serving size: 2 tacos).

CALORIES 270; **FAT** 6.3g (sat 1.6g, mono 2g, poly 1.4g); **PROTEIN** 18.1g; **CARB** 37.1g; **FIBER** 3g; **CHOL** 21mg; **IRON** 1.3mg; **SODIUM** 568mg; **CALC** 95mg

Quick Pickled Cabbage:
Place 3 cups chopped napa cabbage in a medium bowl with 2 crushed garlic cloves. Bring ½ cup rice vinegar, 2 tablespoons lower-sodium soy sauce, 1 tablespoon sugar, and 2 teaspoons chile paste to a boil. Pour hot vinegar mixture over cabbage; toss. Let stand at least 30 minutes. Serves 4 (serving size: ½ cup).

CALORIES 33; **FAT** 0g; **SODIUM** 204mg

KID-FRIENDLY COOKING

TREATS FOR THE TROOP

This month, our Kid in the Kitchen whips up a batch of coconut granola bars and watches them disappear!

Matisse Reid, our food-savvy 11-year-old kitchen blogger—who loves the taste of squid and olives but has friends who may be a little less adventurous—gives a road test to our coconut granola bars. These are perfect for breakfast, car, or snack. Here's what Matisse told us.

—Phoebe Wu

"Chewy Coconut Granola Bars are really easy to make. I whipped them up for my Girl Scout meeting, and everyone loved them (even the adults!). I also took some to school for lunch—yum! They make a great after-school snack and could even be eaten for breakfast if you are in a hurry. The bars are soft and gooey on the inside but have a nice crunch on the outside. I liked the combination of fruit and granola, which created different textures when I bit in. If you are not a big coconut fan, try using organic coconut in place of sweetened. It's not as sweet and the coconut flavor isn't as strong, so it's a great option for those who don't like too much coconut. But both options taste great. Trust me, these bars won't last long, so you might want to double the recipe!"

YOUNGER KIDS CAN USE KITCHEN SCISSORS TO CUT THE FRUIT.

Kid Friendly • Make Ahead

Chewy Coconut Granola Bars

Hands-on time: 15 min. Total time: 35 min.

Cooking spray
2 teaspoons all-purpose flour
3 ounces all-purpose flour (about ⅔ cup)
1.6 ounces whole-wheat flour (about ⅓ cup)
1 teaspoon baking powder
½ teaspoon salt
1¼ cups packed brown sugar
¼ cup canola oil
2 tablespoons fat-free milk
2 large eggs
1½ cups whole-grain granola
¾ cup chopped dried mixed tropical fruit
½ cup flaked sweetened coconut

1. Preheat oven to 350°.
2. Coat a 13 x 9–inch metal baking pan with cooking spray; dust with 2 teaspoons all-purpose flour.
3. Weigh or lightly spoon 3 ounces all-purpose flour and 1.6 ounces whole-wheat flour into dry measuring cups; level with a knife. Combine flours, baking powder, and salt in a small bowl; stir with a whisk. Combine sugar and next 3 ingredients in a large bowl; beat with a mixer at high speed until smooth. Add flour mixture, beating at low speed until blended. Fold in granola and fruit. Spoon batter into prepared pan. Sprinkle with coconut.
4. Bake at 350° for 20 minutes or until golden. Cool completely in pan on a wire rack. Cut into bars. Serves 16 (serving size: 1 bar).

CALORIES 154; **FAT** 5.8g (sat 1.5g, mono 2.5g, poly 1.1g); **PROTEIN** 2.7g; **CARB** 23.4g; **FIBER** 1.7g; **CHOL** 26mg; **IRON** 1mg; **SODIUM** 148mg; **CALC** 36mg

---

THE VERDICT

From the Girl Scout troop:

DEVON (AGE 10):
Gives this recipe a **10/10**

ABIGAIL (AGE 10):
Gives this recipe a **7/10**

MONICA (AGE 10):
Gives this recipe a **10/10**

MATISSE:
This was delicious! **10/10**

MAKE SURE YOU ALLOW THIS TO COOL COMPLETELY BEFORE CUTTING. EXTRA BARS KEEP WELL IN AN AIRTIGHT CONTAINER FOR UP TO TWO WEEKS.

DINNER TONIGHT

Here is a batch of fast weeknight menus from the *Cooking Light* Test Kitchen.

READY IN
40
MINUTES

The
SHOPPING LIST

Shrimp Florentine Pasta
Fettuccine (8 ounces)
Butter
Large raw shrimp (1 pound)
Garlic cloves
Crushed red pepper
Lemon
(6-ounce) package baby spinach

Cherry Tomato Caprese Salad
White wine vinegar
Extra-virgin olive oil
Heirloom cherry tomatoes (1 pint)
Fresh basil leaves (¼ cup)
Miniature mozzarella balls (2.5 ounces)

The
GAME PLAN

While water comes to a boil:
 ■ Prepare salad.
While pasta cooks:
 ■ Cook shrimp.

continued

Shrimp Florentine Pasta

With Cherry Tomato Caprese Salad

Time-Saver: Purchase peeled and deveined shrimp from your fishmonger.
Kid Tweak: Prepare recipe with ¼ teaspoon crushed red pepper, or omit entirely.
Shop Smart: Look for tiny fresh mozzarella balls labeled "pearls."
Lemon juice adds bright acidity and makes all the difference in such a simple dish. Garnish with a slice of lemon to enhance the citrus effect.

8 ounces uncooked fettuccine
2 tablespoons butter
1 pound large shrimp, peeled and deveined
1 tablespoon chopped fresh garlic
1 teaspoon crushed red pepper
1 tablespoon fresh lemon juice
½ teaspoon kosher salt
½ teaspoon freshly ground black pepper
1 (6-ounce) package fresh baby spinach

1. Cook pasta according to package directions, omitting salt and fat. Drain well; set aside, and keep warm.
2. Melt butter in a large nonstick skillet over medium heat. Add shrimp, garlic, and crushed red pepper; cook 4 minutes or until shrimp are done, stirring occasionally. Add cooked pasta, lemon juice, salt, black pepper, and spinach; cook 3 minutes or until spinach starts to wilt, stirring to combine. Serve immediately. Serves 4 (serving size: 1¾ cups).

CALORIES 402; **FAT** 8.6g (sat 4.3g, mono 1.8g, poly 1g); **PROTEIN** 32.1g; **CARB** 49.3g; **FIBER** 4g; **CHOL** 188mg; **IRON** 6mg; **SODIUM** 520mg; **CALC** 107mg

For the Cherry Tomato Caprese Salad:
Combine 1 tablespoon white wine vinegar, 1 tablespoon extra-virgin olive oil, ¼ teaspoon kosher salt, and ¼ teaspoon freshly ground black pepper in a medium bowl, stirring well with a whisk. Add 1 pint halved heirloom cherry tomatoes, ¼ cup fresh basil leaves, and ¼ cup halved miniature mozzarella balls. Toss to combine. Serves 4 (serving size: about ½ cup).

CALORIES 84; **FAT** 6.8g (sat 2.5g); **SODIUM** 132mg

READY IN
40
MINUTES

The
SHOPPING LIST

Seared Scallops and Herb Butter Sauce
Orzo (¾ cup)
Large sea scallops (1.5 pounds)
Dry white wine
White wine vinegar
Shallots (3 medium)
Butter
Fresh parsley
Fresh chives
Fresh thyme

Roasted Green Beans
Haricots verts (8 ounces)
Wax beans (8 ounces)
Olive oil

The
GAME PLAN

While oven preheats:
- Cook orzo.
While beans roast:
- Brown scallops.
- Prepare sauce.

Seared Scallops and Herb Butter Sauce

With Roasted Green Beans

¾ cup uncooked orzo
2 tablespoons chopped fresh parsley, divided
2 tablespoons chopped fresh chives divided
2 teaspoons olive oil
⅛ teaspoon kosher salt
1½ pounds large sea scallops
⅜ teaspoon kosher salt, divided
⅜ teaspoon black pepper, divided
Cooking spray
⅓ cup dry white wine
1 tablespoon chopped shallots
1 tablespoon white wine vinegar
3 tablespoons chilled butter, cubed
1 teaspoon chopped fresh thyme

1. Prepare orzo according to package directions, omitting salt and fat. Drain. Return to pan; stir in 1 tablespoon parsley, 1 tablespoon chives, olive oil, and ⅛ teaspoon salt. Keep warm.
2. Heat a cast-iron skillet over medium-high heat. Sprinkle scallops evenly with ¼ teaspoon salt and ¼ teaspoon pepper; coat scallops with cooking spray. Add scallops; cook 3 minutes on each side or until browned. Remove from pan; keep warm.
3. Combine wine, shallots, and vinegar in a saucepan; bring to a boil. Cook 5 minutes or until liquid reduces to 1 tablespoon. Reduce heat to low. Add butter cubes, 1 at a time, whisking after each addition until butter is fully incorporated. Stir in 1 tablespoon parsley, 1 tablespoon chives, 1 teaspoon thyme, ⅛ teaspoon salt, and ⅛ teaspoon pepper. Serve scallops with sauce and orzo. Serves 4 (serving size: about ½ cup orzo, 3 scallops, and 1½ tablespoons sauce).

CALORIES 382; **FAT** 12.9g (sat 5.9g, mono 4g, poly 1g); **PROTEIN** 32.8g; **CARB** 29g; **FIBER** 1.3g; **CHOL** 79mg; **IRON** 0.7mg; **SODIUM** 577mg; **CALC** 50mg

For the Roasted Green Beans:
Preheat oven to 450°. Combine ½ pound haricots verts, trimmed; ½ pound wax beans, trimmed; ½ cup thinly sliced shallots; 1 tablespoon olive oil; and ¼ teaspoon kosher salt on a foil-lined baking sheet. Roast at 450° for 10 minutes or until crisp-tender. Serves 4 (serving size: about ¾ cup).

CALORIES 84; **FAT** 3.6g (sat 0.5g); **SODIUM** 130mg

READY IN
40
MINUTES

The
SHOPPING LIST

Chinese Noodle Salad with Sesame Dressing
(8-ounce) package uncooked Chinese-style noodles
Sugar snap peas (1 cup)
Peanut oil
Firm water-packed tofu (about 6 ounces)
Cherry tomatoes
Sliced water chestnuts (½ cup)
Green onions (2)
Seasoned rice vinegar
Lower-sodium soy sauce
Dark sesame oil
Chile paste with garlic
Sesame seeds, toasted

Tangy Pickled Cucumber
Brown sugar
Seasoned rice vinegar
English cucumbers (2)

The
GAME PLAN

While water comes to a boil:
■ Prepare cucumber and chill.
While noodles cook:
■ Brown tofu.

Quick & Easy • Vegetarian
Chinese Noodle Salad with Sesame Dressing

With Tangy Pickled Cucumber

Time-Saver: Grab packaged, trimmed snap peas from your produce department. Simple Sub: If you don't have Chinese-style noodles, use spaghetti or rice noodles.

1 (8-ounce) package uncooked dried Chinese-style flat noodles
1 cup sugar snap peas, trimmed
2 teaspoons peanut oil
1 cup cubed firm water-packed tofu (about 6 ounces)
1 cup cherry tomatoes, halved
½ cup drained, sliced water chestnuts
½ cup thinly sliced green onions
3 tablespoons seasoned rice vinegar
1 tablespoon lower-sodium soy sauce
2 teaspoons dark sesame oil
2 teaspoons chile paste with garlic
¼ teaspoon kosher salt
1 tablespoon sesame seeds, toasted and divided

1. Cook noodles according to package directions, omitting salt and fat. Add peas during last 1 minute of cooking. Drain; rinse with cold water.

2. Heat a large nonstick skillet over medium-high heat. Add peanut oil to pan; swirl to coat. Add tofu to pan; cook 5 minutes or until browned, stirring frequently.
3. Combine noodle mixture, tofu, tomatoes, water chestnuts, and onions in a large bowl. Combine vinegar and next 4 ingredients in a small bowl, stirring with a whisk. Add vinegar mixture to noodle mixture, tossing gently to coat. Add 1½ teaspoons sesame seeds; toss to combine. Sprinkle with remaining sesame seeds. Serves 4 (serving size: 2 cups).

CALORIES 351; **FAT** 10.7g (sat 1.3g, mono 2.8g, poly 3.8g); **PROTEIN** 14.8g; **CARB** 55.5g; **FIBER** 10.2g; **CHOL** 0mg; **IRON** 7.3mg; **SODIUM** 489mg; **CALC** 338mg

For the Tangy Pickled Cucumber:
Combine ¼ cup seasoned rice vinegar and 1 tablespoon brown sugar in a medium bowl. Add 2 cups thinly sliced English cucumber, tossing gently to coat. Chill. Serves 4 (serving size: about ½ cup).

CALORIES 27; **FAT** 0.1g (sat 0g); **SODIUM** 225mg

TOASTING SESAME SEEDS INTENSIFIES THEIR FLAVOR.

Garlic-Chipotle Chicken Tacos
Garlic cloves
Chipotle chiles in adobo sauce
Canola oil
Chicken cutlets (1 pound)
Corn tortillas (6-inch), 8 tortillas
Small red bell pepper
Small green bell pepper
Small Vidalia onion
Chili powder
Green leaf lettuce (1 head)

Avocado and Orange Salad
Garlic cloves
Olive oil
Orange (1)
Grape tomatoes (½ cup)
Red onion (1 small)
Avocado (1)

The
GAME PLAN

While grill heats:
 ▪ Prepare rub, and coat chicken.
While chicken grills:
 ▪ Coat vegetables with spices.
While veggies grill:
 ▪ Prepare salad.

REFRIGERATE EXTRA CHIPOTLES AND ADOBO FOR TWO WEEKS IN A SEALED CONTAINER.

Quick & Easy
Garlic-Chipotle Chicken Tacos

With Avocado and Orange Salad

Time-Saver: Chicken cutlets cook up in a flash. Flavor Hit: Vidalia onions bring a welcome hint of sweetness.

1 tablespoon chopped fresh garlic
1 tablespoon minced chipotle chile,
    canned in adobo sauce
2 tablespoons canola oil, divided
1 pound chicken cutlets
¾ teaspoon kosher salt, divided
¾ teaspoon black pepper, divided
Cooking spray
2 teaspoons chili powder
1 small red bell pepper, quartered
1 small green bell pepper, quartered
1 small Vidalia onion, cut into ½-inch
    rings
8 (6-inch) corn tortillas
½ cup shredded green leaf lettuce

1. Preheat grill to medium-high heat.
2. Combine garlic, chipotle, and 1 tablespoon oil; rub evenly over chicken. Sprinkle with ¼ teaspoon salt and ¼ teaspoon black pepper. Place on grill rack coated with cooking spray; grill 3 minutes on each side or until done. Remove from grill; keep warm.
3. Combine remaining 1 tablespoon oil, remaining ½ teaspoon salt, remaining ½ teaspoon black pepper, and chili powder in a large bowl. Add bell peppers and onion; toss gently to coat. Place vegetables on grill rack; grill 5 minutes on each side or until soft and charred. Place tortillas on grill rack coated with cooking spray; grill 30 seconds on each side or until lightly charred. Remove from grill; keep warm.
4. Thinly slice chicken. Divide chicken, bell peppers, onion, and lettuce among tortillas. Serves 4 (serving size: 2 tacos).

CALORIES 312; FAT 9.8g (sat 0.9g, mono 4.8g, poly 2.8g); PROTEIN 29.5g; CARB 27.8g; FIBER 4g; CHOL 66mg; IRON 1.4mg; SODIUM 533mg; CALC 60mg

---

For the Avocado and Orange Salad:
Combine 1 tablespoon minced garlic, 1 teaspoon olive oil, ½ teaspoon black pepper, and ¼ teaspoon kosher salt in a medium bowl. Peel and section 1 orange; squeeze membranes to extract juice into bowl. Stir garlic mixture with a whisk. Add orange sections, ½ cup halved grape tomatoes, ¼ cup thinly sliced red onion, and 1 cup sliced avocado to garlic mixture; toss gently. Serves 4 (serving size: about ½ cup).

CALORIES 119; FAT 8.6g (sat 1.2g); SODIUM 126mg

SUPERFAST

Flavor-packed global ingredients are a weeknight cook's secret weapon. This month, look to fish sauce, Sriracha, and cumin to add depth to dishes.

Quick & Easy
Thai Steak Salad

Cooking spray
1 (1½-pound) flank steak, trimmed
½ teaspoon freshly ground black
    pepper
¼ teaspoon kosher salt
¼ cup fresh lime juice
1 tablespoon brown sugar
2 tablespoons lower-sodium soy sauce
1 tablespoon fish sauce
2 teaspoons minced fresh garlic
1 teaspoon Sriracha (hot chile sauce,
    such as Huy Fong)
1½ cups thinly sliced red cabbage
1¼ cups fresh bean sprouts
¾ cup julienne-cut carrots
⅓ cup fresh mint leaves
⅓ cup fresh cilantro leaves
⅓ cup fresh basil leaves

1. Heat a large grill pan over medium-high heat. Coat pan with cooking spray. Sprinkle steak evenly with pepper and salt. Add steak to pan; cook 6 minutes each side or until desired degree of doneness. Remove steak from pan; let stand 5 minutes. Cut steak diagonally across grain into thin slices.

2. Combine juice and next 5 ingredients in a small bowl; stir with a whisk.

3. Combine cabbage and remaining ingredients in a medium bowl. Add 6 tablespoons juice mixture to cabbage mixture; toss well. Toss steak in remaining 2 tablespoons juice mixture. Add steak to cabbage mixture; toss to combine. Serves 6 (serving size: 3 ounces steak and ⅔ cup salad).

CALORIES 198; **FAT** 6.5g (sat 2.4g, mono 2.2g, poly 0.3g); **PROTEIN** 26.3g; **CARB** 8.4g; **FIBER** 1.5g; **CHOL** 37mg; **IRON** 2.4mg; **SODIUM** 498mg; **CALC** 57mg

---

Kid Friendly • Quick & Easy

Chicken and Bean Burritos

¾ pound chicken breast tenders, cut into 1-inch pieces
½ cup prechopped onion
1½ teaspoons chili powder
½ teaspoon ground cumin
⅛ teaspoon salt
⅛ teaspoon freshly ground black pepper
2 teaspoons canola oil
½ cup lower-sodium canned black beans, rinsed and drained
1 garlic clove, minced
2 (10-inch) flour tortillas
1 ounce preshredded Monterey Jack cheese (about ¼ cup)
Cooking spray
½ cup pico de gallo
¼ cup reduced-fat sour cream

1. Combine first 6 ingredients in a bowl; toss well.

2. Heat a large skillet over medium-high heat. Add oil to pan; swirl to coat. Add chicken mixture; cook 8 minutes or until chicken is done, stirring occasionally. Add beans and garlic; cook 2 minutes or until heated, stirring frequently. Divide chicken mixture

---

evenly among tortillas. Top each burrito with 2 tablespoons cheese. Roll up each burrito jelly-roll fashion.

3. Heat a large skillet over medium-high heat. Coat both sides of burritos evenly with cooking spray. Place burritos in pan; cook 2 minutes on each side or until browned. Cut burritos in half. Top with pico de gallo and sour cream. Serves 4 (serving size: 1 burrito half, 2 tablespoons pico de gallo, and 1 tablespoon sour cream).

CALORIES 287; **FAT** 8.8g (sat 2.6g, mono 3.8g, poly 1.6g); **PROTEIN** 24.7g; **CARB** 25.4g; **FIBER** 2.9g; **CHOL** 57mg; **IRON** 2.4mg; **SODIUM** 499mg; **CALC** 101mg

---

Quick & Easy

Honey Cashew Chicken with Rice

1 cup instant rice
2 (6-ounce) skinless, boneless chicken breast halves, cut into 1-inch cubes
2 tablespoons cornstarch
½ teaspoon salt
½ teaspoon black pepper
1 tablespoon canola oil
1 tablespoon dark sesame oil
2 cups broccoli florets
1 cup frozen shelled edamame (green soybeans)
2 garlic cloves, minced
1 medium yellow onion, finely chopped
1 red bell pepper, sliced
½ cup dry-roasted cashews, unsalted
1 tablespoon rice vinegar
3 tablespoons honey
2 tablespoons lower-sodium soy sauce
1 tablespoon Sriracha (hot chile sauce, such as Huy Fong)

1. Cook rice according to package directions, omitting salt and fat.

2. Combine chicken and next 3 ingredients in a bowl; toss to coat.

3. Heat a large skillet over medium-high heat. Add canola and sesame oils; swirl to coat. Add chicken mixture; sauté 4 minutes or until lightly browned. Increase heat to high; add

---

broccoli and next 4 ingredients. Cook 5 minutes or until vegetables are crisp-tender and chicken is done, stirring frequently. Stir in cashews.

4. Combine vinegar and remaining ingredients in a small bowl; stir with a whisk. Add vinegar mixture to chicken mixture; toss to coat. Serve with rice. Serves 4 (serving size: ½ cup rice and 1 cup chicken mixture).

CALORIES 470; **FAT** 17.6g (sat 2.7g, mono 8.7g, poly 4.2g); **PROTEIN** 29.1g; **CARB** 50.9g; **FIBER** 4.5g; **CHOL** 49mg; **IRON** 3.1mg; **SODIUM** 638mg; **CALC** 66mg

---

Quick & Easy • Make Ahead

Tex-Mex Chicken Soup

1½ tablespoons extra-virgin olive oil
1 cup chopped onion
3 garlic cloves, minced
1 red bell pepper, chopped
1 jalapeño, seeded and minced
1 tablespoon chili powder
1½ teaspoons crushed red pepper
½ teaspoon salt
½ teaspoon ground cumin
½ teaspoon black pepper
3 cups shredded rotisserie chicken
2 cups frozen whole-kernel corn
4 cups lower-sodium chicken broth
2 large tomatoes, chopped
1 (15-ounce) can no-salt-added black beans, rinsed and drained
¼ cup chopped fresh cilantro
3 ounces queso fresco, crumbled
8 lime wedges

1. Heat a Dutch oven over medium-high heat. Add oil, onion, and next 3 ingredients; sauté 3 minutes. Add chili powder and next 4 ingredients; sauté 30 seconds. Add chicken and next 4 ingredients; bring to a boil. Cover, reduce heat, and simmer 6 minutes. Top evenly with cilantro and queso. Serve with lime. Serves 8 (serving size: 1 cup).

CALORIES 186; **FAT** 5.4g (sat 1.3g, mono 2.8g, poly 0.7g); **PROTEIN** 179g; **CARB** 18.4g; **FIBER** 3.9g; **CHOL** 41mg; **IRON** 1.2mg; **SODIUM** 571mg; **CALC** 67mg

Tuna Salad Melt

¹⁄₄ cup walnuts, chopped
¹⁄₄ cup chopped red onion
¹⁄₄ cup canned chickpeas (garbanzo
   beans), rinsed and drained
¹⁄₄ cup canola mayonnaise
1 tablespoon Dijon mustard
1 teaspoon red wine vinegar
¹⁄₄ teaspoon hot pepper sauce
¹⁄₂ teaspoon salt
¹⁄₂ teaspoon freshly ground black
   pepper
1 (12-ounce) can solid white tuna in
   water, drained and flaked
1 garlic clove, minced
6 (1-ounce) slices multigrain bread
1¹⁄₂ ounces shredded Swiss cheese
   (about ¹⁄₃ cup)
12 (¹⁄₄-inch-thick) slices tomato
1 cup baby spinach

1. Preheat broiler to high.
2. Combine first 11 ingredients in a
medium bowl; toss gently to coat.
3. Top bread evenly with cheese;
broil 4 minutes or until bubbly.
Arrange 2 tomato slices and about ¹⁄₃
cup tuna mixture over each bread slice.
Top sandwiches evenly with spinach.
Serves 6 (serving size: 1 sandwich).

Sustainable
Choice

*Solid white tuna is albacore, the
most sustainable choice among
varieties of tuna.*

CALORIES 231; FAT 11.1g (sat 1.9g, mono 2.9g, poly 3.8g);
PROTEIN 15.2g; CARB 18g; FIBER 3.9g; CHOL 21mg;
IRON 1.4mg; SODIUM 500mg; CALC 94mg

Quick & Easy • Make Ahead
Vegetarian

Parsley-Farro Salad

*If you can't find precooked farro, substitute
precooked or boil-in-bag brown rice.*

1 (8.5-ounce) package precooked farro
   (such as Archer Farms)
1¹⁄₂ tablespoons sherry vinegar
1 tablespoon olive oil
1 teaspoon Dijon mustard
¹⁄₂ teaspoon salt
¹⁄₄ teaspoon freshly ground black
   pepper
1 garlic clove, minced
¹⁄₂ cup coarsely chopped fresh parsley

1. Heat farro according to directions.
2. Combine vinegar and next 5 ingredients in a medium bowl; stir with a
whisk.
3. Add cooked farro and parsley to
vinegar mixture; toss to coat. Serves
4 (serving size: ¹⁄₂ cup).

CALORIES 90; FAT 4g (sat 0.5g, mono 2.5g, poly 0.4g);
PROTEIN 2.4g; CARB 14.8g; FIBER 2.2g; CHOL 0mg;
IRON 0.5mg; SODIUM 329mg; CALC 12mg

Variation 1: Tomato and Cucumber

Prepare base recipe through step 2,
substituting 1¹⁄₂ tablespoons fresh
lemon juice for sherry vinegar. Add
cooked farro, ¹⁄₂ cup diced fresh tomato,
¹⁄₂ cup diced cucumber, ¹⁄₄ cup chopped
fresh parsley leaves, ¹⁄₄ cup chopped
fresh mint, and ¹⁄₄ cup chopped green
onions to lemon juice mixture; toss to
coat. Serves 4 (serving size: ³⁄₄ cup).

CALORIES 97; FAT 4g (sat 0.5g); SODIUM 330mg

Variation 2: Basil and Corn

Prepare base recipe through step 2.
Heat a medium skillet over medium-
high heat. Add 1 tablespoon olive oil
to pan; swirl to coat. Add 1 cup fresh
corn kernels (about 2 ears) to pan;
sauté 3 minutes. Add cooked farro,
corn, and ¹⁄₂ cup chopped fresh basil
to vinaigrette; toss to coat. Serves 4
(serving size: about ³⁄₄ cup).

CALORIES 157; FAT 7.9g (sat 1g); SODIUM 332mg

Variation 3: Onion, Feta, and Bell Pepper

Prepare base recipe through step 2,
omitting salt. Heat a medium skillet over
medium-high heat. Add 1 tablespoon
olive oil to pan; swirl to coat. Add ¹⁄₂ cup
diced red onion and ¹⁄₂ cup diced orange
bell pepper to pan; sauté 2 minutes. Add
cooked farro, onion, and bell pepper to
vinaigrette; toss to coat. Fold in ¹⁄₄ cup
crumbled feta cheese. Serves 4 (serving
size: ³⁄₄ cup).

CALORIES 156; FAT 9.4g (sat 2.4g); SODIUM 136mg

Kid Friendly • Quick & Easy

Broiled Pineapple Sundaes

*This sundae also makes a great breakfast
parfait—just substitute plain fat-free Greek
yogurt for frozen.*

3 tablespoons brown sugar
3 tablespoons fresh orange juice
1¹⁄₂ teaspoons honey
¹⁄₂ teaspoon ground cinnamon
¹⁄₂ teaspoon ground ginger
2 cups coarsely chopped fresh
   pineapple
¹⁄₄ cup macadamia nuts, coarsely
   chopped
2 cups vanilla fat-free frozen Greek
   yogurt

1. Preheat broiler to high.
2. Combine first 5 ingredients in a
medium bowl, stirring well with a
whisk. Add pineapple; toss to coat.
3. Spread pineapple mixture in a single
layer on a jelly-roll pan lined with foil.
Broil 5 minutes or until bubbly.
4. Place nuts in a skillet; cook over
medium heat 3 minutes or until lightly
browned, shaking pan frequently. Spoon
¹⁄₂ cup yogurt into each of 4 bowls; top
each with about ¹⁄₄ cup pineapple mixture and 1 tablespoon nuts. Serves 4.

CALORIES 235; FAT 6.4g (sat 1g, mono 4.9g, poly 0.2g);
PROTEIN 11.9g; CARB 34.5g; FIBER 2g; CHOL 0mg;
IRON 0.6mg; SODIUM 54mg; CALC 30mg

BLACKBERRY CURD

It's always a thorny challenge, a real-life *Itchy and Scratchy* adventure: While on a country or edge-of-town stroll, we spot the berries hanging heavy on their canes. Blackberry bushes favor ditches, back roads, power right-of-ways, hedgerows. As summer ripens, the fat fruit turns from raspberry red to an intense inky purple. There's about a six-week window, and it varies a lot across the continent. So when we find some, we have to pick. And no matter how carefully the project is undertaken, the thorns bite back. The more reckless on our staff have returned with a good, two-bucket haul looking like they've been in a back-alley battle with a gang of angry cats: streaks of dried blood on legs and arms. But it's worth it. Blackberries are delicious fresh, and cooking applications abound: cobbler, vinaigrette, and barbecue sauce, to name a few. Our latest obsession is Blackberry Curd: thick, tart, beautiful. Well worth a few nicks.

Kid Friendly • Make Ahead

Blackberry Curd Tart

Hands-on time: 51 min. Total time: 3 hr. 34 min.

4.5 ounces all-purpose flour (about 1 cup)
1/3 cup powdered sugar
1/4 cup almonds, toasted and finely ground
3/8 teaspoon salt, divided
8 tablespoons chilled butter, divided
Baking spray with flour (such as Baker's Joy)
3 cups fresh blackberries
1 3/4 cups granulated sugar, divided
1/4 cup fresh lemon juice
2 tablespoons cornstarch
2 large egg yolks
1/4 teaspoon cream of tartar
3 large egg whites
1/3 cup water

1. Preheat oven to 350°.
2. Weigh or lightly spoon flour into a dry measuring cup; level with a knife. Place flour, powdered sugar, almonds, and 1/8 teaspoon salt in a food processor; pulse to combine. Cut 7 tablespoons butter into small pieces. Add to flour mixture; pulse just until mixture resembles coarse meal. Press in bottom and up sides of a 9-inch round removable-bottom tart pan coated with baking spray. Bake at 350° for 30 minutes or until golden. Cool on a wire rack.
3. Combine berries, 3/4 cup granulated sugar, and juice in a saucepan over medium-high heat; bring to a boil. Reduce heat, and simmer 6 minutes. Place mixture in a blender; let stand 5 minutes. Blend until smooth. Strain mixture through a cheesecloth-lined sieve into a medium bowl, pressing on solids. Discard solids. Wipe pan clean; return mixture to pan. Combine cornstarch and egg yolks, stirring until smooth. Stir yolk mixture into berry mixture; bring to a boil over medium-low heat. Cook 1 minute, stirring constantly. Remove from heat; stir in 1/8 teaspoon salt and remaining 1 table-spoon butter. Scrape mixture into a bowl; cover surface directly with plastic wrap. Chill.
4. Combine 1/8 teaspoon salt, cream of tartar, and egg whites in a large bowl; beat with a mixer at high speed until soft peaks form. Combine remaining 1 cup granulated sugar and 1/3 cup water in a saucepan; bring to a boil. Cook, without stirring, until a candy thermometer registers 250°. Gradually pour hot sugar syrup in a thin stream over egg whites, beating at medium speed, then at high speed until stiff peaks form.
5. Preheat broiler.
6. Spoon curd over crust; top with meringue. Broil 2 minutes or until golden. Serves 12 (serving size: 1 slice).

CALORIES 285; FAT 10.2g (sat 5.3g, mono 3.3g, poly 0.9g); PROTEIN 3.7g; CARB 46.6g; FIBER 2.5g; CHOL 55mg; IRON 0.9mg; SODIUM 90mg; CALC 27mg

A WORD ABOUT CURD: OUR VERSION USES JUICE AND SUGAR THICKENED WITH EGG YOLKS AND CORNSTARCH.

OOPS!
YOUR BLUEBERRIES TAKE A DIVE

Keep the fruit afloat with a starchy coat.

Nothing brightens a bite of a summertime muffin quite like the burst of a fresh-baked blueberry, unless you discover the poor things have sunk to the bottom, where they have congregated into a mush.

The cause of sinkage is in a sense the season itself: In the heart of the summer, fat, ripe berries may be more dense than batter, causing them to drop.

The solution: A dash of flour will help blueberries defy gravity for the very simple reason that the flour makes them stick to the batter and stay put. Just toss blueberries with a tablespoon of flour before folding in. But use flour from the recipe—don't add extra; that will keep your ingredient ratios even.

As always, be gentle when mixing the muffin batter. As batters are over-beaten, they can thin out, exacerbating the problem and producing a poor crumb as well. If your batter does seem a bit thin, try sprinkling some of the berries on top just before baking.

(So sad)

(Just right!)

STEP-BY-STEP GUIDE TO THE BEST SUMMER PARTY GRILLING

With tips and techniques from grill master Steven Raichlen, you can delight a few friends or a crowd with perfect versions of healthy chicken, fish, veggies, and more.

1. **Start with ground buffalo.** It has fewer calories and as much as half the sat fat of 90% lean beef, but boasts big, meaty flavor.

2. **Add some Parmigiano-Reggiano to the patties**—it kicks up the savory umami taste and seasons the burgers from the inside.

3. **Stir in a splash of extra-virgin olive oil.** A little heart-healthy fat added to the patties helps keep the extra-lean burgers moist.

4. **Make a kickin' condiment.** Slow-roast tomatoes to intensify their sweetness. Add a little tangy balsamic vinegar and peppery basil, and then puree the mixture into a ketchup.

5. **Grill the burgers over high heat** to no more than medium so they don't dry out.

6. **Toast the buns on the grill** to add a little crisp texture and some lightly charred flavor.

Kid Friendly

Parmesan Buffalo Burgers with Balsamic Ketchup

Hands-on time: 25 min. Total time: 4 hr.

Burgers:
1 tablespoon extra-virgin olive oil
1/4 teaspoon kosher salt
1/4 teaspoon freshly ground black pepper
1 pound lean ground buffalo or bison
1 ounce grated Parmigiano-Reggiano cheese (about 1/4 cup)
Cooking spray
4 (1 1/2-ounce) hamburger buns, toasted
1 cup baby arugula
4 thin slices red onion
4 tablespoons Balsamic Ketchup (recipe at right)

1. Preheat grill to high heat.
2. Combine first 5 ingredients in a bowl. Divide buffalo mixture into 4 equal portions, gently shaping each into a 1/2-inch-thick patty. Press a nickel-sized indentation in the center of each patty.
3. Place patties on grill rack coated with cooking spray; grill 3 minutes on each side or until desired degree of doneness.
4. Place bottom bun halves on plates. Top each with 1/4 cup arugula, 1 onion slice, and 1 patty. Spread 1 tablespoon ketchup on top half of each bun; place on top of burgers. Serves 4 (serving size: 1 burger).

CALORIES 368; FAT 16.5g (sat 5.6g, mono 7.5g, poly 1.8g); PROTEIN 30.3g; CARB 27.8g; FIBER 1.8g; CHOL 68mg; IRON 4.9mg; SODIUM 555mg; CALC 162mg

Balsamic Ketchup

Hands-on time: 10 min. Total time: 3 hr. 10 min. Refrigerate extra ketchup in an airtight container for up to a week.

1 tablespoon extra-virgin olive oil
3/8 teaspoon kosher salt, divided
2 pounds small tomatoes, quartered
3 tablespoons chopped fresh basil
2 teaspoons balsamic vinegar
1/2 teaspoon sugar
1/4 teaspoon ground red pepper

1. Preheat oven to 325°.
2. Combine oil, 1/4 teaspoon salt, and tomatoes in a large bowl, and toss gently to coat. Arrange tomatoes, skin side down, on a wire rack set inside a jelly-roll pan. Bake at 325° for 3 hours. Cool slightly; peel. Discard peels.
3. Place tomatoes, remaining 1/8 teaspoon salt, basil, and remaining ingredients in a food processor; process until smooth. Serves 16 (serving size: 1 tablespoon).

CALORIES 19; FAT 1g (sat 0.1g, mono 0.7g, poly 0.1g); PROTEIN 0.5g; CARB 2.5g; FIBER 0.7g; CHOL 0mg; IRON 0.2mg; SODIUM 48mg; CALC 7mg

Grilled Chicken Thighs with Ancho-Tequila Glaze

Hands-on time: 1 hr. 10 min. Total time: 1 hr. 10 min. *If you're using a charcoal grill, skip the foil pan and add the chips to the coals. Look for granulated garlic in the spice aisle, or substitute 3/4 teaspoon garlic powder. Amber agave syrup has a deeper flavor than the more neutral, light-colored varieties.*

1 1/2 cups hickory wood chips
1 tablespoon ancho chile powder
1 1/2 teaspoons sugar
1 1/2 teaspoons granulated garlic
1 1/2 teaspoons ground cumin
1 1/2 teaspoons freshly ground black pepper
3/4 teaspoon kosher salt
12 bone-in chicken thighs, skinned (about 2 1/2 pounds)
1 1/2 tablespoons extra-virgin olive oil
6 tablespoons amber agave syrup
3 tablespoons tequila
1 1/2 tablespoons hot sauce
1 1/2 tablespoons butter
1 1/2 tablespoons fresh lime juice
1/4 teaspoon crushed red pepper
Cooking spray
3 tablespoons chopped fresh cilantro (optional)
6 lime wedges

1. Soak wood chips in water 30 minutes; drain well.
2. Preheat grill to medium-high heat using both burners. After preheating, turn the left burner off (leave the right burner on). Pierce the bottom of a disposable aluminum foil pan several times with the tip of a knife. Place pan on heat element on heated side of grill; add wood chips to pan. Let chips stand 15 minutes or until smoking.
3. Combine chile powder and next 5 ingredients in a medium bowl. Add chicken to bowl; toss well. Add oil to bowl; toss well.
4. Place syrup and next 5 ingredients in a small saucepan. Bring to a boil. Cook until mixture is reduced to 1/2 cup and begins to thicken (about 3 minutes). Reserve syrup mixture.
5. Place chicken, meaty side down, on grill rack coated with cooking spray over left burner (indirect heat). Brush chicken with 2 tablespoons syrup mixture; grill 15 minutes. Turn chicken over. Brush with 2 tablespoons syrup mixture; grill 15 minutes. Turn chicken over and move to direct heat; grill 5 minutes or until done. Garnish with cilantro, if desired. Serve with remaining syrup mixture and lime wedges. Serves 6 (serving size: 2 thighs, 2 teaspoons sauce, and 1 lime wedge).

CALORIES 278; FAT 10.8g (sat 3.4g, mono 4.5g, poly 1.6g); PROTEIN 21.7g; CARB 20.5g; FIBER 1.2g; CHOL 97mg; IRON 1.7mg; SODIUM 448mg; CALC 21mg

1. Go with thighs, which have deeper, richer chicken flavor than breast meat. They can withstand the dry heat of the grill and stay moist.

2. Dark meat is fattier than white, so to cut your sat fat intake, take the skin off.

3. Coat the chicken with a bold spice rub to amp up flavor.

4. Grill the chicken over indirect heat. Putting the meat over the cooler side of the grill cooks it slowly, gently, and evenly and ensures the glaze won't scorch.

5. But leave the bone in: It helps the meat stay juicy and makes for more flavorful chicken than boneless cuts.

6. Make a spicy sweet-tart glaze: It's so tasty, you won't miss the skin!

7. Finish it for five minutes over direct heat to add delicious light charring and caramelize the glaze.

Vegetarian

Grilled Corn, Poblano, and Black Bean Salad

Hands-on time: 40 min. Total time: 40 min. *This is a great side for grilled meats and fish.*

2 ears shucked corn
2 tablespoons extra-virgin olive oil, divided
4 green onions
1 avocado, peeled, halved, and pitted
1 large red bell pepper
1 large poblano chile
Cooking spray
1/2 cup chopped fresh cilantro
3 tablespoons fresh lime juice
1 teaspoon ground cumin
1/4 teaspoon salt
1/4 teaspoon freshly ground black pepper
1 (15-ounce) can no-salt-added black beans, rinsed and drained

1. Preheat grill to high heat.
2. Brush corn with 2 teaspoons oil. Place green onions, avocado, bell pepper, poblano, and corn on a grill rack coated with cooking spray. Grill onions 2 minutes on each side or until lightly browned. Grill avocado 2 minutes on each side or until well marked. Grill bell pepper 6 minutes on each side or until blackened; peel. Grill poblano 9 minutes on each side or until blackened; peel. Grill corn 12 minutes or until beginning to brown on all sides, turning occasionally.
3. Cut kernels from ears of corn; place in a large bowl. Chop onions, bell pepper, and poblano; add to bowl. Add remaining 4 teaspoons oil, cilantro, juice, cumin, salt, black pepper, and beans to bowl; toss well. Cut avocado into thin slices; place on top of salad. Serves 6 (serving size: 3/4 cup).

CALORIES 167; FAT 9.9g (sat 1.4g, mono 6.7g, poly 1.3g); PROTEIN 4.6g; CARB 17.8g; FIBER 6g; CHOL 0mg; IRON 1.4mg; SODIUM 209mg; CALC 38mg

1. **Go with a variety of produce** for color and texture contrasts: corn, bell pepper, poblano chile, and green onions.

2. **Add avocado to the mix:** People don't think to grill avocado, but it adds fantastic smoky depth to the buttery fruit.

3. **Crank up the grill.** Heat to high for optimum charring—it's the browned and blackened bits that really make the salad shine.

4. **Watch carefully,** since each item has its own ideal doneness—the green onions need to brown and wilt slightly; the peppers should fully blacken so they can be easily peeled; and the corn has to be turned often so it browns evenly. The avocado gets just a minute or two—it'll grow bitter if cooked too long.

5. **Bring the chopped salad together** with some black beans, a touch of earthy cumin, and fresh lime juice and cilantro to brighten flavors.

Vampire Steak

Hands-on time: 27 min. Total time: 1 hr. 27 min. The marinade features a robust dose of garlic. Score the meat lightly, about ⅛ inch deep.

4 teaspoons minced garlic
1 tablespoon fresh lemon juice
2 teaspoons Spanish smoked paprika
2 teaspoons chopped fresh tarragon
1 (1½-pound) flank steak, trimmed
1 teaspoon kosher salt
½ teaspoon freshly ground black pepper
Cooking spray

1. Combine first 4 ingredients. Score a diamond pattern on both sides of steak; rub juice mixture evenly over both sides. Cover; refrigerate 1 hour.
2. Preheat grill to high heat.
3. Sprinkle both sides of steak evenly with salt and pepper. Place steak on grill rack coated with cooking spray, and grill 6 minutes on each side or until desired degree of doneness. Remove steak from grill; let stand

5 minutes. Cut steak across grain into slices. Serves 6 (serving size: 3 ounces steak).

CALORIES 166; FAT 6.3g (sat 2.4g, mono 2.2g, poly 0.3g); PROTEIN 24.7g; CARB 1.4g; FIBER 0.4g; CHOL 37mg; IRON 2mg; SODIUM 383mg; CALC 34mg

1. **Score the beef lightly** to help the marinade penetrate quickly and keep the steak flat while it cooks.

2. **Keep it juicy and tender by** letting it rest for several minutes after cooking, and then slicing thinly against the grain: Flank steak turns tough if sliced with the grain or into thick pieces.

3. **Add salt just before grilling,** after the steak comes out of the marinade. (If you add salt to a wet marinade, you will lose some of it with the discarded liquid.)

4. **Add smoked paprika** to the spice rub. The steak doesn't spend long on the grill, so paprika boosts its open-fire flavor.

5. **Buy flank steak:** It's lean—with almost 30% less saturated fat than top sirloin—but flavorful.

Vietnamese Pork Tenderloin

Hands-on time: 1 hr. Total time: 1 hr. 23 min.

2 tablespoons sugar
1 teaspoon freshly ground black pepper
2 garlic cloves, peeled
1 shallot, halved
1 (4-inch) piece fresh lemongrass, halved
1 (1-inch) piece peeled ginger, halved
1 tablespoon lower-sodium soy sauce
2½ tablespoons fish sauce, divided
1 tablespoon canola oil
1 (1-pound) pork tenderloin, trimmed and cut crosswise into ¼-inch slices
⅓ cup grated carrot
2 tablespoons sugar
¼ cup fresh lemon juice
¼ cup rice vinegar
1 teaspoon minced garlic

1 Thai or serrano chile, thinly sliced and divided
2 ounces rice vermicelli
Cooking spray
16 Bibb lettuce leaves (about 2 heads)
1 cup cilantro leaves
1 cup sliced English cucumber
1 cup fresh bean sprouts
⅓ cup finely chopped unsalted, dry-roasted peanuts
16 basil leaves
16 mint leaves
2 Thai chiles, thinly sliced

1. Place first 6 ingredients in a mini food processor; pulse until coarsely ground. With processor on, add soy sauce, 1 tablespoon fish sauce, and oil; process until blended. Combine mixture and pork in a zip-top plastic bag; seal and marinate in refrigerator 1 hour, turning occasionally.
2. Combine carrot and sugar in a medium bowl; let stand 10 minutes. Add juice, vinegar, 1½ tablespoons fish sauce, minced garlic, and 1 sliced chile; stir until sugar dissolves.
3. Cook noodles according to package directions, omitting salt and fat. Drain and rinse with cold water; drain well.
4. Preheat grill to high heat.
5. Remove pork from marinade; discard marinade. Thread pork evenly onto 6 (12-inch) skewers. Place skewers on grill rack coated with cooking spray; grill 2 minutes on each side or until lightly charred.
6. Top each lettuce leaf evenly with pork, noodles, and remaining ingredients. Serve with dipping sauce. Serves 4 (serving size: 4 wraps and 3 tablespoons sauce).

CALORIES 343; FAT 9.9g (sat 1.8g, mono 4.7g, poly 2.8g); PROTEIN 29.7g; CARB 36.1g; FIBER 3.3g; CHOL 74mg; IRON 2.8mg; SODIUM 620mg; CALC 53mg

continued

1. **Choose a lean pork cut.** Not all parts of the hog are fat bombs. Go with grill-friendly tenderloin: It's a leaner cut than pork loin chops, saving you as much as 3g sat fat per serving.

2. **But tenderloin is extremely mild-tasting.** This Vietnamese-style dish pairs it with big, strong flavors: salty, umami-rich soy and fish sauces, peppery ginger, tangy rice vinegar, and fiery Thai chiles.

3. **Slice meat into thin medallions** before marinating it. This increases the surface area for the marinade to coat and helps the flavorings fully permeate the pork.

4. **Thread the meat onto skewers** so it's easier to handle on the grill. Then, cook over very high heat; it's how you get those delicious crispy, blackened bits on the edges of the meat, just like the Saigon street vendors do.

5. **Pack the pork up in lettuce wraps** loaded with fresh, crisp veggies, fragrant herbs, and crunchy peanuts: It's the perfect setup for a casual, serve-yourself kind of gathering.

Quick & Easy
Cedar Plank–Grilled Salmon with Mango Kiwi Salsa

Hands-on time: 25 min. Total time: 40 min.

1 large cedar plank
1 cup finely diced peeled ripe mango
1/2 cup diced peeled kiwifruit
2 tablespoons chopped fresh cilantro
1 teaspoon extra-virgin olive oil
1 teaspoon fresh lime juice
1 serrano chile, finely chopped
1/2 teaspoon kosher salt, divided
1/2 teaspoon freshly ground black pepper, divided
4 (6-ounce) sustainable skinless salmon fillets (such as wild Alaskan)

1. Soak plank in water 25 minutes.
2. Preheat grill to medium-high heat.
3. Combine mango and next 5 ingredients. Add 1/4 teaspoon salt and 1/4 teaspoon pepper; set aside.
4. Sprinkle salmon with remaining 1/4 teaspoon salt and remaining 1/4 teaspoon pepper. Place plank on grill rack; grill 3 minutes or until lightly charred. Turn plank over; place fish on charred side. Cover; grill 8 minutes or until desired degree of doneness. Place each fillet on a plate; top each with 1/3 cup mango salsa. Serves 4.

CALORIES 267; **FAT** 7.5g (sat 1.2g, mono 2.5g, poly 2.6g); **PROTEIN** 34.7g; **CARB** 14.8g; **FIBER** 2.2g; **CHOL** 88mg; **IRON** 1.6mg; **SODIUM** 356mg; **CALC** 42mg

1. **Since the skin** won't be in direct contact with the grill to get nice and crisp, go with skinless fillets.

2. **The smoky fish** can stand up to the spicy sweetness of a tropical fruit salsa. Prepare it before the fish so the flavors have time to meld.

3. **Grill on cedar planks:** Rich wood smoke infuses the salmon.

4. **Put the lid on the grill** so the fish bathes in cedar smoke, the main "seasoning."

5. **Choose salmon:** Packed with flavor and heart-healthy fats, it can handle the grill. Flaky fish like cod, sole, and tilapia tend to fall to pieces.

ONLY A VERY HOT GRILL YIELDS TASTY, CHARRED EDGES.

EVERYDAY VEGETARIAN
GREAT TART, SMART CRUST

This fresh entrée features a unique crust, made tender and flaky with olive oil.

Vegetarian
Summer Squash and Ricotta Galette

Hands-on time: 25 min. Total time: 2 hr. *Here's a fantastic crust that you can swap in for a standard butter-based one. You can make the dough in advance, and chill until ready to use.*

7.25 ounces all-purpose flour (about 1 2/3 cups)
1/2 teaspoon salt
1/2 teaspoon baking powder
1/3 cup plus 1 tablespoon extra-virgin olive oil, divided
1/4 cup water
1 medium zucchini, cut crosswise into 1/4-inch-thick slices
1 large yellow squash, cut crosswise into 1/4-inch-thick slices
2 garlic cloves, minced
3/4 cup part-skim ricotta cheese
2 ounces grated fresh Parmesan cheese (about 1/2 cup)
2 teaspoons chopped fresh thyme
1/2 teaspoon grated lemon rind
1 teaspoon fresh lemon juice
1/4 teaspoon freshly ground black pepper
1 large egg, lightly beaten
1/4 teaspoon kosher salt
1 teaspoon water
1 large egg white
1/4 cup fresh basil leaves

1. Weigh or lightly spoon flour into dry measuring cups; level with a knife. Place flour, salt, and baking powder in a food processor; pulse 2 times to combine. Combine ⅓ cup oil and ¼ cup water in a small bowl. With processor on, slowly add oil mixture through food chute; process until dough is crumbly. Turn dough out onto a lightly floured surface. Knead 1 minute; add additional flour, if necessary, to prevent dough from sticking. Gently press dough into a 5-inch disk, and wrap in plastic wrap; chill at least 30 minutes.

2. Preheat oven to 400°.

3. Combine remaining 1 tablespoon oil, zucchini, squash, and garlic in a large bowl. Combine ricotta and next 6 ingredients in a medium bowl, stirring to combine.

4. Unwrap dough, and roll into a 14-inch circle on a lightly floured surface. Place dough on a baking sheet lined with parchment paper. Spread ricotta mixture over dough, leaving a 2-inch border. Arrange zucchini and squash slices alternately, slightly overlapping, in a circular pattern over ricotta mixture. Sprinkle zucchini and squash with kosher salt. Fold edges of dough toward center, pressing gently to seal (dough will only partially cover squash). In a small bowl, whisk together 1 teaspoon water and egg white. Brush dough edges with egg white mixture. Bake at 400° for 40 minutes or until golden brown. Cool 5 minutes; sprinkle with basil. Cool an additional 15 minutes. Cut into 6 wedges. Serves 6 (serving size: 1 wedge).

CALORIES 362; FAT 20.1g (sat 5.5g, mono 12.3g, poly 2g); PROTEIN 13.3g; CARB 31g; FIBER 1.8g; CHOL 53mg; IRON 2.4mg; SODIUM 519mg; CALC 236mg

LITTLE BURGERS, BIG FLAVORS

We tackled the slider craze with the help of *Top Chef All-Stars'* Richard Blais. These baby burgers range from absolutely classic to a beet-based veggie special and a succulent tuna version with a wasabi kick.

Kid Friendly • Quick & Easy

Bacon and Cheddar Sliders

Hands-on time: 20 min. Total time: 30 min.

3 tablespoons shallots, minced
1 teaspoon Dijon mustard
12 ounces ground sirloin
¾ teaspoon freshly ground black pepper, divided
Cooking spray
2 ounces 2% reduced-fat sharp cheddar cheese, shredded (about ½ cup)
8 whole-wheat slider buns
3 tablespoons canola mayonnaise
4 cornichon or other small dill pickles, each cut lengthwise into 4 slices
4 small lettuce leaves, each torn in half
1 small ripe tomato, cut into 8 slices
3 cooked bacon slices, cut into 1-inch pieces

1. Preheat grill to medium-high heat.

2. Gently combine first 3 ingredients and ½ teaspoon pepper in a large bowl, being careful not to overmix. Divide beef mixture into 8 equal portions; gently shape each portion into a ¼-inch-thick patty, taking care not to pack mixture down.

3. Arrange patties on grill rack coated with cooking spray; cook 2 minutes on each side or until desired degree of doneness. Top each patty with about 1 tablespoon cheese during last minute of cooking. Lightly coat cut sides of buns with cooking spray. Place buns, cut sides down, on grill rack. Grill 1 minute or until toasted. Spread about 1 teaspoon mayonnaise on bottom half of each bun; top with 1 patty. Top each slider with 2 pickle slices, ½ lettuce leaf, and 1 tomato slice; sprinkle evenly with remaining ¼ teaspoon pepper. Arrange bacon pieces evenly over tomato. Top with bun tops. Serves 4 (serving size: 2 sliders).

CALORIES 400; FAT 16.9g (sat 4.9g, mono 6.4g, poly 4.2g); PROTEIN 23.8g; CARB 39.8g; FIBER 5.9g; CHOL 48mg; IRON 3.8mg; SODIUM 783mg; CALC 290mg

Butcher's Cut Sliders

Hands-on time: 28 min. Total time: 58 min.

5 tablespoons red wine vinegar, divided
1 teaspoon sugar
½ cup thinly sliced shallots
12 ounces ground sirloin
¼ teaspoon salt
¼ teaspoon freshly ground black pepper
Cooking spray
1 tablespoon extra-virgin olive oil
1 teaspoon Dijon mustard
1 teaspoon lower-sodium soy sauce
1½ cups arugula
1 tablespoon chopped fresh chives
2 tablespoons canola mayonnaise
1 ounce blue cheese, crumbled (about ¼ cup)
8 sourdough slider buns

1. Combine ¼ cup vinegar and sugar, stirring until sugar dissolves. Add shallots to vinegar mixture; toss. Cover and chill 30 minutes. Toss. Drain; set aside.
2. Divide beef into 8 equal portions; gently shape each portion into a ¼-inch-thick patty, taking care not to pack beef. Sprinkle both sides of patties evenly with salt and pepper. Heat a grill pan over medium-high heat. Coat pan with cooking spray. Add patties to pan; cook 2 minutes on each side or until desired degree of doneness; do not press on patties as they cook.
3. Combine remaining 1 tablespoon vinegar, oil, mustard, and soy sauce in a large bowl, stirring with a whisk. Add arugula and chives; toss gently to coat. Combine mayonnaise and cheese in a small bowl. Spread bottom half of each bun with about 2 teaspoons mayonnaise mixture. Top with 1 patty, about ¼ cup arugula mixture, 1 tablespoon pickled shallot, and 1 bun top. Serves 4 (serving size: 2 sliders).

CALORIES 402; **FAT** 17.7g (sat 5g, mono 7.9g, poly 3g); **PROTEIN** 21.4g; **CARB** 41.2g; **FIBER** 6.1g; **CHOL** 47mg; **IRON** 3.6mg; **SODIUM** 756mg; **CALC** 125mg

---

Kid Friendly • Quick & Easy

Italian Meatball Sliders

Hands-on time: 30 min. Total time: 30 min.

¼ cup panko (Japanese breadcrumbs)
1½ tablespoons fresh basil, minced
½ teaspoon kosher salt
12 ounces ground sirloin
1 large egg
1 garlic clove, minced
12 water rolls, halved lengthwise
Cooking spray
4 ounces fresh mozzarella cheese, cut crosswise into 12 thin slices
1 cup lower-sodium marinara sauce (such as McCutcheon's)
12 fresh basil leaves (optional)

1. Preheat broiler to high.
2. Gently combine first 6 ingredients in a large bowl, being careful not to overmix. Divide beef mixture into 24 equal portions; gently shape each portion into a meatball (do not pack). Arrange rolls, cut sides up, on a heavy baking sheet; broil 30 seconds or until very lightly toasted. Remove roll tops from pan.
3. Arrange meatballs on a broiler pan coated with cooking spray; broil 3 minutes or until browned. Turn meatballs over; broil 2 minutes or until desired degree of doneness. Arrange 2 meatballs on bottom half of each roll; top each slider with 1 cheese slice. Broil 1 minute or until cheese melts.
4. Place marinara sauce in a microwave-safe dish; cover and microwave at HIGH 1½ minutes or until thoroughly heated, stirring once. Place 2 sliders on each of 6 plates; spoon about 1½ tablespoons sauce over each slider. Top each slider with 1 basil leaf, if desired, and 1 bun top. Serves 6 (serving size: 2 sliders).

CALORIES 325; **FAT** 13.2g (sat 5.9g, mono 3g, poly 1.5g); **PROTEIN** 16.6g; **CARB** 40.1g; **FIBER** 2.1g; **CHOL** 76mg; **IRON** 1.1mg; **SODIUM** 595mg; **CALC** 12mg

---

Vegetarian

Beet and Brown Rice Sliders

Hands-on time: 49 min. Total time: 49 min.

16 thin slices sourdough bread
Cooking spray
1 cup cooked, cooled whole-grain brown rice blend
¾ cup grated cooked beet (about 1 medium)
½ cup panko (Japanese breadcrumbs)
6 tablespoons chopped walnuts, toasted
¼ cup chopped fresh flat-leaf parsley
2 tablespoons finely chopped shallots
½ teaspoon kosher salt
¼ teaspoon freshly ground black pepper
2 tablespoons Dijon mustard
1 large egg
2 tablespoons olive oil
1 (3-ounce) log goat cheese, sliced crosswise into 8 slices
1 cup watercress

1. Preheat broiler to high.
2. Cut each bread slice into a 3-inch circle using a round cutter; reserve scraps for another use (such as breadcrumbs or croutons). Lightly coat bread rounds with cooking spray. Arrange bread rounds in a single layer on a baking sheet. Broil 2 minutes on each side or until lightly toasted. Cool on a wire rack.
3. Reduce oven temperature to 400°. Place a baking sheet in oven to preheat.
4. Combine rice and next 7 ingredients in a medium bowl. Combine mustard and egg, stirring well. Add egg mixture to rice mixture; stir until well blended. Spoon ⅓ cup rice mixture into a (2½-inch) round cookie cutter; pack mixture down. Remove mold. Repeat procedure 7 times to form 8 patties.
5. Heat a large skillet over medium-high heat. Add 1 tablespoon oil to pan;

swirl to coat. Carefully add 4 patties to pan; cook 2 minutes. Carefully transfer patties to preheated baking sheet, turning patties over and arranging in a single layer. Repeat procedure with remaining 1 tablespoon oil and remaining 4 patties. Place pan in oven; bake patties at 400° for 9 minutes. Top each patty with 1 cheese slice; bake an additional 1 minute or until cheese is soft and patties are set.

6. Place 8 toasted bread rounds on a flat surface; top each round with 1 patty. Divide watercress evenly among sliders; top with remaining toasted bread rounds. Serves 4 (serving size: 2 sliders).

CALORIES 400; FAT 16.9g (sat 4.9g, mono 6.4g, poly 4.2g); PROTEIN 23.8g; CARB 39.8g; FIBER 5.9g; CHOL 48mg; IRON 3.8mg; SODIUM 783mg; CALC 290mg

---

SIDE OF FRIES!

GARLIC AND HERB OVEN FRIES

Preheat a roasting pan and oven to 450°. Cut 2 pounds peeled baking potatoes into 1/4-inch matchsticks; toss with 2 tablespoons canola oil. Arrange in pan; bake at 450° for 5 minutes. Turn oven to broil. Broil 20 minutes or until browned, turning once. Melt 1 1/2 tablespoons butter in a skillet. Add 1 minced garlic clove; sauté 30 seconds. Add fries; cook 1 minute. Toss with 2 tablespoons chopped fresh parsley, 1/2 teaspoon kosher salt, and 1/4 teaspoon freshly ground black pepper. Serves 6 (serving size: about 1 1/2 cups).

CALORIES 209; FAT 7.7g (sat 2.2g); SODIUM 189mg

Quick & Easy

Southwest Crispy Chicken Sliders

Hands-on time: 32 min. Total time: 32 min.

Muffins:

3 ounces all-purpose flour (about 2/3 cup)
2/3 cup yellow cornmeal
3/4 teaspoon baking soda
1/4 teaspoon baking powder
1/4 teaspoon kosher salt
3/4 cup nonfat buttermilk
2 tablespoons butter, melted
1 large egg, lightly beaten
1.5 ounces sharp cheddar cheese, shredded (about 1/3 cup)
1 jalapeño pepper, seeded and minced
Cooking spray

Chicken:

2/3 cup panko (Japanese breadcrumbs)
1/4 cup fat-free milk
1 large egg, lightly beaten
3 (6-ounce) skinless, boneless chicken breast halves
2 tablespoons canola oil, divided

Additional ingredients:

1 ripe, pitted, peeled avocado
2 teaspoons fresh lime juice
2 applewood-smoked bacon slices, cooked and crumbled
12 (1/2-inch-thick) slices small, ripe tomato
1/4 teaspoon kosher salt
1/4 teaspoon freshly ground black pepper

1. Preheat oven to 350°.

2. To prepare muffins, weigh or lightly spoon flour into dry measuring cups; level with a knife. Combine flour, cornmeal, baking soda, baking powder, and 1/4 teaspoon salt in a medium bowl, stirring well with a whisk. Combine buttermilk, butter, and 1 egg, stirring well. Add buttermilk mixture to flour mixture, stirring just until combined. Stir in cheese and jalapeño. Spoon batter into 12 muffin cups coated with cooking spray. Bake at 350° for 17 minutes or until a wooden pick comes out clean. Cool 5 minutes in pan on a wire rack. Remove muffins from pan; cool on wire rack. Cut muffins in half crosswise.

3. To prepare chicken, place panko in a shallow dish. Combine fat-free milk and 1 egg in a shallow dish, stirring well. Split each chicken breast in half lengthwise to form 2 cutlets; cut each piece in half, crosswise, to form 12 pieces. Heat a large skillet over medium-high heat. Add 1 tablespoon oil to pan; swirl to coat. Dip chicken in egg mixture; dredge in panko. Coat panko lightly with cooking spray. Add 6 chicken cutlets to pan; cook 3 minutes on each side or until golden and done. Repeat procedure with remaining 1 tablespoon oil, remaining 6 chicken cutlets, and cooking spray.

4. To prepare additional ingredients, combine avocado and lime juice; mash to desired consistency. Stir in bacon. Place 2 muffin bottom halves on each of 6 plates. Divide avocado mixture evenly among muffins; top each slider with 1 chicken cutlet and 1 tomato slice. Sprinkle tomato evenly with 1/4 teaspoon salt and black pepper; top with muffin tops. Serves 6 (serving size: 2 sliders).

CALORIES 402; FAT 18g (sat 5.7g, mono 8.3g, poly 2.6g); PROTEIN 24.5g; CARB 34.3g; FIBER 3.1g; CHOL 106mg; IRON 2.1mg; SODIUM 576mg; CALC 129mg

Tuna Tartare Sliders with Wasabi Mayo

Hands-on time: 27 min. Total time: 1 hr. 27 min.

3 tablespoons lower-sodium soy sauce, divided
2 tablespoons rice vinegar
16 (¹⁄₈-inch-thick) slices carrot
16 (¹⁄₈-inch-thick) slices cucumber
¼ cup canola mayonnaise
½ teaspoon wasabi paste
1 teaspoon fresh lemon juice
16 thin slices white bread
Cooking spray
2 tablespoons chopped fresh chives
1 teaspoon sambal oelek (ground fresh chile paste)
10 ounces sushi-grade albacore tuna steak, finely chopped
8 green leaf lettuce leaves
1 peeled avocado, halved lengthwise
4 lime wedges (optional)

1. Combine 2 tablespoons soy sauce and vinegar in a medium bowl. Add carrot and cucumber; toss. Cover and chill 1 hour. Toss. Drain; set vegetables aside. Combine mayonnaise, wasabi, and juice in a small bowl, stirring well.
2. Preheat broiler to high.
3. Cut each bread slice into a 3-inch circle using a round cutter; reserve scraps for another use (such as bread-crumbs or croutons). Lightly coat both sides of bread rounds with cooking spray. Place bread rounds on a baking sheet in a single layer; broil 2 minutes on each side or until toasted. Cool on a wire rack.
4. Combine remaining 1 tablespoon soy sauce, chives, chile paste, and tuna in a large bowl; gently mix until blended. Spread about ½ teaspoon mayonnaise mixture on one side of each bread round; top each with 1 lettuce leaf. Divide tuna mixture evenly among sliders, mounding about 2 tablespoons on each. Cut each avocado half into 8 slices. Place 2 avocado slices,

2 cucumber slices, and 2 carrot slices on each slider. Top each slider with remaining bread round, mayonnaise-coated side down. Serve with lime wedges, if desired. Serves 4 (serving size: 2 sliders).

Sustainable Choice | *Buy fresh or frozen Pacific albacore or yellowfin tuna.*

CALORIES 315; FAT 13.9g (sat 1.7g, mono 7.4g, poly 2.4g); PROTEIN 22.2g; CARB 23.7g; FIBER 5.2g; CHOL 33mg; IRON 1.8mg; SODIUM 431mg; CALC 241mg

LESS MEAT, MORE FLAVOR

FINGER-LICKIN' BBQ VEGGIES

By Mark Bittman

Turn up the flavor with saucy grilled eggplant and tofu or braised fennel with pork.

Imagine you're sitting outside at a picnic table eating barbecue. The smell wafting up from your plate is smoky and sweet, slightly charred. There's likely some sauce on your face, and certainly some on your fingers, which you will lick off with great satisfaction. My guess is that the foods you're eating in this scenario are probably not vegetables, and definitely not tofu.

The term *finger-lickin'* is usually reserved for sticky, saucy meats like barbecue chicken, brisket, and ribs. With vegetables, we often grill or broil with olive oil to give them some color and a bit of smokiness, or braise them in wine or stock until tender, saving those seductive barbecue sauces and glazes for meat and chicken. But when you apply them to vegetables—and even tofu—you can capture the essence of great barbecue without relying so heavily on meat.

The first recipe here is a Chinese-style barbecue dish using eggplant and

tofu. I start with firm or extra-firm but squeeze out some of the moisture anyway by putting something heavy on top. While the tofu is getting squeezed, I quickly heat a glaze with hoisin and ketchup—both sweet—as the base, salty soy sauce and sharp rice vinegar to cut the sweetness, and garlic, ginger, and fresh chile because, well, they just make everything taste better.

I cut the tofu and eggplant about ½ inch thick and give them a brush of oil and sprinkle of salt. I put them on the grill (or under the broiler) at first without the sauce so they can begin to cook without burning; then after a few minutes, I start basting and turning until the eggplant is tender, the tofu is firm, and the glaze is beautifully cara-melized. You can eat this as is, but over brown rice with a scattering of scallions and sesame seeds is the best.

The second dish is a nod to low-and-slow Southern barbecue. I start with a pile of fennel and onions, sliced lengthwise so they don't get stringy, and a little bit of pork shoulder in a pot. I cover and cook them without any added fat until the vegetables start to caramelize and stick to the bottom. That's your cue to add liquid; where normally it might be water or stock, here I build the barbecue sauce right into the pot. Cider vinegar provides the trademark tang of North Carolina–style pulled pork, while crushed toma-toes and spices give it a deep color and round out the acidity.

The vegetables and pork simmer in the sauce until meltingly tender. Then, just like pulled pork, they're piled high on a toasted bun, slathered with a mix-ture of Greek yogurt, mayo, and garlic, and topped with shredded cabbage.

This dish is great for casual summer entertaining—and it's not hard to multiply the recipe. Just cook the veg-etable and pork mixture ahead of time (even a day or two before would be fine), and reheat slowly before serving. (You could just as easily slow-bake the tofu and eggplant slices ahead of time, as well.)

One of these dishes cooks fast and furious, the other low and slow, but I guarantee that both will have you lickin' your fingers in no time.

Grilled Eggplant and Tofu Steaks with Sticky Hoisin Glaze

Hands-on time: 45 min. Total time: 45 min.

1 (14-ounce) package extra-firm tofu, drained
1/3 cup ketchup
3 tablespoons hoisin sauce
1 1/2 tablespoons lower-sodium soy sauce
1 1/2 tablespoons rice vinegar
1 1/2 tablespoons minced garlic
1 tablespoon minced peeled ginger
1 serrano chile, finely chopped
2 tablespoons peanut oil
2 (1-pound) eggplants, cut lengthwise into 1/2-inch-thick slices
1/8 teaspoon kosher salt
Cooking spray
1/4 cup sliced green onions
2 teaspoons sesame seeds, toasted

1. Place tofu on paper towels; cover with paper towels. Top with a heavy skillet; let stand 20 minutes. Cut tofu crosswise into 8 (1/2-inch-thick) slices.
2. Combine ketchup and next 6 ingredients in a saucepan; bring to a boil. Reduce heat to medium-low; cook until reduced to 1 cup (12 minutes), stirring occasionally. Set aside 1/2 cup.
3. Preheat grill to medium-high heat.
4. Brush oil over tofu and eggplant; sprinkle with salt. Place eggplant on grill rack coated with cooking spray, and grill 2 minutes. Turn eggplant over, and brush with 2 tablespoons sauce; grill 2 minutes. Turn eggplant over; brush with 2 tablespoons sauce. Cook 2 minutes on each side.

5. Add tofu to grill; grill 3 minutes. Turn tofu over, and brush with 2 tablespoons sauce; grill 3 minutes. Turn tofu over and brush with 2 tablespoons sauce; grill 1 minute on each side. Sprinkle with onions and seeds. Serve with eggplant and 1/2 cup reserved sauce. Serves 4 (serving size: about 3 eggplant slices, 2 tofu slices, and 2 tablespoons sauce).

CALORIES 286; FAT 14.3g (sat 2.6g, mono 4.7g, poly 6.4g); PROTEIN 13.4g; CARB 29.4g; FIBER 8.5g; CHOL 0mg; IRON 2.5mg; SODIUM 630mg; CALC 124mg

GREEN ONION SAVER

Scallions are almost always sold by the bundle. Many recipes only require a few stalks though, so you're left with quickly wilting extras that often end up in the trash. Instead, slice the remaining stalks and store them in a container in the freezer. Although they aren't as tasty as raw, frozen onions perform well in stir-fries, pastas, soups, or any other cooked applications, and they're a great time-saver for the busy cook.

Kid Friendly

Slow-Cooked BBQ Fennel, Onion, and Pork Sandwiches

Hands-on time: 35 min. Total time: 45 min.

8 ounces boneless pork shoulder, trimmed and chopped
2 cups vertically sliced onion
1 large fennel bulb, thinly sliced
1/2 teaspoon kosher salt
1/2 teaspoon chili powder
1/2 teaspoon paprika
1/4 teaspoon ground cumin
1/4 teaspoon freshly ground black pepper
1/4 cup crushed tomatoes
1/4 cup cider vinegar
2 teaspoons extra-virgin olive oil
2 teaspoons cider vinegar
3/4 cup thinly sliced green cabbage
3/4 cup thinly sliced red cabbage
1/3 cup plain 2% Greek yogurt
2 tablespoons canola mayonnaise
1 teaspoon minced garlic
6 (1 1/2-ounce) whole-wheat hamburger buns, toasted

1. Heat a Dutch oven over medium-high heat. Add pork to pan; cook 2 minutes. Add onion and fennel to pan; cover and cook 15 minutes, stirring frequently. Add salt and next 4 ingredients, and cook 1 minute, stirring constantly. Add tomatoes and 1/4 cup vinegar to pan. Reduce heat to medium. Uncover and cook 15 minutes or until pork is tender, stirring frequently.
2. Combine olive oil and 2 teaspoons vinegar in a medium bowl. Add green and red cabbage; toss gently to coat.
3. Combine yogurt, mayonnaise, and garlic in a small bowl. Spread about 1 1/2 teaspoons yogurt mixture onto each bun half. Top bottom half of each bun with 1/4 cup fennel mixture, 1/4 cup cabbage mixture, and top half of bun. Serves 6 (serving size: 1 sandwich).

CALORIES 253; FAT 9.9g (sat 1.9g, mono 4.6g, poly 2.4g); PROTEIN 13.3g; CARB 29.5g; FIBER 5.6g; CHOL 25mg; IRON 2.2mg; SODIUM 470mg; CALC 102mg

TODAY'S LESSON: KEBABS

Food on a stick, over a fire: It's the universal technique of street-chow vendors the world over. Here, we present a simple shrimp and veggie option with a zingy Italian-style blend of fresh herbs. Plus, we include tips on skewer selection and marinating.

Quick & Easy

Shrimp and Fennel Kebabs with Italian Salsa Verde

Hands-on time: 40 min. Total time: 40 min. *Italian salsa verde has a tangy-briny flavor.*

Salsa verde:
⅓ **cup chopped fresh parsley**
⅓ **cup chopped fresh basil**
1½ **tablespoons finely chopped shallots**
2 **tablespoons extra-virgin olive oil**
1½ **tablespoons fresh lemon juice**
1 **tablespoon water**
1½ **teaspoons capers, chopped**
⅛ **teaspoon kosher salt**
⅛ **teaspoon black pepper**
Kebabs:
4 **teaspoons olive oil, divided**
28 **large shrimp, peeled and deveined (about 1½ pounds)**
1 **large fennel bulb, cut into 12 wedges**
1 **large red onion, cut into 12 wedges**
⅜ **teaspoon kosher salt**
⅛ **teaspoon black pepper**
Cooking spray

1. To prepare salsa verde, combine first 9 ingredients in a medium bowl, stirring with a whisk.
2. Preheat grill to medium-high heat.
3. To prepare kebabs, combine 2 teaspoons oil and shrimp; toss to coat. Thread shrimp evenly onto 4 (12-inch) skewers. Thread 3 fennel wedges and 3 onion wedges alternately onto each of 4 (12-inch) skewers. Brush vegetables with remaining 2 teaspoons oil. Sprinkle shrimp and vegetables with ⅜ teaspoon salt and ⅛ teaspoon pepper.
4. Place skewers on a grill rack coated with cooking spray; grill shrimp 1½ minutes on each side or until done. Grill vegetables 12 minutes or until tender, turning occasionally. Serve with salsa verde. Serves 4 (serving size: 1 shrimp kebab, 1 vegetable kebab, and about 1½ tablespoons salsa verde).

CALORIES 320; **FAT** 14.4g (sat 2.1g, mono 8.7g, poly 2.4g); **PROTEIN** 36.1g; **CARB** 11g; **FIBER** 2.8g; **CHOL** 259mg; **IRON** 5.2mg; **SODIUM** 559mg; **CALC** 142mg

SKEWER STRATEGIES

BASIC STICKS
Wooden skewers are cheap and widely available in either round or flat shapes. Soak in water for 30 minutes so they don't ignite. Or opt for reusable metal skewers, available at kitchen shops for a nominal price.

FLEXIBLE OR CURVED SKEWERS
These are great for fitting kebabs into bowls to marinate or store. With rigid skewers, you have to marinate and then thread ingredients onto the skewers, a messier proposition.

KEBAB SET OR SKEWER STATION
For the avid griller, the Weber Kabob Set includes skewers and a rack. Slip skewers in place and place the whole thing on the grill (racks fit most models).

VERY CHERRY

For a fleeting time, all those sweet cherries pile into roadside stands and farmers' markets. Some areas get them as early as May, but the rest of us have to wait until the heart of the season, from June to early August. What beautiful fruits they are, too, firm but surprisingly syrupy and juicy. Anyone who's stood over a sink pitting a bowl-ful with stained hands can attest to the cherry's dangerous squirtability. Sweet, deep-crimson Bing and peachy-colored Rainier are most abundant—and what we use in our recipes—though you might find yellow or inky purple varieties, too. If you live in an area where sour cherries reign, by all means use those; just be sure to balance the tang with a bit more sweetness.

Cherry-Peach Sangria

Hands-on time: 20 min. Total time: 8 hr. 20 min. *We recommend zesty Spanish albariño, but you can use any other refreshing white wine.*

1/4 cup sugar
1/4 cup brandy
2 1/2 cups pitted fresh Rainier cherries
1 (750-milliliter) bottle albariño wine, chilled
1 cup chilled club soda
1 peach, thinly sliced
3 thyme sprigs
1 purple basil sprig (optional)
1 sweet basil sprig (optional)

1. Combine ¼ cup sugar and ¼ cup brandy in a pitcher; stir until sugar dissolves. Add cherries and wine, and chill 8 hours or up to overnight. Just before serving, stir in club soda and remaining ingredients. Serves 8 (serving size: about ⅔ cup).

CALORIES 155; **FAT** 0.2g (sat 0g, mono 0g, poly 0g); **PROTEIN** 0.8g; **CARB** 18.3g; **FIBER** 1.3g; **CHOL** 0mg; **IRON** 0.5mg; **SODIUM** 11mg; **CALC** 18mg

Make Ahead

Bourbon Candied Cherries

Hands-on time: 15 min. Total time: 3 days *The taste of a Manhattan in a fruit snack! Serve these cherries as a fun party nibble, or use in cocktails. Don't toss the soaking liquid—stir it into cocktails, or drizzle over ice cream or pound cake. The cherries taste best after soaking at least three days (we loved them after six days), and they will keep in the refrigerator for up to two weeks.*

1 1/2 pounds fresh Bing cherries with stems
1 cup sugar
1/3 cup fresh lime juice
1/4 cup water
1 cup bourbon or rye whiskey

1. Place cherries in a medium glass bowl or large jar. Combine sugar, juice, and ¼ cup water in a small sauce-pan; bring to a boil. Reduce heat to medium; cook 5 minutes, stirring to dissolve sugar. Add 1 cup bourbon; bring just to a boil. Pour hot bourbon mixture over cherries. Cool completely. Cover and refrigerate at least 3 days before serving. Serves 12 (serving size: about 5 cherries and about 2 table-spoons soaking liquid).

CALORIES 119; **FAT** 0.1g (sat 0g, mono 0g, poly 0g); **PROTEIN** 0.6g; **CARB** 25.3g; **FIBER** 1.1g; **CHOL** 0mg; **IRON** 0.2mg; **SODIUM** 0mg; **CALC** 7mg

Salad with Cherries, Goat Cheese, and Pistachios

Hands-on time: 15 min. Total time: 15 min. *Fruit in salad may not be your thing, but the cherries really work here, offering a sweet, juicy burst to complement peppery greens and tangy cheese. Although we like the color of Rainiers, any cherry variety would be great.*

4 cups arugula
2 cups baby spinach
1/3 cup thinly vertically sliced red onion
1 1/2 tablespoons fresh lemon juice
1/2 teaspoon Dijon mustard
1/2 teaspoon honey
1/4 teaspoon salt
1/4 teaspoon freshly ground black pepper
1 small garlic clove, minced
2 tablespoons extra-virgin olive oil
1 cup pitted halved fresh Rainier cherries
1 ounce crumbled goat cheese (about 1/4 cup)
1/4 cup salted dry-roasted pistachios

1. Combine arugula, spinach, and onion in a large bowl.
2. Combine juice, mustard, honey, salt, black pepper, and garlic in a medium bowl, stirring with a whisk. Gradually drizzle in olive oil, stirring constantly with a whisk. Drizzle dressing over salad, and toss gently to coat. Arrange 1 1/2 cups salad on each of 4 salad plates. Top each serving with 1/4 cup cherries, 1 tablespoon cheese, and 1 tablespoon nuts. Serves 4.

CALORIES 173; **FAT** 12.6g (sat 2.9g, mono 7.3g, poly 1.9g); **PROTEIN** 4.6g; **CARB** 13g; **FIBER** 2.7g; **CHOL** 6mg; **IRON** 1.4mg; **SODIUM** 256mg; **CALC** 80mg

Double-Cherry Upside-Down Cake

(pictured on page 221)

Hands-on time: 35 min. Total time: 1 hr. 20 min. *The batter comes to the top of the pan and threatens to spill over. It shouldn't, but just in case, bake on a foil-lined baking sheet.*

Cooking spray
2 tablespoons butter, melted
1/3 cup packed brown sugar
2 cups pitted fresh Rainier cherries
2 cups pitted fresh Bing cherries
6.75 ounces all-purpose flour (about 1 1/2 cups)
2 teaspoons baking powder
1/4 teaspoon salt
1/4 teaspoon baking soda
3/4 cup granulated sugar
6 tablespoons butter, softened
3 tablespoons canola oil
1 1/2 teaspoons vanilla extract
2 large eggs
1 cup nonfat buttermilk

1. Preheat oven to 350°.
2. Coat a 9-inch springform pan or cake pan with 3-inch sides with cooking spray; line bottom of pan with parchment paper. Coat paper with cooking spray. If using a springform pan, wrap outside and bottom of pan tightly with a double layer of heavy-duty foil.
3. Drizzle melted butter over parchment in bottom of pan; sprinkle with brown sugar. Arrange cherries in a single layer over brown sugar. Place pan on a baking sheet lined with foil.
4. Weigh or lightly spoon flour into dry measuring cups; level with a knife. Combine flour, baking powder, salt, and baking soda, stirring with a whisk; set aside. Place granulated sugar, softened butter, and oil in a large bowl; beat with a mixer at medium speed until well blended (about 3 minutes). Beat in vanilla. Add eggs, 1 at a time, beating well after each addition. Add flour mixture and buttermilk alternately to oil mixture, beginning and ending with flour mixture (batter will be thick). Spread batter evenly over cherries in pan. Bake at 350° for 30 minutes.
5. Reduce oven temperature to 325° (do not remove cake from oven). Bake at 325° for 25 to 30 minutes or until a wooden pick inserted in center comes out clean. Cool 10 minutes in pan on a wire rack. Loosen cake from edges of pan with a knife; invert onto wire rack. Serves 12 (serving size: 1 wedge).

CALORIES 283; **FAT** 12.3g (sat 5.4g, mono 4.6g, poly 1.5g); **PROTEIN** 4.1g; **CARB** 40.3g; **FIBER** 1.5g; **CHOL** 56mg; **IRON** 1.1mg; **SODIUM** 230mg; **CALC** 86mg

JUICES RELEASED FROM THE FRUIT MAKE FOR A MOIST CAKE AND REWARD YOU WITH FRUITY, SUMMERY FLAVOR.

Bing Cherry Sorbet with Prosecco

Hands-on time: 30 min. Total time: 4 hr. 30 min. For extra cherry essence, top with chopped fresh cherries.

1 cup sugar
2/3 cup water
4 cups pitted fresh Bing cherries
  (about 1 1/3 pounds)
3 tablespoons amaretto
2 tablespoons fresh lime juice
2 2/3 cups prosecco or other sparkling
  white wine, chilled

1. Combine 1 cup sugar and 2/3 cup water in a 2-cup glass measuring cup. Microwave at HIGH 2 minutes. Cool completely. Place sugar syrup, cherries, amaretto, and lime juice in a blender; process 1 minute or until smooth. Pour mixture into the freezer can of a tabletop ice-cream freezer; freeze according to manufacturer's instructions. Spoon sorbet into a freezer-safe container; cover and freeze 4 hours or until firm. Pour 1/3 cup prosecco into each of 8 chilled dessert bowls; spoon about 1/3 cup sorbet into each glass or bowl. Serves 8.

CALORIES 214; FAT 0.2g (sat 0g, mono 0.1g, poly 0g); PROTEIN 0.8g; CARB 41g; FIBER 1.6g; CHOL 0mg; IRON 0.3mg; SODIUM 0mg; CALC 11mg

---

Kid Friendly

Fresh Cherry Galette

Hands-on time: 26 min. Total time: 1 hr. 11 min. The galette looks and sounds fancy, but with its free-form shape, it's ridiculously easy. Rainier cherries have pale, creamy flesh and are larger and sweeter than Bing cherries. If you opt for another variety, add an extra tablespoon of sugar.

1/2 (14.1-ounce) package refrigerated
  pie dough (such as Pillsbury)
3 tablespoons granulated sugar,
  divided
1 1/2 teaspoons cornstarch
3 1/2 cups pitted fresh Rainier cherries
  (about 1 1/4 pounds)
1/2 teaspoon grated lemon rind
2 teaspoons fresh lemon juice
1 1/2 tablespoons buttermilk
1 tablespoon turbinado sugar

1. Preheat oven to 400°.
2. Line a baking sheet with parchment paper. Unroll pie dough onto parchment, and roll to a 12 1/2-inch circle. Combine 1 tablespoon sugar and 1 1/2 teaspoons cornstarch, stirring with a whisk. Sprinkle cornstarch mixture over dough, leaving a 2-inch border.
3. Combine cherries, remaining 2 tablespoons granulated sugar, rind, and juice; toss well to coat. Arrange cherry mixture over dough, leaving a 2-inch border. Fold dough border over cherries, pressing gently to seal (dough will only partially cover cherries). Brush edges of dough with buttermilk. Sprinkle turbinado sugar over cherries and edges of dough. Bake at 400° for 25 minutes or until dough is browned and juices are bubbly. Remove from oven; cool on pan at least 20 minutes before serving. Serves 6 (serving size: 1 wedge).

CALORIES 227; FAT 8.9g (sat 3.8g, mono 3.2g, poly 0.6g); PROTEIN 2.3g; CARB 38g; FIBER 1.9g; CHOL 4mg; IRON 0.3mg; SODIUM 177mg; CALC 12mg

---

FIVE CHERRY VARIETIES

1. BRIGHT RED SOUR CHERRIES
(from Cherry Connection in Traverse City, Mich.; cherryconnection.com)

2. BING CHERRIES
(from Melissa's; melissas.com)

3. DARK HUDSON CHERRIES
(from Red Jacket Orchards in N.Y. State; redjacketorchards.com)

4. RAINIER CHERRIES
(from Cherry Connection in Traverse City, Mich.; cherryconnection.com)

5. YELLOW CHERRIES
(from Mair Farm-Taki in Wapato, Wash.; mairtaki.com)

USE RAINIER CHERRIES WHEREVER YOU WANT SOFTER, PEACHY HUES, AS BINGS' CRIMSON JUICE WILL MAKE A BOLDER COLOR STATEMENT.

FRESH SPINS ON SUMMER GAZPACHO

By Rozanne Gold

Blended, chilled soups packed with veggies or fruit make a delicious first course, a zingy entrée, and even a refreshing dessert.

Gazpacho has come a long way since its humble beginnings—the earliest versions, possibly dating back to ancient Rome, contained little more than bread, water, and olive oil mashed into a poor man's porridge. In the Middle Ages, cooks added garlic, vinegar, and nuts to punch up the flavor and enrich the pulverized mixture. Tomatoes and peppers made an appearance in the post-Columbus era when these New World flavors came to the Spanish table. Today, there are countless adaptations.

Yet the dish remains a study in simplicity. Pick your favorite fruits and veggies of the season, blend them together as smooth or chunky as you like, and chill. Try Moroccan Red Gazpacho as a dramatic backdrop for grilled chicken or chilled shrimp. Serve tangy blueberry gazpacho as a vibrant first course, or top with a scoop of lemon sorbet as a grand finale to a summer meal.

Kid Friendly • Make Ahead Vegetarian

"Royal Blueberry" Gazpacho with Lemon and Mint

Hands-on time: 12 min. Total time: 2 hr. 37 min. This twist on gazpacho is an unexpected first course, a new idea for brunch, or a great summer dessert. It is interesting enough just topped with grated lemon zest and snippets of fresh mint, or it can be topped with flake salt or finely diced honeydew and cantaloupe for drama and texture. Diced strawberries and a dollop of Greek yogurt would also be nice.

1 pound dark purple seedless grapes
12 ounces fresh blueberries
1/2 cup white grape juice
2 tablespoons honey
2 teaspoons grated lemon rind
2 tablespoons fresh lemon juice
1/4 teaspoon salt
Small mint leaves (optional)
Grated lemon rind (optional)

1. Remove stems from fruit. Rinse and pat dry with paper towels. Place fruit in a 4-quart saucepan over medium-high heat. Add grape juice and honey; bring to a boil. Reduce heat to medium; simmer 15 minutes, stirring occasionally. Remove from heat; let stand 10 minutes. Place blueberry mixture in a food processor; process until almost smooth. Strain; discard solids. Chill 2 hours.
2. Stir in rind, juice, and salt. Ladle about 1/2 cup into each of 5 chilled bowls, and garnish with mint and additional lemon rind, if desired. Serves 5.

CALORIES 142; FAT 0.4g (sat 0.1g, mono 0g, poly 0.2g); PROTEIN 1.3g; CARB 37.2g; FIBER 2.7g; CHOL 0mg; IRON 0.6mg; SODIUM 124mg; CALC 18mg

---

Make Ahead • Vegetarian

Moroccan Red Gazpacho

Hands-on time: 15 min. Total time: 2 hr. 21 min. Ras el hanout, a spice blend, is available in Middle Eastern stores. Use garam masala in a pinch. Garnish with chopped tomato, red bell pepper, cucumber, onion, hard-cooked egg, or a mix; serve with pita bread.

1 (6½-inch) pita, torn into pieces
1/2 cup boiling water
4 tablespoons extra-virgin olive oil, divided
2 tablespoons sherry vinegar
4 large ripe plum tomatoes, coarsely chopped (about 1 pound)
1 large red bell pepper, seeded and coarsely chopped
1 large cucumber, peeled, seeded, and coarsely chopped (about 8 ounces)
1/4 small yellow onion, chopped
2 cups no-salt-added tomato puree (such as Pomi strained tomatoes)
1 cup cold water
2 teaspoons ras el hanout
3/4 teaspoon salt
1/2 teaspoon ground cumin
1/4 teaspoon ground cinnamon
2 tablespoons chopped fresh cilantro

1. Place pita in a bowl; cover with ½ cup boiling water. Let stand 1 minute. Drain; reserve pita. Place moistened pita, 1 tablespoon oil, and next 5 ingredients in a food processor; pulse until almost smooth. Scrape into a bowl; stir in tomato puree and next 5 ingredients. Cover and chill 2 hours. Ladle about 1 cup soup into each of 8 bowls; top each with about 1 teaspoon oil and ¾ teaspoon cilantro. Serves 8.

CALORIES 128; FAT 7.2g (sat 1g, mono 5g, poly 0.8g); PROTEIN 2.8g; CARB 14.6g; FIBER 2.9g; CHOL 0mg; IRON 1.4mg; SODIUM 281mg; CALC 26mg

PROJECT PO'BOY

We keep the bon temps rolling with crispy shrimp, spicy slaw, and 1,400 fewer calories.

New Orleans turns out one of the world's most exuberant sandwiches and calls it a poor boy: always joking down there, always delicious. An arm's length of crusty French bread piled high with Cajun-battered fried shrimp, lettuce, mayo, and salty pickles can, however, add up to your day's worth of calories and fat, along with today's and tomorrow's salt.

To kick off our po'boy reclamation, we start with an adjustment in portion size. Downsizing by nearly two-thirds, we take a smaller (but still plentiful) portion of a classic French-style loaf and toast it up to get good and crusty. The bread is hollowed out—leaving more room for the tasty fillings—and the insides are turned into breadcrumbs to coat pan-seared shrimp. A spicy rémoulade slaw adds just the right amount of kick and crunch to the sandwich, with no need for salty Cajun seasoning, extra mayo, or ketchup. Delightfully crunchy and deliciously messy, this lighter po'boy delivers classic satisfaction. Food is sacred in New Orleans, but this is not heresy; it's a loving, lighter homage.

CLASSIC	MAKEOVER
1,796 calories per serving	400 calories per serving
64 grams total fat	10.4 grams total fat
4,705 milligrams sodium	736 milligrams sodium

Shrimp Po'boys

Hands-on time: 40 min. Total time: 1 hr.
Crusty, well-toasted bread; crispy pan-seared shrimp; and crunchy slaw make this sandwich worth every bite.

Rémoulade slaw:
3 tablespoons canola mayonnaise
1 tablespoon minced shallots
1 teaspoon fresh lemon juice
1 teaspoon Worcestershire sauce
½ teaspoon Dijon mustard
½ teaspoon prepared horseradish
¼ teaspoon hot pepper sauce
¼ teaspoon grated lemon rind
1 garlic clove, minced
2½ cups packaged cabbage-and-carrot coleslaw
Po'boys:
1 tablespoon cornstarch
½ teaspoon grated lemon rind
¼ teaspoon kosher salt
¼ teaspoon ground red pepper
1 large egg white
1 pound medium shrimp, peeled and deveined
4 (2½-ounce) pieces French bread baguette, split and toasted
3 tablespoons stone-ground cornmeal
¼ teaspoon freshly ground black pepper
2 teaspoons extra-virgin olive oil
8 (¼-inch-thick) slices tomato

1. To prepare rémoulade slaw, combine first 9 ingredients in a medium bowl, stirring with a whisk. Add coleslaw; toss to coat. Cover and chill.

2. To prepare po'boys, combine cornstarch and next 4 ingredients in a medium bowl; whisk until blended. Add shrimp; toss well. Marinate in refrigerator 30 minutes, stirring once.
3. Hollow out top and bottom halves of bread, leaving a ¼-inch-thick shell. Place torn bread in a food processor; process until very fine crumbs form. Set aside ½ cup breadcrumbs; reserve remaining breadcrumbs for another use. Combine ½ cup breadcrumbs, cornmeal, and black pepper in a large zip-top plastic bag; seal and shake to combine.
4. Remove shrimp from bowl; discard marinade. Add shrimp to breadcrumb mixture. Seal and shake to coat.
5. Heat a large nonstick skillet over medium-high heat. Add oil to pan; swirl to coat. Add shrimp; cook 3 minutes on each side or until done.
6. Arrange ½ cup slaw on each bottom half of bread. Top with one quarter of shrimp and 2 tomato slices. Cover with top half of bread. Serves 4 (serving size: 1 sandwich).

CALORIES 400; FAT 10.4g (sat 1.7g, mono 3.9g, poly 2.3g); PROTEIN 32g; CARB 46.5g; FIBER 3.9g; CHOL 172mg; IRON 6mg; SODIUM 736mg; CALC 143mg

PO'BOY POINTERS

PAN-SEARED VS. DEEP-FRIED
The shrimp is marinated, breaded, and then seared in a hot, lightly oiled pan to save 300 calories and 34g of fat per sandwich over the deep-fried version.

A 2½-OUNCE PORTION VS. A 12-INCH LOAF
We cut back on the bread by two-thirds, saving 550 calories and more than 1,000mg sodium per sandwich. The loaves are hollowed out and the insides ground to coat our crispy shrimp.

SPICY SLAW VS. CAJUN SEASONING
We skip the salty Cajun seasonings and heavy fixin's and add zest, flavor, and kick with a spicy rémoulade slaw, saving 100 calories and 1,250mg of sodium per sandwich.

FEED 4 FOR LESS THAN $10

Take dinner cues from the produce section: Fresh fruits, veggies, and herbs add pops of color and bright flavors to summer meals.

Quick & Easy

Melon Salad with Prosciutto

$2.50/serving, $9.99 total

Hands-on time: 40 min. Total time: 40 min. *Salty cheese and ham accent the sweet summer fruit in this refreshing main-dish salad, a perfect meal on a sweltering summer day.*

2 cups sliced seeded watermelon
2 cups sliced seeded honeydew melon
1/3 cup very thinly vertically sliced red onion
1 serrano pepper, very thinly sliced
2 ripe nectarines, pitted and sliced
1/4 teaspoon kosher salt
3 tablespoons fresh lemon juice
2 tablespoons olive oil
1 1/2 tablespoons honey
4 cups arugula
1/4 cup torn fresh mint leaves
3 ounces prosciutto, very thinly sliced
1/2 ounce pecorino Romano cheese, shaved

1. Combine first 5 ingredients in a large bowl; sprinkle with salt. Combine juice, oil, and honey, stirring well. Drizzle dressing mixture over fruit mixture; toss gently. Arrange 1 cup arugula and 1 tablespoon mint on each of 4 plates; top each serving with about 1¾ cups fruit mixture. Divide prosciutto evenly among plates; top evenly with cheese. Serves 4.

CALORIES 232; FAT 10g (sat 2g, mono 5g, poly 0.9g); PROTEIN 8.6g; CARB 31.5g; FIBER 2.8g; CHOL 18mg; IRON 1.3mg; SODIUM 674mg; CALC 62mg

Quick & Easy

Roast Pork Tenderloin with Thyme-Scented Plums

$2.37/serving, $9.49 total

Hands-on time: 13 min. Total time: 35 min. *Broiling the plums intensifies their tangy-sweet flavor. Serve with Couscous Pilaf.*

2 1/2 tablespoons olive oil, divided
1 (1-pound) pork tenderloin
3/4 teaspoon kosher salt, divided
1/2 teaspoon freshly ground black pepper, divided
1 pound small, ripe plums, quartered and pitted (about 6)
2 tablespoons honey
1 garlic clove, minced
2 teaspoons chopped fresh thyme

1. Preheat oven to 500°.
2. Heat a large ovenproof skillet over medium-high heat. Add 1½ tablespoons olive oil to pan; swirl to coat. Sprinkle pork with ½ teaspoon salt and ¼ teaspoon black pepper. Add pork to pan; cook 4 minutes, turning to brown on all sides. Place pan in oven. Cook at 500° for 15 minutes or until a thermometer registers 145°. Remove pork from pan. Let stand 10 minutes; slice crosswise into 12 slices.
3. Preheat broiler to high.
4. Without cleaning pan, arrange plums, cut sides up, in pan. Combine remaining 1 tablespoon oil, honey, and garlic, stirring well; brush plums evenly with honey mixture. Sprinkle with remaining ¼ teaspoon salt and remaining ¼ teaspoon pepper. Broil plums 6 minutes or until lightly charred; sprinkle with chopped thyme. Serve with pork. Garnish with thyme sprigs, if desired. Serves 4 (serving size: 3 ounces pork and 6 plum quarters).

CALORIES 285; FAT 10.9g (sat 2g, mono 7.1g, poly 1.3g); PROTEIN 24.6g; CARB 23.4g; FIBER 1.7g; CHOL 74mg; IRON 1.6mg; SODIUM 421mg; CALC 11mg

Couscous Pilaf:
Cook 2/3 cup couscous in water according to package directions, omitting salt and fat; fluff with a fork. Stir in 1 tablespoon olive oil, ¼ teaspoon salt, ¼ teaspoon freshly ground black pepper, 2 sliced green onions, and 1 ounce toasted sliced almonds. Serves 4.

CALORIES 184; FAT 7.1g (sat 0.8g); SODIUM 153mg

Kid Friendly • Make Ahead

Summer Veggie Rice Bowl

$1.64/serving, $9.56 total

Hands-on time: 12 min. Total time: 1 hr. 15 min. *Fresh tomatoes, zucchini, basil, and toasted pine nuts bring this rice salad to life. Serve it with 1 pound roasted fresh green beans.*

1 1/3 cups cooked brown rice, cooled to room temperature
1 cup frozen shelled edamame (green soybeans), thawed
1 cup grape tomatoes, halved
1/2 cup torn fresh basil
1/4 cup pine nuts, toasted
2 teaspoons grated lemon rind
3 tablespoons fresh lemon juice
1 teaspoon kosher salt
1/4 teaspoon freshly ground black pepper
3 tablespoons olive oil, divided
2 cups chopped zucchini
1/2 ounce fresh Parmesan cheese, shaved

1. Combine first 9 ingredients in a large bowl, and toss until well blended. Heat a medium skillet over medium-high heat. Add 1 tablespoon olive oil to pan; swirl to coat. Add zucchini; sauté 4 minutes, stirring occasionally. Add zucchini and remaining 2 tablespoons oil to rice mixture; toss. Top with shaved Parmesan cheese. Serves 4 (serving size: about 1 cup).

CALORIES 305; FAT 19.1g (sat 2.5g, mono 9.5g, poly 4.3g); PROTEIN 9.6g; CARB 25.4g; FIBER 4.9g; CHOL 3mg; IRON 2mg; SODIUM 570mg; CALC 111mg

MATISSE'S HAWAIIAN HIT

This month, our kid in the kitchen gets rave reviews on pineapple-ham pizza.

To test one of our kid-friendly recipes, we contacted Matisse Reid, a food-savvy 11-year-old who loves to experiment with new flavors. This month, we got her grilling with a ham and pineapple pizza, earning high marks with friends and family. Here's her report.
—Phoebe Wu

"Tonight, I made Grilled Ham and Pineapple Pizza for my best friend and my little brother. This recipe was really easy to make and lots of fun to cook outside on the grill. I like to heat up the grill while I'm getting the ingredients ready. And you can save more time by preparing the crust, sauce, and cheese while the pineapple and ham are cooking. Grilling the ham gives it a nice smoky flavor, and the pineapple is sweet and juicy. Although I used a regular-sized pizza crust, it would also be fun for everyone to have their own small, individual pizzas. I had so much fun making this, I'm definitely going to make it again—soon."

YOUNGER CHILDREN SHOULD HAVE THEIR PARENTS HELP THEM WITH THE GRILL.

THE VERDICT

MEGAN (AGE 11):
It was so good, she added an extra zero.
100/10

FRAANZ (AGE 7):
He's not normally a fan of pineapple but thought it was yummy.
10/10

MATISSE:
I could not stop eating it!
10/10

Kid Friendly • Quick & Easy

Grilled Ham and Pineapple Pizza

Hands-on time: 20 min. Total time: 34 min. *Make sure you watch the pizza while it cooks so that you don't burn the crust.*

2 (1/2-inch-thick) slices fresh pineapple
3 ounces thinly sliced lower-sodium ham (such as Boar's Head)
Cooking spray
1/2 cup spicy tomato and basil pasta sauce
1 (8-ounce) prebaked thin pizza crust
2 ounces shredded part-skim mozzarella cheese (about 1/2 cup)

1. Preheat grill to medium-high heat.
2. Arrange pineapple and ham slices on grill rack coated with cooking spray. Grill ham 1 minute, turning once. Remove ham from grill. Grill pineapple 9 minutes, turning once. Remove from grill; coarsely chop pineapple. Spread sauce evenly over crust, leaving a 1/2-inch border; top evenly with cheese. Arrange pineapple and ham over cheese. Place pizza on grill rack coated with cooking spray; grill 7 minutes or until cheese melts. Cut into 8 slices. Serves 4 (serving size: 2 slices).

CALORIES 292; **FAT** 9.6g (sat 2.7g, mono 2.1g, poly 3.3g); **PROTEIN** 12.7g; **CARB** 38.5g; **FIBER** 2.9g; **CHOL** 17mg; **IRON** 2.1mg; **SODIUM** 575mg; **CALC** 150mg

SUPERFAST

Welcome the height of summer with easy, no-sweat dishes like field pea hash, quick peach crisp, and more.

Quick & Easy

Pork and Tomato Skillet Sauté

(pictured on page 223)

Use heirloom tomatoes to make this dish extra colorful.

4 teaspoons olive oil, divided
4 (6-ounce) bone-in center-cut loin pork chops, trimmed (about 1/2 inch thick)
1/2 teaspoon salt, divided
1/2 teaspoon freshly ground black pepper, divided
1/2 cup thinly sliced shallots
2 tablespoons balsamic vinegar
2 teaspoons minced garlic
2 cups grape tomatoes
3 tablespoons chopped fresh basil

1. Heat a large nonstick skillet over medium-high heat. Add 1 teaspoon oil to pan; swirl to coat. Sprinkle chops evenly with 1/4 teaspoon salt and 1/4 teaspoon pepper. Add pork to pan; cook 3 minutes on each side or until desired degree of doneness. Remove pork from pan. Add remaining 1 tablespoon oil, shallots, vinegar, and garlic to pan; sauté 1 minute, scraping pan to loosen browned bits. Combine tomatoes, remaining 1/4 teaspoon salt, and remaining 1/4 teaspoon pepper in a medium bowl; toss gently to coat. Add tomato mixture to pan; cook 2 minutes or until tomatoes begin to soften. Sprinkle with basil. Serve tomato mixture with pork. Serves 4 (serving size: 1 chop and about 1/2 cup tomato mixture).

CALORIES 255; **FAT** 10.7g (sat 2.4g, mono 5.5g, poly 1.2g); **PROTEIN** 25.3g; **CARB** 15.1g; **FIBER** 1.1g; **CHOL** 71mg; **IRON** 1.6mg; **SODIUM** 348mg; **CALC** 41mg

Sausage and Black-Eyed Pea Hash

This simple one-dish meal is made even more delicious with a fried egg on top of each plate; the yolk creates its own creamy sauce. If you can find fresh peas, use them in place of canned.

8 ounces diced turkey andouille sausage (such as Wellshire Farms)
1 cup sliced celery (about 2 stalks)
1 cup chopped fresh tomato
1 medium-sized red bell pepper, cubed
1 medium-sized yellow squash, cubed
¼ cup water
2 teaspoons chopped fresh thyme
2 teaspoons cider vinegar
2 teaspoons Worcestershire sauce
2 teaspoons Dijon mustard
1 (15-ounce) can no-salt-added black-eyed peas, rinsed and drained
1 tablespoon canola oil
4 large eggs
¼ teaspoon freshly ground black pepper

1. Heat a large nonstick skillet over medium-high heat. Add sausage; sauté 4 minutes or until lightly browned, stirring occasionally. Add celery and next 3 ingredients; sauté 3 minutes, stirring frequently. Add ¼ cup water and next 5 ingredients. Simmer 2 minutes or until peas are thoroughly heated. Remove pea mixture from pan; keep warm. Wipe pan with a paper towel.
2. Return pan to medium heat. Add oil to pan; swirl to coat. Crack eggs into pan; cook 4 minutes or until whites are set. Remove from heat.
3. Place about 1 cup pea mixture onto each of 4 plates; top each serving with one egg. Sprinkle eggs evenly with black pepper. Serves 4.

CALORIES 242; **FAT** 11.3g (sat 3g, mono 4.2g, poly 1.8g); **PROTEIN** 19.7g; **CARB** 17g; **FIBER** 3.9g; **CHOL** 194mg; **IRON** 2.4mg; **SODIUM** 478mg; **CALC** 68mg

Wild Rice and Carrots

(pictured on page 222)

If you can't find precooked wild rice, substitute boil-in-bag or precooked brown rice.

1 (8.5-ounce) package precooked wild rice (such as Archer Farms)
1½ tablespoons unsalted butter
1 cup thinly sliced carrot
1 tablespoon chopped fresh parsley
½ teaspoon freshly ground black pepper
¼ teaspoon salt

1. Prepare rice according to the package directions.
2. Melt butter in a large nonstick skillet over medium heat. Add carrot; cook 8 minutes or until tender, stirring frequently. Stir in rice, parsley, pepper, and salt; cook 1 minute. Serves 4 (serving size: ½ cup).

CALORIES 113; **FAT** 4.6g (sat 2.8g, mono 1.2g, poly 0.3g); **PROTEIN** 2.8g; **CARB** 16.2g; **FIBER** 2.1g; **CHOL** 11mg; **IRON** 0.5mg; **SODIUM** 173mg; **CALC** 16mg

Quick & Easy • Vegetarian
Variation 1: Bell Pepper and Fennel
Prepare rice according to package directions. Heat a large nonstick skillet over medium heat. Add 1½ tablespoons olive oil to pan; swirl to coat. Add ½ cup diced yellow bell pepper and ½ cup diced fennel bulb to pan; cook 8 minutes or until tender, stirring frequently. Stir in rice, 1½ teaspoons chopped fresh oregano, ½ teaspoon freshly ground black pepper, and ¼ teaspoon salt; cook 1 minute. Serves 4 (serving size: about ¾ cup).

CALORIES 116; **FAT** 5.4g (sat 0.7g); **SODIUM** 156mg

Quick & Easy • Vegetarian
Variation 2: Cucumber and Feta
Prepare rice according to package directions. Combine cooked rice, 1 cup diced English cucumber,

1½ tablespoons olive oil, 1 tablespoon fresh lemon juice, and 2 ounces crumbled feta cheese in a medium bowl; toss to coat. Stir in ½ teaspoon pepper and ¼ teaspoon salt. Serves 4 (serving size: about ¾ cup).

CALORIES 149; **FAT** 8.3g (sat 2.9g); **SODIUM** 308 mg

Quick & Easy • Vegetarian
Variation 3: Tomatoes and Pine Nuts
Prepare rice according to package directions. Melt 1½ tablespoons unsalted butter in a large nonstick skillet over medium heat. Add ¼ cup pine nuts and 8 quartered cherry tomatoes to pan; cook 8 minutes or until tomatoes are tender, stirring frequently. Stir in rice, 1 tablespoon chopped fresh basil, ½ teaspoon freshly ground black pepper, and ¼ teaspoon salt; cook 1 minute. Serves 4 (serving size: ½ cup).

CALORIES 163; **FAT** 10.4g (sat 3.2g); **SODIUM** 152mg

Melty Monsieur

Serve fruit with this kid-friendly take on the classic croque monsieur.

4 (1½-ounce) slices multigrain bread
8 teaspoons creamy mustard blend (such as Dijonnaise)
8 Canadian bacon slices (4.8 ounces)
12 (¼-inch-thick) slices tomato
3 ounces shaved Gruyère cheese (about ¾ cup)

1. Preheat broiler to high.
2. Place bread in a single layer on a baking sheet; broil 1½ minutes on each side or until lightly toasted. Spread 2 teaspoons mustard blend on each bread slice. Top each serving with 2 bacon slices, 3 tomato slices, and about 3 tablespoons cheese. Broil 3 minutes or until cheese melts. Serves 4 (serving size: 1 sandwich).

CALORIES 312; **FAT** 16.5g (sat 6.6g, mono 6.6g, poly 2.2g); **PROTEIN** 19.7g; **CARB** 21.9g; **FIBER** 4.5g; **CHOL** 48mg; **IRON** 1.4mg; **SODIUM** 692mg; **CALC** 320mg

Beef Kefta Patties with Cucumber Salad

Cooking spray
1 pound ground sirloin
1/4 cup plus 2 tablespoons chopped fresh flat-leaf parsley, divided
1/4 cup chopped fresh cilantro
1 tablespoon chopped peeled fresh ginger
2 teaspoons ground coriander
1 teaspoon ground cumin
1/2 teaspoon salt
1/2 teaspoon ground cinnamon
2 cups thinly sliced English cucumber
2 tablespoons rice vinegar
1/2 cup plain fat-free Greek yogurt
1 tablespoon fresh lemon juice
1/2 teaspoon freshly ground black pepper
2 (6-inch) pitas, quartered

1. Heat a grill pan over medium-high heat. Coat pan with cooking spray. Combine beef, 1/4 cup parsley, cilantro, and next 5 ingredients in a medium bowl. Divide mixture into 4 equal portions, shaping each into a 1/2-inch-thick patty. Add patties to pan; cook 3 minutes on each side or until desired degree of doneness.
2. Combine cucumber and vinegar in a medium bowl; toss well. Combine yogurt, remaining 2 tablespoons parsley, juice, and pepper in a small bowl; stir with a whisk. Arrange 1 patty and 1/2 cup cucumber mixture on each of 4 plates. Top each serving with about 2 tablespoons yogurt sauce. Serve each with 2 pita wedges. Serves 4.

CALORIES 321; FAT 12.1g (sat 4.7g, mono 5g, poly 0.6g); PROTEIN 28.7g; CARB 22.4g; FIBER 1.8g; CHOL 74mg; IRON 4.1mg; SODIUM 696mg; CALC 85mg

Easy Peach Crisp

1/2 cup low-fat granola without raisins
2 tablespoons unsalted butter
4 large peaches, pitted and sliced
2 tablespoons brown sugar
1/2 teaspoon ground cinnamon
1 cup vanilla low-fat frozen yogurt

1. Preheat broiler to high.
2. Place granola on a jelly-roll pan, spreading evenly. Broil 2 minutes, stirring after 1 minute.
3. Melt butter in a large nonstick skillet over medium heat. Add peaches to pan; cook 3 minutes, stirring occasionally. Add sugar and cinnamon to pan; cook 1 minute or until sugar melts, stirring occasionally. Spoon about 2/3 cup peach mixture in each of 4 shallow bowls. Top each serving with 2 tablespoons granola and 1/4 cup yogurt. Serves 4.

CALORIES 284; FAT 9g (sat 5.1g, mono 1.9g, poly 0.6g); PROTEIN 6.9g; CARB 46.8g; FIBER 3.1g; CHOL 48mg; IRON 0.9mg; SODIUM 57mg; CALC 149mg

WHAT TO COOK RIGHT NOW

SPICY BASIL-BEEF SALAD

There is no more fragrant summer plant than basil, easy to grow in a patio pot or on a windowsill perch. When you have a generous plant, the more leaves you snip off, the more seem to sprout in return. Genovese, with its large green leaves, is the familiar variety. But there are at least 40 types, each with signature flavor notes and shapes: purple basil, citrusy lemon basil, licorice-y Vietnamese and Thai basil, all now appearing in farmers' markets. Here is a Southeast Asian-style salad in which we used the leaves of several varieties to stand in for lettuce.

Spicy Basil-Beef Salad

Hands-on time: 16 min. Total time: 30 min. *It's worth searching out a few varieties of basil, such as purple, Thai, or lemon basil. Using a mix of varieties improves the salad by adding visual interest and nuanced flavors..*

1 tablespoon canola oil
12 ounces hanger steak, trimmed
1/4 teaspoon kosher salt
1/2 teaspoon black pepper
3 tablespoons lower-sodium soy sauce
2 tablespoons rice vinegar
2 tablespoons minced fresh lemongrass
1 tablespoon dark sesame oil
2 teaspoons fish sauce
2 teaspoons sambal oelek (ground fresh chile paste)
1 1/2 cups loosely packed fresh basil leaves
1 cup thinly sliced English cucumber
3 large ripe heirloom tomatoes, cut into wedges
2 medium shallots, thinly sliced

1. Preheat oven to 425°.
2. Heat a large ovenproof stainless-steel skillet over medium-high heat. Add canola oil to pan; swirl to coat. Sprinkle both sides of steak evenly with salt and black pepper. Add steak to pan; sauté 5 minutes or until browned. Turn steak over. Bake at 425° for 8 minutes or until a thermometer inserted into thickest portion of steak registers 135° or until desired degree of doneness. Remove steak from pan; let stand 10 minutes. Slice across grain.
3. Combine soy sauce and next 5 ingredients, stirring well. Combine basil and remaining ingredients. Drizzle dressing mixture over basil mixture; toss gently. Divide salad mixture evenly among 4 plates; divide beef evenly among salads. Serves 4.

CALORIES 226; FAT 11.9g (sat 2.5g, mono 5.5g, poly 2.7g); PROTEIN 17g; CARB 14.6g; FIBER 2g; CHOL 22mg; IRON 1.2mg; SODIUM 585mg; CALC 49mg

DINNER TONIGHT

Here is a batch of fast weeknight menus from the *Cooking Light* Test Kitchen.

READY IN
40
MINUTES

The
SHOPPING LIST

Open-Faced Pimiento Cheese BLTS
Shallot (1)
Baby arugula
Tomatoes (2 large)
Canola mayonnaise
Cider vinegar
Sourdough bread
Bottled diced pimientos
Center-cut bacon (4 slices)
Parmesan cheese (1.25 ounces)
Reduced-fat sharp cheddar cheese
    (4 ounces)

Sweet Potato Fries
Sweet potato (1 large)
Extra-virgin olive oil
Ground red pepper

The
GAME PLAN

While oven preheats:
  ■ Cut and season fries.
While fries bake:
  ■ Prepare pimiento cheese.
  ■ Assemble sandwiches.

Kid Friendly • Quick & Easy
Open-Faced Pimiento Cheese BLTs
With Sweet Potato Fries
(pictured on page 224)

Shopping Tip: Try colorful heirloom tomatoes from your local farmers' market.
Simple Sub: Use green leaf lettuce in place of arugula.
Kid Tweak: Leave the ground red pepper off the fries.

2 tablespoons bottled diced pimientos, drained
1 tablespoon grated peeled shallots
2 tablespoons canola mayonnaise
1 teaspoon cider vinegar
¼ teaspoon freshly ground black pepper
4 ounces shredded reduced-fat sharp cheddar cheese (about 1 cup)
1.25 ounces grated fresh Parmesan cheese (about ⅓ cup)
4 (1-ounce) slices sourdough bread, toasted
12 tomato slices
¼ teaspoon kosher salt
4 center-cut bacon slices, cooked and halved
1 cup baby arugula leaves

1. Combine first 7 ingredients in a large bowl. Spread 3 tablespoons cheese mixture on each bread slice; top each with 3 tomato slices. Sprinkle tomato slices evenly with salt. Top each sandwich with 2 bacon halves and ¼ cup arugula. Serves 4 (serving size: 1 sandwich).

CALORIES 266; **FAT** 14.9g (sat 5.5g, mono 6.1g, poly 2.2g); **PROTEIN** 16.4g; **CARB** 19.3g; **FIBER** 2.2g; **CHOL** 31mg; **IRON** 1.7mg; **SODIUM** 743mg; **CALC** 139mg

For the Sweet Potato Fries:
Preheat oven to 450°. Cut 1 large, peeled sweet potato into ¼-inch strips. Combine sweet potato, 1 tablespoon

---

extra-virgin olive oil, ¼ teaspoon kosher salt, ¼ teaspoon freshly ground black pepper, and ⅛ teaspoon ground red pepper in a large bowl; toss to combine. Arrange in a single layer on a foil-lined jelly-roll pan. Bake at 450° for 25 minutes or until browned, turning occasionally. Serves 4 (serving size: ½ cup).

CALORIES 58; **FAT** 3.4g (sat 0.5g); **SODIUM** 138mg

READY IN
30
MINUTES

The
SHOPPING LIST

Glazed Chicken and Szechuan Noodle Salad
Fresh ginger
Matchstick-cut carrots
Green onions
Lime (1)
Lower-sodium soy sauce
Olive oil
Hoisin sauce
Szechuan sauce
Udon noodles
Reduced-fat creamy peanut butter
Skinless, boneless chicken thighs
    (1.5 pounds)

Sesame Broccoli
(12-ounce) package broccoli florets (1)
Sesame seeds
Dark sesame oil

The
GAME PLAN

While grill preheats:
  ■ Coat chicken in hoisin mixture.
Grill chicken.
While chicken rests:
  ■ Cook noodles.
  ■ Steam broccoli.

Glazed Chicken and Szechuan Noodle Salad

With Sesame Broccoli

Simple Sub: Use whole-wheat linguine in place of udon noodles.
Time-Saver: Look for matchstick-cut carrots in the refrigerated produce section.

1 tablespoon grated peeled fresh ginger
3 tablespoons hoisin sauce
1 teaspoon olive oil
1 teaspoon lower-sodium soy sauce
8 skinless, boneless chicken thighs
   (about 1¹/₂ pounds)
Cooking spray
6 ounces uncooked udon noodles
   (thick, fresh Japanese wheat noodles)
   or whole-wheat linguine
¹/₄ cup bottled Szechuan sauce
1 tablespoon reduced-fat creamy
   peanut butter
2 teaspoons lower-sodium soy sauce
2 teaspoons fresh lime juice
1 cup matchstick-cut carrots
¹/₂ cup matchstick-cut green onions

1. Preheat grill to medium-high heat.
2. Combine first 4 ingredients in a bowl; stir well. Add chicken; toss.
3. Place chicken on grill rack coated with cooking spray; grill 4 minutes on each side or until done. Remove from grill; cover.
4. Cook noodles according to package directions, omitting salt and fat. Drain, and rinse with cold water; drain well. Combine Szechuan sauce, peanut butter, soy sauce, and juice in a large bowl, stirring with a whisk. Add noodles, carrots, and green onions; toss, and serve immediately with chicken. Serves 4 (serving size: 2 chicken thighs and 1 cup noodle salad).

CALORIES 417; FAT 11.3g (sat 2.1g, mono 6.1g, poly 1.8g);
PROTEIN 35.5g; CARB 41.8g; FIBER 4g; CHOL 115mg;
IRON 4mg; SODIUM 556mg; CALC 46mg

For the Sesame Broccoli:

Add water to a large saucepan to a depth of 1 inch; set a large vegetable steamer in pan. Bring water to a boil over high heat. Add 1 (12-ounce) package broccoli florets to steamer. Steam broccoli, covered, 4 minutes or until crisp-tender. Place broccoli in a medium bowl. Add 1 tablespoon toasted sesame seeds, 1 tablespoon dark sesame oil, ¹/₄ teaspoon kosher salt, and ¹/₄ teaspoon freshly ground black pepper to broccoli; toss well. Serves 4 (serving size: 1 cup).

CALORIES 67; FAT 4.9g (sat 0.7g); SODIUM 143mg

READY IN 40 MINUTES

The SHOPPING LIST

Snapper with Zucchini and Tomato
Zucchini (1)
Cherry tomatoes (1 pint)
Fresh basil
Fresh oregano
Lemon (1)
Shallot (1)
Extra-virgin olive oil
Dry vermouth
(6-ounce) snapper fillets (2)

Parsley Orzo
Uncooked orzo
Pine nuts
Fresh parsley

The GAME PLAN

While water comes to a boil:
 ■ Chop produce.
 ■ Toast pine nuts.
While orzo cooks:
 ■ Cook snapper.
 ■ Sauté zucchini mixture.

Snapper with Zucchini and Tomato

With Parsley Orzo

Simple Sub: Dry white wine like sauvignon blanc works in place of vermouth.
Shopping Tip: Avoid large zucchini, which can be bitter.

4 teaspoons extra-virgin olive oil,
   divided
¹/₂ teaspoon kosher salt, divided
¹/₂ teaspoon freshly ground black
   pepper, divided
2 (6-ounce) snapper fillets
2 tablespoons dry vermouth or white
   wine
1 cup diced zucchini
1¹/₂ tablespoons minced shallots
1 teaspoon chopped fresh oregano
1 teaspoon grated lemon rind
1 cup halved cherry tomatoes
1 tablespoon chopped fresh basil
2 teaspoons fresh lemon juice

1. Heat a large nonstick skillet over medium-high heat. Add 1 teaspoon oil to pan; swirl to coat. Sprinkle ¹/₄ teaspoon salt and ¹/₄ teaspoon pepper over fish. Add fish to pan; cook 3 minutes on each side or until desired degree of doneness. Remove fish from pan; keep warm. Add vermouth; cook until liquid almost evaporates. Add zucchini, shallots, oregano, lemon rind, 1 teaspoon oil, and ¹/₈ teaspoon salt; sauté 3 minutes or until zucchini is tender.
2. Combine zucchini mixture, tomato, remaining ¹/₈ teaspoon salt, remaining 2 teaspoons oil, basil, and juice; toss gently. Serve with fish. Serves 2 (serving size: 1 fillet and 1 cup zucchini mixture).

CALORIES 303; FAT 11.8g (sat 1.8g, mono 7.3g, poly 1.8g);
PROTEIN 36.8g; CARB 7.8g; FIBER 1.9g; CHOL 63mg;
IRON 1mg; SODIUM 602mg; CALC 83mg

continued

For the Parsley Orzo:
Cook ½ cup orzo (rice-shaped pasta) according to package directions, omitting salt and fat. Drain. Stir in 2 tablespoons toasted pine nuts, 2 teaspoons chopped fresh parsley, 1 teaspoon extra-virgin olive oil, and ⅛ teaspoon salt. Serves 2 (serving size: about ½ cup).

CALORIES 237; **FAT** 8.9g (sat 0.7g); **SODIUM** 148mg

READY IN
40
MINUTES

The
SHOPPING LIST

Pork Tenderloin Salad and Grilled Nectarines
Nectarines (2)
Fresh tarragon
Garlic
Gourmet salad greens (6 cups)
Red onion (1)
Olive oil
Balsamic vinegar
Maple syrup
(1-pound) pork tenderloin (1)

Goat Cheese Toasts
French bread baguette
Soft goat cheese (2 ounces)
Fresh thyme

The
GAME PLAN

While grill preheats:
- Prepare balsamic mixture.
- Halve and pit nectarines.
- Preheat broiler.

Grill pork and nectarines.

While pork rests:
- Prepare salad.
- Broil toasts.

Quick & Easy
Pork Tenderloin Salad and Grilled Nectarines
With Goat Cheese Toasts

Simple Sub: Peaches can stand in for nectarines.
Prep Pointer: Remove silver skin from tenderloin before grilling.

5 tablespoons olive oil
3 tablespoons balsamic vinegar
2 teaspoons minced fresh tarragon
2 garlic cloves, minced
2 tablespoons maple syrup, divided
1 (1-pound) pork tenderloin, trimmed
½ teaspoon kosher salt
¼ teaspoon freshly ground black pepper
Cooking spray
2 large nectarines, halved and pitted
6 cups gourmet salad greens
½ cup thinly sliced red onion

1. Preheat grill to medium-high heat.
2. Combine first 4 ingredients in a small bowl. Divide mixture in half. Combine half of balsamic mixture and 1 tablespoon maple syrup. Reserve 2 tablespoons maple syrup mixture. Brush remaining maple syrup mixture evenly over pork; sprinkle pork with salt and pepper. Place pork on a grill rack coated with cooking spray, and grill 16 minutes or until a thermometer registers 145°, turning occasionally and brushing with reserved maple syrup mixture. Remove pork from grill, and let stand 10 minutes before slicing.

3. Coat cut sides of nectarines with cooking spray; brush with remaining 1 tablespoon maple syrup. Place, cut sides down, on grill rack; grill 5 minutes or until well marked and tender. Remove from grill; slice into ½-inch wedges.
4. Combine remaining half of balsamic mixture, greens, and onion in a large bowl, tossing to coat. Divide mixture among 4 plates; top with pork and nectarines. Serves 4 (serving size: 1½ cups salad, 3 ounces pork, and 5 nectarine wedges).

CALORIES 366; **FAT** 19.8g (sat 3.2g, mono 13.3g, poly 2.3g); **PROTEIN** 25.9g; **CARB** 22.7g; **FIBER** 3.6g; **CHOL** 74mg; **IRON** 2.4mg; **SODIUM** 335mg; **CALC** 29mg

For the Goat Cheese Toasts:
Preheat broiler. Place 8 (½-inch-thick) slices French bread baguette on a baking sheet. Spread 1½ teaspoons goat cheese over each bread slice. Sprinkle with 1 teaspoon chopped fresh thyme; broil 2 minutes or until toasted. Serves 4 (serving size: 2 toasts).

CALORIES 112; **FAT** 3.6g (sat 2.1g); **SODIUM** 217mg

FLAVOR HIT: GRADE B SYRUP HAS THE STRONGEST MAPLE FLAVOR.

OOPS!

YOUR FISH STICKS TO THE GRILL

Sturdy seafood and a shipshape grill are key.

Grilled fish makes for a delicious, healthy summertime meal, but many backyard chefs give the seafood counter a wide berth for fear of disastrous results: fillets that cling to the grill rack and break into little pieces when you try to flip them. A grimy grill, insufficient heat, and the wrong fish are all often to blame.

(Nonstick fish)

(Calamity)

The solution: Stickage prevention is a process, and it starts at the store. Skip delicate, flaky fish like tilapia, cod, or flounder, and go with firmer-fleshed fish, such as salmon, tuna, or swordfish. Pat the fillets dry with paper towels before grill time.

Now prep the grill. Set the rack over a hot fire for five minutes to burn away lingering debris, and then scrub thoroughly with a grill brush. Carefully lift the rack and coat with cooking spray. Don't spray into the fire; if you can't remove the rack, swab it with oil using wadded paper towels held with tongs. But don't use the tongs for the fish: A spatula is less likely to tear the fillets. Let the fillets cook undisturbed for a few minutes. When they're ready to flip, they'll release cleanly.

THE FOOD LOVER'S GUIDE TO

SUPER SIMPLE COOKING

How to keep the flavor when you're cutting steps, time, and ingredients. You'll feel like a genius!

STRATEGIES & SHOPPING

Simple food, for its own sake, can be a snooze. The holy grail is simple food that has an essential deliciousness that gets to the soul of the ingredients and the dish. Some cooks have a gift for it. But the gift can be learned. Not everything is about shortcuts: Sometimes a special splurge is the key. Not everything is about speed: Sometimes careful prep makes a dish sing. Here are 25 tricks for successful simplicity.

STRATEGY

1. THE SEASONING SECRET. Don't overcomplicate things; have the confidence to season simply. A whole roasting chicken will be delicious with salt, pepper, and lemon rind. Summer tomatoes sparkle with a bit of oil and salt. Play with the idea.

2. THE STANDOUT STRATEGY. Build a meal around one star dish, not several. **The tomato stack salad on page 192,** for example, can be a star, allowing you to pair it with a very basic piece of chicken. Again, it hinges on ingredients.

3. THE BREAD BLESSING. Bread can be far more than the starch of a meal—it can be a star. A standout loaf may require a side trip to a great bakery, but it's always worth it.

4. THE VISUALIZATION TACTIC. Flavor and texture can be compromised if the cooking doesn't come together smoothly. Picture your progress through the steps of a recipe. Become a mental game planner.

SHOPPING

5. THE LET-OTHERS-DO-IT PLOY. Too few cooks take advantage of help at the store. Have the butcher cut, bone, or skin meat; have the fishmonger skin or fillet the fish. Buy precut veggies to save more time.

6. THE EXPLORER'S ROUTE. Specialty markets are full of ingredients that give dishes more punch, such as fresh and dried noodles, sauces, and spices. Asian stores have frozen Indian flatbreads that heat in seconds: Add a simmering sauce—voilà, you've got a great meal.

7. THE SPLURGE. Spend a little more at those specialty stores. Buy beautiful pasta, artisanal cheese, gorgeous finishing salts, or luxury items to keep in the freezer—a nub of pancetta or a tub of demi-glace to make **the tasty sauce on page 192.**

8. THE CONVENIENCE PLAY. Keep these on hand for easy pull-together meals: low-sodium marinara, precooked grains (brown rice, farro), fresh pizza dough.

GETTING AHEAD & INGREDIENTS

GETTING AHEAD

9. THE COOK ONCE, EAT TWICE HABIT. If you're planning to grill four chicken breasts, grill eight. When roasting veggies, do a giant batch—it adds little time. Use extras for salads, pizzas, tacos.

10. THE WEEKEND WARRIOR APPROACH. On a lazy Sunday, make versatile, high-flavor components to simplify cooking on a downstream night: roasted tomatoes, toasted breadcrumbs, roasted garlic. Super-slow-cooked caramelized onions sweeten **the zucchini quiche on page 190.**

11. THE FREEZER PLEASER. Label and store extra portions of sauces, sides, and entrées. That extra cup of pasta sauce would be great for pizza, meatball hoagies, even soup.

12. THE VEG-AHEAD TACTIC. Blanch veggies ahead of time. Trim and boil green beans, cauliflower, butternut squash, and broccoli for a few minutes just to get them softened. Drain and shock in ice water; then drain and store for the week. Or chop ahead. In a few minutes of downtime, you can get those onions, carrots, cauliflower, or broccoli prepped and ready to go. Store in zip-top bags in the fridge.

INGREDIENTS

13. THE IN-SEASON POLICY. Always start with fresh, peak-season ingredients so they won't need much gussying up: Summer tomatoes are sweet and tangy, as are peaches and plums. When winter comes, commit to acorn squash and Brussels sprouts, and explore easy flavor-enhancing techniques such as roasting.

14. THE DOUBLE-DUTY BLESSING. Use foods that offer two flavors or components in one. Citrus gives floral essence from zest and tartness from juice. Fennel provides crunchy bulk from the bulb and feathery greenery from the fronds. Capers yield salt and tang. Even Parmesan rind is a flavor-booster for sauces and soups, a smart use once you grate all the cheese.

15. THE PRECOOKED PROPOSITION. Explore the store for high-quality, no-cook proteins for pasta tosses, salads, pizzas, or sandwiches: jarred sustainable tuna, rotisserie chicken, smoked salmon or trout, or salumi.

16. THE HIGH-FLAVOR MANDATE. Build a repertoire of bold ingredients from which you can pull to turn up some serious flavor, like smoked paprika, sambal oelek, sherry vinegar, chipotle chiles, truffle oil, sweet Indonesian soy sauce, Indian pickles, and dried porcini mushrooms.

17. THE SPECIAL-SAUCE TRICK. Fast-food empires have been built on the power of mayo that's simply jazzed up with a few stir-ins. Secret sauces can make a boring sandwich a signature sandwich and work wonders with chicken or fish. **See page 190 for our favorite combos.**

TECHNIQUES & EQUIPMENT

TECHNIQUES

18. THE BLAZING-HOT PAN PRINCIPLE. Simple cooking often involves stovetop searing of fish or meat and sautéing of vegetables. A good pan, preheated until really hot, delivers the intense flavors you're looking for.

19. THE QUICK-REDUCTION TRICK. A hot pan also reduces a half-cup of good stock, wine, or orange juice to a glaze, and a bit of butter whisked in yields a master sauce.

20. THE EMULSIFICATION PROCLAMATION. Know how to make a well-blended sauce, which can pull a meal together. For vinaigrette, drizzle in oil as you whisk vigorously. **For the beurre blanc on page 191,** we whip cold butter into a warm wine reduction. To coat noodles, churn oil into a bit of boiling pasta water, **as with the pasta at right.**

EQUIPMENT

21. THE SLOW-COOKER SCHEME. Learn a few reliable slow-cooker recipes. Time is not the issue for the simple cook: This is hands-free cooking that can take place while you're at work.

22. THE WEIGHTY MATTER. Use a kitchen scale for measuring ingredients like flour or cheese. It's simpler than spooning into cups and leveling off.

23. THE MICROWAVE MANEUVER. Streamline prep, and cut down on the pots and pans you drag out. You can quickly zap parchment-wrapped beets, soften bell peppers you'll stuff, or bring stock to a boil for soup.

24. THE TOOL RULE. Use gadgets that deliver the textural variety that makes simple food special: julienne peelers, mandolines, and Microplane-style graters.

25. THE EQUIPMENT INVESTMENT. Get some good knives. We've said it before, and we'll say it again: You simplify prep greatly when you have sharp, precise knives and hone your knife skills. Simple food, often sautéed, needs to be cut into even pieces; they're prettier, too. It's often much quicker and less messy to hand-cut than to yank out the food processor.

RECIPES

Kid Friendly • Quick & Easy
Vegetarian

Pasta with Roasted Tomatoes and Garlic
(pictured on page 230)

Hands-on time: 4 min. Total time: 35 min. Principles 13 & 20: Height-of-summer tomatoes burst with flavor and need little embellishment to create a spectacular dish. Churning the oil into boiling liquid emulsifies the mixture, yielding a creamy sauce that coats.

1 tablespoon kosher salt
8 ounces uncooked spaghetti
¼ cup extra-virgin olive oil, divided
2 pints multicolored cherry tomatoes
4 garlic cloves, thinly sliced
½ teaspoon kosher salt
¼ teaspoon freshly ground black pepper
2 ounces fresh Parmigiano-Reggiano cheese, shaved
¼ cup small basil leaves

1. Preheat oven to 450°.
2. Bring a large pot of water to a boil; add 1 tablespoon salt. Add pasta; cook 10 minutes or until al dente. Drain pasta in a colander over a bowl, reserving 6 tablespoons cooking liquid. Return pasta to pan. Combine reserved cooking liquid and 2 tablespoons oil in a small saucepan; bring to a boil. Boil 4 minutes or until mixture measures ⅓ cup. Add oil mixture to pan with pasta; toss to coat.
3. While pasta cooks, combine remaining 2 tablespoons oil, tomatoes, and garlic on a jelly-roll pan, tossing to combine. Bake at 450° for 11 minutes or until tomatoes are lightly browned and begin to burst. Add tomato mixture, ½ teaspoon salt, and pepper to pasta; toss to coat. Top with cheese and basil. Serves 4 (serving size: about 1 cup).

CALORIES 417; FAT 18.4g (sat 4.4g, mono 11.1g, poly 2g); PROTEIN 14.1g; CARB 49.8g; FIBER 3.7g; CHOL 10mg; IRON 2.6mg; SODIUM 599mg; CALC 205mg

SECRET: PROPERLY EMULSIFYING A SIMPLE SAUCE GIVES IT THAT PASTA-CLINGY TEXTURE.

Zucchini and Caramelized Onion Quiche

Hands-on time: 20 min. Total time: 1 hr. 5 min. Principles 10 & 24: *Silky caramelized onions, which you can cook on the weekend, flavor this beautifully simple dish. Use a mandoline to thinly slice the zucchini.*

½ (14.1-ounce) package refrigerated pie dough (such as Pillsbury)
1 tablespoon olive oil
4 cups (⅛-inch-thick) slices zucchini
3 garlic cloves, minced
¾ teaspoon kosher salt, divided
½ cup finely chopped Basic Caramelized Onions
1 cup 1% low-fat milk
1½ tablespoons all-purpose flour
½ teaspoon black pepper
3 large eggs
2 ounces fresh Parmigiano-Reggiano cheese, grated (about ½ cup)

1. Preheat oven to 425°.
2. Roll dough into a 12-inch circle. Fit dough into a 10-inch deep-dish pie plate. Fold edges under; flute. Line dough with foil; arrange pie weights or dried beans on foil. Bake at 425° for 12 minutes or until edges are golden. Remove weights and foil; bake an additional 2 minutes. Cool on a wire rack.
3. Reduce oven temperature to 375°.
4. Heat a large nonstick skillet over medium-high heat. Add oil to pan; swirl to coat. Add zucchini and garlic; sprinkle with ¼ teaspoon salt. Sauté 5 minutes or until crisp-tender. Cool slightly.
5. Arrange Basic Caramelized Onions over bottom of crust; top with zucchini mixture. Combine remaining ½ teaspoon salt, milk, flour, pepper, eggs, and cheese in a medium bowl, stirring well with a whisk. Pour milk mixture over zucchini mixture. Bake at 375° for 35 minutes or until set. Let stand 10 minutes before serving. Serves 6 (serving size: 1 wedge).

CALORIES 314; **FAT** 18.1g (sat 6.2g, mono 7.5g, poly 3.1g); **PROTEIN** 9.6g; **CARB** 28.5g; **FIBER** 1.9g; **CHOL** 119mg; **IRON** 1.1mg; **SODIUM** 564mg; **CALC** 164mg

SECRET:
WEEKEND TIME SPENT CARAMELIZING ONIONS PAYS OFF MIDWEEK.

Make Ahead • Vegetarian

Basic Caramelized Onions

Hands-on time: 7 min. Total time: 1 hr. 22 min. Principle 10: *Make these on the weekend, and use throughout the week—in our quiche, on pizza, or in meat loaf. Although you start with 12 cups of onion, you end up with 2 cups after cooking; the flavor is concentrated, so a little goes a long way.*

3 tablespoons olive oil
1 tablespoon butter
12 cups vertically sliced yellow onion
¼ teaspoon kosher salt

1. Heat a large Dutch oven over medium heat. Add oil and butter; swirl until butter melts. Add onion and salt; cook 15 minutes or until onion begins to soften, stirring occasionally. Reduce heat to medium-low. Cook 50 minutes or until very tender, stirring occasionally. Cook 10 minutes or until browned and caramelized, stirring frequently. Serves 8 (serving size: about ¼ cup).

CALORIES 126; **FAT** 6.7g (sat 1.7g, mono 4.1g, poly 0.6g); **PROTEIN** 1.9g; **CARB** 16.1g; **FIBER** 2.9g; **CHOL** 4mg; **IRON** 0.4mg; **SODIUM** 77mg; **CALC** 40mg

SECRET:
A SIMPLE "SECRET SAUCE" PUTS SANDWICHES INTO NEW TERRITORY.

Quick & Easy

Steak Sandwiches with Pickled Onion and Herb Aioli

Hands-on time: 21 min. Total time: 40 min. Principle 17: *Herbs, garlic, and lemon juice combine with mayo for a sauce that makes the sandwich. Some other favorite secret-sauce ideas to mix with ¼ cup canola mayo: 1 tablespoon pesto; 1 tablespoon Sriracha; 1 tablespoon grated onion and 1 teaspoon chopped capers; or 2 tablespoons chopped cilantro, 1 teaspoon lime juice, and 1 minced garlic clove.*

¼ cup water
¼ cup cider vinegar
2 tablespoons sugar
1 cup thinly sliced red onion
¼ cup canola mayonnaise
1 tablespoon chopped fresh thyme
1 tablespoon chopped fresh tarragon
1 tablespoon fresh lemon juice
1 garlic clove, minced
1 pound flank steak, trimmed
1½ teaspoons olive oil
¼ teaspoon kosher salt
¼ teaspoon black pepper
1 (12-ounce) French bread baguette
1 cup arugula leaves

1. Combine first 3 ingredients in a medium microwave-safe bowl; microwave at HIGH 2 minutes or until boiling. Stir in onion. Let stand at room temperature 30 minutes.

2. Preheat grill to medium-high heat.

3. Combine mayonnaise and next 4 ingredients.

4. Rub steak evenly with oil; sprinkle with salt and pepper. Place steak on grill rack; grill 5 minutes on each side or until desired degree of doneness. Remove from grill; let stand 5 minutes. Cut steak across the grain into thin slices.

5. Cut baguette in half lengthwise. Hollow out top and bottom halves of bread, leaving a ½-inch-thick shell; reserve torn bread for another use. Place bread, cut sides down, on grill rack; grill 1 minute or until toasted.

6. Drain onion mixture; discard liquid. Arrange steak evenly over bottom half of baguette; top evenly with onion and arugula. Spread mayonnaise mixture over cut side of top baguette half; place on sandwich. Cut into 4 pieces. Serves 4 (serving size: 1 sandwich).

CALORIES 403; **FAT** 11.8g (sat 2.5g, mono 5.9g, poly 1.9g); **PROTEIN** 30g; **CARB** 43.4g; **FIBER** 1.8g; **CHOL** 37mg; **IRON** 3.8mg; **SODIUM** 677mg; **CALC** 39mg

SECRET:
A SUPERHOT PAN GIVES SCALLOPS THAT RESTAURANT-TYPE CRUST.

Quick & Easy

Seared Scallops with Summer Vegetables and Beurre Blanc

Hands-on time: 30 min. Total time: 30 min. Principles 18 & 20: *A screaming-hot skillet and baking sheet yield fantastic seared scallops and quick-roasted veggies. The luxurious sauce is little more than butter emulsified into reduced white wine—keep the butter cold and whisk it in gradually for the creamiest sauce.*

½ cup dry white wine
¼ cup chopped shallots
3 tablespoons chilled butter, cut into small pieces
½ teaspoon grated lemon rind
⅝ teaspoon kosher salt, divided
1 medium zucchini
1 medium-sized yellow squash
1 orange bell pepper, cut into 1-inch pieces
1 small red onion, cut into wedges
2 tablespoons olive oil, divided
1 cup grape tomatoes
3 garlic cloves, thinly sliced
½ teaspoon freshly ground black pepper, divided
1½ pounds sea scallops
¼ cup small basil leaves

1. Place a jelly-roll pan in oven. Preheat oven to 500° (leave pan in oven as it preheats).

2. Combine wine and shallots in a small saucepan; bring to a boil. Cook 6 minutes or until mixture is reduced to 2 tablespoons. Strain through a sieve into a bowl; discard solids. Return mixture to pan. Gradually add butter, stirring with a whisk until smooth and emulsified. Stir in rind and ⅛ teaspoon salt; keep warm.

3. Cut zucchini and yellow squash in half lengthwise. Cut each half crosswise into 3 pieces; cut each piece lengthwise into 4 strips. Combine zucchini, squash, bell pepper, onion, and 1 tablespoon oil in a large bowl; toss to coat. Arrange vegetable mixture carefully onto preheated jelly-roll pan. Bake at 500° for 3 minutes. Add tomatoes and garlic; toss gently. Bake at 500° for 4 minutes or until vegetables are lightly browned. Remove from oven; sprinkle with ¼ teaspoon salt and ¼ teaspoon black pepper.

4. While vegetables cook, heat a large cast-iron skillet over high heat. Pat scallops dry with paper towels; sprinkle evenly with remaining ¼ teaspoon salt and ¼ teaspoon black pepper. Add remaining 1 tablespoon oil to pan; swirl to coat. Add scallops to pan; cook 1½ minutes on each side or until scallops are seared and desired degree of doneness. Serve scallops with vegetable mixture and sauce; garnish with basil leaves. Serves 4 (serving size: about 4 ounces scallops, about 1 cup vegetables, and about 1 tablespoon sauce).

CALORIES 345; **FAT** 17g (sat 6.6g, mono 7.3g, poly 1.6g); **PROTEIN** 31.1g; **CARB** 14.9g; **FIBER** 2.5g; **CHOL** 79mg; **IRON** 1.5mg; **SODIUM** 660mg; **CALC** 85mg

Quick & Easy

Tomato Stack Salad with Corn and Avocado
(pictured on page 229)

***Hands-on time: 30 min. Total time: 30 min. Principles 2 & 13:** This salad is the star of the meal; keep the entrée simple.*

2 bacon slices, halved
¼ cup low-fat buttermilk
1 tablespoon finely chopped fresh chives
1 tablespoon finely chopped fresh basil
2 tablespoons canola mayonnaise
2 teaspoons cider vinegar
1 garlic clove, minced
½ teaspoon freshly ground black pepper, divided
2 ears shucked corn
Cooking spray
2 large beefsteak tomatoes, cut into 8 (¹/₂-inch-thick) slices total
2 globe tomatoes, cut into 8 (¹/₂-inch-thick) slices total
¹/₈ teaspoon kosher salt
½ ripe peeled avocado, thinly sliced
4 teaspoons extra-virgin olive oil

1. Preheat grill to high heat.
2. Heat a large nonstick skillet over medium heat. Add bacon to pan; cook 8 minutes or until crisp, tossing occasionally to curl. Drain on paper towels.
3. Combine buttermilk and next 5 ingredients, stirring with a whisk. Stir in ¼ teaspoon pepper.

4. Coat corn with cooking spray. Place corn on grill rack; grill 8 minutes or until well marked, turning occasionally. Remove from grill; cool slightly. Cut corn kernels from cobs.
5. Sprinkle tomato slices evenly with salt. Alternate layers of tomato and avocado on each of 4 plates. Scatter corn evenly onto plates. Drizzle each tomato stack with about 1½ table-spoons dressing and 1 teaspoon oil. Sprinkle remaining ¼ teaspoon black pepper over salads; top each salad with 1 bacon piece. Serves 4.

CALORIES 191; FAT 13g (sat 1.9g, mono 8g, poly 2.2g); PROTEIN 5.1g; CARB 16.1g; FIBER 4.5g; CHOL 5mg; IRON 0.9mg; SODIUM 228mg; CALC 40mg

Quick & Easy

Sablefish with Mild Mustard Glace

***Hands-on time: 20 min. Total time: 25 min. Principle 7:** Here, demi-glace is the base of a rich sauce for buttery sablefish. Serve with Cider-Glazed Carrots; if you can, use a mix of multicolored baby carrots.*

Cooking spray
2 garlic cloves, crushed
³/₄ cup water, divided
1 (1.5-ounce) container roasted chicken demi-glace (such as More Than Gourmet)
³/₄ teaspoon dry mustard
1 teaspoon cider vinegar
½ teaspoon freshly ground black pepper, divided
¼ teaspoon kosher salt
4 (6-ounce) sablefish fillets
1 tablespoon thinly sliced green onions

1. Heat a small saucepan over medium-high heat. Coat pan with cooking spray. Add garlic; sauté 30 seconds or until fragrant, stirring constantly. Add ½ cup water; bring to a simmer. Add demi-glace, stirring with a whisk until combined. Combine remaining ¼ cup water and mustard, stirring with a whisk

until mustard dissolves. Stir mustard mixture, vinegar, and ¼ teaspoon pepper into glace mixture; bring to a boil. Reduce heat, and simmer 3 minutes; strain through a fine sieve over a bowl. Discard solids; keep glace warm.
2. Heat a large heavy skillet over medium-high heat. Sprinkle remaining ¼ teaspoon pepper and salt evenly over fish. Add fish to pan; cook 2½ minutes. Reduce heat to medium; turn fish, and cook 7 minutes or until desired degree of doneness. Sprinkle with green onions, and serve with glace. Serves 4.

CALORIES 350; FAT 25.2g (sat 5.3g, mono 13.2g, poly 3.4g); PROTEIN 25.1g; CARB 2.8g; FIBER 0.2g; CHOL 80mg; IRON 2.6mg; SODIUM 416mg; CALC 64mg

Kid Friendly • Quick & Easy
Vegetarian

Cider-Glazed Carrots

Trim, but don't peel, 2 pounds baby carrots with tops. Cook carrots in boiling water for 5 minutes; drain. Rinse under cold water. Remove skins by rubbing carrots gently with a clean, dry paper towel. Bring ½ cup cider vinegar and 1 teaspoon brown sugar to a boil in a medium skillet; cook 6 minutes or until reduced to ¼ cup. Add carrots; increase heat to high, and cook 2 minutes or until sauce is syrupy and coats carrots. Stir in 1 tablespoon butter and ¼ teaspoon kosher salt. Serves 4.

CALORIES 71; FAT 3.1g (sat 1.9g); SODIUM 201mg

UNDER 300 CALORIES! FULL FLAVOR, NO GUILT

We're not interested in low-calorie eating for low-calorie's sake. The first principle is taste. But with so much fresh produce around, it's a pure pleasure to cook this way.

Kid Friendly • Make Ahead
Chicken, Potato, and Leek Pie

Hands-on time: 22 min. Total time: 1 hr. 5 min. *Fast-food chicken pies can contain 800 calories per serving. We deploy full-flavored chicken thighs and smoky bacon to add depth. Store-bought piecrust keeps prep easy.*

1 smoked bacon slice, chopped
1½ cups cubed red potato (about 8 ounces)
1 cup chopped carrot
6 skinless, boneless chicken thighs, cut into bite-sized pieces
3½ tablespoons all-purpose flour
3 cups sliced leeks (about 2)
½ teaspoon kosher salt
¼ teaspoon freshly ground black pepper
2 cups fat-free, lower-sodium chicken broth
½ (14.1-ounce) package refrigerated pie dough
1 tablespoon fat-free milk
1 large egg white

1. Preheat oven to 450°.
2. Cook bacon in a large Dutch oven over medium heat until almost crisp, stirring frequently. Increase heat to medium-high. Add potato and carrot to pan, and sauté 3 minutes, stirring occasionally. Add chicken; sauté 3 minutes or until lightly browned, stirring occasionally. Stir in flour and next 3 ingredients; sauté 1 minute, stirring frequently.
3. Slowly add broth to pan, stirring constantly; bring to a boil. Cook 2 minutes or until slightly thick, stirring occasionally. Spoon mixture into a 1½-quart glass or ceramic baking dish. Top with dough, folding under and pressing down on edges to seal.
4. Combine milk and egg white; brush mixture over top of dough. Cut small slits in dough to vent. Bake at 450° for 30 minutes or until crust is golden. Let stand 10 minutes. Serves 6 (serving size: about 1¼ cups).

CALORIES 298; **FAT** 11.9g (sat 4.5g, mono 3.6g, poly 3g); **PROTEIN** 18g; **CARB** 31g; **FIBER** 2.2g; **CHOL** 62mg; **IRON** 2.1mg; **SODIUM** 561mg; **CALC** 42mg

Vegetarian
Tomato Tart

Hands-on time: 20 min. Total time: 1 hr. 5 min. *Tomato tarts are creamy, cheesy calorie and sat fat bombs. Ours is meat-free and cream-free, but olives add satisfying richness.*

½ (14.1-ounce) package refrigerated pie dough
Cooking spray
2.5 ounces fontina cheese, shredded (about ⅔ cup)
½ cup pitted kalamata olives, chopped
⅓ cup sliced shallots
3 heirloom tomatoes, seeded and cut into ½-inch-thick slices
3 tablespoons all-purpose flour
1 tablespoon cornmeal
1 tablespoon chopped fresh thyme
1 teaspoon kosher salt, divided
½ teaspoon black pepper
1¼ cups 2% reduced-fat milk
1½ tablespoons grated fresh Parmigiano-Reggiano
3 large eggs
2 tablespoons basil leaves
1 cup cherry tomatoes, quartered

1. Preheat oven to 350°.
2. Roll dough to a 12-inch circle; press into a 9-inch deep-dish tart or springform pan coated with cooking spray. Sprinkle with fontina, olives, and shallots. Arrange half of tomato slices over shallots. Combine flour, cornmeal, and thyme; sprinkle over tomatoes. Top with remaining tomato slices; sprinkle with ¾ teaspoon salt and pepper.
3. Combine milk, Parmigiano-Reggiano, and eggs, and pour into pan. Bake at 350° for 40 minutes or until set; let stand 10 minutes. Top with basil.
4. Combine remaining ¼ teaspoon salt and cherry tomatoes. Slice tart, and serve with cherry tomatoes. Serves 8 (serving size: 1 tart slice and 2 tablespoons cherry tomato mixture).

CALORIES 244; **FAT** 13.9g (sat 6g, mono 5.1g, poly 2.4g); **PROTEIN** 8.9g; **CARB** 22.7g; **FIBER** 1.6g; **CHOL** 96mg; **IRON** 1.1mg; **SODIUM** 596mg; **CALC** 134mg

Sweet and Spicy Shrimp with Rice Noodles

(pictured on page 226)

Hands-on time: 30 min. Total time: 1 hr. *A healthy take on pad thai, this dish stretches 12 ounces of shrimp to feed four and keeps the noodle portions in check. The sauce has some pumped-up kicks, comparable to many restaurant versions. This dish has the starch built in, and because the recipe includes lots of fresh veggies, it qualifies as a one-dish meal.*

1 tablespoon rice vinegar
2¹/₂ teaspoons honey
1 tablespoon sambal oelek (ground fresh chile paste, such as Huy Fong)
1 tablespoon lower-sodium soy sauce
12 ounces peeled and deveined medium shrimp
4 ounces uncooked flat rice noodles (pad thai noodles)
1 tablespoon peanut oil
2 tablespoons chopped unsalted cashews
1 tablespoon thinly sliced garlic
2 teaspoons chopped peeled fresh ginger
1 green Thai chile, halved
12 sweet mini peppers, halved
³/₄ cup matchstick-cut carrot
¹/₄ teaspoon salt
³/₄ cup snow peas, trimmed
³/₄ cup fresh bean sprouts

1. Combine first 4 ingredients in a bowl, stirring well with a whisk. Add shrimp to vinegar mixture; toss to coat. Cover and refrigerate 30 minutes.
2. Cook noodles according to package directions, omitting salt and fat; drain. Rinse with cold water; drain.
3. Heat a large skillet or wok over medium-high heat. Add oil to pan; swirl to coat. Add cashews, garlic, ginger, and chile to pan; stir-fry 1 minute or until garlic begins to brown. Remove cashew mixture from pan with a slotted spoon, and set aside.

4. Increase heat to high. Add sweet peppers, carrot, and salt to pan; stir-fry 2 minutes. Add shrimp mixture (do not drain); stir-fry 2 minutes. Stir in noodles and peas; cook 1 minute, tossing to coat. Return cashew mixture to pan. Add bean sprouts; cook 1 minute or until thoroughly heated, tossing frequently. Serves 4 (serving size: about 1¼ cups).

CALORIES 299; FAT 8.5g (sat 1.5g, mono 3g, poly 2.1g); PROTEIN 21.7g; CARB 34.3g; FIBER 2.9g; CHOL 129mg; IRON 3.4mg; SODIUM 492mg; CALC 84mg

Barbecue Salmon and Snap Pea Slaw

(pictured on page 227)

Hands-on time: 46 min. Total time: 1 hr. 6 min. *Sugar snap peas, radishes, and shallots combine for an interesting twist on slaw.*

2 tablespoons dark sesame oil, divided
3 garlic cloves, crushed
1 (¹/₂-inch) piece fresh ginger, peeled
2 tablespoons fresh lime juice
2 tablespoons lower-sodium soy sauce
1¹/₂ tablespoons ketchup
2 teaspoons dark brown sugar
1 teaspoon sambal oelek (ground fresh chile paste, such as Huy Fong)
4 (6-ounce) fresh or frozen sustainable salmon fillets (such as wild Alaskan), thawed
Cooking spray
2 cups sugar snap peas, trimmed and thinly sliced crosswise
¹/₂ cup grated radishes
¹/₄ cup very thinly vertically sliced shallots
2 teaspoons rice vinegar
¹/₄ teaspoon kosher salt

1. Preheat grill to high heat.
2. Place 1 tablespoon oil, garlic, and ginger in a mini food processor; pulse until finely chopped. Add juice and next 4 ingredients; pulse to combine. Place salmon on a grill rack coated with cooking spray, and brush tops of salmon with half of sauce. Grill

10 minutes; brush with remaining sauce. Grill an additional 10 minutes or until desired degree of doneness.
3. Combine peas, radishes, and shallots. Combine vinegar and remaining 1 tablespoon oil, stirring well; drizzle over pea mixture. Sprinkle with salt; toss. Serve with salmon. Serves 4 (serving size: 1 fillet and about ¾ cup slaw).

CALORIES 268; FAT 11.4g (sat 1.7g, mono 3.9g, poly 4.6g); PROTEIN 27.8g; CARB 12.7g; FIBER 1.8g; CHOL 66mg; IRON 2.1mg; SODIUM 474mg; CALC 49mg

Grilled Skirt Steak and Roasted Tomatillo Sauce

(pictured on page 226)

Hands-on time: 33 min. Total time: 1 hr. 53 min. *Satisfy beef cravings with skirt steak, an ultra-flavorful cut that does well on the grill in no time. The veggie-based sauce with tangy tomatillos is a perfect match for charred beefiness. Serve the steak with halved multicolored cherry tomatoes, which add very few calories.*

1 cup boiling water
1 dried guajillo chile, stemmed
3 tablespoons chopped fresh oregano, divided
2 tablespoons fresh lime juice, divided
1 tablespoon olive oil
1¹/₂ teaspoons ground cumin, divided
8 garlic cloves, divided
1 (1-pound) skirt steak, trimmed
¹/₂ cup sliced onion
8 ounces tomatillos, husks removed
Cooking spray
1 teaspoon kosher salt, divided
³/₄ teaspoon black pepper, divided
Dash of sugar
2 tablespoons chopped fresh cilantro

1. Combine 1 cup boiling water and chile in a small bowl; let stand 10 minutes or until hydrated. Drain; finely chop chile. Combine chile,

1 tablespoon oregano, 1 tablespoon juice, oil, and 1 teaspoon cumin in a zip-top plastic bag. Mince 4 garlic cloves; add to bag. Add steak to bag; seal. Shake to coat; refrigerate 1 hour.
2. Preheat oven to 450°.
3. Crush remaining 4 garlic cloves. Arrange crushed garlic, onion, and tomatillos in a single layer on a baking sheet coated with cooking spray; lightly coat vegetables with cooking spray. Bake at 450° for 20 minutes or until charred. Place tomatillo mixture, remaining 2 tablespoons oregano, remaining 1 tablespoon juice, remaining ½ teaspoon cumin, ½ teaspoon salt, ¼ teaspoon pepper, and sugar in a blender; process until smooth, scraping sides.
4. Preheat grill to high heat.
5. Remove steak from bag; sprinkle both sides of steak evenly with remaining ½ teaspoon salt and remaining ½ teaspoon pepper. Place steak on grill rack coated with cooking spray. Grill 2 minutes on each side or until a thermometer inserted into the thickest portion of steak registers 135° or until desired degree of doneness. Let steak stand 10 minutes. Cut steak diagonally across grain into thin slices. Place 3 ounces steak on each of 4 plates. Top each serving with about 3 tablespoons sauce; sprinkle each serving with 1½ teaspoons cilantro. Serves 4.

CALORIES 227; **FAT** 11.4g (sat 3.3g, mono 6.3g, poly 1g); **PROTEIN** 19.9g; **CARB** 11g; **FIBER** 1.8g; **CHOL** 48mg; **IRON** 3.5mg; **SODIUM** 543mg; **CALC** 58mg

ON THE SIDE

Starchy sides inflate calories quickly, so turn to small servings of whole grains or add a veggie side to round out your plate. Any of these suggestions will keep calories in check:

- Cucumber salad
- Cabbage slaw
- Melon and tomato salad
- Peach and radish salsa
- Tomato and onion toss
- Zucchini ribbons with lemon
- Grilled summer squash
- Broccoli salad

Stone Fruit Chicken-Rice Salad
(pictured on page 226)

Hands-on time: 28 min. Total time: 48 min. *Chicken is pure lean protein (use a good brand for chicken-y flavor). Cherries and nectarines lend a sweet-tart counterpart. Brown rice adds whole-grain goodness. Serve a bitter lettuce, like frisée, or a peppery green, such as watercress or arugula, with this savory-sweet twist on a whole-grain salad.*

3 (6-ounce) skinless, boneless chicken breast halves, trimmed
1 teaspoon salt, divided
½ teaspoon freshly ground black pepper, divided
Cooking spray
2 tablespoons olive oil
1 teaspoon grated lemon rind
2 tablespoons fresh lemon juice
2 teaspoons Dijon mustard
1½ cups pitted, coarsely chopped nectarines
1 cup cooked brown rice, cooled
1 cup coarsely chopped pitted cherries
½ cup sliced green onions
¼ cup dry-roasted almonds, chopped
3 tablespoons torn mint

1. Preheat grill to medium-high heat.
2. Sprinkle both sides of chicken evenly with ½ teaspoon salt and ¼ teaspoon pepper. Place chicken on a grill rack coated with cooking spray; grill 5 minutes on each side or until done. Let stand 5 minutes. Chop chicken.
3. Combine oil, rind, juice, and mustard in a large bowl, stirring well with a whisk. Add chopped, cooked chicken, nectarines, and remaining ingredients; toss well. Serves 4 (serving size: about 1¼ cups).

CALORIES 299; **FAT** 11.4g (sat 1.6g, mono 7.2g, poly 1.9g); **PROTEIN** 23.2g; **CARB** 26.9g; **FIBER** 4.1g; **CHOL** 49mg; **IRON** 1.7mg; **SODIUM** 705mg; **CALC** 53mg\

LESS MEAT, MORE FLAVOR

POTATO SALAD, HOLD THE MAYO
By Mark Bittman

Tangy yogurt-buttermilk ranch and lime vinaigrette offer bolder flavor.

I come to this story with a distinct advantage: I'm just not crazy about potato salad bound with mayonnaise. Never have been. Vinaigrette—in one form or another, though usually laced with mustard—has always been my dressing of choice. Not that there's anything wrong with mayonnaise, but in salads, it quickly becomes dominant. I would rather taste the vegetables, especially the subtle earthiness of the potatoes themselves.

For starters, pick a flavorful potato that will stand up to boiling and tossing (more and more varieties are popping up in supermarkets these days). Yukon golds are a nice departure from russets, and red new potatoes and fingerlings are perfect for salad. And don't forget about sweet potatoes, which are most often overlooked and the best, nutrition-wise.

Start by dressing warm potatoes in a simple vinaigrette (you might be shocked by how good that is), and go from there. Potatoes can stand mostly alone in salads, or they can share the stage with other vegetables, beans, grains, and even bits of meat or seafood (potato and mussel salad is a classic, and potatoes with chopped smoked salmon and dill is also a treat).

Of the two recipes here, one is a spin on a conventional potato salad, and the other is a bit more out-of-the-box; I love both. The more mainstream salad features real, homemade
continued

ranch dressing, which gives you all the creamy richness of mayo without actually using any. I combine equal parts Greek yogurt and buttermilk with Dijon mustard (which is heaven with boiled potatoes) and a lot of black pepper. Buttermilk adds that essential ranch tang.

After that, it's totally straightforward: I toss the dressing with chunks of boiled potatoes, celery, red bell peppers, onion, parsley, dill, and chives. The potatoes are tender and warm, the veggies supercrunchy, and the dressing rich and tangy (better than straight mayo, if you ask me).

The other dish takes potato salad out of the pot and onto the grill. (It's a picnic dish, after all, so why not cook it outside?) The key to cooking potatoes on the grill is to get one side of the grill nice and hot, and leave the other side relatively cool. Here, I use sweet potatoes, which are especially good on the grill. I cut them into half-inch-thick planks, rub them with oil, salt, and pepper, put them on the cool side of the grill, and close the lid. This essentially roasts them without subjecting them to the direct heat that will burn the outsides. Once the sweet potatoes are golden and tender, I move them to the hot side of the grill to char ever so slightly.

I slice the sweet potatoes and toss them with shredded Napa cabbage, slivered red onion, scallions, cilantro, toasted pumpkin seeds, and a lime vinaigrette with a touch of honey for sweetness and a dash of hot sauce for spice. The sweet and smoky potatoes absorb the tart dressing, their tender flesh a perfect foil for the crunchy cabbage and onions.

When was the last time that you described a mayonnaise-y potato salad like that?

Quick & Easy • Make Ahead Vegetarian

Potato and Vegetable Salad with Mustard Ranch

Hands-on time: 10 min. Total time: 20 min. *You could use any waxy potato for this recipe, such as red new potatoes or Yukon gold.*

2 pounds multicolored fingerling potatoes, unpeeled and cut into bite-sized pieces
2 teaspoons kosher salt, divided
¼ cup plain 2% reduced-fat Greek yogurt
¼ cup buttermilk
1 tablespoon Dijon mustard
1 tablespoon fresh lemon juice
¾ teaspoon freshly ground black pepper
½ teaspoon honey
1 garlic clove, minced
1 cup chopped red bell pepper (about 1 medium)
¾ cup chopped celery
½ cup finely chopped onion
½ cup chopped fresh flat-leaf parsley leaves
¼ cup chopped fresh chives
2 tablespoons chopped fresh dill

1. Place potato pieces and 1 teaspoon salt in a medium saucepan, and cover with water. Bring to a boil. Reduce heat, and simmer 20 minutes or until potatoes are tender but still hold their shape. Drain and rinse with cold water. Drain.
2. Combine remaining 1 teaspoon salt, yogurt, and next 6 ingredients in a large bowl, stirring well with a whisk. Add potatoes, bell pepper, and remaining ingredients to yogurt mixture, and toss gently to coat. Serves 8 (serving size: 1 cup).

CALORIES 107; FAT 0.7g (sat 0.3g, mono 0g, poly 0.2g); PROTEIN 3.7g; CARB 22.4g; FIBER 2.8g; CHOL 2mg; IRON 1.2mg; SODIUM 318mg; CALC 35mg

Make Ahead • Vegetarian

Grilled Sweet Potato and Napa Cabbage Salad with Lime Vinaigrette

Hands-on time: 25 min. Total time: 55 min. *To save time, you could also cook the pumpkin seeds in a skillet directly on the grill.*

3 medium sweet potatoes (2 pounds)
5 tablespoons olive oil, divided
¾ teaspoon kosher salt, divided
½ teaspoon black pepper, divided
¼ cup fresh lime juice
2 tablespoons warm water
2 teaspoons honey
Dash of hot sauce (optional)
1 jalapeño pepper, seeded and minced
3 cups shredded napa cabbage
1 cup sliced red onion
⅓ cup pumpkin seeds, toasted
¼ cup chopped green onions
¼ cup chopped fresh cilantro

1. Prepare grill for indirect grilling, heating one side to medium-high and leaving one side with no heat.
2. Peel potatoes, and cut lengthwise into ½-inch-thick slices. Combine potatoes, 1 tablespoon oil, ¼ teaspoon salt, and ¼ teaspoon black pepper; toss.
3. Place potatoes on grill rack over unheated side; close lid. Cook 12 minutes on each side or until tender. Move potatoes to heated side; grill 2 minutes on each side or until charred.
4. Combine ¼ cup oil, ½ teaspoon salt, ¼ teaspoon black pepper, juice, and next 4 ingredients in a large bowl. Slice potato slices into strips. Add potatoes, cabbage, and remaining ingredients to bowl; toss. Serves 6 (serving size: 1⅓ cups).

CALORIES 259; FAT 12g (sat 1.7g, mono 8.4g, poly 1.5g); PROTEIN 3.9g; CARB 34.8g; FIBER 5.7g; CHOL 0mg; IRON 1.2mg; SODIUM 330mg; CALC 55mg

SUMMER'S GOLD

Recipes for all the sweet, crunchy, peak-season corn. This is pure summer, perfectly packaged, quintessentially American. The Europeans, who get weepy about a lot of produce, just don't get as sentimental about chomping into an ear of fresh corn—all that sun-packed sweetness is perhaps a bit gauche. This is our treat, best right now. Peel back a cob and poke a plump kernel with a thumbnail to see the sweet milk. Beyond the whole cob lie these of-the-moment recipes: tangy relishes, savory pancakes, creamy fresh-corn grits, and a frozen corn-milk treat.

Saucy Crawfish with Whole Corn Grits

Hands-on time: 46 min. Total time: 46 min. Substitute shrimp for the crawfish, if you prefer. Microgreens make an elegant garnish.

Grits:
3½ cups 2% reduced-fat milk, divided
1½ cups fresh corn kernels
1 chipotle chile, canned in adobo sauce
1½ cups water
½ teaspoon kosher salt
1 cup uncooked regular grits
2 ounces reduced-fat shredded cheddar cheese (about ½ cup)
3 tablespoons light sour cream

Crawfish:
1½ tablespoons all-purpose flour
2 teaspoons olive oil
¼ cup finely chopped andouille sausage or kielbasa (about 1.5 ounces)
⅔ cup chopped onion
⅔ cup chopped green bell pepper
1 tablespoon minced garlic
2 teaspoons chopped fresh thyme
¼ teaspoon kosher salt
2 teaspoons tomato paste
8 ounces cooked crawfish tail meat (about 1⅔ cups)
1 cup 2% reduced-fat milk
¼ cup light sour cream
¼ cup chopped fresh chives, divided

1. To prepare grits, place ½ cup milk, corn, and chipotle chile in a blender, and process until corn is coarsely chopped.

2. Combine remaining 3 cups milk, 1½ cups water, and ½ teaspoon salt in a medium saucepan; bring to a simmer over medium-high heat. Gradually add grits, stirring with a whisk. Cover, reduce heat, and simmer 11 minutes or until thick, stirring frequently. Add corn mixture; cook an additional 3 minutes, stirring frequently. Remove from heat; add cheese and 3 tablespoons sour cream, stirring until cheese melts. Keep warm.

3. To prepare crawfish, place flour in a large nonstick skillet over medium heat; cook 4 minutes or until lightly browned, stirring frequently. Remove flour from pan; set aside. Wipe pan clean.

4. Return pan to medium heat. Add oil and sausage to pan; cook 3 minutes, stirring occasionally. Add onion, bell pepper, garlic, thyme, and ¼ teaspoon salt; cook 3 minutes, stirring occasionally. Add reserved flour, tomato paste, and crawfish; cook 1 minute, stirring frequently. Stir in 1 cup milk; bring to a simmer, and cook 2 minutes or until sauce thickens, stirring frequently. Remove from heat. Stir in ¼ cup sour cream. Sprinkle 1 tablespoon chives over crawfish mixture. Stir 3 tablespoons chives into grits; serve with crawfish mixture. Serves 6 (serving size: about ½ cup crawfish mixture and ⅔ cup grits).

CALORIES 365; FAT 11.2g (sat 5.8g, mono 2.6g, poly 0.7g); PROTEIN 23.3g; CARB 44g; FIBER 2.4g; CHOL 99mg; IRON 3mg; SODIUM 530mg; CALC 394mg

TOASTING THE FLOUR BRINGS NUTTY FLAVOR TO THE SAUCE, SIMILAR TO A BROWN ROUX.

Corn Pancakes with Smoked Salmon and Lemon-Chive Cream

Hands-on time: 14 min. Total time: 32 min.

¼ cup light sour cream
2 tablespoons chopped fresh chives
1 teaspoon grated lemon rind
2.25 ounces all-purpose flour (about ½ cup)
½ cup yellow cornmeal
1 teaspoon sugar
¼ teaspoon baking soda
¼ teaspoon kosher salt
⅛ teaspoon ground red pepper
1¼ cups fresh corn kernels, divided (about 3 ears)
⅔ cup low-fat buttermilk
3 tablespoons butter, melted
1 large egg
12 thin slices cold-smoked salmon (about 6 ounces)

1. Combine first 3 ingredients in a small bowl; chill.
2. Weigh or lightly spoon flour into a dry measuring cup; level with a knife. Combine flour and next 5 ingredients in a medium bowl. Place 1 cup corn kernels, buttermilk, butter, and egg in a blender; process until coarsely pureed. Add pureed corn mixture to flour mixture, stirring until just combined. Fold in remaining ¼ cup corn.
3. Pour about 2 tablespoons batter per pancake onto a hot nonstick griddle or nonstick skillet; spread gently with a spatula. Cook 3 minutes or until tops are covered with bubbles and edges look cooked. Carefully turn pancakes over; cook 3 minutes or until bottoms are lightly browned. Arrange 2 pancakes on each of 6 plates; top each pancake with 1 slice salmon and 1 teaspoon lemon-chive cream. Serve immediately. Serves 6.

CALORIES 239; FAT 9.7g (sat 5g, mono 2.9g, poly 1g); PROTEIN 10.7g; CARB 27.6g; FIBER 1.8g; CHOL 56mg; IRON 1.7mg; SODIUM 409mg; CALC 59mg

Oaxacan-Style Grilled Corn on the Cob

(pictured on page 228)

Hands-on time: 25 min. Total time: 25 min. Look for crema at Latin markets or by the supermarket's Mexican cheeses. It's slightly tangier than sour cream.

1½ tablespoons queso fresco
1¼ teaspoons chili powder
3 tablespoons Mexican crema or sour cream
½ teaspoon kosher salt
⅛ teaspoon ground red pepper
4 ears shucked corn
4 lime wedges

1. Preheat grill to medium heat.
2. Combine cheese and next 4 ingredients in a small bowl.
3. Place corn on grill rack. Cover and grill 8 minutes or until lightly charred, turning occasionally. Place corn on serving plate; drizzle with crema mixture. Serve with lime wedges. Serves 4 (serving size: 1 corn cob and 1 lime wedge).

CALORIES 112; FAT 3.4g (sat 0.5g, mono 0.5g, poly 0.5g); PROTEIN 4g; CARB 20g; FIBER 3g; CHOL 8mg; IRON 0.5mg; SODIUM 336mg; CALC 18mg

Sweet Corn Ice Cream

Hands-on time: 30 min. Total time: 3 hr. 50 min. Steeping cobs in the cream mixture infuses it with corn flavor. If possible, chill the corn mixture overnight. This lets flavors meld and helps the ice cream to freeze faster. The quicker it freezes, the creamier it will be.

4 ears shucked corn
3 cups 2% reduced-fat milk, divided
¾ cup sugar
¼ teaspoon salt
1 cup half-and-half
6 large egg yolks

1. Cut kernels from ears of corn; set cobs aside. Place kernels and 1 cup milk in a blender; process until smooth. Combine corn mixture, remaining 2 cups milk, sugar, and salt in a medium, heavy saucepan. Cut cobs into thirds; add cobs to pan. Heat corn mixture over medium heat to 180° or until tiny bubbles form around edge (do not boil). Remove from heat; let stand 1 hour. Discard cobs.
2. Return pan to medium heat; heat to 180°. Combine half-and-half and egg yolks in a medium bowl, stirring with a whisk. Gradually add half of hot milk mixture to egg mixture, stirring constantly with a whisk. Pour egg yolk mixture into pan with remaining milk mixture; cook over medium heat 2 minutes or until a thermometer registers 160°, stirring constantly. Pour mixture through a fine sieve over a bowl, pressing lightly with a wooden spoon; discard solids. Place bowl in a large ice-filled bowl. Cool completely, stirring occasionally. Pour mixture into

freezer can of an ice-cream freezer, and freeze according to manufacturer's instructions. Spoon ice cream into a freezer-safe container. Freeze 1 hour or until firm. Serves 8 (serving size: about ½ cup).

CALORIES 237; FAT 9.2g (sat 4.6g, mono 2.2g, poly 0.9g); PROTEIN 7.4g; CARB 33.5g; FIBER 1.2g; CHOL 176mg; IRON 0.6mg; SODIUM 137mg; CALC 156mg

Quick & Easy • Make Ahead

Corn Chowchow

Hands-on time: 11 min. Total time: 28 min. Make a milder relish by seeding the jalapeño.

1 cup champagne or white wine
   vinegar
½ cup sugar
½ cup water
½ teaspoon kosher salt
¼ teaspoon black peppercorns,
   crushed
1 bay leaf
1½ cups fresh corn kernels (about
   2 ears)
1 cup diced red bell pepper
½ cup diced green tomato
½ cup diced tomatillo
3 tablespoons minced shallots
2 tablespoons minced jalapeño
   pepper

1. Place first 6 ingredients in a medium saucepan; bring to a boil. Add corn and remaining ingredients; simmer 15 minutes. Remove and discard bay leaf. Serve chowchow chilled or at room temperature. Serves 6 (serving size: ½ cup).

CALORIES 117; FAT 0.7g (sat 0.1g, mono 0.2g, poly 0.3g); PROTEIN 1.9g; CARB 28.1g; FIBER 2g; CHOL 0mg; IRON 0.6mg; SODIUM 169mg; CALC 8mg

---

A BUYER'S GUIDE TO FRESH CORN

There's no real flavor difference between white and yellow corn—the carotene that colors the kernels is tasteless. Much of the corn you'll find in grocery stores or farmers' markets is bred to be supersweet (in fact, too sweet for some folks, who miss the balancing starch and full corn flavor that's been lost in the process). On the plus side, fresh corn now stays sweet longer after harvesting, so you don't need to race from market to pot before it turns bland and completely starchy. But as always, freshness counts. Here are some pointers:

1. Look for green, moist husks that cling tightly to the corn.

2. Silks should be moist and golden, and not too dark.

3. Peel the husk slightly, and check the top two rows of kernels for plumpness and density.

4. Don't shuck until you're ready to use; eat within two days of purchasing.

WHAT TO COOK RIGHT NOW

AMERICAN LOBSTER

Quick & Easy

Grilled Lobster Tail with Confetti Relish

Hands-on time: 10 min. Total time: 20 min.

¼ cup thinly sliced green onions
2 tablespoons finely chopped shallots
2 tablespoons diced yellow bell pepper
2 tablespoons diced orange bell pepper
2 tablespoons diced red bell pepper
¼ teaspoon freshly ground black
   pepper
⅛ teaspoon salt
⅛ teaspoon sugar
1 teaspoon red wine vinegar
1 teaspoon olive oil
2 tablespoons butter, softened
1 teaspoon chopped fresh thyme
2 small garlic cloves, minced
4 (6-ounce) lobster tails in shells
Cooking spray
4 cups watercress, trimmed

1. Preheat grill to medium-high heat.
2. Combine first 5 ingredients; sprinkle with black pepper, salt, and sugar. Drizzle vinegar and oil over bell pepper mixture, and toss.
3. Combine butter, thyme, and garlic, stirring until well blended. Arrange lobster tails, back sides up, on a cutting board. Carefully cut shells lengthwise, cutting to, but not through, the middle of the meat. Open halves. Arrange tails, cut sides down, on a grill rack coated with cooking spray. Grill 2 minutes. Turn tails over; divide butter mixture evenly among lobster tails, spreading evenly over flesh. Grill 2 minutes or until desired degree of doneness.
4. Arrange 1 cup watercress on each of 4 plates; top each serving with 1 lobster tail and about 2 tablespoons relish. Serves 4.

CALORIES 206; FAT 8.3g (sat 4.1g, mono 2.7g, poly 0.6g); PROTEIN 27.9g; CARB 4.1g; FIBER 0.8g; CHOL 150mg; IRON 0.8mg; SODIUM 552mg; CALC 122mg

LOBSTER CAN BE MESSY BUSINESS. TRY THE TAILS FOR A MEAL THAT'S LESS SPLATTERY.

TODAY'S LESSON: GRANITA

Like a grown-up snow cone, granita hits the spot on a hot summer day. The basic formula starts with a syrupy base that's frozen and scraped until fluffy. And that's the beautiful thing about a granita—anyone can make it, no ice-cream maker needed. Rev up the flavor with booze, herbs, or spices, as we've done here. Sangria goes frosty and sweet, mint refreshes cukes, and ground chile warms up mango.

Freezable • Make Ahead

Sangria Ice

Hands-on time: 30 min. Total time: 5 hr. 30 min.

1 cup 100% Concord grape juice
¼ cup sugar
2 teaspoons finely grated orange rind
1 teaspoon finely grated lemon rind
1¾ cups fruity red wine

1. Combine juice and sugar in a small saucepan over medium-high heat; bring to a boil. Cook 1 minute, stirring until sugar dissolves. Remove from heat. Stir in rinds; cool completely. Strain mixture through a fine sieve into a bowl; discard solids. Stir in wine. Pour into an 11 x 7–inch baking dish. Cover and freeze for about 45 minutes; scrape with a fork. Freeze. Scrape mixture every 45 minutes until completely frozen (about 5 hours). Remove mixture from freezer; scrape mixture with a fork until fluffy. Serves 6 (serving size: about ½ cup).

CALORIES 117; **FAT** 0.1g (sat 0g, mono 0g, poly 0.1g); **PROTEIN** 0.2g; **CARB** 16.6g; **FIBER** 0.2g; **CHOL** 0mg; **IRON** 0.4mg; **SODIUM** 5mg; **CALC** 12mg

---

Freezable • Make Ahead

Cucumber-Lime Granita

Hands-on time: 30 min. Total time: 3 hr. 30 min.

1 tablespoon grated lime rind
½ cup fresh lime juice
¾ cup sugar
1 cup water
¼ teaspoon salt
3 mint sprigs
1 pound chopped English cucumber

1. Combine first 5 ingredients in a small saucepan over medium heat; bring to a boil. Cook 1 minute; remove from heat. Add mint; let stand 10 minutes. Discard mint. Place juice mixture and cucumber in a blender; process until smooth. Cool completely. Pour mixture into an 11 x 7–inch baking dish. Cover and freeze 45 minutes; scrape with a fork. Freeze. Scrape mixture every 45 minutes until completely frozen (about 3 hours). Remove from freezer; scrape with a fork until fluffy. Serves 6 (serving size: about ½ cup).

CALORIES 112; **FAT** 0g; **PROTEIN** 1g; **CARB** 28.9g; **FIBER** 1.1g; **CHOL** 0mg; **IRON** 0mg; **SODIUM** 99mg; **CALC** 5mg

---

Freezable • Make Ahead

Spicy Mango Granita

Hands-on time: 20 min. Total time: 6 hr. 20 min. Garnish with additional red pepper for more kick.

4 cups cubed peeled ripe mango
6 tablespoons sugar
¼ cup fresh orange juice
3 tablespoons fresh lime juice
⅜ teaspoon ground red pepper
Dash of salt

1. Combine all ingredients in a small saucepan; bring to a boil. Reduce heat, and simmer 10 minutes. Remove from heat; let stand 10 minutes. Pour mixture into a blender; process until smooth. Strain through a sieve over a bowl, and discard solids. Pour into an 11 x 7–inch baking dish; cool. Cover and freeze 45 minutes; scrape with a fork. Freeze. Scrape every 45 minutes until completely frozen (about 6 hours). Remove from freezer; scrape with a fork until fluffy. Serves 6 (serving size: about ½ cup).

CALORIES 127; **FAT** 0.3g (sat 0.1g, mono 0.1g, poly 0.1g); **PROTEIN** 0.7g; **CARB** 33.1g; **FIBER** 2.1g; **CHOL** 0mg; **IRON** 0.2mg; **SODIUM** 2mg; **CALC** 13mg

---

TRY THESE SWEET-TART TREATS TO COOL DOWN AFTER A HOT SUMMER DAY.

GLOBAL PANTRY

MORE WAYS WITH MISO

By Naomi Duguid

This thick, fermented soybean paste adds worlds of savory depth to soups, stir-fries, and more.

Most people in North America first encounter miso as a flavoring for soup broth in Japanese restaurants, a starter before the sushi. Miso hails from Japan and, like soy sauce, is a fermented food that adds salty depth of flavor to savory dishes. There are a few versions, all made from soybeans, possibly with rice or barley. The mildest and sweetest, shiro miso, is white to pale yellow in color and is made from rice and soybeans. There are many misos in the middle range, mild to strong, all medium-brown. In Japan this category is known as "red miso" because when used as a marinade it gives an attractive reddish-brown tint to the food. Finally, the darkest miso, brown in color, with a strong, smoky flavor, is known as hatcho miso.

I like to use mild or medium (white or "red") miso to flavor vegetables before grilling them, a good summer use. But miso is also wonderful if I have a soup, a chicken broth, say, that lacks oomph. It gives a satisfying depth, the flavor that we know by the Japanese word "umami." (Umami is often described as a meaty flavor, like that of cooked mushrooms or ripe tomatoes, meat broth or grilled meat.)

Start experimenting by stirring a tablespoon of miso into a little warm water and adding it to a soup or stew as it's cooking. Or add the miso-water mixture to a vegetable stir-fry a minute or two before it's done. Taste after you add it. If you want to add a little more, do so, again dissolving it in water before stirring it in. You'll notice that it gives more substantial flavor; it also adds saltiness, so season the soup or stew or stir-fry only after you've added the miso.

Quick & Easy • Vegetarian

Miso Grilled Vegetables

Hands-on time: 25 min. Total time: 25 min.

The vegetable amounts suggested below are just a guideline; double or triple for a crowd. The important thing to remember is the proportion in the marinade: 1 to 2 tablespoons miso and 1 tablespoon water to about 3 tablespoons olive oil works well.

2 tablespoons red or white/yellow miso (soybean paste)
1 tablespoon lukewarm water
3 tablespoons olive oil
1 pound zucchini, cut lengthwise into ⅓-inch-thick slices
8 ounces Japanese eggplant, cut lengthwise into ⅓-inch-thick slices
1 red bell pepper, cut into 6 pieces
1 orange bell pepper, cut into 6 pieces
1 small red onion, cut into wedges
Cooking spray
2 tablespoons mint leaves
1 lime, cut into wedges

1. Preheat grill to high heat.
2. Combine miso and 1 tablespoon water. Gradually add oil, stirring with a whisk. Place zucchini, eggplant, and bell peppers on a jelly-roll pan. Add 5 tablespoons miso mixture; toss to coat. Brush onion with remaining miso mixture.
3. Place vegetables on a grill rack coated with cooking spray. Grill zucchini, eggplant, and bell pepper 4 minutes on each side or until tender. Grill onion 6 minutes on each side or until tender. Sprinkle with mint. Serve with lime wedges. Serves 6 (serving size: about 3 zucchini pieces, 2 eggplant pieces, 2 bell pepper pieces, and 1 onion wedge).

CALORIES 112; **FAT** 7.1g (sat 1g, mono 4.9g, poly 0.8g); **PROTEIN** 1.8g; **CARB** 11.4g; **FIBER** 4.5g; **CHOL** 0mg; **IRON** 0.6mg; **SODIUM** 221mg; **CALC** 22mg

LIGHTER, BRIGHTER LEMON SQUARES

Creamy, zippy citrus meets nutty cookie goodness.

Refreshingly tangy and buttery-crisp...somehow the puckery citrus makes a good lemon square seem lighter than it really is. Typical recipes call for a full cup of butter and 1½ *pounds* of sugar—adding up to more than 300 calories in one little square.

Lightening was tricky because we didn't want to compromise the two great textures: the creamy filling and the buttery, crumbly crust. For the latter, we kept a touch of butter for rich flavor but traded out the rest for canola oil and toasted pine nuts, whose healthy nut oils help compensate for less saturated fat. The resulting crust was even better than we expected—buttery, crumbly, and irresistibly short.

For the filling, we added just enough sugar to satisfy any sweet tooth while allowing lots of zesty, bright citrus to shine. A couple of eggs and an egg white kept the creaminess we wanted without needless fat.

Mission accomplished: a healthier, lighter lemon square that retains the flavor and soul of the original.

CLASSIC	MAKEOVER
319 calories per square	124 calories per square
11 grams total fat	5 grams total fat
6.3 grams saturated fat	1.3 grams saturated fat

TENDER, SHORT COOKIE CRUST MEETS A DELECTABLY BOLD, TART LEMON FILLING IN THESE LUSCIOUS TREATS.

Kid Friendly • Make Ahead

Lemon Squares

Hands-on time: 15 min. Total time: 3 hr.

3.4 ounces all-purpose flour (about ³/₄ cup)
¼ cup powdered sugar
3 tablespoons pine nuts, toasted and coarsely chopped
¹/₈ teaspoon salt
2 tablespoons chilled unsalted butter, cut into small pieces
2 tablespoons canola oil
Cooking spray
³/₄ cup granulated sugar
2 tablespoons all-purpose flour
1 teaspoon grated lemon rind
¹/₂ cup fresh lemon juice
2 large eggs
1 large egg white
2 tablespoons powdered sugar

1. Preheat oven to 350°.

2. Weigh or lightly spoon flour into dry measuring cups; level with a knife. Place flour, ¼ cup powdered sugar, pine nuts, and salt in a food processor; pulse 2 times to combine. Add butter and canola oil. Pulse 3 to 5 times or until mixture resembles coarse meal. Place mixture into the bottom of an 8-inch square glass or ceramic baking dish coated with cooking spray; press into bottom of pan. Bake at 350° for 20 minutes or until lightly browned. Reduce oven temperature to 325°.
3. Combine granulated sugar and next 5 ingredients in a medium bowl, stirring with a whisk until smooth. Pour mixture over crust. Bake at 325° for 20 minutes or until set. Remove from oven, and cool completely in pan on a wire rack. Cover and chill for at least 2 hours. Sprinkle squares evenly with 2 tablespoons powdered sugar. Serves 16 (serving size: 1 square).

CALORIES 124; FAT 5g (sat 1.3g, mono 2g, poly 1.2g); PROTEIN 2g; CARB 18.5g; FIBER 0.3g; CHOL 30mg; IRON 0.5mg; SODIUM 31mg; CALC 6mg

FOR A LIGHTER LEMON BAR

BUTTER/CANOLA OIL COMBO
We sub heart-healthy canola oil for some of the butter to save 5 grams of saturated fat per serving.

LESS SUGAR
We reduce the sugar by two-thirds and cut another 95 calories per serving.

PINE NUTS
Toasted pine nuts impart a delightful roasted flavor and irresistible crunch to our shortbread crust. Expensive, but we don't use a lot. Buy them in bulk, and keep them stored in your freezer.

BEEFSTEAKS AND EGGS

Sometimes the best "steak" comes in the form of ripe, juicy tomato slices, as in this easy gratin and a simple fried-egg-and-tomato sandwich.

Vegetarian

Tomato, Squash, and Red Pepper Gratin

Hands-on time: 30 min. Total time: 1 hr. 12 min. *Serve with a salad of fresh summer greens.*

5 teaspoons olive oil, divided
2 cups chopped red onion
1½ cups chopped red bell pepper
1 pound yellow squash, cut into ¼-inch thick slices (about 3½ cups)
1 tablespoon minced garlic
½ cup cooked quinoa
½ cup thinly sliced fresh basil, divided
1½ teaspoons chopped fresh thyme
¾ teaspoon salt, divided
½ teaspoon freshly ground black pepper
½ cup 2% reduced-fat milk
3 ounces aged Gruyère cheese, shredded (about ¾ cup)
3 large eggs, lightly beaten
Cooking spray
1½ ounces French bread baguette, torn
1 (12-ounce) beefsteak tomato, seeded and cut into 8 slices

1. Preheat oven to 375°.
2. Heat a large nonstick skillet over medium heat. Add 4 teaspoons oil to pan; swirl to coat. Add onion; cook 3 minutes. Add bell pepper; cook 2 minutes. Add squash and garlic; cook 4 minutes. Place vegetable mixture in a large bowl. Stir in quinoa, ¼ cup basil, thyme, ½ teaspoon salt, and black pepper.
3. Combine remaining ¼ teaspoon salt, milk, cheese, and eggs in a medium bowl, stirring with a whisk. Add milk mixture to vegetable mixture, stirring until just combined. Spoon mixture into an 11 x 7–inch glass or ceramic baking dish coated with cooking spray.
4. Place bread in a food processor; pulse until coarse crumbs form. Return skillet to medium-high heat. Add remaining 1 teaspoon oil to pan; swirl to coat. Add breadcrumbs; cook 3 minutes or until toasted. Arrange tomatoes evenly over vegetable mixture. Top evenly with breadcrumbs. Bake at 375° for 40 minutes or until topping is browned. Sprinkle with remaining ¼ cup basil. Serves 6.

CALORIES 235; **FAT** 12.1g (sat 4.4g, mono 5.3g, poly 1.2g); **PROTEIN** 12.2g; **CARB** 21.2g; **FIBER** 3.9g; **CHOL** 123mg; **IRON** 1.9mg; **SODIUM** 443mg; **CALC** 229mg

STAY FULL LONGER! QUINOA HAS DOUBLE THE PROTEIN AND FIBER OF RICE.

SEEDING TOMATOES

1. Slice the tomato in half using a very sharp knife (a dull one will crush the fruit).

2. Gently squeeze the halves over a bowl; the seeds should slip right out.

3. Slice, chop, or wedge the tomato as the recipe instructs.

Open-Faced Sandwiches with Mushrooms and Fried Eggs

Hands-on time: 25 min. Total time: 25 min.

4 teaspoons extra-virgin olive oil, divided

1 cup thinly sliced shallots, divided

1 (8-ounce) package presliced cremini mushrooms

2 tablespoons dry white wine

½ teaspoon freshly ground black pepper, divided

¼ teaspoon kosher salt

8 teaspoons refrigerated pesto

4 (1½-ounce) slices multigrain bread

2 ounces grated fresh Parmigiano-Reggiano cheese (about ½ cup)

4 large eggs

8 (¼-inch-thick) slices beefsteak tomato

3 tablespoons chopped fresh basil

1. Heat a large nonstick skillet over medium heat. Add 2 teaspoons oil to pan; swirl to coat. Add ⅔ cup shallots; cook 3 minutes. Add mushrooms; cook 4 minutes or until tender, stirring occasionally. Add wine, ¼ teaspoon pepper, and salt; bring to a boil, scraping pan to loosen browned bits. Cook 2 minutes or until liquid almost evaporates, stirring occasionally. Remove mushroom mixture from pan; keep warm.

2. Return pan to medium heat. Add 1 teaspoon oil to pan; swirl to coat. Add remaining ⅓ cup shallots; sauté 5 minutes or until lightly browned. Remove shallots from pan; keep warm.

3. Preheat broiler to high.

4. Spread 2 teaspoons pesto over one side of each bread slice. Top each slice with about 2 tablespoons cheese. Broil 2 minutes or until cheese melts; keep warm.

5. Return pan to medium heat. Add remaining 1 teaspoon oil to pan; swirl to coat. Crack eggs into pan, and cook 4 minutes or until whites are set.

6. Top each bread slice with 2 tomato slices. Divide mushroom mixture evenly among bread slices, and top each serving with 1 egg. Sprinkle with remaining ¼ teaspoon pepper, shallots, and basil. Serves 4 (serving size: 1 sandwich).

CALORIES 378; FAT 19.2g (sat 5.2g, mono 9.2g, poly 2.6g); PROTEIN 20.4g; CARB 31.6g; FIBER 4.9g; CHOL 198mg; IRON 3.5mg; SODIUM 623mg; CALC 234mg

KID-FRIENDLY COOKING

MATISSE GETS A LITTLE FANCY

Our kid in the kitchen goes all cordon bleu on us—to accolades.

To put a kid-friendly recipe to the test, we contacted Matisse Reid, an 11-year-old foodie who loves tinkering around in the kitchen. This month, she whipped up Chicken Cordon Bleu for her brother and sister. Here's her report.
—Phoebe Wu

"This recipe surprised me because I thought it would take a lot of preparation to make, but it was really quick. Rolling up the flattened chicken with the filling might be hard for some children, especially when you're supposed to hold the rolls together with toothpicks. I used a product called The Food Loop to tie the chicken up, but kitchen twine would have been a good substitute. Tying the chicken made the whole job so much easier, and the rolls kept their shape after they were cooked. I was also surprised that the recipe put cheese in the breading—I would have liked more cheese in the middle instead. But the pancetta gave it a nice smoky flavor, and the breadcrumbs were really light and didn't weigh the dish down at all."

Kid Friendly Chicken Cordon Bleu

Hands-on time: 16 min. Total time: 48 min.

4 (6-ounce) skinless, boneless chicken breast halves

½ teaspoon freshly ground black pepper

¼ teaspoon salt

¾ cup panko (Japanese breadcrumbs)

½ cup all-purpose flour

1 tablespoon water

1 large egg

2.5 ounces shredded Gruyère cheese (about 10 tablespoons), divided

1 tablespoon chopped fresh thyme

2 garlic cloves, minced

4 slices pancetta (about 1¼ ounces)

Cooking spray

1. Preheat oven to 350°.

2. Place chicken between 2 sheets of plastic wrap; pound to ¼-inch thickness. Sprinkle chicken evenly with pepper and salt.

3. Heat a skillet over medium heat. Add panko; cook 2 minutes or until toasted, stirring often. Remove from heat. Place flour in a dish. Combine 1 tablespoon water and egg in a bowl; lightly beat. Pour egg mixture into a

DON'T FORGET TO SEASON THE CHICKEN BEFORE FILLING IT.

YOUNGER CHILDREN WILL ENJOY POUNDING THE CHICKEN.

dish. Combine panko, 2 tablespoons cheese, thyme, and garlic in a dish.
4. Working with 1 piece of chicken at a time, dredge in flour. Dip in egg mixture; dredge in panko mixture. Top with 1 pancetta slice and 2 tablespoons cheese. Roll up; secure with a toothpick. Place roll, seam side down, on a wire rack coated with cooking spray. Place rack on a baking sheet. Repeat procedure with remaining ingredients. Bake at 350° for 25 minutes or until chicken is done. Serves 4 (serving size: 1 chicken roll).

CALORIES 414; **FAT** 12.4g (sat 5.5g, mono 2.8g, poly 1g); **PROTEIN** 50.7g; **CARB** 20.6g; **FIBER** 1g; **CHOL** 169mg; **IRON** 2.4mg; **SODIUM** 513mg; **CALC** 213mg

THE VERDICT

KALANI (AGE 14):
Like me, he wanted a bit more cheese, but he said it was really good, which is good coming from him!
7/10

RACHEL (AGE 20):
She really liked the light and super-crunchy breading.
8/10

MATISSE:
The chicken was beautifully tender, and overall, it was very good.
9/10

BUDGET COOKING

FEED 4 FOR LESS THAN $10

You can fit premium-priced ingredients into a budget meal if you use them the right way: Parm on pasta, claw meat in crab cakes.

Quick & Easy • Vegetarian

Fettuccine with Tomato-Cream Sauce

$1.87/serving, $7.47 total

Hands-on time: 25 min. Total time: 25 min.

8 ounces uncooked fettuccine
4 quarts boiling water
1/2 teaspoon kosher salt, divided
1 tablespoon olive oil
3 tablespoons coarsely chopped garlic
1 (28-ounce) can whole peeled tomatoes, drained and crushed
3 ounces 1/3-less-fat cream cheese
1/4 cup oil-cured olives, pitted and coarsely chopped
1/4 teaspoon crushed red pepper
1/4 cup small basil leaves
1/2 ounce fresh Parmigiano-Reggiano cheese, shaved

1. Cook pasta in 4 quarts boiling water with ¼ teaspoon salt 8 minutes or until noodles are almost al dente. Drain pasta through a sieve over a bowl; reserve 1⅓ cups pasta cooking water.
2. Heat a large skillet over medium-low heat. Add oil to pan; swirl to coat. Add garlic; cook 2 minutes or until very fragrant and tender, stirring occasionally. Stir in remaining ¼ teaspoon salt and tomatoes; cook 3 minutes, stirring occasionally. Stir in reserved 1⅓ cups pasta water; bring to a boil. Add cream cheese; stir until smooth. Add pasta, olives, and red

pepper; cook 3 minutes or until pasta is al dente, tossing to coat. Divide pasta mixture among 4 shallow bowls; top each serving with 1 tablespoon basil. Divide Parmigiano-Reggiano evenly among servings. Serves 4 (serving size: 1¼ cups).

CALORIES 383; **FAT** 14.2g (sat 4.5g, mono 7.1g, poly 1.2g); **PROTEIN** 12.9g; **CARB** 52.7g; **FIBER** 3.6g; **CHOL** 18.9mg; **IRON** 3.6mg; **SODIUM** 533mg; **CALC** 142mg

Kid Friendly • Make Ahead

Corn and Crab Cakes

$2.49/serving, $9.97 total

Hands-on time: 40 min. Total time: 1 hr.
Toss 3 cups arugula and 1 cup parsley leaves with fresh lemon juice for a side salad.

Cakes:
1/2 cup fresh yellow corn kernels
1/4 cup chopped red bell pepper
3 tablespoons chopped green onions
3 tablespoons canola mayonnaise
1 teaspoon Dijon mustard
3/4 teaspoon Old Bay seasoning
8 ounces crab claw meat, shell pieces removed
1 large egg, lightly beaten
1 1/2 cups panko (Japanese breadcrumbs), divided
Cooking spray
1 1/2 tablespoons butter, divided
Sauce:
2 tablespoons chopped fresh parsley
1 tablespoon chopped green onions
3 tablespoons canola mayonnaise
2 teaspoons fresh lemon juice
Dash of kosher salt
1 drop hot pepper sauce

1. To prepare cakes, combine first 8 ingredients in a large bowl, stirring until well blended. Stir in ¾ cup panko. Divide mixture into 8 equal portions; shape each into a 1-inch-thick patty. Arrange patties in a single layer on a small baking sheet. Place patties in freezer 20 minutes or until firm.

continued

2. Heat a large skillet over medium-high heat. Coat pan with cooking spray. Add remaining ¾ cup panko to pan; coat panko lightly with cooking spray. Cook 2 minutes or until toasted, stirring frequently. Place toasted panko in a shallow dish; dredge crab cakes in toasted crumbs. Wipe pan clean with paper towels.

3. Melt 2¼ teaspoons butter in a large nonstick skillet over medium-high heat; swirl to coat. Coat both sides of 4 cakes with cooking spray. Add coated cakes to pan; cook 4 minutes on each side or until golden brown. Remove from pan, and keep warm. Repeat procedure with remaining butter, cooking spray, and crab cakes.

4. To prepare sauce, combine parsley and remaining ingredients in a small bowl, stirring well. Serve with cakes. Serves 4 (serving size: 2 cakes and about 1 tablespoon sauce).

CALORIES 279; **FAT** 13.9g (sat 3.3g, mono 5.5g, poly 2.9g); **PROTEIN** 15.6g; **CARB** 20.5g; **FIBER** 1.6g; **CHOL** 109mg; **IRON** 1mg; **SODIUM** 569mg; **CALC** 68mg

Kid Friendly

$2.49/serving, $9.97 total

Maple-Soy Chicken Thighs

Hands-on time: 10 min. Total time: 1 hr. 45 min.

- **¹/₂ cup maple syrup**
- **¹/₄ cup fresh orange juice**
- **2 tablespoons lower-sodium soy sauce**
- **1 tablespoon grated peeled fresh ginger**
- **1 teaspoon dark sesame oil**
- **¹/₂ teaspoon crushed red pepper**
- **2 garlic cloves, minced**
- **8 bone-in chicken thighs, skinned**
- **¹/₂ teaspoon salt**
- **2 tablespoons sliced green onions**

1. Combine first 7 ingredients in a small bowl, stirring with a whisk. Place maple mixture in a large zip-top plastic bag. Add chicken thighs to bag; seal. Marinate in refrigerator 1 hour.

2. Preheat oven to 375°.

3. Remove chicken from bag, reserving marinade. Place marinade in a small saucepan over medium-high heat; bring to a boil. Cook until marinade reduces to ¼ cup (about 5 minutes). Arrange chicken in a single layer on a foil-lined baking sheet. Baste with 2 tablespoons maple mixture; sprinkle evenly with salt. Bake chicken at 375° for 20 minutes. Turn chicken over; baste with remaining 2 tablespoons maple mixture. Bake 15 minutes or until chicken is done; sprinkle with onions. Serves 4 (serving size: 2 thighs).

CALORIES 349; **FAT** 12.6g (sat 3.3g, mono 4.8g, poly 3.1g); **PROTEIN** 27.7g; **CARB** 30.1g; **FIBER** 0.3g; **CHOL** 99mg; **IRON** 2mg; **SODIUM** 587mg; **CALC** 48mg

Citrus Couscous:

Rehydrate ½ cup couscous in water according to package directions, omitting salt and fat. Fluff with a fork. Add sections from 1 orange and ½ ounce toasted, sliced almonds. Sprinkle couscous mixture with ¼ teaspoon kosher salt and ¼ teaspoon freshly ground black pepper; toss. Serves 4 (serving size: about ½ cup).

CALORIES 131; **FAT** 2g (sat 0.2g); **SODIUM** 123mg

SUPER FAST

End-of-summer heat calls for simple, easy dishes, like quick-seared scallops, veggie-packed noodle bowls, and more.

Quick & Easy

Herbed Shrimp and White Bean Salad

- **4 teaspoons sherry vinegar**
- **4 teaspoons extra-virgin olive oil**
- **1 tablespoon chopped fresh thyme**
- **2 teaspoons minced fresh garlic**
- **1 teaspoon chopped fresh rosemary**
- **¹/₂ teaspoon black pepper**
- **2 cups loosely packed arugula**
- **1 cup trimmed watercress**
- **1 cup grape tomatoes, halved**
- **¹/₄ cup chopped fresh flat-leaf parsley**
- **1 (15.5-ounce) can Great Northern beans, rinsed and drained**
- **1 tablespoon honey**
- **1 teaspoon water**
- **24 peeled and deveined medium shrimp (about 1 pound)**
- **Cooking spray**
- **¹/₄ teaspoon salt**

1. Combine first 6 ingredients in a large bowl; stir with a whisk. Add arugula and next 4 ingredients to bowl, and toss gently to coat.

2. Combine honey and 1 teaspoon water in a bowl, stirring with a whisk. Add shrimp to honey mixture; toss to coat. Heat grill pan over medium-high heat; coat pan with cooking spray. Sprinkle shrimp with salt. Add shrimp to pan; cook 2 minutes on each side or until done. Serve with salad. Serves 4 (serving size: 6 shrimp and about 1 cup arugula mixture).

Sustainable Choice

Buy American shrimp farmed in fully recirculating systems or ponds.

CALORIES 276; **FAT** 6.7g (sat 1g, mono 3.6g, poly 1.3g); **PROTEIN** 30g; **CARB** 23.3g; **FIBER** 5.5g; **CHOL** 172mg; **IRON** 4.7mg; **SODIUM** 581mg; **CALC** 147mg

Quick & Easy

Sesame Chicken and Noodles in Mushroom Broth

4 shiitake mushrooms
1 cup fat-free, lower-sodium chicken broth
1 cup water
4 teaspoons lower-sodium soy sauce
2 teaspoons fish sauce
2 garlic cloves, crushed
1 (2-inch) piece fresh ginger, sliced
1 serrano chile, thinly sliced
1 quart water
2 cups uncooked fresh Chinese-style noodles
1 pound chicken cutlets
1/4 teaspoon freshly ground black pepper
1/3 cup toasted sesame seeds
2 teaspoons sesame oil
4 baby bok choy, cut in half lengthwise
1/2 cup (1/4-inch-thick) slices red bell pepper
1 lime, cut into 8 wedges

1. Remove mushroom stems. Thinly slice caps; set caps aside. Bring stems, broth, and next 6 ingredients to a boil in a saucepan. Remove pan from heat.
2. Bring 1 quart of water to a boil in a large saucepan. Add noodles; cook 3 minutes or until done. Drain.
3. Sprinkle chicken with black pepper. Place seeds in a dish. Press seeds into both sides of chicken. Heat a nonstick skillet over medium-high heat. Add oil; swirl to coat. Add chicken; cook 3 minutes on each side or until done. Remove from pan. Add bok choy, cut sides down; cook 3 minutes or until browned. Add reserved mushroom slices and bell pepper. Strain broth mixture through a sieve into pan; cover and cook 2 minutes. Remove vegetables with a slotted spoon.
4. Thinly slice chicken. Place 1/2 cup noodles, about 1/4 cup vegetables, and 4 ounces chicken into 4 shallow bowls. Spoon 1/4 cup broth mixture over each. Garnish each with 2 lime wedges. Serves 4.

CALORIES 338; **FAT** 9.2g (sat 1.5g, mono 3.2g, poly 3.6g); **PROTEIN** 34g; **CARB** 29.5g; **FIBER** 4.2g; **CHOL** 71mg; **IRON** 3.6mg; **SODIUM** 795mg; **CALC** 65mg

Quick & Easy

Seared Scallops with Haricots Verts

2 tablespoons finely chopped shallots
2 tablespoons chopped parsley
1 tablespoon fresh lemon juice
1 tablespoon dry white wine
1/2 teaspoon Dijon mustard
3/8 teaspoon freshly ground black pepper, divided
2 quarts water
12 ounces haricots verts, trimmed
1 1/2 tablespoons butter
2 tablespoons canola oil
1 1/2 pounds sea scallops (about 16)
1/4 teaspoon kosher salt

1. Combine first 5 ingredients in a bowl. Stir in 1/8 teaspoon pepper.
2. Bring 2 quarts water to a boil. Add beans; cook 3 minutes. Drain. Melt butter in a nonstick skillet over medium heat; cook 3 minutes. Add shallot mixture and beans; cook 1 minute. Remove from heat.
3. Heat a large skillet over high heat. Add oil. Pat scallops dry; sprinkle with salt and remaining 1/4 teaspoon pepper. Add scallops to pan; cook 2 minutes on each side or until done. Serve with beans. Serves 4 (serving size: 4 scallops and 3/4 cup beans).

Sustainable Choice *Look for diver-caught sea scallops from Mexico for the most sustainable choice.*

CALORIES 284; **FAT** 12.7g (sat 3.4g, mono 5.6g, poly 2.6g); **PROTEIN** 30.4g; **CARB** 11.7g; **FIBER** 3g; **CHOL** 68mg; **IRON** 1.6mg; **SODIUM** 446mg; **CALC** 79mg

Quick & Easy

Crisp Lamb Lettuce Wraps

Lettuce leaves offer a light, fresh alternative to pita or flatbread. If you can't find red pepper hummus, plain hummus is a welcome substitute.

2 teaspoons canola oil
1 cup finely chopped onion
2 teaspoons minced fresh garlic
1 teaspoon ground cinnamon
3/4 teaspoon kosher salt
1/4 teaspoon freshly ground black pepper
6 ounces lean ground lamb
1/2 cup chopped fresh parsley
1/2 cup chopped tomato
1/2 cup chopped cucumber
1/4 cup plain fat-free Greek yogurt
1/4 cup red pepper hummus (such as Tribe)
8 Boston lettuce leaves
2 tablespoons torn mint leaves
1 tablespoon pine nuts, toasted

1. Heat a large skillet over high heat. Add oil to pan; swirl to coat. Add onion and next 5 ingredients to pan; sauté 5 minutes or until lamb is done. Combine parsley, tomato, and cucumber in a medium bowl. Stir in lamb mixture. Combine yogurt and hummus in a small bowl. Place about 1/4 cup lamb mixture in each lettuce leaf. Top each wrap with 1 tablespoon hummus mixture. Divide mint and pine nuts evenly among wraps. Serves 4 (serving size: 2 wraps).

CALORIES 158; **FAT** 8g (sat 1.2g, mono 3g, poly 1.6g); **PROTEIN** 11.4g; **CARB** 11.3g; **FIBER** 3g; **CHOL** 24mg; **IRON** 2mg; **SODIUM** 488mg; **CALC** 68mg

Kid Friendly • Quick & Easy

Baked Egg-in-a-Hole

These bacon-and-egg toasts make for a fun breakfast or easy dinner.

1 bacon slice
4 (1-ounce) slices multigrain bread, lightly toasted
4 large eggs
4 teaspoons grated fresh pecorino Romano cheese (about 1/4 ounce)
1 teaspoon chopped fresh sage
1/4 teaspoon freshly ground black pepper

1. Position an oven rack in the middle setting. Place a jelly-roll pan on rack. Preheat oven to 400°.
2. Place bacon on heated pan, and cook until crisp (about 4 minutes); crumble. Cut a hole into the center of each toast using a 3-inch biscuit cutter or round cookie cutter. Reserve cutouts.
3. Arrange bread slices on hot pan; crack 1 egg into each hole. Sprinkle eggs evenly with crumbled bacon, cheese, and sage. Bake at 400° for 5 minutes or until egg whites are set. Sprinkle with pepper, and serve with toast cutout. Serves 4 (serving size: 1 egg toast).

CALORIES 167; **FAT** 7.7g (sat 2.5g, mono 2.6g, poly 1.3g); **PROTEIN** 11.3g; **CARB** 12.8g; **FIBER** 2.1g; **CHOL** 216mg; **IRON** 1.7mg; **SODIUM** 273mg; **CALC** 73mg

Quick & Easy • Make Ahead Vegetarian

Lemony Kale Salad

1 tablespoon fresh lemon juice
1 tablespoon olive oil
1/2 teaspoon sugar
1/2 teaspoon freshly ground black pepper
1/4 teaspoon kosher salt
4 cups torn kale leaves

2 cups torn Swiss chard leaves
4 teaspoons unsalted pumpkinseed kernels
1/4 cup sliced green onions (about 2)
1 ounce shaved fresh pecorino Romano

1. Combine first 5 ingredients, stirring until sugar dissolves. Add kale and chard; toss. Let stand 10 minutes.
2. Heat a skillet over medium heat. Add kernels; cook 5 minutes or until brown, stirring frequently. Add kernels, onions, and cheese to greens; toss. Serves 6 (serving size: 1 cup).

CALORIES 65; **FAT** 4g (sat 0.8g, mono 2g, poly 0.8g); **PROTEIN** 2.6g; **CARB** 6.3g; **FIBER** 1.4g; **CHOL** 2mg; **IRON** 1.4mg; **SODIUM** 234mg; **CALC** 87mg

Kid Friendly • Quick & Easy Make Ahead

Cinnamon Crisps with Blackberries and Yogurt

This recipe is just as tasty with fresh blueberries or strawberries. If you can't find wonton wrappers, egg roll wrappers work equally well—just cut them into 3 1/2-inch squares.

8 wonton wrappers, cut in half diagonally
Cooking spray
1 tablespoon sugar
1/4 teaspoon ground cinnamon
1 1/2 cups plain fat-free Greek yogurt
1 cup blackberries
4 teaspoons honey

1. Preheat oven to 400°.
2. Arrange wonton wrappers in a single layer on a baking sheet coated with cooking spray; lightly coat wrappers with cooking spray. Combine sugar and cinnamon in a small bowl. Sprinkle sugar mixture evenly over wrappers; bake at 400° for 3 minutes or until crisp and slightly browned. Set wrappers aside to cool slightly.

3. Layer 6 tablespoons yogurt, 1/4 cup berries, and 1 teaspoon honey into each of 4 bowls. Serve each with 4 wonton crisps. Serves 4.

CALORIES 142; **FAT** 0.6g (sat 0.1g, mono 0.1g, poly 0.2g); **PROTEIN** 9.6g; **CARB** 25.1g; **FIBER** 2.2g; **CHOL** 1mg; **IRON** 0.8mg; **SODIUM** 124mg; **CALC** 76mg

---

FOUR FAST KALE SALADS

1. SPICY SOY

Combine 1 tablespoon rice vinegar, 1 tablespoon lower-sodium soy sauce, 2 teaspoons dark sesame oil, 1/2 teaspoon brown sugar, and 1/4 teaspoon chili garlic sauce in a bowl. Add 4 cups torn kale, 2 cups torn Savoy cabbage leaves, 1 cup shredded carrot, 1 cup sliced red bell pepper, 1/2 cup sliced radish, and 1/4 cup chopped cilantro; toss. Let stand 8 minutes. Serves 6 (serving size: 1 cup).

CALORIES 60; **FAT** 2g (sat 0.3g); **SODIUM** 136mg

2. GREEK-STYLE

Combine 1 tablespoon lemon juice, 1 tablespoon olive oil, 1/2 teaspoon sugar, and 1/2 teaspoon freshly ground black pepper in a bowl, stirring until sugar dissolves. Add 4 cups torn kale and 2 cups torn Swiss chard; toss. Let stand 10 minutes. Add 1 cup chopped English cucumber, 1 ounce crumbled feta cheese, 1/4 cup sliced green onions, and 10 kalamata olives, pitted and quartered. Toss. Serves 6 (serving size: 1 cup).

CALORIES 79; **FAT** 5.3g (sat 1.3g); **SODIUM** 200mg

3. APPLE-WALNUT

Combine 1 tablespoon cider vinegar, 1 tablespoon walnut oil, 1/2 teaspoon kosher salt, 1/2 teaspoon brown sugar, and 1/2 teaspoon freshly ground black pepper. Add 4 cups torn kale and 2 cups torn Swiss chard; toss. Let stand 10 minutes. Add 1 cup sliced Granny Smith apple, 1/2 cup sliced celery, 1/4 cup sliced red onion, 1 ounce crumbled blue cheese, and 2 tablespoons toasted walnuts; toss. Serves 6 (serving size: 1 cup).

CALORIES 94; **FAT** 5.6g (sat 1.3g); **SODIUM** 278mg

Double Plum Baked Chicken,
page 21

Shrimp with Lemon-Saffron Rice, *page 45*

Beef Tenderloin Steaks and Balsamic Green Beans, *page 44*

Cheesy Potato Soup, *page 43*

Chicken Soup with Cabbage and Apple, *page 30*

Pan-Seared Halibut with Bell Pepper Relish, *page 45*

All-American Meat Loaf, *page 60*

Tex-Mex Hash Brown
Casserole, *page 57*

213

**Chicken and Prosciutto Salad with
Arugula and Asiago,** *page 101*

Grilled Sirloin with Anchovy-Lemon Butter and Broccoli Rabe, *page 74*

Pobalano-Jalapeño Chili, *page 64*

Garlicky Meatball Pasta, *page 91*

Creamy Spring Pasta, *page 78*

Salmon with Spinach Salad and Miso Vinaigrette, *page 129*

Reuben Sandwiches, *page 111*

Lemony Snap Peas, *page 129*

Shrimp Fried Rice, *page 114*

Chicken Piccata,
page 20

**Melon and Fig Salad
with Prosciutto and
Balsamic Drizzle,** *page 138*

Champagne Mango Margaritas, *page 132*

Lemon–Earl Grey Squares, *page 141*

Double-Cherry Upside-Down Cake,
page 176

Wild Rice and Carrots, *page 182*

Pork and Tomato Skillet Sauté, *page 181*

Open-Faced Pimiento Cheese BLTs,
page 184

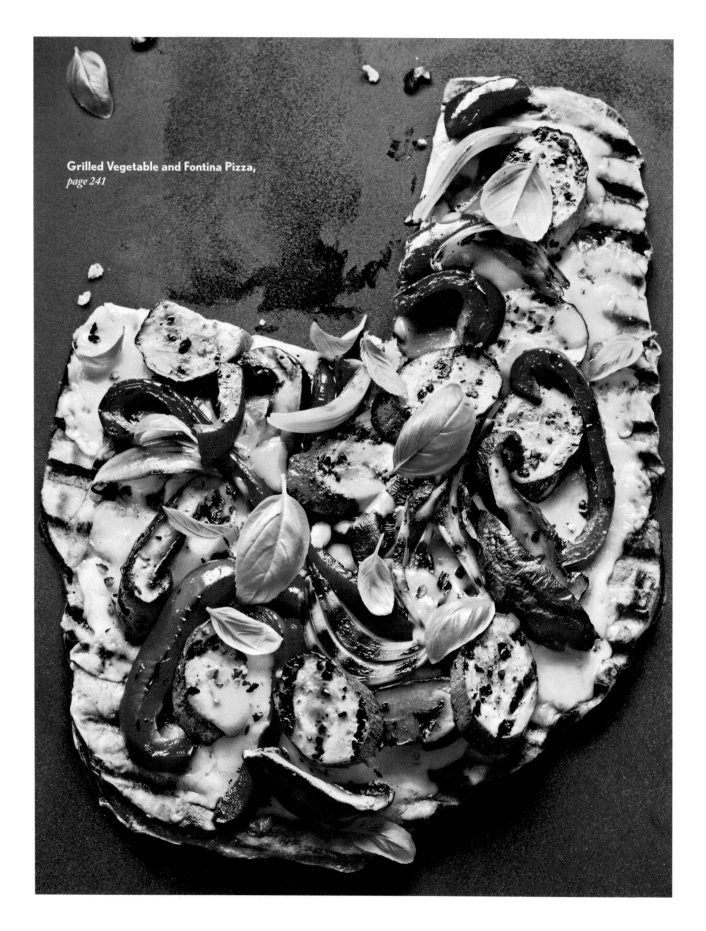

Grilled Vegetable and Fontina Pizza,
page 241

Grilled Skirt Steak and Roasted Tomatillo Sauce, *page 194*

Sweet and Spicy Shrimp with Rice Noodles, *page 194*

Barbecue Salmon and Snap Pea slaw, *page 194*

Stone Fruit Chicken-Rice Salad, *page 195*

Oaxacan-Style Grilled Corn on the Cob, *page 198*

Tomato Stack Salad
with Corn and Avocado,
page 192

**Pasta with Roasted Tomatoes
and Garlic,** *page 189*

Sweet-Spicy Chicken and Vegetable Stir-fry, *page 269*

Sichuan Beef Soup, *page 250*

Mu Shu Pork Wraps, *page 267*

Garbure (French Ham and Vegetable Stew), *page 251*

Kung Pao
Chicken Tacos,
page 272

232

Chicken and Vegetable Soup,
page 286

Carrot Salad with a Hit of Heat,
page 282

234

Sausage and Apple Stuffing, *page 295*

Green Beans with Caramelized Onions and Walnuts, *page 296*

Polenta-Sausage Triangles, *page 294*

Winter Citrus, Escarole, and Endive Salad, *page 296*

Browned Butter Bourbon Mashed Sweet Potatoes, *page 297*

Pumpkin-Hazelnut Cheesecake,
page 310

Fresh Ginger Cake with Candied Citrus Glaze, *page 314*

Endive and Watercress Salad with Bacon-Cider Dressing, *page 321*

Walnut Streusel Bread, *page 279*

Chicken and Sausage Gumbo, *page 301*

Spanish Spaghetti with Olives with Pear, Date, and Manchego Salad, *page 331*

Spicy Maple Turkey Breast with
Quick Pan Sauce, *page 293*

239

Seriously Lemon Tart,
page 306

DINNER TONIGHT

Here is a batch of fast weeknight menus from the *Cooking Light* Kitchen.

READY IN
40
MINUTES

The
SHOPPING LIST

Grilled Vegetable and Fontina Pizza
Portobello mushrooms
Garlic
Red bell pepper
Zucchini
Red onion
Fresh basil
Crushed red pepper
Extra-virgin olive oil
Refrigerated pizza dough
Fontina cheese

Herbed Mediterranean Salad
Lemon
Fresh oregano
Mixed salad greens
Fresh parsley
Fresh basil
Cherry tomatoes
Cucumber
Crushed red pepper
Kalamata olives

The
GAME PLAN

While grill preheats:
- Prep vegetables.

While vegetables cook:
- Make salad.
- Roll out pizza dough.

Assemble and grill pizza.

Quick & Easy
Grilled Vegetable and Fontina Pizza
With Herbed Mediterranean Salad
(pictured on page 225)

Technique Tip: Grilling both sides of the crust cooks the dough through.
Simple Sub: Use Gruyère cheese for fontina.

2 portobello mushroom caps
1 tablespoon chopped garlic
1 large red bell pepper, cut into ½-inch strips
1 medium zucchini, cut diagonally into ½-inch-thick slices
1 red onion, cut into ½-inch wedges (root end intact)
5 teaspoons extra-virgin olive oil
¼ teaspoon kosher salt
¼ teaspoon black pepper
Cooking spray
8 ounces refrigerated fresh pizza dough
4 ounces shredded fontina cheese (about 1 cup)
¼ cup thinly sliced basil leaves
½ teaspoon crushed red pepper

1. Preheat grill to high heat.
2. Remove brown gills from undersides of mushrooms with a spoon; discard. Combine mushrooms and next 5 ingredients in a bowl; toss to coat. Sprinkle with salt and pepper. Arrange vegetables on grill rack coated with cooking spray; grill 8 minutes or just until tender. Slice mushrooms.
3. Roll dough into a 12-inch oval on a lightly floured surface. Place dough on grill rack; grill 2 minutes on each side or until lightly browned.
4. Sprinkle cheese over dough, leaving a ½-inch border around edges. Arrange vegetable mixture over cheese. Grill pizza 3 minutes or until cheese melts. Sprinkle pizza with basil leaves and red pepper; cut into 8 slices. Serves 4 (serving size: 2 slices).

CALORIES 344; **FAT** 16.1g (sat 6g, mono 6.5g, poly 2.2g); **PROTEIN** 14.2g; **CARB** 38g; **FIBER** 3.1g; **CHOL** 31mg; **IRON** 2.6mg; **SODIUM** 693mg; **CALC** 173mg

---

For the Herbed Mediterranean Salad:
Combine 2 tablespoons olive oil, 1 tablespoon fresh lemon juice, 1 teaspoon chopped fresh oregano, and ¼ teaspoon crushed red pepper in a large bowl, stirring with a whisk. Add 4 cups salad greens, 1 cup fresh parsley leaves, ½ cup halved cherry tomatoes, ½ cup sliced peeled cucumber, ¼ cup basil leaves, and 2 tablespoons halved, pitted kalamata olives; toss gently. Serves 4 (serving size: ¾ cup).

CALORIES 103; **FAT** 8.8g (sat 1.2g); **SODIUM** 146mg

READY IN
40
MINUTES

The
SHOPPING LIST

Chicken Tostadas and Avocado Salsa
Limes
Prechopped tomato
Prechopped white onion
Avocado
Green leaf lettuce
Flour tortillas
Fresh cilantro
Extra-virgin olive oil
Ground cumin
Rotisserie chicken breast
15-ounce can no-salt-added black beans
Queso fresco

Chipotle Rice
Chipotle chiles in adobo sauce
Uncooked rice
Butter

The
GAME PLAN

While rice cooks:
- Make salsa.
- Brown tortillas.
- Assemble tostadas.

continued

Kid Friendly • Quick & Easy

Chicken Tostadas and Avocado Salsa

With Chipotle Rice

Flavor Hit: Try roasted cumin for even deeper spice flavor.
Waste Not: Freeze extra chipotle chiles in adobo sauce for later use.
Simple Sub: Use corn tortillas in place of flour.

3 tablespoons fresh lime juice
1½ tablespoons extra-virgin olive oil
½ teaspoon ground cumin
½ teaspoon freshly ground black pepper
¼ teaspoon kosher salt
1 cup prechopped tomato
½ cup prechopped white onion
1 tablespoon chopped fresh cilantro
1 avocado, peeled and diced
1 tablespoon extra-virgin olive oil, divided
4 (6-inch) flour tortillas
2 cups shredded green leaf lettuce
1 (15-ounce) can no-salt-added black beans, rinsed and drained
2 cups shredded, boneless rotisserie chicken breast
¼ cup crumbled queso fresco

1. Combine first 5 ingredients in a medium bowl, stirring with a whisk. Add tomato, onion, cilantro, and avocado; toss gently to coat.
2. Heat a large cast-iron or nonstick skillet over medium heat. Add ¾ teaspoon oil to pan; swirl to coat. Add 1 tortilla to pan; cook 1 minute on each side or until browned. Repeat procedure 3 times with remaining 2¼ teaspoons oil and tortillas.
3. Place 1 tortilla on each of 4 plates. Layer each tortilla with ½ cup lettuce, about ½ cup beans, ½ cup chicken, ¼ cup avocado salsa, and 1 tablespoon cheese. Serves 4 (serving size: 1 tostada).

CALORIES 429; **FAT** 21.6g (sat 4.1g, mono 13.4g, poly 2.7g); **PROTEIN** 26.3g; **CARB** 35g; **FIBER** 8.6g; **CHOL** 55mg; **IRON** 3mg; **SODIUM** 544mg; **CALC** 147mg

For the Chipotle Rice:
Combine 2 cups water; 1 tablespoon butter; 1 tablespoon minced chipotle chile, canned in adobo sauce; ¼ teaspoon salt; and ¼ teaspoon freshly ground black pepper in a small saucepan. Bring to a boil. Add 1 cup rice; stir gently. Cover, reduce heat, and simmer 18 minutes. Stir in 1 tablespoon chopped fresh cilantro. Serves 4 (serving size: ⅔ cup).

CALORIES 197; **FAT** 3.2g (sat 1.9g); **SODIUM** 211mg

READY IN 40 MINUTES

The
SHOPPING LIST

Shrimp Salad Rolls
Butter
Lemon
Boston lettuce
Fresh parsley
Fresh tarragon
Large raw shrimp (about 1 pound)
Hot dog buns
Canola mayonnaise

Roasted Herbed Potatoes
Fresh thyme
Fresh parsley
Refrigerated potato wedges

The
GAME PLAN

While oven preheats:
 ■ Cook shrimp.
While potatoes roast:
 ■ Make shrimp salad.
Toast buns.
Assemble rolls.

Quick & Easy

Shrimp Salad Rolls

With Roasted Herbed Potatoes

Healthy Choice: Canola mayonnaise has less saturated fat than regular mayo.
Flavor Hit: Tarragon gives the salad light licorice taste.
Time-Saver: Refrigerated potato wedges are ready to season and roast.

1 tablespoon butter
20 large shrimp, peeled and deveined (about 1 pound)
¼ cup canola mayonnaise
1 teaspoon grated lemon rind
1 tablespoon fresh lemon juice
2 teaspoons chopped fresh parsley
1½ teaspoons chopped fresh tarragon
½ teaspoon freshly ground black pepper
¼ teaspoon kosher salt
4 (1½-ounce) hot dog buns
8 Boston lettuce leaves

1. Preheat broiler to high.
2. Heat butter in a large nonstick skillet over medium-high heat; swirl to coat. Add shrimp to pan; sauté 4 minutes or until done. Place shrimp on a large plate; chill in refrigerator 10 minutes. Coarsely chop shrimp. Combine chopped shrimp, mayonnaise, and next 6 ingredients in a large bowl.
3. Open buns without completely splitting; arrange, cut sides up, on a baking sheet. Broil 1 minute or until toasted. Place 2 lettuce leaves in each bun; top each serving with ½ cup shrimp mixture. Serves 4 (serving size: 1 sandwich).

CALORIES 370; **FAT** 17.8g (sat 3.7g, mono 7.5g, poly 4.7g); **PROTEIN** 27.4g; **CARB** 23g; **FIBER** 1.2g; **CHOL** 185mg; **IRON** 4.4mg; **SODIUM** 616mg; **CALC** 128mg

For the Roasted Herbed Potatoes:
Preheat oven to 425°. Place 1 (20-ounce) package refrigerated potato wedges (such as Simply Potatoes) on a foil-lined jelly-roll pan coated with cooking spray. Add 2 teaspoons chopped fresh thyme, ¼ teaspoon

kosher salt, and ¼ teaspoon freshly ground black pepper; toss to coat. Arrange potatoes in a single layer on prepared pan. Bake at 425° for 29 minutes, turning once. Remove from oven; sprinkle with 1½ teaspoons chopped fresh parsley. Serves 4 (serving size: ½ cup).

CALORIES 90; **FAT** 0.2g (sat 0g); **SODIUM** 269mg

READY IN 40 MINUTES

The
SHOPPING LIST

Seared Tuna Niçoise
Red potatoes
Haricots verts
Grape tomatoes
Niçoise olives
Extra-virgin olive oil
Red wine vinegar
Dijon mustard
Large eggs
2 (6-ounce) tuna steaks

Lemony White Bean Mash
Celery
Fresh parsley
Lemon
15-ounce can cannellini beans
Olive oil

The
GAME PLAN

While eggs cook:
- Cut potatoes, haricots verts, and tomatoes.
- Cook potatoes and haricots verts.
- Sear tuna.
- Make vinaigrette.
- Prepare mashed beans.

Kid Friendly • Quick & Easy
Seared Tuna Niçoise
With Lemony White Bean Mash

Shopping Tip: Look for multicolored grape tomatoes.
Technique Tip: Start potatoes in cold water to cook them evenly.

3 large eggs
1½ cups quartered small red potatoes
1 cup haricots verts, trimmed
Cooking spray
2 (6-ounce) tuna steaks
½ teaspoon kosher salt, divided
¼ teaspoon freshly ground black pepper
2 tablespoons extra-virgin olive oil
3 tablespoons red wine vinegar
1 teaspoon Dijon mustard
⅔ cup grape tomatoes, halved
¼ cup pitted and quartered niçoise olives

1. Place eggs in a large saucepan. Cover with water to 1 inch above eggs. Bring just to a boil. Remove from heat; cover and let stand 15 minutes. Drain; cool in ice water 5 minutes. Peel eggs; cut each egg into 4 slices.
2. Place potatoes in pan; cover with water. Bring to a boil. Reduce heat; simmer 12 minutes. Add beans, and cook 3 minutes. Drain; plunge beans into ice water 1 minute. Drain well.
3. Heat a large cast-iron skillet over medium-high heat. Coat pan with cooking spray. Sprinkle tuna with ¼ teaspoon salt and pepper. Add tuna to pan; cook 2 minutes on each side or until desired degree of doneness. Cut thinly across the grain.
4. Combine remaining ¼ teaspoon salt, oil, vinegar, and mustard in a small bowl, stirring with a whisk. Add tomatoes and olives; toss. Divide eggs, potatoes, beans, and tuna among 4 plates; top with tomato mixture. Serves 4 (serving size: about 2 ounces tuna, 3 egg slices, ⅓ cup potatoes, ¼ cup beans, and 2 tablespoons tomato mixture).

CALORIES 311; **FAT** 14.7g (sat 2.6g, mono 9.4g, poly 2g); **PROTEIN** 25.7g; **CARB** 16.8g; **FIBER** 2.4g; **CHOL** 175mg; **IRON** 2.7mg; **SODIUM** 596mg; **CALC** 68mg

For the Lemony White Bean Mash:
Place 1 (15-ounce) can rinsed and drained cannellini beans in a bowl; mash with a fork. Add 3 tablespoons chopped celery, 2 tablespoons chopped fresh parsley, 1 tablespoon fresh lemon juice, 2 teaspoons olive oil, and ¼ teaspoon kosher salt; stir to combine. Serves 4 (serving size: ½ cup).

CALORIES 65; **FAT** 2.7g (sat 0.3g); **SODIUM** 142mg

PREP POINTER: SHOCKING BEANS IN ICE WATER SETS THEIR COLOR AND TEXTURE.

OOPS!

YOUR THAWED BERRIES ARE A MUSHY MESS

To prevent waterlogged fruit, give your berries some breathing room.

(Squee!)

(Squish)

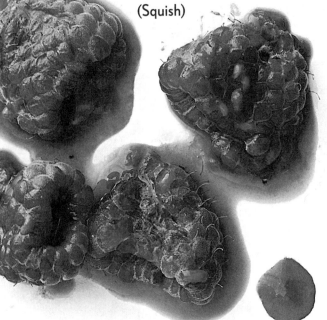

Freezing fresh-picked berries lets you preserve a delightful dose of summer flavor for months after the season is over. But when thawed fruit becomes a squishy clump with juice spilling out, it's barely fit for smoothies. The freezing method is the culprit: If you're putting raspberries, blueberries, and the like in bags to freeze, you're doing it wrong.

The longer it takes food to freeze, the larger the ice crystals will be. These big ice chunks destroy cell walls inside the food, so when it thaws, it loses structural integrity and turns mushy.

Big frozen-food companies use special equipment to flash-freeze berries individually. This makes for small crystals, so the thawed product better retains fresh taste and texture.

To approximate an industrial quick-freeze at home, spread berries in a single layer (not touching) on a baking sheet, and place the sheet in the back of your freezer. The extra space allows more exposure to the cold, freezing the fruit faster and preventing it from clumping. Then transfer the frozen berries to large zip-top freezer bags.

50 BUCKS, 5 MEALS, 4 PEOPLE: DIARY OF A SUPERMARKET TIGHTWAD

We challenged Robin Bashinsky to cook up a week's worth of tasty dinners for four—for just $50.

Budgets always bugged me: cold reminders of all the cool things I couldn't afford to buy or do. But I'm not a big spender, and in truth a budget is just a challenge of the sort I enjoy in the Test Kitchen—such as developing a recipe for seasonal ingredients available in Wyoming in February. And what is a budget, really, but a recipe of a different sort?

But this assignment was a doozy: Could I serve four people five meals for $50—total out-of-pocket expenses, no cheating—and keep the meals interesting? Oh, and could I do that without dipping into my pantry? The only freebies were salt, pepper, flour, sugar, and canola oil. And emphasis, too, on the "keep it interesting" part.

From the get-go, it was obvious that my usual one-stop shopping routine would not keep me on budget, and indeed, shopping turned out to be the key to the whole thing. I also knew, though, that I needed a rough menu plan, one flexible enough to accommodate surprise bargains (hello, mussels) but focused enough to steer me away from impulse purchases.

First up was a morning trip to Birmingham's old-school farmers' market on Finley Avenue, where stalls burst with produce on the cheap and the food is sold by real country folk. Baby new potatoes for 50 cents per pound? Yes, please. There's less variety here than at the more boutique farmers' market, but you save big.

Next stop, an Asian market. Yes, many products here can now be found in supermarkets, but they're often sold and priced as "specialty" foods. Here, I grabbed rice noodles for 89 cents, soy sauce for a buck, and cilantro at less than half the grocery-store price.

There's an embarrassment of cheap, flavorful riches at any supermarket, however. You just need the courage to buy in comically small quantities. I bought half-teaspoons of bulk spices; half a head of garlic; a broken length of ginger. And serranos? Two will run you 6 cents. The same economies of scale apply at not-cheap Whole Foods. Pork shoulder was my economy meat, so I sheepishly asked the butcher to remove a pound and a quarter off the 6-pound honker in the case. He did, without even rolling his eyes.

And at the end of the day, the only real "challenge" was overcoming the small mortification of buying in these small amounts—including a Miller High Life tall boy for steaming mussels purchased at a gas station with my last $1.52.

Following are the recipes from my week of budget cooking. They will save you money, but they will not scrimp on flavor: I guarantee it.

The SHOPPING LIST

Produce
- [ ] Onions (2 large)
- [ ] Collard greens (8 cups)
- [ ] Garlic (14 cloves)
- [ ] Cremini mushrooms (1 ounce)
- [ ] Fresh oregano
- [ ] Baby spinach (6 ounces)
- [ ] Gingerroot (1 small)
- [ ] Serrano chiles (2)
- [ ] Thai chiles (2)
- [ ] Limes (2)
- [ ] Lemon (1)
- [ ] Carrots (2 large)
- [ ] Fresh cilantro (1 bunch)
- [ ] Fennel bulb with stalks (12 ounces)
- [ ] Red potatoes (10 ounces)
- [ ] Green beans (4 ounces)
- [ ] Yellow squash (1 medium)
- [ ] Baby bok choy (6 ounces)

Dry Goods
- [ ] Crushed red pepper
- [ ] Ground cumin (½ teaspoon)
- [ ] Garam masala (½ teaspoon)
- [ ] Curry powder (½ teaspoon)
- [ ] Ground coriander (½ teaspoon)
- [ ] Quick-cooking grits
- [ ] Brown rice (½ cup)
- [ ] Dried small red lentils (¾ cup)
- [ ] No-salt-added chicken stock (such as Swanson 1 [32-ounce] container)
- [ ] Lower-sodium soy sauce
- [ ] Rice vermicelli (4 ounces)
- [ ] No-salt-added whole tomatoes (28.5-ounce can)

Refrigerated
- [ ] Refrigerated fresh pizza dough (1 pound)

Alcohol
- [ ] Beer (1 [16-ounce] can/bottle)

Dairy
- [ ] Fresh mozzarella cheese (3 ounces)
- [ ] Fresh Parmesan cheese (1.5 ounces)

Meats
- [ ] Boneless pork shoulder (Boston butt; 20 ounces)
- [ ] Applewood-smoked bacon (1½ ounces)
- [ ] Skin-on, boneless chicken thighs (4 [4-ounce])
- [ ] Mussels (1½ pounds)

continued

Vegetarian

Red Lentil Dal with Carrot Salad and Coriander Flatbreads

Hands-on time: 35 min. Total time: 53 min. *This is basically an all-out assault on the bulk bins, as well as our modern take on the rice-and-beans dinner. Spices, dried lentils, and rice are cheap ingredients, especially when you buy in these small quantities. Chiles are also a thrifty flavor booster; you should be able to score the two here for 6 cents. Your vegetable peeler will get you nice carrot ribbons. And you'll use your leftover pizza dough to make the flatbread.*
Saving Strategy: *Don't blow all the pizza dough on pizza; save some for grilled flatbreads for dipping into inexpensive dal.*

Dal:
5 cups water, divided
¾ cup dried small red lentils
1 tablespoon canola oil
¾ cup chopped onion
1 tablespoon minced peeled fresh ginger
1 tablespoon minced garlic
1 teaspoon kosher salt
½ teaspoon ground cumin
½ teaspoon garam masala
½ teaspoon curry powder
2 serrano chiles, minced
2 ounces fresh baby spinach (about 4 cups loosely packed)

Salad:
2 tablespoons canola oil
1 teaspoon grated lime rind
1½ tablespoons fresh lime juice
1 teaspoon sugar
4 cups shaved carrot (about 2 large)
1 cup thinly vertically sliced onion
1 cup cilantro leaves
Flatbreads:
4 (1-ounce) pieces refrigerated fresh pizza dough
Cooking spray
½ teaspoon ground coriander
¼ teaspoon kosher salt
Remaining ingredient:
1⅓ cups hot cooked long-grain brown rice

1. To prepare dal, combine 3 cups water and lentils in a bowl. Let stand 20 minutes; drain.
2. Heat a medium saucepan over medium-high heat. Add 1 tablespoon oil; swirl to coat. Add chopped onion; sauté 3 minutes. Add ginger and next 6 ingredients; sauté 30 seconds. Add lentils and remaining 2 cups water to pan. Bring to a boil; reduce heat, and simmer 23 minutes. Stir in spinach; cook 2 minutes or until spinach wilts.
3. To prepare salad, combine 2 tablespoons oil, rind, juice, and sugar in a medium bowl, stirring with a whisk. Add carrot, sliced onion, and cilantro; toss to coat.
4. To prepare flatbreads, shape each dough portion into a 5-inch circle on a lightly floured surface. Coat dough with cooking spray. Heat a grill pan over high heat. Add 2 dough portions to pan; cook 2 minutes on each side or until lightly charred. Repeat procedure with remaining dough. Combine coriander and ¼ teaspoon salt; sprinkle over hot flatbreads. Serve with rice, dal, and salad. Serves 4 (serving size: about ½ cup dal, 1 cup salad, 1 flatbread, and ⅓ cup rice).

CALORIES 410; **FAT** 12.4g (sat 1.4g, mono 7.7g, poly 2.1g); **PROTEIN** 15.5g; **CARB** 60.2g; **FIBER** 10.9g; **CHOL** 0mg; **IRON** 3.5mg; **SODIUM** 768mg; **CALC** 67mg

Vegetarian

Spinach and Onion Pizza

Hands-on time: 15 min. Total time: 55 min. *You'll use the tomatoes reserved from the pork dinner (page 247) here. Purchase one pound of pizza dough and use most of it here; the rest becomes grilled flatbreads for the dal dinner at left.*

12 ounces refrigerated fresh pizza dough
1 tablespoon canola oil, divided
2 cups vertically sliced onion (about ½ large)
6 garlic cloves, thinly sliced
1 (28.5-ounce) can no-salt-added whole tomatoes, well drained and coarsely chopped
2 tablespoons chopped fresh oregano, divided
¾ teaspoon crushed red pepper
¼ teaspoon kosher salt
3 ounces fresh mozzarella cheese, torn into bite-sized pieces
1.5 ounces Parmesan cheese, grated (about ⅓ cup)
4 ounces fresh baby spinach

1. Remove dough from refrigerator. Let stand at room temperature, covered, 30 minutes.
2. Place a heavy baking sheet in oven. Preheat oven to 500° (keep baking sheet in oven as it preheats).
3. Heat a large nonstick skillet over medium heat. Add 1 teaspoon oil to pan; swirl to coat. Add onion; cook 4 minutes or until softened, stirring frequently. Remove onion from pan. Add 1 teaspoon oil to pan; swirl to coat. Add garlic; cook 1 minute, stirring frequently. Add tomatoes, 1 tablespoon oregano, pepper, and salt; cook 4 minutes or until most of liquid evaporates, stirring mixture occasionally.
4. Roll dough into a 13-inch circle on a lightly floured surface; pierce entire surface liberally with a fork.

Carefully place dough on preheated baking sheet. Spread tomato mixture evenly over dough, leaving a ½-inch border. Top with onion and cheeses. Bake at 500° for 12 minutes or until crust is golden and cheese is lightly browned.

5. Heat a large nonstick skillet over medium-high heat. Add remaining 1 teaspoon oil to pan; swirl to coat. Add spinach; sauté 2 minutes or until spinach wilts. Top pizza with remaining 1 tablespoon oregano and spinach. Cut into 8 slices. Serves 4 (serving size: 2 slices).

CALORIES 407; FAT 13.3g (sat 5.1g, mono 4.1g, poly 1.6g); PROTEIN 17.5g; CARB 53.6g; FIBER 9.4g; CHOL 27mg; IRON 3.1mg; SODIUM 716mg; CALC 195mg

---

SAVING STRATEGY

Two uses for one can of tomatoes: The juice is the savory backbone for gravy while the tomatoes go on pizza.

Braised Pork with Slow-Cooked Collards, Grits, and Tomato Gravy

Hands-on time: 40 min. Total time: 2 hr. 40 min. *The greens can simmer while the pork cooks (they can be done ahead and reheated). Start the grits and gravy around the same time; you don't want the grits to sit or they'll get too firm. You'll use the liquid from a can of tomatoes for the gravy here, and then reserve the tomatoes for Spinach and Onion Pizza (page 246).*

1½ tablespoons canola oil, divided
1 (20-ounce) boneless pork shoulder (Boston butt), trimmed (about 1 pound trimmed)
1 teaspoon kosher salt, divided
¾ teaspoon freshly ground black pepper, divided
2 cups water, divided
2 cups no-salt-added chicken stock, divided
1½ teaspoons lower-sodium soy sauce
2 cups vertically sliced onion (about ½ large)
8 cups chopped trimmed collard greens
2 teaspoons sugar
1 (28.5-ounce) can no-salt-added whole tomatoes
1 tablespoon all-purpose flour
⅓ cup finely chopped onion
1 ounce chopped cremini mushrooms
2 garlic cloves, minced
½ cup uncooked quick-cooking grits

1. Preheat oven to 325°.
2. Heat a medium ovenproof saucepan over medium-high heat. Add 1½ teaspoons oil; swirl to coat. Sprinkle pork with ½ teaspoon salt and ½ teaspoon pepper. Add pork to pan; cook 8 minutes, browning on all sides. Discard oil from pan. Add ½ cup water, ½ cup stock, and soy sauce. Cover and bake at 325° for 2 hours or until very tender. Remove pork from pan; reserve liquid. Place pork on a cutting board; cover with foil. Let stand 10 minutes; cut into 4 slices.
3. While pork cooks, heat a Dutch oven over medium heat. Add 1½ teaspoons oil; swirl to coat. Add sliced onion and ¼ teaspoon salt; cook 2 minutes or until golden, stirring occasionally. Add ½ cup water, ½ cup stock, greens, and sugar. Bring to a boil. Cover; reduce heat, and simmer 25 minutes or until tender, stirring occasionally.

4. Remove 1 cup tomato liquid from can; reserve remaining liquid and tomatoes for another use. Combine 1 cup tomato liquid and flour in a medium bowl, stirring with a whisk. Place a zip-top plastic bag inside a 2-cup glass measure. Pour pork cooking liquid into bag; let stand 5 minutes (fat will rise to the top). Seal bag; snip off 1 bottom corner of bag. Drain liquid into tomato mixture, stopping before fat layer reaches the opening; discard fat. Return pan to medium-high heat. Add remaining 1½ teaspoons oil to pan; swirl to coat. Add chopped onion and mushrooms; sauté 2 minutes. Add tomato mixture to saucepan; bring to a boil. Cook until reduced to 1 cup (about 10 minutes).
5. While gravy cooks, bring remaining 1 cup water, 1 cup stock, ¼ teaspoon salt, ¼ teaspoon pepper, and garlic to a boil in a medium saucepan. Gradually add grits, stirring constantly with a whisk. Reduce heat; simmer 5 minutes or until liquid is absorbed, stirring frequently. Serve grits with gravy, pork, and greens. Serves 4 (serving size: about 3 ounces pork, ½ cup greens, ½ cup grits, and ¼ cup gravy).

CALORIES 454; FAT 24.8g (sat 7.4g, mono 11.5g, poly 3.5g); PROTEIN 27.3g; CARB 30.9g; FIBER 4.7g; CHOL 89mg; IRON 3.1mg; SODIUM 771mg; CALC 151mg

START THE GRITS AND GRAVY AT THE SAME TIME; YOU DON'T WANT THE GRITS TO SIT OR THEY'LL GET TOO FIRM.

Quick & Easy

Mussels Steamed with Bacon, Beer, and Fennel

Hands-on time: 25 min. Total time: 25 min. You may not think of seafood as budget-friendly, but mussels certainly are. If you can't find a 16-ounce beer (a "tall boy"), you can use a 12-ounce beer plus ½ cup broth or water. If there's wiggle room in your budget, pick up some crusty bread to dunk into the beer broth.

1 (12-ounce) fennel bulb with stalks
1½ ounces applewood-smoked bacon, cut crosswise into thin strips
10 ounces red potatoes, cut into ½-inch pieces (about 2 cups)
¼ teaspoon kosher salt
¼ teaspoon freshly ground black pepper
1 (16-ounce) can beer
1½ pounds mussels, scrubbed and debearded (about 40)
4 ounces green beans, trimmed and cut into ⅓-inch pieces (about ¾ cup)
1 tablespoon fresh lemon juice

1. Trim tough outer leaves from fennel; mince feathery fronds to measure 2 tablespoons. Remove and discard stalks. Cut fennel bulb in half lengthwise, and discard core. Vertically slice bulb.
2. Cook bacon in a large Dutch oven over medium heat 3 minutes or until crisp, stirring frequently. Add fennel bulb, potatoes, salt, and pepper. Cook 10 minutes or until fennel is lightly browned, stirring occasionally. Increase heat to high. Add beer, scraping pan to loosen browned bits; bring to a boil. Stir in mussels and green beans; cover and cook 4 minutes or until mussels open. Discard any unopened shells. Stir in juice. Divide mussel mixture evenly among 4 bowls, and spoon broth evenly over mussels. Sprinkle each serving with 1½ teaspoons chopped fennel fronds. Serves 4.

CALORIES 237; FAT 7g (sat 2.2g, mono 2.9g, poly 0.9g); PROTEIN 18g; CARB 23.3g; FIBER 3.8g; CHOL 38mg; IRON 5mg; SODIUM 665mg; CALC 73mg

Quick & Easy

Fiery Thai Noodle Bowl with Crispy Chicken Thighs

Hands-on time: 30 min. Total time: 30 min. Using the cilantro stems for the base of the sauce (instead of throwing them in the trash) is a flavorful way to stretch a buck or two. If you can't find skin-on boneless chicken thighs, purchase bone-in and bone them yourself or have the butcher do so.

4 (4-ounce) skin-on, boneless chicken thighs
1 teaspoon kosher salt, divided
¼ teaspoon freshly ground black pepper
1 tablespoon canola oil
4 ounces uncooked rice vermicelli
1½ cups cilantro stems (about 1 bunch)
¼ cup no-salt-added chicken stock
¼ cup water
2 teaspoons minced peeled fresh ginger
3 garlic cloves
2 fresh Thai chiles
1¼ cups chopped yellow squash (about 1 medium)
6 ounces baby bok choy, halved and sliced
1 tablespoon lower-sodium soy sauce
8 lime wedges

1. Preheat oven to 425°.
2. Heat a large stainless steel skillet over high heat. Sprinkle chicken evenly with ¼ teaspoon salt and pepper. Add oil to pan; swirl to coat. Add chicken, skin side down; cook 3 minutes or until skin begins to brown. Remove chicken from pan. Pour oil into a small bowl; reserve oil. Return chicken to pan, skin side down. Place pan in oven; bake chicken at 425° for 4 minutes. Turn chicken over, skin side up, and bake an additional 2 minutes or until done. Remove chicken from pan; place on a cutting board. Let chicken stand, skin side up, 10 minutes. Cut chicken into slices; keep warm.
3. Cook noodles according to package directions, and drain. Sprinkle noodles with ¼ teaspoon salt; toss well to combine.
4. Place ¼ teaspoon salt, cilantro, and next 5 ingredients in a food processor, and process until well blended.
5. Return skillet to medium-high heat. Add reserved oil to pan; swirl to coat. Add squash, bok choy, and remaining ¼ teaspoon salt; sauté 3 minutes or until vegetables are crisp-tender, stirring frequently. Stir in soy sauce. Divide noodle mixture evenly among 4 bowls. Top each serving with ½ cup squash mixture, 1 chicken thigh, and 2 lime wedges. Drizzle sauce evenly over servings. Serves 4.

CALORIES 320; FAT 13.5g (sat 3g, mono 6.1g, poly 3.2g); PROTEIN 19.9g; CARB 28.8g; FIBER 2g; CHOL 59mg; IRON 2.7mg; SODIUM 669mg; CALC 81mg

CUCINA POVERA

Mighty rich flavors for much less money: These global dishes hail from humble but inspired kitchens.

Translated literally, cucina povera means "poor kitchen," but it really refers to the frugal genius of poor Italian cooks who made the most of gardens, forests, oceans, and backyard coops. Anything abundant and affordable became the backbone of a dish; also anything left over, as with the use of bread in salads and soups, or breadcrumbs with pastas. The approach isn't unique to Italy, of course: Every culture has beloved dishes with roots in the flavors of necessity. Here, some global recipes inspired by the original "fresh and local" frugal cooks.

Vegetarian

Whole-Wheat Spaghetti with Kale, Poached Eggs, and Toasted Breadcrumbs

Hands-on time: 55 min. Total time: 55 min. Humble leftover bread is transformed into a crunchy-savory garnish. Tuscan kale, sometimes labeled cavalo nero or lacinato or black kale, has dark leaves that are richly flavored. Abundant in its namesake region, it shows up more and more in American markets and stands out for its deep flavor and easy-to-work-with flat leaves. If you can't find Tuscan kale, you can use regular curly kale. Or try Swiss chard instead and cut the cooking time for the greens in half.

1 (2-ounce) piece whole-wheat baguette, cubed
2 tablespoons extra-virgin olive oil, divided
3 cups sliced onion (about 1 medium)
14 cups stemmed, coarsely chopped Tuscan kale (about 18 ounces)
½ cup water
¼ teaspoon crushed red pepper
4 garlic cloves, chopped
2¼ teaspoons kosher salt
4 large eggs
8 ounces whole-wheat spaghetti
2 ounces pecorino Romano cheese, divided
½ teaspoon coarsely ground black pepper

1. Preheat oven to 400°.

2. Place bread in a food processor; pulse until 1 cup fine breadcrumbs form. Combine breadcrumbs and 2 teaspoons oil on a baking sheet. Bake at 400° for 8 minutes or until toasted, stirring occasionally.

3. Heat a large nonstick skillet over medium-high heat. Add 1 teaspoon oil; swirl to coat. Add onion; sauté 8 minutes or until golden, stirring frequently. Gradually add kale, stirring to wilt after each addition. Stir in ½ cup water, red pepper, and garlic. Reduce heat to medium; cook, uncovered, 12 minutes or until kale is tender, stirring occasionally. Stir in ¼ teaspoon salt. Keep warm.

4. Bring a large pot of water and remaining 2 teaspoons salt to a simmer. Working with 1 egg at a time, crack egg into a small bowl or ramekin. Gently slide eggs into water; cook 3 minutes or until whites are just set. Carefully remove eggs from water with a slotted spoon; set aside. Remove any remaining egg solids from water with a slotted spoon, and discard.

5. Bring water to a boil. Add pasta; cook 10 minutes or until al dente. Drain and place in a large bowl. Grate 1 ounce cheese. Add cheese, remaining 1 tablespoon oil, and black pepper to pasta; toss to coat. Place about ¾ cup kale in bottom of each of 4 shallow bowls. Top each serving with about 1 cup pasta mixture, 1 egg, and ¼ cup breadcrumbs. Shave remaining 1 ounce cheese over servings. Serves 4.

CALORIES 519; FAT 16.4g (sat 4g, mono 7.8g, poly 2.5g); PROTEIN 25.6g; CARB 75.9g; FIBER 13.4g; CHOL 216mg; IRON 7.4mg; SODIUM 569mg; CALC 438mg

PEASANT DISHES SPRING FROM WHAT LAND AND SEA LAVISH ON THE REGION, FROM CREAMY RICE PORRIDGE TO SHIMMERY FISH.

Filipino Arroz Caldo

Hands-on time: 40 min. Total time: 1 hr. 30 min. *Chinese immigrants brought congee—savory rice porridge—to the Philippines, where it was given a new name and adapted to suit the tastes of Spanish colonizers. The golden color of this comforting porridge comes from saffron, whose earthy essence blends well with the Southeast Asian flavors of ginger and fish sauce. True, saffron is the world's most expensive spice, but if you buy in small envelopes, it only costs about $2.50. Rice, chicken, and chicken broth are the other main ingredients, all budget-friendly components. Heat-seekers can dot the porridge with Sriracha, or for milder spice, drizzle with sweet chile sauce.*

Broth:
4 cups fat-free, lower-sodium chicken broth
2 cups water
1 cup cilantro stems (from 1 bunch)
3 (1½-inch) lime rind strips
2 garlic cloves, crushed
1½ pounds bone-in, skin-on chicken breast halves (about 2 large)
1½ ounces (¼-inch-thick) slices ginger
1 small white onion, coarsely chopped
1 small carrot, coarsely chopped
Porridge:
1 tablespoon dark sesame oil
1 medium white onion, vertically sliced
1 cup long-grain white rice
1½ tablespoons minced peeled fresh ginger
⅛ teaspoon crushed saffron threads
6 garlic cloves, minced
2 tablespoons cream sherry
1½ tablespoons fish sauce
¾ cup cilantro leaves
¾ cup sliced green onions
6 large hard-cooked eggs, halved

1. To prepare broth, combine first 9 ingredients in a large Dutch oven. Bring to a boil. Reduce heat to low; simmer 20 minutes or until chicken is just cooked through, skimming off and discarding foam as needed. Strain broth through a fine sieve to yield 5 cups (add additional water as needed to measure 5 cups), and discard solids. Remove chicken meat from bones; shred meat. Discard skin and bones.
2. To prepare porridge, heat a large saucepan over medium heat. Add oil to pan; swirl to coat. Add sliced white onion; cook 5 minutes or until softened, stirring occasionally. Add rice and next 3 ingredients; cook 30 seconds, stirring constantly. Add 5 cups broth and sherry; bring to a boil. Cover and cook 35 minutes or until thick and rice begins to break down, stirring occasionally. (Mixture should be the consistency of rice pudding). Stir in chicken and fish sauce; cook 2 minutes or until thoroughly heated. Spoon about 1 cup porridge into each of 6 bowls. Top each serving with 2 tablespoons cilantro, 2 tablespoons green onions, and 2 egg halves. Serves 6.

CALORIES 385; FAT 15.4g (sat 4.2g, mono 6.3g, poly 3.4g); PROTEIN 24.8g; CARB 29.9g; FIBER 2g; CHOL 260mg; IRON 3.1mg; SODIUM 661mg; CALC 72mg

Sichuan Beef Soup

(pictured on page 231)

Hands-on time: 30 min. Total time: 11 hr. 30 min. *Beef shank, which imbues a broth with rich, meaty essence, is one of those under-appreciated (and fairly priced) cuts of meat. It works beautifully for slow-cooked soups, breaking down during long simmering to render the aromatic broth superbeefy. Shop at an Asian market for Sichuan peppercorns, black bean sauce, and chile sauce.*

3 quarts water
2 pounds (2-inch-thick) bone-in beef shanks
2 teaspoons peanut oil or canola oil
1 cup chopped white onion
2 teaspoons minced peeled fresh ginger
2 garlic cloves, chopped
6 cups water
1 tablespoon chile garlic sauce
1½ teaspoons black bean garlic sauce
1 teaspoon Sichuan peppercorns
3 star anise
1 cup sliced green onions, divided
1 tablespoon brown sugar
2 tablespoons lower-sodium soy sauce
2 plum tomatoes, chopped
2 baby bok choy, cut in half lengthwise
½ pound fresh Chinese-style wheat noodles
¼ cup chopped fresh cilantro

1. Bring 3 quarts water to a boil in a large Dutch oven. Add beef shanks; boil until surface of meat is no longer red (about 6 minutes). Drain shanks; cool slightly. Remove meat from bones; reserve bones. Cut meat into cubes.
2. Rinse pan; wipe clean with paper towels. Heat pan over high heat. Add oil; swirl to coat. Add white onion, ginger, and garlic; stir-fry 4 minutes or until browned. Stir in 6 cups water, chile garlic sauce, and black bean sauce. Place peppercorns and star anise on a double layer of cheesecloth. Gather edges of cheesecloth together; tie securely. Add cheesecloth bag, ½ cup green onions, sugar, and soy sauce to pan. Return meat and bones to pan. Bring to a simmer. Partially cover, and simmer gently 2 hours or until meat is tender. Uncover and simmer 1 hour or until reduced to about 5 cups. Cool to room temperature; cover and chill overnight.
3. Skim fat from soup; discard fat. Discard bones and cheesecloth bag. Bring soup to a simmer. Add tomatoes and bok choy; cook 5 minutes or until bok choy is tender.
4. Cook noodles according to package directions. Place about ½ cup noodles in each of 4 bowls. Ladle 1 cup soup into each bowl, dividing bok choy evenly. Sprinkle each serving with 2 tablespoons green onions and 1 tablespoon cilantro. Serves 4.

CALORIES 408; FAT 8.6g (sat 2.4g, mono 3.5g, poly 1.1g); PROTEIN 40.3g; CARB 4.1g; FIBER 2.9g; CHOL 53mg; IRON 4.5mg; SODIUM 635mg; CALC 97mg

Kid Friendly • Make Ahead

Garbure (French Ham and Vegetable Stew)

(pictured on page 231)

Hands-on time: 25 min. Total time: 9 hr. 30 min. *This hearty peasant stew from Béarn traditionally contained whatever seasonal vegetables were growing in the region. In would go cabbage, beans, potatoes, and turnips—all of which happen to be dirt-cheap in our country. If, like a French rural household might, you can get your hands on a bit of preserved goose, use that instead of pork. The key to the rich flavor of this peasant soup is the smoked ham hock. Be sure to purchase a meaty cross-cut hock (which looks like an osso buco-cut shank); other hocks offer little meat. Or look for a smoked pork shank. The soup-stew is so thick with beans, leeks, root vegetables, and cabbage that you can almost eat it with a fork. And it's the type of dish that gets better with each successive reheating.*

4 ounces dried cannellini or Great Northern beans
1 tablespoon extra-virgin olive oil
1 cup chopped onion
1½ cups thinly sliced leek (about 1 large)
4 garlic cloves, chopped
4 cups no-salt-added chicken stock
½ teaspoon dried herbes de Provence
1 cross-cut smoked ham hock (about 8 ounces)
1 bay leaf
6 ounces red potatoes, cubed
6 ounces turnip, cubed
1 large carrot, cubed
4 cups thinly sliced Savoy cabbage
¼ cup chopped fresh flat-leaf parsley
2 tablespoons chopped fresh thyme
1½ tablespoons cider vinegar
½ teaspoon kosher salt
½ teaspoon freshly ground black pepper
6 (1-ounce) slices country bread, toasted
1 garlic clove, halved
1 tablespoon butter, softened

1. Sort and wash beans. Place in a large Dutch oven. Cover with water to 2 inches above beans. Cover and let stand 8 hours or overnight. Drain.
2. Heat a large Dutch oven over medium heat. Add oil to pan; swirl to coat. Add onion. Cover and cook 8 minutes or until tender, stirring occasionally. Add leek and chopped garlic; cook 2 minutes, stirring occasionally. Add soaked beans, stock, herbes de Provence, ham hock, and bay leaf. Bring to a boil. Cover, reduce heat, and simmer 1 hour or until beans are just tender. Remove ham hock; cool slightly. Pick meat from bones; reserve meat. Discard bones and fat.
3. Add potato, turnip, and carrot to pan; cook 10 minutes or until tender. Stir in cabbage; simmer 4 minutes. Stir in parsley, thyme, vinegar, salt, and black pepper. Remove bay leaf.
4. Rub toast slices with cut sides of garlic clove; spread evenly with butter. Serve toast with soup. Serves 6 (serving size: about 1 cup soup and 1 bread slice).

CALORIES 235; FAT 7.3g (sat 2.4g, mono 2.8g, poly 0.6g); PROTEIN 13.1g; CARB 30.7g; FIBER 6.6g; CHOL 28mg; IRON 2.2mg; SODIUM 645mg; CALC 98mg

Portuguese Sardine and Potato Salad with Arugula

Hands-on time: 35 min. Total time: 35 min. *Skillet-fried sardines are standard fare for fishermen in Portugal, where the plentiful beauties are often served with boiled potatoes and lemony-dressed salad greens. Relatively inexpensive (we found them for $12 per pound), sardines are gorgeous fish to try—as well as a sustainable and nutritional standout. If they are too hard to come by, substitute 2 (4.25-ounce) cans of oil-packed sardine fillets.*

1½ pounds fingerling potatoes, halved lengthwise
5 tablespoons extra-virgin olive oil, divided
1 teaspoon kosher salt, divided
Cooking spray
3 tablespoons fresh lemon juice
2 tablespoons minced shallots
¼ teaspoon smoked paprika
1 large garlic clove, minced
8 fresh whole sardines (about 1 pound)
5 ounces baby arugula
8 lemon wedges
Freshly ground black pepper

1. Preheat oven to 400°.
2. Combine potato, 1 tablespoon oil, and ⅜ teaspoon salt on a baking sheet coated with cooking spray; toss well to coat. Bake at 400° for 15 minutes. Stir potatoes; bake an additional 10 minutes or until golden brown and tender. Combine 2 tablespoons oil, juice, shallots, paprika, garlic, and ¼ teaspoon salt in a large bowl, stirring with a whisk. Add hot potatoes to bowl; toss to coat.
3. Heat a large nonstick skillet over medium-high heat. Pat sardines dry with paper towels, and sprinkle with remaining ⅜ teaspoon salt. Add remaining 2 tablespoons oil to pan; swirl to coat. Add sardines to pan; cook 3 minutes on each side or until crisp and done.
4. Arrange about 1½ cups arugula on each of 4 plates. Remove potatoes from dressing with a slotted spoon; arrange about ¾ cup potatoes on each serving. Drizzle remaining dressing over salads; top each with 2 sardines. Serve each with 2 lemon wedges; sprinkle evenly with pepper. Serves 4.

CALORIES 347; FAT 19.1g (sat 2.7g, mono 14g, poly 2.3g); PROTEIN 9.1g; CARB 33.3g; FIBER 2.6g; CHOL 23mg; IRON 2mg; SODIUM 581mg; CALC 52mg

CRUNCH!
THE ART OF MAKING FOOD THAT'S SATISFYINGLY NOISY

Fight your way down the snack aisle of any American supermarket and the obsession with crunch is manifest—in fact, it's a global obsession.

The ratios of sugar, salt, and fat may vary, but crunch prevails. One theory about the ascendancy of crunch concerns evolution. Crispy-crunchy texture often signals freshness in fruits and vegetables, and, one supposes, in bugs. But the obvious fact is this: Crunch rings a gong in our brains very near to our deepest food-pleasure centers. We all crave crunch. The conundrum was this: Could we make favorite crunchy foods healthier, with less fat and sugar? We started out by devising a crunch-o-meter against which to measure our foods (it's at right), and then got cooking. It was crunch time in our Test Kitchen.

Kid Friendly • Make Ahead

Crunchy Chickpeas

Hands-on time: 15 min. Total time: 1 hr. 55 min.

2 (15½-ounce) cans organic chickpeas (garbanzo beans), rinsed and drained
2 tablespoons canola oil
1 teaspoon ground cumin
¾ teaspoon kosher salt
¼ teaspoon ground red pepper
⅛ teaspoon onion powder
1 garlic clove, minced

1. Preheat oven to 300°.

2. Wrap chickpeas in a towel; lightly roll to loosen skins. Discard skins. Combine chickpeas and remaining ingredients. Arrange on a baking sheet. Bake at 300° for 1 hour and 40 minutes, stirring every 20 minutes. Serves 8 (serving size: ¼ cup).

CALORIES 95; FAT 3.9g (sat 0.5g, mono 2.5g, poly 0.4g); PROTEIN 3.5g; CARB 11.6g; FIBER 2.5g; CHOL 0mg; IRON 0.9mg; SODIUM 195mg; CALC 39mg

CRUNCH-O-METER: 8

CRUNCHY CHICKPEAS: Low and slow is the key to drawing out all the moisture without burning the chickpeas or seasoning. As they cook, the spices mingle and mellow for a rounded flavor.

CRUNCH-O-METER

CRAZY CRUNCH	9	Toffee, Jolly Ranchers, Starlight peppermints
	8	Corn Nuts!
MEDIUM CRUNCH	7	Wasabi peas, the hard edges of melba toast, Grape Nuts cereal, thick hard pretzels
	6	Carrots, celery, bell peppers
	5	Toasted whole almonds, Stacy's pita chips
	4	Superfresh radishes, the crunchiest pickles
	3	Biscotti (except the hard-as-concrete kind), Captain Crunch, Kettle chips
LIGHT CRUNCH	2	Water crackers and thin tortilla chips, such as Xochitl brand
	1	Graham crackers

MY KIND OF *CRUNCH*

CHRISTINA TOSI

Chef and owner, *Momofuku Milk Bar*
NEW YORK

Working side by side with Momofuku owner David Chang pushes the creative envelope on a daily basis. Christina Tosi's desserts are famous for their blunt names and fun ingredients. Crunchy potato chips and pretzels are star ingredients in her Compost Cookies, which are perfectly baked until sugar forms a slight crust on the outside, with crunchy nuggets inside. Tosi likes to play with salty-sweet flavor combos, as well as texture. She explains: "It's not about fluffy extravagance for me. It's about simplicity and a sense of humor."

APRIL BLOOMFIELD

Chef and co-owner,
The Spotted Pig** and **The Breslin
NEW YORK

Crunch alone isn't complete for April Bloomfield, who is really excited about contrasting textures. In her yin-yang terms, crunchy doesn't reach its apex without something soft below. And that's why one potato dish has captured her heart (no, it isn't her popular thrice-fried chips, despite their cult-like following). It's potatoes roasted in magically transformational duck fat. As the potatoes roast, they develop a gorgeous golden exterior, becoming "supercrunchy on the outside, but hav[ing] this creamy interior," she says. "It's a heavenly combination."

ANDY RICKER

Executive chef, *Pok Pok*
PORTLAND, ORE.

Andy Ricker made his name as an American chef cooking great Thai food in Portland, Oregon, and now he's taken NYC by storm. During his extensive travels in Thailand,

Ricker picked up a trick for keeping fruits and vegetables crunchy: a soak in *naam boon sai*, a limestone solution. "It predates modernist molecular cuisine," says Ricker, though science can now explain why this technique works. The solution—made by combining white limestone paste with water—can also be mixed into batter for extra crunch in deep-fried foods.

BRYCE GILMORE

Executive chef and owner, *Barley Swine*
AUSTIN, TEXAS

Bryce Gilmore's flagship Odd Duck Farm to trailer truck may now be closed, but his haute-and-humble style continues at Barley Swine, harmoniously and deliciously. Gilmore confesses that crunchy nuts have always been a favorite of his, dating back to his childhood love of the old-school candy bar, Almond Joy. "Right now, I'm really liking fried nuts," he says. He makes his snack-of-the-moment by boiling nuts (usually pecans) in beer and sugar before frying and seasoning them, resulting in a snack that's sweet, spicy, salty, addictively tasty, and crazy crunchy.

KENJI LOPEZ-ALT

Chief creative officer and author of *The Food Lab: Better Home Cooking Through Science* at SeriousEats.com

"I associate thickness with 'crunchy,' but 'crispy' I see as a more fleeting shatter. If you can bite a few times and continue to get crunchy bits in your teeth, I'd call it crunchy." To bring crunch to battered food, Lopez offers a scientific rationale for adding booze to the batter. Vodka or beer evaporates quickly as food cooks (due to the alcohol), leaving it supercrisp. For a more crunchy mouthfeel, we created a rough panko coating for shrimp (page 256), with lots of nooks and crannies.

CRUNCH-O-METER: 6½

CELERY-APPLE SALAD: Here, crunch derives from ingredients rather than technique. Apples get the noise going, while celery, one of the loudest vegetables on earth, makes this a fresh festival of crunchy goodness.

Kid Friendly • Quick & Easy
Vegetarian

Celery-Apple Salad

Hands-on time: 8 min. Total time: 8 min.

2 tablespoons extra-virgin olive oil
2 tablespoons fresh lemon juice
¼ teaspoon kosher salt
¼ teaspoon freshly ground black pepper
2 cups thinly sliced Honey Crisp apple
2 cups sliced celery
½ cup loosely packed fresh flat-leaf parsley
⅓ cup sliced red onion

1. Combine first 4 ingredients. Add apple and remaining ingredients; toss to combine. Serves 6 (serving size: ⅔ cup).

CALORIES 62; FAT 4.6g (sat 0.7g, mono 3.3g, poly 0.5g); PROTEIN 0.5g; CARB 5.2g; FIBER 1.1g; CHOL 0mg; IRON 0.4mg; SODIUM 110mg; CALC 24mg

CRACKER-CRUST MUSHROOM PIZZA: We set out to maximize the crunch with a crust that basically shatters, deliciously. A small amount of yeast, a thin roll of the dough, and high-heat cooking nailed it. Minimalist toppings prevent sogging, but the center of the pizza still softens to the 3 to 4 range on the crunch-o-meter.

Vegetarian

Cracker-Crust Mushroom Pizza

Hands-on time: 40 min. Total time: 1 hr. 10 min.

Crust:
5 tablespoons warm water (100° to 110°)
1 teaspoon olive oil
¼ teaspoon active dry yeast
3.5 ounces bread flour (about ¾ cup)
3 tablespoons semolina flour
2 teaspoons chopped fresh rosemary
½ teaspoon salt
Cooking spray
Topping:
1 tablespoon extra-virgin olive oil, divided
4 ounces sliced shiitake mushroom caps
¼ teaspoon salt
2 teaspoons minced garlic
⅛ teaspoon crushed red pepper
1 tablespoon cornmeal
¼ cup lower-sodium marinara sauce
2 ounces shredded part-skim mozzarella cheese (about ½ cup)
2 tablespoons grated fresh Parmigiano-Reggiano cheese

1. To prepare crust, combine 5 tablespoons water, 1 teaspoon oil, and yeast in a bowl. Let stand 2 minutes. Weigh or lightly spoon 3.5 ounces bread flour into dry measuring cups; level with a knife. Sprinkle bread flour over yeast mixture. Add semolina flour, rosemary, and salt. Stir until just combined. Turn dough onto counter; knead 1 minute. Place dough in a medium bowl coated with cooking spray, turning to coat top. Cover and place in a warm place, free from drafts, 40 minutes.
2. Position an oven rack in lowest setting. Place a pizza stone on lowest rack. Preheat oven and pizza stone to 500°; leave stone in oven 30 minutes.
3. To prepare topping, heat a nonstick skillet over medium-high heat. Add 2 teaspoons oil to pan; swirl to coat. Add mushrooms to pan; sprinkle with ¼ teaspoon salt. Sauté 2 minutes. Add garlic and pepper; sauté 3 minutes.
4. Turn dough out onto a lightly floured surface. Roll dough out to a thin 14-inch circle. Transfer dough to a baking sheet dusted with cornmeal. Brush dough with 1 teaspoon oil. Slide dough onto the preheated pizza stone, using a spatula as a guide. Reduce oven temperature to 475°; bake 5 minutes. Remove from oven. Spread sauce over crust, leaving a ½-inch border; top with mozzarella cheese, mushroom mixture, and Parmigiano. Bake 4 minutes or until crust is browned. Slice pizza into 8 wedges. Serves 4 (serving size: 2 wedges).

CALORIES 226; FAT 8.3g (sat 2.6g, mono 3.7g, poly 0.7g); PROTEIN 10.2g; CARB 31g; FIBER 1.4g; CHOL 10mg; IRON 1.7mg; SODIUM 577mg; CALC 246mg

SEARED SALMON WITH WILTED SPINACH: Salmon skin cooks to a remarkably crisp exterior that's contrasted by buttery flesh beneath.

Quick & Easy

Seared Salmon with Wilted Spinach

Hands-on time: 17 min. Total time: 17 min. A thicker center-cut salmon fillet will yield best results.

4 (6-ounce) salmon fillets
¾ teaspoon kosher salt, divided
¼ teaspoon black pepper, divided
1 tablespoon canola oil, divided
1 pint grape tomatoes, halved
3 garlic cloves, sliced
1 (9-ounce) package fresh baby spinach
2 tablespoons small basil leaves

1. Preheat oven to 450°.
2. Sprinkle salmon with ½ teaspoon salt and ⅛ teaspoon pepper. Heat a large cast-iron skillet over high heat. Add 2 teaspoons oil to pan; swirl to coat. Add fillets, skin sides down; cook 3 minutes or until skin begins to brown, gently pressing fillets. Place pan in oven. Bake at 450° for 6 minutes or until desired degree of doneness.
3. Heat a nonstick skillet over medium-high heat. Add 1 teaspoon oil to pan; swirl to coat. Add tomatoes; sauté 1 minute. Add garlic; sauté 30 seconds, stirring constantly. Add spinach; remove from heat. Toss until spinach wilts. Stir in remaining ¼ teaspoon salt and remaining ⅛ teaspoon pepper. Place about ½ cup spinach mixture on each of 4 plates; top each serving with 1 fillet and basil. Serves 4.

CALORIES 346; FAT 16.5g (sat 3.6g, mono 8.1g, poly 3.5g); PROTEIN 38.4g; CARB 10.6g; FIBER 4.1g; CHOL 87mg; IRON 2.7mg; SODIUM 545mg; CALC 84mg

Sugar-Crusted Pork Cabbage Wraps

Hands-on time: 25 min. Total time: 2 hr. 20 min. *Coat pork tenderloin in a spiced, sticky sugar rub and roast until it's almost done—avoid overcooking the pork at this stage so it remains moist. Then cool slightly, shred, crisp the outside edges, and cook to desired degree of doneness in a hot skillet.*

1/4 cup granulated sugar
1/4 cup packed dark brown sugar
1 3/4 teaspoons kosher salt
2 teaspoons freshly ground black
 pepper
1/2 teaspoon five-spice powder
1 (1 1/2-pound) pork tenderloin, trimmed
 and silver skin removed
Cooking spray
2 tablespoons canola oil, divided
2 tablespoons dark sesame oil, divided
8 napa cabbage leaves
2 cups thinly sliced cucumber
1 cup (1-inch) green onion pieces
8 teaspoons hoisin sauce
4 teaspoons sambal oelek (ground
 fresh chile paste)

1. Combine first 5 ingredients, stirring well; rub spice mixture evenly over all sides of pork. Place pork in a zip-top plastic bag, and seal. Marinate in refrigerator 1 hour, turning every 20 minutes.

2. Preheat oven to 375°.
3. Remove pork from refrigerator; let stand at room temperature 30 minutes. Remove pork from bag, and discard marinade. Place pork on a broiler pan coated with cooking spray. Bake at 375° for 25 minutes or until a thermometer inserted in thickest portion registers 120°. Remove pork from oven; let stand 10 minutes. Cut pork crosswise into 2-inch pieces, and shred with 2 forks.
4. Heat a large nonstick skillet over medium-high heat. Add 1 tablespoon canola and 1 tablespoon sesame oil to pan; swirl to coat. Add half of shredded pork to pan; sauté 4 minutes or until browned and edges are crisp, stirring occasionally. Repeat procedure with remaining oils and pork. Place 1 cabbage leaf on each of 8 plates; divide pork evenly among leaves. Top each serving with 1/4 cup cucumber and 2 tablespoons green onions. Drizzle 1 teaspoon hoisin over each serving; top each with 1/2 teaspoon sambal oelek. Serves 8.

CALORIES 236; FAT 10g (sat 1.5g, mono 4.4g, poly 2.8g); PROTEIN 18.6g; CARB 18g; FIBER 0.8g; CHOL 55mg; IRON 1.3mg; SODIUM 581mg; CALC 37mg

Kid Friendly • Vegetarian

Tah Dig (Persian Rice)

Hands-on time: 10 min. Total time: 1 hr. 2 min.

4 cups water
1 cup long-grain basmati rice
1/2 cup plain 2% reduced-fat Greek
 yogurt
1 teaspoon kosher salt
1/8 teaspoon crushed saffron threads
1 1/2 tablespoons unsalted butter
2 teaspoons canola oil

1. Place 4 cups water in a saucepan over medium-high heat; bring to a boil. Add rice; cook 10 minutes. Drain. Rinse with cold water; drain.
2. Combine yogurt, salt, and saffron in a medium bowl. Add rice to yogurt mixture, stirring well.
3. Melt butter in a medium nonstick sauté pan over medium heat. Add oil to pan; swirl to coat. Add rice mixture to pan, lightly packing rice down. Wrap a clean, dry dish towel around lid to pan, tying it at the handle; place prepared lid on pan. Cook rice, covered, over medium heat 20 minutes (do not stir or uncover). Reduce temperature to medium-low; cook an additional 20 minutes or until rice is tender on top and a golden crust forms on bottom.
4. Loosen rice crust with a rubber spatula around edges. Place a plate over the top of pan, and invert rice onto plate, browned side up. Cut into 6 wedges, and serve immediately. Serves 6 (serving size: 1 wedge).

CALORIES 172; FAT 4.8g (sat 2.2g, mono 1.7g, poly 0.6g); PROTEIN 3.4g; CARB 31g; FIBER 0.9g; CHOL 9mg; IRON 1mg; SODIUM 327mg; CALC 13mg

Kid Friendly

Crispy Pork Spring Rolls

Hands-on time: 45 min. Total time: 45 min. Serve with spicy Sriracha sauce or sweet red chili sauce.

5 cups peanut oil
1 ounce bean thread noodles
2 medium shallots, peeled and coarsely chopped
2 garlic cloves, chopped
1 stalk peeled fresh lemongrass, coarsely chopped
1 (3.5-ounce) package shiitake mushrooms, stems removed
2 tablespoons dark sesame oil
1 tablespoon fish sauce
1 teaspoon sambal oelek (ground fresh chile paste)
½ teaspoon kosher salt
1 (1-inch) piece fresh ginger, peeled and grated
2½ cups grated carrot (about 3 medium)
1 pound lean ground pork
26 frozen square spring roll pastry wrappers, thawed

1. Place peanut oil in a large Dutch oven or deep fryer. Clip a candy/frying thermometer to the side of pot; heat oil to 385°.
2. Place noodles in a bowl, and pour enough boiling water over to cover by 1 inch. Let stand 20 minutes; drain well. Cut noodles with scissors into 1-inch pieces. Set aside.
3. Place shallots, garlic, and lemongrass in a food processor, and process until finely chopped. Add mushrooms; pulse until finely chopped. Add sesame oil and next 4 ingredients; process until well combined. Combine noodles, mushroom mixture, carrot, and pork in a large bowl, stirring until well blended.
4. Working with 1 spring roll pastry at a time (cover the remaining wrappers with a damp towel so they don't dry out), place the wrapper on a smooth work surface in a diamond pattern, with a corner edge pointing up and another pointing down. Place about 2 tablespoons pork mixture in the middle of pastry. Brush top point of pastry with water. Fold sides of pastry over filling; roll up jelly-roll fashion, starting from bottom. Gently press seam to seal. Repeat procedure with remaining pastry and filling to form 26 rolls.
5. Working in batches, place 5 spring rolls in 385° oil; fry 7 minutes or until golden and crisp, turning as necessary. Make sure oil temperature does not drop below 375°. Remove rolls with a slotted spoon; drain on a rack over paper towels. Return oil to 385°. Repeat procedure with remaining spring rolls and oil, making sure oil temperature does not drop below 375°. Serve immediately. Serves 26 (serving size: 1 roll).

CALORIES 108; FAT 5.5g (sat 1.3g, mono 1.7g, poly 1.4g); PROTEIN 4.6g; CARB 10.5g; FIBER 0.3g; CHOL 13mg; IRON 0.2mg; SODIUM 98mg; CALC 10mg

Kid Friendly • Quick & Easy

Pan-Fried Shrimp

Hands-on time: 25 min. Total time: 25 min.

1 cup panko (Japanese breadcrumbs)
1 tablespoon finely chopped flat-leaf parsley leaves
¼ teaspoon kosher salt
3.5 ounces rice flour (about ¾ cup)
2.25 ounces all-purpose flour (about ½ cup)
½ teaspoon baking soda
12 ounces chilled pilsner beer
6 tablespoons canola oil, divided
1½ pounds peeled, deveined large shrimp

1. Combine first 3 ingredients in a shallow baking dish; toss to combine. Weigh or lightly spoon rice flour and all-purpose flour into dry measuring cups; level with a knife. Combine flours and baking soda in a large bowl, stirring with a whisk. Gradually add beer, stirring with a whisk until smooth.
2. Heat a large skillet over medium-high heat. Add 3 tablespoons oil to pan; swirl to coat. Dip half of shrimp in batter; shake off excess. Dredge shrimp lightly in panko mixture. Place shrimp in a single layer in pan, and cook 2½ minutes on each side or until golden brown. Remove shrimp from pan; drain on paper towels. Repeat procedure with remaining oil, shrimp, batter, and panko mixture. Serves 4 (serving size: about 4½ ounces shrimp).

CALORIES 435; FAT 23.1g (sat 2g, mono 13.6g, poly 6.5g); PROTEIN 30.2g; CARB 22.8g; FIBER 0.9g; CHOL 252mg; IRON 4.3mg; SODIUM 610mg; CALC 52mg

Make Ahead

Chocolate-Almond Toffee

Hands-on time: 35 min. Total time: 1 hr. 35 min. We topped our buttery toffee with chopped whole almonds to add extra crunch. If you use other nuts, toast them first.

1 cup sugar
¼ cup water
4 tablespoons butter, softened
½ teaspoon vanilla extract
Dash of salt
2 ounces bittersweet chocolate, finely chopped
½ cup chopped whole almonds, toasted

1. Combine first 3 ingredients in a small, heavy saucepan over medium-high heat, stirring just until combined; bring to a boil. Cook, without stirring, until a candy thermometer registers 325° or until syrup begins to caramelize. Stir in vanilla and salt. Working carefully and quickly, pour sugar mixture onto a baking sheet covered with parchment paper; spread to desired thickness. Let toffee stand 5 minutes. Sprinkle chocolate over warm toffee; let stand 5 minutes. Spread melted chocolate in a thin, even layer over toffee; immediately sprinkle with chopped almonds. Let stand 1 hour or until completely cool. Break toffee into pieces. Serves 16.

CALORIES 118; **FAT** 6.6g (sat 2.8g, mono 2.1g, poly 0.7g); **PROTEIN** 1.2g; **CARB** 15.4g; **FIBER** 0.8g; **CHOL** 8mg; **IRON** 0.3mg; **SODIUM** 30mg; **CALC** 13mg

LESS MEAT, MORE FLAVOR

CRAB CAKES FOR LESS

By Mark Bittman

These treats and their shrimpy cousins can be made less costly without gaining that too-much-filler texture.

There's nothing quite like a seafood cake: luxurious with crab, shrimp, or fish; crisp and golden on the outside, soft and moist inside; and preferably served with a creamy sauce. They are a delight to eat, as long as you don't think about how much it costs to make them.

Fact is, the seafood that makes the best cakes tends to be the expensive kind: Lump crabmeat can be $25 per pound, and salmon and shrimp easily $15 or more. We gravitate toward these ingredients because they make really fantastic and familiar cakes. Yes, you could do sardine or bluefish cakes on the cheap, but those don't have quite the same allure. The savings solution is not to turn to less appealing seafood or to compromise on the quality of what you buy, but simply to make seafood cakes without using quite so much seafood. By combining seafood with ingredients that both flavor and help bind the cakes—I'm thinking more along the lines of beans and grains than eggs and bread—you can make a little bit of pricey fish go a long way.

The keys to holding the budget crab cakes together are to mash up the lump crabmeat a little before mixing in the rest of the ingredients, and to overcook the quinoa so it releases its starch and sticks together. The trick with the shrimp cakes is to first give some of the shrimp and white beans a whirl in the food processor, where they combine into a rough puree that binds the cakes together. You only need to sacrifice a small amount of each for the puree; the rest of it is lightly pulsed in afterward, along with a little cooked bulgur, so the cakes keep their signature flaky texture. In place of some of the pureed beans or starchy grains, you can also use grated vegetables such as celery root, carrots, or parsnips.

Since the cakes won't be loaded with cracker crumbs or mayonnaise, they're not as sturdy as you might be used to, so they benefit from a little time in the fridge to firm up before cooking. I take the mild anxiety of pan-frying out of play by brushing the cakes with oil and broiling them. They still develop a crust on both sides, but you use little fat.

I serve the crab and quinoa cakes with a simple tartar sauce, which cools down the Cajun-style spice rub. The shrimp and white bean cakes go with a sauce made from Greek yogurt, roasted garlic, and lime juice (the sweet richness of the garlic is a great match for the tang of the yogurt and lime). With flavorful sauces like these, you don't really need bread, but serving the cakes on toasted whole-wheat buns or English muffins is never a bad idea.

Of course, you can replace the shrimp and crab with salmon, scallops, or any good fish fillet you like. Whatever you choose, you'll wind up with seafood cakes that are as light on the stomach as they are on the wallet.

continued

Cajun Crab and Quinoa Cakes

Hands-on time: 34 min. Total time: 1 hr. 24 min.

4 cups water
½ cup uncooked quinoa
1 thyme sprig
½ teaspoon freshly ground black pepper
½ teaspoon paprika
¼ teaspoon ground red pepper
¼ cup plain fat-free Greek yogurt
¼ cup canola mayonnaise
¼ cup chopped sweet pickles
1 teaspoon Dijon mustard
8 ounces lump crabmeat, drained and shell pieces removed
¼ cup finely chopped red bell pepper
¼ cup finely chopped celery
¼ cup chopped green onions
½ teaspoon kosher salt
1 large egg white
2 tablespoons olive oil, divided

1. Combine first 3 ingredients in a saucepan; bring to a boil. Reduce heat; simmer 30 minutes or until mushy. Discard thyme. Drain, pressing to remove excess water. Cool slightly.
2. Combine black pepper, paprika, and red pepper. Combine yogurt, mayonnaise, pickles, and mustard.
3. Place crab in a medium bowl; mash slightly. Add quinoa, ½ teaspoon spice mixture, half of yogurt mixture, bell pepper, and next 4 ingredients; stir gently. Divide mixture into 8 equal portions; gently pat into a 3-inch-wide patty. Place on a parchment-lined plate. Refrigerate 20 minutes.
4. Preheat broiler to high.
5. Brush a jelly-roll pan with 1 tablespoon oil. Arrange chilled cakes on pan; brush tops with remaining 1 tablespoon oil. Sprinkle with half of remaining pepper mixture. Broil 5 minutes or until browned. Turn cakes

over. Brush with oil from pan; sprinkle with remaining spice mixture. Broil 5 minutes or until browned. Serve cakes with remaining sauce. Serves 4 (serving size: 2 cakes and 1 tablespoon tartar sauce).

CALORIES 327; FAT 20.2g (sat 2.2g, mono 11.4g, poly 4.9g); PROTEIN 16g; CARB 19.3g; FIBER 2.3g; CHOL 62mg; IRON 1.9mg; SODIUM 604mg; CALC 102mg

Shrimp and White Bean Cakes with Roasted Garlic Sauce

Hands-on time: 35 min. Total time: 2 hr. 5 min. *A little bit of cooked bulgur helps to bind the ingredients and make the cakes heartier—plus, it adds some whole grain.*

1 whole garlic head
7 teaspoons olive oil, divided
½ cup plain fat-free Greek yogurt
1 teaspoon fresh lime juice
½ teaspoon freshly ground black pepper, divided
¼ teaspoon kosher salt, divided
½ pound peeled and deveined medium shrimp, divided
1 (15-ounce) can cannellini beans or other white beans, rinsed and drained, divided
½ cup cooked bulgur
¼ cup coarsely chopped cilantro leaves

1. Preheat oven to 375°.
2. Remove white papery skin from garlic head (do not peel or separate cloves). Drizzle 1 teaspoon oil over garlic; wrap in foil. Bake at 375° for 1 hour; cool 10 minutes. Separate cloves; squeeze into a small bowl to extract pulp. Discard skins. Mash garlic using the back of a spoon. Stir in yogurt,

juice, ¼ teaspoon pepper, and ⅛ teaspoon salt.
3. Place 3 shrimp and ⅔ cup beans in a food processor; pulse until blended but not quite pureed. Add remaining shrimp, remaining beans, bulgur, cilantro, remaining ¼ teaspoon pepper, and remaining ⅛ teaspoon salt to food processor; pulse until coarsely chopped. Fill a ¼-cup dry measuring cup with shrimp mixture. Invert onto a platter lined with parchment paper; gently pat into a 2½-inch-wide patty. Repeat procedure with remaining shrimp mixture, forming 8 cakes. Refrigerate 20 minutes.
4. Preheat broiler to high.
5. Brush a jelly-roll pan with 1 tablespoon oil. Arrange chilled cakes on pan; brush tops of cakes with remaining 1 tablespoon oil. Broil 5 minutes or until browned. Carefully turn cakes over. Brush tops of cakes with oil from pan. Broil an additional 5 minutes or until browned. Serve cakes with sauce. Serves 4 (serving size: 2 cakes and about 2 tablespoons sauce).

CALORIES 223; FAT 9g (sat 1.3g, mono 5.9g, poly 1.3g); PROTEIN 18.7g; CARB 17.2g; FIBER 3.8g; CHOL 86mg; IRON 2.6mg; SODIUM 364mg; CALC 91mg

THERE'S NOTHING QUITE LIKE A SEAFOOD CAKE: LUXURIOUS WITH CRAB, SHRIMP, OR FISH; CRISP AND GOLDEN ON THE OUTSIDE, SOFT AND MOIST INSIDE.

Kid Friendly

Chicken Nuggets with Crispy Potato Chips and Honey Mustard

Hands-on time: 34 min. Total time: 1 hr. 24 min. *Use a mandoline for quick, uniform potato slices, keeping the purple and white slices separate, as cook times may vary. For speedier prep time, make the chips while the chicken marinates.*

Chicken nuggets:
4 (6-ounce) skinless, boneless chicken breast halves, cut into 1-inch pieces
⅓ cup low-fat buttermilk
⅓ cup dill pickle juice
1½ cups panko (Japanese breadcrumbs)
¼ teaspoon kosher salt
2 tablespoons water
1 large egg, lightly beaten
Potato chips:
1 tablespoon extra-virgin olive oil
¼ teaspoon salt
1 medium purple sweet potato (about 8 ounces), cut crosswise into ⅛-inch-thick slices
1 medium baking potato (about 8 ounces), cut crosswise into ⅛-inch-thick slices
Sauce:
¼ cup canola mayonnaise
¼ cup fat-free plain Greek yogurt
1 tablespoon honey
1 tablespoon yellow mustard
1 teaspoon Dijon mustard

1. To prepare chicken nuggets, combine first 3 ingredients in a large zip-top plastic bag. Marinate in refrigerator 1 hour, turning occasionally.
2. Place panko in a large skillet; cook over medium heat 3 minutes or until toasted, stirring frequently.
3. Preheat oven to 400°.
4. Remove chicken from marinade; discard marinade. Sprinkle chicken evenly with ¼ teaspoon kosher salt. Place panko in a zip-top plastic bag. Combine 2 tablespoons water and egg in a shallow dish; dip half of chicken in egg mixture. Add chicken to bag; seal and shake to coat. Remove chicken from bag; arrange chicken in a single layer on a baking sheet. Repeat procedure with remaining egg mixture, panko, and chicken. Bake chicken at 400° for 12 minutes or until done.
5. To prepare chips, combine oil and ¼ teaspoon salt in a large bowl. Add potatoes; toss gently to coat. Place microwave plate over parchment paper. Cut paper to fit plate. Cover plate with parchment paper; arrange purple potato slices in a single layer over paper. Microwave at HIGH 4 minutes or until potatoes are crisp and begin to brown. Repeat procedure with baking potatoes, reusing parchment paper.
6. To prepare sauce, combine mayonnaise and remaining ingredients in a medium bowl; stir to combine. Serve with chicken nuggets and potato chips. Serves 8 (serving size: about 6 nuggets, about 13 chips, and 1 tablespoon sauce).

CALORIES 241; **FAT** 6.1g (sat 0.7g, mono 3g, poly 1.3g); **PROTEIN** 23.8g; **CARB** 20.5g; **FIBER** 1.7g; **CHOL** 76mg; **IRON** 1.2mg; **SODIUM** 386mg; **CALC** 31mg

CLASSIC	MAKEOVER
660 calories per serving	241 calories per serving
44 grams total fat	6.1 grams total fat
1,000 milligrams sodium	386 milligrams sodium

CALLING ALL KID COOKS

Dip chicken pieces in egg mixture, and then let the kids shake them up in toasted panko. These oven-baked bites are 140 calories and 16g fat lighter than the 6-piece fast-food version.

Adults, slice the potatoes. Have kids lay slices on parchment paper, keeping the two potato types separate. These chips are better than store-bought, saving 261 calories and 251mg sodium per serving.

Put the kids on sauce duty, and stir up some fun. They'll fall in love with this healthier yogurt-based dip, with only 37 calories and 84mg sodium per tablespoon. Try with veggies as a sub for heavy ranch.

TODAY'S LESSON: CORN MUFFINS

The trick with corn muffins is the cornmeal-to-flour ratio, so you have just enough of the former to hearty-up the texture and enough flour and leavening to avoid doorstop density. Flour lends tender structure. Once you master a basic formula, though, you can have fun playing around with flavor variations, as we did here. The base lends itself to sweet or savory directions. Parmesan-chive or bacon-cheddar muffins can be a great pairing with soup or chili, while lightly sweetened raspberry muffins make a great breakfast.

Kid Friendly • Quick & Easy
Freezable • Make Ahead
Vegetarian

Parmesan Corn Muffins

Hands-on time: 15 min. Total time: 28 min.

Real imported Parmigiano-Reggiano cheese is worth the splurge since it tastes best.

1¼ cups nonfat buttermilk
¼ cup olive oil
1 large egg, lightly beaten
4.5 ounces all-purpose flour (about 1 cup)
¾ cup yellow cornmeal
1 tablespoon sugar
2 teaspoons baking powder
¼ teaspoon baking soda
¼ teaspoon salt
⅛ teaspoon ground red pepper
3 ounces grated fresh Parmigiano-Reggiano cheese (about ¾ cup), divided
3 tablespoons finely chopped fresh chives, divided
Cooking spray

1. Preheat oven to 400°.
2. Combine first 3 ingredients in a bowl, stirring with a whisk.
3. Weigh or lightly spoon flour into a dry measuring cup; level with a knife.

Combine flour and next 6 ingredients in a bowl, stirring well with a whisk. Make a well in center of flour mixture. Add milk mixture; stir just until moist.
4. Stir in 2 ounces cheese (about ½ cup) and 2 tablespoons chives. Spoon into 12 muffin cups coated with cooking spray. Sprinkle muffins evenly with remaining 1 ounce cheese and remaining 1 tablespoon chives.
5. Bake at 400° for 13 minutes or until a wooden pick inserted in center comes out with moist crumbs clinging. Remove muffins from tins; cool on a wire rack. Serves 12 (serving size: 1 muffin).

CALORIES 164; FAT 7.1g (sat 1.8g, mono 3.5g, poly 0.7g); PROTEIN 6.3g; CARB 18.5g; FIBER 0.7g; CHOL 20mg; IRON 1mg; SODIUM 300mg; CALC 177mg

Variation 1: Bacon, Onion, and Cheddar Corn Muffins

Cook 2 bacon slices in a skillet over medium heat. Remove bacon, reserving drippings in pan. Drain bacon; crumble. Increase heat to medium-high. Add ¾ cup chopped onion to drippings in pan; sauté 5 minutes. Prepare muffin batter, omitting sugar, cheese, and chives; stir in bacon, onion, and 2 ounces shredded sharp cheddar cheese (about ½ cup). Proceed with step 5. Serves 12 (serving size: 1 muffin).

CALORIES 137; FAT 4.6g (sat 1.5g); SODIUM 217mg

Variation 2: Raspberry-Cornmeal Muffins

Prepare muffin batter, omitting pepper, cheese, and chives. Stir in 1 cup fresh raspberries; spoon batter into prepared muffin cups. Sprinkle batter with 1 tablespoon sugar. Proceed with step 5. Serves 12 (serving size: 1 muffin).

CALORIES 144; FAT 5.1g (sat 0.8g); SODIUM 173mg

MUFFIN METHOD

MIX SEPARATELY
Stir wet ingredients. Separately, combine dry ingredients in a bowl, and make a well in the center.

GENTLY STIR BY HAND
Add milk mixture to the dry ingredients in bowl, and stir just until combined. Overmixing can create tough muffins.

PARTIALLY FILL
Divide batter evenly into prepared muffin tins, filling each cup about two-thirds full. An ice-cream scoop is great for even portioning.

WHAT TO COOK RIGHT NOW

FRESH THREE-BEAN SALAD

Canned beans may be a busy cook's best friend, and dried beans a healthy staple, but for a short window, freshly shelled beans offer a glorious middle ground. These mottled beans cook much quicker than dried, and their flavor and texture are superior to canned. Try fresh chickpeas in our vibrant Three-Bean Salad, where they combine with edamame (conveniently bought shelled and frozen) and slender haricots verts for a lovely side.

Three-Bean Salad

Hands-on time: 40 min. Total time: 56 min.

1 medium red bell pepper
¾ cup frozen shelled edamame (green soybeans), thawed
8 ounces haricots verts, trimmed
1½ cups cooked, shelled fresh chickpeas (garbanzo beans)
½ teaspoon kosher salt
½ teaspoon freshly ground black pepper
¼ cup minced shallots
3 tablespoons flat-leaf parsley leaves
1½ tablespoons fresh oregano leaves
2 tablespoons fresh lemon juice
1 tablespoon Dijon mustard
1 tablespoon extra-virgin olive oil

1. Preheat broiler to high.
2. Cut bell pepper in half lengthwise; discard seeds and membranes. Place pepper halves, skin sides up, on a foil-lined baking sheet; flatten with hand. Broil 10 minutes or until blackened. Place in a paper bag; fold to close tightly. Let stand 10 minutes. Peel and chop. Cook edamame and haricots verts in boiling water 4 minutes; rinse with cold water, and drain.
3. Combine bell pepper, edamame mixture, chickpeas, salt, and pepper in a medium bowl. Combine shallots and remaining ingredients, stirring well with a whisk. Drizzle dressing over bean mixture; toss. Serves 6 (serving size: about ⅔ cup).

CALORIES 255; FAT 6.2g (sat 0.6g, mono 2.3g, poly 1.6g); PROTEIN 12.8g; CARB 38.8g; FIBER 11.5g; CHOL 0mg; IRON 4.2mg; SODIUM 245mg; CALC 90mg

WHAT TO DRINK RIGHT NOW

BROWN SUGAR BOURBON SPARKLER
Combine ¾ cup water and ¼ cup dark brown sugar in a microwave-safe dish; microwave at HIGH 2 minutes, stirring until sugar dissolves. Cool, and then chill. Stir ¼ cup chilled fresh lemon juice and 3 ounces bourbon into chilled sugar syrup mixture. Divide mixture evenly among 4 glasses, and top each serving with about 3 tablespoons chilled dry sparkling wine and 2 to 3 dashes bitters. Serve immediately.

CALORIES 138; FAT 0g; SODIUM 4mg

30-MINUTE VEGGIE MAINS

Less time in the kitchen means more time to linger over cheesy pasta, lentil burgers, and a tasty Thai-style curry.

Quick & Easy • Vegetarian

Tomato and Asparagus "Carbonara"

Hands-on time: 25 min. Total time: 25 min. *Toss the pasta and vegetables immediately after cooking. The heat from the pasta will cook the egg, thickening it into a light, creamy sauce.*

3 quarts water
1 tablespoon extra-virgin olive oil
1 pound (1-inch) diagonally cut trimmed
  asparagus
3 garlic cloves, minced
1 pint cherry tomatoes, halved
2 ounces fresh pecorino Romano
  cheese, finely grated (about ½ cup)
½ teaspoon kosher salt
½ teaspoon freshly ground black pepper
1 large egg
8 ounces uncooked penne pasta
¼ cup basil leaves

1. Bring 3 quarts water to a boil in a Dutch oven.
2. Heat a large nonstick skillet over medium-high heat. Add oil to pan; swirl to coat. Add asparagus; sauté 3½ minutes. Add garlic; sauté 1 minute. Add tomatoes; cook 6 minutes or until tomatoes are tender.
3. Combine cheese, salt, pepper, and egg in a large bowl, stirring with a whisk.
4. Add pasta to boiling water; cook 10 minutes or until al dente. Drain

and toss pasta immediately with egg mixture. Add tomato mixture, tossing until sauce thickens. Place pasta mixture in each of 4 bowls. Sprinkle each serving with 1 tablespoon basil. Serve immediately. Serves 4 (serving size 1¼ cups).

CALORIES 335; FAT 8.7g (sat 3.2g, mono 3g, poly 0.7g); PROTEIN 14.7g; CARB 50.6g; FIBER 5.2g; CHOL 63mg; IRON 4.8mg; SODIUM 447mg; CALC 156mg

---

WINE MATCH

The bright, dry acidity of a sauvignon blanc will complement the grassy asparagus in Tomato and Asparagus "Carbonara" (and won't bring out an unflattering metallic taste). Try a fuller-bodied California wine like Simi Winery's Sonoma County Sauvignon Blanc ($14), with crisp lemon and rich tropical notes.

Quick & Easy • Vegetarian

Mushroom Lentil Burgers

Hands-on time: 28 min. Total time: 28 min. *Make homemade veggie burgers in a snap with precooked lentils. We like the black beluga variety from Archer Farms, with no added salt.*

1 tablespoon extra-virgin olive oil,
  divided
¾ cup chopped onion
2 garlic cloves, chopped
5 regular or whole-wheat hamburger
  buns, toasted and divided
6 ounces presliced cremini mushrooms
1 (8-ounce) pouch precooked black
  beluga lentils (such as Archer Farms)
4 teaspoons Dijon mustard, divided
2 teaspoons chopped fresh thyme
½ teaspoon freshly ground black
  pepper
¼ teaspoon kosher salt
1 large egg, lightly beaten
1 ounce goat cheese, crumbled
1½ tablespoons canola mayonnaise
½ cup baby arugula

1. Preheat broiler.
2. Heat a large nonstick skillet over medium-high heat. Add 1 teaspoon oil to pan; swirl to coat. Add onion and garlic; sauté 3 minutes or until onion is tender. Remove from heat.
3. Place 1 bun in a food processor; process until coarse crumbs form. Remove breadcrumbs from food processor; set aside.
4. Place mushrooms, lentils, 2 teaspoons mustard, and next 3 ingredients in food processor; pulse to combine.
5. Combine onion mixture, breadcrumbs, mushroom mixture, and egg in a large bowl, stirring well. Divide mixture into 4 equal portions, gently shaping each into a ½-inch-thick patty. Heat a large nonstick skillet over medium-high heat. Add remaining 2 teaspoons oil to pan; swirl to coat. Add patties; cook 4 minutes on each side or until browned. Remove patties from pan; arrange in a single layer on a baking sheet. Sprinkle patties evenly with cheese. Place under broiler 2 minutes or until cheese is softened.
6. Combine canola mayonnaise and remaining 2 teaspoons mustard in a small bowl. Spread top half of each of remaining 4 buns with 2 teaspoons mayonnaise mixture. Top each bottom half of bun with 1 patty. Divide arugula evenly among burgers, and top with top half of bun, coated side down. Serves 4 (serving size: 1 burger).

CALORIES 387; FAT 11.4g (sat 2.4g, mono 4.9g, poly 2.4g); PROTEIN 20.1g; CARB 51.4g; FIBER 7.2g; CHOL 56mg; IRON 3.1mg; SODIUM 579mg; CALC 123mg

Quick & Easy • Vegetarian
Jungle Curry with Tofu

Hands-on time: 26 min. Total time: 26 min.

1 cup uncooked jasmine rice
1 (12-ounce) package extra-firm tofu, drained and cut into ¹/₂-inch cubes
2 tablespoons canola oil, divided
2 cups (2-inch) cut haricots verts
1 small eggplant, cut into ¹/₂-inch cubes (about 4 cups)
1 red bell pepper, cut into julienne strips
2 tablespoons green curry paste
1 cup organic vegetable broth
3 tablespoons lower-sodium soy sauce
2 teaspoons brown sugar
2 teaspoons grated lime rind
1 cup thinly sliced fresh basil
Lime wedges (optional)

1. Cook rice according to package directions, omitting salt and fat.
2. Place tofu on several layers of paper towels, and cover with additional paper towels. Let stand 5 minutes, pressing down once.
3. Heat a large nonstick skillet over medium-high heat. Add 1 tablespoon oil to pan; swirl to coat. Add tofu; sauté 4 minutes or until lightly browned, stirring occasionally. Remove from pan; keep warm. Wipe pan clean with a paper towel. Return pan to medium-high heat. Add remaining 1 tablespoon oil to pan; swirl to coat. Add haricots verts, eggplant, and bell pepper; sauté 3 minutes, stirring occasionally. Add curry paste; cook 30 seconds, stirring frequently. Add broth, soy sauce, sugar, and rind; cook 5 minutes, stirring occasionally. Add reserved tofu; cook 1 minute. Place ½ cup rice in each of 4 shallow bowls. Top each with about 1½ cups tofu mixture and ¼ cup basil. Serve with lime wedges, if desired. Serves 4 (serving size: 1 bowl).

CALORIES 292; FAT 12.4g (sat 1g, mono 8.2g, poly 2.6g); PROTEIN 13g; CARB 35.4g; FIBER 6.1g; CHOL 0mg; IRON 3.2mg; SODIUM 686mg; CALC 201mg

RADICALLY SIMPLE COOKING
CHIC SUPPERS ON THE CHEAP

By Rozanne Gold

Create restaurant-worthy meals from everyday ingredients.

Anyone can make delicious recipes using costly, rarefied ingredients. But my greatest inspiration comes from transforming humble foods into enticing meals. Using a bit of ingenuity, I created these budget-friendly dishes, each with an unexpected "grace note" that makes the recipe feel celebratory despite the no-frills approach and simple preparation.

Roasted Cauliflower Fettuccine is a great example of a simple recipe transcending the sum of its parts. Commonplace cauliflower is roasted into addictive nuggets, while a touch of garlic and sunny citrus tie the flavors together. Good Parmigiano-Reggiano is expensive, but just a couple ounces make a big flavor statement. Serve with a romaine salad with cherry tomatoes.

Simple chicken and rice get an Asian transformation with soy, scallions, rice wine, and healthy faux-fried rice, enhanced with the last of summer's fresh corn and a profusion of fragrant basil. Chicken thighs are less expensive and more flavorful than breast meat, so they anchor the dish. A bowl of miso soup would make a delicious beginning to this late-summer meal.

Roasted Cauliflower Fettuccine

Hands-on time: 12 min. Total time: 1 hr. 4 min.

1 head cauliflower, cut into florets
3 tablespoons water
¹/₄ teaspoon kosher salt
¹/₄ teaspoon freshly ground black pepper
4¹/₂ teaspoons olive oil, divided
8 ounces uncooked fettuccine
1¹/₂ ounces pancetta or cured bacon, finely chopped
1¹/₂ teaspoons grated lemon rind
1 tablespoon fresh lemon juice
2 teaspoons chopped fresh thyme
1¹/₂ teaspoons minced fresh garlic
2 ounces fresh Parmigiano-Reggiano cheese, shaved (about ¹/₂ cup)

1. Preheat oven to 400°.
2. Combine first 4 ingredients; drizzle with 2 teaspoons olive oil. Toss. Arrange mixture on a baking sheet; bake at 400° for 40 minutes or until cauliflower is tender and golden, stirring twice. Cook pasta according to package directions, omitting salt and fat. Drain in a colander over a bowl, reserving ½ cup cooking liquid.
3. Heat a large skillet over medium heat. Add pancetta to pan; cook 5 minutes or until crisp, stirring frequently. Remove pancetta; set aside. Add remaining 2½ teaspoons oil to drippings in pan. Add ½ cup reserved cooking liquid to pan; bring to a boil over high heat. Boil 30 seconds or until emulsified, stirring constantly with a whisk. Add rind, juice, thyme, and garlic to pan. Add pasta; toss. Remove from heat. Add cauliflower and pancetta; toss. Top with cheese. Serve immediately. Serves 4 (serving size: 1¼ cups).

CALORIES 410; FAT 13.6g (sat 4.9g, mono 4.9g, poly 0.8g); PROTEIN 19.3g; CARB 55.7g; FIBER 7.7g; CHOL 20mg; IRON 3.1mg; SODIUM 583mg; CALC 222mg

Asian Marinated Chicken with Corn and Basil Faux-Fried Rice

Hands-on time: 45 min. Total time: 2 hr. 45 min.

Chicken:
1/3 cup sliced green onions
3 tablespoons lower-sodium soy sauce
2 tablespoons mirin (sweet rice wine)
2 teaspoons minced garlic (about 2 cloves)
8 skinless, bone-in chicken thighs
1 tablespoon olive oil
Rice:
1/2 cup uncooked basmati rice
1 tablespoon olive oil
2 tablespoons thinly sliced green onions
3/4 cup fresh yellow corn kernels (about 2 small ears)
1 tablespoon lower-sodium soy sauce
1/4 cup chopped fresh basil
1 lime

1. To prepare chicken, place first 4 ingredients in a large zip-top plastic bag. Add chicken to bag; seal. Marinate in refrigerator 2 hours, turning after 1 hour.
2. Preheat oven to 375°.
3. Heat a large ovenproof skillet over medium-high heat. Add 1 tablespoon oil to pan; swirl to coat. Remove chicken from bag; discard marinade. Add chicken to pan, meaty sides down; sauté 3 minutes. Turn chicken over; place skillet in oven. Bake at 375° for 10 minutes or until chicken is done. Let chicken stand 5 minutes.
4. To prepare rice, cook rice 15 minutes in boiling water; drain. Heat a large skillet or wok over medium-high heat. Add 1 tablespoon oil to pan; swirl to coat. Add 2 tablespoons onions to pan; sauté 30 seconds, stirring constantly. Add rice, corn, and 1 tablespoon soy sauce; sauté 5 minutes, stirring occasionally. Remove from heat; stir in basil. Divide rice evenly among 4 plates, and top each serving with 2 chicken thighs. Grate lime rind over chicken. Cut lime into wedges, and serve with chicken. Serves 4.

CALORIES 327; **FAT** 12.5g (sat 2.4g, mono 6.7g, poly 2.2g); **PROTEIN** 30.2g; **CARB** 21g; **FIBER** 1.8g; **CHOL** 115mg; **IRON** 2.1mg; **SODIUM** 515mg; **CALC** 33mg

KID-FRIENDLY COOKING

MATISSE SPICES UP DINNER

Our kid in the kitchen massages chicken and creates a new family fave.

To test one of our kid-friendly recipes, we contacted Matisse Reid, an 11-year-old foodie who loves to cook for her family and friends. This month, she received rave reviews for a flavorful spice rub applied to chicken. Here's her report.

–Phoebe Wu

"This month I tested a rub. I enjoyed measuring and combining all the ingredients. I made a double batch because we also had ribs in the fridge and Mom needed a rub for them, too. Instead of sprinkling the spices over the chicken, I placed the rub, oil, garlic, and chicken in a large zip-top bag and massaged the chicken through the bag (this was fun!). I cooked this on the outdoor grill instead of in a grill pan. The rub was delicious on both the ribs and the chicken. I found it a bit spicy, which is surprising for me, but I thought the flavor was good and liked the garlic in it. My mom, dad, brother, and sister loved it, and Mom wants me to make more to keep on hand for barbecues."

KEEP EXTRA RUB IN THE PANTRY–JUST ADD MEAT WHEN YOU'RE IN A HURRY.

Kid Friendly • Quick & Easy

Spice-Rubbed Grilled Chicken

Hands-on time: 5 min. Total time: 15 min.

1 teaspoon kosher salt
2 teaspoons Hungarian sweet paprika
2 teaspoons ground cumin
1 teaspoon dark brown sugar
1/2 teaspoon Spanish smoked paprika
1/4 teaspoon ground red pepper
1/4 teaspoon celery seeds
4 (6-ounce) skinless, boneless chicken breast halves
2 tablespoons olive oil
3 garlic cloves, minced
Cooking spray

1. Combine first 7 ingredients. Brush both sides of chicken evenly with oil; rub with garlic. Sprinkle spice mixture evenly over chicken; coat with cooking spray. Heat a grill pan over medium-high heat. Coat pan with cooking spray. Add chicken to pan, and grill 5 minutes on each side or until done. Serves 4 (serving size: 1 breast half).

CALORIES 261; **FAT** 9.3g (sat 1.5g, mono 5.5g, poly 1.2g); **PROTEIN** 39.7g; **CARB** 2.4g; **FIBER** 0.5g; **CHOL** 99mg; **IRON** 1.7mg; **SODIUM** 594mg; **CALC** 34mg

THE VERDICT

KALANI (AGE 14)
My brother really liked it! **10/10**

MATISSE
It was a little spicy for me (and my younger brother), but overall, it was very good. **8/10**

SUPERFAST

Zippy, flavorful entrées for less than $2.50 a serving: chicken chili, black bean cakes with eggs, and a fun plate of Mu Shu Pork Wraps.

Kid Friendly • Quick & Easy
Make Ahead

Popcorn Balls

1 tablespoon canola oil
3 tablespoons unpopped popcorn kernels
2 tablespoons unsalted butter
2¼ cups mini marshmallows
1 cup honey-nut toasted oat cereal
1 ounce pretzel sticks, broken into pieces
¼ cup chopped dry-roasted peanuts, salted

1. Heat oil in a Dutch oven over medium-high heat. Add kernels; cover and cook 4 minutes, shaking pan frequently. When popping slows, remove pan from heat. Let stand.
2. Melt butter in a pan over low heat. Add marshmallows; cook 2 minutes.

Remove from heat. Add 3 cups popcorn and remaining ingredients; stir. Cool 2 minutes. Form into 10 (3-inch) balls. Cool 5 minutes. Serves 10 (serving size: 1 ball).

CALORIES 122; **FAT** 5.8g (sat 2g, mono 1.9g, poly 1.5g); **PROTEIN** 2g; **CARB** 16.7g; **FIBER** 1g; **CHOL** 6mg; **IRON** 0.9mg; **SODIUM** 147mg; **CALC** 17mg

Quick & Easy

Chicken with Honey-Beer Sauce

Opt for an inexpensive, full-flavored domestic beer, like Blue Moon wheat ale.

2 teaspoons canola oil
4 (6-ounce) skinless, boneless chicken breast halves
¼ teaspoon freshly ground black pepper
⅛ teaspoon salt
3 tablespoons thinly sliced shallots
½ cup beer
2 tablespoons lower-sodium soy sauce
1 tablespoon whole-grain Dijon mustard
1 tablespoon honey
2 tablespoons flat-leaf parsley leaves

1. Heat a large skillet over medium-high heat. Add oil to pan; swirl to coat. Sprinkle chicken evenly with pepper and salt. Add chicken to pan; sauté 6 minutes on each side or until done. Remove chicken from pan; keep warm. Add shallots to pan; cook 1 minute or until translucent. Combine beer and next 3 ingredients in a small bowl; stir with a whisk. Add beer mixture to pan; bring to a boil, scraping pan to loosen browned bits. Cook 3 minutes or until liquid is reduced to ½ cup. Return chicken to pan; turn to coat with sauce. Sprinkle evenly with parsley. Serves 4 (serving size: 1 breast half and 2 tablespoons sauce).

CALORIES 245; **FAT** 4.5g (sat 0.7g, mono 2g, poly 1.1g); **PROTEIN** 40g; **CARB** 7.8g; **FIBER** 0.2g; **CHOL** 99mg; **IRON** 1.6mg; **SODIUM** 544mg; **CALC** 27mg

Kid Friendly • Quick & Easy
Freezable • Make Ahead

Fast Chicken Chili

1 tablespoon canola oil
1 pound skinless, boneless chicken breast, cut into bite-sized pieces
¾ teaspoon salt, divided
½ cup vertically sliced onion
2 teaspoons minced fresh garlic
2 teaspoons ground cumin
1 teaspoon ground coriander
½ teaspoon dried oregano
¼ teaspoon ground red pepper
3 cups no-salt-added canned cannellini beans, rinsed and drained
1 cup water
2 (4-ounce) cans chopped green chiles, undrained and divided
1 (14-ounce) can fat-free, lower-sodium chicken broth
¼ cup cilantro leaves
1 lime, cut into wedges

1. Heat a Dutch oven over medium-high heat. Add oil to pan; swirl to coat. Sprinkle chicken with ¼ teaspoon salt. Add chicken to pan; sauté 4 minutes. Add onion and next 5 ingredients; sauté 3 minutes. Add 2 cups beans, 1 cup water, remaining ½ teaspoon salt, 1 can chiles, and broth; bring to a boil.
2. Mash 1 cup beans and 1 can chiles in a bowl. Add to soup; simmer 5 minutes. Serve with cilantro and lime. Serves 6 (serving size: 1 cup).

CALORIES 189; **FAT** 4.3g (sat 0.5g, mono 1.8g, poly 1g); **PROTEIN** 22.3g; **CARB** 15.1g; **FIBER** 4.8g; **CHOL** 44mg; **IRON** 2.6mg; **SODIUM** 624mg; **CALC** 67mg

Butter-Pecan Mashed Sweet Potatoes

4 sweet potatoes (about 2 pounds)
1½ tablespoons butter
2 tablespoons fat-free milk
¼ teaspoon salt
¼ cup chopped pecans, toasted

1. Pierce each potato with a fork 3 to 4 times on each side. Wrap each potato in a damp paper towel. Microwave at HIGH 8 minutes, turning after 4 minutes. Cool slightly. Cut potatoes in half; scoop pulp into a bowl. Mash pulp.
2. Heat butter in a small saucepan over medium heat; cook 3 minutes or until browned. Stir butter, milk, and salt into potato pulp. Top with pecans. Serves 4 (serving size: ½ cup).

CALORIES 262; FAT 9.2g (sat 3.2g, mono 3.9g, poly 1.6g); PROTEIN 4.4g; CARB 41.5g; FIBER 7.6g; CHOL 12mg; IRON 1.4mg; SODIUM 304mg; CALC 51mg

Kid Friendly • Quick & Easy
Variation 1: Maple-Bacon
Prepare master recipe through step 1. Stir in 1 tablespoon softened butter, 2 tablespoons fat-free milk, and 4 teaspoons maple syrup. Top mashed sweet potato mixture with 1¼ ounces cooked and crumbled bacon (about 3 slices). Serves 4 (serving size: ½ cup).

CALORIES 268; FAT 6.6g (sat 3.1g); SODIUM 351mg

Quick & Easy • Vegetarian
Variation 2: Chipotle-Lime
Prepare master recipe through step 1. Stir in 1 tablespoon brown sugar, 2 tablespoons fat-free milk, 1 tablespoon fresh lime juice, 1½ teaspoons finely chopped chipotle chile in adobo sauce, ½ teaspoon adobo sauce, and ⅛ teaspoon salt. Serves 4 (serving size ½ cup).

CALORIES 193; FAT 0g (sat 0g); SODIUM 227mg

Quick & Easy • Vegetarian
Variation 3: Parmesan-Sage
Prepare master recipe through step 1. Stir in 1 tablespoon softened butter, 2 tablespoons fat-free milk, ½ teaspoon chopped fresh sage, 1 ounce grated fresh Parmesan cheese (about ¼ cup), and ⅛ teaspoon salt. Serves 4 (serving size: ½ cup).

CALORIES 233; FAT 4.9g (sat 3.1g); SODIUM 328mg

Turkey, Apple, and Swiss Melt

Vary the fruit to suit your kids' preferences— use red- or green-skinned apples or pears.

1 tablespoon Dijon mustard
1 tablespoon honey
8 (1-ounce) slices whole-wheat bread
4 (1-ounce) slices Swiss cheese
5 ounces thinly sliced Granny Smith apple (about 1 small)
8 ounces thinly sliced lower-sodium deli turkey breast
Cooking spray

1. Combine mustard and honey in a small bowl. Spread one side of each of 4 bread slices with 1½ teaspoons mustard mixture. Place 1 cheese slice on dressed side of bread slices; top each with 5 apple slices and 2 ounces turkey. Top sandwiches with remaining 4 bread slices. Coat both sides of sandwiches with cooking spray. Heat a large nonstick skillet over medium-high heat. Add sandwiches to pan. Cook 2 minutes on each side or until bread is browned and cheese melts. Serves 4 (serving size: 1 sandwich).

CALORIES 350; FAT 10.9g (sat 5.5g, mono 3g, poly 0.6g); PROTEIN 27.2g; CARB 34.5g; FIBER 4.3g; CHOL 46mg; IRON 1.9mg; SODIUM 758mg; CALC 287mg

Black Bean Cakes with Mixed Greens and Eggs

3 tablespoons canola oil, divided
5 large eggs, divided
1 (15-ounce) can black beans, rinsed and drained
½ cup panko, divided
¼ cup finely chopped green onions
2 tablespoons chopped fresh cilantro
¾ teaspoon ground cumin
¼ teaspoon kosher salt
¼ teaspoon ground red pepper
1 garlic clove, minced
1½ tablespoons olive oil
1½ teaspoons fresh lime juice
½ teaspoon Dijon mustard
¼ teaspoon kosher salt
¼ teaspoon black pepper
6 cups mixed baby lettuce

1. Place 1 tablespoon canola oil, 1 egg, and beans in a food processor; pulse 20 times or until mixture becomes a coarsely chopped paste. Combine bean mixture, 5 tablespoons panko, onions, and next 5 ingredients in a bowl.
2. Place 3 tablespoons panko in a dish. Divide bean mixture into 4 equal portions. Shape each into a ¾-inch-thick patty; dredge in panko. Heat a nonstick skillet over medium-high heat. Add 4 teaspoons canola oil to pan; swirl to coat. Add patties; cook 3 minutes on each side. Remove from pan. Wipe pan clean. Add remaining 2 teaspoons canola oil; swirl to coat. Crack 4 eggs into skillet. Cover and cook 4 minutes. Remove from heat.
3. Combine olive oil and next 4 ingredients, stirring with a whisk. Add lettuce; toss gently. Arrange 1½ cups salad, 1 black bean patty, and 1 egg on each of 4 plates. Serve immediately. Serves 4.

CALORIES 322; FAT 22.6g (sat 3.4g, mono 12.7g, poly 4.5g); PROTEIN 13.8g; CARB 18.7g; FIBER 5.1g; CHOL 264mg; IRON 3.4mg; SODIUM 602mg; CALC 92mg

Kid Friendly • Quick & Easy

Mu Shu Pork Wraps

(pictured on page 231)

If your butcher is unable to cut an 8-ounce piece of pork loin, buy 1 pound and freeze the remainder for another use. Save the mushroom stems for stocks or broths.

1 small head green or Savoy cabbage
2 tablespoons lower-sodium soy sauce
2 tablespoons dark sesame oil
1 tablespoon hoisin sauce
1 teaspoon cornstarch
1 (8-ounce) boneless pork loin, trimmed
½ cup matchstick-cut carrots
4 mushroom caps, thinly sliced
2 tablespoons canola oil, divided
¾ cup sliced green onions, divided
3 tablespoons water
2 teaspoons minced fresh garlic

1. Reserve 8 cabbage leaves. Shred remaining cabbage to measure 2 cups. Combine soy sauce and next 3 ingredients in a large bowl. Cut pork crosswise into ¼-inch-thick slices. Stack several slices vertically; slice pork into ¼-inch-thick pieces. Repeat procedure with remaining pork. Add pork, carrots, and mushrooms to soy sauce mixture; toss.
2. Heat a large skillet over medium-high heat. Add 1 tablespoon oil to pan; swirl to coat. Add ¼ cup onions to pan; sauté 30 seconds. Add shredded cabbage and water; sauté 2 minutes. Remove cabbage mixture from pan. Add remaining 1 tablespoon oil to pan; swirl to coat. Add remaining ½ cup onions and garlic; sauté 30 seconds. Add pork mixture; sauté 3 minutes or until done. Add cabbage mixture; toss. Place about ⅓ cup pork mixture into each of 8 reserved cabbage leaves. Serves 4 (serving size: 2 wraps).

CALORIES 248; FAT 17.1g (sat 2.4g, mono 8.2g, poly 5.3g); PROTEIN 13.5g; CARB 11.7g; FIBER 3.5g; CHOL 33mg; IRON 1.3mg; SODIUM 386mg; CALC 64mg

---

DINNER TONIGHT

Here is a batch of fast $15 menus to serve four from the *Cooking Light* Test Kitchen.

READY IN 40 MINUTES

The SHOPPING LIST

Lemony Grilled Shrimp Salad
Lemon (1)
Avocado (1)
Jicama (1)
Baby arugula (6 cups)
White wine vinegar
Extra-virgin olive oil
Smoked paprika
Queso fresco (1 ounce)
Extra-large shrimp (24)
Sugar

Spicy Mango
Mango (1)
Ground red pepper
Honey

The GAME PLAN

While grill preheats:
  ■ Combine shrimp and seasonings.
  ■ Slice jicama.
While shrimp grills:
  ■ Make vinaigrette.
  ■ Slice and season mango.
While mango grills:
  ■ Assemble salad.

Quick & Easy

Lemony Grilled Shrimp Salad

With Spicy Mango

Penny Pincher: Queso fresco is cheaper at Mexican markets.

2 teaspoons grated lemon rind
½ teaspoon smoked paprika
½ teaspoon kosher salt, divided
½ teaspoon black pepper, divided
7 teaspoons extra-virgin olive oil, divided
24 extra-large shrimp, peeled and deveined (about 1 pound)
Cooking spray
6 cups baby arugula
1 cup peeled jicama, cut into 2 x ¼-inch strips
1 avocado, peeled and diced
2 tablespoons fresh lemon juice
1 tablespoon white wine vinegar
¼ teaspoon sugar
1 ounce queso fresco, crumbled (about ¼ cup)

1. Preheat grill to high heat.
2. Combine rind, paprika, ¼ teaspoon salt, ¼ teaspoon pepper, 1 teaspoon oil, and shrimp in a medium bowl. Thread 4 shrimp onto each of 6 (10-inch) skewers. Coat grill rack with cooking spray. Grill shrimp 2 minutes on each side or until done.
3. Remove shrimp from skewers. Combine shrimp, arugula, jicama, and avocado in a large bowl; toss gently. Combine remaining 2 tablespoons oil, remaining ¼ teaspoon salt, remaining ¼ teaspoon pepper, lemon juice, vinegar, and sugar in a small bowl, stirring with a whisk. Add juice mixture to shrimp mixture, and toss gently to coat. Divide salad among 4 large plates; sprinkle evenly with queso fresco. Serves 4 (serving size: 2 cups salad and 6 shrimp).

CALORIES 309; FAT 18.4g (sat 3g, mono 11.7g, poly 2.6g); PROTEIN 26g; CARB 11g; FIBER 6g; CHOL 175mg; IRON 3.8mg; SODIUM 430mg; CALC 141mg

For the Spicy Mango:
Preheat grill to high heat. Combine 1 tablespoon extra-virgin olive oil, 1 tablespoon honey, ¼ teaspoon salt, and ¼ teaspoon ground red pepper in a small bowl. Peel 1 large mango, and cut lengthwise into 4 slices; toss with honey mixture. Grill 4 minutes on each side or until lightly charred and softened. Cut crosswise into ½-inch-thick slices. Serves 4 (serving size: ¼ mango).

CALORIES 80; **FAT** 3.5g (sat 0.5g); **SODIUM** 149mg

READY IN
40
MINUTES

The

SHOPPING LIST

Grilled Chicken Florentine Pasta
Garlic
Spinach (4 cups)
(6-ounce) bone-in skinless chicken
    breasts (2)
Canola oil
All-purpose flour
Parmesan cheese (3 ounces)
Whole milk (1 cup)
Fat-free, lower-sodium chicken broth (1 cup)
8 ounces linguine

Grilled Broccolini
Broccolini (1 pound)
Crushed red pepper

The

GAME PLAN

While grill preheats:
  ■ Cook pasta.
  ■ Prep Broccolini.
While Broccolini and chicken grill:
  ■ Make sauce for pasta.

Kid Friendly • Quick & Easy

Grilled Chicken Florentine Pasta
With Grilled Broccolini

Budget Buy: Bone-in chicken breasts cost less than boneless.
Penny Pincher: Asiago tastes like more expensive Parmesan.
Time-Saver: Refrigerated, fresh linguine cooks in under 4 minutes.

2 (6-ounce) bone-in chicken breasts, skinned
¾ teaspoon salt, divided
¾ teaspoon freshly ground black pepper, divided
Cooking spray
8 ounces uncooked linguine
2 tablespoons canola oil
3 tablespoons all-purpose flour
1 teaspoon chopped garlic
1 cup whole milk
1 cup fat-free, lower-sodium chicken broth
3 ounces fresh Parmesan cheese, grated (about ¾ cup)
4 cups fresh spinach leaves

1. Preheat grill to medium-high heat.
2. Sprinkle chicken with ¼ teaspoon salt and ¼ teaspoon pepper. Place chicken on grill rack coated with cooking spray, and grill 8 minutes on each side or until done. Let stand 10 minutes. Carve chicken off bones, and thinly slice.

3. Cook pasta according to package directions. Drain well; keep warm.
4. Heat a large nonstick skillet over medium-high heat. Add oil to pan; swirl to coat. Add flour and garlic; cook until garlic is browned (about 2 minutes), stirring constantly. Add milk and broth, stirring with a whisk; bring to a simmer, and cook 2 minutes or until thickened. Add cheese, stirring until cheese melts. Add remaining ½ teaspoon salt, remaining ½ teaspoon pepper, and spinach; stir until spinach wilts. Add pasta and chicken; toss to combine. Serves 4 (serving size: about 1½ cups).

CALORIES 332; **FAT** 10.3g (sat 3.2g, mono 4.3g, poly 1.7g); **PROTEIN** 24.8g; **CARB** 35g; **FIBER** 2g; **CHOL** 46mg; **IRON** 2.6mg; **SODIUM** 579mg; **CALC** 195mg

For the Grilled Broccolini:
Preheat grill to medium-high. Combine 1 teaspoon canola oil, ½ teaspoon crushed red pepper, ¼ teaspoon salt, and 1 pound trimmed Broccolini in a large bowl; toss to coat. Place in a grill basket; grill 4 minutes on each side or until lightly browned. Serves 4 (serving size: ⅓ cup).

CALORIES 58; **FAT** 1.2g (sat 0.1g); **SODIUM** 181mg

The
SHOPPING LIST

Sweet-Spicy Chicken and Vegetable Stir-Fry

Sugar snap peas (8 ounces)
Red bell pepper (1)
Red onion (1 medium)
Green onions
Dark brown sugar
Cornstarch
Canola oil
Unsalted dry-roasted peanuts
Lower-sodium soy sauce
Fish sauce
Rice vinegar
Sambal oelek
Dark sesame oil
Skinless, boneless chicken breast
  (1 pound)

Double Sesame Rice

Boil-in-bag long-grain rice
Toasted sesame seeds

The
GAME PLAN

While water for rice comes to a boil:
- Cut chicken.
- Prep vegetables.

While rice cooks:
- Cook stir-fry.

Quick & Easy

Sweet-Spicy Chicken and Vegetable Stir-Fry
With Double Sesame Rice
(pictured on page 231)

Budget Buy: Shop for Asian condiments at Asian markets.
Penny Pincher: Boil-in-bag rice is inexpensive; longer cooking rice is even cheaper.
Time-Saver: Choose pretoasted sesame seeds and save a step.

3 tablespoons dark brown sugar
1½ tablespoons lower-sodium soy sauce
1 tablespoon fish sauce
1 tablespoon rice vinegar
1 tablespoon sambal oelek
1 teaspoon dark sesame oil
¾ teaspoon cornstarch
2 tablespoons canola oil, divided
1 pound skinless, boneless chicken breast, cut into bite-sized pieces
8 ounces sugar snap peas
1 red bell pepper, sliced
½ medium-sized red onion, cut into thin wedges
¼ cup sliced green onions
¼ cup unsalted dry-roasted peanuts

1. Combine first 7 ingredients, stirring well; set aside.
2. Heat a large wok or large heavy skillet over high heat. Add 1 tablespoon canola oil to pan; swirl to coat. Add chicken; stir-fry 4 minutes or until browned and done. Remove chicken from pan. Add remaining 1 tablespoon canola oil to pan; swirl to coat. Add sugar snap peas, bell pepper, and red onion; stir-fry 3 minutes or until vegetables are crisp-tender. Stir in brown sugar mixture; cook 1 minute or until thickened. Stir in chicken; toss to coat. Sprinkle with green onions and peanuts. Serves 4 (serving size: 1 cup).

CALORIES 349; **FAT** 14.2g (sat 1.7g, mono 7.5g, poly 4.3g); **PROTEIN** 31g; **CARB** 24.6g; **FIBER** 3.5g; **CHOL** 66mg; **IRON** 2mg; **SODIUM** 576mg; **CALC** 69mg

---

For the Double Sesame Rice:
Cook 1 (3½-ounce) bag boil-in-bag long-grain rice according to package directions; drain. Stir in 1 tablespoon toasted sesame seeds, 2 teaspoons dark sesame oil, and ¼ teaspoon salt. Serves 4 (serving size: ½ cup).

CALORIES 119; **FAT** 3.3g (sat 1.7g); **SODIUM** 148mg

The
SHOPPING LIST

Pork Chops with Roasted Apples and Onions

Gala apples (2)
Fresh thyme
Fat-free, lower-sodium chicken broth
Canola oil
Cider vinegar
All-purpose flour
Butter
Frozen pearl onions
Bone-in, center-cut pork loin chops
  (4 [6-ounce])

Haricots Verts and Mustard Vinaigrette

Microwavable haricots verts
  (2 [8-ounce] packages)
Olive oil
Stone-ground mustard

The
GAME PLAN

While oven preheats:
- Make vinaigrette.
- Cut apples.
- Brown onions.

While apple mixture roasts:
- Cook pork.
- Make pan sauce.
- Steam haricots verts.

continued

Pork Chops with Roasted Apples and Onions

With Haricots Verts and Mustard Vinaigrette

Budget Buy: Purchase bone-in pork chops instead of boneless.
Penny Pincher: Gala apples are less expensive when in season in the fall.
Technique Tip: Use a stainless steel skillet to build flavor for the pan sauce.

2½ teaspoons canola oil, divided
1½ cups frozen pearl onions, thawed
2 cups Gala apple wedges
1 tablespoon butter, divided
2 teaspoons thyme leaves
½ teaspoon kosher salt, divided
½ teaspoon freshly ground black pepper, divided
4 (6-ounce) bone-in center-cut pork loin chops (about ½ inch thick)
½ cup fat-free, lower-sodium chicken broth
½ teaspoon all-purpose flour
1 teaspoon cider vinegar

1. Preheat oven to 400°.
2. Heat a large ovenproof skillet over medium-high heat. Add 1 teaspoon oil to pan; swirl to coat. Pat onions dry with a paper towel. Add onions to pan; cook 2 minutes or until lightly browned, stirring once. Add apple to pan; place in oven. Bake at 400° for 10 minutes or until onions and apple are tender. Stir in 2 teaspoons butter, thyme, ¼ teaspoon salt, and ¼ teaspoon pepper.

3. Heat a large skillet over medium-high heat. Sprinkle pork with remaining ¼ teaspoon salt and ¼ teaspoon pepper. Add remaining 1½ teaspoons oil to pan; swirl to coat. Add pork to pan; cook 3 minutes on each side or until desired degree of doneness. Remove pork from pan; keep warm. Combine broth and flour in a small bowl, stirring with a whisk. Add broth mixture to pan; bring to a boil, scraping pan to loosen browned bits. Cook 1 minute or until reduced to ¼ cup. Stir in vinegar and remaining 1 teaspoon butter. Serve sauce with pork and apple mixture. Serves 4 (serving size: 1 chop, about 1 tablespoon sauce, and ¾ cup apple mixture).

CALORIES 240; **FAT** 10g (sat 3.3g, mono 4.1g, poly 1.4g); **PROTEIN** 24.9g; **CARB** 11g; **FIBER** 1.5g; **CHOL** 84mg; **IRON** 1mg; **SODIUM** 379mg; **CALC** 28mg

For Haricots Verts and Mustard Vinaigrette:
Cook 2 (8-ounce) packages microwave-in-a-bag fresh haricots verts according to package directions. Combine 1½ teaspoons olive oil, 1½ teaspoons cider vinegar, 1 teaspoon stone-ground mustard, ¼ teaspoon kosher salt, and ¼ teaspoon freshly ground black pepper in a medium bowl. Add beans; toss well to coat. Serves 4.

CALORIES 51; **FAT** 1.8g (sat 0.3g); **SODIUM** 143mg

OOPS!
YOUR PUDDING LOOKS LIKE PORRIDGE

Irate over curds in your way? Temper, temper...

So you undertake the decidedly old-school but comforting job of making a pudding. You carefully stir the beaten eggs into the hot milk mixture, but soon you see the dreaded signs of mixture separation. And when it breaks, it breaks fast—and now you've got a watery pile of scrambled eggs suspended in a milky broth. The problem is a failure to temper, the critical heat-control technique that basically acclimates eggs to higher heat.

The solution: Slowly whisk a thin stream of the hot milk mixture into beaten raw eggs in a bowl. Tempering will heat the eggs gradually without cooking them completely. The milk-egg mixture can then be returned to the pan and cooked as the recipe requires. Be patient cooking, though: If you crank up the heat after tempering, you can still wreck things, even with the inclusion of flour or cornstarch helping to stabilize. A small jump in the pudding's temperature can lead to coagulation.

CHICKEN STRUTS ITS STUFF

Fun recipes that put America's favorite bird in bright, new flavor feathers

THE IDEA

This is a riff on coq au vin, the French standard of chicken and veggies simmered in red wine. The coq usually takes on a deep purplish-red cast from the vin, but our modern take cooks the chicken in broth: It tastes lighter and looks much brighter. After the chicken cooks, it's smothered with a delicious Champagne reduction sauce that's enriched with nutty browned butter.

Make Ahead

Champagne-Browned Butter Chicken

Hands-on time: 50 min. Total time: 1 hr. 50 min. Browned-butter flavor, Champagne zing.

2 center-cut bacon slices
²/₃ cup all-purpose flour
6 bone-in chicken thighs, skinned (about 1³/₄ pounds)
6 bone-in chicken drumsticks, skinned (about 1¹/₂ pounds)
1¹/₄ teaspoons kosher salt, divided
³/₄ teaspoon freshly ground black pepper, divided
2 tablespoons canola oil, divided
1 pound red-skinned potatoes, quartered
1 pound button mushrooms, halved
¹/₄ cup brandy
4 shallots, halved

³/₄ cup no-salt-added chicken stock (such as Swanson)
1 tablespoon black peppercorns
3 thyme sprigs
1 bay leaf
¹/₂ bunch fresh flat-leaf parsley
12 baby carrots with tops
1 cup Champagne
3 tablespoons butter
1 teaspoon all-purpose flour
2 tablespoons chopped fresh flat-leaf parsley
2 teaspoons chopped fresh thyme

1. Preheat oven to 300°.
2. Cook bacon in a large Dutch oven over medium heat until crisp; remove bacon from pan, reserving drippings in pan. Reserve bacon for another use. Place ²/₃ cup flour in a shallow dish. Sprinkle chicken evenly with ¾ teaspoon salt and ½ teaspoon pepper. Dredge chicken lightly in flour; shake off excess flour. Increase heat to medium-high. Add 1 tablespoon oil to drippings in pan; swirl to coat. Add half of chicken to pan; cook 5 minutes or until browned. Turn chicken over; cook 2 minutes. Remove from pan. Repeat procedure with remaining 1 tablespoon oil and chicken.
3. Add potatoes to pan; cook 3 minutes or until browned, stirring occasionally. Add mushrooms; sprinkle with ¼ teaspoon salt. Cook 3 minutes, stirring occasionally. Stir in brandy. Cook until liquid almost evaporates (about 30 seconds), stirring occasionally. Return chicken to pan. Add shallots and stock; bring to a boil. Place

peppercorns and next 3 ingredients on a double layer of cheesecloth. Gather edges; tie with butcher's twine. Add bundle to pan. Bake, uncovered, at 300° for 15 minutes.
4. Trim carrot tops to 1-inch; scrub carrots. Add carrots to pan. Bake an additional 45 minutes or until vegetables are tender and chicken is done. Remove chicken and vegetables from pan; keep warm. Discard herb bundle. Place pan over medium-high heat. Add Champagne to pan; bring to a boil, scraping pan to loosen browned bits. Cook until mixture reduces to ²/₃ cup (about 11 minutes).
5. Melt butter in a small saucepan over medium heat. Cook butter 3 minutes or until lightly browned, shaking pan occasionally. Stir in 1 teaspoon flour; cook 1 minute, stirring constantly with a whisk. Gradually add butter mixture to reduced wine mixture, stirring constantly with a whisk. Cook 1 minute or until slightly thick. Stir in remaining ¼ teaspoon salt and ¼ teaspoon pepper. Serve with chicken and vegetables. Garnish with chopped fresh parsley and thyme. Serves 6 (serving size: 1 drumstick, 1 thigh, 2 carrots, about ²/₃ cup mushroom mixture, and about 2 tablespoons sauce).

CALORIES 464; FAT 16.9g (sat 5.7g, mono 6.5g, poly 3.1g); PROTEIN 35.9g; CARB 39.2g; FIBER 3.1g; CHOL 123mg; IRON 4.2mg; SODIUM 658mg; CALC 40mg

BANISH ALL BORING BIRDS: REV UP DINNER WITH TANGY, SMOKY, OR FIERY FLAVORS.

Kung Pao Chicken Tacos

(pictured on page 232)

Hands-on time: 30 min. Total time: 1 hr.

- **6 skinless, boneless chicken thighs, cut into bite-sized pieces**
- **3 tablespoons lower-sodium soy sauce, divided**
- **¼ cup plus 1½ teaspoons cornstarch, divided**
- **¼ teaspoon kosher salt**
- **2 tablespoons canola oil, divided**
- **1½ tablespoons honey**
- **1 tablespoon dark sesame oil**
- **2 teaspoons rice vinegar**
- **1 teaspoon sambal oelek (ground fresh chile paste)**
- **1 large garlic clove, minced**
- **3 tablespoons coarsely chopped dry-roasted peanuts**
- **¾ cup diagonally sliced celery (about 2 stalks)**
- **8 (6-inch) corn tortillas**
- **⅓ cup sliced green onions**
- **½ medium-sized red bell pepper, thinly sliced**
- **4 lime wedges**

1. Place chicken in a large zip-top plastic bag. Add 1 tablespoon soy sauce to bag; seal. Marinate at room temperature 30 minutes. Remove chicken from bag; discard marinade. Place ¼ cup cornstarch in a shallow dish. Sprinkle chicken evenly with salt. Add chicken to cornstarch in dish; toss to coat. Shake off excess cornstarch.
2. Heat a large skillet over medium-high heat. Add 1 tablespoon canola oil to pan; swirl to coat. Add half of coated chicken; sauté 6 minutes or until done, turning to brown. Remove chicken from pan using a slotted spoon; drain on paper towels. Repeat procedure with remaining 1 tablespoon canola oil and coated chicken.
3. Combine remaining 1½ teaspoons cornstarch, remaining 2 tablespoons soy sauce, honey, and next 3 ingredients in a microwave-safe bowl, stirring with a whisk until smooth. Microwave at HIGH 1½ minutes or until slightly thick, stirring twice. Stir in garlic. Combine soy sauce mixture, chicken, peanuts, and celery; toss to coat.
4. Toast tortillas under broiler or on a griddle until lightly blistered, turning frequently. Place 2 tortillas on each of 4 plates; divide chicken mixture evenly among tortillas. Top each taco with green onions and bell pepper strips; serve with lime wedges. Serves 4 (serving size: 2 tacos).

CALORIES 418; FAT 19.1g (sat 2.5g, mono 8.9g, poly 6.1g); PROTEIN 25.2g; CARB 39.3g; FIBER 4g; CHOL 86mg; IRON 1.6mg; SODIUM 531mg; CALC 53mg

Kid Friendly • Quick & Easy

Crisp Chicken Marinara

Hands-on time: 26 min. Total time: 37 min. *Keeping chicken crispy.*

- **2½ tablespoons olive oil, divided**
- **1 cup chopped onion**
- **1 carrot, diced**
- **3 garlic cloves, minced**
- **⅓ cup red wine**
- **1½ cups lower-sodium marinara sauce (such as Amy's)**
- **⅓ cup pitted, coarsely chopped oil-cured olives**
- **5 tablespoons water, divided**
- **4 (6-ounce) skinless, boneless chicken breast halves**
- **1 large egg, lightly beaten**
- **2 ounces fresh Parmesan cheese, divided**
- **½ cup panko (Japanese breadcrumbs)**
- **2 cups hot cooked orzo pasta**
- **2 tablespoons chopped fresh flat-leaf parsley**

1. Heat a saucepan over medium-high heat; add oil to pan, swirl to coat. Add onion and carrot; sauté 3 minutes. Add garlic; sauté 1 minute, stirring constantly. Add wine; cook 2 minutes. Stir in marinara sauce, olives, and ¼ cup water. Reduce heat to medium, and simmer 10 minutes, stirring occasionally. Nestle chicken in sauce. Cover and simmer 15 minutes or until chicken is almost done. Remove chicken from pan.
2. Preheat broiler to high.
3. Combine remaining 1 tablespoon water and egg in a shallow dish. Grate 1 ounce cheese. Combine panko and grated cheese in a shallow dish. Coat chicken with egg mixture, and dredge in panko mixture.
4. Heat an ovenproof skillet over medium-high heat. Add remaining 1½ tablespoons oil to pan; swirl to coat. Place chicken in pan; sauté 2 minutes or until lightly browned. Turn chicken over. Place skillet in oven, and broil chicken 3 minutes or until golden and done. Arrange ½ cup orzo in each of 4 shallow bowls; top with ½ cup sauce and 1 chicken breast half. Garnish evenly with parsley; shave remaining 1 ounce cheese evenly over top of each serving. Serves 4.

CALORIES 516; FAT 19.2g (sat 4.7g, mono 10.3g, poly 1.9g); PROTEIN 45g; CARB 36.9g; FIBER 3g; CHOL 117mg; IRON 3.4mg; SODIUM 611mg; CALC 218mg

THE IDEA

Move over, chicken noodle soup—ramen is the new bowl of comfort. Here, we offer a Japanese-style chicken soup twist, flavored with miso, soy sauce, chile paste, and porcini mushrooms.

Ramen Noodle Bowl

Hands-on time: 1 hr. 8 min. Total time: 1 hr. 8 min.

4 cups boiling water
½ ounce dried porcini mushrooms
1 smoked bacon slice
½ cup chopped onion
1 carrot, coarsely chopped
2 tablespoons yellow miso
2 tablespoons lower-sodium soy sauce
2 cups no-salt-added chicken stock
3 garlic cloves, crushed
1 (½-inch) piece ginger, cut into thin slices
8 ounces fresh Chinese egg noodles or ramen noodles
2 tablespoons dark sesame oil, divided
2 (4-ounce) packages gourmet fresh mushrooms
6 skin-on, boneless chicken thighs
3 large eggs
¾ cup thinly sliced green onion strips
2 tablespoons sambal oelek (ground fresh chile paste)

1. Combine 4 cups boiling water and porcini; let stand 15 minutes. Drain through a sieve over a bowl; reserve porcini and soaking liquid. Slice porcini; set aside.
2. Heat a Dutch oven over medium heat. Add bacon; cook until almost crisp. Increase heat to medium-high. Add onion and carrot; sauté 2 minutes. Combine miso and soy sauce. Add miso mixture, porcini liquid, stock, garlic, and ginger to pan; bring to a boil. Reduce heat, and simmer 20 minutes. Strain mixture through a sieve over a bowl; discard solids. Wipe pan clean. Return broth to pan; bring to a boil. Add noodles; cook 8 minutes or until tender. Remove from heat.
3. Heat a large skillet over medium-high heat. Add 1 tablespoon sesame oil to pan; swirl. Add fresh mushrooms; sauté 8 minutes. Remove from pan; combine porcini and fresh mushrooms. Add remaining 1 tablespoon sesame oil to pan; swirl to coat. Add chicken, skin-side down; sauté 7 minutes or until skin is very crisp and golden brown. Turn chicken over; sauté 2 minutes or until done.
4. Place eggs in a small saucepan; add water to cover. Bring to a boil; cook 1 minute. Remove from heat; let stand 3 minutes. Drain; rinse under cold water. Drain and peel.
5. Divide noodle mixture among 6 bowls; top each serving with 3 tablespoons mushroom mixture, 2 tablespoons green onions, 1 chicken thigh, ½ egg, and 1 teaspoon sambal. Serves 6.

CALORIES 449; FAT 23.9g (sat 6.3g, mono 9.8g, poly 6g); PROTEIN 30g; CARB 28.1g; FIBER 2.6g; CHOL 186mg; IRON 2.7mg; SODIUM 654mg; CALC 56mg

THE IDEA

Thai green curry is a sauce of lemongrass, ginger, chiles, and herbs. It's spicy, fragrant, and wonderful, and turns pedestrian chicken patties into spicy powerhouses that are perfect with crunchy slaw.

Green Curry Fritters

Hands-on time: 25 min. Total time: 1 hr. 5 min. Patties with a curry punch.

⅔ cup panko (Japanese breadcrumbs)
¼ cup diagonally sliced green onions
1 pound ground chicken breast
2 tablespoons canola mayonnaise
1½ tablespoons green curry paste
1 tablespoon dark sesame oil
1 tablespoon lower-sodium soy sauce
2 teaspoons sambal oelek (ground fresh chile paste)
⅜ teaspoon kosher salt
½ teaspoon grated peeled fresh ginger
1 large egg
2 tablespoons canola oil, divided

1. Place first 3 ingredients in a large bowl. Combine mayonnaise and next 7 ingredients. Add mayonnaise mixture to chicken mixture; mix lightly until combined. Divide into 12 equal portions; gently shape each portion into a small patty (do not pack).
2. Heat a large skillet over medium-high heat. Add 1 tablespoon canola oil to pan; swirl. Add 6 patties to pan; cook 2½ minutes on each side or until done. Remove from pan. Repeat procedure with remaining oil and patties. Serve with Cabbage Slaw. Serves 6 (serving size: 2 fritters).

CALORIES 206; FAT 11.9g (sat 1.2g, mono 6.3g, poly 3.4g); PROTEIN 18.4g; CARB 6g; FIBER 0.3g; CHOL 75mg; IRON 0.2mg; SODIUM 368mg; CALC 8mg

Make Ahead • Vegetarian

Cabbage Slaw

Hands-on time: 5 min. Total time: 1 hr. 5 min.

3 cups sliced cabbage
1 tablespoon lime juice
1 tablespoon dark sesame oil
½ teaspoon kosher salt
⅛ teaspoon sugar
¼ cup cilantro leaves
1 jalapeño pepper, very thinly sliced
1 ripe peeled avocado, sliced

1. Combine first 5 ingredients. Chill 1 hour. Add cilantro and jalapeño; toss. Top with avocado. Serve immediately. Serves 6 (serving size: about ½ cup).

CALORIES 84; FAT 7.3g (sat 1.1g, mono 4.3g, poly 1.6g); PROTEIN 1.2g; CARB 5.3g; FIBER 3.2g; CHOL 0mg; IRON 0.4mg; SODIUM 169mg; CALC 19mg

SECRETS OF A SALAD MAN

This Southern star chef shows how a deft hand can make raw vegetables special.

For a very long time the simple salad was an afterthought in American restaurant cooking—anyone could make one, and not a lot of technique was required. At home, too, salads can become something more thrown-together than inspired. The current obsession with seasonal produce is changing that. But a great salad is about more than ingredients; it's about finesse, an understanding of flavor and texture, and a little old-fashioned restraint.

"The tendency among chefs much younger than myself is to overthink it," says Chef Chris Hastings, winner of the 2012 James Beard Best Chef: South award, who's been in the business going on three decades now. "Too often there are too many ingredients. You end up losing the textural or flavor integrity of that beautiful produce. Less is generally more." But what you do with that less is the key.

As a Southern cook, Hastings knows a thing or two about veggies. "The South has a long history of agriculture and clean, healthy, vegetable-directed cooking but doesn't get as much credit for it as the West Coast," he says. Hastings is part of a passionate cadre of Southern chefs—like Charleston's Sean Brock and Hugh Acheson in Athens, Georgia—drawing attention to the region's agricultural heritage. "There's no question that we've moved away from focusing on protein to focusing instead on vegetables," Hastings says.

Hastings builds salads with a Southern accent by combining peak-quality ingredients as if they were a little taste and texture puzzle, with interlocking elements. His Apple, Almond, and Endive Salad, a staple at Hot and Hot Fish Club in the fall, is a great example: It gets crunch from nuts, crispness from endive, sugary notes from Southern heirloom apples, a touch of richness from aioli, and bright, bracing acidity from a blend of vinegar and verjus. "You have to have balance—it's what makes a salad great," Hastings says.

One common mistake: overdressing. "It's where most people go wrong," Hastings warns. Less is more, plain and simple.

WHO
Chris Hastings

WHERE
Hot and Hot Fish Club, Birmingham, Alabama

SIGNATURE FLAVORS
Traditional Southern ingredients deployed with modern flair

STREET CRED
Beat Bobby Flay in an *Iron Chef America* sausage smackdown

Quick & Easy • Vegetarian

Apple, Almond, and Endive Salad with Creamy Herb Dressing

Hands-on time: 15 min. Total time: 15 min. Blond verjus is acidic juice from unripe grapes—look for it in specialtiy stores, or subsitute vinegar.

3 tablespoons canola mayonnaise
2 teaspoons blond verjus
2 teaspoons tarragon vinegar
1¼ teaspoons Dijon mustard
1½ teaspoons finely chopped tarragon
1½ teaspoons finely chopped chives
1½ teaspoons finely chopped fresh flat-leaf parsley
1½ teaspoons finely chopped chervil
¼ teaspoon kosher salt
⅛ teaspoon black pepper
2 medium Cumberland Spur or Fuji apples, cored and thinly sliced
2 heads green endive, trimmed and separated into leaves
2 heads red endive, trimmed and separated into leaves
¼ teaspoon kosher salt
¼ teaspoon black pepper
¼ cup toasted sliced almonds
3 tablespoons flat-leaf parsley leaves

1. Combine first 4 ingredients in a bowl. Stir in tarragon and next 5 ingredients.
2. Combine apples and endives. Add ¼ cup dressing; toss. Add remaining dressing, if needed, to coat. Sprinkle with salt and pepper. Arrange ¾ cup salad mixture on each of 8 salad plates. Top with almonds and parsley. Serves 8.

CALORIES 133; FAT 6.1g (sat 0.6g, mono 3.2g, poly 1.7g); PROTEIN 4.2g; CARB 18.2g; FIBER 9.7g; CHOL 2mg; IRON 2.5mg; SODIUM 235mg; CALC 152mg
Recipe adapted and reprinted with permission from The Hot and Hot Fish Club Cookbook, *copyright 2009 by Chris and Idie Hastings with Katherine Cobbs, Running Press, a member of the Perseus Books Group.*

A POCKET FULL OF YUM

Tucked inside crisp, flaky phyllo dough pastry are tender potato chunks and a perfectly cooked egg.

Vegetarian

Tunisian Brik-Style Eggs

Hands-on time: 45 min. Total time: 55 min. See our step-by-step phyllo folding instructions below.

Harissa:
1 teaspoon caraway seeds
1 teaspoon cumin seeds
1 teaspoon ground ancho chile pepper
3/4 cup chopped bottled roasted red bell pepper
2 tablespoons water
1/2 teaspoon sugar
1 garlic clove, crushed
Brik:
2 cups (1-inch) cubed Yukon gold potato (about 12 ounces)

2 teaspoons extra-virgin olive oil
1/2 teaspoon ground turmeric
1/4 teaspoon kosher salt
1/8 teaspoon ground red pepper (optional)
1/4 cup chopped fresh parsley
1/3 cup thinly sliced green onions
4 (13 x 18-inch) sheets frozen phyllo dough, thawed
Cooking spray
4 large eggs, chilled
2 ounces feta cheese, crumbled (about 1/2 cup)
1/4 teaspoon black pepper
1 large egg white
1 teaspoon water
1/4 cup chopped fresh cilantro

1. To prepare harissa, place caraway and cumin seeds in a small skillet over medium-high heat; cook 1 minute, stirring frequently. Place seed mixture, ancho chile pepper, and next 4 ingredients in a blender; process until smooth.
2. To prepare brik, place potatoes in a saucepan; cover with water, and bring to a boil. Reduce heat; simmer 10 minutes or until just tender. Drain.
3. Preheat oven to 450°.
4. Heat a large nonstick skillet over medium-high heat. Add oil to pan; swirl to coat. Add potatoes, turmeric, salt, and ground red pepper (if desired); sauté 6 minutes or until edges are crisp.

Add parsley and green onions; cook 2 minutes, stirring frequently. Remove from heat; cool 5 minutes.
5. Place 1 sheet of phyllo dough on a large cutting board or work surface (cover remaining phyllo to prevent drying); coat phyllo with cooking spray. Fold sheet in half like a book. Coat bottom third of phyllo with cooking spray (narrow end should be facing you). Fold bottom third up. Arrange 1/4 of the potatoes in a circle in center of the bottom (folded) third of the phyllo, creating a nest for the egg. Crack 1 egg into center of potatoes. Sprinkle 1/4 of feta over egg. Sprinkle with black pepper. Fold top third of phyllo over egg, potatoes, and cheese, folding in sides to form a packet. Place packet on a baking sheet coated with cooking spray. Repeat with remaining phyllo, potatoes, eggs, cheese, and black pepper. Combine egg white and 1 teaspoon water in a small bowl, stirring with a whisk. Brush phyllo packets with egg white mixture. Bake at 450° for 9 minutes or until golden brown and crisp. Spoon harissa evenly over brik, and sprinkle with cilantro. Serves 4 (serving size: 1 phyllo packet, 3 tablespoons harissa, and 1 tablespoon cilantro).

CALORIES 277; FAT 12.4g (sat 4.4g, mono 5g, poly 1.5g); PROTEIN 13.1g; CARB 29.2g; FIBER 3.6g; CHOL 224mg; IRON 3.3mg; SODIUM 612mg; CALC 135mg

HOW TO SHAPE PHYLLO PACKETS

We coat the pastry with cooking spray— it's faster and easier than brushing on butter.

1. Fold a phyllo sheet in half, like you're closing a book.

2. Fold up one-third of the halved phyllo sheet.

3. Spoon on potato nest, leaving a hole in middle for the egg.

4. Fold over the top third of the phyllo sheet.

QUICK SLICE OF HEAVEN

A sweet quick bread for every taste, including two amped-up banana breads, a bejeweled cornmeal loaf, and the nuttiest almond bread ever

Maple-Stout Quick Bread

***Hands-on time: 15 min. Total time: 1 hr. 8 min.** Stout beer—think of Guinness, with its black color and intense richness—gives this bread a slightly bitter background note and gorgeous nut-brown hue.*

7.88 ounces all-purpose flour (about 1¾ cups)
1 teaspoon baking soda
½ teaspoon baking powder
½ teaspoon salt
6 tablespoons butter, softened
¾ cup packed dark brown sugar
2 large eggs
½ teaspoon vanilla extract
½ cup stout beer
½ cup fat-free sour cream
5 tablespoons maple syrup, divided
Baking spray with flour (such as Baker's Joy)
5 tablespoons powdered sugar

1. Preheat oven to 350°.
2. Weigh or lightly spoon flour into dry measuring cups; level with a knife. Combine flour, baking soda, baking powder, and salt, stirring well with a whisk. Place butter and brown sugar in a large mixing bowl; beat with a mixer at high speed until well blended. Add eggs, 1 at a time, beating well after each addition. Beat in vanilla extract. Combine beer, sour cream, and ¼ cup syrup, stirring well with a whisk. Beating at low speed, add flour mixture and beer mixture alternately to butter mixture, beginning and ending with flour mixture; beat just until combined.
3. Scrape batter into a 9 x 5–inch metal loaf pan coated with baking spray. Bake at 350° for 43 minutes or until a wooden pick inserted in center comes out with moist crumbs clinging. Cool 10 minutes in pan on a wire rack. Remove from pan; cool completely on wire rack.
4. Place powdered sugar in a small bowl. Add remaining 1 tablespoon syrup; stir until smooth. Drizzle glaze over cooled bread; let stand until set, if desired. Serves 14 (serving size: 1 slice).

CALORIES 190; FAT 5.7g (sat 3.3g, mono 1.6g, poly 0.4g); PROTEIN 2.9g; CARB 31.9g; FIBER 0.4g; CHOL 40mg; IRON 1mg; SODIUM 247mg; CALC 33mg

THE BOOZY BACK NOTE IS TEMPERED WITH SWEET AMBER SYRUP.

Chocolate-Hazelnut Banana Bread

***Hands-on time: 17 min. Total time: 1 hr. 22 min.** Use a light hand when swirling the batter; too much swirling may lose the stripe effect.*

5 tablespoons chocolate-hazelnut spread (such as Nutella)
3 tablespoons plus 1 teaspoon canola oil, divided
3 tablespoons butter, softened
½ cup packed brown sugar
2 medium-sized ripe bananas, sliced
2 large eggs
6.75 ounces all-purpose flour (about 1½ cups)
¾ teaspoon baking soda
½ teaspoon baking powder
½ teaspoon salt
⅔ cup whole buttermilk
Baking spray with flour (such as Baker's Joy)
¼ cup hazelnuts, coarsely chopped
1 ounce bittersweet chocolate, finely chopped

1. Preheat oven to 350°.
2. Combine chocolate-hazelnut spread and 1 teaspoon oil in a microwave-safe dish; microwave at HIGH 30 seconds or until melted. Stir. Combine 3 tablespoons oil, butter, brown sugar, and banana in a large bowl; beat with a mixer at medium-high speed until well blended. Add eggs, 1 at a time, beating well after each addition.
3. Weigh or lightly spoon flour into dry measuring cups; level with a knife. Combine flour, baking soda, baking powder, and salt. Beating at low speed, add flour mixture and buttermilk alternately to banana mixture, beginning and ending with flour mixture; beat just until combined. Scrape half of batter into a 9 x 5–inch metal loaf pan

coated with baking spray, and top with chocolate-hazelnut spread mixture. Spread remaining batter over chocolate mixture. Using a wooden pick, swirl batter. Sprinkle batter with hazelnuts.

4. Bake at 350° for 55 minutes or until a wooden pick comes out with moist crumbs clinging. Cool 10 minutes in pan on a wire rack. Remove bread; cool on wire rack.

5. Place bittersweet chocolate in a microwave-safe dish; microwave at high 30 seconds. Drizzle bread with chocolate; let stand until set. Serves 16 (serving size: 1 slice).

CALORIES 193; FAT 9.7g (sat 3g, mono 3.5g, poly 1.2g); PROTEIN 3.4g; CARB 24.6g; FIBER 1.2g; CHOL 30mg; IRON 1mg; SODIUM 186mg; CALC 28mg

Kid Friendly • Freezable
Make Ahead • Vegetarian

Caramelized Banana Bread with Browned Butter Glaze

Hands-on time: 31 min. Total time: 1 hr. 31 min. *A few techniques take banana bread to the next level: Cooking ripe banana slices in butter deepens the sweet banana flavor, while browned butter gives the glaze nutty richness.*

4 tablespoons butter, softened and divided
3/4 cup packed dark brown sugar
3 medium-sized ripe bananas, sliced
1/2 cup nonfat buttermilk
3 tablespoons canola oil
2 tablespoons amber or gold rum
2 large eggs
9 ounces all-purpose flour (about 2 cups)
3/4 teaspoon baking soda
1/2 teaspoon salt
Baking spray with flour (such as Baker's Joy)
1/3 cup powdered sugar
2 teaspoons half-and-half

1. Preheat oven to 350°.
2. Melt 3 tablespoons butter in a large skillet over medium-high heat. Add brown sugar and bananas; sauté 4 minutes, stirring occasionally. Remove from heat; cool 10 minutes. Place banana mixture in a large bowl. Beat with a mixer at medium speed until smooth.
3. Combine buttermilk and next 3 ingredients. Weigh or lightly spoon flour into dry measuring cups; level with a knife. Combine flour, baking soda, and salt. Add flour mixture and buttermilk mixture alternately to banana mixture, beginning and ending with flour mixture; beat at low speed just until combined. Scrape batter into a 9 x 5–inch metal loaf pan coated with baking spray. Bake at 350° for 1 hour or until a wooden pick inserted in center comes out with moist crumbs clinging. Cool 10 minutes in pan on a wire rack. Remove bread from pan, and cool on wire rack.
4. Melt remaining 1 tablespoon butter in a small, heavy saucepan over medium-high heat. Cook 3 minutes or until butter begins to brown; remove from heat. Add powdered sugar and half-and-half, stirring with a whisk until smooth. Drizzle glaze over bread. Let stand until glaze sets. Serves 16 (serving size: 1 slice)

CALORIES 190; FAT 6.3g (sat 2.3g, mono 2.7g, poly 1g); PROTEIN 3g; CARB 30.5g; FIBER 1g; CHOL 30mg; IRON 1mg; SODIUM 173mg; CALC 26mg

CHOCOLATE, HAZELNUTS, BANANA: AN INSANELY GOOD COMBO

Kid Friendly • Freezable
Make Ahead • Vegetarian

Almond Bread

Hands-on time: 15 min. Total time: 1 hr. 15 min. *A package of almond paste—which you'll find on the baking aisle—makes this loaf incredibly moist and dense, almost like a pound cake.*

6.75 ounces all-purpose flour (about 1 1/2 cups)
1 1/2 teaspoons baking powder
1/2 teaspoon salt
2/3 cup granulated sugar
2 tablespoons butter, softened
2 tablespoons canola oil
1 (7-ounce) package almond paste
2 large eggs
1/2 teaspoon vanilla extract
1/2 cup plus 1 tablespoon 2% reduced-fat milk, divided
Baking spray with flour (such as Baker's Joy)
1/4 cup sliced almonds
1/3 cup powdered sugar
Dash of salt

1. Preheat oven to 350°.
2. Weigh or lightly spoon flour into dry measuring cups; level with a knife. Combine flour, baking powder, and salt, stirring well with a whisk. Place granulated sugar and next 3 ingredients in a large bowl; beat with a mixer at medium speed until well combined (about 3 minutes). Add eggs, 1 at a time, beating well after each addition; beat in vanilla. Beating at low speed, add flour mixture and 1/2 cup milk alternately to butter mixture, beginning and ending with flour mixture; beat just until combined.
3. Scrape batter into a 9 x 5–inch metal loaf pan coated with baking spray; sprinkle with sliced almonds. Bake at 350° for 50 minutes or until a wooden pick inserted in the center comes out with moist crumbs clinging. Cool in pan on a wire rack 10 minutes. Remove from pan; cool on wire rack.

continued

4. Place powdered sugar in a small bowl. Add remaining 1 tablespoon milk and dash of salt; stir with a whisk until smooth. Drizzle glaze over top of bread; let stand until set. Serves 16 (serving size: 1 slice).

CALORIES 193; FAT 8.2g (sat 1.7g, mono 4.5g, poly 1.6g); PROTEIN 3.7g; CARB 26.9g; FIBER 1.1g; CHOL 27mg; IRON 0.9mg; SODIUM 144mg; CALC 63mg

Kid Friendly • Freezable
Make Ahead • Vegetarian

Kumquat-Cranberry Cornmeal Loaf

Hands-on time: 15 min. Total time: 1 hr. 15 min. *Juicy fruit bakes on the bottom of the bread, which is inverted to reveal a gorgeously jeweled top. Slice off a thin layer of the domed top to create a stable base before you turn out the bread.*

1 cup fresh cranberries
⅓ cup granulated sugar
¼ cup thinly sliced kumquat or 2 tablespoons slivered orange rind strips
1 teaspoon all-purpose flour
½ teaspoon grated lemon rind
Baking spray with flour (such as Baker's Joy)
6.75 ounces all-purpose flour (about 1½ cups)
½ cup yellow cornmeal
¾ teaspoon baking powder
½ teaspoon salt
⅔ cup agave nectar
½ cup extra-virgin olive oil
½ cup whole buttermilk
1 teaspoon grated orange rind
2 large eggs

1. Preheat oven to 350°.
2. Combine first 5 ingredients in a bowl, and toss well. Coat a 9 x 5–inch loaf pan with baking spray; line bottom of pan with wax paper. Coat wax paper with baking spray. Sprinkle bottom of pan with cranberry mixture. Set aside.
3. Weigh or lightly spoon 6.75 ounces flour into dry measuring cups; level with a knife. Combine flour, cornmeal, baking powder, and salt in a large bowl; make a well in center of mixture. Combine agave nectar and remaining ingredients in a bowl, stirring well; add agave mixture to flour mixture, stirring just until combined. Scrape batter into prepared pan over cranberry mixture. Bake at 350° for 50 minutes or until a wooden pick inserted in center comes out with moist crumbs clinging. Cool in pan 10 minutes on a wire rack.
4. Cut dome off bread using a serrated knife. Place a plate upside down on top of bread; invert bread onto plate. Discard wax paper. Cool. Serves 16 (serving size: 1 slice).

CALORIES 198; FAT 7.8g (sat 1.3g, mono 5.2g, poly 0.9g); PROTEIN 2.7g; CARB 30g; FIBER 1.1g; CHOL 24mg; IRON 1mg; SODIUM 112mg; CALC 20mg

CRANBERRIES SPARKLE WITH BRILLIANT COLOR.

Kid Friendly • Make Ahead
Vegetarian

Sweet Potato Bread

Hands-on time: 25 min. Total time: 1 hr. 5 min. *Inspired by carrot cake, we created a cream cheese–frosted bread.*

6.75 ounces all-purpose flour (about 1½ cups)
2 teaspoons baking powder
1 teaspoon ground cinnamon
½ teaspoon baking soda
¼ teaspoon salt
¼ teaspoon ground nutmeg
⅛ teaspoon ground cloves
½ cup plain 2% reduced-fat Greek yogurt
½ cup granulated sugar
¼ cup canola oil
2 large eggs
½ cup packed shredded peeled sweet potato (about 4 ounces)
⅓ cup raisins
⅓ cup chopped pecans, toasted
Baking spray with flour (such as Baker's Joy)
3 ounces ⅓-less-fat cream cheese, softened
⅓ cup powdered sugar
½ teaspoon grated lemon rind
Dash of salt

1. Preheat oven to 350°.
2. Weigh or lightly spoon flour into dry measuring cups; level with a knife. Combine flour and next 6 ingredients in a large bowl, stirring well with a whisk. Combine yogurt, sugar, oil, and eggs. Add yogurt mixture to flour mixture, stirring just until moist. Gently fold in sweet potato, raisins, and pecans.
3. Scrape batter into a 9 x 5–inch metal loaf pan coated with baking spray. Bake at 350° for 40 minutes or until a wooden pick inserted in center comes out with moist crumbs clinging. Cool in pan 10 minutes. Remove bread from pan; cool completely on wire rack.
4. Combine cream cheese and remaining ingredients in a bowl; beat with a mixer at medium speed 2 minutes or until smooth. Spread frosting evenly over bread. Serves 14 (serving size: 1 slice).

CALORIES 191; FAT 8.1g (sat 1.6g, mono 3.9g, poly 1.9g); PROTEIN 3.9g; CARB 26.3g; FIBER 1.1g; CHOL 31mg; IRON 1mg; SODIUM 197mg; CALC 58mg

A FUN TWIST ON CARROT CAKE, COMPLETE WITH CREAM CHEESE FROSTING

Walnut Streusel Bread

(pictured on page 238)

Hands-on time: 15 min. Total time: 1 hr. 15 min.

Streusel:
⅓ cup packed brown sugar
⅓ cup old-fashioned rolled oats
1 tablespoon all-purpose flour
¼ teaspoon ground cinnamon
Dash of salt
2 tablespoons butter, melted
2 tablespoons chopped walnuts
Bread:
9 ounces all-purpose flour (about 2 cups)
½ teaspoon baking soda
½ teaspoon baking powder
½ teaspoon salt
5 tablespoons butter, softened
⅔ cup granulated sugar
3 large eggs
1 teaspoon vanilla extract
1 cup nonfat buttermilk
Baking spray with flour (such as Baker's Joy)

1. Preheat oven to 350°.
2. To prepare streusel, combine first 5 ingredients in a medium bowl. Add 2 tablespoons melted butter, stirring until well combined. Stir in nuts. Set aside.
3. To prepare bread, weigh or lightly spoon 9 ounces flour into dry measuring cups; level with a knife. Combine flour, baking soda, baking powder, and ½ teaspoon salt in a bowl, stirring well with a whisk. Combine 5 tablespoons butter and granulated sugar in a large bowl; beat with a mixer at medium-high speed until well blended. Add eggs, 1 at a time, beating well after each addition; beat in vanilla. Beating at low speed, add flour mixture and buttermilk alternately to sugar mixture, beginning and ending with flour mixture; beat just until combined. Scrape half of batter into a 9 x 5–inch loaf pan coated with baking spray; sprinkle with half of streusel mixture. Spread remaining batter over streusel; swirl. Sprinkle remaining streusel on top of batter. Bake at 350° for 50 minutes or until a wooden pick inserted in center comes out with moist crumbs clinging. Cool 10 minutes in pan on a wire rack. Remove from pan; cool completely on wire rack. Serves 16 (serving size: 1 slice).

CALORIES 187; **FAT** 6.7g (sat 3.5g, mono 1.8g, poly 0.9g); **PROTEIN** 3.9g; **CARB** 27.9g; **FIBER** 0.7g; **CHOL** 47mg; **IRON** 1mg; **SODIUM** 200mg; **CALC** 40mg

WHAT TO COOK RIGHT NOW

SCARY-GOOD TREATS

Adults love Halloween about as much as kids do, and here are recipes to get both groups in an even better, ghastlier frame of mind. Our Black Cat Sandwich Cookies (page 280) are a tasty blend of shortbread-like cookies with a layer of soft chocolate. Or, make the Chocolate-Toffee Apples (at right), which combine the buttery richness of caramel apples with the fun crunch of candied ones—two old standards twisted together. After the kiddies retire to inventory their candy haul, grown-ups can drink from our Black Cauldron (page 280) —a spiked ice-cream float that bubbles and burbles.

Chocolate-Toffee Apples

Hands-on time: 32 min. Total time: 1 hr.

12 small Honeycrisp or other firm red apples
1 cup chopped pecans, toasted
1 cup granulated sugar
⅔ cup packed brown sugar
¼ cup water
2 tablespoons brown sugar corn syrup
2 tablespoons heavy whipping cream
2 tablespoons butter
½ teaspoon vanilla extract
⅛ teaspoon salt
2 ounces bittersweet chocolate, finely chopped

1. Rinse apples; dry well to remove waxy residue. Insert a craft stick into stem end of each apple. Place pecans in a shallow dish.
2. Combine sugars and next 4 ingredients in a small, heavy saucepan over medium-high heat, stirring just until sugar dissolves, and bring to a boil. Cook, without stirring, until a candy thermometer reaches 325° or until syrup begins to caramelize. Remove from heat; stir in vanilla and salt.
3. Working quickly with 1 apple at a time and holding apple by its stick, dip in caramel mixture, tilting pan and turning apple to mostly coat apple; allow excess to drip off. Quickly dip apple in pecans. Place apple, stick side up, on a cooling rack; let stand until set. Place chocolate in a microwave-safe dish; microwave at HIGH 1 minute or until melted, stirring every 20 seconds until smooth. Drizzle chocolate over apples. Let stand until set. Serves 12 (serving size: 1 apple).

CALORIES 311; **FAT** 11.7g (sat 3.4g, mono 4.5g, poly 2.2g); **PROTEIN** 1.6g; **CARB** 55.8g; **FIBER** 4.8g; **CHOL** 9mg; **IRON** 0.6mg; **SODIUM** 49mg; **CALC** 29mg

Black Cat Sandwich Cookies

Hands-on time: 30 min. Total time: 1 hr. 25 min.

Cookies:
8 ounces cake flour (about 2 cups)
½ teaspoon salt
¼ teaspoon baking powder
1 cup powdered sugar
½ cup butter, softened
2 tablespoons 2% reduced-fat milk
1½ teaspoons vanilla extract
Filling:
1½ ounces bittersweet chocolate, finely chopped
2 tablespoons 2% reduced-fat milk
½ cup powdered sugar
2 tablespoons Dutch process cocoa
Dash of salt

1. Preheat oven to 350°.
2. To prepare cookies, weigh or lightly spoon flour into dry measuring cups; level with a knife. Combine flour, ½ teaspoon salt, and baking powder, stirring with a whisk. Place powdered sugar and butter in a large bowl. Beat with a mixer at medium-high speed until well blended. Add 2 tablespoons milk and vanilla; beat 1 minute or until well combined. Add flour mixture; beat on low speed until just combined.
3. Shape dough into a 6-inch disk. Cover tightly with plastic wrap; chill 30 minutes. Discard plastic. Roll dough to a ¼-inch thickness on a lightly floured surface. Cut out 36 (2-inch) round cookies, rerolling scraps as necessary. Using a small decorative cookie cutter, cut a cat-shaped opening in 18 rounds. Place cookies 1 inch apart on baking sheets lined with parchment paper. Bake at 350° for 14 minutes or until lightly browned. Cool on a wire rack.

4. To prepare filling, combine chocolate and 2 tablespoons milk in a microwave-safe dish; microwave at HIGH 1 minute or until melted, stirring every 15 seconds. Stir just until smooth. Combine ½ cup powdered sugar, cocoa, and dash of salt in a bowl, stirring well with a whisk. Add chocolate mixture to sugar mixture; stir just until smooth. (Mixture will thicken as it cools.) Divide chocolate mixture evenly among 18 whole cookies; spread in a thin, even layer. Top each cookie with a cut-out cookie. Serves 18 (serving size: 1 cookie sandwich).

CALORIES 156; **FAT** 6.1g (sat 3.7g, mono 1.6g, poly 0.3g); **PROTEIN** 1.6g; **CARB** 23.9g; **FIBER** 0.5g; **CHOL** 14mg; **IRON** 1.3mg; **SODIUM** 118mg; **CALC** 12mg

WE LIKE SAMUEL SMITH'S OATMEAL STOUT IN THE CAULDRON. IF YOU WANT A MORE BITTER EDGE, YOU CAN TRY A CHOCOLATE STOUT.

Quick & Easy

Black Cauldron

Place ½ cup vanilla ice cream in each of 4 tall glasses. Top each serving with 1 tablespoon vodka, 1 tablespoon brewed espresso, and 6 ounces oatmeal stout beer. Serve immediately. Serves 4 (serving size: 1 float).

CALORIES 264; **FAT** 7.3g (sat 4.5g); **SODIUM** 60mg

CHIP CHIP HOORAY!

The classic chocolate chip treat is made lighter and better with browned butter, dark chocolate, and whole grains.

The chocolate chip cookie—crisp around the edges, soft in the middle, with gooey pockets of melty chocolate—is an almost perfect treat. And it's hardly a huge nutrition offender at just 200 or so calories per cookie. But who can eat just one? Or, put another way, what if you can have the pleasures of the classic with about half the fat and calories? That's what we have delivered here, even sneaking in a few whole grains. And we did not skimp on the rich, buttery cookie or the essential minimum chip-per-cookie ratio.

Saturated fat is cut by swapping in a little canola oil, which soaks up that browned-buttery goodness. Whole-wheat flour gives a nutty twist, and a pinch of salt balances the sweetness of two sugars. For the chocolate lover, we blend classic semisweet chips with our new dark-chocolate favorite, Hershey's Special Dark, for a double hit.

THE BUTTER IS BROWNED TO DRAW OUT A DEEPER, RICHER FLAVOR.

Kid Friendly • Freezable
Make Ahead

Browned Butter Chocolate Chip Cookies

Hands-on time: 17 min. Total time: 42 min. *Butter moves from nutty and brown to bitter and burned quickly, so be sure to take the pan off the heat once it turns amber-brown. To keep cookies from spreading, make sure the cookie sheet is completely cool before starting the next batch.*

6 tablespoons unsalted butter
2 tablespoons canola oil
5.6 ounces all-purpose flour (about 1¼ cups)
3.3 ounces whole-wheat flour (about ¾ cup)
1 teaspoon baking powder
½ teaspoon kosher salt
¾ cup packed light brown sugar
⅔ cup granulated sugar
½ teaspoon vanilla extract
2 large eggs, lightly beaten
½ cup semisweet chocolate chips
⅓ cup dark chocolate chips (such as Hershey's Special Dark)

1. Preheat oven to 375°.
2. Heat butter in a small saucepan over medium heat; cook 5 minutes or until browned. Remove from heat; add oil. Set aside to cool.
3. Weigh or lightly spoon flours into dry measuring cups; level with a knife. Combine flours, baking powder, and salt, stirring with a whisk. Place butter mixture and sugars in a large bowl; beat with a mixer at medium speed until combined. Add vanilla and eggs; beat until well blended. Add flour mixture, beating at low speed until just combined. Stir in chocolate chips.
4. Drop by level tablespoonfuls 2 inches apart onto baking sheets lined with parchment paper. Bake 12 minutes or until bottoms of cookies just begin to brown. Cool slightly. Serves 40 (serving size: 1 cookie).

CALORIES 96; FAT 4g (sat 2g, mono 1.2g, poly 0.4g); PROTEIN 1.2g; CARB 14.8g; FIBER 0.6g; CHOL 14mg; IRON 0.5mg; SODIUM 42mg; CALC 14mg

THIS COOKIE DESERVES A GLASS OF ICE-COLD MILK.

CLASSIC	MAKEOVER
187 calories per serving	96 calories per serving
5.8 grams saturated fat	2 grams saturated fat
9.6 grams total fat	4 grams total fat

FOR AN IRRISISTIBLE COOKIE

Browned Butter
Less becomes more when butter gets browned, which amps up richness and nuttiness. A touch of canola oil comes in to save 3g sat fat per cookie.

A Boost of Whole Grains
We add some whole-wheat flour to make a better, more nutrient-dense treat.

Chocolate Duo
We develop a deeper, more intense chocolate presence with two types of chips: classic semisweet and rich dark chocolate.

COOL USES FOR FIERY SAMBAL

By Naomi Duguid

Meet your new favorite hot sauce—with a range far wider than Asian applications.

Sambal oelek (sometimes written "sambal ulek") is a chile paste made of pounded or chopped fresh red cayenne chiles flavored with salt, a little sugar, and vinegar, but with no garlic or spices—so its taste is that of pure hot chile essence. It's originally from Indonesia, where a "sambal" is a chile-based condiment sauce (there are many kinds of sambal), and "oelek" means mortar or pounded in a mortar.

If you've bought a jar of sambal oelek to use in Indonesian or other Asian food, you'll soon find it has a place in many other parts of your repertoire, from salads (see recipe at right) to sandwiches. One fabulous everyday use that will have you buying more in a hurry is in peanut butter or almond butter sandwiches. (I also love it on cheddar cheese.) Spread the nut butter on your bread or toast; then smear on a little sambal oelek. Top with another slice of bread or toast, or eat open-faced: a very adult peanut butter sandwich!

Sambal oelek is also a versatile kitchen friend. Try tossing in a spoonful to add punch to a soup or to a tomato sauce for pasta, or include some when you are marinating meat (it's particularly delicious in a marinade for lamb). Put some out as a condiment (in a small bowl with a small spoon) with practically any meal; its fresh red color is very decorative.

Quick & Easy • Make Ahead
Vegetarian

Carrot Salad with a Hit of Heat

(pictured on page 234)

Hands-on time: 10 min. Total time: 40 min.
Some like cooked carrots, while others prefer them grated to make a crunchy salad. You can do either with this recipe—just toss steamed carrot coins with the dressing. I suggest a mix of cilantro and mint, but you could use 3 tablespoons of just one or the other, if you wish; minced chives are an optional extra. One teaspoon sambal gives subtle heat; two give a noticeable punch. You can also make this salad with boiled sweet potatoes, peeled and chopped into bite-sized chunks—a delicious version.

3 tablespoons extra-virgin olive oil
1 tablespoon fresh lemon juice
1 teaspoon sambal oelek (ground fresh chile paste)
4 cups coarsely grated carrot (about 1 pound)
3/8 teaspoon kosher salt
2 tablespoons chopped fresh cilantro
1 tablespoon minced fresh mint
1 tablespoon minced fresh chives (optional)

1. Combine first 3 ingredients in a large bowl, stirring with a whisk. Add carrot and salt; toss to coat. Let stand 30 minutes. Just before serving, add cilantro, mint, and chives, if desired; toss to combine. Serves 4 (serving size: 1 cup).

CALORIES 138; FAT 10.4g (sat 1.4g, mono 7.4g, poly 1.2g); PROTEIN 1.1g; CARB 11.5g; FIBER 3.2g; CHOL 0mg; IRON 0.4mg; SODIUM 259mg; CALC 39mg

FIVE MORE EVERYDAY USES FOR SAMBAL OELEK

Keep in mind this stuff is pretty potent. If you're sensitive to heat, start with small amounts.

1 Dot on top of scrambled eggs or omelets, as you would Tabasco.

2 Deploy it as your secret weapon for a three- or four-alarm chili.

3 Mash it into softened butter to make a feisty topping for bread, roasted vegetables, or steak.

4 Stir into the meat mixture for burgers or meat loaf; double the heat by adding some to the ketchup topping.

5 Wake up pizza by adding sambal to the tomato sauce.

THE SWEETNESS OF THE CARROTS IS BALANCED BY THE FRESH BITE OF THE SAMBAL OELEK AND CHOPPED HERBS.

FEED 4 FOR LESS THAN $10

Dress up basic rice or pasta with big, bold sauces: spicy tomato cream on penne, roasted tomatillo on rice.

**Kid Friendly • Quick & Easy
Make Ahead**

Chicken and Orzo Skillet Dinner

$2.50/serving, $9.99 for four

Hands-on time: 35 min. Total time: 35 min. *Combine 4 cups romaine lettuce with 2 tablespoons chopped red onion and bottled vinaigrette for a quick side.*

- 1 pound skinless, boneless chicken breast halves, cut into bite-sized pieces
- 8 cups water
- 12 ounces uncooked orzo
- 2 cups chopped tomato (about 2 medium)
- 2 teaspoons no-salt-added tomato paste
- 1/2 teaspoon salt
- 1/2 teaspoon crushed red pepper
- 1/4 teaspoon black pepper
- 3 cups baby spinach leaves
- 3 ounces feta cheese, crumbled (about 3/4 cup)

1. Heat a nonstick skillet over medium-high heat. Add chicken. Sauté 6 minutes, turning to brown all sides. Remove chicken from pan; keep warm.
2. Bring 8 cups water to a boil in a large saucepan. Add orzo; cook 8 minutes or until orzo is al dente. Drain in a colander over a bowl, reserving 1/4 cup cooking liquid.
3. Add reserved cooking liquid, chopped tomato, tomato paste, 1/2 teaspoon salt, and peppers to skillet; cook

over medium-high heat 2 minutes. Add chicken, pasta, and 3 cups spinach leaves, stirring until spinach wilts. Remove from heat; sprinkle with cheese. Serves 4 (serving size: 2 cups).

CALORIES 486; **FAT** 7.5g (sat 3.6g, mono 1.4g, poly 0.5g); **PROTEIN** 39.8g; **CARB** 62.6g; **FIBER** 4.5g; **CHOL** 85mg; **IRON** 1.8mg; **SODIUM** 641mg; **CALC** 138mg

Make Ahead

Penne Rigate with Spicy Sausage and Zucchini in Tomato Cream Sauce

$1.96/serving, $7.83 for four

Hands-on time: 25 min. Total time: 45 min.

- 8 ounces uncooked penne rigate pasta
- 6 ounces hot turkey Italian sausage, casings removed
- 12 ounces zucchini, quartered lengthwise and cut into 1/2-inch slices
- 1 1/2 teaspoons dried oregano
- 1 teaspoon dried thyme
- 1/4 teaspoon crushed red pepper
- 3 garlic cloves, minced
- Dash of sugar
- 2 tablespoons red wine vinegar
- 1 (28-ounce) can no-salt-added whole tomatoes
- 2 tablespoons heavy whipping cream
- Cooking spray
- 3 ounces part-skim mozzarella cheese, shredded and divided (about 3/4 cup)
- 1 ounce Parmigiano-Reggiano cheese, grated and divided (about 1/4 cup)

1. Preheat oven to 375°.
2. Cook pasta according to package directions, omitting salt and fat. Drain; set aside.
3. Heat a large nonstick skillet over medium-high heat. Add sausage to pan, and sauté 5 minutes or until browned, stirring to crumble. Using

a slotted spoon, remove sausage from pan. Wipe drippings from pan with a paper towel. Add zucchini to pan; sauté 3 minutes or until crisp-tender, stirring frequently. Add oregano and next 4 ingredients; sauté 1 minute, stirring constantly. Add vinegar; cook 30 seconds or until liquid evaporates. Drain tomatoes in a sieve over a bowl, reserving 1 cup tomato liquid. Crush tomatoes with hands, and add to zucchini mixture. Add reserved 1 cup tomato liquid; bring to a boil. Reduce heat, and simmer 5 minutes, stirring occasionally. Remove pan from heat; stir in cream. Add pasta and sausage to tomato mixture; stir to combine.
4. Spoon half of pasta mixture into an 11 x 7–inch glass or ceramic baking dish, or divide half evenly among 4 individual dishes coated with cooking spray. Sprinkle 1 ounce mozzarella and 2 tablespoons Parmigiano-Reggiano over pasta. Top with remaining pasta mixture; sprinkle evenly with remaining 2 ounces mozzarella and remaining 2 tablespoons Parmigiano-Reggiano. Bake at 375° for 20 minutes or until browned and bubbly. Serves 4 (serving size: about 1 1/2 cups).

CALORIES 450; **FAT** 14.1g (sat 6.8g, mono 3.8g, poly 1.5g); **PROTEIN** 26.9g; **CARB** 55.6g; **FIBER** 5g; **CHOL** 60mg; **IRON** 5.2mg; **SODIUM** 508mg; **CALC** 347mg

KITCHEN SECRET: UNTANGLING PASTA

For the busy cook, pasta makes a fast meal—sauce and noodles can cook concurrently and be combined just before serving. But once cooked, pasta has a short lifespan: If left undressed or allowed to cool down, the shapes and strands clump together, creating a tangled mess. To combat this problem, some cooks like to toss pasta with oil, but this method gives the pasta a slick surface, making it difficult for béchamel and ragù to cling to each bite. Instead, simply rinse clumpy pasta under hot tap water, tousling it with fingers or tongs to loosen knots and break up clusters. Drain, and immediately toss with sauce.

Roasted Chili Verde with Pork and Rice

$2.15/serving, $8.59 for four

Hands-on time: 40 min. Total time: 1 hr. 25 min. *Charring the tomatillos gives this verde sauce a smoky flavor.*

1 1/2 **pounds tomatillos, husks and stems removed**
Cooking spray
1 **cup chopped onion, divided**
1/4 **cup chopped cilantro leaves**
1 **teaspoon sugar**
2 **garlic cloves, chopped**
1 **jalapeño pepper, chopped**
2 **tablespoons canola oil, divided**
1 **pound boneless pork shoulder (Boston butt), trimmed, cut into 1-inch pieces**
1/2 **teaspoon kosher salt, divided**
1/4 **teaspoon black pepper**
1 **cup uncooked long-grain rice**
1 **(10-ounce) can mild diced tomatoes and green chiles, undrained**
1 **cup water**
1 **jalapeño pepper, sliced (optional)**
Cilantro leaves (optional)

1. Preheat broiler to high.
2. Place tomatillos on a baking sheet or jelly-roll pan coated with cooking spray. Broil 8 inches from broiler 15 minutes or until skins blacken and tomatillos are soft.
3. Place tomatillos, pan juices, 3/4 cup onion, and next 4 ingredients in a blender or a food processor; process until sauce is almost smooth.
4. Heat a Dutch oven over medium-high heat. Add 1 tablespoon oil to pan; swirl to coat. Sprinkle pork evenly with 1/4 teaspoon salt and black pepper. Add pork to pan. Sauté 6 minutes, turning to brown on all sides. Add tomatillo mixture to pan; bring to a boil. Cover, reduce heat, and simmer 1 hour or until pork is very tender, stirring occasionally.
5. Heat a large saucepan over medium-high heat. Add remaining 1 tablespoon oil to pan; swirl to coat. Add remaining 1/4 cup onion; sauté 2 minutes or until soft. Add rice; sauté 3 minutes, stirring frequently. Add remaining 1/4 teaspoon salt, tomatoes, and 1 cup water to pan; bring to a boil. Cover and simmer 15 minutes or until liquid evaporates and rice is tender; do not stir. Divide rice among 4 plates. Top with pork mixture; garnish with sliced jalapeño and cilantro leaves, if desired. Serves 4 (serving size: about 3/4 cup chili verde and 1/2 cup rice).

CALORIES 496; FAT 17.4g (sat 3.7g, mono 8.5g, poly 3.7g); PROTEIN 28.3g; CARB 56.1g; FIBER 5.3g; CHOL 76mg; IRON 5mg; SODIUM 585mg; CALC 68mg

KID-FRIENDLY COOKING

MATISSE STIRS UP A CLASSIC

Our kid in the kitchen charms a picky eater and offers us a few pointers.

We asked Matisse Reid, our favorite 11-year-old foodie, to tackle a risotto.
—Phoebe Wu

"Today, I cooked Tomato and Mozzarella Risotto. I invited my friend Alex to come over. I was excited to use my new bag of Arborio rice. The recipe is pretty time-consuming, so we were a bit bored stirring the rice even though we took turns—what can I say, we're kids! Alex is pretty picky when it comes to food (she doesn't usually like garlic, onion, or spinach), but she liked this dish. She thought that it tasted a bit like lasagna, and it does. It was a little bit bland for my taste, so the next time I make it, I might use spicy canned tomatoes instead of regular tomatoes or chicken stock instead of vegetable stock to add more flavor. Overall, this recipe was easy to make and is a great dish to eat on its own or as a side."

TEST THE RICE TO MAKE SURE IT'S COOKED—YOU MAY NEED MORE VEGETABLE BROTH IF IT'S NOT.

Kid Friendly • Quick & Easy
Vegetarian

Tomato and Mozzarella Risotto

Hands-on time: 32 min. Total time: 32 min.

3 1/4 **cups organic vegetable broth**
1 **tablespoon unsalted butter**
1/2 **cup finely chopped onion**
1 **tablespoon minced garlic**
1 1/4 **cups uncooked Arborio rice**
3/4 **cup canned crushed tomatoes**
2 **ounces chopped fresh mozzarella cheese (about 1/2 cup)**
1/4 **teaspoon black pepper**
1/8 **teaspoon kosher salt**
2 **cups torn fresh baby spinach**
1/4 **cup finely chopped fresh basil**
4 **teaspoons extra-virgin olive oil, divided**

1. Bring vegetable broth to a simmer in a medium saucepan (do not boil). Keep warm over low heat.
2. Melt butter in a large saucepan over medium heat. Add onion and garlic to pan; sauté 2 minutes or until onion is tender, stirring frequently. Add rice to pan; cook 1 minute, stirring constantly. Add 1/2 cup broth to rice mixture; cook 5 minutes or until liquid is nearly absorbed, stirring constantly. Reserve 1/3 cup broth. Add remaining broth, 1/4 cup at a time, stirring constantly until each portion of broth is absorbed before adding the next (about 22 minutes

total). Stir in tomatoes, and cook 1 minute. Add cheese, pepper, and salt to rice mixture, stirring constantly until cheese melts. Remove from heat, and stir in reserved ⅓ cup broth, spinach, and basil. Place 1 cup risotto in each of 4 shallow bowls. Drizzle 1 teaspoon oil over each serving. Serves 4.

CALORIES 362; FAT 11.5g (sat 4.5g, mono 4.1g, poly 0.6g); PROTEIN 8.8g; CARB 57.5g; FIBER 4.4g; CHOL 19mg; IRON 1.4mg; SODIUM 599mg; CALC 113mg

---

THE VERDICT

ALEX (AGE 11)
This score is pretty good, considering she was not impressed with some of the ingredients! **6/10**

MATISSE
I'd give this an 8/10 or 9/10 with spicy tomatoes. **6/10**

KICK UP THE HEAT: MATISSE SUGGESTS USING SPICY CANNED TOMATOES TO ADD MORE FLAVOR.

SUPERFAST

Kid-Friendly Edition! The bluntest judgments always come from the kids' side of the table. We invited a tasting panel, ages 5 to 13, to tell us which fast entrées made the grade.

SHOPPING LIST

Italian Sausage Hoagies
- ☐ Prechopped onion
- ☐ Garlic
- ☐ Red bell pepper (1)
- ☐ 2-ounce hoagie rolls (4)
- ☐ Lower-sodium marinara sauce
- ☐ Sweet turkey Italian sausage (9 ounces)
- ☐ Shredded part-skim mozzarella cheese (2.25 ounces)

Kid Friendly • Quick & Easy

Italian Sausage Hoagies

4 (2-ounce) hoagie rolls, halved lengthwise
9 ounces sweet turkey Italian sausage, cut into 1-inch-thick pieces
½ cup prechopped onion
1 teaspoon minced garlic
1 cup lower-sodium marinara sauce (such as Amy's)
1 small red bell pepper, thinly sliced
¼ teaspoon freshly ground black pepper
2.25 ounces shredded part-skim mozzarella cheese (about ½ cup)

1. Preheat broiler to high.
2. Hollow out top halves of rolls. Arrange rolls, cut sides up, on a baking sheet. Broil 1½ minutes or until toasted. Set aside.
3. Heat a large skillet over medium-high heat. Add sausage to pan; cook 2 minutes or until lightly browned,

---

stirring occasionally. Add onion and garlic; cook 1 minute. Add marinara, bell pepper, and black pepper; bring to a boil. Reduce heat, and simmer 6 minutes or until bell pepper is crisptender.
4. Arrange about ¾ cup sausage mixture over bottom half of each roll; sprinkle each serving with about 2 tablespoons cheese. Place on a baking sheet; broil 2 minutes or until cheese melts. Top with top halves of rolls. Serves 4 (serving size: 1 hoagie).

CALORIES 309; FAT 7g (sat 4.4g, mono 0.9g, poly 0.1g); PROTEIN 20.7g; CARB 28.5g; FIBER 2.5g; CHOL 51mg; IRON 1.8mg; SODIUM 588mg; CALC 182mg

---

"IT TASTES LIKE MEATBALLS. I WANT ANOTHER ONE!" EVAN, AGE 9

THE VERDICT
The hearty filling garnered rave reviews from our kid panel, and Evan, who usually avoids vegetables, didn't even notice the sliced bell pepper.

The
SHOPPING LIST

Beef and Broccoli Bowl
- ☐ Broccoli florets (2 cups)
- ☐ Red onion (1)
- ☐ Carrots
- ☐ Green onions
- ☐ Boil-in-bag long-grain rice (1 [3½-ounce] bag)
- ☐ Lower-sodium soy sauce
- ☐ Cornstarch
- ☐ Hoisin sauce
- ☐ Canola oil
- ☐ Dark sesame oil
- ☐ Boneless sirloin steak (12 ounces)

continued

Beef and Broccoli Bowl

1 (3½-ounce) bag boil-in-bag long-grain rice
¼ cup lower-sodium soy sauce
1 tablespoon cornstarch
1 tablespoon hoisin sauce
1 (12-ounce) boneless sirloin steak, cut into thin strips
2 teaspoons canola oil
2 cups broccoli florets
1 cup vertically sliced red onion
1 cup chopped carrot
½ cup water
2 teaspoons dark sesame oil
⅓ cup sliced green onions

1. Cook rice according to package directions.
2. Combine soy sauce, cornstarch, and hoisin in a medium bowl. Add beef; toss to coat. Heat a large skillet over high heat. Add oil to pan; swirl to coat. Remove beef, reserving marinade. Add beef to pan; cook 2 minutes or until browned, stirring occasionally. Remove beef from pan. Add broccoli and next 4 ingredients to pan; cook 4 minutes or until broccoli is crisp-tender, stirring occasionally. Add reserved marinade to pan; bring to a boil. Cook 1 minute. Add beef to pan; cook 1 minute or until thoroughly heated. Sprinkle with green onions. Serve over rice. Serves 4 (serving size: 1 cup stir-fry and about ½ cup rice).

CALORIES 311; FAT 9.3g (sat 2g, mono 3.9g, poly 2g); PROTEIN 23.5g; CARB 32.5g; FIBER 3g; CHOL 36mg; IRON 3.2mg; SODIUM 529mg; CALC 71mg

"THAT WAS THE BEST THING I'VE EVER HAD IN MY LIFE!" GRADIE, AGE 6

THE VERDICT
This stir-fry was a hit, and several tasters even went back for seconds. A flavorful sweet-salty sauce helps make the veggie-packed dish easy to love. "The juice coming from the meat is really good!" reported John.

PREP POINTERS
Vary the vegetables to appeal to tastes. Snow peas, green beans, or leafy greens such as spinach would all work nicely here. Young cooks will also enjoy measuring out the marinade ingredients.

The SHOPPING LIST

Chicken and Vegetable Soup

☐ Onion (1)
☐ Carrots
☐ Garlic
☐ Fresh thyme
☐ Green beans (5 ounces)
☐ Extra-virgin olive oil
☐ Fat-free, lower-sodium chicken broth (3 cups)
☐ 14.5-ounce can no-salt-added, fire-roasted diced tomatoes
☐ Orzo or pastina (tiny star-shaped pasta)
☐ Rotisserie chicken breast
☐ Parmesan cheese (2 ounces)

Chicken and Vegetable Soup

(pictured on page 233)

1½ tablespoons extra-virgin olive oil
1 cup chopped onion
½ cup chopped carrot
1 tablespoon minced fresh garlic
½ teaspoon black pepper
¼ teaspoon salt
1 thyme sprig
3 cups fat-free, lower-sodium chicken broth
1 (14.5-ounce) can no-salt-added, fire-roasted diced tomatoes, undrained
½ cup uncooked orzo (rice-shaped pasta) or pastina (tiny star-shaped pasta)
5 ounces green beans, cut into 1-inch pieces (about 1 cup)
1 cup shredded skinless, boneless rotisserie chicken breast
2 ounces fresh Parmesan cheese, grated (about ½ cup)

1. Heat a Dutch oven over medium-high heat. Add oil to pan; swirl to coat. Add onion and next 5 ingredients to pan; sauté 4 minutes. Add broth and tomatoes; bring to a boil. Add pasta and beans; cook 5 minutes. Stir in chicken, and sprinkle with cheese. Discard thyme. Serves 6 (serving size: 1 cup soup and 4 teaspoons cheese).

CALORIES 257; FAT 7.3g (sat 2.5g, mono 3.5g, poly 0.6g); PROTEIN 15.4g; CARB 32.8g; FIBER 3g; CHOL 25mg; IRON 2mg; SODIUM 552mg; CALC 145mg

"THIS SOUP WAS MY FAVORITE— I REALLY LIKE ALL THE VEGETABLES IN IT." MINA, AGE 10

THE VERDICT
For adventuresome eaters like Mina, this soup was a welcome change from the usual chicken noodle. A variety of veggies and the shredded chicken kept our tasters interested.

PREP POINTERS
Tiny pasta stars will up the fun factor. Or try orzo, alphabet, ditalini, or another small pasta. Swap in your kids' favorite veggies—spinach or zucchini are good options. Don't skip the nutty Parmesan, which adds extra depth to the soup's broth.

Raspberry Chocolate Parfaits
- ☐ Fresh raspberries (2 [6-ounce] packages)
- ☐ Sugar
- ☐ Bittersweet chocolate (1 ounce)
- ☐ Fresh orange juice
- ☐ Vanilla frozen Greek yogurt

Kid Friendly • Quick & Easy

Raspberry Chocolate Parfaits

2 (6-ounce) packages fresh raspberries, divided
1/4 cup sugar
2 tablespoons fresh orange juice
1 cup vanilla frozen Greek yogurt
1 ounce shaved bittersweet chocolate (about 1/4 cup)

1. Combine 1 package raspberries, sugar, and juice in a small saucepan over medium-high heat; bring to a boil. Reduce heat, and simmer 8 minutes, stirring occasionally to break up berries. Place raspberry mixture and remaining package raspberries in a medium bowl; cool 5 minutes in freezer.
2. Place 2 tablespoons yogurt in each of 4 glasses. Top each serving with 3 tablespoons raspberry mixture and 1½ teaspoons chocolate shavings. Repeat procedure with remaining ½ cup yogurt, ¾ cup raspberry mixture, and 2 tablespoons chocolate. Serves 4 (serving size: 1 parfait).

CALORIES 198; **FAT** 3.2g (sat 1.7g, mono 0.1g, poly 0.3g); **PROTEIN** 5.9g; **CARB** 38.9g; **FIBER** 6.2g; **CHOL** 3mg; **IRON** 1.1mg; **SODIUM** 31mg; **CALC** 26mg

---

"MOM, CAN YOU MAKE THIS AT HOME?" MACLAINE, AGE 5

THE VERDICT
Sweet raspberries and creamy frozen yogurt replace traditional ice cream—a much lower-fat swap that went unnoticed by Maclaine, one of our toughest critics.

Panko-Crusted Fish Sticks
- ☐ Panko (Japanese breadcrumbs)
- ☐ Canola oil
- ☐ Canola mayonnaise
- ☐ Bread-and-butter pickles
- ☐ Capers
- ☐ 2% reduced-fat milk
- ☐ Large eggs (2)
- ☐ Light sour cream
- ☐ Halibut fillets (1 pound)

Kid Friendly • Quick & Easy

Panko-Crusted Fish Sticks

1 tablespoon 2% reduced-fat milk
2 large eggs, lightly beaten
1 pound halibut fillets, cut into 20 (1-inch) strips
1 cup panko (Japanese breadcrumbs)
3/8 teaspoon kosher salt, divided
3/8 teaspoon freshly ground black pepper, divided
2 tablespoons canola oil, divided
1/4 cup light sour cream
3 tablespoons canola mayonnaise
2 tablespoons finely chopped bread-and-butter pickles
2 teaspoons minced capers

---

1. Combine milk and eggs in a large bowl; stir with a whisk. Add fish, and toss gently to coat. Place panko, ¼ teaspoon salt, and ¼ teaspoon pepper in a large zip-top bag. Add fish to panko mixture; seal bag. Shake bag gently to coat fish.
2. Heat a large nonstick skillet over medium-high heat. Add 1 tablespoon oil to pan; swirl to coat. Add half of fish; cook 4 minutes or until done, turning occasionally to brown all sides. Repeat procedure with remaining 1 tablespoon oil and remaining fish.
3. Combine sour cream, mayonnaise, pickles, capers, remaining ⅛ teaspoon salt, and remaining ⅛ teaspoon pepper in a small bowl. Serve sauce with fish. Serves 4 (serving size: 5 fish sticks and about 1½ tablespoons sauce).

CALORIES 382; **FAT** 22.1g (sat 2.9g, mono 12g, poly 5.9g); **PROTEIN** 29.5g; **CARB** 13.2g; **FIBER** 0.6g; **CHOL** 136mg; **IRON** 1.5mg; **SODIUM** 463mg; **CALC** 97mg

---

"THE HOMEMADE TARTAR SAUCE IS SURPRISINGLY GOOD!" JOHN, AGE 13

PREP POINTERS
Young cooks will enjoy breading the fish sticks and stirring together the tartar sauce. Look for wild-caught Pacific halibut at your fish counter for the most sustainable choice. Avoid Atlantic halibut. For tilapia, buy American farm-raised.

THE VERDICT
We tried this recipe first with cod, a more delicate fish. John, our oldest taster, liked the flavor but thought the fish was "really squishy." We swapped out cod for halibut, equally mild but much firmer. A less expensive alternative would be tilapia.

DINNER TONIGHT

Fast weeknight menus from the *Cooking Light* Test Kitchen.

READY IN
40
MINUTES

The
GAME PLAN

While oven preheats:
- Brown chicken.
- Prep potatoes and beans.
While chicken and vegetables roast:
- Chop onion and thyme.

Kid Friendly • Quick & Easy

Roasted Chicken Thighs with Mustard-Thyme Sauce with Roasted Potatoes and Green Beans

Kid Tweak: Add a little honey to the pan sauce.
Crowd Pleaser: High-temp roasting makes the skins French-fry crisp.

1 tablespoon olive oil
8 bone-in chicken thighs, skinned (about 2½ pounds)
½ teaspoon salt, divided
½ teaspoon freshly ground black pepper, divided
1 tablespoon butter
½ cup chopped onion
2 teaspoons chopped fresh thyme
1 cup no-salt-added chicken stock (such as Swanson), divided
4 teaspoons flour
1 teaspoon Dijon mustard

1. Preheat oven to 425°.
2. Heat a large nonstick skillet over medium-high heat. Add oil to pan; swirl to coat. Sprinkle chicken with ¼ teaspoon salt and ¼ teaspoon pepper. Add chicken to pan; cook 4 minutes on each side or until lightly browned.

Remove chicken from pan; place in an 11 x 7–inch glass or ceramic baking dish. Bake at 425° for 16 minutes or until a thermometer registers 165°. Remove chicken from dish; reserve drippings.
3. Return skillet to medium-high heat. Add butter; swirl to coat. Add onion and thyme; sauté 5 minutes or until tender. Combine 3 tablespoons stock and flour in a small bowl, stirring with a whisk until smooth. Add flour mixture, remaining stock, and reserved drippings to pan, scraping pan to loosen browned bits. Bring to a boil, and cook 2 minutes or until slightly thickened. Remove from heat, and add mustard, remaining ¼ teaspoon salt, and remaining ¼ teaspoon pepper, stirring with a whisk. Serve sauce with chicken. Serves 4 (serving size: 2 thighs and 3 tablespoons sauce).

CALORIES 246; FAT 11.7g (sat 3.7g, mono 4.9g, poly 1.8g); PROTEIN 28.9g; CARB 4.6g; FIBER 0.5g; CHOL 122mg; IRON 1.8mg; SODIUM 498mg; CALC 27mg

For the Roasted Potatoes and Green Beans:
Preheat oven to 425°. Combine 1 tablespoon olive oil; ¼ teaspoon salt; ¼ teaspoon black pepper; 1 pound fingerling potatoes, halved lengthwise; 10 ounces trimmed haricots verts; and 2 thinly sliced garlic cloves on a jelly-roll pan coated with cooking spray; toss to coat. Bake at 425° on bottom rack for 25 minutes, stirring once. Serves 4 (serving size: 1 cup).

CALORIES 145; FAT 3.7g (sat 0.5g); SODIUM 158mg

TECHNIQUE TIP: LETTING THE STOCK MIXTURE COOK DOWN THICKENS THE SAUCE.

The SHOPPING LIST

Apple and Rosemary Pork Roulade
Olive oil
(8-ounce) package prechopped onion (1)
Fuji apple
Garlic
Fresh rosemary
Cider vinegar
(1-pound) pork tenderloin
Unfiltered apple cider
No-salt-added chicken stock
Dijon mustard

Roasted Brussels Sprouts
Hazelnuts
Canola oil
Maple syrup
Brussels sprouts (1 pound)

The GAME PLAN

While oven preheats:
- Cook apple mixture.
- Prepare Brussels sprouts.

While apple mixture cools:
- Roast Brussels sprouts.
- Cut open and flatten pork.

Kid Friendly • Quick & Easy

Apple and Rosemary Pork Roulade with Roasted Brussels Sprouts

Feed A Family: Substitute green beans for bitter Brussels sprouts.
Prep Pointer: Cut pork open, and then again from the middle outward.

1 teaspoon olive oil
³/₄ cup prechopped onion
³/₄ cup chopped Fuji apple
2 teaspoons minced fresh garlic
1 tablespoon cider vinegar
1 teaspoon chopped fresh rosemary
1 (1-pound) pork tenderloin, trimmed
½ teaspoon kosher salt, divided
¼ teaspoon freshly ground black pepper
Cooking spray
⅓ cup no-salt-added chicken stock (such as Swanson)
3 tablespoons unfiltered apple cider
1 teaspoon Dijon mustard

1. Preheat oven to 425°.
2. Heat a large ovenproof skillet over medium-high heat. Add oil; swirl to coat. Add onion, apple, and garlic; sauté 5 minutes or until tender. Add vinegar and rosemary; cook 1 minute. Place apple mixture in a small bowl. Wipe pan clean.
3. Slice pork lengthwise, cutting to, but not through, other side. Open halves, laying pork flat. Starting from the center, slice each half lengthwise, cutting to, but not through, other side; open so pork is flat. Place plastic wrap over pork; pound to an even thickness using a meat mallet or small heavy skillet. Sprinkle evenly with ⅜ teaspoon salt and pepper. Spread apple mixture on pork. Roll up, jelly-roll fashion.
4. Return pan to medium-high heat. Coat pan with cooking spray. Add pork, seam side down; cook 4 minutes or until browned, carefully turning occasionally. Place pan in oven. Bake at 425° for 15 minutes or until a thermometer inserted in the center registers 145°. Remove pork from pan; let stand 5 minutes before slicing.
5. Return pan to medium-high heat; add stock, cider, mustard, and remaining ⅛ teaspoon salt, stirring with a whisk. Bring to a boil; cook 2 minutes. Serve over pork. Serves 4 (serving size: about 3 ounces pork and 2 tablespoons sauce).

CALORIES 181; FAT 4.1g (sat 1g, mono 1.7g, poly 0.6g); PROTEIN 24.7g; CARB 9.6g; FIBER 1g; CHOL 74mg; IRON 1.3mg; SODIUM 343mg; CALC 17mg

For the Roasted Brussels Sprouts:
Preheat oven to 425°. Combine ¼ cup chopped hazelnuts, 2 teaspoons canola oil, 1½ teaspoons maple syrup, ½ teaspoon black pepper, ¼ teaspoon salt, and 1 pound halved Brussels sprouts on a jelly-roll pan. Bake at 425° for 17 minutes, stirring once. Serves 4 (serving size: about ½ cup).

CALORIES 122; FAT 7.1g (sat 0.6g); SODIUM 176mg

READY IN
40
MINUTES

The SHOPPING LIST

Poblano-Turkey Sausage Chili

Canola oil
(8-ounce) package prechopped onion (1)
Garlic
8 ounces sweet turkey Italian sausage
Chili powder
Dried oregano
Ground cumin
Poblano chiles (2)
Bay leaf
No-salt-added chicken stock
28-ounce can diced tomatoes
15-ounce can no-salt-added black beans
15-ounce can no-salt-added pinto beans
Flour
Fresh cilantro
Reduced-fat sour cream
Radishes (optional)

Corn Bread Sticks

Flour
Cornmeal
Baking powder
Reduced-fat buttermilk
Butter
Canola oil
Large egg (1)

The GAME PLAN

While oven preheats:
- Prepare chili.

While chili simmers:
- Make corn bread batter.
- Bake corn bread.

Quick & Easy • Make Ahead

Poblano-Turkey Sausage Chili with Corn Bread Sticks

Family-Friendly: Use milder green bell peppers in place of poblanos.
Kid-Pleaser: Corn bread stick molds make fun shapes.
Make-Ahead Tip: Cook and freeze the chili up to two months in advance.

2 teaspoons canola oil
1 cup prechopped onion
1 tablespoon minced fresh garlic
8 ounces sweet turkey Italian sausage
1 tablespoon chili powder
½ teaspoon dried oregano
½ teaspoon ground cumin
2 poblano chiles, seeded and finely chopped
1 bay leaf
1 cup plus 2 tablespoons no-salt-added chicken stock (such as Swanson), divided
1 (28-ounce) can diced tomatoes, undrained
1 (15-ounce) can no-salt-added black beans, rinsed and drained
1 (15-ounce) can no-salt-added pinto beans, rinsed and drained
2 tablespoons all-purpose flour
½ cup coarsely chopped fresh cilantro
½ teaspoon freshly ground black pepper
¼ cup reduced-fat sour cream
Sliced radishes (optional)

1. Heat a large Dutch oven over medium-high heat. Add oil to pan; swirl to coat. Add onion and garlic; sauté 4 minutes or until browned. Remove casings from sausage; add sausage to pan. Stir in chili powder, oregano, cumin, poblanos, and bay leaf; cook 4 minutes or until sausage is browned, stirring to crumble sausage.
2. Add 1 cup stock, tomatoes, and beans. Bring to a boil; reduce heat, and simmer 25 minutes or until slightly thickened. Combine flour and remaining 2 tablespoons stock in a small bowl, stirring with a whisk to form a slurry. Add slurry to chili, stirring with a whisk. Bring to a boil; cook 1 minute or until thickened. Remove from heat; stir in cilantro and black pepper. Discard bay leaf. Serve with sour cream and sliced radishes, if desired. Serves 6 (serving size: about 1 cup chili and 2 teaspoons sour cream).

CALORIES 218; FAT 3.5g (sat 1.7g, mono 1.3g, poly 0.5g); PROTEIN 14.3g; CARB 25.7g; FIBER 5.7g; CHOL 29mg; IRON 2.4mg; SODIUM 449mg; CALC 132mg

For the Corn Bread Sticks:
Place a cast-iron corn bread stick mold pan in oven. Preheat oven to 400°. Weigh or lightly spoon 3 ounces all-purpose flour (about ⅔ cup) into a dry measuring cup; level with a knife. Combine flour, ½ cup cornmeal, 1 teaspoon baking powder, and ¼ teaspoon salt. Stir in ½ cup reduced-fat buttermilk, 1 tablespoon melted butter, 1 tablespoon canola oil, and 1 large egg, beaten. Remove pan from oven; divide batter among 6 corn bread stick molds. Bake at 400° for 12 minutes or until lightly browned on top. Serves 6 (serving size: 1 corn bread stick).

CALORIES 161; FAT 5.7g (sat 2.1g); SODIUM 209mg

READY IN
30
MINUTES

The

SHOPPING LIST

Spiced Lentils and Poached Eggs
Dried small red lentils
Bay leaf
Olive oil
Onion (1)
Tomatoes (2)
Curry powder
Ground cumin
Ground red pepper
Garlic
White vinegar
Eggs (4)
Plain low-fat Greek yogurt
Fresh cilantro

Cumin-Scented Carrots
Baby carrots (1 pound)
Olive oil
Ground cumin

The

GAME PLAN

While oven preheats:
- Cook lentils.
While carrots roast:
- Sauté veggies.
- Poach eggs.

Kid Friendly • Quick & Easy
Vegetarian

Spiced Lentils and Poached Eggs with Cumin-Scented Carrots

Feed A Family: Adults and kids can enjoy eggs for dinner.
Shopping Tip: Look for red lentils in the rice and grains aisle.

1 cup dried small red lentils
3 cups water
1 bay leaf
2 teaspoons olive oil
1 cup chopped onion
1 cup chopped tomato
1 teaspoon curry powder
¼ teaspoon ground cumin
½ teaspoon salt, divided
⅛ teaspoon ground red pepper
1 garlic clove, minced
1 tablespoon white vinegar
4 large eggs
¼ teaspoon freshly ground black pepper
¼ cup plain low-fat Greek yogurt
2 tablespoons chopped fresh cilantro

1. Combine first 3 ingredients in a large saucepan. Bring to a boil. Cover, reduce heat, and simmer 20 minutes or until lentils are tender. Drain; discard bay leaf.

2. Heat a nonstick skillet over medium-high heat. Add oil to pan; swirl to coat. Add onion and tomato; sauté 8 minutes or until onion is tender. Add curry, cumin, ¼ teaspoon salt, red pepper, and garlic; sauté 2 minutes. Add lentils; cook 1 minute. Remove from heat.

3. Add water to a large skillet, filling two-thirds full; bring to a boil. Reduce heat; simmer. Add vinegar to pan. Break eggs into custard cups. Gently pour eggs into pan; cook 3 minutes or until desired degree of doneness. Carefully remove eggs from pan using a slotted spoon. Place about ¾ cup lentil mixture on each of 4 plates; top each serving with 1 poached egg. Sprinkle evenly with remaining ¼ teaspoon salt and black pepper. Top each serving with 1 tablespoon yogurt and 1½ teaspoons cilantro. Serves 4.

CALORIES 291; FAT 6.8g (sat 1.7g, mono 3.6g, poly 1.1g); PROTEIN 20.5g; CARB 35.1g; FIBER 4g; CHOL 181mg; IRON 2.7mg; SODIUM 379mg; CALC 74mg

For the Cumin-Scented Carrots:
Preheat oven to 425°. Combine 2 teaspoons olive oil; ¼ teaspoon salt; ⅛ teaspoon ground cumin; and 1 pound peeled, trimmed baby carrots, halved lengthwise. Bake at 425° for 15 minutes or until tender and lightly browned. Serves 4 (serving size: about ½ cup).

CALORIES 74; FAT 2.3g (sat 0.3g); SODIUM 208mg

KID TWEAK: OMIT THE CURRY POWDER FOR MILDER LENTILS.

(Beautiful broth)

OOPS!

YOUR SOUP SPORTS AN OIL SLICK

A little pot maneuvering helps you get rid of the grease.

When a bowl of soup leaves lips as slick as if they'd just been slathered with balm, it's a bummer. This problem occurs most often with brothy, meaty soups, such as chicken noodle and beef barley. Fat from the meat—along with oil or butter used to sauté the veggies—rises as the broth simmers. The problem comes when this fat isn't removed. But even if you stand with your skimming spoon at the ready or try the messy and potentially scalding trick of dabbing the surface with a paper towel, you may still leave enough grease there to annoy.

The solution: Skim smarter. Move the soup pot halfway off the burner every 15 minutes or so, and skim from the edge that's tilted off the heat. Impurities and fat gather at the coolest spot—in this case, the side of the pan off the burner. Tilt the pan slightly as you skim to avoid taking off too much broth. Simmer the soup gently, and never boil: That just churns fat into the broth, making an oily, unappetizing emulsion. If time allows, chill the soup overnight. Fat will solidify on top; simply spoon it off before you reheat.

(Greasy film)

THE HOLIDAY COOKBOOK

Thanksgiving is not exactly a time to overhaul the entire menu, any more than Christmas is a time to roll out a whole new set of carols. Tradition trumps innovation. Tinkering, though, keeps this labor of love fresh for the cook.

TWO TURKEYS AND ALL THE TRIMMINGS

If you're up for a new word on the bird, we've got two great approaches. If it's sides you'd like to play with this holiday, we have a whole mess of them—stuffing to sprouts.

We came up with a turkey recipe that yields a gorgeous whole-bird result, and a quicker one for roasted breast for smaller gatherings.

All along the edge of the turkey-focused table are side dishes, and it's there that you can stretch a bit, play with the menu's notes even as the melody stays the same. Here, we offer up a variety of sides, ranging from a traditional sausage and sourdough stuffing punched up with a touch of cider, to a creamy parsnip soup topped with smoky bacon crumbles, to a crunchy, bittersweet salad of winter greens and bright citrus that will contrast beautifully with the old standards. Some dishes can be made ahead, while others come together quickly in real time.

Spicy Maple Turkey Breast with Quick Pan Sauce

(pictured on page 239)

Hands-on time: 10 min. Total time: 1 hr.
If you don't want to spend your entire Turkey Day in the kitchen, this is the entrée for you. A bold spice rub gives the meat big flavor and gorgeous color.

Turkey:
3 tablespoons maple syrup
1 tablespoon olive oil
2 teaspoons ground cumin
1 teaspoon kosher salt
1 teaspoon dried oregano
1 teaspoon smoked paprika
1/2 teaspoon ground coriander
1/2 teaspoon freshly ground black pepper
2 (1 1/2-pound) skinless, boneless turkey breast halves
Cooking spray
Sauce:
2 teaspoons olive oil
2/3 cup chopped onion
1 teaspoon minced garlic
1 1/4 cups no-salt-added chicken stock (such as Swanson)
1 tablespoon flour
1/4 teaspoon kosher salt
1/4 teaspoon freshly ground black pepper

1. Preheat oven to 450°.
2. To prepare turkey, combine first 8 ingredients in a large bowl; add turkey, turning to coat. Marinate at room temperature 20 minutes. Remove turkey from marinade; discard marinade. Place a rack inside a roasting pan; coat rack lightly with cooking spray. Arrange turkey breasts on rack. Bake at 450° for 25 minutes or until a thermometer inserted in thickest part registers 155°. Remove from oven. Let stand 10 minutes; cut turkey diagonally across the grain into 16 slices.
3. To prepare sauce, heat a medium nonstick skillet over medium-high heat. Add 2 teaspoons oil; swirl to coat. Add onion and garlic to pan; sauté 4 minutes, stirring occasionally. Combine stock and flour in a bowl, stirring with a whisk. Add stock mixture to onion mixture, stirring with a whisk. Bring to a boil; cook 2 minutes or until slightly thick, stirring constantly. Remove from heat; stir in 1/4 teaspoon salt and 1/4 teaspoon pepper. Serve sauce with turkey. Serves 8 (serving size: 2 turkey slices and 2 tablespoons sauce).

CALORIES 205; FAT 3.9g (sat 0.7g, mono 2.2g, poly 0.6g); PROTEIN 36.6g; CARB 7.9g; FIBER 0.7g; CHOL 79mg; IRON 2.1mg; SODIUM 385mg; CALC 33mg

Roast Turkey with Sage Pan Gravy

***Hands-on time: 1 hr. Total time: 2 hr. 50 min.** This classic bird and its rich gravy can easily anchor any traditional holiday feast.*

1 (12-pound) fresh or frozen turkey, thawed
3 tablespoons chopped fresh sage, divided
2 tablespoons extra-virgin olive oil
2 tablespoons unsalted butter, softened
1¼ teaspoons kosher salt, divided
½ teaspoon freshly ground black pepper, divided
1 lemon, halved crosswise
6 garlic cloves, peeled
3 carrots, coarsely chopped
3 celery stalks, coarsely chopped
2 medium onions, coarsely chopped
1 bay leaf
3 cups no-salt-added chicken stock (such as Swanson), divided
2 cups water
3 tablespoons white wine
3 tablespoons all-purpose flour

1. Preheat oven to 325°.
2. Remove giblets and neck from turkey; discard liver. Reserve turkey neck and giblets. Pat turkey dry with paper towels; trim and discard excess fat. Starting at neck cavity, loosen skin from breast and drumsticks by inserting fingers, gently pushing between skin and meat.
3. Combine 2 tablespoons sage, olive oil, butter, 1 teaspoon salt, and ¼ teaspoon black pepper. Rub sage mixture under the loosened skin and over breasts and drumsticks. Squeeze juice from 1 half of lemon over turkey; place remaining lemon half in cavity. Tie legs together with kitchen string. Place reserved giblets, neck, garlic, carrots, celery, onion, and bay leaf in the bottom of a large roasting pan. Add 1 cup stock and 2 cups water to pan. Place roasting rack in pan. Arrange turkey, breast side up, on roasting rack. Bake turkey at 325° for 1 hour and 20 minutes, rotating pan every 30 minutes. Increase oven temperature to 425° (do not remove turkey from oven). Bake turkey an additional 30 minutes or until a thermometer inserted into meaty part of thigh registers 165°. Remove turkey from pan; place on a cutting board. Let stand 30 minutes. Carve turkey; discard skin.
4. Place a large zip-top plastic bag inside a 4-cup glass measure. Strain pan drippings through a colander into bag; discard solids. Let drippings stand 10 minutes. Seal bag; snip off 1 bottom corner of bag. Drain pan drippings into a medium saucepan, stopping before fat layer reaches the opening. Add remaining 1 tablespoon sage, remaining ¼ teaspoon salt, remaining ¼ teaspoon black pepper, 1½ cups chicken stock, and wine to drippings in pan; bring to a boil. Cook 15 minutes or until reduced to 2½ cups. Combine flour and remaining ½ cup chicken stock in a small bowl, stirring with a whisk until smooth. Stir flour mixture into stock mixture in pan; bring to a boil. Boil 1 minute or until slightly thick, stirring gravy constantly. Serve gravy with turkey. Serves 12 (serving size: about 6 ounces turkey and ¼ cup gravy).

CALORIES 315; FAT 8.8g (sat 3g, mono 3.3g, poly 1.6g); PROTEIN 51.9g; CARB 3.2g; FIBER 0.4g; CHOL 172mg; IRON 3.6mg; SODIUM 349mg; CALC 49mg

Polenta-Sausage Triangles

(pictured on page 235)

***Hands-on time: 25 min. Total time: 4 hr. 40 min.** Prepare polenta through step 2 up to two days ahead. Before serving, let the dish stand at room temperature one hour, cut polenta into triangles, and toast them at mealtime.*

Cooking spray
8 ounces reduced-fat pork sausage
¾ cup finely chopped yellow onion
¾ cup finely chopped celery
3 garlic cloves, minced
1½ cups water
1¼ cups 1% low-fat milk
1 cup instant polenta
½ teaspoon kosher salt
2 tablespoons olive oil, divided

1. Heat a large saucepan over medium-high heat. Coat pan with cooking spray. Add sausage; cook 2 minutes or until sausage begins to brown, stirring to crumble. Add onion, celery, and garlic; sauté 8 minutes or until vegetables are tender.
2. Add 1½ cups water and milk to sausage mixture in pan, and bring to a boil. Gradually add polenta, stirring constantly with a whisk. Stir in salt. Cook 3 minutes or until thick, stirring constantly. Spoon polenta into an 11 x 7–inch glass or ceramic baking dish coated with cooking spray. Cool to room temperature; cover and refrigerate at least 4 hours.
3. Cut chilled polenta into 8 squares; cut each polenta square diagonally into triangles. Heat a large nonstick skillet over medium-high heat. Add 1 tablespoon oil to pan; swirl to coat. Place 8 triangles in pan; cook 2 minutes on each side or until browned. Repeat procedure with remaining oil and polenta. Serves 8 (serving size: 2 triangles).

CALORIES 190; FAT 9g (sat 2.5g, mono 2.6g, poly 0.4g); PROTEIN 7.8g; CARB 14.8g; FIBER 2.3g; CHOL 22mg; IRON 0.5mg; SODIUM 325mg; CALC 55mg

Sausage and Apple Stuffing

(pictured on page 235)

Hands-on time: 45 min. Total time: 1 hr. 30 min. *Sweet Italian sausage, chopped fresh fennel, and apple combine with tangy sourdough for a classic Thanksgiving stuffing.*

8 cups 1-inch sourdough bread cubes (about 12 ounces)
6 ounces mild Italian breakfast sausage
1½ cups chopped onion
1¼ cups chopped fennel bulb
1 cup chopped celery
3 cups chopped peeled Golden Delicious apple (about 2 medium)
6 garlic cloves, minced
3 tablespoons chopped fresh sage
⅓ cup chopped fresh flat-leaf parsley
1¼ cups no-salt-added chicken stock
¼ cup unfiltered apple cider
2 large eggs, lightly beaten
½ teaspoon black pepper
Cooking spray

1. Preheat oven to 350°.
2. Arrange bread cubes in a single layer on a large baking sheet or jelly-roll pan. Bake at 350° for 20 minutes or until golden. Cool slightly. Place in a large bowl.
3. Heat a large nonstick skillet over medium-high heat. Add sausage to pan; cook 5 minutes or until browned, stirring frequently to crumble. Add sausage to bread in bowl.
4. Return pan to medium-high heat. Add onion, fennel, and celery to pan; sauté 7 minutes or until crisp-tender, stirring occasionally. Stir in apple and garlic; sauté 5 minutes or until vegetables are tender. Add sage to pan; cook 1 minute, stirring occasionally. Remove from heat; stir in parsley. Add onion mixture to bread mixture; toss well.
5. Combine chicken stock, apple cider, eggs, and black pepper in a medium bowl, stirring with a whisk. Add egg mixture to bread mixture, stirring gently to combine. Spoon bread mixture into an 11 x 7–inch glass or ceramic baking dish coated with cooking spray. Bake at 350° for 45 minutes or until top of stuffing is browned. Serves 12 (serving size: about ¾ cup).

CALORIES 166; **FAT** 6g (sat 1.8g, mono 2.7g, poly 0.9g); **PROTEIN** 7g; **CARB** 22.1g; **FIBER** 2.3g; **CHOL** 41mg; **IRON** 1.9mg; **SODIUM** 310mg; **CALC** 62mg

Mushroom and Leek Stuffing

Hands-on time: 23 min. Total time: 1 hr. 8 min. *This delicious yet budget-friendly dish comes to $1.15 per serving. Look for a poultry herb blend in the produce section—one package contains all the herbs you need.*

9 cups ½-inch Italian bread cubes (about 12 ounces)
3 tablespoons olive oil
2½ cups chopped leek (about 2 medium)
1½ cups chopped celery
1 cup chopped carrot
2 tablespoons minced fresh sage
1 tablespoon chopped fresh thyme
4 garlic cloves, minced
1 pound sliced cremini mushrooms
1 cup no-salt-added chicken stock (such as Swanson)
1 cup water
½ teaspoon freshly ground black pepper
¼ teaspoon kosher salt
2 large eggs, lightly beaten
Cooking spray

1. Preheat oven to 350°.
2. Arrange bread cubes in a single layer on a large baking sheet or jelly-roll pan. Bake at 350° for 18 minutes or until golden. Cool slightly.
3. Heat a large nonstick skillet over medium-high heat. Add olive oil to pan; swirl to coat. Add leek and next 5 ingredients; sauté 10 minutes or until leek begins to brown, stirring occasionally. Stir in mushrooms; sauté 8 minutes or until mushrooms are tender, stirring occasionally. Place mushroom mixture in a large bowl. Add toasted bread cubes, chicken stock, and remaining ingredients except cooking spray. Toss mixture gently to combine. Spoon mixture into an 11 x 7–inch glass or ceramic baking dish coated with cooking spray. Bake at 350° for 45 minutes or until browned. Serves 10 (serving size: about ¾ cup).

CALORIES 179; **FAT** 6.6g (sat 1.2g, mono 3.6g, poly 1.2g); **PROTEIN** 6.8g; **CARB** 24.1g; **FIBER** 2.4g; **CHOL** 42mg; **IRON** 2.1mg; **SODIUM** 302mg; **CALC** 65mg

Sautéed Broccolini with Tomatoes

Hands-on time: 16 min. Total time: 16 min. *This speedy, simple stovetop dish saves you oven space and can be prepared at the very last minute, and then brought to the holiday table. Roma or plum tomatoes are the best choice this time of year.*

2 teaspoons olive oil
1 large shallot, thinly vertically sliced
1 pound Broccolini, trimmed
¼ cup dry white wine
1 large plum tomato, seeded and finely chopped
⅓ cup no-salt-added chicken stock
¼ teaspoon kosher salt
¼ teaspoon freshly ground black pepper

1. Heat a large skillet over medium-high heat. Add oil to pan; swirl to coat. Add shallot; sauté 2 minutes or until tender, stirring frequently. Add Broccolini; cook 2 minutes. Add wine and tomato. Cover, reduce heat to medium, and cook 3 minutes. Add stock, salt, and pepper; cook, uncovered, 4 minutes or until Broccolini is crisp-tender. Serves 8 (serving size: 2 ounces).

CALORIES 44; **FAT** 1.1g (sat 0.2g, mono 0.8g, poly 0.1g); **PROTEIN** 2.4g; **CARB** 5.2g; **FIBER** 0.8g; **CHOL** 0mg; **IRON** 0.6mg; **SODIUM** 83mg; **CALC** 43mg

Winter Citrus, Escarole, and Endive Salad

(pictured on page 235)

Hands-on time: 35 min. Total time: 35 min. *This bright, fresh salad of winter greens and sweet-tangy citrus is studded with red pomegranate arils: It's a dramatic, holiday-worthy plate and a welcome course for vegetarians.*

6 cups torn escarole
2 cups thinly sliced Belgian endive (about 2 heads)
1 cup thinly sliced radicchio
1 cup pink grapefruit sections
1 cup navel orange sections
3/4 cup blood orange sections
1/4 cup minced shallots
2 tablespoons extra-virgin olive oil
2 tablespoons orange juice
1 tablespoon white wine vinegar or champagne vinegar
1 1/2 teaspoons honey
1/2 teaspoon kosher salt
1/4 teaspoon freshly ground black pepper
1/2 cup pomegranate arils
2 tablespoons pistachios, toasted

1. Combine first 3 ingredients in a large bowl. Add grapefruit, orange, and blood orange sections; toss gently.
2. Combine shallots and next 6 ingredients in a small bowl, stirring well with a whisk. Drizzle dressing over salad; toss gently to coat. Divide salad evenly among 6 plates. Divide pomegranate arils and toasted pistachios evenly among servings. Serves 6 (serving size: about 1¼ cups).

CALORIES 159; **FAT** 6.3g (sat 0.9g, mono 3.9g, poly 1.1g); **PROTEIN** 4.6g; **CARB** 24.3g; **FIBER** 9.7g; **CHOL** 0mg; **IRON** 2.5mg; **SODIUM** 220mg; **CALC** 164mg

Green Beans with Caramelized Onions and Walnuts

(pictured on page 235)

Hands-on time: 33 min. Total time: 46 min. *Here's a crowd-pleasing side that's easy on the pocketbook: just 67 cents per serving! If money is no object, consider finishing with a flourish of white truffle oil.*

1 1/2 pounds green beans, trimmed
1/2 cup chopped walnuts
2 tablespoons extra-virgin olive oil, divided
4 cups thinly vertically sliced onion
1 teaspoon chopped fresh thyme
2 teaspoons white balsamic vinegar
1/2 teaspoon kosher salt
1/4 teaspoon freshly ground black pepper

1. Cook green beans in boiling water 2 minutes. Drain and rinse with cold water, and drain well.
2. Place walnuts in a large nonstick skillet; cook over medium heat 7 minutes or until lightly browned, shaking pan frequently. Remove walnuts from pan; set aside. Add 4 teaspoons oil to pan; swirl to coat. Add onion and thyme to pan; cook 17 minutes or until onion is very tender and golden brown, stirring occasionally. Remove onion mixture from pan; keep warm.
3. Return pan to medium-high heat. Add remaining 2 teaspoons olive oil to pan; swirl to coat. Add green beans; cook 2 minutes or until thoroughly heated, stirring frequently. Add onion mixture and vinegar; cook 2 minutes or until thoroughly heated, tossing to combine. Remove from heat. Sprinkle with nuts, salt, and pepper. Serve immediately. Serves 8 (serving size: ¾ cup).

CALORIES 130; **FAT** 8.4g (sat 1g, mono 3.4g, poly 3.8g); **PROTEIN** 3.3g; **CARB** 12.8g; **FIBER** 4.4g; **CHOL** 0mg; **IRON** 1.4mg; **SODIUM** 128mg; **CALC** 55mg

Romano-Topped Brussels Sprouts

Hands-on time: 10 min. Total time: 30 min. *Simple roasted Brussels sprouts get a big flavor boost from one simple addition: salty pecorino Romano cheese, which punctuates the traditional fall veggie dish with meaty umami notes. You can also use subtler Asiago or Parmigiano-Reggiano cheese, if you prefer. Quarter the larger sprouts so they are about the same size as halved smaller ones, and spread them in a single layer in two different roasting pans so they brown nicely and evenly.*

3 tablespoons olive oil
1/2 teaspoon kosher salt
1/4 teaspoon freshly ground black pepper
2 1/2 pounds Brussels sprouts, trimmed and halved lengthwise
Cooking spray
1 ounce fresh pecorino Romano cheese, shaved (about 1/3 cup)

1. Preheat oven to 425°.
2. Combine olive oil, salt, black pepper, and Brussels sprouts in a medium bowl; toss well to coat. Divide Brussels sprouts mixture evenly between 2 small roasting pans or jelly-roll pans coated with cooking spray. Bake at 425° for 20 minutes or until Brussels sprouts are browned and crisp-tender, rotating pans after 10 minutes. Remove from oven. Sprinkle Brussels sprouts evenly with cheese. Serve immediately. Serves 8 (serving size: 1 cup Brussels sprouts and about 2 teaspoons cheese).

CALORIES 122; **FAT** 6.8 (sat 1.5g, mono 4.1g, poly 0.7g); **PROTEIN** 5.5g; **CARB** 12.7g; **FIBER** 5.4g; **CHOL** 3mg; **IRON** 2mg; **SODIUM** 215mg; **CALC** 92mg

Browned Butter Bourbon Mashed Sweet Potatoes

(pictured on page 235)

Hands-on time: 25 min. Total time: 35 min. *Sweet potatoes laced with bourbon, butter, and cream—what could be better?*

1 tablespoon minced garlic
3 pounds sweet potatoes, peeled and coarsely chopped
2 tablespoons butter
2 tablespoons bourbon
1 tablespoon brown sugar
³⁄₄ teaspoon kosher salt
¹⁄₂ teaspoon freshly ground black pepper
¹⁄₂ cup half-and-half

1. Place garlic and potatoes in a Dutch oven, and cover with water; bring to a boil. Reduce heat; simmer 18 minutes or until tender. Drain. Place potatoes in a large bowl.
2. Return pan to medium-high heat. Add butter; cook 2 minutes or until browned and fragrant. Stir in bourbon and sugar; bring to a simmer. Return potato mixture to pan. Stir in salt and pepper; mash with a potato masher until smooth. Remove from heat; stir in half-and-half. Serves 8 (serving size: ¹⁄₂ cup).

CALORIES 208; **FAT** 4.7g (sat 2.9g, mono 1.3g, poly 0.2g); **PROTEIN** 3.2g; **CARB** 37g; **FIBER** 5.2g; **CHOL** 13mg; **IRON** 1.1mg; **SODIUM** 301mg; **CALC** 72mg

> TINKERING IS WHAT KEEPS THANKSGIVING FRESH AND ENJOYABLE FOR THE COOK—AND IT'S PERFECT FOR SIDES, WHERE THERE'S ALREADY LOTS OF CHOICE.

Make Ahead

Parsnip and Apple Soup

Hands-on time: 25 min. Total time: 55 min. *For convenience, you can prepare the soup up to two days ahead and chill. Reheat and garnish just before serving. Tangy yogurt and smoky bacon provide a nice counterpoint.*

2 tablespoons unsalted butter
5 cups chopped peeled parsnip (about 2 pounds)
3 cups chopped peeled Fuji apple (about 1 pound)
1¹⁄₂ cups chopped onion
2 teaspoons chopped peeled fresh ginger
1¹⁄₂ teaspoons ground coriander
¹⁄₂ teaspoon ground cumin
¹⁄₂ teaspoon kosher salt
¹⁄₄ teaspoon ground white pepper
2 garlic cloves
3 cups no-salt-added chicken stock (such as Swanson)
2 cups water
1 tablespoon cider vinegar
¹⁄₂ cup plain low-fat yogurt
2 tablespoons chopped fresh flat-leaf parsley
2 bacon slices, cooked and crumbled

1. Melt butter in a large saucepan over medium-high heat. Add parsnip and next 8 ingredients; sauté 8 minutes. Add stock, 2 cups water, and vinegar; bring to a boil. Cover, reduce heat, and simmer 30 minutes or until parsnips are tender. Remove from heat; uncover. Let mixture stand 10 minutes.
2. Place half of parsnip mixture in a blender. Remove center piece of blender lid (to allow steam to escape); secure blender lid on blender. Place a clean towel over opening in blender lid (to avoid splatters). Blend until smooth. Strain mixture through a sieve into a bowl, and discard solids. Pour into a large bowl. Repeat procedure with remaining parsnip mixture. Top each serving with 1 tablespoon yogurt. Sprinkle evenly with parsley and bacon. Serves 8 (serving size: 1 cup).

CALORIES 154; **FAT** 4.1g (sat 2.2g, mono 1.2g, poly 0.3g); **PROTEIN** 4.8g; **CARB** 26.3g; **FIBER** 5.8g; **CHOL** 10mg; **IRON** 0.9mg; **SODIUM** 235mg; **CALC** 71mg

Cranberry Sauce with Cassis and Dried Cherries

Hands-on time: 18 min. Total time: 2 hr. 18 min. *This essential trimming can be made up to a week ahead. Cassis is black currant–flavored liqueur. If you can't find it, substitute orange liqueur.*

1 tablespoon canola oil
½ cup finely chopped shallots
⅔ cup dried tart cherries
½ cup crème de cassis (black currant-flavored liqueur)
¾ cup sugar
1 (12-ounce) package fresh cranberries
1½ teaspoons grated fresh lemon rind

1. Heat a medium saucepan over medium heat. Add oil; swirl to coat. Add shallots; sauté 4 minutes or until tender, stirring occasionally. Increase heat to medium-high. Add cherries, crème de cassis, sugar, and cranberries; bring to a boil. Reduce heat, and simmer 8 minutes or until cranberries begin to pop, stirring occasionally. Remove from heat; stir in rind. Cool to room temperature. Serves 12 (serving size: ¼ cup).

CALORIES 143; FAT 1.2g (sat 0.1g, mono 0.7g, poly 0.4g); PROTEIN 0.5g; CARB 27.2g; FIBER 2.2g; CHOL 0mg; IRON 0.3mg; SODIUM 3mg; CALC 18mg

OOPS!

COMMON TURKEY BLUNDERS

1. INSUFFICIENT LEG ROOM
Your turkey should fit the roasting pan with room to spare, or it won't cook properly. Use a heavy-duty pan, not the disposable foil kind that may collapse.

2. OVERCOOKED TURKEY
Use a probe thermometer that stays in the bird. Remove from oven at 160°. Emergency fix: Revive dried-out meat by soaking slices in hot broth or stock.

3. RAGGED CARVING
Do it in the proper order: First, remove the leg quarters. Second, take both breast halves off the bird, and then slice them crosswise (against the grain).

4. UNRESTED BIRD
Let the cooked bird stand 20–30 minutes before carving—it helps keep meat juicy.

SOME SIDE DISH BOO-BOOS

5. GREEN VEG TURNS BROWN
Cook your green veggies only to al dente (slightly crisp), and don't add acids like vinegar or lemon juice until just before serving.

6. LIMP SALAD
Don't overdress. Add your dressing to the sides of the salad bowl just before serving, and toss gently.

7. LUMPY GRAVY
Whisk flour with water to make a slurry; then whisk the slurry into the hot broth mixture. Still lumpy? Strain through a sieve.

YET MORE TURKEY-DAY SNAFUS

8. BURNED SOUP
Stir soup every few minutes so solids don't stick to the bottom. If something has stuck and burned, don't dislodge it: Transfer soup to a new pot; leave the scorched stuff behind.

9. GLUEY MASHED POTATOES
Start with baking or Yukon gold potatoes, not waxy spuds. Electric mixers overwork them, so mash by hand. Better still, use a ricer or food mill.

10. APPROACHING MELTDOWN
This tends to happen when cooks try to do more than they can handle. Ask for help, especially with prep. Keep wine handy. Apply cautiously, as needed.

BEST FAST DISHES EVER

If there's one thing we've heard consistently over the past 25 years, it's this: You want your healthy food fast. The quick recipe that really satisfies is cherished above all others. Sometimes it's a recipe that uses inherently fast-cooking ingredients. But even more dazzling is one that uses smart techniques to infuse a dish with the rich flavors that usually require hours on the stove. Every recipe devised for this challenge had to receive one of our top scores. These were the champs. Prepare to be amazed.

Quick & Easy

30-Minute Filet Bourguignonne with Mashed Potatoes

Hands-on time: 30 min. Total time: 30 min. *An earthy red, such as pinot noir, is the wine traditionally used in Burgundy, where the classic time-consuming stew was born. Serve with mashed potatoes, as the recipe directs, or opt for pappardelle pasta, if you prefer.*

1 pound baking potato, peeled and cut into 1-inch pieces
1 cup frozen pearl onions
1 pound beef tenderloin, cut into 2-inch pieces
½ teaspoon kosher salt, divided
½ teaspoon freshly ground black pepper, divided
5 teaspoons butter, divided
1 bacon slice, finely chopped
1 (8-ounce) package mushrooms, quartered
1 garlic clove, finely chopped
½ teaspoon chopped fresh thyme
½ teaspoon sugar
2 teaspoons no-salt-added tomato paste
½ cup earthy red wine
1 cup fat-free, lower-sodium beef broth
2 tablespoons water
2 teaspoons all-purpose flour
3 tablespoons 2% reduced-fat milk
Thyme sprigs (optional)

1. Place potato in a saucepan over high heat; cover with cool water. Bring to a boil; cook 10 minutes or until very tender. Drain. Return potato to pan; keep warm.

2. While potato cooks, place onions in a microwave-safe bowl; cover with a paper towel. Microwave at HIGH 4 minutes. Finely chop 1 (2-inch) cube of tenderloin, and set aside. Pat remaining beef cubes dry with a paper towel; sprinkle evenly with ¼ teaspoon salt and ¼ teaspoon pepper.

3. Heat a 12-inch cast-iron skillet over medium-high heat. Melt 1 tablespoon butter in pan; swirl to coat. Add seasoned beef cubes; sauté 3 minutes, turning to brown on all sides. Remove beef from pan. Add finely chopped beef and bacon to pan; sauté 3 minutes, stirring occasionally. Add mushrooms; sauté 5 minutes or until mushrooms brown, stirring occasionally. Add garlic, chopped thyme, and sugar; sauté 1 minute, stirring constantly. Add tomato paste; cook 1 minute, stirring constantly. Add wine, and bring to a boil, scraping pan to loosen browned bits. Cook 2 minutes or until liquid is reduced by half.

4. Add onions and broth; bring to a boil. Cook 1 minute. Combine 2 tablespoons water and flour in a bowl, stirring with a whisk until smooth. Add flour mixture to pan; cook 1 minute, stirring constantly. Return browned beef cubes to pan; cook 2 minutes or until thoroughly heated and cooked to medium-rare or desired degree of doneness.

5. Add remaining ¼ teaspoon salt, remaining ¼ teaspoon pepper, remaining 2 teaspoons butter, and milk to potatoes in saucepan; mash with a potato masher until desired consistency. Serve beef and sauce over potatoes; garnish with thyme sprigs, if desired. Serves 4 (serving size: ½ cup potatoes and about ¾ cup stew).

CALORIES 382; FAT 13.4g (sat 6.2g, mono 4.6g, poly 0.7g); PROTEIN 31.1g; CARB 28.4g; FIBER 2.7g; CHOL 91mg; IRON 3.5mg; SODIUM 505mg; CALC 65mg

Quick & Easy

Creamy Lobster Pappardelle

Hands-on time: 29 min. Total time: 29 min. *An admittedly pricey ingredient, lobster fancies up any dinner. Opt for lobster tails—versus whole live lobsters—to bring the cost down.*

1 (8-ounce) package uncooked
   pappardelle (wide ribbon pasta)
2 cups dry white wine
½ cup no-salt-added chicken stock
   (such as Swanson)
1 thyme sprig
3 (5-ounce) American lobster tails
¼ cup extra-virgin olive oil
¾ teaspoon kosher salt
¼ teaspoon freshly ground black
   pepper
2 tablespoons heavy whipping cream
2 tablespoons fresh parsley
1 teaspoon thyme leaves

1. Cook pasta according to package directions, omitting salt and fat; drain.
2. While pasta cooks, bring wine, stock, and thyme sprig to a boil in a large skillet. Add lobster. Cover, reduce heat, and simmer 5 minutes or until done. Remove lobster from pan, and cool slightly. Remove meat from lobster tails; coarsely chop.
3. Add oil, salt, and pepper to wine mixture in pan; bring to a boil. Cook 14 minutes or until reduced to ½ cup. Discard thyme sprig. Stir in cream. Add lobster meat and pasta to sauce. Cook 1 minute or until sauce coats pasta, and toss. Sprinkle with parsley and thyme. Serve immediately. Serves 4 (serving size: 1 cup).

Sustainable Choice | *Look for tails from American lobsters trapped off the New England or eastern Canadian shores.*

CALORIES 481; **FAT** 17.9g (sat 4g, mono 10.9g, poly 1.7g); **PROTEIN** 24.6g; **CARB** 44.8g; **FIBER** 1.9g; **CHOL** 91mg; **IRON** 2.5mg; **SODIUM** 637mg; **CALC** 68mg

Quick & Easy

Butternut Squash and Mushroom Tart with Gruyère

Hands-on time: 30 min. Total time: 30 min. *If you can't find prepared ingredients, using fresh will add only about 15 minutes to the prep time.*

Crust:
5.6 ounces all-purpose flour (about
   1 cup plus 2 tablespoons)
¼ teaspoon kosher salt
¼ teaspoon freshly ground black
   pepper
¼ teaspoon baking powder
¼ cup extra-virgin olive oil
3 tablespoons ice water
Cooking spray
Filling:
3 cups precubed peeled butternut
   squash
2 tablespoons extra-virgin olive oil,
   divided
¾ cup prechopped onion
2.5 ounces aged Gruyère cheese,
   shredded and divided (about ⅔ cup)
2 large eggs
½ teaspoon kosher salt, divided
½ teaspoon freshly ground black
   pepper, divided
1½ ounces prechopped pancetta
5 ounces presliced shiitake mushroom
   caps
¼ cup dry white wine

1. Preheat oven to 425°.
2. To prepare crust, weigh or lightly spoon flour into a dry measuring cup and spoons; level with a knife. Place flour and next 3 ingredients in a food processor; pulse 2 times or until combined. Combine ¼ cup oil and 3 table-spoons ice water in a small bowl. With processor on, slowly add oil mixture through food chute, and process until dough is crumbly. Sprinkle dough into a 9-inch pie plate coated with cooking spray. Quickly press dough into an even layer in bottom and up sides of pie plate. Place crust into preheating oven, and bake 10 minutes.
3. To prepare filling, place cubed squash in food processor (do not clean from dough), and process 1 minute or until squash is finely chopped. Heat a large nonstick skillet over medium-high heat. Add 1 tablespoon oil to pan; swirl to coat. Add squash and onion to pan; and sauté 9 minutes, stirring occasionally.
4. While squash cooks, combine half of cheese (about ⅓ cup), eggs, ¼ teaspoon salt, and ¼ teaspoon pepper in a large bowl; stir in squash mixture. Remove crust from oven; spoon squash mixture over crust, and spread evenly. Return tart to 425° oven; bake 9 minutes.
5. Return pan to medium-high heat. Add remaining 1 tablespoon oil to pan; swirl to coat. Add pancetta; cook 1 minute or until beginning to brown. Add mushrooms; cook 7 minutes or until browned. Stir in remaining ¼ teaspoon salt and ¼ teaspoon pepper. Add wine; cook 1 minute or until liquid almost evaporates. Remove tart from oven. Arrange mushroom mixture evenly over top of tart; sprinkle with remaining ⅓ cup cheese. Return tart to 425° oven. Bake 3 to 5 minutes or until cheese melts. Serves 6 (serving size: 1 wedge).

CALORIES 368; **FAT** 21.8g (sat 5.7g, mono 11.7g, poly 2g); **PROTEIN** 11.1g; **CARB** 31.6g; **FIBER** 2.8g; **CHOL** 89mg; **IRON** 2.3mg; **SODIUM** 442mg; **CALC** 183mg

Quick & Easy • Freezable
Make Ahead

Chicken and Sausage Gumbo

(*pictured on page 238*)

Hands-on time: 30 min. Total time: 30 min.

6 ounces andouille sausage, finely
  chopped
2 tablespoons butter
2 tablespoons canola oil
1.5 ounces all-purpose flour (about
  1/3 cup)
8 ounces skinless, boneless chicken
  thighs, cut into bite-sized pieces
1 cup chopped onion
3/4 cup chopped green bell pepper
  (about 1 medium)
1/2 cup thinly sliced celery
1 tablespoon salt-free Cajun/Creole
  seasoning
1/2 teaspoon salt
5 garlic cloves, minced
3 cups no-salt-added chicken stock
  (such as Swanson)
1 (14.5-ounce) can no-salt-added whole
  tomatoes, drained and crushed
1 cup frozen cut okra
3 cups bagged precooked brown rice

1. Heat a Dutch oven over medium-high heat. Add sausage to pan; sauté 5 minutes, turning to brown on all sides. Remove sausage from pan using a slotted spoon, and drain on paper towels. Melt butter in drippings in pan. Add oil to pan; swirl. Weigh or lightly spoon flour into a dry measuring cup; level with a knife. Stir flour into butter mixture; cook 3 minutes or until flour mixture starts to brown, stirring constantly with a whisk. Add chicken; sauté 4 minutes, stirring frequently. Add chopped onion and next 5 ingredients to pan, and sauté 6 minutes or until vegetables are tender, stirring occasionally. Add stock and tomatoes to pan; bring to a boil. Return sausage to pan; stir in okra. Reduce heat, and simmer 6 minutes, stirring occasionally. Serve over rice. Serves 6 (serving size: 1 cup gumbo and 1/2 cup rice).

CALORIES 367; FAT 16.1g (sat 5.6g, mono 7.3g, poly 2.7g); PROTEIN 19g; CARB 36.8g; FIBER 4.2g; CHOL 57mg; IRON 2.6mg; SODIUM 559mg; CALC 70mg

Kid Friendly • Quick & Easy

Cassoulet in a Flash

Hands-on time: 30 min. Total time: 30 min. *Toasted walnut oil in the topping adds a delicate, sweet backnote of flavor to this hearty dish. If you can't find walnut oil, substitute a fruity extra-virgin olive oil.*

3 ounces duck sausage, casings
  removed (such as D'Artagnan)
2 ounces center-cut bacon, cut into
  1/4-inch pieces
1/3 cup chopped onion
1/3 cup chopped celery
1/3 cup chopped carrot
1 tablespoon chopped fresh thyme
2 garlic cloves, minced
1 (3-ounce) boneless duck breast half
Cooking spray
2 (15.5-ounce) cans no-salt-added
  white beans, rinsed, drained, and
  divided
2 tablespoons no-salt-added tomato
  paste
1 1/4 cups no-salt-added chicken stock
  (such as Swanson)
1/2 teaspoon freshly ground black
  pepper
1/2 cup panko (Japanese breadcrumbs)
1 tablespoon chopped fresh flat-leaf
  parsley
2 tablespoons walnut oil

1. Preheat broiler to high.
2. Heat a large skillet over medium heat. Add sausage and bacon to pan; cook 5 minutes or until lightly browned, stirring occasionally to crumble sausage. Remove mixture from pan using a slotted spoon; place in a bowl. Reserve 1 tablespoon drippings in pan; reserve remaining drippings for another use. Increase heat to medium-high. Add onion and next 4 ingredients to drippings in pan; sauté 3 minutes, stirring occasionally. Add onion mixture to sausage mixture.
3. Remove skin from duck breast; discard skin. Cut breast into 1/2-inch pieces. Return pan to medium-high heat. Lightly coat pan with cooking spray. Add duck breast; sauté 3 minutes, turning to brown on all sides. Remove from heat.
4. Place 1/2 cup beans, tomato paste, and stock in a food processor; process until smooth. Add pureed bean mixture, sausage mixture, remaining beans, and pepper to pan with duck; bring to a boil over medium-high heat. Cook 2 minutes. Spoon 1 cup bean mixture into each of 4 (8-ounce) ramekins lightly coated with cooking spray. Combine panko, parsley, and oil in a small bowl; toss. Divide panko mixture evenly among ramekins. Place ramekins on a baking sheet; broil 2 minutes or until browned. Serves 4 (serving size: 1 ramekin).

CALORIES 383; FAT 21.7g (sat 6.1g, mono 7.8g, poly 5.7g); PROTEIN 20.7g; CARB 26.9g; FIBER 6.4g; CHOL 66mg; IRON 4.5mg; SODIUM 615mg; CALC 66mg

White Sea Bass with Orange-Fennel Relish

Hands-on time: 20 min. Total time: 20 min.

2 tablespoons extra-virgin olive oil
1 tablespoon fresh lemon juice
1 tablespoon fresh orange juice
¹/₂ teaspoon grated orange rind
³/₈ teaspoon kosher salt, divided
³/₈ teaspoon black pepper, divided
1 (12-ounce) fennel bulb
1 cup fresh orange sections
¹/₄ cup thinly sliced red onion
2 ounces halved Castelvetrano olives (about ¹/₂ cup)
4 (6-ounce) white sea bass fillets
1¹/₂ teaspoons butter

1. Combine first 4 ingredients, ⅛ teaspoon salt, and ⅛ teaspoon black pepper in a medium bowl, stirring with a whisk. Remove fronds from fennel bulb; chop fronds to measure 2 tablespoons. Remove and discard stalks. Cut fennel bulb in half lengthwise; discard core. Thinly slice fennel bulb. Add sliced fennel, orange sections, onion, and olives to orange juice mixture; toss gently to coat. Stir in fennel fronds.
2. Heat a large nonstick skillet over medium-high heat. Sprinkle fish with remaining ¼ teaspoon salt and remaining ¼ teaspoon pepper. Add butter to pan; swirl until butter melts. Add fish to pan; cook 4 minutes on each side or until desired degree of doneness. Serve with relish. Serves 4 (serving size: 1 fillet and about 1 cup relish).

Sustainable Choice

Choose U.S. white sea bass—not to be confused with Chilean sea bass.

CALORIES 274; **FAT** 13.4g (sat 2.5g, mono 5.9g, poly 1.7g); **PROTEIN** 25.2g; **CARB** 13.1g; **FIBER** 3.9g; **CHOL** 56mg; **IRON** 1.1mg; **SODIUM** 605mg; **CALC** 76mg

---

Rainbow Trout with Smoked Tomato Salsa

Hands-on time: 30 min. Total time: 30 min.

1 cup cherry wood chips
4 plum tomatoes, halved and seeded
2 tablespoons chopped shallots
1 tablespoon chopped fresh thyme
1 tablespoon extra-virgin olive oil
¹/₂ teaspoon grated lemon rind
1¹/₂ tablespoons fresh lemon juice
1 large garlic clove, minced
¹/₄ teaspoon kosher salt, divided
¹/₄ teaspoon black pepper, divided
4 (6-ounce) rainbow trout fillets, dressed
Cooking spray

1. Pierce 10 holes on one side of the bottom of a 13 x 9–inch disposable aluminum foil pan. Place holes over element on cooktop; place wood chips over holes inside pan. Arrange tomato halves, cut sides up, on opposite end of pan. Heat element under holes to medium-high; let burn 1 minute or until chips begin to smoke. Carefully cover pan with foil. Reduce heat to low; smoke tomatoes 20 minutes. Remove from heat.
2. While tomatoes smoke, combine shallots and next 5 ingredients in a medium bowl; stir in ⅛ teaspoon salt and ⅛ teaspoon pepper. Chop tomatoes, and stir into shallot mixture.
3. Heat a large cast-iron skillet over medium-high heat. Sprinkle remaining ⅛ teaspoon salt and ⅛ teaspoon pepper evenly over trout. Lightly coat trout with cooking spray. Arrange fillets, skin side down, in pan; cook 5 minutes or until fish flakes easily when tested with a fork. Serve with salsa. Serves 4 (serving size: 1 fillet and ¼ cup salsa).

CALORIES 200; **FAT** 7.9g (sat 1.4g, mono 3.9g, poly 2g); **PROTEIN** 26.9g; **CARB** 4.3g; **FIBER** 0.9g; **CHOL** 75mg; **IRON** 1.3mg; **SODIUM** 164mg; **CALC** 99mg

---

Rich Chicken Soup with Fresh Noodles

Hands-on time: 26 min. Total time: 26 min.

1 tablespoon butter
4 (4-ounce) skinless, boneless chicken thighs, trimmed
³/₄ teaspoon kosher salt, divided
¹/₂ teaspoon pepper, divided
2 cups sliced onion
1 cup diagonally sliced carrots
1 tablespoon white miso (soybean paste)
¹/₂ cup dry white wine
1 (1-ounce) package fresh poultry mix herbs
5 cups no-salt-added chicken stock
1 cup sliced celery
1 (8-ounce) skinless, boneless chicken breast half, cut into bite-sized pieces
6 ounces fresh lasagna noodles, chopped
3 tablespoons chopped green onions

1. Melt butter in a Dutch oven over medium-high heat. Sprinkle chicken thighs evenly with ½ teaspoon salt and ¼ teaspoon pepper. Add chicken thighs to pan; sauté 3 minutes on each side or until browned. Remove chicken thighs. Add onion, carrot, and miso to pan; sauté 2 minutes, stirring occasionally. Add wine; cook 1 minute, scraping pan to loosen browned bits. Chop chicken thighs into bite-sized pieces; return chicken thighs to pan. Tie twine around herbs to secure. Add herbs, stock, celery, and chicken breast to pan; bring to a boil. Reduce heat, and cook 5 minutes. Add remaining ¼ teaspoon salt, ¼ teaspoon pepper, and pasta; simmer 2 minutes or until pasta is done. Discard herbs. Sprinkle with green onions. Serves 6 (serving size: about 1½ cups).

CALORIES 287; **FAT** 4.7g (sat 2g, mono 1.2g, poly 0.7g); **PROTEIN** 27.1g; **CARB** 30g; **FIBER** 3.1g; **CHOL** 65mg; **IRON** 2.5mg; **SODIUM** 549mg; **CALC** 60mg

---

New England Clam Chowder

Hands-on time: 30 min. Total time: 30 min. Bring the half-and-half as close to room temperature as possible before adding to the chowder to help keep it from breaking.

2 cups refrigerated diced potatoes with onion (such as Simply Potatoes)
2¼ cups water, divided
50 littleneck clams, scrubbed
2 thyme sprigs
1 bay leaf
1 applewood-smoked bacon slice, finely chopped
½ cup finely chopped celery
3 tablespoons all-purpose flour
1 (8-ounce) bottle clam juice
1 teaspoon chopped fresh thyme
1 cup half-and-half
¼ teaspoon kosher salt
¼ teaspoon black pepper
1 tablespoon chopped fresh chives
½ cup oyster crackers

1. Combine potatoes and 1¼ cups water in a microwave-safe measuring cup. Microwave at HIGH 8 minutes or until potatoes are tender. Set aside.
2. While potatoes cook, combine remaining 1 cup water, clams, thyme sprigs, and bay leaf in a Dutch oven; bring to a boil over medium-high heat. Cover, reduce heat, and simmer 6 minutes or until shells open. Remove clams from pan using a slotted spoon, and discard any unopened shells. Strain cooking liquid through a fine mesh sieve over a bowl; discard solids. Cool clams slightly. Remove meat from shells, and chop. Discard shells.
3. Heat a medium saucepan over medium heat. Add bacon to pan; cook 4 minutes or until browned and crisp, stirring occasionally. Remove bacon from pan using a slotted spoon. Increase heat to medium-high. Add celery to drippings in pan; sauté 3 minutes or until tender, stirring occasionally.

4. Combine flour and bottled clam juice in a small bowl, stirring with a whisk until smooth. Add clam juice mixture and reserved cooking liquid to pan. Bring mixture to a boil; cook 1 minute, stirring constantly with a whisk. Add reserved potato mixture and chopped thyme to pan; reduce heat, and simmer 5 minutes, stirring occasionally. Remove from heat. Stir in chopped clams, half-and-half, and salt. Divide chowder evenly among 4 bowls; sprinkle evenly with bacon, pepper, and chives. Serve with crackers. Serves 4 (serving size: about 1½ cups chowder and 2 tablespoons crackers).

CALORIES 336; FAT 10.4g (sat 5.1g, mono 2.8g, poly 1.2g); PROTEIN 28.8g; CARB 30.2g; FIBER 2.1g; CHOL 88mg; IRON 26.5mg; SODIUM 629mg; CALC 164mg

Fast Shepherd's Pie

Hands-on time: 30 min. Total time: 30 min. Save the lamb bones to enrich a soup or pot of beans.

1 (24-ounce) bag frozen mashed potatoes
½ cup 2% reduced-fat milk
2 tablespoons butter
¾ teaspoon kosher salt, divided
1 tablespoon olive oil
6 lamb loin chops, meat removed from bones and cut into bite-sized pieces
½ teaspoon freshly ground black pepper
1 cup chopped onion
1 (6-ounce) microwavable bag peeled baby carrots
1 tablespoon tomato paste
⅓ cup dry red wine
2 tablespoons all-purpose flour
2 cups fat-free, lower-sodium beef broth
1 cup frozen English peas
1½ tablespoons chopped fresh thyme
1½ teaspoons chopped fresh rosemary

1. Preheat broiler to high.
2. Microwave potatoes according to package directions; stir in milk, butter, and ¼ teaspoon salt.
3. While potatoes cook, heat a Dutch oven over medium-high heat. Add oil to pan; swirl to coat. Sprinkle lamb evenly with remaining ½ teaspoon salt and pepper. Add lamb to pan; sauté 4 minutes, turning to brown on all sides. Remove lamb from pan with a slotted spoon. Add onion to pan, and sauté 4 minutes, stirring occasionally.
4. While onion cooks, microwave carrots at HIGH 1½ minutes. Remove carrots from bag; slice diagonally into ½-inch pieces. Stir tomato paste into onion in pan; cook 1 minute, stirring frequently. Add wine; cook 2 minutes or until liquid almost evaporates, scraping pan to loosen browned bits. Add flour; cook 1 minute, stirring constantly. Gradually add broth, stirring constantly. Stir in sliced carrots, peas, and herbs. Bring to a boil; cook 4 minutes or until slightly thick, stirring occasionally. Remove from heat; stir in browned lamb.
5. Spoon lamb mixture into a 2-quart broiler-safe ceramic casserole dish; top with mashed potato mixture. Broil 4 minutes or until lightly browned on top. Serves 6 (serving size: about ¾ cup lamb mixture and ¾ cup potatoes).

CALORIES 377; FAT 13.7g (sat 5.2g, mono 4.3g, poly 0.8g); PROTEIN 20.2g; CARB 39.9g; FIBER 5.7g; CHOL 59mg; IRON 2.9mg; SODIUM 536mg; CALC 59mg

OUR HAPPIEST RECIPES EVER

The creamiest, beefiest, tangiest, funkiest, spiciest, even booziest recipes we've cooked up.

Quick & Easy • Vegetarian
Pappardelle with Mushrooms

Hands-on time: 12 min. Total time: 40 min. *When this recipe first appeared in the magazine, it was made with hollow bucatini noodles. For the version shown here, we switched to ribbony pappardelle. In truth, any pasta would work well.*

1/2 cup dried porcini mushrooms (about 1/2 ounce)
2/3 cup boiling water
8 ounces uncooked pappardelle pasta or bucatini
3 1/4 teaspoons salt, divided
1 tablespoon olive oil
1/4 cup finely chopped shallots
2 (4-ounce) packages exotic mushroom blend, sliced or coarsely chopped
2 garlic cloves, minced
2 tablespoons dry sherry
2 ounces fresh Parmigiano-Reggiano cheese, divided
1/4 cup heavy whipping cream
1 teaspoon finely chopped fresh sage
1/2 teaspoon cracked black pepper
1 teaspoon truffle oil
Sage leaves (optional)

1. Rinse porcini thoroughly. Combine porcini and 2/3 cup boiling water in a bowl; cover and let stand 30 minutes. Drain in a sieve over a bowl, reserving 1/4 cup soaking liquid. Chop porcini.
2. Cook pasta with 1 tablespoon salt in boiling water 10 minutes or until al dente; drain in a colander over a bowl, reserving 1/4 cup cooking liquid.
3. Heat a large skillet over medium-high heat. Add oil to pan; swirl to coat. Add shallots, mushroom blend, and garlic; sauté 5 minutes, stirring frequently. Stir in porcini, sherry, and remaining 1/4 teaspoon salt; cook 1 minute or until liquid evaporates.
4. Finely grate 1 ounce cheese; crumble remaining cheese. Reduce heat to medium. Stir pasta, 1/4 cup reserved cooking liquid, 1/4 cup reserved porcini soaking liquid, 1/4 cup grated cheese, cream, chopped sage, and pepper into mushroom mixture; toss well to combine. Drizzle with truffle oil; toss. Place about 1 1/4 cups pasta mixture on each of 4 plates; top each serving with about 1 tablespoon crumbled cheese. Garnish with sage leaves, if desired. Serves 4.

CALORIES 393; FAT 14.2g (sat 6.1g, mono 4.3g, poly 0.9g); PROTEIN 15.8g; CARB 49.3g; FIBER 3.4g; CHOL 38mg; IRON 3.1mg; SODIUM 585mg; CALC 201mg

BOOZIEST–NOVEMBER 2012
Freezable • Make Ahead
Cranberry-Whiskey Sour Slush

Hands-on time: 16 min. Total time: 8 hr. 16 min. *Our garnet-colored slush has all the qualities of an intensely delicious cocktail—a not-too-sweet, well-balanced combination of high-quality liquor and fruity tang. Make sure to steer clear of above-80-proof bourbon; it won't freeze solid enough to become slushy. Garnish with any fresh herb.*

1 1/2 cups water
1 cup granulated sugar
Dash of salt
4 cups fresh cranberries (about 1 pound)
1 1/3 cups 80-proof bourbon
3 tablespoons fresh lemon juice

1. Combine water, sugar, and salt in a microwave-safe dish; microwave at HIGH 3 minutes. Stir until sugar dissolves. Place sugar syrup and cranberries in a blender; process until smooth. Strain mixture through a sieve lined with a double layer of cheesecloth over a bowl; press mixture to extract all liquid possible. Discard solids.

2. Combine cranberry mixture, bourbon, and lemon juice in a freezer-safe bowl, stirring well. Freeze mixture overnight or until partially frozen. Scrape mixture with a fork until slushy; serve immediately. Serves 8 (serving size: ½ cup).

CALORIES 210; **FAT** 0.1g (sat 0g, mono 0g, poly 0.1g); **PROTEIN** 0.2g; **CARB** 32.6g; **FIBER** 0.6g; **CHOL** 0mg; **IRON** 0.2mg; **SODIUM** 21mg; **CALC** 7mg

SPICIEST–JULY 2010
Singapore Barbecue Squid (Sotong Bakar)

Hands-on time: 20 min. Total time: 3 hr. 20 min. Thirteen firecracker-fierce Thai chiles blend into a sauce that is beautifully complex, with sweet, fragrant, and salty refrains along with serious heat. To tame the flame, you can use less of the Thai chiles and add extra-mild bell pepper.

1½ pounds whole cleaned skinless squid tubes
⅓ cup chopped red bell pepper
13 fresh red Thai chiles, stemmed
6 large garlic cloves
3 large peeled shallots, coarsely chopped
1 (1-inch) piece peeled fresh ginger, coarsely chopped
6 tablespoons sugar
2 tablespoons lower-sodium soy sauce
1½ teaspoons black pepper
¼ teaspoon kosher salt
Cooking spray

1. Score squid by making 4 (½-inch) crosswise cuts in each tube.
2. Place bell pepper and next 4 ingredients in a food processor; process until finely ground. Stir in sugar, soy sauce,

black pepper, and salt. Combine squid and ⅔ cup chile mixture in a large zip-top plastic bag; seal. Marinate in refrigerator 3 hours, turning bag occasionally. Reserve remaining ⅔ cup chile mixture for dipping sauce.
3. Preheat grill to medium heat.
4. Remove squid from bag; discard marinade. Arrange squid in a single layer on grill rack coated with cooking spray. Grill 2 minutes on each side or until charred and squid begins to curl around edges. Serve with reserved sauce. Serves 4 (serving size: 4½ ounces squid and about 2½ tablespoons sauce).

CALORIES 263; **FAT** 2.6g (sat 0.6g, mono 0.2g, poly 1g); **PROTEIN** 28.1g; **CARB** 30.9g; **FIBER** 1.1g; **CHOL** 396mg; **IRON** 1.8mg; **SODIUM** 466mg; **CALC** 75mg

CHICKENIEST–AUGUST 2011
Fantastic Bourbon Smoked Chicken

Hands-on time: 20 min. Total time: 20 hr. 35 min. Prepare to be amazed: This bird is so beautifully brown—almost as if lacquered—and so wonderfully moist and full of sweet whiskey depth that it will have you firing up the grill year-round. The best flavor, we've found, comes from chickens that have not been injected with salt brine; we like Bell & Evans air-chilled birds.

2 quarts water
9 tablespoons bourbon, divided
¼ cup packed dark brown sugar
3 tablespoons kosher salt
2 quarts ice water
1 tablespoon black peppercorns
1 tablespoon coriander seeds
3 bay leaves
3 garlic cloves, peeled
1 small onion, quartered
1 small Fuji apple, cored and quartered
1 lemon, quartered
1 (4-pound) whole chicken
2 cups applewood chips
½ teaspoon freshly ground black pepper
Cooking spray
1 tablespoon butter, melted

1. Combine 2 quarts water, ½ cup bourbon, sugar, and kosher salt in a large Dutch oven; bring to a boil, stirring until salt and sugar dissolve. Add 2 quarts ice water and next 7 ingredients; cool to room temperature. Add chicken to brine; cover and refrigerate 18 hours, turning chicken occasionally.
2. Soak wood chips in water for 1 hour; drain.
3. Remove chicken from brine; pat chicken dry with paper towels. Strain brine through a sieve; discard brine, and reserve 2 apple quarters, 2 lemon quarters, 2 onion quarters, and garlic. Discard remaining solids. Sprinkle chicken cavity with pepper; add reserved apple, lemon, onion, and garlic to chicken cavity. Lift wing tips up and over back; tuck under chicken. Tie legs.
4. Remove grill rack; set aside. Prepare grill for indirect grilling, heating one side to high heat and leaving one side with no heat. Carefully pierce the bottom of a disposable aluminum foil pan several times with the tip of a knife. Place pierced pan on heat element on heated side of grill; add 1 cup wood chips to pan. Place another disposable aluminum foil pan (do not pierce pan) on unheated side of grill. Pour 2 cups water in pan. Let chips stand 15 minutes or until smoking; reduce grill heat to medium-low. Maintain grill temperature at 275°.
5. Coat grill rack with cooking spray; place rack on grill. Place chicken, breast side up, on grill rack over foil pan on unheated side. Combine remaining 1 tablespoon bourbon and butter; baste chicken with bourbon mixture. Close grill lid; cook chicken 2 hours at 275° or until thermometer inserted into meaty part of thigh registers 165°. Add remaining 1 cup wood chips halfway through cooking time. Place chicken on a platter; cover loosely with foil. Let stand 15 minutes. Discard skin before serving. Serves 4 (serving size: about 5 ounces meat).

CALORIES 299; **FAT** 12.6g (sat 4.4g, mono 4.3g, poly 2.3g); **PROTEIN** 35.8g; **CARB** 6.2g; **FIBER** 1g; **CHOL** 114mg; **IRON** 1.8mg; **SODIUM** 560mg; **CALC** 30mg

Make Ahead

Bourbon-Caramel Truffles

Hands-on time: 30 min. Total time: 2 hr. 38 min. *Cane syrup and evaporated milk keep these truffles extra-creamy without relying on heavy cream. Our lighter recipe cuts half the fat and about two-thirds of the saturated fat from a classic truffle.*

3 tablespoons brown sugar
2 tablespoons evaporated whole milk
1 tablespoon golden cane syrup
Dash of salt
1 tablespoon bourbon
½ teaspoon vanilla extract
3.5 ounces bittersweet chocolate, finely chopped
1.75 ounces milk chocolate, finely chopped
2 tablespoons unsweetened cocoa

1. Combine first 4 ingredients in a saucepan over medium-high heat; bring to a boil. Cook 1 minute or until sugar dissolves. Remove from heat. Stir in bourbon and vanilla. Add chocolates; let stand 1 minute. Stir until smooth. Pour into a shallow dish; cover and chill 2 hours. Heat a tablespoon measuring spoon with hot water; pat dry. Scoop chocolate mixture with spoon; dip in cocoa. Roll into balls. Refrigerate until ready to serve. Serves 19 (serving size: 1 truffle).

CALORIES 60; **FAT** 2.7g (sat 1.6g, mono 0.5g, poly 0g); **PROTEIN** 0.8g; **CARB** 8g; **FIBER** 0.7g; **CHOL** 1mg; **IRON** 0.2mg; **SODIUM** 14mg; **CALC** 12mg

Make Ahead

Seriously Lemon Tart

(pictured on page 240)

Hands-on time: 25 min. Total time: 5 hr. *We mean business with this ultratart tart. It's intensely sour, drawing winks from folks after one bite (and, from those with really sweet tooths, winces). A lemon quadruple-threat—juice, rind, sections, and slices—creates this effect. If you prefer a bit less tang, omit the lemon juice. Try to get the thinnest lemon slices you can for the top of the dessert; a mandoline or very sharp serrated knife will do the trick.*

Cooking spray
½ (14.1-ounce) package refrigerated pie dough (such as Pillsbury)
1½ cups granulated sugar
1 cup lemon sections (about 4 large lemons), seeds removed
2 teaspoons grated lemon rind
2 tablespoons fresh lemon juice
2 teaspoons cornstarch
½ teaspoon salt
3 large egg whites, lightly beaten
2 large eggs, lightly beaten
12 very thin lemon slices, seeds removed
2 tablespoons brown sugar

1. Preheat oven to 450°.
2. Coat bottom of a 9-inch round removable-bottom tart pan with cooking spray. Press dough into bottom and up sides of pan. Line bottom of dough with a piece of aluminum foil; arrange pie weights or dried beans on foil. Bake at 450° for 10 minutes. Remove pie weights and foil. Bake an additional 5 minutes. Cool on a wire rack.
3. Reduce oven temperature to 350°.
4. Combine granulated sugar and next 5 ingredients in a medium non-aluminum saucepan over medium heat, stirring with a whisk. Bring to a boil; cook 30 seconds. Combine egg whites and eggs in a large bowl, stirring well with a whisk. Gradually add hot lemon mixture to egg white mixture, stirring constantly with a whisk, and pour into prepared piecrust. Arrange lemon slices on custard. Bake at 350° for 15 minutes. Sprinkle tart evenly with brown sugar. Bake an additional 10 minutes. Remove from oven.
5. Preheat broiler.
6. Broil about 1½ minutes or until lightly browned. Cool on wire rack 1 hour. Chill 3 hours or until set. Serves 8 (serving size: 1 wedge).

CALORIES 295; **FAT** 8g (sat 3.2g, mono 3.1g, poly 1g); **PROTEIN** 4.2g; **CARB** 55.5g; **FIBER** 1.1g; **CHOL** 56mg; **IRON** 0.4mg; **SODIUM** 317mg; **CALC** 20mg

Kid Friendly • Freezable
Make Ahead

Banana Split Ice-Cream Sandwiches

Hands-on time: 51 min. Total time: 3 hr. *A darling dessert that captures the lovable flavors of a classic banana split between two crisp-chewy cookies. You can make the sandwiches through step 4 and stash in the freezer for up to a month. Let them sit out at room temperature to soften a bit before adding toppings.*

Cookies:
7 tablespoons powdered sugar
6 tablespoons all-purpose flour
¼ teaspoon vanilla extract
1 large egg
Filling:
2 cups vanilla low-fat ice cream, softened
¾ cup ripe mashed banana (about 1½ medium bananas)
6 tablespoons coarsely chopped dry-roasted peanuts, divided
Remaining ingredients:
6 tablespoons frozen fat-free whipped topping, thawed
3 tablespoons chocolate syrup
6 maraschino cherries, drained

1. To prepare cookies, combine sugar and flour, stirring with a whisk. Add vanilla and egg; beat with a mixer at medium speed 2 minutes. Cover and refrigerate 2 hours.

2. Preheat oven to 350°.

3. Cover a large baking sheet or jelly-roll pan with parchment paper. Draw 6 (3-inch) circles onto parchment paper. Turn paper over; secure onto pan with masking tape. Spoon about 1 tablespoon batter into center of each drawn circle; spread batter to outside edge of each circle. Bake at 350° for 7 minutes or until edges begin to brown. Carefully remove cookies from paper, and cool completely on wire racks. Repeat procedure with remaining batter, reusing the parchment paper.

4. To prepare filling, combine softened ice cream and banana in a chilled bowl, stirring mixture well. Place ¼ cup peanuts in a shallow bowl. Place 1 cookie on each of 6 plates. Carefully spread about ⅓ cup ice cream mixture over flat side of each cookie. Top with remaining cookies, flat sides down, pressing gently to adhere. Lightly roll the sides of each sandwich in ¼ cup peanuts in bowl.

5. Top each sandwich with 1 tablespoon whipped topping, 1½ teaspoons chocolate syrup, remaining 1 teaspoon peanuts, and 1 cherry. Serve sandwiches immediately. Serves 6 (serving size: 1 sandwich).

CALORIES 267; FAT 7g (sat 1.6g, mono 3.1g, poly 1.6g); PROTEIN 6.6g; CARB 45g; FIBER 2.4g; CHOL 39mg; IRON 0.8mg; SODIUM 128mg; CALC 80mg

FUNKIEST–MAY 2004

Vegetarian

Wild Mushroom Pizza with Truffle Oil

Hands-on time: 22 min. Total time: 1 hr. 15 min. The earthy pleasures of mushrooms, fontina cheese, and truffle oil are all here, delivering a whiff of damp wood, nuts, and meat in a vegetarian dish. The homemade pizza dough, made with quick-rise yeast, takes just 30 minutes to rise and double in size, but you can also start with store-bought dough to speed things up.

1 teaspoon sugar
1 package quick-rise yeast (about 2¼ teaspoons)
½ cup warm water (100° to 110°)
6.7 ounces all-purpose flour, divided (about 1½ cups)
½ teaspoon salt, divided
Cooking spray
2 teaspoons cornmeal
2 teaspoons olive oil
2 cups thinly sliced shiitake mushroom caps (about 4 ounces)
2 cups sliced cremini mushrooms (about 4 ounces)
1½ cups (¼-inch-thick) slices portobello mushrooms (about 4 ounces)
⅔ cup (about 2½ ounces) shredded fontina cheese, divided
2 teaspoons chopped fresh thyme
½ teaspoon truffle oil
¼ cup (1 ounce) grated fresh Parmesan cheese
¼ teaspoon sea salt or flake salt

1. Dissolve sugar and yeast in warm water in a large bowl; let stand 5 minutes. Weigh or lightly spoon 5.6 ounces (about 1¼ cups) flour into dry measuring cups; level with a knife.

Add flour and ¼ teaspoon salt to yeast mixture; stir until a soft dough forms. Turn dough out onto a lightly floured surface.

2. Knead until smooth and elastic (about 10 minutes); add enough of remaining 1.1 ounces (about ¼ cup) flour, 1 tablespoon at a time, to prevent dough from sticking to hands (dough will feel tacky).

3. Place dough in a large bowl coated with cooking spray, turning to coat top. Cover surface of dough with plastic wrap lightly coated with cooking spray; let rise in a warm place (85°), free from drafts, 30 minutes or until doubled in size. (Gently press two fingers into dough. If indentation remains, dough has risen enough.) Punch dough down; cover and let stand 5 minutes. Line a baking sheet with parchment paper; sprinkle with cornmeal. Roll dough into a 12-inch circle on a floured surface. Place dough on prepared baking sheet. Crimp edges of dough with fingers to form a rim; let rise 10 minutes.

4. Preheat oven to 475°.

5. While dough rises, heat a large nonstick skillet over medium heat. Add olive oil to pan; swirl to coat. Add remaining ¼ teaspoon salt and mushrooms; cook 7 minutes or until mushrooms soften and moisture almost evaporates, stirring frequently.

6. Sprinkle ¼ cup fontina evenly over dough; arrange mushroom mixture evenly over fontina. Sprinkle with thyme; drizzle evenly with truffle oil. Sprinkle remaining fontina and Parmesan cheese evenly over top. Bake at 475° for 15 minutes or until crust is lightly browned. Slide pizza onto a cutting board; sprinkle with sea salt. Cut into 8 slices. Serve immediately. Serves 4 (serving size: 2 slices).

CALORIES 331; FAT 10.6g (sat 4.9g, mono 4.2g, poly 0.8g); PROTEIN 14.8g; CARB 42.8g; FIBER 3.1g; CHOL 25mg; IRON 3.5mg; SODIUM 693mg; CALC 180mg

Kid Friendly • Vegetarian

Creamy Four-Cheese Macaroni

Hands-on time: 29 min. Total time: 59 min. *There's something about the way plain old macaroni cooks to a soft, silky texture that enhances the creaminess of this dish. Each hollow noodle gets coated inside and out with luscious sauce. Though we rarely use processed cheese, here it's the key to a super-creamy texture that does not rely on heavy cream. We tested lots of mac and cheese recipes, and none was as velvety as this one. It has half the fat and calories of traditional versions with no loss of cheesy richness.*

1.5 ounces all-purpose flour (about ⅓ cup)
2⅔ cups 1% low-fat milk
½ cup (2 ounces) shredded fontina cheese or Swiss cheese
½ cup (2 ounces) grated fresh Parmesan cheese
½ cup (2 ounces) shredded extra-sharp cheddar cheese
3 ounces light processed cheese (such as light Velveeta)
6 cups cooked elbow macaroni (about 3 cups uncooked)
½ teaspoon salt
¼ teaspoon freshly ground black pepper
Cooking spray
⅓ cup crushed melba toasts (about 12 pieces)
1 tablespoon canola oil
1 garlic clove, minced

1. Preheat oven to 375°.
2. Weigh or lightly spoon flour into a dry measuring cup; level with a knife. Place flour in a saucepan. Gradually add milk, stirring with a whisk until blended. Cook over medium heat until thick (about 8 minutes), stirring constantly with a whisk. Remove from heat; let stand 4 minutes or until sauce cools to 155°. Add cheeses; stir until cheese melts. Stir in macaroni, salt, and pepper.

3. Spoon mixture into a 2-quart glass or ceramic baking dish coated with cooking spray. Combine crushed toasts, oil, and garlic in a small bowl; stir until well blended. Sprinkle over macaroni mixture. Bake at 375° for 30 minutes or until bubbly. Serves 8 (serving size: about 1 cup).

CALORIES 347; FAT 11.5g (sat 5.9g, mono 3.4g, poly 1.4g); PROTEIN 17.4g; CARB 43.8g; FIBER 1.9g; CHOL 29mg; IRON 1.7mg; SODIUM 607mg; CALC 346mg

Lamb Shanks Braised in Tomato

Hands-on time: 15 min. Total time: 2 hr. 30 min. *Only five ingredients—not including salt, pepper, and cooking spray—cook slow, undisturbed in a bubbling bath until the lamb reaches meltingly tender, fall-off-the-bone greatness. For more comforting joy, serve over basic creamy polenta: Bring 4 cups water to a boil in a medium saucepan. Stir in 1 cup uncooked polenta and ¾ teaspoon salt; reduce heat to medium, and simmer 5 to 10 minutes or until thick, stirring occasionally.*

Cooking spray
4 (12-ounce) lamb shanks, trimmed
½ teaspoon salt
½ teaspoon freshly ground black pepper
4 garlic cloves, minced
¾ cup dry red wine
2 (14.5-ounce) cans diced tomatoes with basil, garlic, and oregano
¼ cup chopped fresh parsley

1. Heat a large Dutch oven over medium-high heat. Coat pan with cooking spray. Sprinkle lamb with salt and pepper. Add lamb to pan; cook 4 minutes on each side or until browned. Remove from pan. Add garlic to pan; sauté 15 seconds. Add wine to pan; cook 2 minutes, scraping pan to loosen browned bits. Stir in tomatoes; cook 2 minutes. Return lamb to pan. Cover pan, reduce heat, and simmer 1 hour.

Turn lamb over; simmer 1 hour or until meat is done and very tender.
2. Place lamb on a plate; cover loosely with foil. Skim fat from surface of sauce. Bring to a boil; cook 10 minutes or until thickened. Return lamb to pan; cook 4 minutes or until lamb is thoroughly heated. Stir in parsley. Serves 4 (serving size: 1 shank and ¾ cup sauce).

CALORIES 254; FAT 11.4g (sat 4.8g, mono 4.8g, poly 0.8g); PROTEIN 25.9g; CARB 11.7g; FIBER 3.5g; CHOL 89mg; IRON 2.9mg; SODIUM 439mg; CALC 64mg

Kid Friendly

Simple, Perfect Fresh-Ground Brisket Burgers

Hands-on time: 35 min. Total time: 1 hr. 18 min. *Beefy bliss comes when you start with a flavor-packed cut like brisket and grind the meat yourself. Yes, it's absolutely worth doing this because the meat is simply more juicy. See our tips on page 309. To keep the meat from drying out, don't cook beyond medium. Show restraint with condiments and toppings, as we did, so you don't cover up that meaty flavor: This is a burger for purists.*

1 (1-pound) flat-cut beef brisket, trimmed and cut into 1-inch pieces
2 tablespoons olive oil
¼ teaspoon kosher salt
⅛ teaspoon freshly ground black pepper
Cooking spray
4 (½-ounce) slices cheddar cheese
4 (1½-ounce) hamburger buns or water rolls, toasted
8 teaspoons canola mayonnaise
4 green leaf lettuce leaves
4 (⅛-inch-thick) slices tomato

1. To prepare meat grinder, place the feed shaft, blade, and ¼-inch die plate in freezer 30 minutes or until well chilled. Assemble grinder just before grinding the meat.

2. Arrange meat pieces in a single layer on a jelly-roll pan, leaving space between each piece. Freeze meat 15 minutes or until meat is firm but not frozen. Combine meat and oil in large bowl, tossing to coat. Pass meat through meat grinder completely. Immediately pass meat through grinder a second time. Divide mixture into 4 equal portions, gently shaping each into a ½-inch-thick patty. Press a nickel-sized indentation in center of each patty. Cover and chill patties until ready to grill.

3. Preheat grill to medium-high heat.

4. Sprinkle chilled patties with salt and pepper. Place patties on a grill rack coated with cooking spray; grill 2 minutes or until grill marks appear. Carefully turn patties; grill 3 minutes. Top each patty with 1 cheese slice; grill 1 minute or until cheese melts and beef reaches desired degree of doneness. Remove patties from grill; let patties rest 5 minutes. Spread 2 teaspoons mayonnaise on bottom half of each bun. Place 1 patty on bottom half of each bun; top each sandwich with 1 lettuce leaf, 1 tomato slice, and top half of bun. Serves 4 (serving size: 1 burger).

CALORIES 407; **FAT** 23.6g (sat 5.8g, mono 11.6g, poly 3g); **PROTEIN** 25.3g; **CARB** 21g; **FIBER** 2g; **CHOL** 53mg; **IRON** 2mg; **SODIUM** 549mg; **CALC** 126mg

GRINDING YOUR OWN BEEF

It seems like work, but believe us: Fresh-ground beef yields a juicier burger. At home, a grinder attachment for your stand mixer is ideal, or an old-fashioned hand grinder. If you use a food processor, work in small batches, pulsing the meat 8 to 10 times or until the meat is finely chopped but not pureed. Keep meat and grinding equipment as cold as possible. Warm meat smears, yielding a mashed texture. Put the meat and grinding equipment in the freezer for 15 to 30 minutes beforehand for optimum results. If you don't have the gear, get your butcher to grind the beef for you—as short a time before grilling as possible.

NEW GIFTS FROM THE DESSERT GODDESS

We have a secret weapon in our Test Kitchen: Deb Wise, an experienced baker who gets the science and loves the challenge of making light sweets with sublime texture and glorious flavor. Here, Deb's wisest offerings yet.

Kid Friendly • Make Ahead

Almond-Mocha Mousse

Hands-on time: 28 min. Total time: 2 hr. 28 min.

Nutrition Note: If you substitute an equivalent amount of whipped cream for the whipped topping in this recipe, you will add 41 calories, 5.8g fat, and 3.2g sat fat to each serving.

3 tablespoons 2% reduced-fat milk
3 ounces bittersweet chocolate, finely chopped
1½ teaspoons instant espresso granules
1 tablespoon amaretto (almond-flavored liqueur)
3 large egg whites
½ cup sugar, divided
2 tablespoons water
Dash of salt
1 cup frozen reduced-calorie whipped topping, thawed
6 chocolate wafer cookies
2 tablespoons coarsely chopped almonds, toasted

1. Combine first 3 ingredients in a large microwave-safe bowl. Microwave at HIGH 45 seconds or until chocolate melts, stirring after 20 seconds; stir until smooth. Stir in liqueur.

2. Place egg whites in a bowl; beat with a mixer at medium-high speed until soft peaks form. Combine ¼ cup sugar, 2 tablespoons water, and salt in a saucepan; bring to a boil. Cook, without stirring, until candy thermometer registers 240°. Gradually pour hot sugar syrup in a thin stream over egg whites, beating at medium speed. Increase speed to high, beating until stiff peaks form.

3. Fold half of egg white mixture into chocolate mixture. Fold in remaining egg white mixture. Gently fold in whipped topping. Divide evenly among 6 bowls. Cover surface of mousse with plastic wrap; chill at least 2 hours.

4. Place wafers 2 inches apart on parchment paper, flat side down. Top each with 1 teaspoon nuts. Place remaining ¼ cup sugar in a clean, small, heavy saucepan; cook over medium heat until sugar dissolves and is golden (about 3 minutes). Do not stir. Drizzle sugar evenly over wafers. Let stand 5 minutes or until set. Remove plastic wrap from dishes; top each serving with 1 wafer. Serves 6.

CALORIES 228; **FAT** 9.8g (sat 4.9g, mono 3.1g, poly 0.8g); **PROTEIN** 4.4g; **CARB** 34.4g; **FIBER** 1.5g; **CHOL** 2mg; **IRON** 0.7mg; **SODIUM** 110mg; **CALC** 26mg

Baked Alaskas

Hands-on time: 1 hr. 2 min. Total time: 5 hr. 22 min.

Cake:
2 ounces cake flour (about 1/2 cup)
3 tablespoons dark unsweetened cocoa (such as Hershey's Special Dark)
1/4 teaspoon salt
6 large egg whites
1/4 teaspoon cream of tartar
1/2 cup sugar
1/4 teaspoon vanilla extract
Cooking spray
3 cups fat-free frozen Greek chocolate yogurt
Meringue:
6 large egg whites
9 tablespoons sugar
1/4 teaspoon cream of tartar
Dash of salt

1. Preheat oven to 350°.
2. To prepare cake, weigh or lightly spoon flour into a dry measuring cup; level with a knife. Sift together flour, cocoa, and 1/4 teaspoon salt.
3. Place 6 egg whites and 1/4 teaspoon cream of tartar in a large bowl; beat with a mixer at medium-high speed until soft peaks form. Add 1/2 cup sugar, 2 tablespoons at a time, beating until stiff peaks form (do not underbeat). Beat in vanilla. Sift flour mixture over egg white mixture, 1/4 cup at a time, folding flour mixture into egg white mixture. Spoon batter into an ungreased 10-inch tube pan, spreading evenly. Break air pockets in batter by cutting through batter with a knife. Bake at 350° for 20 minutes or until cake springs back when lightly touched. Invert pan; cool completely.

Loosen cake from sides of pan using a narrow metal spatula. Invert cake onto a plate.
4. Split cake horizontally into 3 even layers using a serrated knife. Working with 1 cake layer at a time, cut with a 3-inch round cutter into 4 rounds. Repeat procedure with remaining 2 cake layers; discard remaining cake, or reserve for another use.
5. Coat 6 (8-ounce) ramekins with cooking spray. Line each ramekin with plastic wrap, allowing the plastic wrap to extend over edges. Spoon 1/4 cup frozen yogurt into bottom of each ramekin, spreading evenly; top each with 1 cake round. Spread 1/4 cup frozen yogurt over each cake layer, spreading evenly; top each with 1 cake round. Cover with plastic wrap; freeze 4 hours or overnight.
6. To prepare meringue, combine 6 egg whites and remaining ingredients in top of a double boiler. Cook over simmering water 2 minutes or until candy thermometer registers 150°, stirring constantly with a whisk. Remove from heat. Beat egg mixture with a mixer at medium speed until soft peaks form; beat at high speed until stiff peaks form.
7. Invert ramekins, cake sides down, onto a baking sheet. Discard plastic wrap. Divide meringue evenly among servings; spread evenly over each dome (domes should be completely covered with meringue). Holding a kitchen torch about 3 inches from domes, heat meringue, moving the torch back and forth until lightly browned. Transfer to individual plates; serve immediately. Serves 6.

CALORIES 252; **FAT** 0.3g (sat 0.1g, mono 0g, poly 0.1g); **PROTEIN** 12g; **CARB** 51.2g; **FIBER** 1.3g; **CHOL** 2mg; **IRON** 1.3mg; **SODIUM** 187mg; **CALC** 154mg

Pumpkin-Hazelnut Cheesecake

(pictured on page 236)

Hands-on time: 50 min. Total time: 9 hr. 55 min. Sometimes hazelnut flour is sold as meal. If you find toasted nut flour (or meal), skip Step 2.

Nutrition Note: If you substitute an equivalent amount of whipped cream for the whipped topping to garnish, you will add 10 calories, 1.6g fat, and 1g sat fat to each serving.

Cake:
2.25 ounces hazelnut flour (about 1/2 cup)
1/2 cup sugar
2 tablespoons canola oil
2 tablespoons butter, at room temperature
2 large egg whites
1 tablespoon Frangelico (hazelnut liqueur)
1.5 ounces all-purpose flour (about 1/3 cup)
1/4 teaspoon baking powder
Dash of salt
Baking spray with flour
Cheesecake:
1 1/2 cups 1/3-less-fat cream cheese, softened
1/2 cup part-skim ricotta cheese
3/4 cup sugar
1 teaspoon vanilla extract
1/2 teaspoon ground cinnamon
1/2 teaspoon ground allspice
1/4 teaspoon salt
2 large eggs
2 large egg yolks
1 cup unsweetened pumpkin
Brittle:
2 tablespoons hazelnuts, toasted and chopped
1/3 cup sugar
1/2 cup frozen fat-free whipped topping, thawed

1. Preheat oven to 350°.
2. To prepare cake, sprinkle hazelnut flour evenly on a rimmed baking sheet.

Bake at 350° for 10 minutes or until the color of peanut butter, stirring once. Cool.

3. Combine ½ cup sugar, oil, and butter in a large bowl; beat with a mixer at medium speed until well blended. Add egg whites; beat until well blended. Add liqueur; beat 1 minute.

4. Weigh or lightly spoon all-purpose flour into a dry measuring cup; level with a knife. Combine hazelnut flour, all-purpose flour, baking powder, and dash of salt in a bowl. Add flour mixture to sugar mixture. Beat at low speed 1 minute. Spoon batter evenly into a 9-inch springform pan coated with baking spray. Bake at 350° for 15 minutes or until a wooden pick inserted in center comes out clean. Cool completely in pan on a wire rack.

5. Reduce oven temperature to 300°.

6. To prepare cheesecake, place cream cheese and ricotta cheese in a bowl. Beat with a mixer at medium-high speed until smooth (about 3 minutes). Add ¾ cup sugar and next 6 ingredients; beat at low speed until smooth. Add pumpkin; stir gently until combined. Pour cheesecake batter over top of cooled cake. Bake at 300° for 1 hour or until cheesecake center barely moves when pan is touched. Remove cheesecake from oven. Run a knife around outside edge. Cool on a wire rack. Cover and chill 8 hours or overnight.

7. To prepare brittle, cover a large baking sheet with parchment paper. Draw a 14 x 2–inch area on paper; sprinkle nuts inside marked space. Place ⅓ cup sugar in a small, heavy saucepan over medium heat; cook until sugar dissolves, stirring gently as needed to dissolve sugar (about 2 minutes). Continue cooking 1 minute or until golden (do not stir). Drizzle caramelized sugar over nuts. Let stand 10 minutes or until firm; break into 14 pieces. Slice cheesecake into 14 slices; top each serving with about 1½ teaspoons whipped topping and 1 piece brittle. Serves 14.

CALORIES 284; FAT 14.6g (sat 5.3g, mono 6.5g, poly 1.6g); PROTEIN 6.4g; CARB 31.9g; FIBER 1.3g; CHOL 77mg; IRON 1mg; SODIUM 175mg; CALC 79mg

Make Ahead

Cranberry Sherbet in Tuile Cups

Hands-on time: 31 min. Total time: 4 hr. 21 min. Work quickly as you remove tuiles from the baking sheet so they'll mold easily into a cup. Although you can make the sherbet up to a day ahead, the tuiles don't keep well—make them a few hours ahead, garnish, and then store in an airtight container.

Sherbet:
1½ cups water
⅓ cup granulated sugar
3 tablespoons light-colored corn syrup
⅛ teaspoon salt
1 (12-ounce) package fresh cranberries
1 tablespoon Chambord (raspberry-flavored liqueur)
2 teaspoons fresh lime juice
¼ cup heavy whipping cream
Tuiles:
6 tablespoons granulated sugar
6 tablespoons all-purpose flour
1 tablespoon cornstarch
1 teaspoon grated orange rind
Dash of salt
3 tablespoons 2% reduced-fat milk
¼ teaspoon vanilla extract
1 large egg white, lightly beaten
1 tablespoon canola oil
1 tablespoon butter, melted
Baking spray with flour (such as Baker's Joy)
1 ounce semisweet or white chocolate, finely chopped
2 tablespoons sparkling sugar

1. To prepare sherbet, combine first 4 ingredients in a medium saucepan. Bring to a boil; cook 1 minute or until sugar dissolves. Remove from heat. Place pan in a large ice-filled bowl for 15 minutes or until mixture chills, stirring occasionally.

2. Place sugar mixture, cranberries, liqueur, and juice in a food processor or blender; process until smooth. Press cranberry mixture through a fine sieve over a bowl; discard solids. Add cream to cranberry mixture in bowl; stir well.

3. Pour mixture into the freezer can of an ice-cream freezer; freeze according to manufacturer's instructions. Spoon sherbet into a freezer-safe container; cover and freeze at least 3 hours or until firm.

4. Preheat oven to 350°.

5. To prepare tuiles, combine 6 tablespoons sugar and next 4 ingredients in a bowl, stirring with a whisk. Add milk, vanilla, and egg white; stir until smooth. Add oil and butter, stirring until well combined.

6. Coat a baking sheet with baking spray. Using your finger, draw 3 (6-inch) circles about 5 inches apart on baking sheet. Spoon 2 tablespoons batter onto each circle, spreading to edges of circles using back of a spoon. Bake at 350° for 15 minutes or until browned. Loosen edges of tuiles with a spatula; remove from baking sheet. Working quickly, gently shape each tuile over a 4-inch-tall spice jar or small juice glass to form a shallow scalloped cup; cool completely. (Tuiles are delicate; handle carefully when shaped.) Repeat procedure with remaining batter.

7. Place chocolate in a microwave-safe bowl; microwave at HIGH 1 minute or until chocolate almost melts, stirring until smooth. Place sparkling sugar in a shallow bowl. Gently coat edges of tuiles with melted chocolate using a small brush; sprinkle chocolate with sparkling sugar. Let stand 5 minutes or until firm. Spoon ½ cup sherbet into each tuile. Serve immediately. Serves 6 (serving size: 1 filled tuile).

CALORIES 307; FAT 9.8g (sat 4.7g, mono 3.5g, poly 1g); PROTEIN 2.4g; CARB 54g; FIBER 2.9g; CHOL 20mg; IRON 0.5mg; SODIUM 116mg; CALC 34mg

Chocolate Cake with Fluffy Frosting

Hands-on time: 33 min. Total time: 1 hr. 31 min.

Cake:
¼ cup Dutch process cocoa
⅓ cup boiling water
1½ ounces bittersweet chocolate, finely chopped
6.7 ounces cake flour (about 1⅔ cups)
1½ teaspoons baking powder
½ teaspoon baking soda
¼ teaspoon salt
⅔ cup granulated sugar
⅔ cup nonfat buttermilk
⅓ cup canola oil
3 large egg whites
¼ teaspoon cream of tartar
Baking spray with flour (such as Baker's Joy)

Frosting:
¾ cup (6 ounces) cream cheese, softened
1 (8-ounce) package ⅓-less-fat cream cheese, softened
2 tablespoons cake flour
1 teaspoon vanilla extract
⅛ teaspoon salt
3 cups powdered sugar
1 cup marshmallow creme

1. Preheat oven to 350°.
2. To prepare cake, combine first 3 ingredients in a small bowl; let stand 1 minute. Stir until smooth; set aside.
3. Weigh or lightly spoon flour into dry measuring cups; level with a knife. Combine flour, baking powder, baking soda, and ¼ teaspoon salt in a bowl, stirring with a whisk. Place granulated sugar, buttermilk, and oil in a large bowl; beat with a mixer at low speed until blended. Add chocolate mixture; beat at low speed 1 minute. Add flour mixture; beat at low speed just until combined.
4. Combine egg whites and cream of tartar in a medium bowl. Using clean, dry beaters, beat egg white mixture with a mixer at high speed until stiff peaks form (do not overbeat). Gently stir one-third of egg white mixture into chocolate mixture. Fold in remaining egg white mixture. Divide batter evenly between 2 (8-inch) round metal cake pans coated with baking spray. Bake at 350° for 18 minutes or until a wooden pick inserted in center comes out with moist crumbs clinging. Cool 10 minutes in pans on a wire rack; remove cake from pans. Cool completely on wire rack.
5. To prepare frosting, place cream cheeses, 2 tablespoons flour, vanilla, and ⅛ teaspoon salt in a large bowl. Beat with a mixer at medium speed 2 minutes or until smooth. Add powdered sugar; beat 1 minute or until well combined. Gently stir in marshmallow creme just until combined.
6. Place 1 cake layer on a plate; spread with 1 cup frosting, leaving a ½-inch border around edge. Top with remaining cake layer. Spread remaining frosting over top and sides of cake. Refrigerate cake until ready to serve. Serves 16 (serving size: 1 wedge).

CALORIES 315; FAT 13.2g (sat 5g, mono 3.9g, poly 1.5g); PROTEIN 4.1g; CARB 52.3g; FIBER 0.5g; CHOL 22mg; IRON 1.3mg; SODIUM 248mg; CALC 58mg

Pecan Cake with Caramel Mousse and Brown Sugar Topping

Hands-on time: 45 min. Total time: 1 hr. 25 min.

¾ cup granulated sugar
6 tablespoons unsalted butter, softened
2 tablespoons canola oil
3 large eggs
1 teaspoon vanilla extract
7.5 ounces all-purpose flour (about 1⅔ cups)
½ cup ground toasted pecans
1 teaspoon baking powder
½ teaspoon baking soda
¼ teaspoon salt
¾ cup low-fat buttermilk
Baking spray with flour
¼ cup granulated sugar
½ cup 2% reduced-fat milk, warmed
1 teaspoon unsalted butter, melted
1 tablespoon cornstarch
1 tablespoon water
2 teaspoons bourbon
¼ teaspoon vanilla extract
Dash of salt
¾ cup frozen reduced-calorie whipped topping, thawed
½ cup packed brown sugar
3 tablespoons unsalted butter
1 tablespoon canola oil
1 tablespoon dark corn syrup
½ teaspoon fresh lemon juice
Dash of salt
¼ cup chopped pecans, toasted
¼ teaspoon vanilla extract

1. Preheat oven to 350°.
2. Place first 3 ingredients in a bowl; beat with a mixer at medium speed until light and fluffy (about 4 minutes). Add eggs, 1 at a time, beating well after each addition. Beat in 1 teaspoon vanilla. Weigh or lightly spoon flour into dry measuring cups; level with a knife.

SOFT, FINE-CRUMBED CAKE GIVES WAY WITH EACH FORKFUL, ALLOWING CREAMY FROSTING TO DRAPE EVERY BITE.

Combine flour and next 4 ingredients, stirring well with a whisk. Add flour mixture and buttermilk alternately to sugar mixture, beginning and ending with flour mixture; beat just until incorporated.

3. Divide batter evenly between 2 (8-inch) round metal cake pans coated with baking spray. Bake at 350° for 20 minutes or until a wooden pick inserted in center comes out with moist crumbs clinging. Cool in pans 10 minutes on a wire rack; remove from pans. Cool completely on wire rack.

4. Place ¼ cup granulated sugar in a medium, heavy saucepan over medium-high heat; cook until sugar dissolves, stirring gently as needed to dissolve sugar evenly (about 4 minutes). Carefully stir in milk and 1 teaspoon melted butter (mixture will bubble and caramelized sugar will harden and stick to spoon); cook 1 minute or until sugar melts. Combine cornstarch and 1 tablespoon water in a bowl. Add cornstarch mixture to pan; bring to a boil. Cook until thick and bubbly (about 1 minute), stirring constantly. Remove from heat; stir in bourbon, ¼ teaspoon vanilla, and dash of salt. Pour into a bowl; cover and chill 20 minutes. Uncover; fold in one-third of whipped topping. Gently fold in remaining whipped topping.

5. Place 1 cake layer on a plate. Spread mousse over cake, leaving a 1-inch border around outside edge. Top with remaining cake layer.

6. Place brown sugar and next 5 ingredients in a small, heavy saucepan over medium heat; bring mixture to a boil, stirring frequently. Cook until a candy thermometer registers 234° (about 3 minutes), stirring frequently. Remove from heat; stir in chopped pecans and ¼ teaspoon vanilla. Drizzle over top of cake, spreading it out over edges. Let stand until topping is set. Serves 16 (serving size: 1 wedge).

CALORIES 279; **FAT** 14.6g (sat 5.6g, mono 6g, poly 2.3g); **PROTEIN** 3.8g; **CARB** 33.7g; **FIBER** 0.9g; **CHOL** 53mg; **IRON** 1mg; **SODIUM** 156mg; **CALC** 58mg

THIS SINFULLY DELICIOUS MOUSSE IS AS RICH AND SATISFYING AS ANY CHOCOLATE DESSERT YOU'LL FIND.

Kid Friendly • Make Ahead

Baked Chocolate Mousse

Hands-on time: 15 min. Total time: 8 hr. 52 min. *Be patient as you whip the egg mixture. Because there are a couple of yolks in the mix, it takes a full 5 minutes to reach soft peak stage. Dollop with whipped topping and serve with raspberries.*

Or Use Whipped Cream: *If you substitute an equal amount of whipped cream for the whipped topping, you'll add 62 calories, 6.7g fat, and 4.2g sat fat to each serving. You will also need to bake the mousse about 5 minutes longer.*

½ cup water
⅓ cup Dutch process cocoa
1 teaspoon instant espresso granules
4 ounces bittersweet chocolate, finely chopped
1 ounce unsweetened chocolate, finely chopped
1 tablespoon brandy
½ teaspoon vanilla extract
2 large eggs
2 large egg whites
⅓ cup sugar
Dash of salt
1½ cups frozen reduced-calorie whipped topping, thawed
Baking spray with flour (such as Baker's Joy)

1. Preheat oven to 350°.

2. Bring ½ cup water to a boil in a small saucepan. Add cocoa and espresso, stirring until smooth. Remove pan from heat. Add chocolates; gently stir until mixture is smooth. Stir in brandy and vanilla. Pour chocolate mixture into a large bowl. Let stand 10 minutes; stir occasionally.

3. Combine eggs, egg whites, sugar, and salt in the top of a double boiler, stirring with a whisk. Cook over simmering water until a thermometer reaches 115° (about 2 minutes), stirring constantly with a whisk. Place egg mixture in a medium bowl; beat with a mixer at high speed until ribbony, soft peaks form (about 5 minutes).

4. Gently stir one-third of egg mixture into chocolate mixture; gently fold in remaining egg mixture. Gently fold in whipped topping. Spoon batter into an 8-inch springform pan coated with baking spray, spreading evenly. Bake at 350° for 27 minutes or until almost set (center will not be firm but will set as it chills). Cool to room temperature on a wire rack. Cover and chill at least 8 hours or overnight. Serves 10 (serving size: 1 slice).

CALORIES 151; **FAT** 9.3g (sat 5.1g, mono 2.8g, poly 0.5g); **PROTEIN** 3.5g; **CARB** 17.5g; **FIBER** 1.8g; **CHOL** 36mg; **IRON** 1.9mg; **SODIUM** 49mg; **CALC** 22mg

WE FULLY EMBRACE THE PEPPERY PUNCH OF FRESH GINGER, WHICH GIVES THIS MOIST CAKE A SURPRISING TINGLE.

Make Ahead

Fresh Ginger Cake with Candied Citrus Glaze

(pictured on page 237)

Hands-on time: 52 min. Total time: 1 hr. 30 min. If you remember 7UP pound cake, this is a gussied-up twist on that theme. And if you can find fresh yuzu—Japanese citrus—or Buddha's Hand citrus, you can slice and candy either of those instead of kumquats for the delicious glaze.

Cake:
11.25 ounces all-purpose flour (about 2 1/2 cups)
1 teaspoon baking powder
1/2 teaspoon baking soda
1/4 teaspoon salt
2/3 cup canola oil
2/3 cup golden cane syrup (such as Lyle's Golden Syrup)
1/2 cup granulated sugar
1/2 cup reduced-fat sour cream
3 large eggs
3 tablespoons grated peeled fresh ginger
2/3 cup ginger ale, at room temperature
Baking spray with flour (such as Baker's Joy)
Glaze:
1 cup kumquats, thinly sliced and seeded
1/2 cup granulated sugar
1/2 cup water
1 cup powdered sugar
Dash of salt

1. Preheat oven to 350°.
2. To prepare cake, weigh or lightly spoon flour into dry measuring cups; level with a knife. Combine flour, baking powder, baking soda, and salt, stirring with a whisk.
3. Combine oil and next 4 ingredients in a large bowl. Beat with a mixer at medium speed 2 minutes or until well combined. Stir in ginger. Add flour mixture and ginger ale alternately to sugar mixture, beginning and ending with flour mixture, beating just until combined. Scrape batter into a 12-cup Bundt pan coated with baking spray. Bake at 350° for 38 minutes or until a wooden pick inserted in center comes out clean. Cool in pan 15 minutes on a wire rack. Invert cake onto a plate.
4. To prepare glaze, place kumquats, 1/2 cup granulated sugar, and 1/2 cup water in a saucepan; bring to a boil. Simmer, uncovered, 15 minutes, stirring occasionally. Strain kumquat mixture through a sieve into a bowl, reserving sugar syrup and kumquats.
5. Combine powdered sugar, dash of salt, and 3 tablespoons reserved syrup, stirring with a whisk until smooth; reserve remaining syrup for another use. Stir in kumquats. Spoon warm glaze over warm cake. Serves 16 (serving size: 1 slice).

CALORIES 284; FAT 11.3g (sat 1.5g, mono 6.6g, poly 2.9g); PROTEIN 3.6g; CARB 46.9g; FIBER 1g; CHOL 37mg; IRON 1.2mg; SODIUM 175mg; CALC 36mg

SUPERFAST: READER FAVORITES

No recipes are more popular than our fastest weeknight successes. Here, the best of the best, according to you.

Quick & Easy

Lemony Chicken Saltimbocca

Serve this Italian favorite with sautéed broccoli rabe or haricots verts.

"This dish will be a regular in our household. Fancy enough for company, yet so simple to make!"

—emculp1

4 (4-ounce) chicken cutlets
1/8 teaspoon salt
12 fresh sage leaves
2 ounces very thinly sliced prosciutto, cut into 8 thin strips
4 teaspoons extra-virgin olive oil, divided
1/3 cup fat-free, lower-sodium chicken broth
1/4 cup fresh lemon juice
1/2 teaspoon cornstarch
4 lemon wedges (optional)

1. Sprinkle chicken cutlets evenly with salt. Place 3 sage leaves on each chicken cutlet; wrap 2 prosciutto slices around each cutlet, securing the sage leaves in place.
2. Heat a large skillet over medium heat. Add 1 tablespoon oil to pan; swirl to coat. Add wrapped chicken cutlets to pan; cook cutlets 2 minutes on each side or until cutlets are done. Remove chicken cutlets from pan to a platter, and keep warm.
3. Combine chicken broth, lemon juice, and 1/2 teaspoon cornstarch in

a small bowl; stir with a whisk until cornstarch mixture is smooth. Add cornstarch mixture and remaining 1 teaspoon extra-virgin olive oil to pan; bring to a boil, stirring constantly with a whisk. Cook mixture 1 minute or until sauce is slightly thickened, stirring constantly. Spoon sauce over chicken. Serve wtih lemon wedges, if desired. Serves 4 (serving size: 1 cutlet and 2 tablespoons sauce).

CALORIES 202; **FAT** 7.5g (sat 1.5g, mono 4.3g, poly 0.9g); **PROTEIN** 30.5g; **CARB** 2.3g; **FIBER** 0.2g; **CHOL** 77mg; **IRON** 1.1mg; **SODIUM** 560mg; **CALC** 18mg

Quick & Easy

Chicken and Mushrooms in Garlic White Wine Sauce

If you can't find exotic mushrooms, sliced button or cremini mushrooms are a good substitute.

"The tarragon in this recipe absolutely makes it. Don't substitute!"

—*redsox19762*

4 ounces uncooked wide egg noodles
1 pound skinless, boneless chicken breast halves
2 tablespoons all-purpose flour, divided
1/2 teaspoon salt, divided
1/4 teaspoon freshly ground black pepper, divided
2 tablespoons olive oil, divided
1 tablespoon minced fresh garlic
1 (8-ounce) package presliced exotic mushroom blend (such as shiitake, cremini, and oyster)
1/2 cup dry white wine
1/2 cup fat-free, lower-sodium chicken broth
1 teaspoon chopped fresh tarragon
1 ounce fresh Parmesan cheese, shaved (about 1/4 cup)

1. Cook noodles according to package directions, omitting salt and fat. Drain and keep warm.
2. Cut chicken into 1-inch pieces. Place chicken pieces in a shallow dish. Combine 1 tablespoon flour, 1/4 teaspoon salt, and 1/8 teaspoon pepper in a small bowl. Sprinkle flour mixture over chicken; toss to coat.
3. Heat a large nonstick skillet over medium-high heat. Add 1 tablespoon oil to pan; swirl to coat. Add chicken; cook 4 minutes, turning to brown on all sides. Remove chicken from pan. Add remaining 1 tablespoon oil to pan. Add garlic and mushrooms; cook 3 minutes or until liquid evaporates. Add wine; cook 1 minute. Add remaining 1 tablespoon flour; cook 1 minute, stirring constantly. Add broth, remaining 1/4 teaspoon salt, and remaining 1/8 teaspoon pepper; cook 1 minute or until slightly thick, stirring frequently.
4. Return chicken to pan; cover and simmer 2 minutes. Uncover; cook 1 minute or until chicken is done. Stir in noodles and tarragon; cook 1 minute or until thoroughly heated. Place about 1½ cups chicken mixture on each of 4 plates; top each serving with 1 tablespoon Parmesan cheese. Serves 4.

CALORIES 350; **FAT** 11.1g (sat 2.6g, mono 6.2g, poly 1.4g); **PROTEIN** 34.3g; **CARB** 26.5g; **FIBER** 1.2g; **CHOL** 99mg; **IRON** 2.5mg; **SODIUM** 502mg; **CALC** 91mg

Kid Friendly • Quick & Easy

Lemon Pepper Shrimp Scampi

If you choose to peel your own shrimp, save the shells to flavor a homemade seafood stock.

"Great recipe with amazing results every time! The lemon brightens the flavor in a huge way."

—*cwpinatl1*

1 cup uncooked orzo
2 tablespoons chopped fresh parsley
1/2 teaspoon salt, divided
7 teaspoons unsalted butter, divided
1½ pounds peeled and deveined jumbo shrimp
2 teaspoons minced fresh garlic
2 tablespoons fresh lemon juice
1/4 teaspoon freshly ground black pepper

1. Cook orzo according to package directions, omitting salt and fat. Drain. Place orzo in a medium bowl. Stir in parsley and 1/4 teaspoon salt; cover and keep warm.
2. While orzo cooks, melt 1 tablespoon butter in a large nonstick skillet over medium-high heat. Sprinkle shrimp with remaining 1/4 teaspoon salt. Add half of shrimp to pan; sauté 2 minutes or until shrimp are almost done. Transfer shrimp to a plate. Melt 1 teaspoon butter in pan. Add remaining shrimp to pan; sauté 2 minutes or until almost done. Transfer shrimp to plate.
3. Melt remaining 1 tablespoon butter in pan. Add garlic to pan; cook 30 seconds, stirring constantly. Add shrimp, juice, and pepper to pan; cook 1 minute or until shrimp are done. Serves 4 (serving size: ½ cup orzo mixture and about 7 shrimp).

CALORIES 403; **FAT** 10.4g (sat 4.8g, mono 2.2g, poly 1.4g); **PROTEIN** 40.1g; **CARB** 34.7g; **FIBER** 1.7g; **CHOL** 276mg; **IRON** 4.3mg; **SODIUM** 549mg; **CALC** 97mg

Mongolian Beef

"Just like takeout, but healthier (and much less expensive)!"

—CaraCook

2 tablespoons lower-sodium soy sauce
1 teaspoon sugar
1 teaspoon cornstarch
2 teaspoons dry sherry
2 teaspoons hoisin sauce
1 teaspoon rice vinegar
1 teaspoon sambal oelek (ground fresh chile paste)
1/4 teaspoon salt
2 teaspoons peanut oil
1 tablespoon minced peeled fresh ginger
1 tablespoon minced fresh garlic
1 pound sirloin steak, thinly sliced across the grain
16 medium green onions, cut into 2-inch pieces

1. Combine first 8 ingredients; stir with a whisk until smooth.
2. Heat a large nonstick skillet over medium-high heat. Add peanut oil to pan; swirl to coat. Add ginger, garlic, and beef; sauté 2 minutes or until beef is browned. Add onions; sauté 30 seconds. Add soy sauce mixture; cook 1 minute or until thickened, stirring constantly. Serves 4 (serving size: 1 cup).

CALORIES 237; FAT 10.5g (sat 3.5g, mono 4.3g, poly 1.1g); PROTEIN 26g; CARB 9.1g; FIBER 1.7g; CHOL 60mg; IRON 2.7mg; SODIUM 517mg; CALC 67mg

Spiced Pork Tenderloin with Sautéed Apples

The sautéed apples are a great side dish on their own. This spice mixture would also make a wonderful rub for lamb.

3/8 teaspoon salt
1/4 teaspoon ground coriander
1/4 teaspoon freshly ground black pepper
1/8 teaspoon ground cinnamon
1/8 teaspoon ground nutmeg
1 pound pork tenderloin, trimmed and cut crosswise into 12 pieces
Cooking spray
2 tablespoons butter
2 cups thinly sliced unpeeled Braeburn or Gala apple
1/3 cup thinly sliced shallots
1/8 teaspoon salt
1/4 cup apple cider
1 teaspoon fresh thyme leaves

1. Heat a large cast-iron skillet over medium-high heat. Combine 3/8 teaspoon salt, coriander, pepper, cinnamon, and nutmeg in a small bowl; sprinkle spice mixture evenly over pork, gently patting surface to coat. Coat skillet with cooking spray. Add pork to pan; cook 3 minutes on each side or until desired degree of doneness. Remove pork from pan; keep warm.
2. Melt butter in skillet, swirling to coat pan. Add apple slices, sliced shallots, and 1/8 teaspoon salt. Cook 4 minutes or until apple starts to brown, stirring occasionally. Add apple cider to pan; cook 2 minutes or until apple slices are crisp-tender. Stir in thyme leaves. Serve apple mixture with pork. Serves 4 (serving size: 3 pork medallions and about 1/2 cup apple mixture).

CALORIES 234; FAT 9.7g (sat 5g, mono 3.2g, poly 0.7g); PROTEIN 24.4g; CARB 12.3g; FIBER 1.5g; CHOL 89mg; IRON 1.7mg; SODIUM 394mg; CALC 18mg

Loaded Potato Soup

Serve this kid-friendly soup with a mixed greens salad for a light dinner.

4 (6-ounce) red potatoes
2 teaspoons olive oil
1/2 cup prechopped onion
1 1/4 cups fat-free, lower-sodium chicken broth
3 tablespoons all-purpose flour
2 cups 1% low-fat milk, divided
1/4 cup reduced-fat sour cream
1/2 teaspoon salt
1/4 teaspoon freshly ground black pepper
3 bacon slices, halved
1.5 ounces cheddar cheese, shredded (about 1/3 cup)
4 teaspoons thinly sliced green onions

1. Pierce potatoes with a fork. Microwave at HIGH 13 minutes or until potatoes are tender. Cut potatoes in half; cool slightly.
2. While potatoes cook, heat a large saucepan over medium-high heat. Add olive oil to pan; swirl to coat. Add onion to pan; sauté 3 minutes, stirring frequently. Add broth to pan. Combine flour and 1/2 cup milk in a small bowl, stirring until smooth; add flour mixture to pan with remaining 1 1/2 cups milk. Bring soup to a boil, stirring frequently. Cook 1 minute. Remove soup from heat; stir in sour cream, salt, and pepper.
3. Arrange bacon on a paper towel on a microwave-safe plate. Cover with another paper towel; microwave at HIGH 4 minutes. Crumble bacon.
4. Discard potato skins. Coarsely mash potatoes into soup. Top with shredded cheddar cheese, green onions, and crumbled bacon. Serves 4 (serving size: about 1 1/4 cups).

CALORIES 325; FAT 11.1g (sat 5.2g, mono 4.5g, poly 0.8g); PROTEIN 13.2g; CARB 43.8g; FIBER 3g; CHOL 27mg; IRON 1.3mg; SODIUM 670mg; CALC 261mg

Chicken & Summer Vegetable Tostadas

Be sure to use fat-free tortillas for the crispest results.

2 teaspoons canola oil
1 teaspoon ground cumin
¼ teaspoon kosher salt
¼ teaspoon black pepper
12 ounces chicken breast tenders
1 cup chopped red onion (about 1)
1 cup fresh corn kernels (about 2 ears)
1 cup chopped zucchini
½ cup salsa verde
3 tablespoons chopped fresh cilantro, divided
4 (8-inch) fat-free flour tortillas
Cooking spray
3 ounces Monterey Jack cheese, shredded (about ¾ cup)

1. Preheat broiler.
2. Heat a large nonstick skillet over medium-high heat. Add oil to pan; swirl to coat. Combine cumin, salt, and pepper in a bowl. Sprinkle spice mixture evenly over chicken. Add chicken to pan; sauté 3 minutes. Add onion, corn, and zucchini to pan; sauté 2 minutes or until chicken is done. Stir in salsa and 2 tablespoons cilantro. Cook 2 minutes or until liquid almost evaporates, stirring frequently.
3. Working with 2 tortillas at a time, arrange tortillas on a baking sheet; lightly coat with cooking spray. Broil 3 minutes or until lightly browned, turning after 1½ minutes. Spoon about ¾ cup chicken mixture on each tortilla; sprinkle each serving with about 3 tablespoons cheese. Broil 2 minutes or until cheese melts. Repeat procedure with remaining tortillas, chicken mixture, and cheese. Sprinkle each serving with about ¾ teaspoon cilantro. Serves 4 (serving size: 1 tostada).

CALORIES 371; **FAT** 11g (sat 4.6g, mono 3.7g, poly 1.3g); **PROTEIN** 30.8g; **CARB** 36.4g; **FIBER** 3.9g; **CHOL** 68mg; **IRON** 1.3mg; **SODIUM** 740mg; **CALC** 182mg

MISSISSIPPI CHINESE LADY GOES HOME TO KOREA

She loves kimchi as much as chowchow, but our Southern-born and -raised food editor, Ann Taylor Pittman, had never been to the birth country of her mother.

It's a spring day in Korea, and I am here with my brother, Tim, enjoying time with some wonderful people I've just met. They are my family. By being here, by being connected to these lovely people, 7,000 miles from home, by the mere fact of it, Tim and I are finally Korean. Gratitude for this feeling takes me back to the moment, six months earlier, that led to my decision to come here. I was sitting in an elementary school cafeteria in Birmingham, Alabama, with my 6-year-old twin boys. An older child looked at us on his way to put up his tray. He grinned and said, "Hey, Chinese lady!" It was a stab to the heart, not much different from words I sometimes heard as a 7-year-old girl growing up in the Mississippi Delta, sitting in my own elementary school cafeteria, listening to friends who puzzled over my otherness. They knew white and they knew black, but they certainly did not know what I was. Nor, exactly, did I.

I am the daughter of a beautiful woman from Busan, South Korea, and a blonde-haired, blue-eyed farmer's son from Mississippi. They met on a blind date in 1967 while my dad was stationed in Korea with the Army. That, anyway, was half of the story. Turns out that the date, arranged by a friend of my father's, was more serendipitous than blind. My mom, as it happened, was my father's barber, so they had met before. Now they really talked for the first time. "I knew within the first minute of talking to her that I was going to marry her," says my dad, and they did. Then they moved to the States, where they would raise my brother and me in small towns in which there simply weren't many others like my mom.

Southern to the bone, I don't look it. I look Korean or, as I sometimes still overhear in the South, "some kind of Chinese." But I speak no Korean and, before going on my pilgrimage, knew embarrassingly little of the culture. To me, Korean heritage was mostly about food: the traditional dishes my mom would cook every now and then, after driving up to Memphis for ingredients at the closest Asian market. We loved some of the dishes she made—especially sweet-salty marinated meat and any kind of noodle dish. But she also made funky soups, always in this little gold-colored pot. The rest of us wouldn't join her, wary of the burly flavors.

Food, of course, is used everywhere to signify the bonds between people, but these people, this food, this place: It all had huge significance to me. Bulgogi, dumplings, raw fish, and milky-sweet confusing rice beer felt as much a part of my DNA as field peas and boiled peanuts did back home.

Shrimp Mandu (Shrimp Dumplings)

Hands-on time: 49 min. Total time: 57 min. *At a fantastic dumpling stand in the Insadong area of Seoul, I had dumplings like these. The little shrimp tails poking out of the dumplings are an adorable cue to the filling within.*

30 medium shrimp, unpeeled
½ cup chopped shiitake mushroom caps
½ cup chopped green onions
2 garlic cloves, chopped
3 ounces trimmed boneless pork loin chop, chopped
3 ounces water-packed soft tofu, drained
2 teaspoons dark sesame oil
¼ teaspoon freshly ground black pepper
⅛ teaspoon salt
30 gyoza skins
6 large napa cabbage leaves
5 tablespoons Korean Dipping Sauce (recipe on page 319)

1. Peel shrimp, leaving tails intact. Butterfly shrimp by cutting each along its back, cutting to, but not through, inside curve of shrimp. Remove and discard vein. Place butterflied shrimp on a paper towel–lined plate; refrigerate until ready to use.
2. Place mushrooms, onions, and garlic in a mini food processor; pulse until minced. Place mushroom mixture in a medium bowl. Place pork in processor; pulse until ground. Add pork to mushroom mixture. Add tofu, oil, pepper, and salt to mushroom mixture; toss well to combine.
3. Working with 1 gyoza skin at a time (cover remaining skins to prevent drying), moisten outside edge of gyoza with water. Place 1 shrimp on skin, cut side down, so tail slightly points up; allow tail to hang over outside edge of skin. Spoon about 1 teaspoon filling over shrimp. Fold gyoza skin over shrimp so edges meet on top; press edges to seal. Moisten one side of seam with water; pleat seam 5 or 6 times. Place dumpling, seam side up, on a baking sheet lined with damp paper towels; cover with damp paper towels to prevent drying. Repeat procedure with remaining gyoza skins, shrimp, and filling.
4. Line 2 trays of a bamboo steamer with cabbage leaves; top with steamer lid. Add water to a large skillet to a depth of 1 inch; bring to a boil. Place steamer in pan; steam cabbage 4 minutes or until cabbage wilts. Arrange dumplings in trays on top of cabbage; steam 8 minutes or until done. Serve with Korean Dipping Sauce. Serves 5 (serving size: 6 dumplings and 1 tablespoon sauce).

CALORIES 212; FAT 5.3g (sat 0.9g, mono 2g, poly 1.5g); PROTEIN 16.6g; CARB 22.3g; FIBER 1.4g; CHOL 72mg; IRON 2.7mg; SODIUM 544mg; CALC 70mg

AUTHENTIC KOREAN FLAVOR IS MADE EASY FOR DINNER AT HOME.

Boribap (Rice and Barley with Vegetables)

Hands-on time: 32 min. Total time: 47 min. *Korean doenjang (fermented soybean paste) adds the most authentic flavor, but it can be hard to find; white or yellow miso works well in its place. There is a definite method to cooking Asian short-grain rice that mothers teach to their daughters. It involves rinsing several times and cooking in less water than traditional ratios.*

½ cup uncooked whole-grain barley
⅔ cup short-grain white rice
5 teaspoons dark sesame oil, divided
1 medium carrot, peeled and julienned
1 small zucchini, julienne-cut
⅔ cup sliced shiitake mushroom caps
⅔ cup fresh bean sprouts
½ (5-ounce) package fresh baby spinach
1½ tablespoons shiro miso
1½ tablespoons gochujang (Korean chile sauce, such as Annie Chun's)
1 cup microgreens
1 tablespoon roasted ground sesame seeds

1. Cook barley in a large pot of boiling water for 35 minutes or until tender-chewy. Drain.
2. While barley cooks, place rice in a small saucepan; cover with water to 2 inches above rice. Swirl rice with hand in pan to agitate; drain. Repeat procedure 2 more times. Add ⅔ cup water to drained rice in pan. Bring to a boil over medium-high heat. Cover, reduce heat, and simmer 15 minutes. Remove from heat; let stand 10 minutes. Combine rice and barley in a large bowl.
3. Heat a medium nonstick skillet over medium-high heat. Add 1 teaspoon oil to pan; swirl to coat. Add carrot; sauté 2 minutes or until crisp-tender. Remove from pan. Add 1 teaspoon oil and zucchini to pan; sauté 1 minute or until crisp-tender. Remove from pan. Add 1 teaspoon oil and mushrooms to pan; sauté 2 minutes or until tender. Remove from pan. Add 1 teaspoon oil and bean sprouts to pan; sauté 1 minute or until bean sprouts wilt. Remove from pan. Add remaining 1 teaspoon oil and spinach to pan; sauté 1 minute or until spinach wilts. Arrange vegetables in separate piles over rice mixture. Dollop with miso and gochujang; top with microgreens. Sprinkle with sesame seeds. Mix together at the table. Serves 6 (serving size: 1 cup).

CALORIES 212; FAT 5.5g (sat 0.8g, mono 2.1g, poly 2.4g); PROTEIN 5.4g; CARB 36.4g; FIBER 4.9g; CHOL 0mg; IRON 2.4mg; SODIUM 305mg; CALC 39mg

Bulgogi Jungol (Korean Bulgogi Soup)

Hands-on time: 35 min. Total time: 1 hr. 35 min. *This is my version of the lunch I enjoyed with my relatives. It is a specialty of the Hapcheon area—a soup take on the popular Korean dish bulgogi (grilled marinated beef). In Hapcheon, the soup was cooked on the table, and we monitored the cooking. At home, you'll need to watch closely so the broth doesn't boil; you want it at a bare simmer, or else the meat will get tough and the broth cloudy.*

1 pound trimmed boneless rib-eye steak (1.25 pounds untrimmed)
¼ cup lower-sodium soy sauce
2 tablespoons sugar
2 tablespoons soju, sake, or sherry
1 tablespoon dark sesame oil
1 teaspoon freshly ground black pepper
8 garlic cloves, minced
4 ounces sweet potato noodles or cellophane noodles
7 ounces enoki mushrooms
2 medium carrots
6 cups no-salt-added beef stock (such as Swanson)
2 ounces shiitake mushrooms, stemmed and sliced
8 ounces water-packed extra-firm tofu, drained and cubed
1 red jalapeño pepper, sliced
1 bunch green onions, trimmed and cut into 2-inch pieces
³⁄₈ teaspoon salt

1. Place beef in freezer 20 minutes. Remove from freezer; cut across the grain into very thin slices. Place beef in a medium bowl. Add soy sauce and next 5 ingredients; toss well to combine. Marinate in refrigerator 1 hour.
2. Soak noodles in cold water 30 minutes; drain (noodles will not be tender). Cut noodles with kitchen scissors 2 or 3 times.
3. Trim roots from enoki mushrooms; separate mushrooms into several large clumps. Cut carrots crosswise into thirds; cut each piece lengthwise into ⅛-inch-thick slices.
4. Heat a Dutch oven over high heat. Add beef mixture to pan; stir-fry 2 minutes. Arrange noodles over beef mixture; add stock. Reduce heat to medium-high. Top noodles with enoki, carrots, shiitake, tofu, jalapeño, and onions. Bring mixture just to a simmer; simmer gently 5 minutes or until noodles are tender. Stir in salt. Serves 6 (serving size: about 1⅔ cups).

CALORIES 332; FAT 11g (sat 3.3g, mono 4.2g, poly 2.6g); PROTEIN 24.1g; CARB 32.6g; FIBER 3g; CHOL 45mg; IRON 3.4mg; SODIUM 597mg; CALC 76mg

---

Quick & Easy • Make Ahead Vegetarian

Korean Dipping Sauce

Hands-on time: 3 min. Total time: 3 min. *Look for roasted ground sesame seeds at Korean markets. They're not ground to a powder but crushed a bit. You can make your own by toasting sesame seeds until deeply golden, allowing them to cool, and crushing with a mortar and pestle. Serve this sauce with Scallion Pancakes and Shrimp Mandu.*

¼ cup lower-sodium soy sauce
3 tablespoons water
1 tablespoon rice vinegar
1½ teaspoons sugar
1½ teaspoons roasted ground sesame seeds
2 tablespoons thinly sliced green onions
1 red jalapeño pepper, sliced

1. Combine first 5 ingredients in a bowl, stirring until sugar dissolves. Add onions and jalapeño. Serves 8 (serving size: about 1 tablespoon).

CALORIES 12; FAT 0.3g (sat 0g, mono 0.1g, poly 0.1g); PROTEIN 0.6g; CARB 1.7g; FIBER 0.2g; CHOL 0mg; IRON 0.1mg; SODIUM 196mg; CALC 3mg

---

Quick & Easy • Vegetarian

Scallion Pancakes

Hands-on time: 3 min. Total time: 12 min. *These simple savory pancakes were a part of several meals I enjoyed—one of many banchan (side dishes) scattered about the table. The secrets to crisp pancakes are ice-cold water, a hot pan, and enough oil. Look for small green onions; they work best.*

6 green onions, trimmed and halved to form 5-inch pieces
3 ounces all-purpose flour (about ⅔ cup)
1 teaspoon sugar
¼ teaspoon salt
½ cup ice water
2 tablespoons canola oil, divided
2 tablespoons Korean Dipping Sauce (recipe at left)

1. Cut white portion of each green onion in half lengthwise; combine with green portions. Divide onion pieces into 4 even piles. Set aside.
2. Weigh or lightly spoon flour into a dry measuring cup; level with a knife. Combine flour, sugar, and salt in a medium bowl. Add ice water, stirring with a whisk until almost smooth.
3. Heat a large nonstick skillet over medium-high heat. Add 1 tablespoon oil to pan; swirl to coat. Arrange 2 onion piles, about 4 inches apart, in pan, keeping onion pieces parallel. Spoon a scant ¼ cup batter over each onion pile, spreading gently into a circle that covers onions. Cook 3 minutes on each side or until crisp and golden. Repeat procedure with remaining oil, onion pieces, and batter. Serve immediately with Korean Dipping Sauce. Serves 4 (serving size: 1 pancake and 1½ teaspoons sauce).

CALORIES 155; FAT 7.4g (sat 0.6g, mono 4.5g, poly 2.1g); PROTEIN 2.9g; CARB 19.4g; FIBER 1.2g; CHOL 0mg; IRON 1.4mg; SODIUM 249mg; CALC 21mg

Simple Sesame Salad

Hands-on time: 5 min. Total time: 7 min.
I was served this side salad at a few restaurants and loved its nutty flavor and utter simplicity. The key is roasted ground sesame seeds (see note about these in the Korean Dipping Sauce recipe on page 319).

1¹/₂ tablespoons roasted ground sesame seeds
1 tablespoon coarsely ground Korean chile (gochugaru)
1¹/₂ tablespoons dark sesame oil
1¹/₂ tablespoons rice vinegar
1¹/₂ teaspoons lower-sodium soy sauce
¹/₄ teaspoon kosher salt
6 cups torn romaine lettuce
¹/₃ cup slivered red onion

1. Combine first 6 ingredients in a large bowl, stirring with a whisk. Add lettuce and onion; toss to coat. Serve immediately. Serves 4 (serving size: about 1⅓ cups).

CALORIES 83; **FAT** 7.1g (sat 1g, mono 2.8g, poly 3.1g); **PROTEIN** 1.8g; **CARB** 4.9g; **FIBER** 2.5g; **CHOL** 0mg; **IRON** 1.1mg; **SODIUM** 177mg; **CALC** 32mg

---

Tongin Market Tteokbokki (Spicy Rice Cakes)

Hands-on time: 7 min. Total time: 22 min. *In Korea, tteokbokki (tech-boke-ee) comes in many guises. The ubiquitous street-food version consists of rice cakes floating in a sweet-spicy sauce made with corn syrup and gochujang (Korean chile paste). This take, served in only one particular market in Seoul, was the simplest and most delicious I had—crisp on the outside and chewy within. You'll find rice cakes for tteokbokki at Korean markets; they're about the size of a thumb. There really is no substitute for gochugaru (Korean ground chile). It's earthier and far less spicy than many other ground chiles.*

14 ounces rice cakes for tteokbokki (about 2¹/₂ cups)
2 tablespoons coarsely ground Korean chile (gochugaru)
1 tablespoon lower-sodium soy sauce
1 teaspoon sugar
2 teaspoons dark sesame oil
1 tablespoon canola oil

1. Bring a large saucepan of water to a boil. Add rice cakes; boil 2 minutes or just until rice cakes float. Drain and rinse well with cold water. Drain.
2. Place rice cakes in a medium bowl. Add chile, soy sauce, sugar, and sesame oil; let stand at room temperature 15 minutes, tossing occasionally.
3. Heat a large nonstick skillet over medium-high heat. Add canola oil to pan; swirl to coat. Add rice cake mixture; sauté 5 minutes or until rice cakes are crisp and evenly blistered, stirring frequently. Serves 4 (serving size: about ¾ cup).

CALORIES 264; **FAT** 7.2g (sat 0.7g, mono 3.7g, poly 2.5g); **PROTEIN** 3.3g; **CARB** 499g; **FIBER** 1.7g; **CHOL** 0mg; **IRON** 1.2mg; **SODIUM** 254mg; **CALC** 5mg

---

Kimchi Jjigae (Kimchi-Pork Soup)

Hands-on time: 9 min. Total time: 44 min. *At many restaurants, this soup comes to the table boiling hot—literally bubbling in a stone pot for a few minutes. The broth is tangy and slightly spicy, flavored by the kimchi. Good, strong, very fermented kimchi makes for the best soup; if your kimchi seems mild, let it sit out of the fridge for a day to gain a little more fermenty funk.*

1 pound bone-in center-cut pork loin chop
2 tablespoons coarsely ground Korean chile (gochugaru)
1 tablespoon minced fresh garlic
1 tablespoon dark sesame oil
1¹/₂ cups chopped kimchi (with juice)
3 cups water
1 (14-ounce) package water-packed extra-firm tofu, drained
¹/₂ cup diagonally sliced green onions

1. Cut bone from pork; reserve bone. Cut meat across the grain into very thin slices. Place pork in a medium bowl. Add chile, garlic, and oil; toss well to coat. Let stand at room temperature 10 minutes.
2. Heat a large saucepan over medium-high heat. Add pork mixture; sauté 3 minutes or until pork is lightly browned, stirring frequently. Remove pork from pan. Add reserved bone and kimchi to pan; cook 2 minutes, stirring frequently. Add 3 cups water; bring to a boil. Reduce heat, and simmer, uncovered, 20 minutes.
3. Cut tofu into ½-inch-thick slices; cut slices crosswise into ¾-inch pieces.
4. Remove bone from soup. Return pork mixture to soup. Add tofu to soup; simmer 5 minutes. Sprinkle with green onions. Serves 4 (serving size: about 1¼ cups soup and 2 tablespoons green onions).

CALORIES 302; **FAT** 16.7g (sat 3.8g, mono 5.6g, poly 5.8g); **PROTEIN** 27.6g; **CARB** 8.7g; **FIBER** 3.1g; **CHOL** 59mg; **IRON** 2.9mg; **SODIUM** 559mg; **CALC** 222mg

THREE STUNNING STARTERS

By Rozanne Gold

Colorful combos add zing to the Thanksgiving table.

Pumpkins, corn, and other native foods typically show up on Turkey Day, but I like to give my Thanksgiving meal a tasty twist by blending traditions. Italy's prized cheeses, Belgium's bitter lettuces, Chinese five-spice powder, and flaky Greek phyllo make for delicious and sophisticated holiday starters that still marry beautifully with the more traditional dishes that are likely to fill the table. And because Thanksgiving is the official kickoff of the busy holiday season, radically simple ideas are most welcome. That's why all these dishes can be made ahead or whipped up quickly.

Phyllo cups filled with ricotta, chèvre, and thyme are the perfect crispy-creamy predinner nibble to offer guests along with a flute of fizzy Champagne as they settle in.

When it's time to sit down to dinner, start with either soup or salad. The brilliant orange soup blends pumpkin, sweet potato, and red bell peppers until silky and finishes with a pat of butter for creamy flavor. Add texture by garnishing with toasted nuts, if you like. And the colorful salad, tinged with smoke and sweetness, is sure to be a favorite all winter long.

Make Ahead • Vegetarian

Creamy Pumpkin-Red Pepper Soup

Hands-on time: 30 min. Total time: 1 hr. *The soup can be topped with a variety of things: I love Parmigiano-Reggiano and rosemary, but savory sprinkles like chopped smoked almonds or toasted pecans would be lovely. This tastes even better the next day ... or the day after.*

3 cups chopped peeled fresh pumpkin
2½ cups chopped red bell pepper
1½ cups chopped peeled sweet potato
¼ cup chopped green onions
1 teaspoon five-spice powder
1 teaspoon ground cumin
2 teaspoons olive oil
1 teaspoon minced fresh garlic
³⁄₈ teaspoon salt, divided
5 cups no-salt-added chicken stock (such as Swanson)
1 tablespoon unsalted butter
1 tablespoon rosemary leaves (optional)

1. Preheat oven to 400°.
2. Combine first 8 ingredients in a large bowl. Sprinkle with ⅛ teaspoon salt; toss well. Place vegetable mixture in a single layer on a jelly-roll pan. Bake at 400° for 30 minutes or until tender, stirring once.
3. Combine vegetables, stock, and remaining ¼ teaspoon salt in a large saucepan; bring to a boil. Reduce heat; simmer 5 minutes. Place half of vegetable mixture in a blender. Remove center piece of blender lid (to allow steam to escape); secure blender lid on blender. Place a clean towel over opening in blender lid (to avoid splatters). Process until smooth. Pour into a large bowl. Repeat procedure with remaining vegetable mixture. Stir in butter. Top with rosemary, if desired. Serves 6 (serving size: 1 cup).

CALORIES 120; **FAT** 3.8g (sat 1.5g, mono 1.6g, poly 0.3g);
PROTEIN 6.2g; **CARB** 16.2g; **FIBER** 2.9g; **CHOL** 5mg;
IRON 1.7mg; **SODIUM** 279mg; **CALC** 56mg

Quick & Easy

Endive and Watercress Salad with Bacon-Cider Dressing

(pictured on page 238)

Hands-on time: 24 min. Total time: 24 min. *Smoky bacon, tangy Dijon, and maple syrup cut the bitter and pepper notes of the lettuces. Quality ingredients make all the difference in this simple salad, so splurge on extra-virgin olive oil, real maple syrup, and real-wood-smoked bacon.*

4 center-cut bacon slices
3 tablespoons extra-virgin olive oil
2½ tablespoons cider vinegar
2 tablespoons maple syrup
1 teaspoon Dijon mustard
¼ teaspoon kosher salt
¼ teaspoon freshly ground black pepper
1 garlic clove, minced
4 cups (½-inch) diagonally cut Belgian endive
3 cups chopped radicchio
1 cup trimmed watercress

1. Heat a medium nonstick skillet over medium heat. Add bacon to pan; cook until crisp. Remove bacon from pan, reserving 2 teaspoons drippings in pan; coarsely chop bacon. Combine 2 teaspoons drippings, oil, and next 6 ingredients in a large bowl, stirring with a whisk. Add remaining ingredients; toss well. Sprinkle with chopped bacon. Serves 6 (serving size: about 1¼ cups).

CALORIES 108; **FAT** 8.2g (sat 1.6g, mono 4.9g, poly 0.8g);
PROTEIN 2.1g; **CARB** 7.5g; **FIBER** 1.9g; **CHOL** 5mg;
IRON 0.3mg; **SODIUM** 195mg; **CALC** 25mg

Make Ahead • Vegetarian

Phyllo Cups with Ricotta, Chèvre, and Thyme

Hands-on time: 40 min. Total time: 1 hr. 48 min. *Start making the phyllo stacks about 30 minutes after you put the cheese mixture in the refrigerator. Or make the cheese mixture a day ahead, and assemble before guests arrive.*

1 cup fat-free ricotta cheese
   (such as Calabro)
⅓ cup finely chopped green onions
1 tablespoon finely chopped fresh
   thyme
3 ounces chèvre, crumbled (about ¾
   cup)
1 ounce fresh Parmigiano-Reggiano
   cheese, grated (about ¼ cup)
2 tablespoons canola oil
1 tablespoon unsalted butter, melted
8 (14 x 9–inch) sheets frozen phyllo
   dough, thawed
Cooking spray

1. Combine first 5 ingredients, stirring until smooth. Cover and chill 1 hour.
2. Preheat oven to 375°.
3. Combine oil and butter. Place 1 phyllo sheet on a work surface (cover remaining phyllo to prevent drying); lightly brush phyllo with oil mixture. Repeat layers 3 times, ending with oil mixture; press gently on stack. Repeat procedure with remaining 4 phyllo sheets and oil mixture to form two phyllo stacks. Cut each phyllo stack crosswise into 4 (3½ x 9–inch) strips. Cut strips into thirds to form 24 (3½ x 3–inch) rectangles. Press 1 rectangle into each of 24 mini muffin cups coated with cooking spray. Divide cheese mixture evenly among prepared cups. Bake at 375° for 8 minutes or until phyllo is golden. Serves 12 (serving size: 2 cups).

CALORIES 98; **FAT** 5.7g (sat 2.2g, mono 2.3g, poly 0.8g); **PROTEIN** 4.6g; **CARB** 6.2g; **FIBER** 0.2g; **CHOL** 11mg; **IRON** 0.5mg; **SODIUM** 108mg; **CALC** 78mg

9 SIMPLE PRINCIPLES OF *THE NEW WAY TO COOK LIGHT*

On the occasion of our 25th anniversary, our new cookbook serves up more than 400 recipes that reflect our Test Kitchen's freshest approaches and most exciting techniques. The recipes follow nine easy concepts that guide us today: great ingredients, reliable recipes, and, when possible, smart shortcuts that can open up a world of healthy cooking for both weeknights and weekends. Here's an excerpt.

Aromatic Slow-Roasted Tomatoes

PRINCIPLE
7

Hands-on time: 5 min. Total time: 7 hr. 35 min. *As if by magic, all-day slow roasting takes ho-hum winter tomatoes and turns out fruit with summery concentrated sweetness and intense tomato essence. Serve as a side dish alongside roast beef or lamb, seared steak, or fish. Or puree the tomatoes with an additional splash of olive oil, and toss with pasta.*

1 tablespoon sugar
1 tablespoon extra-virgin olive oil
½ teaspoon salt
½ teaspoon dried basil
½ teaspoon dried oregano
¼ teaspoon freshly ground black
   pepper
4 pounds plum tomatoes, halved
   lengthwise (about 16 medium)
Cooking spray

1. Preheat oven to 200°.
2. Combine sugar, extra-virgin olive oil, salt, basil, oregano, pepper, and tomatoes in a large bowl, tossing gently to coat tomatoes. Arrange tomatoes, cut sides up, on a baking sheet coated with cooking spray. Roast at 200° for 7½ hours. Serves 8 (serving size: 4 tomato halves).

CALORIES 63; **FAT** 2.2g (sat 0.3g, mono 1.3g, poly 0.4g); **PROTEIN** 2g; **CARB** 10.6g; **FIBER** 2.8g; **CHOL** 0mg; **IRON** 0.7mg; **SODIUM** 157mg; **CALC** 26mg

9 SIMPLE PRINCIPLES

PRINCIPLE **1**

Embrace the new variety.
Eating many different foods is the best way to enjoy a healthy diet. The global pantry and the local farmers' market are open, expanding, and inspiring. Supermarkets and food companies are rapidly wising up to the American appetite for new flavors.

PRINCIPLE **2**

Cook more often.
All the talk about Americans being too busy to cook obscures a truth about millions of them. Our readers report that cooking is a stress reliever, a bit of "me time" in a frantic world. Every meal cooked is a bit of control regained. Like any habit, cooking begets more of itself.

PRINCIPLE **3**

Eat more whole foods.
The fewer foods in your kitchen with long ingredient lists, the better. Whole foods contain the widest array of nutrients. This is not a ban on packaged foods but a judicious pruning of those that offer the false convenience of excessive processing.

PRINCIPLE **4**

Favor the healthy fats.
That means more plant oils, more servings of certain oily fish, and less saturated fat from meat and dairy. The good news is that the percentage of fat in your diet is less significant than the source of those fats.

PRINCIPLE **5**

Eat less meat, more plants.
Push vegetables, fruits, and whole grains to the center of your plate, and push meat in smaller quantities, to the side.

PRINCIPLE **6**

Cook seasonally and, when possible, locally.
This means enjoying the natural peak of peas and asparagus in spring, tomatoes in summer, apples in fall, root vegetables in winter—and taking advantage of imported foods that actually hold their flavor, like citrus. Out of season, visit the frozen-foods aisle for many vegetables, such as peas and corn, that retain not only their nutrients but also much of their sweet nature.

PRINCIPLE **7**

Learn new cooking techniques.
Kitchen proficiency is its own joy, but it's essential for the daily cook. Confidence comes with practice. Attention to method will break old habits. There are technique and shortcut tips throughout the book.

PRINCIPLE **8**

Buy the best ingredients you can afford.
Not necessarily the most expensive ingredients, but the best and most flavorful. Shopping in most cities is a great adventure. Find that perfect olive oil, that most intense aged cheddar.

PRINCIPLE **9**

Cook and eat mindfully and responsibly.
Healthy eating is about savoring every bite, being mindful of where food comes from (there are lots of sustainability notes in the book's fish chapter), preparing it with care, and sharing it joyfully with friends and family. It's hard not to feel reverence for a farmer's perfect tomato or a baker's perfect boule—and then enjoy sharing it with people who also care.

Quick & Easy

PRINCIPLES 1 2

Soy-Citrus Scallops with Soba Noodles

Hands-on time: 10 min. Total time: 20 min. Robust Japanese buckwheat noodles and seared scallops get coated with a marinade that has been reduced to a glaze. Serve with still-crunchy snow peas or sugar snap peas. You can toss them right in with the noodles.

3 tablespoons lower-sodium soy sauce
1 tablespoon fresh orange juice
1 tablespoon rice vinegar
1 tablespoon honey
1/2 teaspoon minced peeled fresh ginger
1/4 teaspoon chili garlic sauce
1 tablespoon dark sesame oil, divided
1 pound large sea scallops
4 cups hot cooked soba (about 6 ounces uncooked buckwheat noodles)
1/8 teaspoon salt
1/4 cup thinly sliced green onions

1. Combine first 6 ingredients and 1 teaspoon oil in a shallow baking dish. Add scallops to dish in a single layer; marinate at room temperature 4 minutes on each side.
2. Heat a large skillet over medium-high heat. Add remaining 2 teaspoons oil to pan; swirl to coat. Remove scallops from dish, reserving marinade. Add scallops to pan; sauté 1 minute on each side or until almost done. Remove scallops from pan; keep warm. Place reserved marinade in pan; bring to a boil. Return scallops to pan; cook 1 minute.
3. Combine noodles, salt, and onions in a large bowl. Place 1 cup noodle mixture on each of 4 plates. Top each serving with about 3 scallops; drizzle with 1 tablespoon sauce. Serves 4.

CALORIES 315; **FAT** 4.5g (sat 0.6g, mono 1.5g, poly 1.5g); **PROTEIN** 28g; **CARB** 42.7g; **FIBER** 1.9g; **CHOL** 37mg; **IRON** 1.3mg; **SODIUM** 653mg; **CALC** 41mg

Honey-Wheat Pizza with Pear-Prosciutto Salad

PRINCIPLES 3 6

Hands-on time: 24 min. Total time: 2 hr. 8 min. *We like to make a lot of what we call salad pizzas—topping baked crust with a fresh salad. This is a salty, fruity, delicious example. A showy, crimson-skinned pear is beautiful here, but any pear variety will work.*

1 cup warm water (100° to 110°)
1 tablespoon honey
2 tablespoons extra-virgin olive oil, divided
1½ teaspoons dry yeast
9 ounces all-purpose flour (2 cups)
2. 38 ounces whole-wheat flour (½ cup)
¾ teaspoon kosher salt
Cooking spray
6 ounces goat cheese, crumbled (about 1½ cups)
1 tablespoon cornmeal
4 cups fresh mâche or baby spinach
2 teaspoons chopped fresh thyme
2 teaspoons fresh lemon juice
½ teaspoon freshly ground black pepper
3 ounces sliced prosciutto, chopped
2 ripe red pears, cored and sliced

1. Combine 1 cup warm water, honey, and 1 teaspoon oil in a small bowl. Stir in yeast; let stand 10 minutes. Weigh or lightly spoon flours into dry measuring cups; level with a knife. Place flours and salt in a food processor; pulse 2 times or until blended. Add yeast mixture, pulsing to combine (dough will feel sticky). Turn dough out onto a floured surface; knead 3 to 4 times.
2. Place dough in a large bowl coated with cooking spray, turning to coat top. Cover and let rise in a warm place (85°), free from drafts, 1 hour or until doubled in size. (Gently press two fingers into dough. If indentation

remains, dough has risen enough.) Punch dough down; cover and let rest 10 minutes.
3. Preheat oven to 450°.
4. Place a baking sheet in oven. Roll dough into a 14-inch circle on a floured surface. Brush dough with 1 tablespoon oil; sprinkle evenly with cheese. Place dough on a baking sheet sprinkled with cornmeal. Transfer dough carefully to preheated pan; bake at 450° for 12 minutes or until crust is crisp and golden. Combine remaining 2 teaspoons oil, mâche, and remaining ingredients; toss to combine. Arrange salad over crust. Serves 6 (serving size: 1 slice).

CALORIES 393; **FAT** 12.7g (sat 5.2g, mono 5.3g, poly 0.9g); **PROTEIN** 18.1g; **CARB** 56.8g; **FIBER** 5.3g; **CHOL** 21mg; **IRON** 3.7mg; **SODIUM** 559mg; **CALC** 95mg

---

Quick & Easy
Make Ahead • Vegetarian

PRINCIPLE 8

Chickpeas and Spinach with Smoky Paprika

Hands-on time: 10 min. Total time: 40 min. *Do not make this until you have real sherry vinegar (nutty and complex) and Spanish smoked paprika (bacon-y).*

1 tablespoon olive oil
4 cups thinly sliced onion
5 garlic cloves, thinly sliced
1 teaspoon Spanish smoked paprika
½ cup dry white wine
¼ cup organic vegetable broth
1 (14.5-ounce) can fire-roasted diced tomatoes, undrained
1 (15-ounce) can chickpeas (garbanzo beans), rinsed and drained
1 (9-ounce) package fresh spinach
2 tablespoons chopped fresh parsley
2 teaspoons sherry vinegar

1. Heat a Dutch oven over medium heat. Add oil; swirl to coat. Add onion and garlic; cover and cook 8 minutes

or until tender, stirring occasionally. Stir in paprika; cook 1 minute, stirring constantly. Add wine, broth, and tomatoes; bring to a boil. Add chickpeas. Reduce heat, and simmer until sauce thickens slightly (about 15 minutes); stir occasionally. Add spinach; cover and cook 2 minutes or until spinach wilts. Stir in parsley and vinegar. Serves 10 (serving size: about ⅔ cup).

CALORIES 86; **FAT** 1.9g (sat 0.2g, mono 1g, poly 0.2g); **PROTEIN** 3.1g; **CARB** 14.6g; **FIBER** 3.5g; **CHOL** 0mg; **IRON** 1.8mg; **SODIUM** 168mg; **CALC** 64mg

---

Quick & Easy
Make Ahead

PRINCIPLE 5

Simmered Cabbage with Beef, Shan Style

Hands-on time: 17 min. Total time: 37 min.

2 tablespoons peanut oil
1 cup thinly vertically sliced shallots
1 teaspoon salt
1 teaspoon turmeric
½ teaspoon ground red pepper
¼ pound ground sirloin
4 cups shredded cabbage
1 cup thin plum tomato wedges
⅓ cup coarsely chopped unsalted, dry-roasted peanuts

1. Heat a wok or Dutch oven over medium heat. Add oil; swirl to coat. Add shallots, salt, turmeric, and red pepper; cook 3 minutes or until shallots are tender, stirring frequently. Add beef; cook 2 minutes or until beef begins to brown. Add cabbage and tomato; toss. Reduce heat to medium-low; cover and cook 10 minutes or until cabbage wilts. Stir in peanuts; cover and cook 10 minutes or until cabbage is tender. Serves 4 (serving size: 1 cup).

CALORIES 238; **FAT** 15.9g (sat 3.2g, mono 7.4g, poly 4.3g); **PROTEIN** 10.9g; **CARB** 15.7g; **FIBER** 3.4g; **CHOL** 18mg; **IRON** 2.1mg; **SODIUM** 629mg; **CALC** 59mg

Stuffed Whole Roasted Yellowtail Snapper

PRINCIPLES 4 9

Hands-on time: 8 min. Total time: 40 min. *Many home cooks avoid whole fish, thinking it's tricky. It's not. Just as cooking meat on the bone makes for richer flavor and extra succulence, so does cooking fish this way. Make a sustainable choice by selecting U.S. wild-caught yellowtail snapper (also called rainbow snapper).*

2 (1½-pound) whole cleaned yellowtail snappers (heads and tails intact)
2 tablespoons extra-virgin olive oil, divided
¼ cup fresh lemon juice, divided
½ teaspoon salt
¼ teaspoon freshly ground black pepper
Cooking spray
6 tablespoons sliced onion
2 tablespoons sliced fennel bulb
4 rosemary sprigs
4 oregano sprigs

1. Preheat oven to 400°.
2. Score skin of each fish with 3 diagonal cuts. Rub inside flesh of each fish with 2½ teaspoons oil; drizzle fish with 4½ teaspoons juice. Sprinkle flesh evenly with salt and pepper. Place fish on a rimmed baking sheet coated with cooking spray. Place 3 tablespoons onion, 1 tablespoon fennel, 2 rosemary sprigs, and 2 oregano sprigs inside each fish. Rub skin of each fish with ½ teaspoon remaining oil, and drizzle each with 1½ teaspoons remaining juice.
3. Roast at 400° for 30 minutes or until fish flakes when tested with a fork. Serves 4 (serving size: 5 ounces fish and 2 tablespoons vegetables).

CALORIES 251; **FAT** 9.2g (sat 1.5g, mono 5.4g, poly 1.6g); **PROTEIN** 37.5g; **CARB** 2.7g; **FIBER** 0.4g; **CHOL** 67mg; **IRON** 0.4mg; **SODIUM** 378mg; **CALC** 63mg

EVERYDAY VEGETARIAN

FALL HARVEST DINNERS

Brussels sprouts, beets, potatoes, and pumpkin: The full flavors of the season make for a happy table.

Quick & Easy • Vegetarian

Cavatappi with Browned Brussels Sprouts and Buttery Breadcrumbs

Hands-on time: 25 min. Total time: 25 min.

8 ounces uncooked cavatappi pasta
2 teaspoons unsalted butter
¼ cup panko (Japanese breadcrumbs)
4 teaspoons olive oil
12 ounces Brussels sprouts, trimmed and thinly sliced
1 cup thinly sliced onion
1 teaspoon minced garlic
⅔ cup organic vegetable broth
½ teaspoon grated lemon rind
1 tablespoon fresh lemon juice
2 teaspoons thyme leaves
¼ teaspoon salt
¼ teaspoon freshly ground black pepper
2 ounces fresh pecorino Romano cheese, shaved (about ½ cup)
2 tablespoons pine nuts, toasted

1. Cook pasta according to package directions, omitting salt and fat. Drain and transfer to a large bowl; keep warm.
2. Melt butter in a small skillet over medium heat; swirl to coat. Add panko to pan; cook 3 minutes or until browned, stirring frequently.
3. Heat a large nonstick skillet over medium-high heat. Add oil to pan; swirl to coat. Add Brussels sprouts to pan; cook 2 minutes, stirring occasionally. Add onion and garlic; cook 3 minutes or until onion is tender and Brussels sprouts are lightly browned. Add broth and next 5 ingredients. Cover and cook 2 minutes or until Brussels sprouts are crisp-tender. Add Brussels sprouts mixture to pasta; toss well. Sprinkle with cheese, pine nuts, and panko. Serve immediately. Serves 4 (serving size: 1½ cups).

CALORIES 377; **FAT** 12g (sat 3.3g, mono 4.6g, poly 2.1g); **PROTEIN** 13.1g; **CARB** 56.8g; **FIBER** 5.9g; **CHOL** 10mg; **IRON** 3.4mg; **SODIUM** 361mg; **CALC** 103mg

CUT THE SPROUTS LENGTHWISE TO KEEP THEIR SHAPE, ABOUT FOUR SLICES PER SPROUT. THEY'LL BE THIN ENOUGH TO GET A DEEP CARAMELIZED SEAR QUICKLY BUT STILL KEEP A GOOD CRUNCH.

Red Lentil-Pumpkin Soup

Hands-on time: 28 min. Total time: 28 min.

2 teaspoons canola oil
1 cup chopped onion
1 teaspoon minced garlic
3½ cups organic vegetable broth, divided
1 cup dried small red lentils
1 teaspoon ground cumin
¼ teaspoon salt
¼ teaspoon ground cinnamon
⅛ teaspoon ground red pepper
1 cup water
¾ cup canned pumpkin
1 tablespoon grated peeled fresh ginger
1 tablespoon fresh lemon juice
3 tablespoons plain low-fat yogurt
¼ cup unsalted pumpkinseed kernels, toasted
¼ cup chopped fresh cilantro

1. Heat a large Dutch oven over medium-high heat. Add oil to pan; swirl to coat. Add onion and garlic; sauté 4 minutes. Stir in 3 cups broth, lentils, and next 4 ingredients; bring to a boil. Cover, reduce heat, and simmer 10 minutes or until lentils are tender. Place lentil mixture in a blender. Remove center piece of blender lid (to allow steam to escape); secure blender lid on blender. Place a clean towel over opening in blender lid (to avoid splatters). Blend until smooth. Return lentil mixture to pan over medium heat. Add remaining ½ cup broth, 1 cup water, and pumpkin; cook 3 minutes or until thoroughly heated. Stir in ginger and lemon juice. Ladle 1½ cups soup into each of 4 bowls; top each with about 2 teaspoons yogurt, 1 tablespoon pumpkinseeds, and 1 tablespoon cilantro. Serves 4.

CALORIES 291; FAT 7.5g (sat 1g, mono 2.7g, poly 2.2g); PROTEIN 17g; CARB 41.1g; FIBER 9.8g; CHOL 1mg; IRON 4.2mg; SODIUM 648mg; CALC 74mg

Golden Beet, Greens, and Potato Torta

Hands-on time: 45 min. Total time: 2 hr.
Sophisticated and delicious—make this tall, flaky pie the centerpiece of the holiday table.

Crust:
7.9 ounces all-purpose flour (about 1¾ cups)
¾ teaspoon black pepper
½ teaspoon salt
3 tablespoons chilled unsalted butter, cut into small pieces
2 tablespoons chilled vegetable shortening, cut into small pieces
8½ tablespoons ice water
Filling:
1½ pounds golden beets with greens
½ pound Yukon gold potatoes
Cooking spray
1 large onion, chopped
1 tablespoon minced garlic
1 (5-ounce) bag fresh spinach
¾ teaspoon salt, divided
½ teaspoon black pepper, divided
4 large eggs
1 large egg white
2.25 ounces fontina cheese, shredded (about ⅔ cup)
1 ounce fresh Parmigiano-Reggiano cheese, grated (about ¼ cup)

1. To prepare crust, weigh or lightly spoon flour into dry measuring cups; level with a knife. Combine flour, ¾ teaspoon pepper, and ½ teaspoon salt in a large bowl; cut in butter and shortening with a pastry blender or 2 knives until mixture resembles coarse meal. Gradually add ice water, 1 tablespoon at a time; toss with a fork until flour mixture is just moist. Divide dough into 3 equal portions. Roll 1 portion into a ball (about 5 ounces). Combine remaining 2 portions; roll into a larger ball (about 9 ounces). Gently press each portion into a 5-inch circle on plastic wrap. Cover with additional plastic wrap. Chill at least 30 minutes.

2. Preheat oven to 425°.

3. To prepare filling, remove greens from beets; discard stems. Chop greens; set aside. Wrap beets and potatoes in foil. Bake potatoes at 425° for 1 hour or until tender. Bake beets at 425° for 1 hour and 20 minutes or until tender. Cool completely. Reduce oven temperature to 400°. Peel and slice beets and potatoes into ¼-inch-thick rounds.

4. Heat a large Dutch oven over medium-high heat. Coat pan with cooking spray. Add onion; sauté 4 minutes. Add garlic; sauté 1 minute. Add beet greens, spinach, ¼ teaspoon salt, and ¼ teaspoon pepper; sauté 8 minutes or until liquid evaporates. Place spinach mixture in a large bowl. Cool completely.

5. Combine eggs and egg white in a medium bowl, stirring with a whisk. Reserve 2 tablespoons egg mixture. Add remaining ½ teaspoon salt, remaining ¼ teaspoon pepper, and cheeses to bowl, stirring well.

6. Unwrap and place larger portion of dough on a lightly floured surface. Roll dough into a 14-inch circle. Press dough into bottom and 2 inches up sides of a 9-inch springform pan coated with cooking spray. Arrange half of beets and half of potatoes over dough. Top with half of spinach mixture and half of cheese mixture. Repeat layers with remaining beets, potatoes, spinach, and cheese mixture.

7. Unwrap and place smaller portion of dough on a lightly floured surface. Roll dough into a 10-inch circle. Place dough over filling; press edges together. Cut several slits in top of dough to allow steam to escape. Brush top of dough with reserved 2 tablespoons egg mixture. Bake at 400° for 40 minutes or until crust is browned. Let stand 10 minutes. Serves 8 (serving size: 1 wedge).

CALORIES 312; FAT 13.4g (sat 6.4g, mono 3.8g, poly 1.7g); PROTEIN 11.9g; CARB 36.4g; FIBER 4g; CHOL 116mg; IRON 3.1mg; SODIUM 561mg; CALC 129mg

FRESH FROM L.A.

Superhot Los Angeles chef Ricardo Zarate slips us a recipe for one of his signature dishes.

WHO
Ricardo Zarate

WHERE
Picca and Mo-Chica, Los Angeles

SIGNATURE FLAVORS
Peruvian small plates, sometimes with a Japanese influence

STREET CRED
His incredible success stateside began in a food-court stall.

"Peruvian food has been around for 500 years," Ricardo Zarate says. "It's ready to be exported to the world." We've heard that before, of course; Peruvian cuisine always seems to be a bridesmaid at the foodie table, never the bride. But it definitely deserves attention: It's a genuine melting pot, with Asian, African, Spanish, and native ingredients in the mix, boasting aggressive, forward flavors that surprise and delight. And if anyone is making the case in the U.S. for Peruvian food, it's Zarate and his Los Angeles restaurant Picca.

Zarate's ambitious, boldly flavored Peruvian dishes have made Picca hotter than an *aji* chile, and it's been getting local, national, and global press. It's a small-plates cantina, offering traditional fare like *anticucho corazon* (skewered grilled beef heart) and *causa*, a layered dish of mashed potatoes and fish salad. Traditional, but updated: Zarate puts his own spin on causa by forming the cooked potatoes into little bundles, and then topping them with raw fish and serving like nigiri sushi. And, of course, ceviches: At Picca, Zarate plays masterfully with textures as well as flavors, so he may add sweet potato, dried corn, or even fried calamari to the dish's usual elements.

Ceviche, consisting of fish chunks "cooked" in an acidic marinade, is a dish many cooks are wary of trying at home. But it can be a stunner, with "nice, bold flavors," and the only real necessity is knowing a good fishmonger.

"I cannot say it enough: fresh, fresh, fresh fish," says Zarate. Ask your fish seller for sashimi-quality fish, which has been deemed suitable for raw preparations: The marinade does alter the texture and color of the fish, but it doesn't really cook it. The other absolute: "Fresh lime juice is always the best, too—never use bottled lime or lemon."

In Picca's signature Ceviche Criollo, Zarate marinates the fish in a Leche de Tigre—tiger's milk—mixture of pureed fish, aromatics like garlic and ginger, lime juice, and spicy chiles. "It has good acidity and blending of flavors," Zarate says, "but it's always very light, so it's good for you."

PERUVIAN CUISINE IS A GENUINE MELTING POT, WITH ASIAN, AFRICAN, SPANISH, AND NATIVE INGREDIENTS IN THE MIX.

Ceviche Criollo with Leche de Tigre

Hands-on time: 20 min. Total time: 50 min. *Rocoto peppers are available at many Latin markets. You can substitute a red jalapeño or Fresno pepper.*

1 rocoto pepper, stem removed
25.25 ounces striped sea bass, divided
¼ cup chopped red onion
¾ cup fresh lime juice (about 5 limes)
½ teaspoon kosher salt
2 garlic cloves
1 (2-inch) piece celery
1 (1-inch) length peeled fresh ginger, sliced
1 cup thinly vertically sliced red onion
1 tablespoon chopped fresh cilantro

1. Boil rocoto pepper 1 minute; drain. Repeat twice. Place 1¼ ounces pepper flesh (reserve remaining pepper for another use) and 1 teaspoon pepper seeds, 1¼ ounces fish, ¼ cup chopped red onion, juice, salt, garlic, celery, and ginger in a blender. Process until smooth. Chill rocoto mixture 20 minutes.
2. Combine chilled rocoto mixture, remaining 24 ounces sea bass, sliced red onion, and cilantro in a bowl; toss to combine. Serve in chilled bowls or glasses. Serves 8 (serving size: ½ cup).

CALORIES 150; **FAT** 2.5g (sat 0.6g, mono 0.5g, poly 0.9g); **PROTEIN** 22.9g; **CARB** 9.3g; **FIBER** 1g; **CHOL** 49mg; **IRON** 0.6mg; **SODIUM** 249mg; **CALC** 32.7mg

NEW USES FOR TURMERIC

By Naomi Duguid

Add bright color and subtle, earthy flavor to everyday dishes.

While working on my recently released Burma cookbook, I developed a turmeric habit: I add a pinch of it to cooking oil before adding aromatics such as garlic or onions. My friends are used to seeing me use it this way, or stirring it into hot lentils, but they were surprised when I tossed it into hot oil before cooking an omelet. I guess it's because omelets come from a classic French tradition, in which turmeric plays no role. But in fact people all over the world make omelets, and many cooks in India and Nepal use turmeric with their egg dishes.

If you find fresh turmeric, you'll see that it's a rhizome, like ginger—though it's smaller, about the size of a baby finger, with a tawny skin and a bright orange, crisp interior. But you'll most often find it dried and ground to a bright golden powder that can stain hands and clothing. It's a common misunderstanding that turmeric adds only color; in fact it has a subtle earthy flavor. It is an essential ingredient in many parts of the Indian subcontinent, as well as in Burma, and it's used in many Indian spice blends, most notably curry powders.

There's a little more to turmeric, too. It's an anti-inflammatory, cancer researchers tell us, and antibacterial. I like the thought that a pinch of health is going into each dish I add it to, and the hint of color is also welcome.

Quick & Easy • Vegetarian

Omelet with Turmeric, Tomato, and Onions

Hands-on time: 10 min. Total time: 10 min.
Nutrition Note: *This runs a little high in dietary cholesterol but is well within our fat and calorie guidelines.*

4 large eggs
³/₈ teaspoon kosher salt
1 tablespoon olive oil
¼ teaspoon brown mustard seeds
⅛ teaspoon turmeric
2 green onions, finely chopped
¼ cup diced plum tomato
Dash of freshly ground black pepper

1. Whisk together eggs and salt.
2. Heat a large cast-iron skillet over medium-high heat. Add oil to pan; swirl to coat. Add mustard seeds and turmeric; cook 30 seconds or until seeds pop, stirring frequently. Add onions; cook 30 seconds or until soft, stirring frequently. Add tomato; cook 1 minute or until very soft, stirring frequently.
3. Pour egg mixture into pan; spread evenly. Cook until edges begin to set (about 2 minutes). Slide front edge of spatula between edge of omelet and pan. Gently lift edge of omelet, tilting pan to allow some uncooked egg mixture to come in contact with pan. Repeat procedure on the opposite edge. Continue cooking until center is just set (about 2 minutes). Loosen omelet with a spatula, and fold in half. Carefully slide omelet onto a platter. Cut omelet in half, and sprinkle with black pepper. Serves 2 (serving size: 1 omelet half).

CALORIES 216; **FAT** 16.9g (sat 4.1g, mono 8.8g, poly 2.1g); **PROTEIN** 13.3g; **CARB** 3.4g; **FIBER** 0.9g; **CHOL** 370mg; **IRON** 2.3mg; **SODIUM** 504mg; **CALC** 70mg

FOUR MORE EVERYDAY USES FOR TURMERIC

Ground turmeric has more of a color impact than a flavor one, though it does convey subtly earthy and slightly musty notes.

1 Whisk ¼ to ½ teaspoon into the dry flour mixture for pie or pizza dough.

2 Add ¼ teaspoon to vinaigrette for vibrant color.

3 "Bloom" the spice in oil (as we do in this omelet recipe), and use the golden oil for sautéing potato cubes or onions.

4 Mix with softened butter, cumin, and red pepper; rub under chicken skin before roasting.

FEED 4 FOR LESS THAN $10

Twists take dishes from ho-hum to yes, please. Poached eggs enrich grits, chicken and rice go Persian, and grilled cheese meets saltimbocca.

Kid Friendly • Quick & Easy

$2.49/serving, $9.97 total

Pigs in a Poke

Hands-on time: 32 min. Total time: 32 min. *Combine 6 cups torn escarole, 1 tablespoon olive oil, 2 teaspoons fresh lemon juice, 1 slice crumbled bacon, and 1 ounce shaved Parmigiano-Reggiano for a side salad.*

1¹/₂ teaspoons butter
1 ounce andouille sausage, diced
3 cups 2% reduced-fat milk
¹/₂ teaspoon salt, divided
1 cup uncooked stone-ground grits
¹/₂ teaspoon black pepper, divided
1.5 ounces Gouda cheese, shredded (about ¹/₃ cup)
8 cups water
2 tablespoons white vinegar
4 large eggs
2 teaspoons chopped fresh parsley

1. Melt butter in a small saucepan over medium-high heat. Add sausage; sauté 3 minutes, stirring occasionally. Stir in 3 cups milk and ¼ teaspoon salt; bring to a boil. Add grits; reduce heat, and simmer 20 minutes or until tender, stirring frequently. Remove from heat; stir in ¼ teaspoon pepper and cheese.
2. Bring 8 cups water and vinegar to a simmer in a large saucepan. Crack each egg into a small bowl. Gently slide eggs into water; cook 3 minutes or until whites are just set. Remove eggs from water with a slotted spoon.
3. Divide grits evenly among each of 4 bowls. Top each serving with 1 poached egg; sprinkle eggs evenly with remaining ¼ teaspoon salt, ¼ teaspoon pepper, and parsley. Serves 4.

CALORIES 365; **FAT** 13.9g (sat 6.8g, mono 4.1g, poly 1g); **PROTEIN** 19.2g; **CARB** 37.5g; **FIBER** 2.1g; **CHOL** 216mg; **IRON** 2.6mg; **SODIUM** 595mg; **CALC** 317mg

Fiery Chicken Thighs with Persian Rice

$2.15/serving, $8.59 total

Hands-on time: 40 min. Total time: 1 hr. *Pay close attention to the rice as it cooks over medium-low heat—when you hear it begin to crackle, turn the heat down to low. Continue to cook until the bottom side of the rice develops a golden crust. Serve with 1 pound fresh green beans sautéed in 1 tablespoon butter. Toss with 3 tablespoons toasted sliced almonds and fresh parsley. Although the buttery rice cuts through the heat of the chicken, use less chile paste if you are not a fan of spicy foods.*

5 cups water
³/₄ cup long-grain white rice
2¹/₂ tablespoons canola oil, divided
³/₄ cup chopped onion
1¹/₂ teaspoons ground cumin, divided
1 teaspoon kosher salt, divided
¹/₂ teaspoon ground turmeric
¹/₂ cup plain 2% reduced-fat Greek yogurt
1¹/₂ tablespoons butter
1 tablespoon sambal oelek (ground fresh chile paste)
1 tablespoon minced fresh garlic
¹/₄ teaspoon ground coriander
4 bone-in, skin-on chicken thighs
Cooking spray

1. Bring 5 cups water to a boil in medium saucepan. Add rice, and boil 10 minutes. Drain. Rinse rice, and drain.
2. Heat a medium, heavy-bottomed skillet over medium heat. Add 1½ teaspoons oil to pan; swirl to coat. Add onion, and cook 5 minutes. Stir in 1 teaspoon cumin, ¾ teaspoon salt, and turmeric; cook 1 minute. Combine rice, onion mixture, and yogurt in a bowl.
3. Return pan to medium-high heat. Add butter and 1 tablespoon oil to pan; swirl until butter melts. Add rice mixture to pan, lightly packing rice down. Reduce heat to medium-low. Wrap a clean, dry dish towel around the lid, tying it at the handle; place prepared lid on pan. Cook rice, covered, over medium-low heat 10 minutes (do not stir or uncover). Reduce temperature to low; cook an additional 20 minutes or until rice is tender on top and a golden crust forms on bottom.
4. Loosen rice crust with a rubber spatula around edges. Place a plate over top of pan, and invert rice onto plate, browned side up.
5. While rice cooks, preheat broiler to high.
6. Combine remaining 1 tablespoon oil, remaining ½ teaspoon cumin, sambal oelek, garlic, and coriander in a small bowl, stirring well. Scrape spice paste into a zip-top plastic bag. Add chicken to bag; seal. Toss to coat. Let stand 20 minutes. Remove chicken from bag; discard marinade. Sprinkle chicken evenly with remaining ¼ teaspoon salt.
7. Place chicken, skin-side up, on a foil-lined broiler pan coated with cooking spray. Broil 8 minutes or until browned. Turn chicken over; broil an additional 4 minutes or until done. Serve with rice. Serves 4 (serving size: about ½ cup rice and 1 chicken thigh).

CALORIES 439; **FAT** 23.9g (sat 6.5g, mono 10.6g, poly 4.8g); **PROTEIN** 21.1g; **CARB** 33.7g; **FIBER** 1.4g; **CHOL** 71mg; **IRON** 2.8mg; **SODIUM** 547mg; **CALC** 56mg

Grilled Ham, Chicken, and Gruyère Sandwiches

$2.24/serving, $8.95 total

Hands-on time: 28 min. Total time: 28 min.

2 (6-ounce) skinless, boneless chicken breast halves
Cooking spray
¼ teaspoon freshly ground black pepper
1½ ounces prosciutto, cut into 4 thin slices
8 (¾-ounce) slices sourdough bread
4 teaspoons butter, softened and divided
2 ounces Gruyère cheese, shredded (about ½ cup)
2 tablespoons Dijon mustard
2 cups arugula leaves
3 tablespoons thinly sliced shallots
2 teaspoons fresh lemon juice
1 large red-skinned pear, sliced

1. Split each chicken breast in half lengthwise to form 2 cutlets. Heat a large skillet over medium-high heat. Coat pan with cooking spray. Sprinkle chicken evenly with pepper. Add chicken to pan; cook 4 minutes on each side or until done. Remove chicken from pan. Wrap 1 prosciutto slice around each chicken cutlet.
2. Return pan to medium heat. Coat pan with cooking spray. Spread one side of each bread slice evenly with ½ teaspoon butter. Place 4 bread slices, buttered side down, in pan. Top each bread slice in pan with 2 tablespoons cheese; toast bread 2 minutes or until underside is toasted and cheese melts. Remove bread from pan. Recoat pan with cooking spray. Place remaining 4 bread slices, buttered side down, in pan; toast 2 minutes or until toasted. Remove from pan.

3. Top each cheese-topped bread slice with 1 chicken cutlet. Spread 1½ teaspoons mustard over untoasted side of each remaining bread slice. Combine arugula, shallots, and juice in a bowl; toss. Divide mixture evenly among sandwiches; top each sandwich with 1 bread slice, mustard side down. Serve with pear slices. Serves 4 (serving size: 1 sandwich and ¼ pear).

CALORIES 371; FAT 11.5g (sat 6g, mono 3.3g, poly 1.2g); PROTEIN 31.9g; CARB 34.4g; FIBER 2.6g; CHOL 81mg; IRON 2.6mg; SODIUM 750mg; CALC 197mg

KID-FRIENDLY COOKING

BRING ON THE SPICE CAKE

Matisse gets to know molasses and earns her highest rating yet.

We asked Matisse Reid, our favorite 11-year-old foodie, to bake up a snack cake. Here's her report.

—Phoebe Wu

"Today I made a sweet treat called Sticky Ginger Cake. Before you begin, you will want to gather all the ingredients together, as you might not have some of them on hand. The ginger in this cake really balances out the richness from the sweet glaze, which is a nice addition at the end. I had not cooked with molasses before, but I really enjoyed it in this recipe. I also used a round cake tin instead of a square pan, which worked really well and gave us nice, thin wedges—just make sure to watch the cake closely as it bakes so it doesn't overcook. Although this recipe is one of the more complicated cakes I have ever made, follow the recipe and you will do just fine. This cake turned out really well for me and is nice and moist—definitely worth the work!"

KEEP FRESH GINGER IN THE FREEZER; IT'S MUCH EASIER TO GRATE WHEN FROZEN.

Sticky Ginger Cake

Hands-on time: 20 min. Total time: 45 min.

Cooking spray
4.5 ounces all-purpose flour (about 1 cup)
1 teaspoon baking soda
1 teaspoon ground ginger
1 teaspoon ground cinnamon
½ teaspoon ground allspice
¼ teaspoon salt
1 cup low-fat buttermilk
2 large eggs, beaten
5 tablespoons honey, divided
5 tablespoons molasses, divided
¼ cup dark brown sugar
2 tablespoons butter
2 teaspoons grated fresh ginger
1 tablespoon water
1 teaspoon powdered sugar

1. Preheat oven to 400°.
2. Lightly coat an 8-inch square metal baking pan with cooking spray. Set prepared pan aside.
3. Weigh or spoon flour into a dry measuring cup; level with a knife. Combine flour and next 5 ingredients; stir with a whisk. Combine buttermilk and eggs. Combine ¼ cup honey, ¼ cup molasses, brown sugar, butter, and fresh ginger in a pan over medium heat. Stir constantly until sugar melts. Remove pan from heat, and cool

5 minutes. Add egg mixture to honey mixture, stirring with a whisk. Add egg mixture to flour mixture; stir until well combined.

4. Pour batter into pan. Bake at 400° for 25 minutes. Place on a rack; pierce surface with a skewer. Combine 1 tablespoon honey, 1 tablespoon molasses, and 1 tablespoon water; brush over hot cake. Cool. Dust with powdered sugar. Serves 16 (serving size: 1 piece).

CALORIES 209; **FAT** 2.5g (sat 1.2g, mono 0.7g, poly 0.3g); **PROTEIN** 5g; **CARB** 41.7g; **FIBER** 1.1g; **CHOL** 27mg; **IRON** 2.1mg; **SODIUM** 155mg; **CALC** 45mg

THE VERDICT

BAILEY (AGE 11)
He said, "It tastes good!" **8/10**

FRAANZ (AGE 7)
I guess my brother likes ginger. **2,000/10**

MATISSE
It was like a party in my mouth! **10/10**

NO BUTTERMILK? USE REGULAR MILK, AND SUBSTITUTE 1 TABLESPOON WHITE VINEGAR FOR 1 TABLESPOON OF THE MILK.

DINNER TONIGHT

Our best-ever fast weeknight meals.

READY IN
40
MINUTES

The SHOPPING LIST

Spanish Spaghetti with Olives
Onion (1 large)
Garlic
Fresh parsley
(8-ounce) package thin spaghetti (1)
Lower-sodium marinara sauce
Pimiento-stuffed olives
Capers
Olive oil
Dried oregano
Celery salt
Crushed red pepper
Saffron threads
Dry sherry
Extra-lean ground beef (8 ounces)

Pear, Date, and Manchego Salad
(5-ounce) package gourmet salad greens (1)
Bosc pears (2)
Lemon (1)
Pitted dates
Walnuts
Extra-virgin olive oil
Sherry vinegar
Manchego cheese (1 ounce)

The GAME PLAN

While water for pasta comes to a boil:
- Chop onion.
- Mince garlic.
- Slice olives.

While sauce simmers:
- Prepare salad.

"THIS WAS THE BEST SPAGHETTI SAUCE I HAD EVER HAD. THE SAFFRON AND THE SHERRY REALLY MADE IT SPECIAL."
–LSTILPHEN

Quick & Easy

Spanish Spaghetti with Olives

With Pear, Date, and Manchego Salad

(pictured on page 238)

Shopping Tip: Look for less-expensive envelopes of saffron.
Flavor Hit: Capers add a bright, briny note to the sauce.
Technique Tip: Squeeze lemon on the cut pear to keep it from browning.

8 ounces uncooked thin spaghetti
1 tablespoon olive oil
2 cups chopped onion
2 teaspoons minced garlic
1 teaspoon dried oregano
1/2 teaspoon celery salt
1/4 teaspoon crushed red pepper
1/4 teaspoon freshly ground black pepper
1/4 teaspoon crushed saffron threads (optional)
8 ounces extra-lean ground beef
1 2/3 cups lower-sodium marinara sauce (such as Amy's)
2 ounces pimiento-stuffed olives, sliced (about 1/2 cup)
1/4 cup dry sherry
1 tablespoon capers
1/4 cup chopped fresh parsley, divided
continued

1. Cook pasta according to package directions, omitting salt and fat; drain.
2. Heat a large skillet over medium-high heat. Add oil to pan; swirl to coat. Add onion to pan; sauté 4 minutes or until tender. Add garlic; sauté 1 minute. Stir in oregano, celery salt, red pepper, black pepper, and saffron, if desired. Add ground beef; cook 5 minutes or until beef is browned, stirring to crumble. Stir in marinara sauce, olives, dry sherry, capers, and 3 tablespoons parsley; bring to a boil. Reduce heat, and simmer 15 minutes.
3. Add spaghetti to sauce mixture. Cook 2 minutes or until thoroughly heated. Sprinkle with remaining 1 tablespoon parsley. Serves 4 (serving size: about 1¾ cups).

CALORIES 407; FAT 9.3g (sat 2g, mono 4.6g, poly 0.8g); PROTEIN 21g; CARB 57.1g; FIBER 4.6g; CHOL 30mg; IRON 4.9mg; SODIUM 606mg; CALC 69mg

For the Pear, Date, and Manchego Salad:

Arrange 1 cup gourmet salad greens on each of 4 plates. Finely chop 2 ripe Bosc pears; toss with 2 teaspoons fresh lemon juice. Divide pear, 6 finely chopped pitted dates, and 2 tablespoons chopped walnuts evenly among salads. Combine 1½ tablespoons extra-virgin olive oil, 2 teaspoons sherry vinegar, ¼ teaspoon salt, and ⅛ teaspoon black pepper, stirring with a whisk. Drizzle evenly over salads. Top each salad with ¼ ounce shaved Manchego cheese. Serves 4 (serving size: about 1½ cups salad).

CALORIES 182; FAT 10.3g (sat 2.8g); SODIUM 212mg

READY IN
40
MINUTES

The
SHOPPING LIST

Roast Chicken with Balsamic Bell Peppers
Red bell peppers (2)
Yellow bell pepper (1)
Shallot (1 large)
Fresh rosemary
Fennel seeds
Garlic powder
Dried oregano
Olive oil
Balsamic vinegar
Fat-free, lower-sodium chicken broth
4 (6-ounce) skinless, boneless chicken breast halves

Mascarpone Mashed Potatoes
Yukon gold potatoes (1 pound)
1% low-fat milk
Mascarpone cheese

The
GAME PLAN

While oven preheats:
  ■ Cook potatoes.
  ■ Prepare spice rub.
While chicken browns:
  ■ Slice bell peppers and shallot.
While chicken roasts:
  ■ Cook bell pepper mixture.
  ■ Mash potatoes.

"IT'S QUICK AND EASY BUT TASTES LIKE IT TOOK HOURS TO MAKE! I'LL COOK THIS ONE AGAIN."
-LIZARDSTEW

Quick & Easy
Roast Chicken with Balsamic Bell Peppers
With Mascarpone Mashed Potatoes

Flavor Hit: Fennel seeds add licorice notes to the chicken.
Simple Sub: Substitute red onion if you don't have shallots.
Shopping Tip: Look for tubs of mascarpone with the gourmet cheeses.

⅝ **teaspoon salt, divided**
¾ **teaspoon fennel seeds, crushed**
½ **teaspoon freshly ground black pepper, divided**
¼ **teaspoon garlic powder**
¼ **teaspoon dried oregano**
4 **(6-ounce) skinless, boneless chicken breast halves**
2 **tablespoons olive oil, divided**
Cooking spray
2 **cups thinly sliced red bell pepper**
1 **cup thinly sliced yellow bell pepper**
½ **cup thinly sliced shallots (about 1 large)**
1½ **teaspoons chopped fresh rosemary**
1 **cup fat-free, lower-sodium chicken broth**
1 **tablespoon balsamic vinegar**

1. Preheat oven to 450°.

2. Heat a large skillet over medium-high heat. Combine ½ teaspoon salt, fennel seeds, ¼ teaspoon black pepper, garlic powder, and oregano. Brush chicken with 1½ teaspoons oil; sprinkle spice rub over chicken. Add 1½ teaspoons oil to pan; swirl to coat. Add chicken; cook 3 minutes or until browned. Turn chicken over; cook 1 minute. Arrange chicken in an 11 x 7–inch glass or ceramic baking dish coated with cooking spray. Bake at 450° for 10 minutes or until done.

3. Return pan to medium-high heat. Add remaining 1 tablespoon oil; swirl to coat. Add bell peppers, shallots, and rosemary; sauté 3 minutes. Stir in broth, scraping pan to loosen browned bits. Reduce heat, and simmer 5 minutes. Increase heat to medium-high. Stir in vinegar, remaining ⅛ teaspoon salt, and ¼ teaspoon pepper. Cook 3 minutes, stirring frequently. Serve bell pepper mixture over chicken. Serves 4 (serving size: 1 breast half and about ½ cup bell pepper mixture).

CALORIES 292; FAT 9.3g (sat 1.5g, mono 5.5g, poly 1.3g); PROTEIN 40.9g; CARB 8.8g; FIBER 1.7g; CHOL 99mg; IRON 2mg; SODIUM 599mg; CALC 40mg

For the Mascarpone Mashed Potatoes:
Place 1 pound cubed peeled Yukon gold potatoes in a large saucepan; cover with water. Bring to a boil, reduce heat, and simmer 15 minutes or until tender. Drain. Return potatoes to pan. Add ¼ cup 1% low-fat milk, 2 tablespoons mascarpone cheese, and ½ teaspoon salt. Mash to desired consistency. Serves 4 (serving size: about ½ cup).

CALORIES 156; FAT 6.7g (sat 3.6g); SODIUM 315mg

READY IN 40 MINUTES

The SHOPPING LIST

Walnut and Rosemary Oven-Fried Chicken
Fresh rosemary
Dijon mustard
Panko (Japanese breadcrumbs)
Chopped walnuts
4 (6-ounce) chicken cutlets
Low-fat buttermilk
Parmigiano-Reggiano cheese

Toasted Garlic Escarole
(1½-pound) head escarole (1)
Garlic
Lemon (1)
Olive oil

The GAME PLAN

While oven preheats:
- Coat chicken with buttermilk mixture.
- Toast panko.

While chicken bakes:
- Prepare escarole.

Kid Friendly • Quick & Easy

Walnut and Rosemary Oven-Fried Chicken
With Toasted Garlic Escarole

Flavor Hit: Golden garlic balances the slightly bitter escarole.
Simple Sub: If you can't find escarole, substitute chopped endive.
Budget Buy: Asiago is less expensive than Parm-Regg.

¼ cup low-fat buttermilk
2 tablespoons Dijon mustard
4 (6-ounce) chicken cutlets
⅓ cup panko (Japanese breadcrumbs)
⅓ cup finely chopped walnuts
2 tablespoons grated fresh Parmigiano-Reggiano cheese
¾ teaspoon minced fresh rosemary
¼ teaspoon kosher salt
¼ teaspoon freshly ground black pepper
Cooking spray
Rosemary leaves (optional)

1. Preheat oven to 425°.

2. Combine buttermilk and mustard in a shallow dish, stirring with a whisk. Add chicken to buttermilk mixture, turning to coat.

3. Heat a small skillet over medium-high heat. Add panko to pan; cook 3 minutes or until golden, stirring frequently. Combine panko, nuts, and next 4 ingredients in a shallow dish. Remove chicken from buttermilk mixture; discard buttermilk mixture. Dredge chicken in panko mixture.

4. Arrange a wire rack on a large baking sheet; coat rack with cooking spray. Arrange chicken on rack; coat chicken with cooking spray. Bake at 425° for 13 minutes or until chicken is done. Garnish with rosemary leaves, if desired. Serves 4 (serving size: 1 cutlet).

CALORIES 292; FAT 9.6g (sat 1.6g, mono 1.6g, poly 5.1g); PROTEIN 42.7g; CARB 6.8g; FIBER 0.9g; CHOL 101mg; IRON 1.6mg; SODIUM 471mg; CALC 66mg

For the Toasted Garlic Escarole:
Cut a 1½-pound escarole head crosswise into 1-inch strips; place in a large bowl. Heat a small skillet over medium-high heat. Add 1½ tablespoons olive oil; swirl to coat. Add 4 thinly sliced garlic cloves to pan; sauté 2 minutes or until golden. Remove pan from heat; add 1½ tablespoons fresh lemon juice, ¼ teaspoon kosher salt, and ¼ teaspoon freshly ground black pepper, stirring to combine. Drizzle garlic mixture over the escarole; toss to coat. Serves 4 (serving size: about ⅔ cup).

CALORIES 80; FAT 5.4g (sat 0.8g); SODIUM 158mg

READY IN
40
MINUTES

Cheesy Meat Loaf Minis
Onion (1)
Garlic
Fresh parsley
Sliced white bread
Ketchup
Prepared horseradish
Dijon mustard
Dried oregano
Lean ground sirloin (1½ pounds)
White cheddar cheese (3 ounces)
Parmesan cheese
Egg (1)

Salad with Balsamic Vinaigrette
(5-ounce) package herb salad mix (1)
Carrots (2)
Red onion (1)
Shallot (1)
Olive oil
Balsamic vinegar
Dijon mustard
Sugar

The
GAME PLAN

While oven preheats:
- Toast breadcrumbs.
- Chop onion and garlic.

While onion and garlic sauté:
- Dice cheddar cheese.
- Chop parsley.

While meat loaves cook:
- Prepare salad.

Kid Friendly • Quick & Easy
Cheesy Meat Loaf Minis
With Salad with Balsamic Vinaigrette

Prep Pointer: Diced cheese melts into gooey pockets as the loaves cook.
Equipment Tip: A broiler pan lets grease drain away from the loaves.
Flavor Hit: Horseradish adds a welcome, pungent kick to the beef.

1 ounce fresh breadcrumbs (about ½ cup)
Cooking spray
1 cup chopped onion
2 garlic cloves, chopped
½ cup ketchup, divided
¼ cup chopped fresh parsley
2 tablespoons grated fresh Parmesan cheese
1 tablespoon prepared horseradish
1 tablespoon Dijon mustard
¾ teaspoon dried oregano
¼ teaspoon salt
¼ teaspoon freshly ground black pepper
3 ounces white cheddar cheese, diced
1½ pounds lean ground sirloin
1 large egg, lightly beaten

1. Preheat oven to 425°.
2. Heat a skillet over medium-high heat. Add breadcrumbs; cook 3 minutes or until toasted, stirring frequently.
3. While breadcrumbs cook, heat a large skillet over medium-high heat. Coat pan with cooking spray. Add onion and garlic; sauté 3 minutes.

Combine onion mixture, breadcrumbs, ¼ cup ketchup, and remaining ingredients. Shape into 6 (4 x 2–inch) loaves on a broiler pan coated with cooking spray; spread 2 teaspoons ketchup over each. Bake at 425° for 25 minutes or until done. Serves 6 (serving size: 1 meat loaf).

CALORIES 254; FAT 11.4g (sat 5.6g, mono 3.8g, poly 0.9g); PROTEIN 28.3g; CARB 11.1g; FIBER 0.9g; CHOL 112mg; IRON 2.6mg; SODIUM 607mg; CALC 150mg

For the Salad with Balsamic Vinaigrette:
Combine 2 tablespoons balsamic vinegar, 2 tablespoons olive oil, 1 tablespoon minced shallots, and ½ teaspoon Dijon mustard in a large bowl, stirring with a whisk. Stir in ¼ teaspoon sugar and ⅛ teaspoon salt. Add 1 (5-ounce) package herb salad mix, 1 cup carrot ribbons, and ½ cup thinly sliced red onion; toss to combine. Serves 6 (serving size: about 1 cup).

CALORIES 63; FAT 4.6g (sat 0.6g); SODIUM 94mg

"I WOULD RECOMMEND DOUBLING THE RECIPE BECAUSE ONCE YOU TASTE IT, YOU CAN'T GET ENOUGH!"
-LOLABRIDGIT

2012 TAKE ON '87 PIE

Could new kitchen techniques improve on one of our very first recipes? Yes, with a secret ingredient in the crust.

One of our first apple pies after launching this magazine had an interesting walnut crust, filled with healthy fats and nutty flavor. But to save 300 calories, the Test Kitchen had simply removed the bottom crust, yielding a sort of cobbler.

We liked and kept the walnuts but decided we were willing to serve up a few more calories if we could get back that bottom crust. We started by using butter for the crust instead of margarine—just enough for improved texture and rich flavor, while keeping sat fat low. We also used a bit of vodka, a surprise ingredient we first turned to for our Peach "Fried" Pies (May 2012). Vodka inhibits gluten formation, which leads to tough crusts; it vaporizes during baking and leaves no alcohol taste. What remain are beautifully flaky layers—so good you'll definitely want two. Yes, there are a few more calories than in 1987, but our new pie still has only half those in a typical bakery pie.

The lesson? Recipes evolve, techniques improve, and there's always something new to try in a busy test kitchen.

Kid Friendly • Make Ahead

Walnut-Crusted Apple Pie

Hands-on time: 40 min. Total time: 1 hr. 50 min.

1 pound Pink Lady apples (about 2), peeled, cored, and thinly sliced
1 pound Golden Delicious apples (about 2), peeled, cored, and thinly sliced
1/4 cup packed brown sugar
1/4 cup granulated sugar
2 tablespoons all-purpose flour
2 tablespoons fresh lemon juice
1/4 teaspoon salt
1/4 teaspoon ground cinnamon
1/2 cup coarsely chopped walnuts
6.75 ounces all-purpose flour (1 1/2 cups)
3 tablespoons packed brown sugar
1/4 teaspoon salt
5 tablespoons cold butter, cut into pieces
3 tablespoons ice-cold vodka
Cooking spray
1 tablespoon 2% reduced-fat milk
1 large egg yolk

1. Combine first 8 ingredients in a large bowl; toss to coat.
2. Place nuts in a food processor; process until finely ground. Weigh or lightly spoon 6.75 ounces flour into dry measuring cups; level with a knife. Add flour, 3 tablespoons brown sugar, and 1/4 teaspoon salt to food processor; pulse 5 times. Add butter; pulse 6 times or until mixture resembles coarse meal. With processor on, slowly add vodka through food chute, processing just until combined (do not form a ball). Turn dough out onto a lightly floured surface. Knead 3 to 4 times.

Divide dough into 2 equal portions. Gently press each portion into a 4-inch circle on plastic wrap. Cover with plastic wrap; chill 30 minutes.
3. Preheat oven to 425°.
4. Unwrap and place 1 dough piece on plastic wrap. Cover with 2 sheets of overlapping plastic wrap. Roll dough, still covered, into a 10-inch circle. Place into a 9-inch pie plate coated with cooking spray. Spoon apple mixture into pie plate.
5. Unwrap and place remaining portion of dough on plastic wrap. Cover with 2 sheets of overlapping plastic wrap. Roll dough, still covered, into a 12-inch circle. Place over apple mixture. Press edges of dough together. Fold edges under; flute. Cut slits in top of dough to allow steam to escape.
6. Combine milk and egg yolk, stirring with a whisk. Gently brush top of dough with milk mixture. Place pie plate on a foil-lined baking sheet; bake at 425° for 20 minutes in the lower third of oven. Shield edges of piecrust with foil. Reduce oven temperature to 350° (do not remove pie from oven); bake an additional 30 minutes or until browned. Cool on a wire rack. Serves 10 (serving size: 1 wedge).

CALORIES 281; FAT 10.4g (sat 4.2g, mono 2.3g, poly 3.2g); PROTEIN 3.7g; CARB 43.1g; FIBER 2.2g; CHOL 34mg; IRON 1.3mg; SODIUM 122mg; CALC 28mg

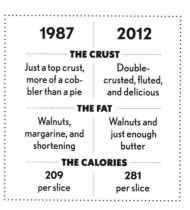

1987	2012
THE CRUST	
Just a top crust, more of a cobbler than a pie	Double-crusted, fluted, and delicious
THE FAT	
Walnuts, margarine, and shortening	Walnuts and just enough butter
THE CALORIES	
209 per slice	281 per slice

7 SECRETS OF HEALTHY HOLIDAY INDULGENCE

Savor the delights of cheese, chocolate, caramel, and meat in light, smart, delicious ways.

Roast Stuffed Pork Loin with Port Sauce

Hands-on time: 35 min. Total time: 1 hr. 45 min. *Pretty spirals of pork stuffed with a fruity-herby filling make for a lovely centerpiece dish. Depending on the intensity of your port, the sauce may be darker or lighter. To make toasted breadcrumbs, pulse 2 ounces bread in a food processor. Spread the fresh breadcrumbs on a jelly-roll pan and bake at 300° until browned, or toast in a skillet over medium heat.*

Our secret: *A healthy portion of pork is 4 ounces raw, which cooks down to about 3 ounces. A 3-ounce serving of the holiday centerpiece could look puny on the plate, but we beef up our dish with a tasty filling featuring licorice-like fennel, tangy dried cherries, and lots of herbs. Thin slices of the finished roast look prettier (and larger), and the port wine sauce that drapes over the meat is lick-your-plate satisfying. All this, and the entrée is well under 300 calories!*

1 cup tawny port
½ cup dried cherries, coarsely chopped
2 tablespoons canola oil, divided
¾ cup finely chopped fennel bulb
½ cup finely chopped onion
2 large garlic cloves, minced
1 cup sourdough breadcrumbs, toasted
2 tablespoons butter, divided
2½ cups no-salt-added chicken stock (such as Swanson), divided
1 tablespoon chopped fresh sage, divided
1½ teaspoons chopped fresh thyme
1½ teaspoons kosher salt, divided
1¼ teaspoons freshly ground black pepper, divided
1 (3-pound) boneless pork loin, trimmed
Cooking spray
2 thyme sprigs
2 sage leaves
1 shallot, peeled and quartered
1 tablespoon all-purpose flour
2 tablespoons water

USE THE GORGEOUS FLAVORS OF DRIED CHERRIES, PUNGENT HERBS, AND RICH PORT WINE TO KEEP SERVINGS SMALL BUT SATISFYING.

1. Preheat oven to 400°.
2. Combine port and cherries in a small saucepan over medium heat; bring to a boil. Reduce heat; simmer 4 minutes. Remove from heat; let stand 10 minutes. Drain cherries in a sieve over a bowl, reserving cherries and port.
3. Heat a medium skillet over medium heat. Add 1 tablespoon oil to pan; swirl to coat. Add fennel and onion; cook 10 minutes or until vegetables are almost tender, stirring occasionally. Add garlic; cook 1 minute, stirring frequently. Combine fennel mixture, cherries, and breadcrumbs in a large bowl. Melt 1 tablespoon butter in pan. Drizzle melted butter and ¼ cup stock over bread mixture; toss. Stir in 2 teaspoons chopped sage, chopped thyme, ¼ teaspoon salt, and ¼ teaspoon pepper.
4. Cut horizontally through center of pork, cutting to, but not through, other side using a sharp knife; open flat as you would a book. Place pork between 2 sheets of plastic wrap; pound to an even ½-inch thickness using a meat mallet or small heavy skillet. Brush 1½ teaspoons oil over inside of pork; sprinkle with ¼ teaspoon salt and ¼ teaspoon pepper. Spread bread mixture evenly over pork, leaving a ½-inch margin around outside edges. Roll up pork, jelly-roll fashion, starting with short side. Secure at 2-inch intervals with twine. Brush outside of pork with remaining 1½ teaspoons oil; sprinkle all sides of pork evenly with ¾ teaspoon salt and ½ teaspoon pepper.
5. Heat a large skillet over high heat. Add pork to pan; cook 8 minutes, turning to brown on all sides. Place pork on a roasting rack coated with cooking spray; place rack in a roasting pan. Pour remaining 2¼ cups stock in bottom of roasting pan. Roast pork at 400° for 45 minutes or until a thermometer inserted in center registers 138°. Remove pork from pan; let stand 15 minutes. Cut crosswise into 24 slices.

6. Place roasting pan over medium-high heat; add reserved port, thyme sprigs, sage leaves, and shallot; bring to a boil. Cook until liquid reduces to 1 cup (about 10 minutes). Combine flour and 2 tablespoons water in a small bowl, stirring with a whisk. Add flour mixture to port mixture, stirring with a whisk; cook 5 minutes or until port mixture begins to thicken. Add remaining 1 tablespoon butter, stirring until butter melts. Strain sauce; discard solids. Stir in remaining 1 teaspoon chopped sage, remaining ¼ teaspoon salt, and remaining ¼ teaspoon pepper. Serve sauce with pork. Serves 12 (serving size: 2 pork slices and about 1½ tablespoons sauce)

CALORIES 262; **FAT** 10.2g (sat 3.1g, mono 4.1g, poly 1.4g); **PROTEIN** 23.3g; **CARB** 12.6g; **FIBER** 1.2g; **CHOL** 72mg; **IRON** 1.2mg; **SODIUM** 362mg; **CALC** 41mg

Two-Potato Gratin

Hands-on time: 30 min. Total time: 1 hr. 40 min. *A starch lover's delight—layers of baking potatoes and sweet potatoes bathed in a creamy, savory cheese sauce.*

Our secret: *The indulgent "cream" sauce for this gratin is actually a low-fat white sauce made from 2% milk thickened with flour—not a speck of cream or butter in sight. The flavor gets seriously delicious when good aged Gruyère cheese, nutty and salty, melts in. Our gratin is wildly delicious, hitting all those comforting starchy-creamy-cheesy notes, and has roughly half the calories and 83% less saturated fat than a classic gratin.*

2 medium baking potatoes, peeled and cut into ¼-inch-thick slices (about 3 cups)
2 medium sweet potatoes, peeled and cut into ¼-inch-thick slices (about 4 cups)
2 quarts no-salt-added chicken stock (such as Swanson)
2 tablespoons canola oil
3 tablespoons all-purpose flour
2 garlic cloves, crushed
1½ cups 2% reduced-fat milk

2 thyme sprigs
¾ teaspoon kosher salt, divided
¼ teaspoon freshly ground black pepper
3 ounces aged Gruyère cheese, shredded (about ¾ cup)
Cooking spray
2 tablespoons chopped fresh chives, divided
1½ teaspoons chopped fresh thyme
1 ounce fresh Parmigiano-Reggiano cheese, grated (about ¼ cup)

1. Preheat oven to 350°.
2. Place potatoes in a large stock pot; cover with stock. Bring mixture to a boil; cook 4 minutes. Remove from heat. Carefully remove potatoes from pot using a slotted spoon, reserving cooking liquid. Arrange potato slices in a single layer on a jelly-roll pan; set aside. Strain cooking liquid through a fine-mesh sieve over a bowl; reserve 1 cup cooking liquid. Discard solids and remaining cooking liquid.
3. Heat a medium saucepan over medium heat. Add oil to pan. Sprinkle flour over oil; cook 1 minute, stirring constantly with a whisk. Add garlic; cook 2 minutes, stirring frequently. Combine milk and reserved 1 cup cooking liquid. Gradually pour milk mixture into flour mixture in pan, stirring constantly with a whisk. Add thyme sprigs to pan. Bring mixture to a boil; cook 4 minutes or until slightly thick, stirring frequently. Remove from heat. Strain mixture through a fine-mesh sieve over a bowl, reserving sauce; discard solids. Stir ½ teaspoon salt, pepper, and Gruyère cheese into sauce.
4. Spread ½ cup sauce into a broiler-safe 2-quart ceramic baking dish. Arrange a single, flat layer of sweet potato and then baking potato slices over sauce. Over flat layer, alternate baking potato and sweet potato slices, in shingle-like fashion, into dish; sprinkle evenly with remaining ¼ teaspoon salt. Sprinkle potato mixture with 1 tablespoon chives and thyme; pour remaining sauce over potato mixture. Sprinkle with Parmigiano-Reggiano cheese. Bake at 350° for 1 hour or until potatoes are tender when pierced with a knife.
5. Remove gratin from oven. Preheat broiler to high.
6. Place gratin in oven. Broil gratin 3 minutes or until browned. Sprinkle with remaining 1 tablespoon chives. Serves 8.

CALORIES 218; **FAT** 9g (sat 3.5g, mono 3.8g, poly 1.3g); **PROTEIN** 9.3g; **CARB** 25.2g; **FIBER** 2.7g; **CHOL** 18mg; **IRON** 1.2mg; **SODIUM** 339mg; **CALC** 228mg

WHEN YOU START WITH NUTTY-INTENSE GRUYÈRE AND PARMIGIANO-REGGIANO CHEESES, THEN TOSS IN SOME EARTHY SWEET POTATOES, YOU DON'T NEED HEAVY CREAM OR BUTTER TO YIELD A DELICIOUS DISH.

PICK ONE INDULGENT STAR, AND SURROUND IT WITH LOW-FAT EMBELLISHMENTS. HERE, MILKY-OOZY BURRATA BAKES INSIDE CRISP PHYLLO DOUGH AND GETS A BRIGHT FLAVOR BOOST FROM GARLICKY ROASTED TOMATOES.

Baked Burrata

Hands-on time: 19 min. Total time: 9 hr. 29 min. If you can't find burrata, you can use whole-milk mozzarella, though it won't be quite as rich. Serve with toasted bread or crackers.

Our secret: The key with this decadent appetizer is to choose one rich ingredient and keep the other ingredients light. In our updated version of the classic puff pastry-wrapped Brie cheese, the star is burrata, an indulgent cheese that's made up of a thin "skin" of mozzarella encasing a runny center of mozzarella and cream. No need to go heavy with the pastry since the cheese itself is so divine. You'll save about 40% of calories, total fat, and saturated fat.

1 (8-ounce) ball burrata
5 teaspoons olive oil, divided
½ teaspoon chopped fresh thyme
¼ teaspoon kosher salt
¼ teaspoon chopped fresh rosemary
¼ teaspoon freshly ground black pepper
3 large ripe plum tomatoes, halved
2 large garlic cloves, crushed
6 (14 x 9-inch) sheets frozen phyllo dough, thawed
Cooking spray

1. Unwrap burrata; pat dry. Wrap burrata in several layers of plastic wrap to preserve the "ball" shape. Freeze 8 hours or until completely frozen.
2. Preheat oven to 425°.

3. Combine 2 teaspoons oil and next 6 ingredients in a medium bowl; toss to combine. Arrange tomatoes, cut sides up, on a foil-lined baking sheet. Bake at 425° for 40 minutes or until blistered and liquid almost evaporates. Cool. Chop tomato mixture.
4. Reduce oven temperature to 350°.
5. Working with 1 phyllo sheet at a time (cover remaining phyllo to prevent it from drying), lay 1 sheet on a flat surface; lightly coat with cooking spray. Stack another phyllo sheet at a slight angle over the first; lightly coat with cooking spray. Repeat procedure with remaining phyllo and cooking spray, continuing to angle each piece of phyllo slightly over the previous. Using a slotted spoon, spoon tomato mixture in center of phyllo stack; discard any remaining liquid. Unwrap burrata; place frozen burrata on tomato mixture. Fold phyllo edges over to enclose cheese and tomato mixture, pressing to seal. Turn ball over with tomato mixture on top; place on a foil-lined baking sheet coated with cooking spray. Brush phyllo with remaining 1 tablespoon oil. Bake at 350° for 30 minutes. Remove from oven.
6. Preheat broiler to high.
7. Broil cheese ball 2 minutes or until golden brown. Serve immediately. Serves 16 (serving size: about 1½ tablespoons).

CALORIES 68; FAT 4.6g (sat 2.2g, mono 1.8g, poly 0.3g); PROTEIN 2.5g; CARB 2.9g; FIBER 0.2g; CHOL 10mg; IRON 0.2mg; SODIUM 80mg; CALC 81mg

Pan-Fried Oysters with Tangy Crème Fraîche

Hands-on time: 40 min. Total time: 40 min. Place cleaned oyster shells in the oven on the lowest heat setting possible. This will keep them dry and warm, like a little heated plate for each oyster. Shopping tip: Many stores sell a poultry or seafood herb mix that contains both thyme and tarragon, so you purchase just one package.

Our secret: Oysters always feel like a special treat, even when served simply raw and on the half shell. But to make them superindulgent, we embellish with some lavish touches. The oysters get pan-fried in panko breading so they're crispy on the outside, tender and juicy inside. And the oyster liquid is cooked down with wine and herbs to a delicious sauce that's made silky with crème fraîche. A final crown of sparkling fish roe takes this into sexy new territory. A happy portion of three has less than 130 calories.

18 large, fresh oysters in shells
⅔ cup dry white wine
¼ cup chopped shallots
1 tablespoon champagne vinegar or white wine vinegar
2 thyme sprigs
1 tarragon sprig
3 tablespoons crème fraîche
⅔ cup panko (Japanese breadcrumbs)
2 tablespoons canola oil
2¼ teaspoons sustainable American caviar or fish roe
2 teaspoons thyme leaves

1. Preheat oven to 170°.
2. Carefully shuck oysters over a small, heavy saucepan. Sever oyster meat from shells; remove oysters from shells into a fine mesh sieve set over pan, capturing oyster liquor in pan. Place oysters in a small bowl; chill. Discard top halves of shells. Scrape adductor muscle from bottom halves of shells; discard muscle. Scrub bottom halves of shells clean. Arrange bottom halves of shells on a jelly-roll pan; place in oven.

3. Add wine and next 4 ingredients to saucepan with oyster liquor, and cook over medium heat 9 minutes or until reduced to 3 tablespoons. Strain through a fine mesh sieve lined with cheesecloth, and discard solids. Whisk crème fraîche into liquid. Keep warm.

4. Place panko in a shallow dish. Heat a small nonstick skillet over medium-high heat. Add 1 tablespoon oil to pan; swirl to coat. Dredge 9 oysters in panko; shake off excess. Arrange coated oysters in a single layer in pan; sauté 2 minutes on each side or until golden. Remove oysters from pan; place 1 cooked oyster in each of 9 warm shells. Keep warm. Repeat procedure with remaining 1 tablespoon oil, 9 oysters, panko, and shells. Top each oyster with 1½ teaspoons sauce and ⅛ teaspoon caviar. Sprinkle with thyme leaves; serve immediately. Serves 6 (serving size: 3 oysters).

CALORIES 128; **FAT** 8.5g (sat 2.2g, mono 3.1g, poly 1.7g); **PROTEIN** 3.7g; **CARB** 6.6g; **FIBER** 0.2g; **CHOL** 29mg; **IRON** 2.8mg; **SODIUM** 124mg; **CALC** 26mg

MAKE AN ALREADY INDULGENT HEALTHY TREAT EXTRA SPECIAL WITH A COUPLE OF LUXURIOUS TOPPINGS—CRÈME FRAÎCHE SAUCE AND A JEWEL-LIKE GARNISH OF SALTY FISH ROE.

IF YOU'RE GOING TO INDULGE IN CHOCOLATE, AT LEAST MAKE SURE IT'S GOOD. FOR ABOUT THE SAME CALORIES AND SAT FAT AS A GENERIC MINI CANDY BAR, YOU CAN SAVOR THESE DECADENT TWO-BITE CONFECTIONS.

Chocolate-Triple Hazelnut Truffles

Hands-on time: 20 min. Total time: 6 hr. 20 min. Mild milk chocolate allows the triple-hit of nutty goodness to come forward in these creamy truffles. To speed up prep, chill the chocolate mixture for 1 hour or until completely set; let stand at room temperature for 30 minutes to soften before scooping.
***Our secret:** The best way to enjoy chocolate is to indulge in good chocolate. Here, creamy milk chocolate gets a hazelnut kick from Nutella, Frangelico, and the nuts themselves. While you can certainly enjoy two or three truffles without going overboard calorie-wise, we suggest serving one perfect treat on the saucer with a cup of coffee or espresso.*

3 tablespoons hazelnut-chocolate spread (such as Nutella)
2½ tablespoons Frangelico (hazelnut-flavored liqueur)
1 tablespoon light-colored corn syrup
½ teaspoon vanilla extract
Dash of salt
5 ounces milk chocolate, finely chopped
⅓ cup finely chopped salted hazelnuts, toasted

1. Combine first 6 ingredients in the top of a double boiler. Cook over simmering water until chocolate melts (about 2 minutes), stirring constantly. Spoon mixture into a shallow dish. Let stand at room temperature 6 hours or up to overnight.

2. Scoop about 1 tablespoon chocolate mixture with a spoon. Dredge in nuts; roll into balls. Repeat procedure with remaining chocolate mixture and nuts. Serves 21 (serving size: 1 truffle).

CALORIES 79; **FAT** 4g (sat 1.7g, mono 1.4g, poly 0.2g); **PROTEIN** 0.8g; **CARB** 9.8g; **FIBER** 0.4g; **CHOL** 2mg; **IRON** 0.1mg; **SODIUM** 13mg; **CALC** 15mg

BAKING INDIVIDUAL DESSERTS IN A MUFFIN PAN IS A SMART WAY TO PRE-PORTION. EACH SERVING IS STILL FULL OF BIG SWEET-SALTY PLEASURES.

Salted Caramel Cheesecakes

Hands-on time: 40 min. Total time: 4 hr. 40 min. *There's something so special about your own individual dessert. For the biggest impact, sprinkle on a beautiful flake salt at the end; if you don't have that, sea salt will work, too.*

Our secret: *Portion control is perhaps the hardest thing about eating healthfully, especially when the food is so yummy. Here, pre-portioning is key. Single-serving cheesecakes bake in muffin tins, so there's no guesswork about the serving size. Our individual desserts don't feel skimpy, except with their numbers—each has about half the calories and one-fourth the sat fast of a typical (not restaurant-gargantuan) caramel cheesecake.*

30 vanilla wafers
2 tablespoons canola oil
Cooking spray
²/₃ cup packed light brown sugar
²/₃ cup plain fat-free Greek yogurt
12 ounces ¹/₃-less-fat cream cheese, softened
1¹/₂ teaspoons vanilla extract
¹/₈ teaspoon table salt
2 large eggs
¹/₂ cup granulated sugar
2 tablespoons water
1 tablespoon butter
¹/₂ cup evaporated milk
³/₈ teaspoon flake salt

1. Preheat oven to 300°.
2. Place cookies in a food processor; process until finely ground crumbs measure about 1 cup. Add oil; pulse to combine. Coat a 12-cup muffin tin well with cooking spray. Spoon about 1 packed tablespoon crumb mixture into each muffin cup; press crumbs firmly into bottom. Bake at 300° for 7 minutes or until lightly browned. Remove from oven; cool.
3. Wipe food processor clean. Place brown sugar, yogurt, and cream cheese in processor; process until smooth. Add vanilla, table salt, and eggs; process until smooth. Spoon about 3 tablespoons batter into each muffin cup. Bake at 300° for 18 minutes or until center of cheesecakes barely move when pan is touched. Remove pan from oven; cool on a wire rack to room temperature. Cover pan; refrigerate cheesecakes 3 hours or until well chilled.
4. Run a thin knife around outside edge of each cheesecake. Carefully remove cheesecakes from pan; place on a platter. Chill cheesecakes until ready to serve.
5. Combine granulated sugar and 2 tablespoons water in a medium, heavy saucepan over medium-high heat; cook until sugar dissolves, stirring gently as needed to dissolve sugar evenly (about 3 minutes). Continue cooking 12 minutes or until the color of light brown sugar (do not stir). Remove from heat; carefully stir in butter and milk (caramelized sugar will harden and stick to spoon). Place pan over medium-high heat until caramelized sugar melts. Bring to a boil; cook 1 minute. Remove pan from heat; cool caramel to room temperature. Cover and chill 1 hour or until slightly thickened. Spoon about 1 tablespoon caramel over each cheesecake. Sprinkle cheesecakes evenly with flake salt. Serves 12 (serving size: 1 cheesecake).

CALORIES 254; FAT 12.7g (sat 5.5g, mono 4.3g, poly 1.1g); PROTEIN 5.7g; CARB 30.1g; FIBER 0.3g; CHOL 64mg; IRON 0.6mg; SODIUM 256mg; CALC 89mg

Roasted Pine Nut Butter
Indulgent Gift: *Homemade roasted pine nut butter is insanely delicious and easy to make—as well as ridiculously expensive, with pine nuts costing around $35 per pound. You should start with pine nuts toasted to medium-brown, enough to taste deeply roasted. But be careful, as you don't want to burn these pricey guys!*

To make butter, place 1 pound toasted pine nuts in a food processor. Add 1 tablespoon of neutral-flavored oil (canola or peanut oil works nicely) and ¼ teaspoon kosher salt. Process until smooth. This will give you 2 cups of the richest, most wonderful nut butter. Since it's such an indulgent treat, you're OK to give in small quantities—look for little 2- or 3-ounce jars. To the lucky recipients, send a note to hoard this precious gift, and offer serving suggestions, such as smearing a smidge onto good chocolate, dolloping onto butternut squash soup, or elevating the PB&J to new heights by pairing with plum preserves. Serves 32 (serving size: 1 tablespoon).

CALORIES 99; FAT 10.1g (sat 0.7g); SODIUM 15mg

SPLURGE ON AN EXPENSIVE INGREDIENT FOR A SIGNATURE HOLIDAY GIFT YOUR FRIENDS WILL TRULY THANK YOU FOR.

CHRISTMAS MORNING BREAKFAST

Convenient, delicious make-ahead casseroles: a present to both the cook and her family.

Give yourself the well-deserved gift of time: These make-ahead breakfast casseroles can be assembled the day before and refrigerated. Come Christmas morning, all you need to do is heat and serve, leaving you to hang in your jammies and tear open presents while wonderful home-cooked aromas—warm cinnamon and sweet apples, smoky bacon and eggs—fill your home. Recipes like Egg and Hash Brown Casserole give you just about everything you could want in a breakfast, all in one convenient dish. Our zingy winter fruit salad, which only improves upon macerating overnight, makes a great complement to all.

Apple-Stuffed Strata

Hands-on time: 24 min. Total time: 9 hr. 12 min. *Last-minute prep couldn't be simpler in this dish: Just add a dusting of sugar and chopped nuts. Pecans add a little crunch to this fruit-filled casserole.*

2 teaspoons butter
4 cups sliced peeled Golden Delicious apple (about 2 apples)
6 tablespoons granulated sugar, divided
Cooking spray
12 (1-ounce) slices cinnamon-swirl bread (such as Pepperidge Farm), cut in half diagonally
³/₄ cup chopped pecans, divided
1¹/₂ cups 1% low-fat milk
¹/₂ teaspoon ground cinnamon
5 large eggs
1 tablespoon turbinado or granulated sugar

1. Melt butter in a large nonstick skillet over medium-high heat. Add apple and 1 tablespoon granulated sugar to pan; sauté 8 minutes or until apple is tender and lightly browned. Remove from heat; cool 5 minutes.
2. Coat an 11 x 7–inch glass or ceramic baking dish with cooking spray. Arrange half of bread in dish. Spread apple mixture evenly over bread; top evenly with ¹/₂ cup pecans. Arrange remaining bread over pecans.
3. Combine remaining 5 tablespoons granulated sugar, milk, cinnamon, and eggs in a medium bowl, stirring with a whisk. Pour milk mixture over bread, pressing down to submerge. Cover and chill overnight.
4. Preheat oven to 350°.
5. Uncover dish. Sprinkle remaining ¹/₄ cup pecans and turbinado sugar evenly over bread. Bake at 350° for 48 minutes or until a knife inserted in center comes out clean. Serves 8.

CALORIES 337; FAT 15.8g (sat 3.3g, mono 5.7g, poly 2.7g); PROTEIN 11.1g; CARB 40.1g; FIBER 4.5g; CHOL 137mg; IRON 2mg; SODIUM 246mg; CALC 82mg

Pineapple and Orange Salad with Toasted Coconut

Hands-on time: 23 min. Total time: 23 min. *Serve this all-purpose side with any of our casseroles. Assemble the salad the night before, but stir in and sprinkle the coconut just before serving so it retains its texture. Red pepper gives a tiny amount of heat here—omit if you prefer a very mild mix.*

2 cups orange sections (about 4 oranges)
4 sliced peeled kiwifruit
1 (4-pound) pineapple, peeled and cut into 1-inch cubes
1 teaspoon grated lime rind
1 tablespoon fresh lime juice
1 tablespoon fresh orange juice
¹/₈ teaspoon ground red pepper
¹/₂ cup flaked sweetened coconut, toasted and divided

1. Combine first 3 ingredients in a medium bowl. Combine rind and next 3 ingredients in a small bowl. Gently stir lime mixture into fruit mixture; cover and chill.
2. Just before serving, stir ¹/₄ cup coconut into pineapple mixture. Sprinkle with remaining ¹/₄ cup coconut. Serves 8 (serving size: about ³/₄ cup).

CALORIES 140; FAT 1.9g (sat 1.4g, mono 0.1g, poly 0.2g); PROTEIN 1.9g; CARB 32.3g; FIBER 4.8g; CHOL 0mg; IRON 0.6mg; SODIUM 18mg; CALC 59mg

Egg and Hash Brown Casserole

Hands-on time: 35 min. Total time: 9 hr. 10 min. *This dish is like enjoying an omelet stuffed with spinach, gooey Swiss cheese, and mushrooms, with hearty sides of smoky bacon and golden hash browns, all in one convenient package.*

8 center-cut bacon slices
1½ cups chopped onion
8 ounces sliced shiitake mushroom caps
3 garlic cloves, minced
2 cups shredded hash brown potatoes (such as Simply Potatoes)
¼ cup no-salt-added chicken stock (such as Swanson)
5 cups fresh baby spinach
2 tablespoons thinly sliced fresh basil
½ teaspoon kosher salt, divided
½ teaspoon freshly ground black pepper, divided
3 ounces reduced-fat Swiss cheese, finely chopped
Cooking spray
½ cup 1% low-fat milk
6 large eggs, lightly beaten

1. Cook bacon in a large nonstick skillet over medium heat until crisp. Remove bacon from pan; crumble. Increase heat to medium-high. Add onion, mushrooms, and garlic to drippings in pan; sauté 6 minutes. Add potatoes and stock to pan; cook 6 minutes, stirring frequently. Add spinach, basil, ¼ teaspoon salt, and ¼ teaspoon pepper; cook 2 minutes or until spinach wilts. Remove from heat; let stand 10 minutes. Stir in crumbled bacon and cheese. Place mushroom mixture in an 11 x 7–inch broiler-safe glass or ceramic baking dish coated with cooking spray. Cover and refrigerate overnight.
2. Preheat oven to 350°.
3. Uncover dish. Combine remaining ¼ teaspoon salt, remaining ¼ teaspoon pepper, milk, and eggs in a medium

bowl. Pour egg mixture over mushroom mixture. Bake at 350° for 28 minutes.
4. Turn broiler on high; remove dish while broiler heats. Broil 3 minutes or until top is browned and just set. Let stand 5 minutes. Serves 6.

CALORIES 238; FAT 9.5g (sat 4.3g, mono 2.7g, poly 0.9g); PROTEIN 16.9g; CARB 21.3g; FIBER 2.8g; CHOL 199mg; IRON 2mg; SODIUM 618mg; CALC 188mg

Streusel-Topped French Toast Casserole with Fruit Compote

Hands-on time: 35 min. Total time: 9 hr. 35 min. *This dish is guaranteed to make your house smell delicious Christmas morning, fragrant with cinnamon, vanilla, and cider. A deep-dish pie plate works best here; you may need to trim the bread so it fits well. Make sure to use unfiltered cider, which gains velvety body as it reduces.*

1 cup unfiltered apple cider
⅓ cup dried cranberries
¼ cup golden raisins
1 cup fat-free milk
½ cup granulated sugar
1 tablespoon vanilla extract
1¼ teaspoons ground cinnamon, divided
¾ teaspoon kosher salt, divided
4 large eggs, lightly beaten
Cooking spray
8 (1½-ounce) slices sourdough bread, crusts removed (such as Pepperidge Farm)
6 tablespoons all-purpose flour
⅓ cup old-fashioned rolled oats
⅓ cup walnuts, chopped
¼ cup brown sugar
3 tablespoons chilled butter, cut into small pieces

1. Bring cider to a boil in a small saucepan. Cook until reduced to ⅔ cup

(about 4 minutes). Add cranberries and raisins; let stand 10 minutes.
2. Combine milk, granulated sugar, vanilla, ½ teaspoon cinnamon, ½ teaspoon salt, and eggs in a medium bowl, stirring with a whisk.
3. Coat a 9-inch deep-dish pie plate with cooking spray. Line bottom of pan with half of bread slices in a single layer. Pour half of egg mixture over bread; let stand 1 minute. Spread cranberry mixture evenly over bread. Top with remaining bread slices; pour remaining egg mixture over bread. Cover and refrigerate overnight.
4. Combine remaining ¾ teaspoon cinnamon, remaining ¼ teaspoon salt, flour, oats, walnuts, and brown sugar in a small bowl; cut in butter with a pastry blender or 2 knives until mixture resembles coarse meal. Cover and refrigerate overnight.
5. Preheat oven to 350°.
6. Uncover bread mixture and flour mixture. Sprinkle flour mixture evenly over bread mixture. Bake at 350° for 1 hour or until golden brown. Let stand 5 minutes. Cut into 8 wedges. Serves 8.

CALORIES 376; FAT 10.1g (sat 3.8g, mono 2.7g, poly 2.9g); PROTEIN 10.4g; CARB 61.5g; FIBER 2.3g; CHOL 102mg; IRON 2.5mg; SODIUM 492mg; CALC 86mg

Sausage and Polenta Breakfast Casserole

Hands-on time: 25 min. Total time: 9 hr. 15 min. *Andouille sausage and a touch of hot sauce add a little spicy kick to the creamy polenta.*

2 teaspoons olive oil
10 ounces diced chicken andouille sausage
2 cups sliced green onions (about 5)
1 tablespoon chopped fresh thyme
4 garlic cloves, minced
4½ cups fat-free milk

1½ cups uncooked quick-cooking
  polenta
¼ teaspoon salt
4 ounces cheddar cheese, shredded
  (about 1 cup)
1.75 ounces fresh Parmigiano-Reggiano
  cheese, grated (about ⅓ cup)
2 teaspoons hot pepper sauce (such as
  Tabasco)
4 large eggs, beaten
Cooking spray

1. Heat a large nonstick skillet over
medium-high heat. Add oil to pan;
swirl to coat. Add sausage; sauté 3
minutes or until lightly browned.
Add onions, thyme, and garlic; sauté
5 minutes. Remove from heat.
2. Bring milk to a simmer in a large
saucepan over high heat. Reduce
heat to medium-low. Stir in polenta
and salt; simmer 7 minutes, stirring
frequently with a whisk. Remove from
heat. Stir in cheeses, stirring until
cheeses melt. Place polenta mixture
in a large bowl; let stand 15 minutes,
stirring occasionally. Add hot pepper
sauce and eggs; stir well. Add sausage mixture to polenta mixture; stir
to combine. Spread polenta mixture
into an 11 x 7–inch glass or ceramic
broiler-safe baking dish coated with
cooking spray. Cool to room temperature. Cover surface with plastic wrap;
refrigerate overnight.
3. Preheat oven to 425°.
4. Uncover dish. Bake at 425° for 25
minutes or just until set.
5. Turn broiler on high; remove dish
while broiler preheats. Broil 2 minutes
or until top is lightly browned. Let
stand 5 minutes. Serves 8.

CALORIES 339; FAT 12.7g (sat 6g, mono 3.7g, poly 0.7g);
PROTEIN 21.7g; CARB 26.4g; FIBER 3.9g; CHOL 167mg;
IRON 1.8mg; SODIUM 580mg; CALC 418mg

SHARE THE LOVE

MIXING UP A SIGNATURE COCKTAIL

Mixologists from all corners of the country
show you how to blend a jigger of this and
shake of that to yield a coupe of Christmas
cheer.

Haymarket

Hands-on time: 2 min. Total time: 4 min.

Simple syrup:
2 tablespoons sugar
¼ cup water
Cocktail:
1 (1-inch) piece cucumber
2 tablespoons Suze (bitter, French
  liquor)
1½ tablespoons fresh lime juice
3 ounces pale ale (such as Titan's Great
  Divide)
1 slice cucumber

1. To prepare simple syrup, combine
sugar and ¼ cup water in a microwave-
safe dish; microwave at HIGH 2 minutes. Stir until sugar dissolves; cool.
2. To prepare cocktail, place cucumber
piece in a martini shaker; muddle. Add
Suze, juice, and 1½ tablespoons syrup;
reserve remaining syrup for another
use. Cover and shake. Strain mixture
into a highball glass with ice. Top with
beer; garnish with cucumber slice.
Serves 1.

CALORIES 172; FAT 0g; PROTEIN 0.6g; CARB 20.4g;
FIBER 0.1g; CHOL 0mg; IRON 0mg; SODIUM 3mg;
CALC 4mg

The Sun Also Rises Cocktail

Hands-on time: 2 min. Total time: 45 min.

Simple syrup:
2 tablespoons sugar
¼ cup water
Cocktail:
3 ounces Prosecco or other dry
  sparkling wine
1½ tablespoons Plymouth Sloe Gin
1½ tablespoons fresh lemon juice
1½ teaspoons absinthe
3 drops Peychaud's bitters

1. To prepare simple syrup, combine
sugar and ¼ cup water in a microwave-
safe dish; microwave at HIGH 2 minutes. Stir until sugar dissolves; cool.
2. To prepare cocktail, pour sparkling
wine into a Champagne flute. Combine
sloe gin, juice, and absinthe in a martini
shaker with ice; add 1½ teaspoons
simple syrup. Reserve remaining simple
syrup for another use. Shake. Strain
into flute; top with bitters. Serves 1.

CALORIES 168; FAT 0g; PROTEIN 0.1g; CARB 13.1g;
FIBER 0.1g; CHOL 0mg; IRON 0mg; SODIUM 1mg;
CALC 2mg

The G Word

Hands-on time: 5 min. Total time: 5 min.

1½ tablespoons Nardini almond grappa
1½ tablespoons Pages Verveine du
  Velay Extra Liqueur
1½ tablespoons Luxardo Maraschino
  Liqueur
1½ tablespoons fresh lime juice

1. Combine all ingredients in a martini
shaker with ice; shake vigorously.
Strain into a chilled cocktail glass.
Serves 1.

CALORIES 182; FAT 0g; PROTEIN 0.2g; CARB 16.8g;
FIBER 0.1g; CHOL 0mg; IRON 0.1mg; SODIUM 1mg;
CALC 3mg

Pear-Cinnamon Cocktail

Hands-on time: 3 min. Total time: 34 min.

¼ cup sugar
2 tablespoons water
1 cinnamon stick, broken into pieces
2 (1-inch) slices Comice pear
1 ounce Karlsson's Gold Vodka
½ ounce Clear Creek Pear Eau de Vie
¾ ounce fresh lemon juice
Pear slices (optional)

1. Combine sugar, 2 tablespoons water, and cinnamon in a small saucepan over medium heat. Cook 4 minutes, stirring to dissolve sugar. Remove from heat. Let stand 30 minutes; strain. Cover and keep refrigerated in a glass container, 3 to 4 weeks.
2. Place pear slices and ½ ounce cinnamon syrup in a martini shaker; reserve remaining cinnamon syrup for another use. Muddle pear mixture. Add ice, vodka, eau de vie, and lemon juice; shake. Strain into a cocktail glass. Garnish with additional pear slices, if desired. Serves 1.

CALORIES 169; FAT 0g; PROTEIN 0.2g; CARB 19g; FIBER 1g; CHOL 0mg; IRON 0.1mg; SODIUM 1mg; CALC 4mg

---

SHARE THE LOVE

HOST AN APPETIZER SWAP

Four tasty starters for this twist on a classic cookie swap.

The concept is simple: Guests bring enough batches of a festive appetizer to snack and swap before leaving with their favorites complete with recipes for each. It's just like its cookie counterpart, but better for cocktail hour.

Be sure to give guests plenty of notice: Send out invites a month in advance. Have them tell you what they'll bring beforehand to guard against duplicate dishes. Partygoers should print enough copies of their recipe to share: They can make cute recipe cards in a snap at skiptomylou.org/recipe-card-maker. They can also share their recipes online at weeatt.com.

Keep portability in mind, and stick with recipes that can be served—and stand—at room temperature without wilting or withering. Make a couple of batches so there's plenty to both nibble and send home. Guests should bring airtight plastic containers so they can pack up what they want. It's also smart for the host to have extra foil, plastic wrap, and parchment on hand for the occasion.

Apricot-Blue Cheese Angels

Hands-on time: 1 hr. Total time: 1 hr. 15 min. Bake and freeze these bites up to a week in advance. Try a trio of flavors like a fig-jam and goat-cheese filling or finely chopped apples tossed with honey and cinnamon.

1 cup boiling water
1 (7-ounce) package dried apricots, chopped (about 1 cup)
½ cup chopped walnuts, toasted
1 tablespoon honey
2 teaspoons fresh lemon juice
¼ teaspoon ground cinnamon
2 ounces crumbled blue cheese (about ½ cup)
2 sheets frozen puff pastry dough, thawed
1 large egg, lightly beaten

1. Preheat oven to 400°.
2. Combine 1 cup boiling water and apricots in a medium bowl; let stand 10 minutes. Drain in a colander over a bowl, reserving 2 tablespoons soaking liquid. Place apricots, reserved 2 tablespoons soaking liquid, walnuts, honey, juice, and cinnamon in a food processor; pulse until coarsely ground. Add cheese to processor; pulse 3 times or until blended.
3. Place 1 sheet pastry dough on a work surface lightly dusted with flour. Gently roll into a 12½-inch square. Cut dough into 25 (2½-inch) squares. Top each dough piece with about 1 teaspoon apricot mixture. Working with 1 dough piece at a time, bring corners up to center and pinch closed. Place angels on a baking sheet lined with parchment paper. Repeat procedure with remaining dough and apricot mixture, placing formed angels on a second baking sheet lined with parchment paper. Brush each angel evenly with egg. Bake at 400° for 15 minutes or until golden. Serves 25 (serving size: 2 angels).

CALORIES 157; FAT 9.9g (sat 1.7g, mono 2.2g, poly 5.5g); PROTEIN 2.8g; CARB 15.1g; FIBER 1.1g; CHOL 9mg; IRON 0.8mg; SODIUM 85mg; CALC 22mg

Creamy Wild Mushroom and Goat Cheese Cups

***Hands-on time: 40 min. Total time: 40 min.** The filling can be made and refrigerated up to a day in advance, and then brought to room temperature before filling the cups. Phyllo shells come conveniently prebaked, so they're ready to fill once thawed.*

2 tablespoons extra-virgin olive oil
½ cup chopped shallots (about 2 large)
2 tablespoons chopped fresh sage
³⁄₈ teaspoon kosher salt, divided
⅛ teaspoon freshly ground black
  pepper
1 pound exotic mushrooms (such
  as shiitake, cremini, and oyster),
  chopped
1½ tablespoons minced garlic
⅓ cup dry sherry
1 teaspoon lower-sodium soy sauce
3 tablespoons light sour cream
3 tablespoons half-and-half
2 ounces goat cheese (about ¼ cup)
2 (2.1-ounce) packages frozen mini
  phyllo shells (such as Athens),
  thawed
2 tablespoons chopped fresh chives

1. Heat a large nonstick skillet over medium-high heat. Add oil to pan; swirl to coat. Add shallots; sauté 1 minute. Add sage, ¼ teaspoon salt, pepper, and mushrooms; sauté 4 minutes. Add garlic; sauté until mushrooms are lightly browned and liquid almost evaporates (about 5 minutes). Stir in sherry and soy sauce; cook 30 seconds or until liquid almost evaporates. Place mushroom mixture in a medium bowl. Stir in remaining ⅛ teaspoon salt, sour cream, half-and-half, and goat cheese. Spoon about 2 teaspoons mushroom mixture into each phyllo shell. Garnish with chives. Serves 10 (serving size: 3 filled phyllo shells).

CALORIES 139; FAT 8.6g (sat 2.2g, mono 4.5g, poly 0.9g); PROTEIN 3.3g; CARB 10.1g; FIBER 0.5g; CHOL 8mg; IRON 0.5mg; SODIUM 160mg; CALC 38mg

Spicy Avocado Rolls with Ponzu Sauce

***Hands-on time: 57 min. Total time: 57 min.** Crushed wasabi peas give the sushi rolls a pop of color. For milder rolls, use just 1 teaspoon Sriracha.*

1¼ cups uncooked short-grain white
  rice
1⅓ cups water
3 tablespoons rice vinegar
2 teaspoons sugar
2 tablespoons canola mayonnaise
2 teaspoons Sriracha (hot chile sauce,
  such as Huy Fong)
3 tablespoons finely crushed wasabi
  peas
3 tablespoons sesame seeds, toasted
1 tablespoon fresh lemon juice
1 medium-sized ripe peeled avocado,
  cut into 12 slices
3 nori (seaweed) sheets, halved
  crosswise
12 (¼ x 3½-inch) slices red bell pepper
6 (¼ x 7-inch) slices julienne-cut
  English cucumber
¼ cup lower-sodium soy sauce
3 tablespoons fresh orange juice
1½ tablespoons fresh lemon juice
1 teaspoon sugar
1 teaspoon rice vinegar

1. Place rice in a fine mesh sieve. Rinse under cold water, stirring rice until water runs clear (about 1 minute). Combine rice and 1⅓ cups water in a medium saucepan. Bring to a boil over medium-high heat; cover and cook 2 minutes. Reduce heat to low; simmer 5 minutes. Increase heat to high; cook 30 seconds. Remove from heat; let stand, covered, 10 minutes.
2. Combine 3 tablespoons vinegar and 2 teaspoons sugar in a small microwave-safe bowl. Microwave at HIGH 1 minute or until sugar dissolves. Sprinkle vinegar mixture over rice, tossing gently with a wooden spoon. Let stand 10 minutes.

3. Combine mayonnaise and Sriracha in a small bowl. Combine wasabi peas and sesame seeds in a small bowl. Combine 1 tablespoon lemon juice and avocado in a small bowl, tossing gently to coat.
4. Place 1 nori sheet half, shiny side down, on a sushi mat covered with plastic wrap, with long end toward you. Pat about ½ cup rice mixture evenly over entire nori sheet with moist hands. Sprinkle 1 tablespoon wasabi pea mixture evenly over rice. Spread about 1½ teaspoons mayonnaise mixture lengthwise down middle of nori sheet. Arrange 2 avocado pieces, 2 pepper pieces, and 1 cucumber piece over mayonnaise mixture. Using the sushi mat, lift edge of nori closest to you; fold over filling. Continue rolling to top edge; press mat to seal sushi roll. Let rest, seam side down, 5 minutes. Slice crosswise into 8 pieces. Repeat procedure with remaining nori sheet halves, rice, wasabi pea mixture, Sriracha mixture, avocado, pepper, and cucumber.
5. Combine soy sauce and remaining ingredients in a small bowl, stirring with a whisk. Serve sauce with sushi rolls. Serves 12 (serving size: 4 sushi pieces and about 2 teaspoons sauce).

CALORIES 154; FAT 5.7g (sat 0.8g, mono 3.1g, poly 1.3g); PROTEIN 3g; CARB 22.7g; FIBER 2.6g; CHOL 0.8mg; IRON 1.5mg; SODIUM 188mg; CALC 35mg

Sweet and Spicy Nut and Pretzel Mix

Hands-on time: 20 min. Total time: 34 min. *Make sure to set a timer to remind you of the nuts toasting in the oven.*

3 tablespoons brown sugar
2 teaspoons chopped fresh thyme, divided
3/4 teaspoon kosher salt
1/2 teaspoon ground cinnamon
1/4 to 1/2 teaspoon ground red pepper
1/2 cup pecans
1/2 cup blanched almonds
1 1/2 tablespoons butter
3 cups tiny unsalted pretzels
1 cup crispy rice cereal squares (such as Rice Chex)
2 tablespoons maple syrup

1. Preheat oven to 350°.
2. Combine sugar, 1 teaspoon thyme, salt, cinnamon, and pepper in a small bowl.
3. Combine pecans and almonds on a jelly-roll pan. Bake at 350° for 10 minutes or until nuts begin to brown. Combine pecan mixture and butter in a medium bowl, stirring until butter melts. Gently stir in pretzels, cereal, and syrup. Sprinkle sugar mixture evenly over pretzel mixture; toss gently to coat. Spread pretzel mixture in a single layer on jelly-roll pan. Bake at 350° for 10 minutes, stirring once. Sprinkle with remaining 1 teaspoon thyme. Cool completely. Serves 16 (serving size: about 1/3 cup).

CALORIES 142; **FAT** 5.5g (sat 1.1g, mono 2.9g, poly 1.3g); **PROTEIN** 3.1g; **CARB** 21.4g; **FIBER** 0.9g; **CHOL** 3mg; **IRON** 0.9mg; **SODIUM** 156mg; **CALC** 26mg

SHARE THE LOVE

A LITTLE BIT OF LOVE IN A JAR

Make an introduction and leave an impression with this velvety-rich spread.

Cranberry Curd

Hands-on time: 35 min. Total time: 1 hr. 35 min.

Like a rich cream, soft and silky, curd is a decadent treat. Tart-fresh cranberries are mellowed with the sweet notes of sugar, a touch of butter, and a hint of Grand Marnier. This recipe makes about 2 1/2 cups and can easily be doubled, but your curd will take longer to thicken. Fill decorative little glass jars, seal, and share with friends.

1/2 cup water
2 tablespoons fresh lemon juice
1 (12-ounce) package fresh cranberries
2/3 cup granulated sugar
1/4 cup packed brown sugar
2 tablespoons unsalted butter, softened
2 large egg yolks
1 large egg
1 1/2 teaspoons cornstarch
1/8 teaspoon salt
1 tablespoon Grand Marnier (orange-flavored liqueur)

1. Combine first 3 ingredients in a medium saucepan; bring to a boil. Reduce heat; simmer 5 minutes or until cranberries pop. Place cranberry mixture in a blender or food processor; process until smooth. Strain cranberry mixture through a fine sieve over a bowl; discard solids.
2. Combine sugars and butter in a bowl; beat with a mixer at medium speed until well combined. Add egg yolks and egg, 1 at a time, beating well after each addition. Stir in cranberry mixture,

cornstarch, and salt. Place mixture in the top of a double boiler. Cook over simmering water until a thermometer registers 160° and mixture thickens (about 10 minutes), stirring frequently. Remove from heat; let stand 5 minutes. Stir in liqueur. Cover and chill. Serves 20 (serving size: 2 tablespoons).

CALORIES 67; **FAT** 1.9g (sat 1g, mono 0.6g, poly 0.2g); **PROTEIN** 0.7g; **CARB** 12.1g; **FIBER** 0.8g; **CHOL** 35mg; **IRON** 0.2mg; **SODIUM** 20mg; **CALC** 8mg

SHARE THE LOVE

LEARN A NEW HOLIDAY DISH: TAMALES

Set aside a weekend to catch up with a loved one and cook up a batch together.

In Texas, tamales are as much a part of Christmas as trees, wreaths, and, well, presents, which is a result of the state's proximity to Mexico. Especially in West Texas, borders are just lines on a map. And across these lines Mexican, American, New Mexican, and Texan influences blend naturally and easily, especially at the table.

For thousands of years, tamales have been prepared roughly the same way: A moistened corn masa mixture is pressed into a husk or leaf of some sort, filled with spiced bits of meat, sealed, and cooked. A time-consuming task, no doubt, but well worth the effort. It's a labor of love that's all the better if you have helping hands in the kitchen, which makes fun of the work and makes preparation faster.

If you're casting about for just the right gift for friends and family on your list this year, consider tackling the challenge of tamale making. Gather a group of friends or loved ones (there are even jobs for kids!), roll up your sleeves, and dive into this centuries-old tradition.

Chipotle Pork Tamales with Cilantro-Lime Créma

Hands-on time: 1 hr. Total time: 4 hr. 55 min. Although the flavor and texture are optimal immediately out of the oven, you can make these delicious little bundles up to a month ahead. Prepare, assemble, and steam them, cool, and freeze in an airtight container. The best way to reheat is to steam the tamales again briefly just until heated. If pressed for time, you can also wrap the frozen tamales in a damp cloth and microwave.

Créma:
3 tablespoons chopped fresh cilantro
2 tablespoons no-salt-added chicken stock (such as Swanson)
1 tablespoon fresh lime juice
¼ teaspoon salt
1 (8-ounce) container light sour cream
1 large garlic clove, minced
Filling:
1 tablespoon olive oil
1 (3-pound) Boston butt (pork shoulder roast), trimmed
½ teaspoon kosher salt
1 cup chopped onion
9 smashed garlic cloves
1 teaspoon cumin seeds, toasted
6 canned chipotles chile peppers (packed in adobo), chopped
1 cup no-salt-added chicken stock (such as Swanson)
1 teaspoon grated orange zest
1 teaspoon unsweetened cocoa powder
¼ teaspoon ground coffee

Masa:
2½ cups unsalted chicken stock (such as Swanson)
2 ancho chiles
1 cup fresh or frozen corn kernels, thawed
4 cups instant masa harina
1¼ teaspoons salt
1½ teaspoons baking powder
½ cup chilled lard
Remaining ingredient:
Dried corn husks

1. To make créma, combine first 6 ingredients in a small bowl, stirring well. Chill until ready to serve.
2. Preheat oven to 300°.
3. To prepare filling, heat a Dutch oven over medium-high heat. Add oil to pan; swirl to coat. Sprinkle pork evenly with ½ teaspoon salt. Add pork to pan; sauté 10 minutes, turning to brown on all sides. Remove pork from pan. Add onion and garlic; sauté 3 minutes, stirring occasionally. Stir in cumin and chipotle chiles; sauté 1 minute. Stir in 1 cup stock and next 3 ingredients; bring to a boil. Return pork to pan; cover. Bake at 300° for 3 hours or until pork is fork-tender. Remove pork from pan; let stand 10 minutes. Shred pork with two forks. Return pork to sauce; keep warm.
3. Increase oven temperature to 450°.
4. To prepare masa, combine 2½ cups stock and ancho chiles in a microwave-safe bowl. Microwave at HIGH 2 minutes or until chiles are tender; cool slightly. Remove stems from chiles. Place hot stock, chiles, and corn in a blender; process until smooth. Lightly spoon masa harina into dry measuring cups; level with a knife. Combine masa harina, 1¼ teaspoons salt, and baking powder, stirring well with a whisk. Cut in lard with a pastry blender or two knives until mixture resembles coarse meal. Add ancho mixture to masa mixture; stir until a soft dough forms. Turn dough out onto a lightly floured surface; knead dough until smooth and pliable. (If dough is dry and crumbly, add water, 1 tablespoon at a time, until a moist dough forms.)
5. To prepare tamales, immerse corn husks in water; weight with a plate. Soak 30 minutes; drain.
6. Working with 1 husk at a time (or overlap 2 small husks to allow enough space), place about 3 tablespoons masa mixture in center of husk, about 1 inch from top of husk; press dough into a 4-inch-long by 3-inch-wide rectangle. Spoon about 1 heaping tablespoon pork mixture down one side of dough. Using corn husk as your guide, fold husk over tamale, being sure to cover filling with dough; use husk to seal masa around filling. Tear 3 or 4 corn husks lengthwise into strips; tie ends of tamale with strips. Place tamale, seam side down, on rack of a broiler pan lined with a damp towel. Repeat procedure with remaining husks, masa mixture, and pork mixture. Cover filled tamales with another damp towel. Pour 2 cups hot water in bottom of a broiler pan; top with prepared rack.
7. Steam tamales at 450° for 25 minutes. Remove and rewet top towel; add 1 cup water to bottom of pan. Turn tamales over; top with damp cloth. Bake an additional 20 minutes or until set. Let tamales stand 10 minutes. Serve with créma. Serves 14 (serving size: 2 tamales and about 2½ teaspoons créma).

CALORIES 374; FAT 17.3g (sat 6g, mono 6.9g, poly 1.8g); PROTEIN 23.6g; CARB 32.5g; FIBER 4g; CHOL 72mg; IRON 3.8mg; SODIUM 516mg; CALC 120mg

READY, SET, DOUGH

The ultimate holiday gift: an afternoon sans little ones.

Deb Wise, *Cooking Light's* resident expert baker, is also a friend and grandmother extraordinaire. Grand Deb, as she's known to Nyya, her precious 18-month-old grandchild, has a holiday gift tradition that's worth sharing. "If you really want to give a thoughtful gift, give your family, friends, and neighbors an afternoon off," says Deb. Did we mention Deb's also a genius?

Each year she invites family and neighborhood children into her home for a holiday cookie- and treat-baking bonanza, organized with military precision, of course. The length of time she'll have the little helpers determines her approach to preparing for the day. Either way, it's (minimally) controlled chaos, "so just be ready," Deb cautions.

The first scenario: Mom just needs a couple of hours for Santa detail or to pamper herself. This instance requires the most pre-planning and work ahead. "With limited time, you don't want to leave anything to chance: Have everything done and ready for the kids to get right down to business," Deb advises. She has batches of dough prepared ahead and chilled, so the children can roll up their sleeves and get busy right away. "It's also important, especially with younger tikes, to avoid hot pans and too much downtime," so she makes a couple of batches of cookies and cupcakes, which she has at ready for decorating. "I just put out buckets of frosting and give each child a few little Dixie cups, craft sticks, and food coloring paste, so they can all mix their favorite colors." And finally, have plenty of decorations: bowls of holiday candies, sprinkles, colored sugar, and anything else you like. And let the kids have at it. If you want to be really organized, purchase small cellophane bags and pretty ribbon from a craft store, and you can let the children wrap up their masterpieces to take home.

Less work, more time scenario: "If you have the whole afternoon, you don't have to do as much work ahead," says Deb. Sometimes, especially with older children, you can let the children do all the work, from start to finish. This option means you'll have to plan for downtime, though, so Deb fills in the gaps with mugs of hot cocoa, children's Christmas movies, and sometimes a holiday sing-along.

Mini Almond Cupcakes

Hands-on time: 33 min. Total time: 46 min. If you're preparing these tasty little cupcakes for an adult gathering, they look beautiful with simple white frosting and a light sprinkling of sparkly sugar. You can also get fancy with a garnish of sugared rosemary or introduce a pop of color by scattering pomegranate arils atop the mini cakes. For children, use colored food paste to tint the frosting—this preserves the nice texture of the frosting.

Cupcakes:

2¹/₂ ounces almond paste
¹/₃ cup sugar
1 large egg white
¹/₄ cup 2% reduced-fat milk
2 tablespoons canola oil
3 ounces all-purpose flour (about ²/₃ cup)
1 teaspoon baking powder
¹/₄ teaspoon salt
Baking spray with flour (such as Baker's Joy)

Icing:

2 ounces ¹/₃-less-fat cream cheese, at room temperature
1 tablespoon butter, softened
1 cup powdered sugar
¹/₄ teaspoon vanilla extract
Dash of salt

1. Preheat oven to 350°.

2. To prepare cupcakes, place almond paste and sugar in a medium bowl. Beat at medium speed until mixture is sandy, about 2 minutes. Add egg white; beat 1 minute or until well combined. Add milk and oil; beat 1 minute or until well combined.

3. Weigh or lightly spoon flour into dry measuring cups; level with a knife. Combine flour, baking powder, and ¼ teaspoon salt, stirring with a whisk. Add flour mixture to almond mixture; beat at low speed 1 minute or until combined. Divide batter evenly among 24 miniature muffin cups coated with baking spray (a scant 2 teaspoons batter per muffin cup). Bake at 350° for 8 minutes or until a wooden pick inserted in center comes out clean. Cool in pan 5 minutes on a wire rack. Remove from pan; cool completely on wire rack.

4. To prepare icing place cream cheese and butter in a bowl; beat with a mixer at medium speed until smooth, about 2 minutes. Add remaining ingredients; beat 2 minutes or until well combined and smooth. Tint frosting, if desired. Top each cupcake with about 1½ teaspoons icing. Serves 12 (serving size: 2 cupcakes).

CALORIES 158; **FAT** 6.1g (sat 1.7g, mono 2.8g, poly 1.1g); **PROTEIN** 2.1g; **CARB** 24.4g; **FIBER** 0.5g; **CHOL** 6mg; **IRON** 0.4mg; **SODIUM** 128mg; **CALC** 41mg

Madeleines

Hands-on time: 20 min. Total time: 2 hrs. *A wonderful year-round recipe takes on a holiday guise when you bake the batter in Christmas-themed cookie mold pans. If using dark, nonstick pans, start checking a minute sooner than you would with an aluminum pan. You can make the batter up to 24 hours in advance and let it chill until you're ready to make the Madeleines.*

¾ cup sugar
2 teaspoons fresh lemon juice
1 teaspoon vanilla extract
¼ teaspoon salt
2 large eggs
2 large egg whites
6 ounces cake flour (about 1½ cups)
⅓ cup butter, melted and cooled
Baking spray with flour (such as Baker's Joy)
3 tablespoons powdered sugar

1. Combine first 6 ingredients in a large bowl. Beat with a mixer at medium speed 5 minutes or until thick and pale. Sift flour over egg mixture, ½ cup at a time; fold in. Fold in butter. Cover and refrigerate at least 1 hour.
2. Preheat oven to 350°.
3. Spoon 2 teaspoons batter into each of 12 madeleine molds coated with baking spray. Bake at 350° for 8 minutes or until golden around edges. Cool in pan on a wire rack 2 minutes. Remove from pan and cool completely on wire rack. Repeat procedure twice with remaining batter to yield 36 Madeleines. Dust Madeleines with powdered sugar. Serves 18 (serving size: 2 Madeleines).

CALORIES 112; **FAT** 3.9g (sat 2.3g, mono 1.1g, poly 0.3g); **PROTEIN** 1.9g; **CARB** 17.3g; **FIBER** 0.2g; **CHOL** 29mg; **IRON** 0.8mg; **SODIUM** 71mg; **CALC** 6mg

Gingerbread People

Hands-on time: 29 min. Total time: 1 hr. 12 min. *Our recipe calls to decorate the cookies with white piping icing. If you want to dress the cookies up, use mini chocolate or red hot candies for buttons and currants for eyes. Of course, if you opt to decorate with candies or dried fruit, press those into the dough cut-outs before they're baked.*

Cookies:
11¼ ounces all-purpose flour (about 2½ cups)
1 tablespoon ground ginger
1 teaspoon baking soda
¼ teaspoon ground cinnamon
¼ teaspoon salt
¾ cup packed dark brown sugar
½ cup butter, at room temperature
¼ cup golden cane syrup (such as Lyle's Golden Syrup)
2 tablespoons molasses
1 large egg
Icing:
½ cup powdered sugar
2 teaspoons 2% reduced-fat milk

1. To prepare cookies, weigh or lightly spoon flour into dry measuring cups; level with a knife. Combine flour, ginger, baking soda, cinnamon, and salt, stirring with a whisk.
2. Place brown sugar and butter in a bowl. Beat with a mixer at medium speed 2 minutes or until light and fluffy. Add cane syrup, molasses, and egg, and beat 1 minute or until well combined. Add flour mixture; beat on low speed 1 minute or until just combined. Gently press mixture into a disc; wrap in plastic wrap. Chill 30 minutes.
3. Preheat oven to 350°.
4. Divide dough in half. Roll each portion of dough to a ⅛-inch-thickness on a lightly floured work surface; cut with 5-inch gingerbread cutters to form 26 cookies. (Reroll scraps, as necessary.) Place cookies 1 inch apart on a baking sheet covered with parchment paper. Bake at 350° for 8 minutes or until lightly browned. Let cool on baking sheet 5 minutes. Remove cookies from baking sheet; cool completely on a wire rack.
5. To prepare icing, combine powdered sugar and milk, stirring with a whisk until smooth. Spoon mixture into a small zip-top plastic bag. Snip a tiny hole off one corner of the bag. Pipe icing onto cookies as desired. Serves 26 (serving size: 1 cookie).

CALORIES 124; **FAT** 3.8g (sat 2.3g, mono 1g, poly 0.2g); **PROTEIN** 1.6g; **CARB** 22.1g; **FIBER** 0.4g; **CHOL** 16mg; **IRON** 0.8mg; **SODIUM** 112mg; **CALC** 13mg

GOLDEN CANE SYRUP ADDS CARAMEL FLAVOR AND MAKES TENDER COOKIES. LOOK FOR IT ON THE BAKING AISLE AT MOST SUPERMARKETS.

CREAMY SOUPS

Creamy soups are a snap to make delicious when saturated fat and calories are not a concern. Take away the magic weapons—butter and heavy cream—and you'll have to get a bit more creative to turn out similarly silky soups with the same gorgeous mouthfeel and comforting flavor as the traditional standards. Good news: We know the route to healthy, satisfying results. And we're sharing. Start with your favorite veggies, and follow our three simple steps to success.

Curried Butternut Squash Soup with Toasted Coconut

Hands-on time: 23 min. Total time: 1 hr. 18 min. *This red curry–spiced soup makes a delicious prelude to any meal of roasted meat, or pair it with a hearty salad or sandwich for a main.*

1 (2½-pound) butternut squash, peeled, seeded, and cut into 2-inch cubes
4 teaspoons canola oil, divided
¾ teaspoon kosher salt, divided
1 cup chopped onion
3 cups no-salt-added chicken stock (such as Swanson)
4 teaspoons red curry paste
1½ tablespoons fresh lime juice
1 (13.5-ounce) can light coconut milk
¼ cup cilantro leaves
¼ cup flaked unsweetened coconut, toasted
2 small Thai red chiles, thinly sliced

1. Preheat oven to 450°.
2. Line a rimmed baking sheet with parchment paper. Place squash in a bowl; drizzle with 1 tablespoon oil. Sprinkle with ¼ teaspoon salt; toss. Arrange on prepared baking sheet. Bake at 450° for 35 minutes or until golden and tender.
3. Heat remaining 1 teaspoon oil in a large saucepan over medium heat; swirl to coat. Add onion; cook 5 minutes, stirring occasionally. Add squash mixture, stock, and curry paste. Sprinkle with remaining ½ teaspoon salt; bring to a boil. Reduce heat, and simmer 15 minutes, stirring occasionally. Remove from heat; stir in lime juice and coconut milk. Let stand 15 minutes.
4. Place half of squash mixture in a blender; blend until smooth. Pour soup into a bowl. Repeat. Divide soup among 8 bowls; top with cilantro, coconut, and chile slices. Serves 8 (serving size: about ¾ cup soup, 1½ teaspoons cilantro, 1½ teaspoons coconut, and ¼ chile).

CALORIES 127; FAT 4.3g (sat 1.8g, mono 1.5g, poly 0.8g); PROTEIN 4g; CARB 21g; FIBER 3.7g; CHOL 0mg; IRON 1.4mg; SODIUM 284mg; CALC 83mg

KITCHEN TIP: LINE YOUR BAKING SHEET WITH PARCHMENT PAPER FOR QUICK AND EASY CLEANUP.

Spiced Beet and Carrot Soup

Hands-on time: 16 min. Total time: 1 hr. 26 min. *This entrée soup is tart, just sweet enough, and hearty, though not a protein powerhouse. To pump up the protein, increase the walnuts or serve with a substantial salad of greens, nuts, and some tangy goat cheese.*

1 pound small red beets, peeled and quartered
½ pound large carrots, peeled and halved lengthwise
2½ teaspoons olive oil, divided
¼ teaspoon salt
1½ cups diced peeled apple
¾ cup chopped yellow onion
½ teaspoon garam masala
2 cups organic vegetable broth
2 cups water
1½ teaspoons fresh lemon juice
¾ cup plain 2% reduced-fat Greek yogurt
½ cup chopped walnuts, toasted
⅓ cup watercress

1. Preheat oven to 400°.

2. Line a rimmed baking sheet with parchment paper. Place beets and carrots in a bowl. Drizzle with 1½ teaspoons oil; sprinkle with ¼ teaspoon salt. Toss. Arrange vegetables on prepared pan. Bake at 400° for 40 minutes or until tender, stirring once. Remove from oven; cool slightly. Cut beets and carrots into 1-inch pieces.

3. Heat a Dutch oven over medium heat. Add remaining 1 teaspoon oil; swirl to coat. Add apple, onion, and garam masala to pan; cook 1½ minutes. Add beet mixture, broth, and 2 cups water; bring to a boil. Reduce heat, and simmer 30 minutes. Remove from heat; let stand 15 minutes.

4. Place half of beet mixture in a blender; blend until smooth. Pour soup into a bowl. Repeat. Stir in lemon juice. Ladle about 1¼ cups soup into each of 4 bowls; top each serving with 3 tablespoons yogurt, 2 tablespoons walnuts, and about 1 tablespoon watercress. Serves 4.

CALORIES 247; FAT 12.3g (sat 1.8g, mono 3.2g, poly 6.4g); PROTEIN 8.4g; CARB 29.5g; FIBER 6.8g; CHOL 3mg; IRON 1.6mg; SODIUM 577mg; CALC 91mg

CREAMY SOUP BASICS

1. Roast veggies at high heat so they develop lovely golden edges and intensely delicious flavor.

2. Build nuanced layers in the soup by starting with a flavorful base. Turn to healthier options, like unsalted cooking stock—our new favorite ingredient—to impart depth without adding unwanted saturated fat and calories and excess sodium.

3. If you have time, let the soup stand off the heat for about 15 minutes to cool slightly before pureeing. In a pinch, pour the hot mixture straight in the blender, remove the round cap on the lid, cover with a clean kitchen towel, and blend away.

RECIPE MAKEOVER

A FRESH TAKE ON FRUITCAKE

We trade in the brightly candied, doorstopper cake for a tasty treat made with real fruit, whole grains, and lots of love.

There's a love-hate relationship that exists with the unforgettable neon-colored, brandy-soaked holiday treat we all know as fruitcake. Each year, the arrival of this classic reveals a range of emotions, from pure, genuine excitement, to complete and total dread—a tradition either way. Heavily packed with candied and dried fruits, nuts, and a stick or two of butter, there's more reason than just bright-green cherries and a never-ending shelf life to avoid this brick of a cake, packed with more than 575 calories and 17 grams of fat.

This season, we thought we'd bake up a cake that's both lighter (in calories and heft) and tastier than the original—something for everyone to enjoy. Candied fruit, heavily sugared and expensive, gets swapped for a combo of fresh fruit, dates, golden raisins, and tart dried cherries. Wholewheat flour, citrus zest, and a trio of spices build a warm, hearty base, while low-fat buttermilk and the bright, crisp flavor of apple brandy keeps our cake moist. A light glaze of brandy, brown sugar, and butter is just icing on the cake—a rich treat with nearly 300 fewer calories than the original. We've turned this foodie faux pas into a new family favorite—and a gift you'll be proud to share.

Fruitcake

Hands-on time: 25 min. Total time: 2 hr. *This cake uses a combination of fresh pears and apples, and dried fruit soaked in Calvados. For a less pronounced apple flavor, substitute regular brandy.*

½ cup dried tart cherries
½ cup chopped pitted dates
⅓ cup golden raisins
¾ cup Calvados (apple brandy), divided
5.6 ounces unbleached all-purpose flour (about 1¼ cups)
4.75 ounces whole-wheat flour (about 1 cup)
1 teaspoon baking powder
¾ teaspoon ground cinnamon
½ teaspoon baking soda
½ teaspoon salt
¼ teaspoon ground nutmeg
¼ teaspoon allspice
5 tablespoons butter, divided
2 tablespoons canola oil
½ cup granulated sugar
¾ cup packed brown sugar, divided
2 large eggs
1 large egg white
1 teaspoon grated peeled fresh ginger
½ teaspoon grated orange rind
⅔ cup low-fat buttermilk
½ cup chopped peeled Pink Lady apple
½ cup chopped peeled pear
½ cup chopped pecans, toasted
Baking spray with flour (such as Baker's Joy)

1. Preheat oven to 350°.
2. Combine first 3 ingredients and ½ cup brandy in a medium glass bowl. Microwave at HIGH 2 minutes, stirring after 1 minute. Set aside.
3. Weigh or lightly spoon flours into dry measuring cups; level with a knife. Combine flours and next 6 ingredients in a bowl, stirring well with a whisk.
4. Place 4 tablespoons butter, oil, granulated sugar, and ½ cup brown sugar in a large bowl; beat with a mixer at medium speed until well blended. Add eggs and egg white, one at a time, beating well after each addition. Add ginger and orange rind; beat 30 seconds or until well blended. Add flour mixture and buttermilk alternately to sugar mixture, beginning and ending with flour mixture. Fold in cherry mixture, apple, pear, and pecans.
5. Spoon batter into a 10-inch tube pan coated with baking spray; smooth top with a spatula. Bake at 350° for 50 minutes or until a wooden pick inserted in center comes out clean. Cool in pan 20 minutes on a wire rack. Remove from pan; cool completely on wire rack.
6. Combine remaining ¼ cup brandy, remaining ¼ cup brown sugar, and remaining 1 tablespoon butter in a small saucepan over medium heat; bring to a boil. Cook 2 minutes or until reduced to ¼ cup, stirring frequently. Drizzle over cake. Serves 16 (serving size: 1 slice).

CALORIES 283; FAT 8.9g (sat 2.9g, mono 3.7g, poly 1.6g); PROTEIN 4.2g; CARB 42.4g; FIBER 2.8g; CHOL 33mg; IRON 1.3mg; SODIUM 202mg; CALC 59mg

THE CLASSIC	THE MAKEOVER
574 calories per serving	283 calories per serving
17 grams total fat	8.9 grams total fat
8 grams saturated fat	2.9 grams saturated fat

MAD FOR MEATBALLS

Our kid in the kitchen wins over her picky brother.

We asked Matisse Reid, our favorite 11-year-old foodie, to shape some meatballs. Here's her report.

—Phoebe Wu

"I was really excited to make these meatballs because my most favorite meat in the world is lamb. And lamb with mint? Even better! This recipe was really easy to make, and we already had most of the ingredients on hand. To mix the ingredients together, wash your hands and dig in; or, if you aren't comfortable with touching raw meat, you can wear plastic disposable gloves. The tomato sauce for this recipe is really good and is spiced (not spicy!), so I think you will love it as much as I did. The meatballs were flavorful enough without the sauce, too. My family could not resist the smell while I was cooking and all piled into the kitchen. Next time, I will double the recipe because it was gobbled up in no time!"

MATISSE'S TIP: YOUNGER KIDS CAN USE KITCHEN SCISSORS TO CUT THE MINT.

Meatballs with Spiced Tomato Sauce

Hands-on time: 18 min. Total time: 50 min. Make fresh breadcrumbs from an extra pita round. To serve, you can stuff meatballs into the pita halves or simply arrange the bread alongside for dipping.

1 tablespoon olive oil
2 tablespoons finely chopped onion
1 teaspoon minced fresh garlic
1/2 cup fresh breadcrumbs
1/4 cup chopped fresh mint
1/2 pound ground lamb
1/2 pound 90% lean ground beef
1 teaspoon kosher salt, divided
1/2 teaspoon freshly ground black pepper, divided
1 large egg, lightly beaten
1/2 cup chopped onion
1 teaspoon ground ginger
1 teaspoon ground cumin
1 teaspoon ground cinnamon
1 (15-ounce) can crushed tomatoes
1/4 cup water
3 (6-inch) whole-wheat pitas, halved and warmed
Small mint leaves

1. Heat a large skillet over medium-high heat. Add oil to pan; swirl to coat. Add finely chopped onion and garlic; cook 1 minute, stirring constantly. Cool slightly. Remove onion mixture from heat; cool slightly. Combine onion mixture, breadcrumbs, and mint in a large bowl; add lamb, beef, 1/2 teaspoon salt, 1/4 teaspoon pepper, and egg; stir gently to combine. Shape meat mixture into 30 (1-inch) meatballs.

2. Return pan to medium-high heat; add meatballs. Cook 4 minutes, turning to brown on all sides. Remove meatballs from pan; set aside. Add chopped onion to pan, and sauté 2 minutes. Add ginger, cumin, cinnamon, and crushed tomatoes, and simmer 5 minutes. Stir in 1/4 cup water, remaining 1/2 teaspoon salt, and remaining 1/4 teaspoon pepper. Return meatballs to pan; simmer 20 minutes or until done. Serve with pitas. Sprinkle with mint leaves. Serves 6 (serving size: 1 pita half and 5 meatballs).

CALORIES 339; **FAT** 14.9g (sat 5.2g, mono 6.4g, poly 1.7g); **PROTEIN** 20.7g; **CARB** 32.3g; **FIBER** 4.9g; **CHOL** 78mg; **IRON** 3.6mg; **SODIUM** 708mg; **CALC** 55mg

THE VERDICT

FRAANZ (AGE 8)
He usually doesn't eat lamb, but I didn't tell him the meatballs had lamb in them. Shhh—don't say anything. **10/10**

KALANI (AGE 14)
Wow! Now that is saying something, coming from him. **10/10**

MATISSE
I love the way the lamb and mint flavors marry together. The smell of these cooking reminded me of a Sunday roast. **10/10**

MATISSE'S TIP: USE A SMALL ICE-CREAM SCOOP TO MAKE SURE ALL THE MEATBALLS ARE THE SAME SIZE.

SUPERFAST

Hearty seafood stew, curry-spiced soup, steak with creamy polenta, and other comforting dishes for a delicious end to the year.

Quick & Easy
Halibut and Chorizo Stew with Garlic Toasts

Firm-fleshed halibut works best in this stew, but cod would also be a tasty, more delicate, choice.

2 teaspoons olive oil, divided
2 ounces Spanish chorizo sausage, diced
1 cup chopped onion
3 garlic cloves, sliced
1/2 cup dry sherry
1/2 cup fat-free, lower-sodium chicken broth
1 1/2 tablespoons chopped fresh flat-leaf parsley
1/4 teaspoon kosher salt
1/4 teaspoon freshly ground black pepper
1 (28-ounce) can no-salt-added diced tomatoes, drained
1 (15-ounce) can no-salt-added chickpeas (garbanzo beans), rinsed and drained
4 (5-ounce) skinless halibut fillets
4 (1/2-ounce) slices ciabatta bread
1 garlic clove, halved

1. Preheat broiler to high.
2. Heat a large sauté pan over medium heat. Add 1 teaspoon oil to pan; swirl to coat. Add chorizo; sauté 3 minutes or until lightly browned. Add onion; sauté 3 minutes or until just tender. Add sliced garlic; sauté 1 minute. Add sherry; cook 1 1/2 minutes, stirring to scrape up browned bits. Stir in broth and next 5 ingredients; stir to combine. Nestle halibut fillets into stew; spoon tomato mixture over fillets. Cover and simmer 5 minutes or until fish flakes easily with a fork or desired degree of doneness.
3. Place ciabatta slices on a baking sheet. Broil 1 minute or until toasted. Brush toasts with remaining 1 teaspoon oil; rub toasts with cut sides of halved garlic clove. Serve toasts with stew. Serves 4 (serving size: 1 fillet, about 1 1/4 cups stew, and 1 toast).

Sustainable Choice *Choose wild-caught Pacific halibut for the most sustainable choice. Avoid Atlantic halibut.*

CALORIES 422; FAT 12.4g (sat 2.9g, mono 5.8g, poly 1.8g); PROTEIN 39.2g; CARB 31.2g; FIBER 4.8g; CHOL 58mg; IRON 3.8mg; SODIUM 702mg; CALC 126mg

Quick & Easy
Skirt Steak with Gorgonzola Polenta

Serve this dish with blanched haricots verts or a mixed greens salad.

2 cups plus 1 tablespoon fat-free, lower-sodium chicken broth, divided
1 cup 2% reduced-fat milk
2/3 cup quick-cooking polenta
1 ounce Gorgonzola cheese, crumbled (about 1/4 cup)
1/2 teaspoon kosher salt, divided
1/2 teaspoon freshly ground black pepper, divided
Cooking spray
1 pound skirt steak, trimmed and cut into 4 pieces
1 teaspoon unsalted butter
1 tablespoon finely chopped shallots
1/2 cup dry red wine
1 teaspoon chopped fresh thyme
1 1/2 teaspoons honey
1/4 teaspoon cornstarch

1. Combine 2 cups broth and milk in a medium saucepan over medium heat; bring to a boil. Gradually whisk polenta into broth mixture, stirring constantly. Reduce heat to medium-low; cook 4 minutes, stirring frequently. Remove from heat. Stir in cheese, 1/4 teaspoon salt, and 1/4 teaspoon pepper. Cover; let stand 5 minutes.
2. Heat a large skillet over medium-high heat. Coat pan with cooking spray. Sprinkle steak evenly with remaining 1/4 teaspoon salt and remaining 1/4 teaspoon pepper. Add steak to pan; cook 3 minutes on each side or until desired degree of doneness. Transfer to a cutting board; cover loosely with foil.
3. Melt butter in skillet over medium-high heat. Add shallots; sauté 1 minute. Add wine, thyme, and honey; bring to a boil. Cook until reduced by half (about 2 minutes). Combine remaining 1 tablespoon broth and cornstarch in a small bowl, stirring with a whisk. Add cornstarch mixture to skillet; cook 1 minute or until sauce slightly thickens. Cut steak diagonally across grain into thin slices. Spoon 1/2 cup polenta onto each of 4 plates. Top each serving with 3 ounces steak and 2 tablespoons sauce. Serves 4.

CALORIES 367; FAT 13.7g (sat 6.5g, mono 5.4g, poly 0.5g); PROTEIN 30g; CARB 20.4g; FIBER 2.9g; CHOL 78mg; IRON 2.7mg; SODIUM 670mg; CALC 123mg

Kid Friendly • Quick & Easy
Peanut Butter Hummus with Cucumber Dippers

3 tablespoons creamy peanut butter
3 tablespoons fresh lemon juice
1 tablespoon plus 2 teaspoons olive oil
1/2 teaspoon ground cumin
1/2 teaspoon freshly ground black pepper
3/8 teaspoon kosher salt
1 (15 1/2-ounce) can chickpeas (garbanzo beans), rinsed and drained
1 garlic clove, minced
7 tablespoons water
1 English cucumber, cut into 48 1/4-inch-thick slices

1. Place peanut butter in a small microwave-safe bowl; microwave on HIGH 20 seconds. Place peanut butter and next 7 ingredients in a food processor. With food processor running, slowly drizzle water into chickpea mixture; process until smooth. Serve hummus with cucumber rounds. Serves 8 (serving size: 2 tablespoons hummus and 6 cucumber slices).

CALORIES 93; FAT 6.3g (sat 1g, mono 3.5g, poly 1.2g); PROTEIN 3.1g; CARB 7.1g; FIBER 1.7g; CHOL 0mg; IRON 0.5mg; SODIUM 194mg; CALC 14mg

Quick & Easy

Pork Medallions with Whiskey-Cumberland Sauce and Haricots Verts

Try serving with roasted new potatoes to round out the meal.

2 tablespoons finely chopped shallots
2 tablespoons Scotch whiskey or bourbon
2 tablespoons red currant jelly
1 tablespoon fresh orange juice
1 tablespoon fresh lemon juice
1/2 teaspoon dry mustard
1/4 teaspoon ground ginger
1 tablespoon olive oil
5/8 teaspoon kosher salt, divided
1/2 teaspoon freshly ground black pepper, divided
1 (1-pound) pork tenderloin, trimmed and cut crosswise into 12 pieces
2 (8-ounce) packages microwave-in-a-bag fresh haricots verts
1 tablespoon butter

1. Combine first 7 ingredients in a microwave-safe bowl. Microwave at HIGH 1 minute or until thoroughly heated.
2. Heat a large skillet over medium-high heat. Add oil to pan; swirl to coat. Sprinkle 1/4 teaspoon salt and 1/4 teaspoon pepper evenly over both sides of pork. Add pork to pan; cook 3 minutes on each side or until desired degree of doneness. Remove from pan; keep warm. Add whiskey mixture to pan; bring to a boil. Cook until reduced to 1/4 cup (about 1 minute).
3. Cook haricots verts according to package directions. Combine beans, butter, remaining 3/8 teaspoon salt, and remaining 1/4 teaspoon pepper in a medium bowl; toss well to coat. Place 3 pork medallions and 4 ounces beans on each of 4 plates; top pork with 1 tablespoon sauce. Serves 4.

CALORIES 256; FAT 9g (sat 3.1g, mono 4.1g, poly 1g); PROTEIN 26.2g; CARB 16.5g; FIBER 4g; CHOL 81mg; IRON 2.4mg; SODIUM 388mg; CALC 53mg

Quick & Easy

Broccoli Rabe with Garlic and Golden Raisins

1 pound broccoli rabe (rapini)
1 tablespoon extra-virgin olive oil
1/8 teaspoon crushed red pepper
3 garlic cloves, thinly sliced
1/4 cup golden raisins
1/4 teaspoon kosher salt
1/4 teaspoon freshly ground black pepper

1. Bring 8 cups of water to a boil in a large saucepan. Cut broccoli rabe into 2-inch pieces. Cook broccoli rabe in boiling water 2 minutes; drain.
2. Heat a large nonstick skillet over medium heat. Add oil to pan; swirl to coat. Add red pepper and garlic to pan; cook 30 seconds. Add rabe and raisins to pan; cook 2 minutes. Stir in salt and pepper. Serves 4 (serving size: about 2/3 cup).

CALORIES 95; FAT 3.4g (sat 0.5g, mono 2.5g, poly 0.4g); PROTEIN 4.5g; CARB 13.4g; FIBER 0.5g; CHOL 0mg; IRON 1.2mg; SODIUM 155mg; CALC 63mg

Variation 1: Broccoli Rabe with Polenta Croutons

Prepare base recipe, omitting raisins. Cut four 1-inch slices of refrigerated tube polenta; cut slices into 1-inch cubes. Heat a large cast-iron skillet over medium-high heat. Add 1 tablespoon extra-virgin olive oil to pan; swirl to coat. Add polenta; cook 8 minutes, turning to brown on all sides. Top broccoli rabe with croutons. Serves 4 (serving size: about 2/3 cup).

CALORIES 137; FAT 6.8g (sat 0.9g); SODIUM 253mg

Variation 2: Broccoli Rabe with Sesame and Soy

Prepare base recipe, keeping rabe whole, mincing garlic, substituting 2 teaspoons peanut oil for olive oil, and omitting raisins. Gently toss sautéed rabe in 1 tablespoon lower-sodium soy sauce, 1 teaspoon rice wine vinegar, 1/2 teaspoon sugar, and 1/2 teaspoon toasted sesame oil. Sprinkle with 1 teaspoon toasted sesame seeds. Serves 4 (serving size: about 2/3 cup).

CALORIES 71; FAT 3.2g (sat 0.5g); SODIUM 251mg

Variation 3: Broccoli Rabe with White Beans and Parmesan

Prepare base recipe, increasing oil to 2 tablespoons, increasing red pepper to 1/4 teaspoon, increasing garlic to 5 cloves, omitting raisins, and increasing black pepper to 1/2 teaspoon. Stir in 1 (15-ounce) can rinsed and drained cannellini beans; cook 1 minute or until thoroughly heated. Top with 1 ounce shaved fresh Parmesan cheese. Serves 6 (serving size: about 3/4 cup).

CALORIES 119; FAT 5.9g (sat 1.4g); SODIUM 273mg

Chicken Yakitori Rice Bowl

Mirin is a rice wine low in alcohol, and most of it cooks off in this recipe. For a nonalcoholic substitute, use a mixture of equal parts rice vinegar and sugar.

- 2 (3.5-ounce) bags boil-in-bag basmati rice
- ¼ cup lower-sodium soy sauce
- ¼ cup mirin (sweet rice wine)
- 3 tablespoons sugar
- 1 tablespoon rice vinegar
- 2 tablespoons fat-free, lower-sodium chicken broth
- 3 teaspoons peanut oil, divided
- 1 pound skinless, boneless chicken thighs
- 8 ounces snow peas, halved crosswise diagonally
- 1 bunch green onions, cut into 1-inch pieces

1. Cook rice according to package instructions, omitting salt and fat.
2. Combine soy sauce and next 4 ingredients in a small saucepan; bring to a boil. Reduce heat; simmer 3 minutes. Remove from heat.
3. Heat a large nonstick skillet over medium-high heat. Add 2 teaspoons oil to pan; swirl to coat. Add chicken thighs to pan; cook 3 minutes on each side or until browned. Transfer to a cutting board; cool slightly. Cut into (1-inch) strips.
4. Return pan to medium-high heat; add remaining 1 teaspoon oil to pan. Add snow peas and onions; sauté 2 minutes. Add soy sauce mixture and chicken to pan; cook 2 minutes or until liquid is syrupy and chicken is thoroughly heated, stirring frequently. Place 1 cup rice in each of 4 shallow bowls; top each serving with 1 cup chicken mixture. Serves 4.

CALORIES 441; FAT 8g (sat 1.7g, mono 3g, poly 2.3g); PROTEIN 29.4g; CARB 59.9g; FIBER 2.6g; CHOL 94mg; IRON 3.2mg; SODIUM 511mg; CALC 71mg

Curried Lentil Soup with Yogurt and Cilantro

Look for prepackaged lentils without salt or fat added.

- 1 tablespoon canola oil
- 1 cup prechopped onion
- 1 tablespoon minced garlic
- 1 tablespoon minced peeled fresh ginger
- 1½ tablespoons curry powder
- ⅛ teaspoon ground red pepper
- 3 cups fat-free, lower sodium chicken broth
- 1½ tablespoons balsamic vinegar
- 2 (8-ounce) packages steamed lentils
- 2 cups fresh baby spinach
- ¼ teaspoon kosher salt
- ¼ teaspoon black pepper
- ¼ cup chopped fresh cilantro, divided
- ¼ cup plain 2% reduced-fat Greek yogurt

1. Heat a medium saucepan over medium heat. Add oil to pan; swirl to coat. Add onion; sauté 3 minutes. Add garlic and ginger; sauté 1 minute. Add curry powder and red pepper; cook 30 seconds, stirring constantly. Add broth, vinegar, and lentils. Increase heat to high; bring to a boil. Reduce heat; simmer 5 minutes.
2. Place half of lentil mixture in a blender. Remove center piece of blender lid (to allow steam to escape); secure blender lid on blender. Place a clean towel over opening in blender lid (to avoid splatters). Blend until smooth. Add blended lentil mixture, spinach, salt, and pepper to pan; stir until spinach wilts. Stir in 2 tablespoons cilantro. Serve with yogurt and remaining 2 tablespoons cilantro. Serves 4 (serving size: about 1½ cups soup, 1 tablespoon yogurt, and 1 tablespoon cilantro).

CALORIES 221; FAT 5g (sat 0.6g, mono 2.4g, poly 1.3g); PROTEIN 13.3g; CARB 31.7g; FIBER 11g; CHOL 1mg; IRON 5mg; SODIUM 488mg; CALC 62mg

DINNER TONIGHT

Fast weeknight menus from the Cooking Light Test Kitchen.

READY IN 40 MINUTES

The
SHOPPING LIST

Creamy Butternut, Blue Cheese, and Walnut Cavatappi
(8-ounce) package prechopped onion (1)
1 large butternut squash
Garlic
Olive oil
Chopped walnuts
All-purpose flour
8 ounces cavatappi
Blue cheese, crumbled (2 ounces)
2% reduced-fat milk
Eggs (2)

Garlic Haricots Verts
Haricots verts (1.5 pounds)
Garlic
Olive oil

The
GAME PLAN

While squash bakes:
- Trim and season haricots verts.
- Cook pasta.
- Chop garlic.

While haricots verts cook:
- Prepare sauce.
- Assemble pasta.

Creamy Butternut, Blue Cheese, and Walnut Cavatappi
With Garlic Haricots Verts

Make Ahead Tip: Roast squash up to a week in advance and reheat before tossing with pasta. Flavor Hit: Toasted walnuts add a crunchy contrast to the creamy pasta.

4 cups (1/2-inch) cubed peeled butternut squash (about 1 1/3 pounds)

2 1/2 teaspoons olive oil, divided

1/2 teaspoon kosher salt, divided

1/2 teaspoon freshly ground black pepper, divided

Cooking spray

8 ounces uncooked cavatappi

1 cup prechopped onion

1 tablespoon minced garlic

1 cup 2% reduced-fat milk, divided

1 teaspoon all-purpose flour

2 large egg yolks

2 ounces blue cheese, crumbled (about 1/2 cup)

3 tablespoons chopped walnuts, toasted

1. Preheat oven to 425°.

2. Combine squash, 1 1/2 teaspoons oil, 1/4 teaspoon salt, and 1/4 teaspoon pepper on a jelly-roll pan coated with cooking spray. Bake at 425° for 24 minutes or until tender, stirring once.

3. Cook pasta according to package directions, omitting salt and fat. Drain; keep warm.

4. Heat a medium saucepan over medium-high heat. Add remaining 1 teaspoon oil to pan; swirl to coat. Add onion and garlic; sauté 3 minutes. Reduce heat to medium-low. Stir in 1/2 cup milk, remaining 1/4 teaspoon salt, and remaining 1/4 teaspoon pepper. Combine remaining 1/2 cup milk, flour, and yolks in a small bowl, stirring with a whisk. Slowly add egg mixture to pan, stirring constantly with a whisk. Cook 5 minutes or until thickened, stirring frequently with a whisk.

5. Combine squash, pasta, and milk mixture in a large bowl; toss gently to coat. Sprinkle with cheese and nuts. Serves 6 (serving size: about 1 cup).

CALORIES 307; FAT 10g (sat 3.5g, mono 3.3g, poly 2.3g); PROTEIN 11.3g; CARB 45.3g; FIBER 3.8g; CHOL 80mg; IRON 2.3mg; SODIUM 318mg; CALC 169mg

For the Garlic Haricots Verts:
Preheat oven to 425°. Combine 1 teaspoon olive oil, 1/4 teaspoon kosher salt, 1/4 teaspoon freshly ground black pepper, 4 sliced garlic cloves, and 1 1/2 pounds trimmed haricots verts on a baking sheet; toss to coat. Bake at 425° for 15 minutes or until tender, stirring once. Serves 6 (serving size: about 1 cup).

CALORIES 45; FAT 0.9g (sat 0.1g); SODIUM 87mg

KID TWEAK: SUBSTITUTE MILDER GOAT CHEESE FOR THE BLUE CHEESE.

READY IN
40
MINUTES

The SHOPPING LIST

Pumpkin-Shiitake Risotto with Pancetta and Pine Nuts

Onion (1 large)

Shiitake mushroom caps (4 ounces)

Garlic

Fresh sage

Fresh chives

Pine nuts

Arborio rice

Ground red pepper

Unsalted chicken stock

Dry white wine

15-ounce can pumpkin

Mascarpone cheese

Pancetta

Pear and Winter Lettuce Salad

Comice pear (1 large)

2 heads Belgian endive

1 small head radicchio

White balsamic vinegar

Extra-virgin olive oil

Dijon mustard

The GAME PLAN

While broth mixture comes to a simmer:
- Toast pine nuts.
- Chop onion and garlic.
- Prepare salad dressing.
- Slice endive, radicchio, and pear.
- Cook risotto.
- Toss salad.

continued

Pumpkin-Shiitake Risotto with Pancetta and Pine Nuts

With Pear and Winter Lettuce Salad

Simple Sub: Use bacon instead of pancetta.
Budget Buy: Crimini mushrooms are less expensive than shiitake.
Flavor Swap: Use milder romaine lettuce in place of bitter endive.

3 cups unsalted chicken stock (such as Swanson)
½ cup water
Cooking spray
2 ounces chopped pancetta
2 cups sliced shiitake mushroom caps (about 4 ounces)
1½ cups chopped onion
1 tablespoon minced garlic
1 cup uncooked Arborio rice
2 teaspoons chopped fresh sage
½ cup dry white wine
½ teaspoon kosher salt
1 cup canned pumpkin puree
2 tablespoons mascarpone cheese
2 tablespoons chopped fresh chives
¼ teaspoon ground red pepper
2 tablespoons pine nuts, toasted

1. Bring stock and ½ cup water to a simmer in a medium saucepan (do not boil). Keep warm over low heat. Set aside ¼ cup of warm stock mixture.
2. Heat a large, heavy-bottomed saucepan over medium heat. Coat pan with cooking spray. Add pancetta; cook 5 minutes or until crisp, stirring frequently. Add mushrooms, onion, and garlic; cook 6 minutes or until tender, stirring occasionally. Stir in rice and sage; cook 1 minute, stirring frequently. Add wine; cook 30 seconds or until liquid is absorbed. Stir in 1¼ cups stock mixture and salt; cook 4 minutes or until liquid is nearly absorbed, stirring constantly. Add remaining stock mixture, ¾ cup at a time, stirring constantly until each portion of stock is absorbed before adding more (about 22 minutes total). Remove rice mixture from heat; stir in pumpkin, mascarpone, chives, and pepper. Stir in reserved ¼ cup stock mixture as needed, 1 tablespoon at a time, until risotto is desired consistency. Spoon 1 cup risotto into each of 4 bowls; sprinkle evenly with pine nuts. Serve immediately. Serves 4.

CALORIES 409; FAT 15g (sat 5.9g, mono 0.8g, poly 1.5g); PROTEIN 13.8g; CARB 52.4g; FIBER 5.4g; CHOL 28mg; IRON 2mg; SODIUM 587mg; CALC 76mg

For the Pear and Winter Lettuce Salad: Combine 2 tablespoons extra-virgin olive oil, 1 tablespoon white balsamic vinegar, 1 teaspoon Dijon mustard, ¼ teaspoon salt, and ¼ teaspoon freshly ground black pepper in a large bowl, stirring with a whisk. Add 2 heads thinly sliced Belgian endive, 1 small head thinly sliced radicchio, and 1 large sliced Comice pear; toss to combine. Serves 4 (serving size: ¾ cup).

CALORIES 103; FAT 7g (sat 1g); SODIUM 188mg

READY IN
40
MINUTES

The SHOPPING LIST

Peppercorn-Crusted Beef Tenderloin
Fresh parsley
Fresh cilantro
Fresh oregano
Garlic
Lemon (1)
Canola oil
Crushed red pepper
4 (4-ounce) beef tenderloin steaks

Herb Roasted Potatoes
Red potatoes (1.25 pounds)
Fresh parsley
Fresh thyme
Olive oil

The GAME PLAN

While oven preheats:
■ Quarter and season potatoes.
While potatoes bake:
■ Cook steaks.
■ Prepare gremolata.

Peppercorn-Crusted Beef Tenderloin with Gremolata

With Herb-Roasted Potatoes

Flavor Hit: Parsley, cilantro, and oregano make a bright, fresh sauce for the steaks.
Budget Buy: Use sirloin in place of tenderloin.
Kid Tweak: Omit the crushed red pepper in the gremolata.

4 (4-ounce) beef tenderloin steaks,
   trimmed (about 1 inch thick)
Cooking spray
2 teaspoons cracked black pepper
½ teaspoon kosher salt, divided
4 teaspoons canola oil, divided
¼ cup chopped fresh flat-leaf parsley
3 tablespoons chopped fresh cilantro
1½ teaspoons chopped garlic
1 teaspoon chopped fresh oregano
½ teaspoon grated lemon rind
1 tablespoon fresh lemon juice
¼ teaspoon crushed red pepper

1. Coat each steak with cooking spray;
sprinkle evenly with pepper and ¼
teaspoon salt. Heat a large ovenproof
skillet over medium-high heat. Add 1
teaspoon oil; swirl to coat. Add steaks
to pan; cook 3 minutes or until desired
degree of doneness.
2. Combine remaining 1 tablespoon
oil, remaining ¼ teaspoon salt, parsley,
and remaining ingredients in a small
bowl, stirring with a whisk. Serve with
steak. Serves 4 (serving size: 1 steak
and about 3 tablespoons gremolata).

CALORIES 224; FAT 12.3g (sat 3.1g, mono 5.9g, poly 1.7g);
PROTEIN 25.4g; CARB 1.8g; FIBER 0.5g; CHOL 76mg;
IRON 2.2mg; SODIUM 306mg; CALC 41mg

For the Herb-Roasted Potatoes:
Preheat oven to 425°. Combine 1
tablespoon olive oil, 1 tablespoon
chopped fresh thyme, ¼ teaspoon
salt, ¼ teaspoon freshly ground black
pepper, and 1¼ pounds quartered red
potatoes in a medium bowl; toss to
coat. Place potatoes on a jelly-roll
pan coated with cooking spray. Bake
at 425° for 28 minutes, stirring once.
Sprinkle with 2 teaspoons chopped
fresh flat-leaf parsley. Serves 4 (serving
size: ⅔ cup).

CALORIES 132; FAT 3.7g (sat 0.5g); SODIUM 156mg

READY IN 40 MINUTES

The SHOPPING LIST

**Sautéed Flounder with Spicy
Rémoulade**
Fresh parsley
Lemon (1)
Extra-virgin olive oil
Orzo
All-purpose flour
Cornichons
Capers
Canola mayonnaise
Whole-grain Dijon mustard
Sriracha
4 (6-ounce) flounder fillets

Bacon-Scented Broccoli
12 ounces broccoli florets
2 center-cut bacon slices

The GAME PLAN

While water for orzo comes to a boil:
  ■ Prepare rémoulade.
While orzo cooks:
  ■ Cook broccoli.
  ■ Dredge and cook fish.

Sautéed Flounder and Spicy Rémoulade
With Bacon-Scented Broccoli

*Prep Pointer: A fish spatula works best to flip
these thin, delicate fillets.*
*Flavor Hit: Sriracha, or hot chile sauce, adds a
spicy kick to the rémoulade.*

¾ cup uncooked orzo
3 tablespoons chopped fresh flat-leaf
   parsley, divided
¾ teaspoon freshly ground black
   pepper, divided
½ teaspoon kosher salt, divided
¼ cup canola mayonnaise
1 tablespoon chopped cornichons
1 tablespoon fresh lemon juice
2 teaspoons whole-grain Dijon mustard
2 teaspoons Sriracha (such as Huy
   Fong)
1 teaspoon chopped capers
2 tablespoons extra-virgin olive oil,
   divided
3 tablespoons all-purpose flour
4 (6-ounce) flounder fillets

1. Cook orzo according to package
directions, omitting salt and fat.
Drain; stir in 2 tablespoons parsley, ¼
teaspoon pepper, and ¼ teaspoon salt.
2. Combine remaining 1 tablespoon
parsley, mayonnaise, and next 5 ingredients in a small bowl.
3. Heat a large nonstick skillet over
medium-high heat. Add 1 tablespoon
oil; swirl to coat. Place flour in a shallow dish. Sprinkle fillets evenly with
remaining ½ teaspoon pepper and remaining ¼ teaspoon salt; dredge fillets
in flour. Add 2 fillets to pan; cook 1½
minutes on each side or until desired
degree of doneness. Remove fish from
pan. Repeat procedure with remaining 1 tablespoon oil and 2 fillets. Serve
with rémoulade and orzo. Serves 4
(serving size: 1 fillet, 1 tablespoon
rémoulade, and about ⅓ cup orzo).

Sustainable Choice | *Look for flounder wild-caught in
the U.S. Pacific.*

CALORIES 461; FAT 20.4g (sat 2.4g, mono 11.3g, poly 4.3g);
PROTEIN 36.8g; CARB 29.7g; FIBER 1.6g; CHOL 87mg;
IRON 1.2mg; SODIUM 603mg; CALC 38mg

continued

For the Bacon-Scented Broccoli:
Place 12 ounces broccoli florets in a large saucepan of boiling water. Cook 3 to 4 minutes or until crisp-tender; drain. Heat a medium nonstick skillet over medium-high heat. Add 2 slices center-cut bacon; cook until crisp. Remove bacon slices from pan with a slotted spoon; crumble. Add broccoli, bacon, ¼ teaspoon freshly ground black pepper, and ⅛ teaspoon salt to drippings in pan; cook 1 minute, tossing to coat broccoli. Serves 4 (serving size: ½ cup).

CALORIES 37; FAT 1.3g (sat 0.6g); SODIUM 164mg

WHAT TO COOK RIGHT NOW

GELÉES

Gelées are trendy in America right now. You'll see sparkly sugared versions on dessert plates and delicious savory interpretations atop foie gras and other delicacies in some of the nation's finest restaurants. Here, we offer a sweet, fruit-based recipe you can make in your home kitchen. Package these beauties in a small box with festive holiday tissue, and tie it with pretty ribbon for a special, homemade holiday gift this year.

Pomegranate Gelée

Hands-on time: 23 min. Total time: 10 hr. 23 min.

Use your favorite flavor fruit puree or concentrate—we made the recipe using Meyer lemon, tangerine, cranberry, and blood orange. You can order various flavors from www.perfect-puree.com.

Cooking spray
1½ cups sugar, divided
¾ cup pomegranate puree or concentrate
¼ cup unsweetened applesauce
¼ cup light-colored corn syrup
1 (3-ounce) package liquid fruit pectin (such as Certo)
1 teaspoon fresh lemon juice

1. Coat a 9 x 5–inch loaf pan with cooking spray; line with plastic wrap. Coat plastic with cooking spray. Place 1¼ cups sugar, fruit puree, applesauce, and corn syrup in a medium, heavy saucepan over medium-high heat; bring to a boil. Cook until a thermometer registers 224° (about 10 minutes), stirring frequently. Add pectin; bring to a boil. Cook 1 minute, stirring frequently. Remove pan from heat. Stir in juice. Pour mixture into prepared pan; cool to room temperature. Cover, and let stand at room temperature overnight.
2. Sprinkle top evenly with 1 tablespoon sugar. Invert gelée onto a cutting board. Discard plastic. Cut into 32 pieces. Place remaining 3 tablespoons sugar in a shallow dish; gently roll gelée in sugar. Serves 32 (serving size: 1 piece).

CALORIES 61; CARB 16g; FIBER 0g; CHOL 0mg; IRON 0.1mg; SODIUM 2mg; CALC 1mg

BUDGET COOKING

FEED 4 FOR LESS THAN $10

Use everyday ingredients as the base for extraordinary meals: An orange marmalade glaze coats pork, a soy sauce and chile–infused broth enlivens a stir-fry, and humble winter squash goes uptown.

Stir-Fried Spicy Rice Cakes

$2.45/serving, $9.81 total

Hands-on time: 29 min. Total time: 29 min. Ovalettes, chewy sliced rice cakes, are a Korean staple and are often available at Asian markets. If you buy more than you need, they freeze well. If you can't find them, simply substitute 2 cups cooked rice. Serve this rich, spicy stew with a side of sliced fresh cabbage tossed with fresh lime juice, 1 tablespoon canola oil, salt, and pepper.

2 tablespoons dark sesame oil, divided
4 cups sliced rice cakes (rice ovalettes), divided
1 bunch green onions, trimmed and cut into 1-inch pieces
12 ounces lean ground pork
½ cup chopped onion
¼ teaspoon kosher salt
3 large garlic cloves, minced
2 teaspoons cornstarch
2 cups no-salt-added chicken stock (such as Swanson)
3 tablespoons lower-sodium soy sauce
1 tablespoon sambal oelek (ground fresh chile paste)
4 lime wedges

1. Heat a wok or large skillet over medium-high heat. Add 1 tablespoon oil to pan; swirl to coat. Add 2 cups rice cakes; stir-fry 3 minutes or until blistered, turning to brown on both sides. Remove rice cakes from pan; place in a large bowl. Add remaining 1 tablespoon oil; swirl to coat. Add remaining 2 cups rice cakes; stir-fry 2 minutes. Add green onions to pan; stir-fry 1 minute or until rice cakes are blistered, turning to brown on both sides. Remove rice cake mixture from pan; add to cooked rice cakes.

2. Add pork to pan; sauté 4 minutes or until browned, stirring to crumble. Stir in chopped onion and salt; sauté 3 minutes, stirring occasionally. Add garlic; sauté 30 seconds, stirring constantly. Stir in cornstarch. Gradually add stock; bring to a boil. Stir in soy sauce and sambal; cook 1 minute, stirring frequently. Divide rice cake mixture among 4 shallow bowls; top each serving with ¾ cup pork mixture. Serve with lime wedges. Serves 4 (serving size: about 1 cup rice cake mixture, ¾ cup pork mixture, and 1 lime wedge).

CALORIES 504; FAT 14.1g (sat 3.8g, mono 4.9, poly 5g); PROTEIN 26.5g; CARB 68.6g; FIBER 2.6g; CHOL 64mg; IRON 3mg; SODIUM 552mg; CALC 41mg

Sausage and Rice Acorn Squash

$2.49/serving, $9.95 total

Hands-on time: 30 min. Total time: 1 hr. *You can also use two larger squashes; just cut in half before roasting, and serve one half per person. Serve with garlicky haricots verts. Cook 1 pound haricots verts in boiling water 3 to 4 minutes, place in ice water, and drain. Sauté with 1 tablespoon olive oil and 1 tablespoon minced garlic; toss with chopped fresh chives.*

4 small acorn or sweet dumpling squashes (about 10 ounces each)
2 (4-ounce) links sweet Italian sausage, casings removed
1 tablespoon canola oil
1 cup finely chopped onion
⅓ cup chopped celery

1½ tablespoons minced garlic
1½ cups cooked brown rice
⅓ cup dried cranberries
3 tablespoons chopped fresh chives
½ teaspoon kosher salt
¼ teaspoon freshly ground black pepper
1 ounce fresh Parmesan cheese, grated (about ¼ cup)
1 ounce Swiss cheese, shredded (about ¼ cup)

1. Preheat oven to 425°.
2. Place whole squashes in a roasting pan. Bake at 425° for 30 minutes or until just tender. Let stand 15 minutes. Halve squashes; scoop out seeds and squash pulp, leaving a ¾-inch-thick shell. Discard seeds; reserve squash pulp for another use.
3. Preheat broiler to high.
4. Heat a large skillet over medium-high heat. Add sausage to pan; sauté 5 minutes or until browned, stirring to crumble. Remove sausage from pan; drain on paper towels. Wipe drippings from pan with a paper towel. Return pan to heat. Add oil to pan; swirl to coat. Add onion; sauté 4 minutes, stirring occasionally. Add celery; sauté 3 minutes, stirring occasionally. Add garlic; sauté 1 minute, stirring constantly. Stir in sausage, rice, and next 5 ingredients. Divide rice mixture evenly among squash halves. Sprinkle evenly with Swiss cheese. Arrange squash halves on a baking sheet; broil 4 minutes or until golden and cheese is melted. Serves 4 (serving size: 1 stuffed squash).

CALORIES 403; FAT 12.6g (sat 4.4g, mono 5.4g, poly 1.9g); PROTEIN 16.7g; CARB 61g; FIBER 7.1g; CHOL 27mg; IRON 3.1mg; SODIUM 636mg; CALC 284mg

Honey-Orange Pork Tenderloin

$1.51/serving, $6.04 total

Hands-on time: 7 min. Total time: 40 min. *This recipe is a study in elegant simplicity, and although very inexpensive, it's fit for company. For a simple side, steam 1 pound halved Brussels sprouts for 4 minutes; pat dry. Heat a skillet over medium-high heat. Add 2 teaspoons olive oil to pan; swirl. Add steamed Brussels sprouts; sauté 6 minutes or until lightly browned and crisp-tender. Sprinkle with ¼ teaspoon kosher salt and ¼ teaspoon freshly ground black pepper.*

⅓ cup orange marmalade
3 tablespoons cider vinegar
3 tablespoons lower-sodium soy sauce
1½ tablespoons minced fresh garlic
1½ teaspoons honey
2 tablespoons canola oil
1 (1-pound) pork tenderloin, trimmed
¼ teaspoon kosher salt
½ teaspoon freshly ground black pepper

1. Preheat oven to 350°.
2. Combine first 5 ingredients, stirring well with a whisk. Reserve 2 tablespoons marmalade mixture. Heat an ovenproof skillet over medium-high heat. Add oil; swirl to coat. Sprinkle pork with salt and pepper. Add pork to pan; cook 5 minutes or until browned. Turn pork over; brush with ¼ cup marmalade mixture. Bake at 350° for 10 minutes. Turn pork over; brush with ¼ cup marmalade mixture. Bake an additional 10 minutes or until a thermometer registers 150°. Remove pork from pan; brush with reserved 2 tablespoons marmalade mixture. Let stand 10 minutes; slice. Serves 4 (serving size: 3 ounces pork).

CALORIES 275; FAT 9.5g (sat 1.3g, mono 5.3g, poly 2.4g); PROTEIN 24.8g; CARB 21.9g; FIBER 0.3g; CHOL 74mg; IRON 1.4mg; SODIUM 609mg; CALC 25mg

SECRETS OF SIMPLE COOKING

One of Portland's top toques shows the benefits of streamlining.

In Portland, Oregon, a city where you can't hurl a pair of tongs without beaning an acclaimed chef, Jenn Louis has come to stand out partly for her lack of cheffiness. She takes a refreshingly simple, less-is-more approach to cooking. Consider her baked eggs, a signature dish at Lincoln: eggs, a little cream, some fruity, briny castelvetrano olives, and breadcrumbs. That's all. Her pork scallopine? Six ingredients.

"I like to keep a very restrained hand with my food," she says. "When dishes have too many ingredients, the quality or subtlety of some of those ingredients gets lost."

It behooves the home cook to stick to basics for many reasons—time, cost, ease. But Louis's food shows how delectable—even impressive—simple cooking can be, so long as it heeds a few key guidelines.

First, when you're cooking with just a few ingredients, quality is critical. This doesn't necessarily mean expensive, Louis notes—freshness is the prime concern. Still, it's smart to have a few top-notch ingredients, like premium extra-virgin olive oil, that you can lean on to elevate dishes: a drizzle on top of weeknight (perhaps leftover) soup can make a world of difference.

When constructing a dish, Louis aims for balance. A greens salad may get fresh orange juice in the vinaigrette and orange sections for additional sweetness, some red onion for a little peppery bite, pine nuts for earthy crunch, and some olives for briny notes. Once she's harmonized the flavors and textures, she's done.

Of course there's a line, and you can pare back a dish too much. Louis gives the example of a plate of gorgeously ripe sliced tomatoes topped with Maldon sea salt and a drizzle of good olive oil: pure deliciousness. But without the salt? Not good. "Know what's going to highlight your main ingredient," she says.

WHO
Jenn Louis

WHERE
Lincoln Restaurant and Sunshine Tavern,
Portland, Oregon

Baked Eggs with Chickpeas, Spinach, and Tomato

Hands-on time: 14 min. Total time: 29 min. Use farm-fresh eggs to make this quick, one-skillet supper really shine.

1 tablespoon olive oil
3 tablespoons thinly sliced shallots (about 1)
1 teaspoon chopped fresh rosemary leaves
Dash of crushed red pepper
1 garlic clove, thinly sliced
½ cup lower-sodium marinara sauce
1 (14-ounce) can chickpeas (garbanzo beans), undrained
2 cups fresh baby spinach
¼ teaspoon kosher salt
⅛ teaspoon freshly ground black pepper
4 large eggs
2 ounces fresh pecorino Romano cheese, shredded (about ½ cup)

1. Heat a large skillet over medium heat. Add oil to pan; swirl to coat. Add shallots, rosemary, red pepper, and garlic; cook 2 minutes or until shallots are tender, stirring constantly. Add marinara and chickpeas; bring to a simmer. Stir in spinach, salt, and black pepper. Break eggs evenly over marinara mixture. Simmer gently 15 minutes (do not stir) or until egg whites are almost set. Cover; cook 1 minute or until egg white is set (yolks should still be runny). Sprinkle with cheese. Serves 4 (serving size: 1 egg and about ⅓ cup chickpea mixture).

CALORIES 259; FAT 13.6g (sat 3.1g, mono 6.8g, poly 1.5g); PROTEIN 12.3g; CARB 20.8g; FIBER 4.1g; CHOL 185mg; IRON 2.8mg; SODIUM 543mg; CALC 104mg

HANUKKAH GOES MODERN

By Rozanne Gold

Celebrate the festival of lights with unique twists on traditional dishes.

Hanukkah is a holiday filled with illuminating rituals: Eight nights of candle lighting and gifts, and foods fried in olive oil! The former refers to the miracle that happened during the rededication of The Temple in Jerusalem in 165 BC, when a tiny bit of oil, enough to last only one night, lasted eight. The latter are edible expressions of the miracle: Crispy potato pancakes, known as latkes, and jelly doughnuts (known as *sufganiyot*), traditionally top the list. But this year, a few new dishes will grace our table at home: nuggets of cauliflower fried in olive oil and served with tahini and pomegranate seeds, and radically simple latkes made with three root vegetables.

Crispy Root Vegetable Latkes with Beet Puree

Hands-on time: 1 hr. Total time: 1 hr.

Beet puree:
1 (8-ounce) package precooked red beets, drained
1 cup chopped Fuji apple (about 3 ounces)
3 tablespoons water
1 tablespoon extra-virgin olive oil
1/4 teaspoon kosher salt
1/8 teaspoon ground red pepper
Latkes:
8 ounces grated peeled sweet potato (about 2 cups)

5 ounces grated peeled baking potato (about 2 cups)
3 ounces grated peeled parsnip (about 1 cup)
3 ounces all-purpose flour (about 2/3 cup)
1/2 teaspoon ground cumin
1/2 teaspoon kosher salt, divided
2 large eggs
4 ounces grated onion (about 1 cup)
2 tablepoons olive oil, divided
1 tablespoon chopped fresh dill (optional)

1. Preheat oven to 325°.
2. To prepare beet puree, place first 6 ingredients in a food processor; process until smooth, scraping sides of bowl occasionally. Set aside.
3. To prepare latkes, combine sweet potato, baking potato, and parsnip in a bowl. Place sweet potato mixture on paper towels; squeeze until barely moist. Lightly spoon flour into a dry measuring cup; level with a knife. Place flour, cumin, 1/4 teaspoon salt, eggs, and onion in a bowl; beat with a mixer at medium speed until blended. Add sweet potato mixture; beat at low speed until combined.
4. Heat a large nonstick skillet over medium heat. Add 2 teaspoons oil to pan; swirl to coat. Spoon 3 tablespoons sweet potato mixture loosely into a dry measuring cup. Pour mixture into pan; flatten slightly. Repeat procedure 5 times to form 6 latkes. Reduce heat to medium-low; cook 6 minutes on each side or until golden brown and thoroughly cooked. Place latkes on a baking sheet; keep warm in oven. Repeat procedure twice with remaining oil and sweet potato mixture to yield 18 latkes total. Sprinkle cooked latkes with remaining 1/4 teaspoon salt. Sprinkle with dill, if desired. Serve with beet puree. Serves 6 (serving size: 3 latkes and about 2½ tablespoons beet puree).

CALORIES 232; FAT 8.4g (sat 4.9g, mono 1.4g, poly 1.1g); PROTEIN 5.5g; CARB 33g; FIBER 4.5g; CHOL 60mg; IRON 1.6mg; SODIUM 297mg; CALC 37mg

Fried Cauliflower with Tahini and Pomegranate Seeds

Hands-on time: 12 min. Total time: 35 min. The presence of olive oil is what symbolically matters. I've reduced the amount of oil by giving the cauliflower a jumpstart in the frying pan, and then roasting in the oven. Cilantro leaves give it a bright taste and lovely color.

1/3 cup cilantro leaves, packed
1/3 cup tahini (roasted sesame seed paste)
3 tablespoons fresh lemon juice
2 garlic cloves
6 tablespoons water, as needed
1/2 teaspoon salt, divided
2 tablespoons extra-virgin olive oil
6 cups cauliflower florets (about 1 large head)
1/4 teaspoon freshly ground black pepper
1/3 cup pomegranate seeds

1. Preheat oven to 375°.
2. Place first 4 ingredients in a food processor; process until smooth. Add water, 1 tablespoon at a time, until mixture is the consistency of a creamy salad dressing. Add 1/4 teaspoon salt; pulse once to combine.
3. Heat a large nonstick skillet over medium heat. Add oil to pan; swirl to coat. Add cauliflower to pan; sauté 10 minutes or until lightly browned, stirring occasionally. Place cauliflower on a jelly-roll pan lined with foil. Roast cauliflower at 375° for 18 minutes or until tender, turning once. Sprinkle with remaining 1/4 teaspoon salt and pepper. Add pomegranate seeds; toss to combine. Serve with tahini mixture. Serves 6 (serving size: about 3/4 cups cauliflower mixture and 1½ tablespoons tahini mixture).

CALORIES 166; FAT 11.7g (sat 1.6g, mono 6g, poly 3.6g); PROTEIN 5.2g; CARB 13.6g; FIBER 4.2g; CHOL 0mg; IRON 1.3mg; SODIUM 244mg; CALC 52mg

FESTIVE HOLIDAY CAKE

To our lightened yet luscious coconut cake we added a merry twist—a bright red ribbon of tangy-fruity raspberry filling.

Coconut Cake with Raspberry Filling

Hands-on time: 35 min. Total time: 2 hr. 10 min. *A little coconut flour—which you'll find with other specialty flours in large supermarkets—adds toasty, nutty flavor to the cake layers. But don't get overzealous and sub in more for additional coconut taste; because it lacks the gluten of wheat-based cake flour, using more will wreck the structure of the cake. If you can't find coconut flour, use all cake flour.*

Filling:
2 pints fresh raspberries (12 ounces)
1/3 cup sugar
2 tablespoons water
1/8 teaspoon salt
3 tablespoons cornstarch
3 tablespoons Chambord (raspberry-flavored liqueur)
Cake:
Baking spray with flour
8 ounces cake flour (about 2 cups)
2 ounces coconut flour (such as Bob's Red Mill; about 1/2 cup)
2 teaspoons baking powder
1/2 teaspoon salt
1 1/2 cups sugar, divided
1/3 cup canola oil
2 tablespoons butter, softened
1 teaspoon vanilla extract
1 cup coconut water (such as Goya)
6 large egg whites
Frosting:
3 large egg whites
1/4 teaspoon cream of tartar
1/2 cup sugar
3 tablespoons water
1/8 teaspoon salt
1/2 cup unsweetened coconut flakes, toasted

1. To prepare filling, combine raspberries, 1/3 cup sugar, 2 tablespoons water, and 1/8 teaspoon salt in a saucepan; bring to a boil. Cook over medium heat 5 minutes, stirring frequently until berries break down. Combine cornstarch and liqueur in a small bowl; stir with a whisk until smooth. Add cornstarch mixture to raspberry mixture, stirring with a whisk; return to a boil. Cook 1 minute or until very thick, stirring constantly. Spoon mixture into a bowl; cover and refrigerate until needed.
2. Preheat oven to 350°.
3. To prepare cake, coat 3 (8-inch) cake pans with baking spray; line bottoms of pans with wax paper. Coat wax paper with baking spray; set aside.
4. Weigh or lightly spoon flours into dry measuring cups; level with a knife. Combine flours, baking powder, and salt in a bowl; stir with a whisk. Place 1 1/4 cups sugar, oil, butter, and vanilla in a large bowl. Beat with a mixer at medium speed for 5 minutes or until fluffy. Add coconut water; beat at low speed 1 minute or until combined. Add flour mixture; beat at low speed 1 minute or until well combined.
5. Place 6 egg whites in a large, clean bowl. Beat with a mixer at high speed until medium peaks form using clean, dry beaters. Add 1/4 cup sugar, 1 tablespoon at a time; beat 1 minute. Stir one-fourth of egg white mixture into batter; gently fold in remaining egg white mixture. Divide batter evenly among prepared pans. Bake at 350° for 19 minutes or until a wooden pick inserted in center comes out clean. Cool in pans on a wire rack for 10 minutes. Remove from pans; cool completely on wire rack.
6. To prepare frosting, place 3 egg whites and cream of tartar in a large bowl; beat with a mixer at high speed until medium peaks form, using clean, dry beaters. Combine 1/2 cup sugar, 3 tablespoons water, and 1/8 teaspoon salt in a saucepan; bring to a boil. Cook, without stirring, until candy thermometer registers 250°. With mixer on low speed, pour hot sugar syrup in a thin stream down the side of mixing bowl. Gradually increase speed to high; beat 3 minutes or until thick and cool.
7. To assemble cake, place 1 cake layer on a serving plate; spread with one-half of filling (about 1 cup), leaving a 1/2-inch border. Top with another cake layer. Spread with remaining filling, leaving a 1/2-inch border. Top with remaining cake layer. Spread frosting over top and sides of cake. Gently press coconut flakes into sides of cake. Serves 16 (serving size: 1 slice).

CALORIES 292; **FAT** 8.4g (sat 3g, mono 3.4g, poly 1.5g); **PROTEIN** 4.1g; **CARB** 49.9g; **FIBER** 3.6g; **CHOL** 4mg; **IRON** 1.4mg; **SODIUM** 209mg; **CALC** 43mg

CONTRIBUTORS

Tiziana Agnello
Elana Beth Altman
Patty Alvarez
Sang An
Simon Andrews
Alison Attenborough
Charlotte Autry
Johnny Autry
Iain Bagwell
Lisa Bell
Amy Berkley
Roscoe Betsill
Mark Bittman
Richard Blais
Jeremy Bolen
David Bonom
Philippa Brathwaite
Doris Brautigan
Katherine Brooking, RD
Levi Brown
Christine Burns Rudalevige
Maureen Callahan, MS, RD
Mary Clayton Carl
Caleb Chancey
Katherine Cobbs
Helena Corzan
Ruth Cousineau
Nigel Cox
Helen Crowther
Lisa Dalsimer
Claudia De Almeida
Mary Drennen
Thom Driver
Abby Duchin Dinces
Naomi Duguid
Melanie Dunea
Katie Dunn
Derek Eng
Karen Evans
Michele Faro

Mel Ferro Cole
Molly Findlay
Allison Fishman
Caroline Ford
Rozanne Gold
Evelyn Good
Heloise Goodman
Victoria Granof
Christopher Griffith
Rachel Haas
Christopher Hirsheimer
Daniela Hritcu
Dennis Huynh
Lauryn Ishak
Liza Jernow
Kate Johnson
Telia Johnson
Scott Jones
Wendy Kalen
Jeanne Kelley
Ana Kelly
Jamie Kimm
Jessica Landy
Frances Largeman-Roth, RD
Barbara Lauterbach
Karen Levin
J. Kenji Lopez-Alt
Lindsey Lower
Nai Lee Lum
Ivy Manning
Phil Mansfield
Erik Marinovich
Claudia P. Marulanda
Gunter Marx Photography/Corbis
Joe McKendry
Jill Melton, MS, RD
Jackie Mills, MS, RD
Krista Ackerbloom Montgomery
Jackie Newgent
Marcus Nilsson

Violet Oon
Kate Parham
Laraine Perri
Marge Perry
José Picayo
Con Poulous
Steven Raichlen
Nicole Rees
Gretchen Roberts
Lucinda Rogers
Leigh Ann Ross
Christine Burns Rudalevige
Amelia Saltsman
Mark Scarbrough
Bernard Scharf
Robert Schueller
Jeffrey Selden
Mary Britton Senseney
Patricia Weigel Shannon
Marcia Whyte Smart
Sarah Smart
Susan Sugarman
Peter Tannenbaum
Jennifer Taylor
Kiyoshi Togashi
Kenji Toma
Lara Tomlin
Francesco Tonelli
John Von Pamer
Lauren Wade
Jason Wallis
Bruce Weinstein
Hannah Whitaker
Scott White
Brian Woodcock
Romulo Yanes
Drea Zacharenko
Laura Zapalowski
Tanya Zuckerbrot, RD

NUTRITION MADE EASY

2012'S PATH TO HEALTHY EATING...

GRAB A CART

PRODUCE
[LOAD UP!]
One calculation estimates that it takes 1.5 pounds of produce per person to yield the recommended 5 to 9 servings per day. Real point: Most people fall short.

DELI COUNTER
[TIME-SAVER]
Deli meats tend to be supersalty. Instead, double up on rotisserie chickens—one for dinner tonight, one for lunches later. More tips on page 368.
SAVE: 260mg sodium per sandwich

CEREAL AISLE
[WHOLE GRAINS]
Secret of oats: Even the instant variety qualifies as whole grain. And cheap: $3 for a container.
GAIN: 16g of your 48g daily whole-grains goal—at breakfast

PRODUCE
[TIME-SAVER]
Prewashed arugula and spinach are year-round salad stars. You pay more but save a lot of washing. Avoid bags with greens that are bruised or starting to blacken. But read labels of those creamy salad dressings—they can be fat bombs.
GAIN: 1 more of any day's veggie servings

COFFEE & TEA
[ANTIOXIDANTS, CAFFEINE]
Unless you're a bean-sourcing fanatic, most supermarkets have made great strides in coffee and tea variety and quality.
GAIN: Wakey-wakey. The health attacks on coffee haven't stuck.

CRACKERS & COOKIES
[WHOLE GRAINS]
This can be a major temptation station, but new emphasis on whole-grain labeling, though tricky, shows some bright spots, like Triscuits.
GAIN: 22g more whole grains

CONDIMENTS
[HEALTHY FATS]
Olive and nut oils bring heart-healthy fats and delicious flavors to homemade vinaigrettes.
SAVE: About 370mg sodium per salad vs many commercial dressings

... starts at the grocery store. With 40,000 items, nutrition-smart navigating is the foundation of healthy cooking. More fruits, vegetables, and whole grains; less sat fat and sodium; and smarter spending, whether the budget priority is calories or cash. Here, a simple guide.

ROUNDING THE CORNER

Try this sampling tactic: If a product is not healthy, sample it and enjoy—but don't join the 47% of shoppers who are more likely to actually *buy* it.
GAIN: A little tasty indulgent treat en route, without a bagful more to take home

MEAT COUNTER
[SAT FAT SAVINGS]

New meat labels make it easier to pick lower-fat cuts. Pay attention to portion size. For example, one Brobdingnagian 12-ounce chicken breast is 3 servings!

FREEZER SECTION
[SAT FAT SAVINGS]

Don't bypass! Out-of-season peas taste almost field-fresh; 1 cup frozen strawberries is a serving.
GAIN: Puts you closer to that hard 5-to-9-servings-per-day goal.

CANNED GOODS
[FIBER, CONVENIENCE]

Canned beans are a fast and healthy staple for quick soup recipes, but buy low-sodium. House brands can save money.
GAIN: Fiber

DAIRY CASE
[CALCIUM]

Low-fat doesn't mean less calcium, and 8 ounces of 1% milk have 3g less sat fat than full-fat.
GAIN: 290mg calcium per serving

CHIPS & SOFT DRINKS
[WHOLE GRAINS, HEALTHY FATS]

Popcorn is a whole grain—but get the low-fat microwave variety, or just air-pop at home. Nuts are healthy-fat, satiating snacks. Avoid soda: Try seltzer.
GAIN: Fiber, good fats, even more whole grains

CHECKOUT

People who wait 25% longer than average are up to 25% more likely to make an impulse buy.
AVOID: Need a treat? Swap the high-fat candy bars for something longer-lasting, like chewing gum.

GROCERY SHOPPING GUIDE

HOW COLD CUTS STACKUP

The curing of meat was traditionally done to preserve a precious food, and that food, being precious, was not served in mile-high deli sandwiches. It's the portion, not the pastrami, that can be unhealthy these days. Still, even in a modest 1- or 2-ounce serving, sodium can add up. To dodge some of the salt, get your slices fresh from the deli for up to 50% sodium savings over presliced. Opt for reduced-sodium versions when you can. Here's the scoop on some favorites:

PROSCIUTTO
Per ounce: Supersalty at 650mg, but that's two of these paper-thin slices, versus one of most other meats.

OVEN-ROASTED CHICKEN BREAST
Per ounce: As lean as you'd expect—less than 1g sat fat. But not salt-free: same as some pastramis, about 243mg sodium. Lower-sodium versions have about 175mg.

BEEF PASTRAMI
Per ounce: Seasoned brisket or round is leaner (0.5g or less sat fat) with lower sodium (242mg) than you might think.

SMOKED TURKEY BREAST
Per ounce: Similar to chicken—no sat fat and about 260mg sodium (170mg in lower-sodium versions).

HONEY-CURED HAM
Per ounce: Just as pork tenderloin can be almost as lean as skinless chicken breast, so too deli ham. A smidge more sodium than the bird, though—265mg.

SOFT & HARD SALAMIS
Per ounce: Starting at 110 calories, 3g sat fat, and 320mg sodium, these options are similar to sausage.

ROAST BEEF
Per ounce: It's easy to forget how lean beef can be, and it's a salt-savvy option (166mg), too. Reduced-sodium versions have even less—just 40mg.

TURN OVER AN OLD LEAF

Old-fashioned dark leafy greens are having their moment in the culinary sun. Boy, are they good for you.

KALE
All-star nutrient: Vitamin A
Body benefit: Vision health
Hard to believe how soft and silky this crinkly, supercrisp leaf turns when cooked. One cup offers more than a day's worth of A (481mcg), nearly double the amount in most other greens.

BEET GREENS
All-star nutrient: Potassium
Body benefit: Blood pressure balance
When cooked, a cup contains almost a third (1,309mg) of the potassium you need in a day. But you don't have to cook: These burgundy–veined beauties are softer in texture than other hearty greens and can be eaten raw.

CHARD
All-star nutrient: Vitamin K
Body benefit: Better bone health
Sturdy candy-colored ribs have an almost celery-like texture, while the leaves are earthy and slightly sweet. A cup of cooked greens has six times your daily recommended intake (572mcg) of vitamin K. Chard is also naturally high in sodium, so use less salt when cooking.

SPINACH
All-star nutrient: Iron
Body benefit: Fatigue fighter
You get a lot of concentrated goodness in a very small serving: A pound of fresh, mild-flavored raw leaves (tender babies or tougher adults) cooks down to 1 cup, boasting a third (6.4mg) of a day's recommended iron.

BUY BETTER BREAD

If a dense artisanal loaf won't cut it with the kids, you can still find good choices in the supermarket.

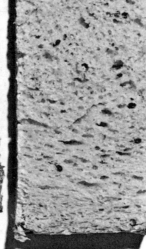

GO FOR 100% WHOLE GRAIN

Step one to getting better bread into kids' lunch boxes: Look for "100% Whole Grain" on the label, and make sure the first ingredient is a 100% whole-grain flour, whether it's wheat, oat, rye, amaranth, etc. "Whole Grain" or "Whole Wheat" is not enough. Those may contain only 51% whole-grain flour (and 49% refined).

SORT OUT GRAIN SERVINGS

There are plenty of whole-grain breads that deliver one serving of whole grains—16g of the 48g recommended each day. A quick way to find them: Look for the Whole Grains Council 100% stamp. In fact, 16g is on the lower end of the spectrum, and more is better. Since one serving is usually one slice, a PB&J can give a kid two-thirds of his or her daily whole grains.

WATCH OUT FOR HIDDEN SODIUM

Salt is there for flavor, of course, but it also helps bread rise evenly, courtesy of baking soda (aka sodium bicarbonate) and baking powder, which also contains baking soda. Among these three sources, sodium can add up fast—and that's before high-sodium foods like deli slices and cheese are piled on top. Stick to breads with 150mg or less per slice.

A LITTLE SUGAR WON'T HURT

A bit of sugar (or honey) lends sweetness that may appeal, and it makes bread tender. It can also be used to supply a caramel hue—a trick used by less-than-whole "brown" breads. Most whole-grain breads have a reasonable 2g to 3g per slice, but there's no need for more.

A PRIMER FOR PASTA

A 2-ounce pasta portion is about 200 calories. Beyond that, there's lots to explore on today's noodle shelves.

SOBA NOODLES
A tasty, thin Japanese noodle made with buckwheat, which isn't wheat, but it's usually blended with wheat so not gluten-free. Check the label—can be high in sodium.

8g protein, 0g fiber, 450mg sodium

DURUM SEMOLINA SPAGHETTI
The Italian classic, made from a high-gluten, high-protein, hard wheat called durum that yields that beautiful al dente texture. Look for 100% semolina on labels.

7g protein, 2g fiber, 4mg sodium

GLUTEN-FREE BROWN RICE SPAGHETTI
A rare whole-grain option among gluten-free noodles made from corn and potato starch; similar nutrition to semolina.

5g protein, 2g fiber, 0mg sodium

WHOLE-WHEAT SPAGHETTI
The nutty, slightly sweet flavor and chewy texture pair well with a robust, chunky sauce. Tops for fiber, and counts as a whole-grain serving.

8g protein, 7g fiber, 5mg sodium

VEGGIE-ENHANCED SPAGHETTI
Dried vegetable powders add color, but only trace vitamins and minerals. In other words, buy if you like the color or flavor, but for vegetables, you'll have to put those in the sauce.

7.5g protein, 6g fiber, 20mg sodium

UDON NOODLES
A thick, ropy Japanese wheat noodle that stands up well in a rich broth.

8g protein, 3g fiber, 82mg sodium

THE PERFECT YOGURT!

With zillions of options, we set out to define the ideal blend of nutrition, creaminess, and flavor.

③ CONSIDER DIFFERENT CULTURES & FLAVORS

Look for the National Yogurt Association seal, signaling live cultures for digestive health. Then turn to creamy texture and real taste: Our ideal yogurt delivers the sensual satisfaction of a rich dessert, with lots of culture tang. The new flavor frontiers are chile spice, rich coffee, deep chocolate, caramel, and honey.

④ CONTEMPLATE THE CALORIES

A healthy, right-sized snack is about 100 to 150 calories, and most single-serving fat-free or 2% yogurts (plain or flavored) fall within that window. The higher-calorie yogurts tend to be higher-fat, as well.

Our perfect yogurt

Small producers are pushing the flavor envelope, like Atlanta Fresh in the South. Their fat-free Vanilla & Caramel is tart, creamy, and intensely flavorful: indulgent while meeting the fat, calorie, and sugar numbers outlined here.

② THEN MULL THE SUGAR

Milk contains sugar, so most yogurt contains at least 7g of natural sugars per 6-ounce serving. Anything else is added—sugar, honey, fruit, syrup. For a convenient treat, we love an exotic-flavored yogurt. When buying that, look for 18g of sugars or less.

① START WITH THE FAT

Fat in yogurt comes from milk, and most of it's saturated. Read the label for total fat in a single serving: We recently saw one with 25g! Fat-free is good, but for creamy goodness we like as much as 2%—but no more than 2g sat fat per serving.

ICE-CREAM DECODER

There are a number of label terms for light ice cream. See if they induce brain freeze.

LOW-FAT
Simple enough: A half-cup serving must contain no more than 3g total fat. Ice creams that don't meet that standard can still be called "reduced-fat" or "light" if they meet those definitions.

WHIPPED
Not a nutrition claim but a process that often indicates less fat. Air is added during the churning process—a technique long used to reduce fat and calories—but new technologies reduce the size of fat globules and ice crystals, yielding a creamy consistency. Total fat tends to be in the 3g to 4g zone—somewhere between low-fat and light.

REDUCED-FAT
Contains 25% less total fat than a brand's original version. The more fat in the original version, the more in the reduced-fat version. We found a reduced-fat version with 6g total fat and 4g sat fat per half-cup. Another had 5g total fat and 3g sat fat.

LIGHT
How's this for confusing: Light ice creams may contain either 50% less total fat *or* 33% fewer calories than the brand's original version. For example: One brand's full-fat ice cream contains 180 calories and 9g fat, while the light version has 140 calories and 4.5g fat. Most manufacturers swap some whole milk or low-fat milk for cream to earn the term.

FAT-FREE
Technically, a fat-free ice milk (it's not an ice cream if it's less than 5% fat) can have up to 0.5g of fat in it—manufacturers can round down. For creamy texture, thickeners and stabilizers (like carrageenan and cellulose gum) are added.

HEALTHY EATING STRATEGIES

Healthy eating is about rebalancing the foods in your diet—more plants, less meat—and it's also about portion size.

1. BIG PLATE, BIG PORTIONS

We took recipes from April's fast-cooking section, and then scaled them up for an oversized, 13-inch charger. You can see that a whopping 9-ounce cooked chicken breast looks suitably in scale, and there's space to double up on starch. Check out the resulting calories when you do that.

MENU*

Grill Pan Chicken
Serving: 9 ounces
Brown Rice with Sesame
Serving: 1 cup rice
Mushroom Sauce
Serving: 6 tablespoons
Mixed Greens Salad
Serving: 1/2 cup
Butter-Roasted Carrots
Serving: 1/4 cup
Wheat Roll with Orange Butter
Serving: 1 roll, 1/2 teaspoon butter

**TOTAL CALORIES
830**

Studies show that when given larger portions, people eat up to 30% more.

* ALL THESE RECIPES can be found in our 40 Meals Under 40 Minutes section, starting on page 77.

THE SECRET TO PERFECT PORTIONS

Plates vary dramatically, and if you have a fill-the-plate, clean-the-plate approach, it really helps to start with right-sized dinnerware. Here, in three steps, we downsize the servings, and then the plate.

Surface area shrinks 62% with the 8-inch plate, leaving less room for food.

2. BIG PLATE, HEALTHY PORTIONS

Right-sizing the portions leaves the meal looking a little stingy.

WHAT'S DIFFERENT

The chicken breast is downsized *to a more reasonable 4½-ounce portion. Less chicken needs less sauce—3 tablespoons instead of 6.* **We cut back on starch,** *halving the rice and removing the roll.* **We upped the vegetables** *to ½ cup of carrots and 1½ cups of greens because they're delicious and healthy, and fill the space vacated by the extra starch.*

TOTAL CALORIES 443

Studies also show that the size of our plate does affect how much we choose to eat.

3. SMALLER PLATE, HEALTHY PORTIONS

With the same healthy portions as on the big plate, the meal now looks satisfying.

WHAT'S DIFFERENT

We used an 8-inch dinner plate. *The advantage of a smaller plate is that it automatically guides you to smaller portions—here, almost 50% less than the big plate. Even if you go for seconds, they'll be smaller.*

TOTAL CALORIES 443

CUT 1 CUP SUGAR IN 1 DAY

You may not have this person's sweet tooth, but being sugar-savvy can still yield big savings.

START HERE

BREAKFAST

5:30 A.M.
So long, sweetened vanilla soy milk. Hello, unsweetened. Savings in a cup:
-6g

5:32 A.M.
Try a bowl of Cheerios instead of the more heavily sweetened flake and cluster combo kind.
-13g

7:45 A.M.
Use 1 sugar packet instead of 2 in my coffee. Not much of a savings, actually.
-3g

7:46 A.M.
Had a good morning workout, but not good enough to burn off a slice of reduced-fat coffee cake. Skip it.
-40g

LUNCH

12:00 P.M.
Order a large half-sweet/ half-unsweet iced tea with my deli sandwich.
-17g

12:03 P.M.
Resist the cookie, grab a banana. Fruit has sugar, too, but it comes with other good-for-you stuff.
-14g

4:30 P.M.
Who calls a meeting at 4:30? Resist temptation to dip into mood-boosting mini candy bar supply.
-7g

6:15 P.M.
Headed to pot-luck cookout. Glad I made coleslaw with my own vinaigrette instead of buying ready-made.
-5g

6:45 P.M.
Margarita from a mix? I'll just have a beer. Only 0.32g in 12 ounces.
-22g

DINNER

3:15 P.M.
If the office-fridge thieves haven't hit, there's a Greek yogurt waiting for me—with blueberries instead of honey.
-13g

7:30 P.M.
BBQ! Avoid extra sauce on the sandwich: Sugar is the first ingredient in many sauces.
-8g

7:31 P.M.
Skip the molasses-y baked beans.
-13g

8:30 P.M.
Cut the caramel sauce from an already-sweet treat.
-27g

1 CUP SUGAR SAVED!

728 CAL. TOTAL!

SMOOTHIES UNDER 250 CALORIES

Smoothie joints can pack 400 calories in a 20-ounce cup. Here's how to downsize while getting lots of fresh fruit and flavor.

Bingo: Press a button and serve up most of your family's daily fruit intake. The recommended goal is 2 cups of fruit a day, and these 12-ounce blends go a long way toward that; some have a few veggies, too. If there's a picky eater in your house, well, he or she doesn't need to know you mixed beets in with the berries—until after they serve up a big smile.

WATERMELON WITH A HINT OF MINT
2 cups seedless watermelon + 2 tablespoons fresh mint + ⅓ cup 2% plain Greek yogurt
98 CALORIES

PEANUT BUTTER BERRY
¼ cup 1% low-fat milk + ½ medium banana + 1 tablespoon creamy peanut butter + 1 cup fresh or frozen raspberries + ½ cup crushed ice
237 CALORIES

BERRIES & BEETS
1 cup fresh blueberries + ½ cup fresh or frozen raspberries + ⅓ cup sliced, cooked beets + ¼ cup nonfat Greek yogurt + ¼ cup fresh orange juice + 1 teaspoon light agave nectar
219 CALORIES

GINGER, BERRIES & OATS
¼ cup prepared oatmeal + ¼ cup 1% low-fat milk + ½ teaspoon grated fresh ginger + 1 cup fresh blackberries + ½ cup sliced fresh strawberries + 1 teaspoon honey + ½ cup ice
179 CALORIES

PEACHES & CREAM
1½ cups sliced fresh peaches + ½ cup nonfat buttermilk + ½ medium banana + 2 teaspoons honey + ½ cup crushed ice
231 CALORIES

PINEAPPLE PIÑA COLADA
½ medium banana + ¼ cup light coconut milk + 1 cup chopped fresh pineapple + ¼ cup chilled pineapple juice + ½ cup crushed ice
203 CALORIES

SMOOTHIE SAVVY

ADD ICE LAST Adding ice first may cause you to overblend, leaving you with a watery drink.

IF YOU USE FROZEN FRUIT You may not need as much ice. Frozen fruit is as nutrient-packed as fresh—just choose those with no added sugars.

NOT A FAN OF DAIRY? Most milk alternatives (soy, rice) have roughly the same calories as 1% milk—about 100 per cup.

CREAMY MANGO, AVOCADO & LIME
¼ cup sliced avocado + 1 cup sliced Champagne mango + 1 tablespoon fresh lime juice + 1 tablespoon fresh mint + 1 teaspoon honey + 2 cups crushed ice
191 CALORIES

GREEN MACHINE
1 cup fresh baby spinach leaves + 1½ cups chopped fresh honeydew + ⅓ cup nonfat vanilla Greek yogurt
162 CALORIES

200-CALORIE PIZZA SLICES

Roll a 1-pound ball of fresh dough into a 14-inch base. Top with one of these tasty topping combinations, bake, and divide by 8. *Buon appetito!*

THE BAGEL-AND-LOX TREATMENT
Base: 1 tablespoon fresh lemon juice + $\frac{1}{2}$ cup $\frac{1}{3}$-less-fat cream cheese
Toppers: 4 ounces sliced smoked salmon + $\frac{1}{3}$ cup thinly sliced red onion + 1 tablespoon chopped fresh dill

THE CHICKEN PESTO PARTY
Base: $\frac{1}{4}$ cup prepared pesto
Toppers: $\frac{3}{4}$ cup shredded roasted chicken breast + $\frac{1}{2}$ cup sliced red bell pepper + $\frac{1}{3}$ cup grated fresh Parmigiano-Reggiano cheese

THE CAN'T-BEET-THIS COMBO
Base: $1\frac{1}{2}$ tablespoons olive oil
Toppers: 8 ounces sliced roasted beets + $\frac{1}{3}$ cup toasted walnut halves + $\frac{1}{3}$ cup crumbled goat cheese + 2 tablespoons chopped fresh flat-leaf parsley

THE HAPPY HAWAIIAN
Base: $\frac{1}{2}$ cup lower-sodium marinara sauce
Toppers: 4 ounces turkey pepperoni slices + 1 cup pineapple chunks (fresh or canned) + $\frac{1}{2}$ cup shredded part-skim mozzarella cheese

THE FARMERS' MARKET
Base: $\frac{1}{3}$ cup part-skim ricotta cheese
Toppers: 2 cups fresh cut asparagus + $\frac{1}{2}$ cup fresh spring peas + $1\frac{1}{2}$ tablespoons olive oil + 2 tablespoons grated lemon rind + $\frac{1}{2}$ cup fresh grated Parmigiano-Reggiano cheese

THE GREEK AUSTERITY CURE
Base: $\frac{3}{4}$ cup ready-made Greek-style hummus
Toppers: 6 sliced plum tomatoes + $\frac{1}{3}$ cup black olives + $\frac{1}{2}$ cup crumbled feta cheese + $\frac{1}{2}$ cup chopped fresh basil

THE BBQ YARDBIRD
Base: $\frac{1}{2}$ cup ready-made barbecue sauce
Toppers: $\frac{1}{2}$ cup sliced roasted chicken breast + $\frac{1}{2}$ cup shredded cheddar cheese + $\frac{1}{2}$ cup sliced red onion + $\frac{1}{2}$ cup chopped fresh cilantro

THE PEPPERY PIG
Base: $1\frac{1}{2}$ tablespoons olive oil
Toppers: 4 ounces sliced prosciutto + $\frac{1}{2}$ cup shaved fresh Parmigiano-Reggiano cheese + 4 cups fresh baby arugula + cracked black pepper

HOW THE DELIVERY STACKS UP

All that cheesy cheesiness promoted in TV ads adds calories to single plain slices of hand-tossed—mostly from cheese.

Little Caesars
250 CALORIES
Domino's
290 CALORIES
Papa John's
290 CALORIES
Godfather's
313 CALORIES
Pizza Hut
320 CALORIES

TACOS FOR 200 CALORIES OR LESS

Start with a warm 6-inch corn tortilla. Pick from these tasty topping combos. They're so healthy and delicious—you'll want two.

MAHI & MANGO
1 tablespoon sliced red onion + 2 tablespoons mango + 2 tablespoons avocado + 2 ounces grilled mahimahi fillet

WAKEY BREAKY
1 tablespoon roasted poblano peppers + 1 tablespoon queso fresco + 1 tablespoon diced tomato + 1 large egg, scrambled + 2 tablespoons hash brown potatoes

BLACK BEAN FIESTA
1½ tablespoons feta cheese + ¼ cup black beans + ¼ cup sautéed zucchini + 2 tablespoons charred corn + 1 tablespoon fresh salsa

CLASSIC
1 tablespoon light sour cream + 1 tablespoon Monterey Jack cheese + ¼ cup shredded lettuce + 1.5 ounces seasoned lean ground beef

MAINE-MEX
2 ounces steamed lobster + ¼ cup sliced Napa cabbage + 2 tablespoons Monterey Jack cheese + 2 tablespoons fresh salsa

WHAT THE TACO TRUCKS SERVE UP

Popular choices get their meltingly tender meat from fattier, slow-roasted cuts—but the good news is that portions tend to be small. Here's what a 2-ounce pull of meat contains (minus other fixings):

Pork Carnitas
153 CALORIES

Barbecued Brisket
229 CALORIES

Korean Short Rib
267 CALORIES

FAJITA-STYLE STEAK
1.5 ounces grilled flank steak + 1 tablespoon guacamole + 1 tablespoon pepper Jack cheese + ¼ cup grilled peppers and onions

CRUSTACEAN CRUNCH
2 tablespoons pico de gallo + ¼ cup shredded red cabbage + 2 ounces lime-grilled shrimp + 1 tablespoon salsa verde

QUINOA COMBOS FOR 250 CALORIES

Fear not this grain: Quinoa is fast-cooking and makes tasty salads. You can cook on Sunday, chill, eat over the next few days, and tote to work.

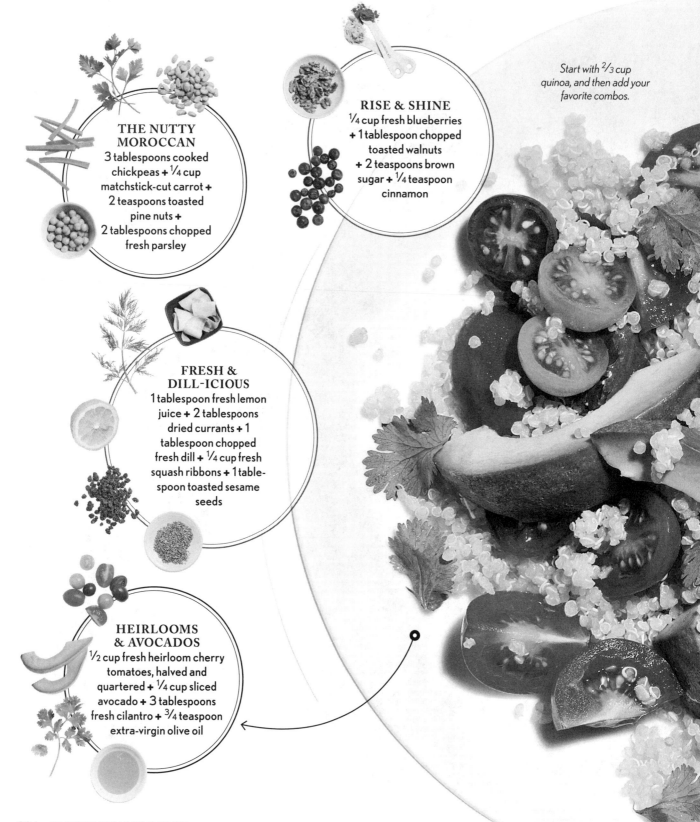

Start with ²/₃ cup quinoa, and then add your favorite combos.

THE NUTTY MOROCCAN
3 tablespoons cooked chickpeas + ¼ cup matchstick-cut carrot + 2 teaspoons toasted pine nuts + 2 tablespoons chopped fresh parsley

RISE & SHINE
¼ cup fresh blueberries + 1 tablespoon chopped toasted walnuts + 2 teaspoons brown sugar + ¼ teaspoon cinnamon

FRESH & DILL-ICIOUS
1 tablespoon fresh lemon juice + 2 tablespoons dried currants + 1 tablespoon chopped fresh dill + ¼ cup fresh squash ribbons + 1 tablespoon toasted sesame seeds

HEIRLOOMS & AVOCADOS
½ cup fresh heirloom cherry tomatoes, halved and quartered + ¼ cup sliced avocado + 3 tablespoons fresh cilantro + ¾ teaspoon extra-virgin olive oil

WHY QUINOA IS SO GOOD

Ready in about 20 minutes, whole-grain, and gluten-free. Here's how $2/3$ cup compares to other whole grains.

Quinoa
148 CALORIES, 5.4G PROTEIN, 3.5G FIBER

Brown Rice
144 CALORIES, 3.4G PROTEIN, 2.3G FIBER

Farro
133 CALORIES, 5.3G PROTEIN, 4.7G FIBER

Barley
129 CALORIES, 2.4G PROTEIN, 4G FIBER

Bulgur
101 CALORIES, 3.7G PROTEIN, 5.5G FIBER

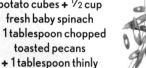

ROOTS, GREENS & SHOOTS
$1/4$ cup roasted sweet potato cubes + $1/2$ cup fresh baby spinach + 1 tablespoon chopped toasted pecans + 1 tablespoon thinly sliced green onions

MINT FOR SUMMER
$1/3$ cup fresh summer corn + $1/2$ ounce ricotta salata cheese + 2 tablespoons fresh mint + $1/4$ cup grated fresh yellow squash

RED, WHITE & GREEN CRUNCH
$1/4$ cup thinly sliced fresh radishes + 2 tablespoons thinly sliced fresh snow peas + 1 ounce goat cheese, crumbled + 1 tablespoon fresh lime juice

STRAWBERRY FIELDS
$1/3$ cup fresh sliced strawberries + 1 tablespoon chopped toasted hazelnuts + $1/4$ cup fresh baby arugula + $1/2$ ounce goat cheese, crumbled

NUTRITIONAL ANALYSIS

What the Numbers Mean For You

Glance at the end of any *Cooking Light* recipe, and you'll see how committed we are to helping you make the best of today's light cooking. With chefs, registered dietitians, home economists, and a computer system that analyzes every ingredient we use, *Cooking Light* gives you authoritative dietary detail like no other magazine. We go to such lengths so you can see how our recipes fit into your healthful eating plan. If you're trying to lose weight, the calorie and fat figures will probably help most. But if you're keeping a close eye on the sodium, cholesterol, and saturated fat in your diet, we provide those numbers, too. And because many women don't get enough iron or calcium, we can help there, as well. Finally, there's a fiber analysis for those of us who don't get enough roughage.

Here's a helpful guide to put our nutritional analysis numbers into perspective. Remember, one size doesn't fit all, so take your lifestyle, age, and circumstances into consideration when determining your nutrition needs. For example, pregnant or breast-feeding women need more protein, calories, and calcium. And women older than 50 need 1,200mg of calcium daily, 200mg more than the amount recommended for younger women.

IN OUR NUTRITIONAL ANALYSIS, WE USE THESE ABBREVIATIONS

sat	saturated fat	**CHOL**	cholesterol
mono	monounsaturated fat	**CALC**	calcium
poly	polyunsaturated fat	**g**	gram
CARB	carbohydrates	**mg**	milligram

Daily Nutrition Guide

	WOMEN ages 25 to 50	WOMEN over 50	MEN ages 25 to 50	MEN over 50
CALORIES	2,000	2,000*	2,700	2,500
PROTEIN	50g	50g	63g	60g
FAT	65g*	65g*	88g*	83g*
SATURATED FAT	20g*	20g*	27g*	25g*
CARBOHYDRATES	304g	304g	410g	375g
FIBER	25g to 35g	25g to 35g	25g to 35g	25g to 35g
CHOLESTEROL	300mg*	300mg*	300mg*	300mg*
IRON	18mg	8mg	8mg	8mg
SODIUM	2,300mg*	1,500mg*	2,300mg*	1,500mg*
CALCIUM	1,000mg	1,200mg	1,000mg	1,000mg

NUTRITIONAL VALUES USED IN OUR CALCULATIONS EITHER COME FROM THE FOOD PROCESSOR, VERSION 10.4 (ESHA RESEARCH) OR ARE PROVIDED BY FOOD MANUFACTURERS.
*Or less, for optimum health.

METRIC EQUIVALENTS

The information in the following charts is provided to help cooks outside the United States successfully use the recipes in this book. All equivalents are approximate.

Cooking/Oven Temperatures

	Fahrenheit	Celsius	Gas Mark
Freeze Water	32° F	0° C	
Room Temp.	68° F	20° C	
Boil Water	212° F	100° C	
Bake	325° F	160° C	3
	350° F	180° C	4
	375° F	190° C	5
	400° F	200° C	6
	425° F	220° C	7
	450° F	230° C	8
Broil			Grill

Liquid Ingredients by Volume

¼ tsp	=				1 ml	
½ tsp	=				2 ml	
1 tsp	=				5 ml	
3 tsp	=	1 tbl	=	½ fl oz	=	15 ml
2 tbls	=	⅛ cup	=	1 fl oz	=	30 ml
4 tbls	=	¼ cup	=	2 fl oz	=	60 ml
5⅓ tbls	=	⅓ cup	=	3 fl oz	=	80 ml
8 tbls	=	½ cup	=	4 fl oz	=	120 ml
10⅔ tbls	=	⅔ cup	=	5 fl oz	=	160 ml
12 tbls	=	¾ cup	=	6 fl oz	=	180 ml
16 tbls	=	1 cup	=	8 fl oz	=	240 ml
1 pt	=	2 cups	=	16 fl oz	=	480 ml
1 qt	=	4 cups	=	32 fl oz	=	960 ml
				33 fl oz	=	1000 ml = 1 l

Dry Ingredients by Weight

(To convert ounces to grams, multiply the number of ounces by 30.)

1 oz	=	¹⁄₁₆ lb	=	30 g
4 oz	=	¼ lb	=	120 g
8 oz	=	½ lb	=	240 g
12 oz	=	¾ lb	=	360 g
16 oz	=	1 lb	=	480 g

Length

(To convert inches to centimeters, multiply the number of inches by 2.5.)

1 in	=			2.5 cm	
6 in	=	½ ft	=	15 cm	
12 in	=	1 ft	=	30 cm	
36 in	=	3 ft	= 1 yd =	90 cm	
40 in	=			100 cm	= 1 m

Equivalents for Different Types of Ingredients

Standard Cup	Fine Powder (ex. flour)	Grain (ex. rice)	Granular (ex. sugar)	Liquid Solids (ex. butter)	Liquid (ex. milk)
1	140 g	150 g	190 g	200 g	240 ml
¾	105 g	113 g	143 g	150 g	180 ml
⅔	93 g	100 g	125 g	133 g	160 ml
½	70 g	75 g	95 g	100 g	120 ml
⅓	47 g	50 g	63 g	67 g	80 ml
¼	35 g	38 g	48 g	50 g	60 ml
⅛	18 g	19 g	24 g	25 g	30 ml

MENU INDEX

A topical guide to all the menus that appear in *Cooking Light Annual Recipes 2013*. See page 402 for the General Recipe Index.

DINNER TONIGHT

30-Minute Dinners

POULTRY

(page 184)
serves 4
Glazed Chicken and Szechuan Noodle Salad
Sesame Broccoli

(page 269)
serves 4
Sweet-Spicy Chicken and Vegetable Stir-Fry
Double Sesame Rice

VEGETARIAN

(page 291)
serves 4
Spiced Lentils and Poached Eggs
Cumin-Scented Carrots

40-Minute Dinners

BEEF

(page 43)
serves 4
Enchilada Casserole
Spicy Black Beans

(page 44)
serves 4
Beef Tenderloin Steaks and Balsamic Green Beans
Parmesan Potatoes

(page 331)
serves 4
Spanish Spaghetti with Olives
Pear, Date, and Manchego Salad

(page 334)
serves 6
Cheesy Meat Loaf Minis
Salad with Balsamic Vinaigrette

(page 358)
serves 4
Peppercorn-Crusted Beef Tenderloin with Gremolata
Herb-Roasted Potatoes

FISH & SHELLFISH

(page 42)
serves 4
Seafood Cioppino
Garlic Sourdough

(page 71)
serves 4
Crispy Herbed Shrimp with Chive Aioli
Roasted Asparagus and Tomatoes

(page 125)
serves 4
Crispy Flounder and Roasted Tomatoes
Fennel-Potato Hash

(page 127)
serves 4
Grilled Salmon and Brown Butter Couscous
Grilled Summer Squash

(page 157)
serves 4
Shrimp Florentine Pasta
Cherry Tomato Caprese Salad

(page 158)
serves 4
Seared Scallops with Herb Butter Sauce
Roasted Green Beans

(page 185)
serves 2
Snapper with Zucchini and Tomato
Parsley Orzo

(page 242)
serves 4
Shrimp Salad Rolls
Roasted Herbed Potatoes

(page 243)
serves 4
Seared Tuna Nicoise
Lemony White Bean Mash

(page 267)
serves 4
Lemony Grilled Shrimp Salad
Spicy Mango

(page 359)
Serves 4
Sautéed Flounder and Spicy Rémoulade
Bacon-Scented Broccoli

PORK

(page 42)
serves 4
Cheesy Potato Soup
Mini Ham Sandwiches

(page 72)
serves 6
Italian Meatball Sliders
Spinach and Mozzarella Salad

(page 184)
serves 4
Open-Faced Pimiento Cheese BLTs
Sweet Potato Fries

Meals Under 40 Minutes

CHICKEN DINNERS

RECIPE TITLE INDEX

An alphabetical listing of every recipe title that appeared in the magazine in 2012. See page 402 for the General Recipe Index.

MONTH-BY-MONTH INDEX

A month-by-month listing of every food story with recipe titles that appeared in the magazine in 2012. See page 402 for the General Recipe Index.

GENERAL RECIPE INDEX

A listing by major ingredient and food category for every recipe that appeared in the magazine in 2012.